Wissenschaftliche Untersuchungen
zum Neuen Testament · 2. Reihe

Herausgegeben von
Martin Hengel und Otfried Hofius

103

Geoffrey R. Treloar

Lightfoot the Historian

The Nature and Role of History in the Life and
Thought of J. B. Lightfoot (1828–1889) as
Churchman and Scholar

Mohr Siebeck

GEOFFREY R. TRELOAR, born 1951; 1970–74 studied history and education at the University of Sydney; 1975–77 secondary school teacher; 1978–82 and 1986–89 teacher in N.S.W. Department of Technical and Further Education; 1983–85 doctoral student at the University of Sydney; 1990–95 Lecturer at the Sydney Institute of Technology; since 1996 Dean, and Academic Dean of the School of Christian Studies, at Robert Menzies College, Macquarie University.

Die Deutsche Bibliothek – CIP-Einheitsaufnahme

Treloar, Geoffrey R.:
Lightfoot the historian : the nature and role of history in the life and thought of J. B. Lightfoot (1828–1889) as churchman and scholar / Geoffrey R. Treolar. – Tübingen : Mohr Siebeck, 1998
  (Wissenschaftliche Untersuchungen zum Neuen Testament : Reihe 2 ; 103)
  ISBN 3-16-146866-X

The book was printed by Druck Partner Rübelmann GmbH in Hemsbach on non-aging paper from Papierfabrik Niefern and bound by Buchbinderei Schaumann in Darmstadt. Printed in Germany.

ISSN 0340-9570

For Linda

Acknowledgements

This book is a somewhat revised version of a doctoral thesis accepted by the University of Sydney in November 1996. First thanks go to my supervisors. Mr Marlay Stephen watched over the early stages with wry urbanity. Professor Deryck Schreuder took the project through the middle period with characteristic verve. Towards the end, Dr Geoffrey Oddie took over responsibility for a project well outside his own field of expertise and cheerfully guided it to completion. Dr D.M. Thompson (Fitzwilliam College, Cambridge), Professor F.M. Turner (Yale) and Mr A.E. Cahill (University of Sydney) were searching and constructive examiners.

For his generous encouragement over an extended period, leading to acceptance of this book in the *W.U.N.T.* series, I am deeply appreciative of Professor Martin Hengel.

My debts to many others are also keenly felt. During my archival term in Durham Professor W.R. Ward acted as associate supervisor and furnished a salutary warning not to become "another worshipper at the Lightfoot shrine". Dr Sheridan Gilley, Mr Gerald Bonner and Professor (now Bishop) Stephen Sykes also took an interest in my research and read some early drafts. I owe a special debt to the incomparable Roger Norris, Assistant Librarian at the Dean and Chapter Library, Durham Cathedral, and his assistant, Ms Wendy Stevenson, for their help and encouragement in innumerable ways. For their permission to use the unpublished papers in their care I should like to thank the authorities of all the bodies listed in the first part of the bibliography, in particular the Dean and Chapter of Durham, the Master and Fellows of Trinity College, Cambridge, and the Keeper of the Cambridge University Archives. The Bishop of Durham granted permission to quote from the Lightfoot Papers.

Other scholars, colleagues and friends have played important parts along the way. These include Bruce Kaye, Greg Horsley, Bob Linder, Edwin Judge, Robert Banks, Sarah Paddle, Stephen Pickard, Rod Hacking, Kim Robinson, John Pryor, Eunice Lovell, Frank and Irene Nelsson, Brian and Maureen Newman, and Kim and Malcom Sinclair.

Several colleagues at Robert Menzies College, Macquarie University, furnished invaluable assistance. The indefatigable Mark Hutchinson put his formidable computing skills at my disposal. The Rev. Richard Quadrio kept me at it with his importunate, "How's the Bishop?" Diane Parkes shared the proof reading load. The College's Master, Dr Stuart Piggin, has been constant in friendly support and sagacious counsel. I owe him a special debt.

My heaviest obligation, however, is to the members of my family. Paul and Glen have taken a bemused interest in my progress. Kelly, James, Bethany and Edward cannot remember a time when Bishop Lightfoot was not part of their lives. As always, my mother and my late father were 'there' for me.

My wife Linda is 'in a class of her own'. For all that she has contributed it is right that this book be dedicated to her. Nobody could deserve it more.

Robert Menzies College
Macquarie University, N.S.W.
31 March 1998

Geoffrey R. Treloar

Table of Contents

Abbreviations

1. Unpublished Sources and their Locations

BLL	Benson Papers, Lambeth Palace Library, London
BLO	Bodleian Library, Oxford
CPO	Church Papers, Pusey House, Oxford
CUA	Cambridge University Archives
CUL	Cambridge University Library
CUR	Cambridge University Register
DGC	Davies Papers, Girton College, Cambridge
DUL	Durham University Library
FCC	Farrar Papers, Canterbury Cathedral Library
GBL	Gladstone Papers, British Library, London
GEC	Gwatkin Papers, Emmanuel College, Cambridge
JBO	Jowett Papers, Balliol College Library, Oxford
LAC	Lightfoot Papers, Auckland Castle
LDC	Lightfoot Papers, Dean and Chapter Library, Durham Cathedral
LKO	Liddon Papers, Keble College Library, Oxford
LPO	Liddon Papers, Pusey House, Oxford
LRO	Liverpool Record Office
PLAB	Private Letters of Archbishop Benson
SDS	Selwyn Divinity School, Cambridge
SPL	St Paul's Cathedral Library, London
TCC	Wren Library, Trinity College, Cambridge
TLL	Tait Papers, Lambeth Palace Library, London

2. Other Printed Sources and Biographies

Alumni	Venn, *Alumni Cantabrigienses*
BL	*Bishop Lightfoot*
Crockfords	*Crockford's Clerical Directory*
DCB	*Dictionary of Christian Biography*
DDC	*Durham Diocesan Calendar*
DDG	*Durham Diocesan Gazette*
DDM	*Durham Diocesan Magazine*
DNB	*Dictionary of National Biography*
LB	*The Life of Edward White Benson*
LD	*Lightfoot of Durham*
LH	*Life and Letters of Fenton J.A. Hort*
LT	*Life of Archibald Campbell Tait, Archbishop of Canterbury*
LW	*Life and Letters of Brooke Foss Westcott*
PP	Parliamentary Papers
RCC	*Report of the Church Congress*
Reporter	*Cambridge University Reporter*

RV   *Revised Version of the Bible*
YJC   *York Journal of Convocation*

3. *Lightfoot's Published Writings*

AF   *The Apostolic Fathers*
BE   *Biblical Essays*
C   *St Paul's Epistle to the Colossians and to Philemon*
Ch   *A Charge Delivered to the Clergy of the Diocese of Durham*
ClR   *The Epistles of S. Clement of Rome*
ClRA   *S. Clement of Rome. Appendix*
CP   *Christian Progress*
CS   *Cambridge Sermons*
DJCS   *An Address Delivered to the Durham Junior Clerical Society*
EWSR   *Essays On a Work Entitled Supernatural Religion*
G   *The Epistle of St Paul to the Galatians*
HE   *Historical Essays*
IACC   *Inaugural Address. Delivered at the Cooperative Congress ... 1880*
IP   *The Increasing Purpose of God*
LA   *Address on the Distribution of Scholarships and Prizes of the Liverpool*
              Council of Education
LNC   *Leaders of the Northern Church*
LO   *Living Oracles*
LS   "J.B. Lightfoot On Strauss and Christian Origins"
MD   *Manifesto on Disestablishment*
MSL   *The Mustard Seed and the Leaven*
NEP   *Notes on the Epistles of St Paul*
NTI   "J.B. Lightfoot and New Testament Interpretation: An Unpublished Manuscript
              of 1855"
OA   *Ordination Addresses*
OFR   *On a Fresh Revision of the New Testament*
OSCG   "On the Style and Character of Galatians"
P   *St Paul's Epistle to the Philippians*
PC   *Primary Charge*
PH   "Papias of Hierapolis"
RE   "Recent Editions of St Paul's Epistles"
RRH   "Results of Recent Historical and Topographical Research Upon the Old and
              New Testament Scriptures"
S   *Sermons*
SCEG   "On the Style and Character of the Epistle to the Galatians"
SMPW   *Strength Made Perfect in Weakness*
SSP   *Sermons in St Pauls*
SSO   *Sermons On Special Occasions*
THCH   "They That Are of Caesar's Household"
TTT   *The Three Temples*
UC   *The Unity of the Church*
WCA   *An Address to Members of the White Cross Army*
WDWI   *What Disestablishment Would Involve. A Warning*

Prefatory Note

Apart from those specifically assigned to other locations, all manuscript sources referred to in the notes belong to the Lightfoot Papers housed in the Dean and Chapter Library, Durham Cathedral. Manuscript sermons are cited by an abbreviated title and the year in which they were first delivered. The word(s) used for citation purposes are italicized in the bibliography where the sermons are listed in chronological order.

In his unpublished writings Lightfoot's punctuation was often unconventional or incomplete. In particular, he tended to use dashes instead of full stops. As the story told about his sending rough versions of manuscripts to the printers suggests, and as the extant manuscripts confirm, he seems to have left the work of tidying up the formal aspects of his writings to compositors. In quotations, except where there is scope for misreading or misunderstanding, the punctuation and spelling is that of the original document.

Part I

Introduction

Chapter One

Lightfoot the Historian

"There is nothing sufficient on ... Lightfoot." So declared G.S.R. Kitson Clark, then doyen of the historians of Victorian England, in the Scott Lectures for 1964.[1] At one level his observation regrets the absence of a *Life and Letters*, the customary monument to, and basis for subsequent reflection upon, a notable Victorian life. This was probably due to a lack of suitable materials rather than the reasons usually given, Lightfoot's "own earnest desire",[2] and the lack of a widow or child to carry out the conventional act of filial piety.[3] Certainly such a work was contemplated,[4] and in the "sons of the house" at Auckland Castle there were suitable workers for the task.[5] But it did not come to fruition. The absence of a *Life and Letters* — and the preservation of valuable diary entries and revealing personal letters — should not therefore be lamented. Such materials do not seem to have existed in a sufficient quantity for a biography of the kind — massive and adulatory — the Victorians liked to write.[6]

---

[1]   G.S.R. Kitson Clark, *An Expanding Society 1830-1900* (Melbourne & Cambridge: Melbourne University Press/Cambridge Univerity Press, 1967) 98. Cf. G.M. Young, *Portrait of an Age. Victorian England* (annotated edition by G.S.R. Kitson Clark; London: Oxford University Press, 1977) 299.

[2]   LD 149.

[3]   Eg. M.L. Loane, "Joseph Barber Lightfoot Bishop of Durham 1828-1889," *Three Faithful Servants* (Blackwood, South Australia: New Creation Publications, 1991) 91.

[4]   J.R. Harmer to E.A. Macmillan, 30 May 1893, indicating that the Lightfoot Trustees were interested in the publication of a biography. An appeal for letters appeared in *The Times* on 2 June 1893. A. Hort to J.R. Harmer, 18 May & 22 May 1893, indicating that there were not many letters of Lightfoot's among his late father's papers.

[5]   For the Auckland Brotherhood, see 225-6 below.

[6]   On the characteristics and assumptions of Victorian biography, see R.D. Altick, *Lives and Letters. A History of Literary Biography in England and America* (Westport, Connecticut: Greenwood Press, 1979 [originally published, 1965]) esp. ch. VI & VII; and R. Hoberman, *Modernizing Lives. Experiments in English Biography, 1918-1939* (Carbondale and Edwardsville: Southern Illinois University Press, 1987) ch. II.

At a second level Clark's observation registers the absence of a substantial scholarly study of Lightfoot's life and work. For Clark this was a matter of some importance. His observation was made in the context of a dual protest: against the depreciation of Victorian religion by historians of the twentieth century; and against their canonization on the basis of abiding interest and importance of a handful of eminent thinkers as representative of the spiritual and intellectual history of nineteenth century Britain, to the exclusion of others "of considerable intelligence and also ... great power".[7] Joseph Barber Lightfoot (1828-1889), successively Hulsean and Lady Margaret Professor of Divinity at Cambridge University (1861 to 1879), Bishop of Durham (from 1879 until his death), and allegedly the greatest English language commentator of all time on New Testament texts,[8] was among those who, according to Clark, warranted detailed consideration if the Victorians were to be understood on their own terms and the variety and complexity of the period duly appreciated. In the ensuing thirty years much has taken place to rectify the situation of which Clark complained. The place of religion in Victorian society is now better appreciated in secular historiography,[9] and many of the individuals nominated have received the attention for which he called. B.F. Westcott, mentioned by Clark in the same sentence as Lightfoot, has been — to take the particularly pertinent example of his close friend, colleague, collaborator, and successor as Bishop of Durham — the subject of at least two major studies.[10] Yet the position with

---

[7]   A more recent plea for genuinely historical treatment of Victorian intellectual and cultural figures occurs in F.M. Turner, *Contesting Cultural Authority. Essays in Victorian Cultural Life* (Cambridge: University Press, 1993).

[8]   See J.D.G. Dunn, *Testing the Foundations. Current Trends In New Testament Study* (Durham: University of Durham, 1984) 1; & "Lightfoot the Critic," *A Christian Heritage - a Collection of Addresses in Honour of the 900th Anniversary of Durham Cathedral* (ed. C. Yeats; Bangor: Headstart History, 1993) 59.

[9]   Eg. D. Thompson, "The Making of the English Religious Classes," *The Historical Journal* 22.2 (1979) 477-91; D. Bebbington, "Religion and Society in the Nineteenth Century," *The Historical Journal* 32.4 (1989) 997-1004, esp. 1004; & H. McLeod, "Varieties of Victorian Belief," *Journal of Modern History* 64.2 (1992) 321-37.

[10]   W.G. O'Dea, "Westcott the Theologian" (unpublished M.Litt. thesis; Cambridge University, 1972). F. Olofsson, *Christus Redemptor Et Consummator. A Study in the Theology of B.F. Westcott* (trans. by N. Tomkinson assisted by J. Gray; Studia Doctrinae Christianae Upsaliensia 19; Stockholm: Almquist & Wiksell, 1979). There have also been several studies of the third member of the Cambridge 'triumvirate', F.J.A. Hort. See I.M. Bubb, "The Theology of F.J.A. Hort, In Relation to Nineteenth Century Thought" (unpublished Ph.D. thesis; Manchester University; 1956): & the two works by G.A. Patrick, "A Study of the Writings of F.J.A. Hort, and an Assessment of Him as a Biblical Scholar" (unpublished Ph.D. thesis; London University, 1978); & *F.J.A. Hort Eminent Victorian* (Sheffield: Almond Press, 1987).

Lightfoot is unaltered. More than a century after his death there is still "nothing sufficient on ... Lightfoot".[11]

Not all would agree that this is an important need. Of Lightfoot's contemporaries, F.W. Farrar, a pupil and a friend, doubted that the predictable biography would be of much use.[12] There was little to reveal of a character so simple and straightforward, and of a public life so uneventful. Lightfoot's books would be sufficient monument to his life and thought.[13] But this perspective assumes that the meaning and significance of the books is self-evident, a proposition which, a century later, is doubtful. Nor was Farrar a close associate (although an ex-pupil and regular correspondent), so that he takes much for granted. His, moreover, was a typically nineteenth century perspective on the function of biography. No longer concerned with memorializing, historical biography has moved on and aims rather at a critical appreciation of a life and the issues it raises in relation to its times in order to explain the individual, and to bring out both what he reflects of wider social developments, and also the contribution he made to the course of events and character of the times.[14] Lightfoot's life has not yet been approached in this manner.

Among contemporary scholars, the iconoclastic John Kent claims that the significance of Lightfoot has been exaggerated. This is because of the place assigned to him by the "Anglican Mythology" which, "largely formed in the Victorian period in Anglican circles", attributed to Lightfoot, Westcott and Hort "something like the intellectual salvation of Christianity".[15] But this only indicates the need for the tradition to be reassessed. The influence of which Kent complains is precisely the point that needs to be explained. Moreover, the implication that Lightfoot was orthodox and conservative is based on later standards, not those of his own day, and therefore requires revision. There has also been a questionable tendency to see Lightfoot in

---

[11] A desire for a biography is expressed again by C.S. Rodd, "Commentator Supreme," *Expository Times* 104 (January 1993) 128.

[12] F.W. Farrar, "Bishop Lightfoot," *Contemporary Review* 57 (February 1890) 170-1.

[13] R.H. Malden, "Bishop Lightfoot 1828-1889," *Great Christians* (ed. R.S. Forman; London: Nicholson & Watson, 1933) 335, says exactly the opposite:

It is a matter for regret that one of his greatest predecessors, and his only namesake, Joseph Butler, lives for us only in his books. Beyond what they reveal, nothing is known about him. It would have been lamentable had similar oblivion been allowed to overtake Lightfoot.

[14] See D. Beales, *History and Biography. An Inaugural Lecture* (Cambridge: University Press, 1981).

[15] J. Kent, "The Study of Ecclesiastical History Since 1930," *The Pelican Guide to Modern Theology* (eds J. Daniélou, A.H. Couratin and J. Kent; Harmondsworth: Penguin Books, 1969) 304.

terms of Westcott and Hort.[16] To be sure, he was (at least outwardly) less concerned with theology than either, but the implication that he had no theology to speak of is misleading. Lightfoot must surely rank among those noteworthy Anglicans who, according to Kent in later works, are due for scholarly reassessment.[17] A critical study will partly redress this larger deficiency as well as offer a much needed revaluation of a prominent Victorian Church leader.

This is not to say that Lightfoot has been entirely neglected. From among contemporaries F.J.A. Hort and H.W. Watkins furnish narrative outlines of his life. Hort poured out what was left of his own life on the *Dictionary of National Biography* entry.[18] A friend and fellow student at Trinity College, collaborator in theological projects, and colleague in the Cambridge Divinity faculty and professoriate, Hort is most informative on the University and scholarly aspects: the episcopate he knew mainly by report. These positions are reversed for Watkins' memoir.[19] Brought to Durham from St Augustine's, Canterbury, to be Archdeacon of Northumberland, he rapidly became Lightfoot's chief *aide de camp*, and in the eyes of some, the real bishop of Durham.[20] Both men were well placed to observe closely one or other of the two main phases in the public career, and they wrote soon after the events recounted. Minor errors apart, their complementary accounts provide a narrative framework which, so far as it goes, it is unnecessary to challenge.

Less satisfactory is the volume which has served as the main source for Lightfoot's life over the last sixty years. In 1932 members of the Auckland Brotherhood published *Lightfoot of Durham: Memories and Appreciations.*[21]

---

[16] Eg. L. Elliott-Binns, *Religion in the Victorian Era* (2nd ed.; London: Lutterworth Press, 1946) ch. 15; & *English Thought 1860-1900. The Theological Aspect* (London: Longmans, Green & Co., 1956) esp. 119-20.

[17] J. Kent, *The Unacceptable Face of the Church. The Modern Church in the Eyes of the Historian* (London: S.C.M., 1987) 82-106; & *William Temple. Church, State and Society in Britain, 1880-1950* (Cambridge: University Press, 1992).

[18] F.J.A. Hort, "Lightfoot, Joseph Barber," *DNB* XI.1111-1119. For the personal significance of Hort's article, see D.L. Edwards, *Leaders of the Church of England 1828-1944* (London: Oxford University Press, 1971) 190.

[19] "Bishop Lightfoot," *Quarterly Review* 176 (January 1893) 73-105. Republished as *Bishop Lightfoot. Reprinted From the Quarterly Review, With a Prefatory Note by B.F. Westcott* (London: Macmillan, 1894), to which future reference is made. For the attribution, *The Wellesley Index to Victorian Periodicals 1824-1900* (ed. W.E. Houghton; Toronto & London: University of Toronto Press/Routledge & Kegan Paul, 1966) I.774.

[20] Watkins was "both hand & eye" to Lightfoot. Lightfoot to Watkins, 24 February 1880 (DUL, Ad'l MS 132). Also Lightfoot to Gladstone, 29 December 1882 (GBL, 44 478, f. 289). H.H. Henson, *More Letters of Hensley Henson* (ed. E.F. Braley; London: S.P.C.K., 1954) 70.

[21] G.R. Eden & F.C. Macdonald (eds), *Lightfoot of Durham. Memories and Appreciations* (Cambridge: University Press, 1932). Not all contributors had been members of the Brotherhood, but all had come under Lightfoot's influence when they were young men.

Written on a larger scale than either Hort or Watkins, it preserves much detail about what might be called the "inside history" of the Durham episcopate, as well as many revealing personal anecdotes. On the other hand, the account reproduces the teleology implicit in the title. More than three quarters of the book are on the last decade. This suggests that the life at Durham is what made Lightfoot significant. All else was prelude to this. As a result the treatment is unbalanced, with the longer period at Cambridge and the eight years at St Paul's in London being skated over. Most serious was the embarrassingly eulogizing tone which perpetuated the Lightfoot myth. At several points indeed Lightfoot's mien seems to resemble that of Jesus, and the response of his "Sons", that of the disciples.[22] In fact the book is really about those who wrote it. The chief significance of *Lightfoot of Durham* is its documentation of the main influence in the formation of a number of Church leaders of the interwar period.[23]

Some of these failings are reproduced in the one attempt to date at a scholarly life. D.J. Wilson's Edinburgh doctoral thesis (of which Clark was evidently unaware) broke some new ground in its use of previously unknown letters by Lightfoot, and by relating his career to the history of ministerial training in the nineteenth century.[24] The specific concern of this study necessarily involved restoring the Cambridge period of Lightfoot's life to proper prominence, while Wilson also gave the first account of Lightfoot's theology.[25] Nevertheless, something of the older teleology survives. The Durham episcopate, and in particular the creation of the Auckland Brotherhood, is regarded as the high point of Lightfoot's life. Moreover, some significant episodes in Lightfoot's previous career, such as the Revised Version and the canonry at St Paul's, are again overlooked. This was mainly due to Wilson's heavy reliance on *Lightfoot of Durham* which he described as "an admirable book".[26] His account was therefore similarly unrepresentative of the ca-

---

[22] LD 43, 44, 80.

[23] Men such as G.R. Eden (1853-1940), Bishop of Wakefield, 1897-1928; J.R. Harmer (1857-1944), Bishop of Adelaide, 1895-1905, and of Rochester, 1905-30; J. Armitage Robinson (1858-1940), Norrisian Professor of Divinity, 1893-9, Dean of Westminster, 1902-11, Dean of Wells, 1911-33; & H.E. Savage (1854-1939), Dean of Lichfield, 1909-39. See further Appendix B, in LD 166-73.

[24] D.J. Wilson, "The Life of J.B. Lightfoot (1829 [sic]-89), with special reference to the training of the ministry" (unpublished Ph.D. thesis; Edinburgh University, 1956). See also the attempt to provide "an orderly chronological narrative" in Loane, "Lightfoot," 91-119 (92 for the quotation).

[25] Curiously, however, he did not give any account of Lightfoot's scholarship as such.

[26] Wilson, "Life," 111. Cf. "the excellent book of reminiscences", *ibid.*, 167. Wilson also made only a limited use of the main deposit of Lightfoot Papers at Durham Cathedral, while his account is marred by several errors of fact (for which, see the body of the study below).

reer as a whole, and while several criticisms were ventured, no fresh perspective was developed. These deficiencies are mostly traceable to its function as a "theological" biography. It aimed to abstract a system of thought,
and gave insufficient recognition to the importance of the environment out
of which the system emerged.

Students of the New Testament and early church, particularly those working in the Cambridge-Durham tradition,[27] have also evinced a significant
interest in Lightfoot as a scholar they readily acknowledge as a progenitor.[28]
Much of this has been eulogistic,[29] but in recent years C.K. Barrett has led a
welcome shift to a more critical perspective.[30] Yet these studies are written
from an internalist standpoint, and are characterized by the "whiggism" which
inevitably arises from a concern with the "state of the question". Thus their
purpose is to establish what Lightfoot contributed to the discipline as it is
currently practised.[31] There have been two important results for the interpretation of Lightfoot's life and work.

For one thing it has meant that the accepted setting for Lightfoot's scholarship remains the debate over the interpretation of early Christian literature
provoked by the Tübingen School between 1830 and 1860. Within this line
of study two issues have emerged. On the one hand, the image of Lightfoot
as "the slayer of Tübingen" has persisted. However, the extent and effectiveness of Lightfoot's engagement with Tübingen has been challenged.
Barrett pointed out that the number of direct references to the Tübingen writers is not so considerable as the received view would suggest and require.
Barrett's re-appraisal, which assumes that Lightfoot conducted his case in a
certain manner, attracted a powerful reply from Martin Hengel in relation to

---

[27] On which see the dedication of M. Hengel, *The Johannine Question* (London &
Philadelphia: S.C.M./Trinity International, 1989). In explanation Hengel says, "I dedicate
this book in gratitude to the theological faculties of the universities of Cambridge and
Durham. A great scholar, Bishop Joseph Barber Lightfoot, worked in both of them, in the
former as a professor, in the latter as a great church leader; our discipline owes much to
him for his study of the second century and thus also of the Johannine corpus, and this
year is his centenary."

[28] The culmination is J.D.G. Dunn (ed.), *The Lightfoot Centenary Lectures To Commemorate the Life and Work of Bishop J.B. Lightfoot (1828-89), Durham University Journal*, extra complimentary number for subscribers (January 1992).

[29] Eg. W.F. Howard, *The Romance of New Testament Scholarship* (London: Epworth,
1949) ch. 3.

[30] C.K. Barrett, "Joseph Barber Lightfoot," *Durham University Journal* LXIV.3 (June
1972) 193-204; "Quomodo Historia Conscribenda Sit," *New Testament Studies* 28.3 (July
1982) 303-20; & "J.B. Lightfoot as Biblical Commentator," in Dunn (ed.), *The Lightfoot
Centenary Lectures*, 53-70.

[31] A striking recent example is J.D.G. Dunn, "Lightfoot in Retrospect," his contribution to Dunn (ed.), *The Lightfoot Centenary Lectures*, 71-94.

the Fourth Gospel.[32] A full account of Lightfoot's scholarly career taking into consideration his actual mode of working will help to settle this question of the importance of the Tübingen School in his concerns as a New Testament scholar.

More interesting is the matter of how well Lightfoot answered Tübingen and whether the encounter had a reflexive effect on his own perspective. Barrett argues that Lightfoot's achievement was to destroy the dating of the Tübingen reconstruction and provide a solid chronological framework within which the New Testament documents can be placed. The effect was not to negate the conflicts said to be characteristic of earliest Christianity but inadvertently to push them and their consequences back into the first century.[33] Though he admitted conflict in the early church, Lightfoot did not face up to the issues this raised.

The second result of the internalist perspective is the use of the leader of the Tübingen School, F.C. Baur, as the yardstick by which to identify Lightfoot's distinctive characteristics as a scholar and to measure his achievement. Again this is best exemplified in Barrett. He contrasts Lightfoot's combination of a vigorous scholarship and an apparently timid attitude towards the New Testament documents with Baur's willingness to interrogate the evidence more radically in order to penetrate beneath the surface statements. For Barrett, Baur shows what sort of questions need to be asked, and Lightfoot how to answer them.[34] But this kind of comparison with (arguably) the most original and daring New Testament scholar of the day leads to the impression that Lightfoot was a theological conservative. He and Baur then become symbols in contemporary debate for different approaches to New Testament study.[35] For those wishing to justify and bolster a conservative view of the New Testament as the basis for Christian faith and practice, Lightfoot is a hero,[36] while those with more radical or strictly scholarly agendas tend to exalt Baur.[37] Either way the impression is left behind

---

[32] M. Hengel, "Bishop Lightfoot and the Tübingen School on the Gospel of John and the Second Century," in Dunn (ed.), *The Lightfoot Centenary Lectures*, 23-51.

[33] This is the basis of Dunn's use of Lightfoot and Baur in J.D.G. Dunn, *The Parting of the Ways Between Christianity and Judaism and Their Significance for the Character of Christianity* (London & Philadelphia: S.C.M./Trinity Press, 1991) 1-4.

[34] Barrett, "Quomodo," 318.

[35] Eg. W.W. Gasque, *A History of the Criticism of the Acts of the Apostles* (Grand Rapids: William B. Eerdmans, 1975) esp. ch. 6; & "Nineteenth-century Roots of Contemporary New Testament Criticism," *Scripture, Tradition and Interpretation* (eds W.W. Gasque & W.S. La Sor; Grand Rapids: Eerdmans, 1978) 146-56.

[36] Eg. W.W. Wiersbe, "Lightfoot: a Devoted Scholar," *Moody Monthly* 76 (April 1976) 127-31; & F.F. Bruce, "J.B. Lightfoot (died 1889): Commentator and Theologian," *Evangel* 7 (Summer 1989) 10-12.

[37] Eg. P.C. Hodgson, *The Formation of Historical Theology. A Study of Ferdinand Christian Baur* (New York: Harper & Row, 1966).

that Lightfoot himself was a conservative and held to a conservative view of the New Testament.

There is some tension for both points of view in this use of Lightfoot. He is freely recognized as a guarded protagonist of the new critical methods of Biblical study pioneered in Germany, and therefore the harbinger of important changes in the English approach.[38] This makes him more or less conservative depending on one's presuppositions. Moreover, the clear assumption in this debate is that 'conservative' meant the same thing in his day as in our own. Most importantly, therefore, it may be questioned whether juxtaposition with Baur is the appropriate method for appreciating Lightfoot's life and work. Against the background of the Victorian Church he does not look like a conservative. This is a term more aptly assigned, for example, to High Churchmen like J.W. Burgon and H.P. Liddon with whom Lightfoot disagreed on questions of text and exegesis.[39] Given the well known resistance to German methods among Victorian Churchmen,[40] Lightfoot's 'Germanizing' does not fit the categorization of 'conservative' either. Nor were the results of his early church studies universally acceptable to contemporaries.[41] Yet his work was not so unsettling as that of another product of Birmingham's King Edward's School, Edwin Hatch.[42] The ideological use of Lightfoot has obscured his standing as a New Testament scholar in his own day.

Their internalist perspective notwithstanding, the work of these writers has not been without important results. In particular they have raised the important question of the relation of Lightfoot's scholarship to the contemporary English context. Once more it was Barrett who took the lead by inquiring into the theological setting in which Lightfoot did his work in order to explain the differences to be discerned between between him and Baur. Relying on an essay by John Rogerson, he claimed that Lightfoot was typical of the philosophical climate of contemporary English theology, with its emphasis upon the externality of the sources of knowledge, and the concomitant minimization of the role of the perceiving subject which has been

---

[38] J.A.T. Robinson acclaimed Lightfoot as "The Champion of Critical Scholarship", MS sermon preached at St Botolph's Church, Cambridge, 7 November 1976 [copy in the Wren Library, TCC]. Also his *The Roots of a Radical* (London: S.C.M., 1980) 155-61.

[39] Lightfoot might also be contrasted with an evangelical like Charles Perry with whom he disagreed strongly on ecclesiological matters. See Chapter 9 below. For Perry, see S. Piggin, "Perry, Charles," *The Australian Dictionary of Evangelical Biography* (ed. B. Dickey; Sydney: Evangelical History Association, 1994) 303-6.

[40] J.S. Andrews, "German Influence on English Religious Life in the Victorian Era," *Evangelical Quarterly* 44 (Oct.-Dec. 1972) 218-33.

[41] See 333, 355-6, & 369-70 below.

[42] On whom, see N.F. Josaitis, *Edwin Hatch and Early Church Order* (Gembloux: Éditions J. Duculot, S.A., 1971) esp. Chapters 4 and 5.

described as a "Lockean sort of supernaturalism".[43] According to this view, Lightfoot was predisposed religiously and epistemologically to a methodology which stressed the accumulation of evidence from received documents, and the derivation of conclusions from it. Since this approach was said to be controlled by the application of "ordinary sense", Barrett has characterized Lightfoot as a "common sense empiricist".[44]

Clearly this is a legitimate and much needed line of inquiry, but its initial results involve several difficulties. It has to be said, first, that Barrett has oversimplified the intellectual context of English theology in the period.[45] A Lockean epistemology *was* widespread and influential in theology, especially in the 'evidences' approach. But it was not in undisputed possession of the field. S.T. Coleridge — regarded ever since John Stuart Mill as one of the two seminal minds of the age — had put up an alternative which was influential at Cambridge among Lightfoot's contemporaries (especially those with whom he was an undergraduate and Fellow at Trinity College in the late 1840s and 1850s).[46] *A priori* there is at least the possibility that Lightfoot was similarly aligned.

Second, the combination of "common sense" and "empiricist" is unfortunate. In fairness to Barrett, it should be allowed that he used the term in a non-technical sense as that inductive process which is natural to the inquiring mind, untroubled by the complications of metaphysics or methodology.[47] Yet placed against the backdrop of the period it is confusing, even a contradiction in terms. "Common sense" was a philosophy of intuitive knowledge developed in Scotland in the eighteenth century in reaction to the scepticism of David Hume.[48] It was carried forward into the nineteenth century by Sir William Hamilton and developed into an intuitionist philosophy by William Whewell, the Master of Lightfoot's Cambridge college. By this time the "empiricism" descended from Locke and Hume was represented by John

[43] J.W. Rogerson, "Philosophy and the Rise of Biblical Criticism: England and Germany," *England and Germany: Studies in Theological Diplomacy* (ed. S. Sykes; Frankfurt Am Main: Verlag Peter D. Lang, 1982) 63-79.

[44] Barrett, "Quomodo," 318.

[45] The standard accounts are V.F. Storr, *The Development of English Theology in the Nineteenth Century 1800-1860* (London: Longmans, Green & Co., 1913); & B.M.G. Reardon, *From Coleridge to Gore. A Century of Religious Thought in Britain* (London: Longman, 1971).

[46] See below 51-7. The influence of Mill at Cambridge was perhaps not so unchallenged as Noel Annan suggests in *Leslie Stephen. His Thought and Character in Relation to his Time* (London: MacGibbon & Kee, 1951) ch. IV.

[47] This attitude was available among contemporaries in the thought of Macaulay. T.B. Macaulay, "Francis Bacon," *Edinburgh Review* lxv (1837) 1-104, esp. 81-92.

[48] S.A. Grave, *The Scottish Philosophy of Common Sense* (Oxford: Clarendon Press, 1960). For an historical account, G.E. Davie, *The Democratic Intellect. Scotland and her Universities in the Nineteenth Century* (Edinburgh: University Press, 1961).

Stuart Mill. His *System of Logic* sought to establish the logic of the natural and social sciences together and held out the promise of such a progress of knowledge that a complete science of society would be possible in time. Throughout the early Victorian period a controversy raged between the two perspectives.[49] Both looked to induction as the method of discovery but differed on how discovery actually takes place. Whereas the empiricist Mill maintained that knowledge was derived as a generalization from particular instances, Whewell claimed the meaning of particular instances was perceived from the innate fundamental ideas of the observer which derive ultimately from the mind of God.[50] Victory in the battle is often said to have gone to empiricism, and Mill became influential in Cambridge in the 1850s and 1860s.[51] By using "common sense" as he does, Barrett puts Lightfoot closer to Mill than to Whewell, an unlikely contingency. While his formulation has the great advantage of locating Lightfoot in one of the key debates of the period, he seems to put Lightfoot on the wrong side. Some other characterization, and some other explanation of Lightfoot's handling of New Testament texts, will have to be found.

The question of Lightfoot's relation to the setting of his own times was raised in another way by one of Barrett's colleagues at Durham. In his own attempt to differentiate Lightfoot from Baur, B.N. Kaye asked what wider social and ecclesiastical interests Lightfoot's scholarship served, and thereby raised the question of how it was affected by the situation of the contemporary English Church.[52] This was a valuable contribution because it impugned the validity of the monocausal interpretation of Lightfoot's life and work implicit in the use of the Tübingen School as the frame of reference. But Kaye did not follow up the question at any length. While he touched on Lightfoot's treatment of the ministry in particular, the matter in general was left for others to pursue. Kaye's question is therefore still on the agenda. With it goes its reciprocal: what role did Lightfoot's scholarship play in contemporary Church life? The question of the relation of his scholarship to its intellectual, social and ecclesiastical context remains to be settled.

----

[49] E.W. Strong, "William Whewell and John Stuart Mill: Their Controversy About Scientific Knowledge," *Journal of the History of Ideas* XVI.2 (April 1955) 209-31. The controversy is a major theme of A. Ryan, *J.S. Mill* (London & Boston: Routledge & Kegan Paul, 1974).

[50] This combination of thought with things in the generation of knowledge may be regarded as 'empiricalism'.

[51] N. Annan, *Leslie Stephen. The Godless Victorian* (New York: Random House, 1984) ch. 6.

[52] B.N. Kaye, "Lightfoot and Baur on Early Christianity," *Novum Testamentum* 26 (1984) 193-224. Now General Secretary of the General Synod of the Anglican Church of Australia, Dr Kaye was Senior Tutor at St John's College, Durham, when the paper was composed.

Questions of this sort are of interest to historians who are concerned with past lives and the issues they raise. But among recent historians of nineteenth century British Christianity only Owen Chadwick, writing in the same tradition, has paid significant attention to Lightfoot.[53] He was in fact one of the heroes of Chadwick's story of the recovery of the Church of England, because of the part he took in strengthening its understanding of the Bible and adjusting its teaching to new historical perceptions. Indeed Lightfoot is said to have created "almost unsupported, the standards of scholarship which hitherto could be found only in the universities of Germany" (recognition in passing that Lightfoot was not quite the conservative that early church scholars believe him to have been).[54] On the other hand, the Durham episcopate was overlooked, in spite of its obvious relevance to the second of Chadwick's themes, the adjustment of the churches to new social conditions created by industrialization and population increase. This is an omission Lightfoot would have felt. In his view it was in Durham where these problems were faced most acutely that the work of the Church of England was being done.[55] In historiography, too, the treatment of Lightfoot remains fragmentary and incomplete.

The first aim of the present study therefore is the provision of a strictly historical account of Lightfoot's life and thought, understood as a comprehensive and integrated recovery as far as possible of what he actually thought and did throughout his public career. The setting will not be confined to the debate with Baur and the Tübingen School but broadened to the life of the contemporary English church and society. In taking this approach the intention is to establish the range and variety of Lightfoot's concerns, the basis of his hopes and aspirations and the character of his thought, and to reach an assessment of his significance in his own day.

In making this claim it needs to be stressed that the investigation is not intended to be a personal biography but the preliminary to one. While observations on Lightfoot's character and motives will be offered where they can be substantiated, the sources do not permit that probing of the "inner man" which has become the hallmark of latter twentieth-century biography. To a large extent this was intentional. It was part of Lightfoot's piety not to speak of himself,[56] and much material bearing on his personal life seems to have been systematically destroyed.[57] As a result it is mostly the public

---

[53] O. Chadwick, *The Victorian Church* (Pt II, 2nd ed.; London: Adam & Charles Black, 1972) esp. 46-55 & 68-71.

[54] O. Chadwick, *Creighton on Luther* (Cambridge: University Press, 1959) 2.

[55] See 221 below.

[56] Cf. "All this is dreadfully egotistical; and I don't know that I ever said or wrote so much about myself before." Lightfoot to Tait, 22 November 1867 (TLL, vol. 283, f. 266).

[57] See the introduction to the Bibliography, 394-5 below.

figure who is on display in the materials out of which an account of his life must be written. For such an historical or intellectual biography, focusing on Lightfoot's social concerns and ideas, the Lightfoot Papers, investigated thoroughly for the first time for the present study, yield a great deal of new information. The thousands of letters, particularly the correspondence with Westcott, which ranges over the whole of Lightfoot's adult life, provides something of the previously unknown private setting for his public career as well as revealing numerous unsuspected aspects. Some occasional pieces ignored by his literary executors disclose the interest in D.F. Strauss and J.S. Mill, which is important for understanding the formation and development of his thought. Also important are the 230 manuscript sermons, written out in full, which provide a continual expression of his characteristic theological ideas and religious conceptions over the period 1854 to 1889. Since sermons are counsels of perfection, they also indicate the ideals Lightfoot placed before his people in each of the constituencies where he attempted to direct opinion and conduct. Thus the attempt at a genuine historical presentation gives rise to a more varied and deeper picture than would have appeared had Lightfoot's books been taken (with Farrar) as sufficient monument to his life and thought.

The specific means to this biographical end is the stereotype purveyed in the literature. Stephen Neill is typical of attempts to differentiate the writings and temperaments of Lightfoot, Westcott and Hort, the three men who constituted the so-called "Cambridge Triumvirate":

> Though all shared many gifts in common, Lightfoot was primarily the historian, Hort the philosopher, and Westcott the exegete.[58]

As usually presented, this characterization of "Lightfoot the historian" implies that ideas in general, and theology in particular, were of no great interest. What counted with Lightfoot was the accumulation of the facts of early Christian history through unremitting toil, and their dispassionate presentation in big books which by their very scale were authoritative. Lightfoot in this perspective becomes a representative in theology of that hopeful but naive positivism which was characteristic of much Victorian intellectual endeavour.

The pervasiveness of this stereotype conceals the fact that Lightfoot's credentials as an historian were once doubted. William Sanday — for a short time Lightfoot's Examining Chaplain, and (arguably) England's leading New Testament scholar of the next generation — once observed:

> Bishop Lightfoot wrote nothing that would come exactly under the popular designation "history". He was an historian lost to his craft. From the point of view of the historical critic, his writings are a series of *disjecta membra*, which were never gath-

---

[58] S. Neill, *The Interpretation of the New Testament 1861-1961* (London: Oxford University Press, 1964) 34. Cf. Reardon, *From Coleridge to Gore*, 346-55, esp. 346-7.

ered together into a connected or articulated whole. The history in them comes in by the way; it is not the first object.[59]

As a result Sanday wrote to secure the proper appreciation of a mentor's achievement in a quarter where it might be overlooked. While the historical component was more substantial than Sanday recognized — the works published posthumously were not yet available — he has drawn attention to a cardinal feature of Lightfoot's writings. His books were editions, albeit executed with introductions and dissertations on a scale quite new in the English study of earliest Christianity, in which the composition of historical narrative was not the leading priority. Moreover, neither of the projected histories was ever written. Clearly Lightfoot's first concern as a scholar was with documents, the provision of a reliable text and its elucidation. This was due partly to the requirements of the subject matter, and partly to the effects of the rise of the higher criticism of the New Testament. But temperament also played a part. In fact, it was to Sanday that Lightfoot wrote:

> if there is any lucidity in my writing, I owe it ... to a natural want of fluency, which obliges me to choose my words.[60]

It appears that he was happier when dealing with the empirical record — determining the text, writing critical notes, and establishing specific facts — than with the more adventurous work of constructing and synthesizing to produce a narrative, although the work was done when necessary, and done well.

It does not follow, however, that Lightfoot was not writing history. In making the failure to write a connected narrative his criterion, Sanday reveals that his expectations were still controlled by the historiography of mid-century. The rise of "scientific history", characterized by the rigorously critical treatment of documents as an integral part of the historical enterprise, made available another perspective on Lightfoot's work. In 1886 no less an authority than Lord Acton made the particularly pertinent observation:

> When Germans assert that their real supremacy rests with their historians, they mean it ... in the sense in which the Bishop of Durham and Sir Henry Maine take the lead in England, the sense in which M. Fustel de Coulanges calls history the most arduous of the sciences. A famous scholar, enumerating the models of historical excellence, named Humboldt, Savigny, Grimm and Ritter, not one of whom had ever written history proper, in the common, classical, literary use of the term.[61]

On another occasion Acton associated Lightfoot and Henry Maine with F.W. Maitland — another who completed large works of historical erudition —

---

[59] W. Sanday, "Bishop Lightfoot as an Historian," *English Historical Review* V.viii (April 1890) 208-20 (the quotation is on 209).

[60] Lightfoot to Sanday, 17 July 1886 (BLO, MSS Eng.misc.d.124 (i), ff. 165-6).

[61] J.E.E. Dalberg-Acton, *Historical Essays and Studies* (ed. J.N. Figgis & R.V. Laurence; London: Macmillan, 1907) 344-5.

as "our three Cambridge historians".[62] Acton himself, of course, also wrote no large historical narrative but became the chief spokesman for the view that historical records speak meaningfully and definitively of the past and by themselves alone establish what actually happened. Very importantly, therefore, Lightfoot is claimed as a member (or at least a precursor) of the positivist school of historians that emerged at Cambridge in the closing decades of the nineteenth century and included such other notable scholars as Mandell Creighton and J.B. Bury.[63]

From within his own field of expertise, moreover, there were scholars who passed a judgment directly opposed to Sanday's. The great Adolf von Harnack not only took Lightfoot's standing as an historian for granted but regarded him as a master of the craft:

> If all investigators in the department of Ancient Church History would go to work with the same specialist acquirements and the same circumspection as Lightfoot, the number of points which are now the subject of controversy would be wonderfully reduced.[64]

To A.C. Headlam, possibly Lightfoot's greatest admirer among the next generation of English early church scholars, it seemed that Lightfoot alone deserved credit for the existence of "solid attainable facts even in Early Church History".[65] Contemporary practitioners continue to regard Lightfoot as the pioneer in England of the historical method in their field of study.[66] What the more widely recognized William Stubbs was attempting at the time for the Middle Ages, Lightfoot essayed for the history of earliest Christianity. While his books do not exhibit the full range of the historian's activities, he was not an historian lost to his craft. Rather Lightfoot was an historian of distinction in a new tradition: in fact, England's first "scientific" historian of the early church.

Statements sown broadcast throughout his *oeuvre* where the word 'history' is used in all its ambiguity indicate that he was an historian in other senses.[67] In speaking of "this world's history", for example, Lightfoot was referring to its life course, or the sum of experience. The same sense could be applied to all the entities of history, so that he could speak of "the history

---

[62] Quoted in H.A.L. Fisher, *F.W. Maitland* (Cambridge: University Press, 1910) 174.

[63] The term 'positivist' does not require any commitment to Positivism. Indeed Lightfoot spurned Comtism. Lightfoot to Stanley, 3 July 1869 (GBL, 44 318, f. 83). For Bury, see D. Goldstein, "J.B. Bury's Philosophy of History: A Reappraisal," *American Historical Review* 82 (1977) 896-919. On Creighton, see 60-1 below.

[64] A. von Harnack, "Bishop Lightfoot's *Ignatius and Polycarp*," *The Expositor* 3rd series II (1885) 401-2. For Harnack's appreciation of Lightfoot's early church scholarship, see further in Appendix 3 below.

[65] A.C. Headlam, "Lightfoot's Apostolic Fathers," *Quarterly Review* 182 (October 1895) 372.

[66] Barrett, "Quomodo," 303, 318.

[67] The examples which follow were chosen more or less at random. They have numerous parallels.

of the nation",[68] "the Apostolic history",[69] "the history of chivalry"[70] and "the history of ... vice".[71] While he also tended to distinguish "past history"[72] and "future history",[73] all were components of history as experience. It was built up by a continuous sequence of presents which could be referred to as "contemporary history".[74] A reference to "the one great crisis in the history of the Church, on the issue of which was staked her future progress and triumph",[75] indicated that each present was a moment for action requiring choice before the openness of the future. Such moments took place in the midst of all the pressures of social existence which included the legacy of the past. They held out the opportunity to influence the future and to change the world. This was history lived and made. For Lightfoot its possibilities for manifestly meaningful action were encapsulated in the expression "the stage of the world's history".[76]

The connotations of the related notion of "the drama of this world's history"[77] and other similar literary conceptions —[78] in particular, author, plot, theme and denouement — also imply Lightfoot's belief in an interpretation of history itself. This was a possibility he was happy to affirm, but he did not underestimate the difficulty of discerning it:

> All history is a parable of God's dealings; and we must learn the interpretation of the parable.[79]

That Lightfoot believed himself to have succeeded is evident in references to "universal history"[80] and "progressive history",[81] with their implication of unity and purposive movement in "the history of the world".[82] That he made out patterns is shown in the claim, "History was destined to repeat itself".[83] Such utterances almost invariably occur incidentally, and the immediate context seldom clarifies meaning. Yet they seem to be reflections of an understanding of history which there has been no substantial previous

---

[68]   Attracting Power, 1874, 3.
[69]   God's Witness, 1875, 1.
[70]   Edifying, 1869, 19.
[71]   Moral Freedom, 1873, 27-8.
[72]   SSP 203.
[73]   Eagles, 1873, 6-7.
[74]   SSP 258.
[75]   G 292.
[76]   Old Things, 1872, 1; Vanity, 1878, 30; Sudden Coming, 1881, 15; SSO 227; LNC 60.
[77]   Charge, 1880, 8.
[78]   Eg. "the pages of history" in Eagles, 1873, 23.
[79]   CS 310.
[80]   CS 131, 132.
[81]   Attracting Power, 1874, 1.
[82]   Triumph, 1874, 24.
[83]   Valley, 1873, 3. Cf. "Will not history repeat itself?" RCC (1881) 16.

attempt to examine. To a large extent, the function of the investigation is to assign these expressions to their contexts and to trace their consequences in Lightfoot's life and thought.

Its second aim, then, is to expound the stereotype "Lightfoot the Historian" by following the lines of enquiry implicit in the ambiguity of the word 'history'. That Lightfoot practised the discipline of history may now be taken as axiomatic. Less certain is his status and character as an historical thinker.[84] If it can be shown that he was one who attempted to comprehend all that happens in time, and especially to connect the present moment with the larger process of which it is part as a guide to thought and conduct, much will have been accomplished towards, first, explaining his life and achievement and, second, assigning him his place in the English intellectual and ecclesiastical tradition. If, moreover, it can be shown that this was fundamental to his career as Churchman and scholar, the way will be open to the composition of that critical biography which is still a desideratum in the historiography of the Victorian Church.

While in this concentration on the man and his thought the investigation has obvious affinities with the history of ideas, the interest in Lightfoot as a Churchman and scholar operating in a larger social situation identifies it as primarily a contribution to the religious history of Victorian England. According to one of its major organs, religious history is that branch of social history which seeks to understand religious aspiration and its significance in the culture in which it takes place.[85] Thus it is not historical theology, which is concerned with how men of different eras have thought about the problems of formal doctrine. Nor is it ecclesiastical history, as traditionally conducted a branch of administrative history concerned with the Church as an institution. Both approaches, of course, will be involved, and, at times, basic to the discussion. But the scope of religion, and therefore of religious history, is wider and deeper than both. By examining how men have formed and answered the ultimate questions about themselves and the universe, the study of religion goes beyond the appearances of ecclesiastical and social machinery, and behind the subtleties of ratiocination about metaphysical entities, to the complex domain of human consciousness.[86] As a result, the data of religious history consist of beliefs, values and sentiments, together with their results in behavioural and organizational terms, viewed in relation to the forces at work in society at large. This is by no means to reduce

---

[84] See the introduction to Part II, 60-2 below.

[85] B. Mansfield, "J.R.H. - A Memoir at Twenty Years," *Journal of Religious History* XI.1 (June 1980) 5-6. Cf. C. Brooke et. al., "What is Religious History?" *History Today* 35 (August 1985) 43-52.

[86] For this understanding of religion, see E.J. Sharpe, *Understanding Religion* (London: Duckworth, 1983).

them to something else. Indeed religious history affirms the importance of religion in past human experience and of the religious factor in human understanding and motivation. But it also recognizes that wider influences, often secular and material, help to shape religious consciousness and experience. As originally developed by the *Annales* school, this methodology was directed more to the study of groups than individuals.[87] Nevertheless, it has obvious advantages for understanding intellectuals like Lightfoot who were also self-consciously religious leaders.[88] Their space-time experience provided the social co-ordinates in which specific Christian thinking and teaching took place. In Lightfoot's case, the perspective of religious history discloses what he himself believed and did as a devoutly religious man, and what as a religious leader he thought others should believe and do, in response to the social setting of mid- and late-Victorian England.

The importance of this approach for understanding Lightfoot's career was grasped by Hensley Henson, Bishop of Durham from 1920 to 1939, in commenting on the projected volume *Lightfoot of Durham*.[89] There was a need, he claimed, for a "very careful description of the actual milieu in which he worked". Henson in fact thought that so favourable were the conditions of the time that Lightfoot had had an "easy run". Part of his point, that the Lightfoot phenomenon was not so amazing as was commonly supposed, was that his munificence was made possible by low costs and few taxes. No doubt in this assessment there was some of the irritation the dyspeptic Henson was inclined to feel at having to live in the shadow of a "golden age" during a time of industrial decline and economic depression. But the importance of contemporary conditions in Lightfoot's success is a point that can be made many times over. The much vaunted Lightfoot Scholarship for Ecclesiastical History, for example, was made possible by the evidently ample returns on his investments. In other words, Lightfoot was a beneficiary of the prosperity of the mid-Victorian economy, and in particular of its railway boom. No more than other intellectuals was he exempt from Keith Robbins' point that they "would have had little impact without the ability to correspond with each other and their readers through the post on the one hand, and to publish their articles and books on the other".[90] Both were greatly facili-

---

[87] B. Mansfield, "Lucien Febvre and the Study of Religious History," *Journal of Religious History* I.2 (December 1960) 102-11.

[88] See the caveats of E.R. Norman & P. Collinson in Brooke et. al., "Religious History," 45, 46.

[89] H.H. Henson to F.C. Macdonald, 29 January 1931, *More Letters of Hensley Henson*, 69-72. Cf. H.H. Henson, "Bishop Lightfoot," *Bishoprick Papers* (London: Oxford University Press, 1946) 133-40. Henson's observations are behind LD xiv-v. See also O. Chadwick, *Hensley Henson. A Study in the Friction Between Church and State* (Oxford: Clarendon Press, 1983).

[90] K. Robbins, *Nineteenth-Century Britain. Integration and Diversity* (Oxford: Clarendon Press, 1988) 156.

tated in his day. In any account of Lightfoot personal factors are important. But so are the circumstances of time and place.

Very important therefore are the major social and cultural forces that affected Christianity and the Church in Lightfoot's lifetime. For English Christians the so-called 'age of equipoise' — the period from around 1850 to about 1870, when Lightfoot came to maturity as a Churchman and scholar — was fraught with ambivalence and tension.[91] Three developments in particular are illuminating for presenting Lightfoot's life and thought and explaining his influence.

The first was the changing place of the Church in English society. Driven by industrialization and demographic change, a series of reforms from 1828 dismantled the privileged position of the Church of England and plunged it into a situation in which it had to compete with Dissent, Roman Catholicism and infidelity for the allegiance of the English people.[92] This effective denominationalization of the established Church had two almost contradictory effects. By about 1850, recognition of the challenges to its status and function from both government and people had produced such organizational reform and inner renewal that the Church had achieved a measure of recovery, although the Census of 1851 showed how far there was to go.[93] At the same time this new vitality also produced an almost unprecedented internal disputation that wasted effort and discredited the Church.[94] These developments left an ambivalent legacy to Churchmen of Lightfoot's generation. In a competitive situation, they had to determine, on the one hand, how best to woo their constituency and whether the establishment was worth retaining. On the other hand, they had to decide whether conflict inside the Church was worth what it cost and, if not, what could be done about it.

The changing place of the established Church in English society was paralleled by the changing place of Christianity itself. In the first half of Victoria's reign, its assumed role as the religious basis of public life was under greater strain than at any time since the Deist controversy of the previous

---

[91] See W.L. Burn, *The Age of Equipoise. A Study of the Mid-Victorian Generation* (London: George Allen & Unwin, 1964); W.O. Chadwick, *The Victorian Church* (Pt I, 3rd ed.; & Pt II, 2nd ed.; London: Adam & Charles Black, 1971 & 1972).

[92] See esp. A. Gilbert, *Religion and Society in Industrial England. Church, Chapel and Social Change 1740-1914* (London & New York: Longman, 1976).

[93] See the summaries of G. Parsons, "Reform, Revival and Realignment: The Experience of Victorian Anglicanism," *Religion in Victorian Britain. Vol I. Traditions* (ed. G. Parsons; Manchester: University Press, 1988) 14-66; & S. Gilley, "The Church of England in the Nineteenth Century," *A History of Religion in Britain. Practice and Belief From Pre-Roman Times to the Present* (eds S. Gilley & W.J. Sheils; Oxford & Cambridge, Massachusetts: Blackwell, 1994) 291-305.

[94] S.W. Sykes & S.W. Gilley, " 'No Bishop, No Church!' The Tractarian Impact on Anglicanism," *Tradition Renewed. The Oxford Movement Conference Papers* (ed. G. Rowell; Alison Park, Pennsylvania: Pickwick Publications, 1986) 120-39.

century. This was caused by such forces as religious experimentation, scientific naturalism and aesthetic subjectivism, all of which arose within Anglicanism itself.[95] To these were added from outside the rationalist empiricism of John Stuart Mill's *System of Logic*, and the irruption of foreign ideas long held at bay by the combined effects of geographical isolation and fear of revolution. One result was the breakdown of the "common context" which had held together religious faith and scientific inquiry in the first half of the century.[96] At the same time the morality of the Evangelical Revival impacted unfavourably on the religion that had nurtured it.[97] For some the effect of these pressures was a 'crisis of faith' in which they wondered whether Christianity was true or even desirable.[98] Others came out in opposition to a system of belief which, to them, was incompatible with the results of rational inquiry. Alongside these reactions was a creeping secularization which changed how religion itself was perceived,[99] and produced something of a 'paradigm shift', from the 'age of atonement' to the less strident 'age of incarnation'.[100] Out of this ferment arose competition among the representatives of the various outlooks for social and cultural dominance.[101] For the community at large in the 1860s and 1870s this raised the question of whether Christianity, or even religion, was necessary for organizing its public life. The challenge for the Church was to retain its position when Christianity as a "public doctrine" was under such attack.[102]

---

[95]   Turner, *Contesting Cultural Authority*, ch. 2.

[96]   See A. Brown, *The Metaphysical Society: Victorian Minds in Crisis, 1869-1880* (New York: Columbia University Press, 1947); & R.M. Young, "Natural Theology, Victorian Periodicals and the Fragmentation of a Common Context," *Darwin to Einstein. Historical Studies on Science and Belief* (eds C. Chant & J. Fauvel; Burnt Mill, Harlow, Essex & New York: Longman in association with the Open University Press, 1980) 69-107.

[97]   M. Bartholomew, "The Moral Critique of Christian Orthodoxy," & G. Parsons, "On Speaking Plainly: 'Honest Doubt' and the Ethics of Belief," *Religion in Victorian Britain. Volume II. Controversies* (ed. G. Parsons; Manchester: University Press, 1988) 166-90 & 191-219.

[98]   See the range of responses examined in R.J. Helmstadter & B. Lightman (eds), *Victorian Faith in Crisis. Essays on Continuity and Change in Nineteenth-Century Religious Belief* (London: Macmillan, 1990).

[99]   A.D. Gilbert, *The Making of Post-Christian Britain. A History of the Secularization of Modern Society* (London & New York: Longman, 1980).

[100]   On which see B. Hilton, *The Age of Atonement. The Influence of Evangelicalism on Social and Economic Thought, 1795-1865* (Oxford: Clarendon Press, 1988) esp. Part III.

[101]   This is the argument of Turner, *Contesting Cultural Authority*.

[102]   The assault on Christianity as public doctrine, and the responses to it, is the theme of M. Cowling, *Religion and Public Doctrine in Modern England* (2 vols; Cambridge: University Press, 1980-85). "A public doctrine," he writes, "adumbrates the assumptions that constitute the framework within which teaching, writing and public action are conducted." See *ibid.*, I.xi; and for the relevance to Lightfoot, II.xv & 289.

It had to do this in what may be regarded as an age of science and history. In an increasingly complex society, these were the primary forces shaping intellectual life and its institutional relations in the mid-Victorian years.[103] One side of this effect was methodological. The success of its empirical method in both natural science and technology gave the scientific approach jurisdiction in almost every area of human understanding. Even in history only duly accredited material could hope to be taken seriously if it aspired to winning popular assent. Scientific knowledge and its processes also seemed to offer a method for systematically improving the world. Similarly, the science of history held out the possibility of being able to direct rationally and constructively the course taken by society. Science loomed as a better basis than religion for organizing the English community.

The other side of this effect was perspectival. In science, the received natural theology, which offered a view of the world characterized by order and design, came under serious challenge, particularly after the publication of *The Origin of Species* in 1859. In its place emerged a different chronology and explanation of organic life. The doctrine of the regularity of nature seemed to render divine intervention both impossible and unnecessary. The rival picture of the world as competitive and randomly open-ended was appealing because of its correspondence with the apparent nature of industrial society.

In history there was a similar move away from a religious framework as people studied and explained it with reference to its own processes. This outlook tended to reduce Christianity to a mere phase in the human story which was interpreted partly as a liberation from its authoritarian influence. As the Victorians thought more generally about the meaning of their own times within time, many adopted a doctrine of progress, but uncertainty and despair also spawned theories of regress and even meaninglessness.[104] No consensus 'philosophy of history' emerged, but as rival ideologies competed for the sanction of history there were few educated Victorians who did not feel the power of the historical.

The interest of the Victorians in history is a matter that has attracted considerable scholarly attention in recent years. The historians themselves remain the axis of this concern,[105] with some new faces having been added to

---

[103] T.W. Heyck, *The Transformation of Intellectual Life in Victorian England* (London & Canberra: Croom Helm, 1982) esp. ch 3-5.

[104] See J.H. Buckley, *The Triumph of Time: A Study of the Victorian Concepts of Time, History, Progress and Decadence* (Cambridge, Massachusetts: Harvard University Press, 1967).

[105] The outstanding studies are J.W. Burrow, *A Liberal Descent. Victorian Historians and the English Past* (Cambridge: University Press, 1981); R. Jann, *The Art and Science of Victorian History* (Columbus, Ohio: Ohio State University Press, 1985); & C. Parker, *The English Historical Tradition Since 1850* (Edinburgh: John Donald, 1990).

the pantheon.[106] At the same time the ambit has been widened to include other individuals and groups.[107] There have also been studies of the meaning for the Victorians of different periods and episodes, while in a few cases specific uses of history have been traced.[108] However, Churchmen and their uses of history have not figured much in this interest.[109] Attention has been drawn more to those who used history to challenge the religion in which they had been nurtured.[110] Because of the role of history in the Victorian reaction against Christianity, this is an important line of enquiry.[111] But the result has been to obfuscate the resilience and grounds of belief in later Victorian society.[112] Certainly from the 1830s history had been a problem for the received understanding of Christianity as naturalistic modes of understanding furnished alternative explanations of life, weakened the credibility of miracles and challenged the oracular status of the Biblical writings.[113] But the fact that Bishop Stubbs and Mandell Creighton of the first order historians were also clergymen suggests that history was also important to those able to remain inside the Church. Their interest was, of course, broader than the formal discipline. This was because, in the language of social theory, the Church was a "traditional society" confronted by a constellation of modernizing forces which challenged not only the position in English society bequeathed to it by the past, but also its *raison d'être* in historical events of the first century.[114] As a group, therefore, Churchmen represent an interest-

---

[106] Eg. D. Wormell, *Sir John Seeley and the Uses of History* (Cambridge: University Press, 1980).

[107] Eg. P. Levine, *The Amateur and the Professional. Antiquarians, Historians, and Archaeologists in Victorian England, 1838-1886* (Cambridge: University Press, 1986).

[108] Most notably by F.M. Turner, *The Greek Heritage in Victorian Britain* (New Haven & London: Yale University Press, 1981). On the much studied nineteenth century mediaeval revival, see C. Dellheim, *The Face of the Past. The Preservation of the Medieval Inheritance in Victorian England* (Cambridge: University Press, 1982). Two recent examples are B.W. Young, "Knock-Kneed Giants: Victorian Representations of Eighteenth-Century Thought," & R. Samuel, "The Discovery of Puritanism, 1820-1914: A Preliminary Sketch," *Revival and Religion Since 1700. Essays for John Walsh* (eds J. Garnett & C. Matthew; London & Rio Grande, Ohio: Hambledon Press, 1993) 79-93 & 201-47.

[109] An exception is P. Hinchliff, *God and History. Aspects of British Theology 1875-1914* (Oxford: Clarendon Press, 1992). It represents a beginning of what might be achieved by this line of investigation.

[110] J. von Arx, *Progress and Pessimism. Religion, Politics, and History in Late Nineteenth Century Britain* (Cambridge, Massachusetts & London: Harvard University Press, 1985).

[111] Heyck, *Intellectual Transformation*, 104-5.

[112] For the continuing importance of religious belief in later Victorian society, see J. Harris, *Private Lives Public Spirit. A Social History of Britain 1870-1914* (Oxford: University Press, 1993) ch. 6.

[113] On these developments, see Hinchliff, *God and History*, ch. 1.

[114] S.N. Eisenstadt, *Tradition, Change and Modernity* (New York: Wiley, 1973) ch. 14.

ing case study of those seeking to maintain a tradition under tremendous strain.

Of course, they did not all hold the same view of what the tradition meant or what was required in adhering to it. By the time Lightfoot completed his education the existence of three major divisions inside the Church - 'high', 'low' and 'broad' - was well recognized.[115] While acknowledging the importance of these differences, historians have not been satisfied with the received terminology for describing them. For one thing, the main defining categories are not mutually exclusive. A 'broad' Churchman like Hort, for example, held to a 'high' ecclesiology. It has been thought preferable, therefore, to speak in terms of overlapping subcultures within the one Anglican culture.[116] From this perspective, another way of differentiating Churchmen is by their attitude to the tradition they shared.[117] As members of a body which claimed continuity with the ancient catholic church but which had been separated and defined by the conflicts of the sixteenth and seventeenth centuries, all felt the normative power of the past. But they differed greatly over what this should mean in the present. There were traditionalists, conservative Anglicans like E.B. Pusey and G.A. Denison, who sought continuity with the past without change. To the right of them were ultratraditionalists, reactionary Anglicans such as A.H. Mackonochie and Charles Lowder, who wanted to restore old practices. To the left were the modifiers, liberal Anglicans like Thomas Arnold and Julius Hare, who wanted change within continuity. Finally, there were opponents of the Anglican tradition, men like Leslie Stephen and J.R. Green, both of whom gave up their orders. Within these groups further divisions might be made according to how far each attitude was taken.

The important attitude for understanding Lightfoot was that of the modifiers.[118] Anglican in their commitment to the national Church, they were liberals because of their reliance on the conscience as the basis of religious life, advocacy of an inclusive ecclesiology, and openness to cultural and theological innovation. But as a group they were no more homogeneous than the other groups. Virtually from the beginning liberal Anglicanism had

---

[115] The classic description is W.J. Conybeare, "Church Parties," *Edinburgh Review* xcviii (October 1853) 273-342.

[116] P. Avis, "The Tractarian Challenge to Consensus and the Identity of Anglicanism," *King's Theological Review* 9 (1986) 14-17; Kent, *Unacceptable Face*, 80, 82-99; & Parsons, "Reform, Revival and Realignment," 31-47.

[117] See E. Shils, *Tradition* (London: Faber & Faber, 1981).

[118] For the account which follows, see R. Brent, *Liberal Anglican Politics. Whiggery, Religion, and Reform 1830-1841* (Oxford: Clarendon Press, 1987); & A.J. Pickard, "Liberal Anglicanism 1847-1902. A Study of Class and Cultural Relationships in Nineteenth Century England" (unpublished Ph.D. thesis; University of Birmingham, 1982).

evinced two lines of development corresponding to the two ancient universities.[119]

What might be called the left wing appeared at Oxford. Centring first on
Oriel College in the 1820s and subsequently at Balliol, it was outwardly
Aristotelian, strictly inductive in method and insisted that Christianity must
be rational in order to warrant belief.[120] It was temporarily eclipsed by the
rise of Tractarianism but came into its own following the defection of
Newman in 1845.[121] This second stage culminated in 1860 with the publication of *Essays and Reviews*, an event that produced such a reaction that all
that Oxford liberal Anglicanism represented seemed to have been defeated.[122]
Following the reverses of the 1860s and the apparent triumph of the High
Churchmen, it was laicized when T.H. Green and Matthew Arnold took up
its ideals. Largely under the influence of the former, these ideals were then
incorporated into the perspective of the new generation of High Churchmen
who decided they must be liberals as well as catholics. *Lux Mundi* in 1889
was the statement of their platform.[123] At each stage of its development it
was this side of the liberal Anglican subculture that challenged the boundaries of acceptable opinion within the Church of England.

Centring on Trinity College, the right wing emerged at Cambridge at about
the same time as its left wing counterpart at Oxford. Openly Platonic, it
sought reconciliation with the knowledge of the age on the basis of inductive reasoning in harness with the faculty of faith.[124] Of a different intellectual temper in a different kind of university, its course was relatively untroubled. Because its history was less spectacular, it has remained in the shadow
of developments emanating from the sister university. Only historians of
science, who have shown that it promoted the modernization,
professionalization and internationalization of English intellectual endeavour, have appreciated its achievement.[125] However, its development after

---

[119] The influential D. Forbes, *The Liberal Anglican Idea of History* (Cambridge: University Press, 1952) is flawed by its treatment of Liberal Anglicanism as a monolithic
phenomenon and by the failure to recognize that it changed over time.

[120] The main outlines are presented in P. Corsi, *Science and Religion. Baden Powell
and the Anglican Debate, 1800-1860* (Cambridge: University Press, 1988).

[121] W.R. Ward, *Victorian Oxford* (London: Cass, 1965) ch. VII.

[122] For *Essays and Reviews*, see 63 below.

[123] C. Gore (ed.), *Lux Mundi. A Series of Studies in the Religion of the Incarnation*
(London: John Murray, 1889, 1890[4]). On which, see R. Morgan (ed.), *The Religion of the
Incarnation. Anglican Essays in Commemoration of "Lux Mundi"* (Bristol: Bristol Classi-
cal Press, 1989).

[124] N.M. Distad, *Guessing at Truth. The Life of Julius Charles Hare (1795-1855)*
(Shepherdstown: Patmos Press, 1979).

[125] S.F. Cannon, *Science in Culture. The Early Victorian Period* (New York: Science
History Publications, 1978) ch. 2.

1860 remains to be charted.[126] Lightfoot's career is part of that story.

In order to find the basis for writing his life, the investigation elaborates the stereotype "Lightfoot the Historian" against this background. Its main question is: what was Lightfoot's understanding of history and its consequences in his career as a Churchman and scholar? As the introductions to Parts II-IV explain, the answer to this question follows from the answers to a sequence of smaller questions which arise out of the different senses of 'history'. Did Lightfoot have a theory of history, and, if so, what was it like? What was the place of history as ideology in his approach to the institutional life of the Church of which he was a part? What was his understanding of the nature and purpose of the method for obtaining historical knowledge?

The structure of the investigation reflects its argument. The next two chapters in Part I provide an account of the milieu in which Lightfoot grew to maturity at Liverpool, Birmingham and Trinity College, Cambridge. Their purpose is to establish the basis of his thought and career aspirations, and to characterize his general intellectual position. In Part II Lightfoot's understanding of history as "the increasing purpose of God" is reconstructed (Chapter 4), traced to its sources in the Bible and contemporary life and culture (Chapter 5), and analyzed as the basis for thought and conduct (Chapter 6). The result is to reveal Lightfoot's perception of the challenges facing the Church and the nation and what broad response was required. Part III traces the bearings of this way of thinking about history and its disclosures in his career at Cambridge University (Chapter 7), St Paul's Cathedral in London and the diocese of Durham (Chapter 8), and in the life of his Church in general (Chapter 9). Because the idea of history was not the only determinant of action in these spheres, its interaction with other key notions — of the University, the ministry, and the Church of England — is examined. In the first systematic account of Lightfoot's scholarship, Part IV concentrates on history as a method of knowing in the study of the writings which survive from the period of earliest Christianity. Separate chapters survey Lightfoot's use of the method in each of the main areas of his scholarly interest. The outcome of this treatment is the proposition that his understanding of history was fundamental to his life and thought as Churchman and scholar. His interpretation of the world was a function of a theology of divine immanence. In this perspective all history, including his own life, was part of the outworking in the material sphere of metaphysical entities usually categorized as theological. This belief provided the major impulse to Lightfoot's

---

[126] The impression is sometimes given that this line of development ended with F.D. Maurice. Eg. P. Avis, *Anglicanism and the Christian Church. Theological Resources in Historical Perspective* (Edinburgh: T. & T. Clark, 1989) esp. ch. 15 & 16.

career. The effect was the characteristic socio-religious use of historical knowledge in each of the main spheres of his activity. On the basis of this understanding it will be possible to write a properly historical account of his life.

Chapter 2

Liverpool and Birmingham

I

Born at Liverpool on 13 April 1828, the immediate origins of Joseph Barber Lightfoot are of greater historical than biographical interest.[1] His family was obscure, hailing from Wensley Dale and the neighbouring dales of western Yorkshire.[2] Family tradition said Lightfoot's grandfather, William Keppel Lightfoot, one of a family of 21 children, was the first to leave the district; but contemporary sources indicate that he was born at Liverpool, in August, 1769.[3] At that time his father, Bernard Lightfoot, once a brewer, was listed as a "Gentleman".[4] The inclusion of "Keppel" in his son's name was due to the engagement of his daughter to Admiral Keppel, a relation of the Albemarle family.[5]

This seems to represent a peak of respectability from which the family's fortunes later fell. The marriage into the Keppel family did not come off and, in adulthood, William worked for a living, taking advantage of Liverpool's burgeoning port life by going to sea.[6] After his disappearance from local record, his wife, Alice — presumably now a widow — appears in her own right from 1805: as a boarding house proprietor in 1813 and 1814; and then as a milliner in 1818.[7]

---

[1]   On the social backgrounds of nineteenth century Cambridge graduates and Anglican bishops, see H.W. Becher, "The Social Origins of Post Graduate Careers of a Cambridge Intellectual Elite, 1830-1860," *Victorian Studies* 28.1 (1984) 97-127; W.T. Gibson, "The Social Origins and Education of an Elite: The Nineteenth-Century Episcopate," *History of Education* 20.2 (1991) 95-105, & "The Professionalization of an Elite: The Nineteenth Century Episcopate," *Albion* 23.3 (1991) 459-82; & H. Jenkins & D. Caradog Jones, "Social Class of Cambridge University Alumni of the 18th and 19th Centuries," *British Journal of Sociology* 1 (1950) 93-116.

[2]   J.R. Harmer to N.K. Lightfoot, 29 August 1888. Harmer explained that Lightfoot himself could not trace his family lineage beyond his great grandfather, Bernard Lightfoot, the family pedigree having been lost in a fire.

[3]   Baptism Register of St Nicholas' Church, Liverpool (LRO).

[4]   *Ibid.* He had lived at Liverpool at least since 1766, the year of the first Liverpool Directory, in which he is listed as a brewer.

[5]   J.R. Harmer to N.K. Lightfoot, 29 August 1888.

[6]   Baptism Register of St Nicholas' Church, Liverpool (LRO). G. Chandler, *Liverpool* (London: B.T. Batsford, 1957) ch. 6.

[7]   Liverpool City Directories, 1805-1824.

By 1824 her son, John Jackson Lightfoot (1796-1843), was established as an accountant.[8] He associated with the local intelligentsia as a member of the Liverpool Literary and Philosophical Society,[9] and married the sister of another member, Charles Barber, who was also a teacher at the Royal Institution, a co-founder of the Architectural and Archaeological Association, and a friend of such dignitaries as Thomas Traill and William Roscoe.[10] While otherwise undistinguished, John Lightfoot seems to have prospered in his work.[11] When Joseph (his second son) was born, the family resided in the still not unfashionable Duke Street.[12] Subsequently, the Lightfoots moved outwards from the town centre to Edge Hill; and, in 1841, away from "the monotony of the town", across the Mersey to Tranmere.[13] Two years later John Lightfoot added "architect" to his professional listing.[14] He was, moreover, ambitious for his sons. Rightly identifying education as a mechanism for advancement for members of the middle class,[15] he insisted that they have a college education, an objective to which his widow gave up all her property.[16] When the boys became clergymen their lives conformed to a familiar pattern in the history of the Victorian middle-class. The sons of a father who had done well in business escaped through education to a traditional (and now resurgent) profession to which they brought the values of their class.[17] Thus Lightfoot's background was urban (if provincial),[18] bourgeois and commercial, increasingly well-off and aspiring.

---

[8] *Baines History and Directory of Liverpool*, 1824, 284. The statement in LD 1, that Lightfoot's father was a Yorkshireman, may be incorrect. He was baptized on 20 March 1796 in St Nicholas' Church, Liverpool.

[9] MS Minute Book of the Liverpool Literary and Philosophical Society for the period 1817-1823 (LRO).

[10] DNB I.1066. He was subsequently treasurer, secretary and president of the Liverpool Academy of Art (1847-1854). The family association was evidently close. Alice Lightfoot named Charles Barber as executor of her will. Probate of the Will of Alice Lightfoot, 18 March 1851 (LRO).

[11] J. Lodge to Lightfoot, 3 March 1879 (LAC).

[12] On Duke Street, see J.A. Picton, *Memorials of Liverpool. Historical and Topographical Including a History of the Dock Estate* (2 vols; 2nd ed.; Liverpool: G.G. Walmsley; & London: Longmans, Green & Co., 1875) II.266-77.

[13] For Lightfoot's recollection of Tranmere, see P. Sulley, *The Hundred of the Wirral* (Birkenhead: B. Haram & Co., 1889) 387.

[14] *Gore's Liverpool Directory 1843*, 310.

[15] On its importance in the careers of bishops, see Gibson, "Social Origins," 101-5.

[16] E.A. Lightfoot to J.R. Harmer, 14 February & 3 April no year [1893?].

[17] P. Butler, *Gladstone, Church, State and Tractarianism: A Study of his Religious Ideas and Attitudes, 1809-1859* (Oxford: Clarendon Press, 1982) 14-5, for the wish to escape the business world of Liverpool, and the interest in upward social mobility. Also M.J. Wiener, *English Culture and the Decline of the Industrial Spirit, 1850-1980* (Cambridge: University Press, 1981) Part 1. A. Haig, *The Victorian Clergy* (Beckenham & Sydney: Croom Helm, 1984).

[18] I have been able to find no evidence that Lightfoot's being from the north was a

In view of the distinction Lightfoot achieved as a student of early Christian literature, an exception to this lack of biographical lustre would be a family connection with the seventeenth century Hebraist and theologian, John Lightfoot (1602-1675).[19] It is a possibility he himself liked to contemplate. When W.I. Lightfoot of Staplehurst in Kent set out to trace the pedigree of the earlier scholar, Lightfoot brought to light a tradition that his famous namesake had sprung from his own family.[20] In the ensuing investigation, nothing was discovered to authenticate a familial link between the two scholars.[21] When a commemorative tablet in honour of John Lightfoot was placed in the Church of Great Munden, where he had been rector from 1644 until his death, it was a memorial not to a relative but to an esteemed namesake and intellectual ancestor.[22]

Most of what can be recovered of Lightfoot's Liverpool life concerns his education. A sickly child, he was first taught at home by a private tutor.[23] Not until he was 13 did he attend the school of the Royal Institution, which had been founded in 1814 to provide professional and liberal education for the middle class of Liverpool.[24] After only a week Lightfoot was promoted to the Headmaster's class. So intense was his application to his studies he often had to be touched to break his concentration. On one occasion a friend watched him stand in a puddle while examining a book with the Rev. William Spencer, the Second Master,[25] and then walk on, still in conversation, without having noticed either the puddle or the friend.[26] The results of this devotion were precocious, for it is to this period of his life that many stories of

---

consideration in his being raised to the episcopate, as is implied by Gibson, "Social Origins," 99.

[19] On whom, see DNB XI.1108-10.

[20] Sixteen letters by W.I. Lightfoot to Lightfoot between 18 May 1859 & 4 May 1861. The allusion to the tradition occurs in the letter of 31 May 1859.

[21] BL 7. Nor is there any connection with the twentieth century New Testament scholar R.H. Lightfoot, the study of whom is now reaching the stage represented by *Lightfoot of Durham*, viz. recollection and appreciation by pupils and friends. Eg. D. Nineham, "R.H. Lightfoot and the Significance of Biblical Criticism," *Theology* 88 (1985) 97-105.

[22] Lightfoot used the Hebraist's work in his own first piece of serious New Testament scholarship and frequently referred to it thereafter. LS 199. Also 'S. John. Notes. II. St John II. 1.29 - IV.5,' 34, 52, 57, 59, 62, 64, 68; 'Acts I - VII.43,' 9, 12, 19; 'Acts XV.1 - [XVII.14],' 11, 17; 'Acts XVII.16 - [XIX.20],' 65, 70; 'Acts XIX.21 - [XXI.39],' 112, 122; 'Acts of the Apostles. External Evidence. SR,' 13; 'I Corinthians IX.34 - XI.8,' 135, 136; 'I Corinthians XII.8 - XIV.20,' 179, 187 a; 'Ephesians I.10 - III end,' 9, 10, 13; & 'First Peter. Introduction,' 3, 5, 23, 30, 31.

[23] DNB XI.1111.

[24] T. Kelly, *For Advancement of Learning. The University of Liverpool 1881-1981* (Liverpool: University Press, 1981) 18-22.

[25] On Spencer, see Venn, *Alumni* II.V.605.

[26] Enclosure with E.A. Lightfoot to J.R. Harmer, 3 April n.y. [1893?].

exceptional early intellectual achievement are assigned.[27] By the time he
left the Royal Institution, he had acquired a solid grounding in Mathematics
and Classics,[28] and risen to become head boy.[29]

Too little is known of Lightfoot's family life to make confident judgments about its effect on the man to come. Nevertheless, it seems to have
been important. The fact that his older brother William (1823 [?]-1881)[30]
entered on a clerical career immediately after completing his formal education points to a pious home — although his love of dancing suggests it was
not of the strictest sort.[31] It may also be that his commitment to hard work,
self-discipline and methodical habits as the path to mental and moral improvement owes something to his family background. In addition to the
example of his father, his maternal grandfather is said to have established
his own drawing school in Birmingham "after several years of difficulty"
and to have run it "with unremitting industry".[32] Although grist to the mill
of ecclesiastical diplomacy, Lightfoot also liked to recall his great grandfather, who had been a bookseller in Newcastle-upon-Tyne.[33] More apparent
is the artistic influence. His mother came from a family of artists of minor
distinction.[34] The interest which Lightfoot always showed in art and archi-
tecture,[35] while a pervasive feature of Victorian church life, seems to go
back to this source.

II

Lightfoot's father died early in 1843, when the young student was 15 years
old. To be near his mother's relations, the family moved to Birmingham in

---

[27] BL 7-8. Cf. Farrar, "Bishop Lightfoot," 174.

[28] W. Spencer to Lightfoot, 22 October 1845.

[29] The recollection of Lightfoot as head boy occurs in G. Iliff to Lightfoot, 21 March
1877 (LAC.). Iliff's father was the Headmaster.

[30] Venn, *Alumni* II.IV.170.

[31] For the anecdote about dancing, Mrs Johnson to Elizabeth Lightfoot, 28 January
n.y., enclosure in E. Lightfoot to J.R. Harmer, 2 February n.y. [1893?].

[32] DNB I.1068.

[33] LD 1-2.

[34] Her father, Joseph Barber (1757-1811), was a well known landscape artist in Birmingham. *Ibid.*, & "Obituary; with Anecdotes of Remarkable Persons," *The Gentleman's
Magazine* 81 (1811) 285. Both her brothers, Charles Barber (1784-1854) and John Vincent Barber (1787-1838), exhibited at the Royal Academy. S. Redgrave, *A Dictionary of
Artists of the English School* (Amsterdam: G.W. Hissink & Co., 1970 [originally published in 1878]) 21-2. Lightfoot's father, too, was something of an antiquarian. His two
papers to the Liverpool Literary and Philosophical Society were "The Varieties of Gothic
Arch," 6 February 1818; & "The Present and Ancient States of Kenilworth Castle," 4 May
1821. Minute Book of the Literary and Philosophical Society 1817-23 (LRO).

[35] Eg. LNC 17; RCC (1881) 458; SSO 171-3, 303; SSP 200-1, 284-5.

the following year.[36] An important centre of political Liberalism, the city to which Lightfoot came was in the grip of the Anti-Corn Law League agitation.[37] Unlike B.F. Westcott, with whom he was later closely associated, he seems to have taken only a perfunctory interest in local affairs.[38] The significant influences in this new setting were personal.

One was E.W. Benson, subsequently first Bishop of Truro (1877-83) and Archbishop of Canterbury (1883-96). Younger by a year, and also now fatherless, Benson was the chief among a circle of classmates who were enthusiastic for the same things at King Edward VI's Grammar School.[39] The obvious focus for their friendship was schoolwork, which generated a friendly rivalry.[40] On holidays they undertook long walks during which they discussed Classical texts, and other subjects of mutual interest.[41] Most important was the discovery, in Benson, of a confidant and support for his own religious aspirations. They read the canonical hours, and later contemplated the formation of a society for holy living. Their friendship suggested continuing the association beyond school days, working as clergymen in the same parish church, serving the poor and studying together.[42] The plan itself came to nothing, but the vision of glory through service remained with both into adulthood, although somewhat redirected by worldly success.

At this stage, however, much more important in Lightfoot's personal formation was the influence of his new Headmaster. With Benson he shared an attachment to James Prince Lee (1804-69) so deep that it is scarcely an exaggeration to see in him the father figure of their adolescent lives.[43] The

---

[36] DNB XI.1111.

[37] For a record of contemporary events, J.A. Langford, *Modern Birmingham and its Institutions: A Chronicle of Local Events, From 1841 to 1871* (2 vols; Birmingham & London, 1873). Also A. Briggs, *Victorian Cities* (Harmondsworth: Penguin, 1968).

[38] Lightfoot once mentioned the creditable outcome of the 1844 by election. Lightfoot to Benson, Saturday 3rd 1844 [sic] (PLAB 1842-1848, TCC). For Westcott, LW I.ch. 1. There is some confusion about whether Lightfoot and Westcott were acquainted before the former went up to Cambridge. According to Westcott himself, they were. Testimonial for Lightfoot, 1854.

[39] The school boy correspondence between Lightfoot and Benson now held at TCC has been analyzed by D. Newsome, *Godliness and Good Learning. Four Studies of a Victorian Ideal* (London: John Murray, 1961) 105-18, esp. 112-17.

[40] LB I.27-8. For the significance of such friendships, see J.R.S. de S. Honey, *Tom Brown's Universe. The Development of the Victorian Public School* (London: Millington Books, 1977) 186-9.

[41] DNB XI.1112. LB I.31-2.

[42] Benson to Lightfoot, 31 October 1847 (PLAB 1842-1848, TCC). For a comment on the idea, see D. Edwards, *Leaders of the Church of England 1828-1944* (London: Oxford University Press, 1971) 192, 193.

[43] Most of the evidence comes from Benson, but see Prince Lee to Lightfoot, 5 November 1847; and the Appendix to E.W. Benson, *ΣΑΛΠΙΣΕΙ. A Memorial Sermon, Preached After the Death of the Right Reverend James Prince Lee ... With Appendix Containing*

man who inspired this devotion was recalled at Cambridge as "One of the most distinguished classical scholars ever known in the University".[44] Not an Apostle himself, he was associated with them as a proponent of the new philology in the Etymological and Philological Societies.[45] Like his more famous Cambridge contemporaries, he was a man of wide culture and awareness, with a highly developed interest in art, modern and foreign literature, and also the discoveries of science.[46]

To his Cambridge connections Lee owed his appointment in 1830 to Thomas Arnold's Rugby.[47] Although there were important differences between them, Lee found the eight-year association with Arnold congenial.[48] They shared a similar approach to the Classics — though Lee was the better scholar —[49] and espoused the same moral ideals. Lee seems to have admired Arnold's innovations at Rugby, particularly the reliance on the boys of the Headmaster's own house and form to set a moral tone for the school.[50] Circumstances did not allow the duplication of Rugby in the commercial Midlands, even if this had been Lee's wish;[51] but, in a letter of farewell, he acknowledged how much he had learned from Arnold, and hoped "that what you

---

Memorial Notices of the Late Bishop (2nd ed.; London: Macmillan; & Manchester: Howell & Roworth, 1870) 38-9. The importance Lightfoot attached to Lee's influence is indicated by the scene intended to "set forth the power of oral teaching" in the lowest medallion of the centre lancet of the west window of St Ignatius', Hendon Docks (for which, see 230 below); which depicts Lightfoot as a boy under Lee's instruction, together with Benson and Westcott. G.F. Browne, *A Description of the Series of Stained Glass Windows To Be Placed in the Church of S. Ignatius, the Martyr, Sunderland, Built By the Late Bishop of Durham, The Right Rev. J.B. Lightfoot, D.D., As a Thankoffering For God's Mercies Vouchsafed to Him During Seven Years of His Episcopate, 1879-86* (Sunderland: privately printed, no date [1889]) 7-8. The windows were designed by Browne, a Cambridge friend and colleague, but the choice of subjects was Lightfoot's. G.F. Browne, *The Recollections of a Bishop* (London: Smith, Elder & Co., 1915) 240.

[44] Venn, *Alumni* II.IV.132. DNB XI.799-800.

[45] H. Aarsleff, *The Study of Language in England, 1780-1860* (Princeton: University Press, 1967) 217-18. For the Apostles, see P. Allen, *The Cambridge Apostles* (Cambridge: University Press, 1978).

[46] Benson, ΣΑΛΠΙΣΕΙ, 31.

[47] He was recommended by Julius Hare. A.P. Stanley, *The Life and Correspondence of Thomas Arnold* (single volume edition; London: Ward, Lock & Co., no date) 163.

[48] On Lee's enthusiasm for Arnold's work, see Westcott to C.J. Vaughan in Benson, ΣΑΛΠΙΣΕΙ, 28. Lee presented his bust of Arnold to the National Portrait Gallery. *Ibid.*, 33-4. For the differences, see LW I.249. The evidence was destroyed, but it is not improbable that these differences were in theological matters where Lee's outlook was traditional and conservative.

[49] de Honey, *Tom Brown's Universe*, 13.

[50] Benson, ΣΑΛΠΙΣΕΙ, 35. Newsome, *Godliness*, 41-2.

[51] For the local circumstances, see C. Gill, *A History of Birmingham. Volume I. Manor and Borough to 1865* (London: Oxford University Press, 1952) 388-91.

have taught I may be aided to persist in".[52]   When in 1838 Lee came to his own school, recently retrieved from decrepitude by Francis Jeune, he brought with him the new scholarship and the religious earnestness of the rising middle classes.[53]

J.R. de S. Honey described the effect of Lee on his leading pupils as "a personal spell".[54] There is support for this in Lightfoot's own appreciation of lessons on Butler:

> I have sometimes thought that, if I were allowed to live one hour only of my past life over again, I would choose a Butler lesson under Lee. His rare eloquence was never more remarkable than during these lessons. I have heard many great preachers since, but I do not recollect anything comparable in its kind to his oratory, when leaning back in his chair and folding his gown about him, he would break off at some idea suggested by the text, and pour forth an uninterrupted flood of eloquence for half an hour or more, the thought keeping pace with the expression all the while, and the whole marked by a sustained elevation of tone which entranced even the idlest and most careless among us.[55]

Although Butler was important to him,[56] evidently Lightfoot was struck more by the expositor than the subject matter.

This did not mean that Lee's influence was without intellectual and moral content. Already devoted to study, Lightfoot was ideally suited to benefit from the most conspicuous result of Lee's headmastership — the establishment of the school as a place of learning.[57] As at Rugby, the curriculum was dominated by Classics. The teaching which laid the foundations of successive university triumphs was based on "an intense belief in the exact force of language", and therefore characterized by a strict attention to words, their history and nuances, and illustration from an author's other writings.[58] Lightfoot extolled the approach as

> most irregular in one respect, and yet rigorously exact in another, irregular in form, but strict in enforcing habits of precise observation and analysis. There was a singular absence of special rules, but a constant recurrence to broad principles.[59]

Here was the basis of the inductive method of independent study which Lee promoted. It was not as old fashioned as A.C. Benson thought. The range of

---

[52] Quoted in Newsome, *Godliness*, 99.

[53] *Ibid.,* 4, 34-5, for the link between the middle classes and the older public and grammar schools. For Jeune, see T.W. Hutton, *King Edward's School Birmingham 1552-1952* (Oxford: Basil Blackwell, 1952) 81-6.

[54] Honey, *Tom Brown's Universe*, 31.

[55] Benson, *ΣΑΛΠΙΣΕΙ*, 40-1.

[56] See 35 & 52 below.

[57] Thirteen of his pupils achieved a first class in the Cambridge Classical Tripos. Five were Senior Classic, and four Senior Chancellor's medallist. Newsome, *Godliness*, 104-5. Lightfoot was in each category.

[58] B.F. Westcott, *Teacher and Scholar: A Memory and a Hope* (Birmingham: Cornish Brothers, 1893) 6-7. LB I.37-8. Benson, *ΣΑΛΠΙΣΕΙ,* 47-8.

[59] *Ibid.*, 39.

texts covered was unusual,[60] and the interest in that to which the text pointed was an innovation.[61] On the one hand, this combination of the new and the old nurtured in Lee's pupils the best of the Cambridge tradition of close textual study with the more recent attention to subject matter in relation to the history of humankind, which created a legacy of severe linguistic discipline, cultural appreciation and philosophical training.[62] On the other, it produced excesses in the convoluted prose of Benson, and the over-imaginative scholarship of Westcott.[63] In avoiding both extremes, Lightfoot was recognized as its best representative.

Although traditional in this devotion to Classics, the teaching at King Edward's was broader than was common in the schools of the day.[64] Lee's own Mathematics were notoriously weak, but in the Rev. John Abbott he found a man capable of teaching the subject at a proper standard;[65] and some attempt was made to apply this knowledge by surveying tracts of Birmingham parkland.[66] To direct instruction, Lee added his own individual influence. He encouraged pupils to share his interests in art, geography and scientific devices.[67] He also urged attendance at local lectures, on scientific, artistic and antiquarian subjects, in order to promote an awareness of what was going on around and the wider relevance of schoolwork.[68] The whole programme was drawn together by wide reading outside the classroom. Lee granted pupils access to his own books, and in Lightfoot's case directed that he be given the run of the town library.[69] Lightfoot recalled how

---

[60] In a single term, for example, the boys read, for poetry, Sophocles' *Antigone*, Euripides' *Orestes*, Horace's *Odes* and *Georgic* III; and for prose, Herodotus IX, Thucydides III, Plato's *Menexenus*, and Cicero's *In Verrum* II. Almost all were new texts for schoolboy study. See E.W. Benson to his uncle, the Rev. William Jackson, 30 November 1844 (PLAB 1842-1848, TCC). For the general situation in the public schools, J.W. Adamson, *English Education 1789-1902* (Cambridge: University Press, 1964) 239-40.

[61] Benson, *ΣΑΛΠΙΣΕΙ*, 13.

[62] Newsome, *Godliness*, 63.

[63] LB I.37-8. Also LW I.26-8; & A.C. Benson, *The Leaves of the Tree. Studies in Biography* (London: Smith, Elder & Co., 1911) 36.

[64] Adamson, *English Education*, ch. IX. On curriculum innovation, E.C. Mack, *Public Schools and British Opinion* (London: Methuen, 1938) 268-9.

[65] Lightfoot was advised to benefit as much as possible from Lee's Classical expertise and leave his Mathematics for college. W. Spencer to Lightfoot, 22 October 1845. The simultaneous equations with which he teased Benson indicates that this side of his studies was not entirely neglected. Lightfoot to Benson, Monday PM 1844 (PLAB 1842-1848, TCC); & Newsome, *Godliness*, 113.

[66] Benson, *ΣΑΛΠΙΣΕΙ*, 41-2.

[67] *Ibid.*, 36, 37-8.

[68] Westcott, *Teacher and Scholar*, 7-8.

[69] Benson, *ΣΑΛΠΙΣΕΙ*, 40.

we were not forced to study, but encouraged to read and remember. We learnt by experience that any knowledge we might acquire would be brought out some time or other to illustrate our regular school-work, and we felt amply rewarded by the eager delight with which our master would hail such indications of private reading.[70]

He himself responded by reading in the Church Fathers, and sharing in the enthusiasm for modern literature which the regime engendered.[71] From Lee's encouragement, therefore, came the rich powers of illustration evident in Lightfoot's later writings, and his extensive knowledge of poetry in particular.[72]

It was not only intellectual, but, of course, also a religious and moral formation at which Lee aimed. He endeavoured to show the reality of religion for life, and its application to behaviour. Lightfoot later attributed Lee's influence to "this singular combination of intellectual vigour and devotional feeling".[73]

The basis of the religious instruction in the Classical School was the "Bible. Greek and English".[74] Its importance in Lee's outlook and teaching was noted by another pupil, J.F. Wickenden:

> For all his reading he might, more truly than almost any man, be called a man *unius libri*. The New Testament in Greek was his one book.[75]

Indeed, Lee himself claimed that its proper study was what he wished to achieve in his pupils above all else.[76] This is why it is often said that Lightfoot owed to his Headmaster his commitment to New Testament study.[77] In fact, he did not choose so to specialize until 1861, and even then Church History was his preference.[78] What he did acquire from Lee was the recognition of the centrality of the New Testament to every other subject; and, when the time came to make it his vocation, the basis of a method. For Lee had insisted, first, that his boys become acquainted with the sources for the construction of the text; and, second, that in its exegesis they begin with a sys-

[70]   *Ibid.*

[71]   R.A., "Joseph Barber Lightfoot, Bishop of Durham," *The Cambridge Review* (January 16 1890) 134. The author was Richard Appleton who had been an Examining Chaplain to Lightfoot. Benson, *ΣΑΛΠΙΣΕΙ*, 40. Benson, *Leaves of the Tree*, 257, recalled the experience of watching Lightfoot read *Alice In Wonderland*. A newspaper clipping among the Lightfoot Papers indicates that at one point Lightfoot was suspected of being its author, but the report is hopelessly confused.

[72]   Quotations throughout his *oeuvre* indicate that his favourite poets were Wordsworth, Tennyson, Keble and Browning. See 120 below for the importance of poetry in the formation of Lightfoot's outlook.

[73]   Benson, *ΣΑΛΠΙΣΕΙ*, 13, 41.

[74]   Prince Lee to J.W. Croker, 10 June 1845 (BLO, MS.Eng.Lett.d.368, ff. 62-7).

[75]   Benson, *ΣΑΛΠΙΣΕΙ*, 47. Cf. *ibid.*, 14, 26.

[76]   *Ibid.*, 14.

[77]   Eg. LD 3.

[78]   See 50 below. LH I.448.

tematic study of the usage of the language.[79] In none of them was the outcome more fruitful than in Lightfoot.[80]

The teaching from revelation was supplemented by natural theology. Among the set authors was William Paley.[81] More significantly, as the first schoolmaster to include *The Analogy* in the curriculum, Lee introduced his pupils to the Butler renaissance in contemporary English theology.[82] Lightfoot came to regard *The Analogy* as "the greatest work of English theology".[83] Its influence is reflected in later life by the continual appeal to the principle of analogy,[84] the rule of probability, and the cumulative weight of evidence.[85] More fundamentally, he acquired a grounding in that natural theology which regarded all aspects of life as manifestations of the work of God, and therefore to be interpreted by the revelation given in Christianity.[86]

Two moral ideals stand out in Lee's teaching and practice. One was truthfulness. Like Arnold, Lee acted in the conviction that the basis of all right conduct is truth. Accordingly his special objective was the elimination of falsehood from the school.[87] Even as he was about to leave King Edward's for the See of Manchester, he could still make a public spectacle of a boy caught lying.[88] While to a later generation this seems obsessive, in its own day it was effective. Looking back after Lee's death Benson averred, "it was not so much the teaching he infused as the ardour he aroused, as the truth-seeking spirit he created, in those who were worthy".[89] Thus the model furnished by their Headmaster made truthfulness the main object of their own moral and intellectual aspiration, and Christianity its chief satisfaction.

---

[79] Benson, *ΣΑΛΠΙΣΕΙ*, 26-7.

[80] LB I.38.

[81] Prince Lee to J.W. Croker, 10 June 1845 (BLO, MS.Eng.Lett.d.368, ff. 62-7). The works by Paley were *Horae Paulinae, Evidences of Christianity*, and *Natural Theology*.

[82] For which, see H.F.G. Swanston, *Ideas of Order: The Mid-Nineteenth Century Revival of Anglican Theological Method* (Assen, The Netherlands: Van Gorcum & Comp. B.V., 1974) 1-13.

[83] SSO 108.

[84] Eg. "Acts I-VIII," ff. 85r-86r. CS 74-5. See 345-6 below.

[85] BE 428-9, 48-9. EWSR ix. 'Witnessing,' 1879, 3. The reference to "historic probability" is omitted from the published version in SSO 120 where it should occur. CS 306. LNC 5, 24-5.

[86] On natural theology, see R. Yeo, "Natural Theology and the Philosophy of Knowledge in Britain, 1819-1869" (unpublished Ph.D. thesis; University of Sydney, 1977).

[87] Newsome, *Godliness*, 46-9.

[88] LB I.45. Significantly, while at Rugby, Lee was the chief witness to the March incident. T.W. Bamford, *Thomas Arnold* (London: Cresset Press, 1960) 50.

[89] Benson, *ΣΑΛΠΙΣΕΙ*, 13, 41. For an example of Benson's own ardour as a headmaster, see D. Newsome, *A History of Wellington College 1859-1959* (London: John Murray, 1959) 108-10.

At the end of his life as an ecclesiastical statesman and Christian scholar Lightfoot hoped to have been found συνεργὸς τῇ ἀληθείᾳ.[90]

The second ideal was manliness. Benson commented on Lee's refusal further to punish "N — " after his public humiliation, "Was it not nobly done?" He was moved by the coupling of integrity with compassion and mercy. This combination of morality and chivalry was common before the ideal was overrun by athleticism later in the century.[91] It was in this early sense that Lightfoot endorsed manliness. In him it produced the same earnestness tempered by sympathy.

The teaching and influence of Lee formed a vision for life similar to that imparted by Arnold.[92] In 1870 Westcott spoke for all Lee's leading pupils when he claimed that contact with their Headmaster

> revealed to us in every lesson that intellectual and moral warmth which is the evidence and source of the highest life ... He made us feel that there was something which we could do, and not only something which we could receive ... He enabled us to see that scholarship is nothing less than one method of dealing with the whole problem of human existence, in which art and truth and goodness are inextricably combined.[93]

He also recalled that because of Lee's influence "our souls were touched, and we felt a little more the claims of duty, a little more of the possibilities of life, a little more of the pricelessness of opportunity".[94] In turn, this engendered the conviction that in adulthood there was "work to be done, work to be done in the face of formidable difficulties, work to be done in faith in God".[95] As a result, a number of Lee's pupils, Lightfoot among them, left the school imbued with a combative Christianity which linked deep religious conviction and rigorous Classical scholarship with a sense of social responsibility.

David Newsome has epitomized this outlook in the apt phrase, "godliness and good learning".[96] Lightfoot's adherence to it is signified not only by the tenor of his subsequent career, but also by his explicitly purveying "all sound learning and all godly living" as an ideal of college life at Cambridge.[97] If it is remembered that this ideal had been revivified at Rugby, and brought to Birmingham by Lee, then Lightfoot's secondary education

---

[90]   EWSR ix.

[91]   N. Vance, "The Ideal of Manliness," in *The Victorian Public School* (B. Simon & I. Bradley eds; Dublin: Gill & Macmillan, 1975) 115-28.

[92]   F.J. Woodward, *The Doctor's Disciples* (London: Oxford University Press, 1954). And the caveat of Mack, *Public Schools*, 239-40.

[93]   Benson, ΣΑΛΠΙΣΕΙ, 25-6.

[94]   Westcott, *Teacher and Scholar*, 5.

[95]   *Ibid.*, 10.

[96]   Newsome, *Godliness*, 56-7.

[97]   CS 125.

was Arnoldian.[98] By his initiation into this tradition, he was prepared for the part he would play in bringing its influence to bear on the life of the Church later in the century. In the short term, it left him well prepared for the next stage in his education at the University of Cambridge.

---

[98] A caveat against the loose use of the term is issued in G.M. Young, *Portrait of an Age* (annotated edition by G.S.R. Kitson Clark; London: Oxford University Press, 1977) 294-5. On the importance of the Arnoldian outlook in the making of Victorian England, see G.S.R. Kitson Clark, *Churchmen and the Condition of England 1832-1885* (London: Methuen, 1973) 76.

Chapter 3

Trinity College, Cambridge

Towards the end of 1847 Lightfoot 'went up' to Cambridge. In the last of its 'unreformed' days before the Royal Commission of 1850 began its work, the University purported to be a seminary of sound learning and religious education.[1] In fact, the reality fell a long way short of the theory, although peacemeal attempts at reform occurred periodically.[2] The general standard of instruction in the Colleges was poor, a deficiency which encouraged an unofficial system of private tuition or 'coaching', and very little was done for teaching Theology. Poor provision was matched by undergraduate expectations. Most did not come seeking academic success. They were content with the 'poll' or pass degree, and were happy to spend the bulk of their time in various sporting and social pursuits. Yet, while it functioned much like a finishing school for sons of the nobility and aspiring professional men, Cambridge still produced hard workers and scholars of renown. Lightfoot was determined to be among them.

I

For his College Lightfoot chose Trinity, entering as a 'pensioner' in October 1847.[3] It had been Prince Lee's College, as well as being the largest and most distinguished in Cambridge.[4] At a time when it was still unusual, Trinity evinced a strong commitment to teaching, and boasted a number of reputable and earnest Tutors. Lightfoot felt the benefits of the system when he was assigned to the 'side' of William Hepworth Thompson, formerly a pupil of Julius Hare and Connop Thirlwall, and subsequently Regius Professor of

---

[1]   See, for example, the defence of the ancient universities in Oxoniensis, *An Apology for the Universities* (Oxford,1841).

[2]   The standard accounts are D.A. Winstanley, *Early Victorian Cambridge* (Cambridge: University Press, 1940); & J.P.C. Roach, "The University of Cambridge," in *A History of the County of Cambridgeshire and the Isle of Ely. Vol III. The City and University of Cambridge* (ed. J.P.C. Roach; London: Oxford University Press, 1959) 235-65. See also M.M. Garland, *Cambridge Before Darwin* (Cambridge: University Press, 1980).

[3]   A 'pensioner' was a student who paid his own expenses as an ordinary student without scholarship aid. J.R. Tanner, *The Historical Register of the University of Cambridge* (Cambridge: University Press, 1917) 13.

[4]   For Trinity College in Lightfoot's time as a student, see R. Robson, "Trinity College in the Age of Peel," in *Ideas and Institutions of Victorian Britain* (R. Robson ed.; London: Bell, 1967) 312-15.

Greek and Master of the College.[5] Although sharp tongued, he was said to be an admirable Tutor, firm but just in discipline, and able to make his pupils feel that he really was *in loco parentis*. As the College's Classical Lecturer he performed his duties "exceeding well".[6] While Lightfoot's response to him goes unrecorded, Thompson was perhaps one reason for his high expectations of College life not being disappointed.[7]

Intent on being a 'reading man' — still the exception in contemporary Cambridge — Lightfoot soon settled down to work. No doubt he followed the kind of routine described by C.A. Bristed, who had left Cambridge only the year before.[8] The day began with chapel at 7. After breakfast, the morning and early afternoon were given over to tuition. At 2 there was a break of about two hours for exercise before dinner at 4. This was followed by a "lounging time" until evening chapel at 6. The evening was then devoted to study, often until very late. Lightfoot's efforts were spurred on at first by perceived shortcomings in Latin prose composition and the spectre of College examinations.[9] But his sights were set on "the *real* honours of the Tripos examinations", which, he averred to Benson, "indeed are worth having".[10] At the beginning of his second year Lightfoot employed a 'coach', at the time the *sine qua non* of examination success.[11] His choice fell on another Birmingham man, B.F. Westcott, Senior Classic and Chancellor's Medallist in 1848. Just prior to the publication of his triumph in the Tripos Lightfoot had written to Benson:

> The object of my greatest admiration is Westcott. I shall not attempt to tell you all his good qualities, for that would not be very possible, but imagine to yourself one of the most gentlemanly, quietest, humblest, and most conscientious of mankind! (to say nothing of cleverness) and you have my opinion of him.[12]

Six months later Lightfoot became his pupil.

Usually the pupil came to the 'coach' for instruction either daily or every second day, and Lightfoot later recalled with pleasure the many hours spent

---

5   Thompson (1810-1886) was Tutor at Trinity (1844-1853); Regius Professor of Greek (1853-1866); & Master of Trinity (1866-86). Venn, *Alumni* II.VI.168. *DNB* XIX.708-10. J. Willis Clark, *Old Friends at Cambridge and Elsewhere* (London: Macmillan, 1900) 302-13. LB I.97, 121-2.

6   LH I.45.

7   "Thank you for your account of the Lecture Room, and the Sermon, and Mr Thompson." Benson to Lightfoot, 29 October 1847 (PLAB 1842-1848, TCC). Edward Purbrick to Lightfoot, 8 January 1848.

8   C.A. Bristed, *Five Years in an English University* (2nd ed.; New York: Putnam, 1852) 15-22.

9   Lightfoot to Benson, 8 March & 29 April 1848 (PLAB 1842-1848, TCC).

10   Lightfoot to Benson, 19 July 1848 (*ibid.*). The emphasis is Lightfoot's.

11   On the significance of the 'coach', see S. Rothblatt, *The Revolution of the Dons. Cambridge and Society in Victorian England* (London: Faber, 1968) 198-208.

12   Lightfoot to Benson, 8 March 1848, in LB I.55.

in this way.[13] The staple of their work together was in Classics. The pupil was expected to read the authors by himself and rely on his 'coach' for translation and composition. Westcott also provided guidance in Mathematics and (as Lightfoot prepared for the College Fellowship examination) Philosophy.[14] As was not uncommon the relationship became quite friendly, with Westcott providing counsel in matters outside the curriculum as well as jibing his pupil for elementary errors in Mathematics and threatening "heavy penance for unexecuted composition".[15] But his devotion to his pupils was such that it earned the admiration of the College authorities, and Lightfoot had no doubt that he owed his eventual success to his "only private tutor".[16] Westcott's manifest character combined with his scholarship to consolidate the moral and intellectual influence of Prince Lee.[17]

While diligent in his studies Lightfoot was not entirely single-minded, at least in the early part of his undergraduate career.[18] Politics claimed some of his attention, with the events of the 1848 revolution in France at the forefront of his interest.[19] Contemporary Church questions such as the Hampden and baptism controversies were also of concern.[20] In the vacations he visited his brother, who was hard at work as a curate in a Lambeth parish. He also found time for friends, although most of his 'set' were Birmingham men and of a similar caste of mind. A measure of their earnestness was the engagement with Benson, after he came up the following year, to breakfast together every Sunday morning and afterwards to read the Fathers. "This," according to A.C. Benson, "was my father's first introduction to Cyprian whose *De Unitate* they read and discussed."[21] Benson's *Cyprian* which appeared in 1897 was but one outcome of this College friendship for the Victorian Church.

Apart from his studies, the religious question was uppermost in Lightfoot's mind at this time. There was no question of losing his faith. Against a background of some indifference in Cambridge he cultivated his spiritual

---

[13] Lightfoot to Westcott, 12 March 1852 (LAC). The background information in this paragraph is based on Bristed, *Five Years in an English University*, 145-56.

[14] Westcott to Lightfoot, 30 July [1851].

[15] Westcott to Lightfoot, undated in LW I.164; & 5 October [1850].

[16] LW I.108, 124-5.

[17] For Lightfoot's assessment of Westcott, see LW I.124-7. For Westcott's subsequent influence, see further 46-7, 76-7 & 125 below.

[18] See LH I.72 for sharp criticism of somebody who was.

[19] A.A. Ellis to Lightfoot, 3 July 1848; Lightfoot to Benson, 8 March 1848 (PLAB 1842-1848, TCC).

[20] Lightfoot to Benson, 14 January 1848 (PLAB 1842-1848, TCC); J.F. Wickenden to Lightfoot, 7 October 1849.

[21] LB I.74-5.

life, keeping the canonical hours as much as possible.[22] How and where to direct this religiosity was the problem. To Benson he confided:

> I am not at all settled in my Church views, that is, in matters of the so-called high and low Church parties; the more I read on the subject the less fixed I become, and I should be heartily thankful if I saw any prospect of coming to a decided conclusion on such points — yet I hope it may be so.[23]

On the one hand, he castigated Benson for taking part in a schismatical and heretical act of worship by going to hear Newman preach.[24] On the other hand, while admiring the pietism of the Evangelicals, soon after going up to Cambridge he reacted "against the absurdities of the evangelical system, particularly the exaltation of preaching to the detriment of praying".[25] If there were only a choice between Tractarianism and Evangelicalism, it was the former he would have taken unhesitatingly.[26] But he did not make the choice, because the line taken by the Tractarians over Hampden's elevation to the episcopate seemed "inseparable from the system, and there must be something wrong in that belief which excites such feelings in men otherwise good and exemplary".[27] This attitude was modified by a visit to Cambridge by W.F. Hook, Vicar of Leeds, whose "sacrifice of self and selfish desires to his principles" typified "the spirit which animates the High Churchman generally" and offered "the greatest regenerating element among us, the only one ... which will be able to withstand the assaults of Romanism and Protestant Dissent".[28] But Lightfoot felt no necessity to choose between the major Church 'parties'. It was sufficient to show charity to all and maintain inward moral purity.[29] Religious and moral substance mattered more than outward appearance or organization.[30]

---

[22] Lightfoot to Benson, 8 March 1848 (PLAB 1842-1848, TCC). Winstanley, *Early Victorian Cambridge*, 405-6; & Roach, "University of Cambridge," 249-50.

[23] Lightfoot to Benson, 8 March 1848, in LB I.56.

[24] Lightfoot to Benson, 29 April & 19 July 1848 (PLAB 1842-1848, TCC).

[25] J. Pollock, *A Cambridge Movement* (London: John Murray, 1953) 12, alleges the influence on Lightfoot of William Carus, Simeon's successor at Holy Trinity. No source is cited for this claim, and none has been traced. No relationship of any kind is implied in W. Carus to Lightfoot, 31 January 1861. On Simeon, see H.E. Hopkins, *Charles Simeon of Cambridge* (London: Hodder & Stoughton, 1977); & on Carus, A. Pollard, "Carus, William," *The Blackwell Dictionary of Evangelical Biography 1730-1860* (2 vols; ed. D.M. Lewis; Oxford: Blackwell, 1995) I.204.

[26] Lightfoot to Benson, 29 April 1848 (PLAB 1842-1848, TCC).

[27] Lightfoot to Benson, 8 March 1848 (*ibid.*).

[28] Lightfoot to Benson, 19 July 1848 (*ibid.*). On Hook, see W.R. Stephens, *The Life and Letters of Walter Farqhar Hook* (London: Bentley & Son, 1880).

[29] Lightfoot to Benson, 8 March 1848 (PLAB 1842-1848, TCC).

[30] Hinchliff, *God and History*, 77 & 79, comments on the difficulty of classifying the churchmanship of Lightfoot and his friends. He goes on to make the interesting suggestion that they continued "the attitudes and sympathies of the old pre-Tractarian High Church tradition". *Ibid.*, 80. Lightfoot's learning, commitment to the Establishment and restrained

According to Hort, a slightly senior contemporary, Lightfoot "matured slowly" as a student.[31] This probably referred to his lack of success in the University and Craven Scholarship examinations,[32] and evidently he was not considered for election as an Apostle.[33] In every other respect his academic record was distinguished. He was placed in the first class in each College exam (usually at the top of the list),[34] and in the vexatious Previous Examination set by the University early in 1849.[35] The same year he was elected a Scholar of Trinity, as soon as he became eligible.[36] Following the disappointment of the Scholarship examinations, Lightfoot toiled away in preparation for the Tripos finals which he was due to take early in 1851. The results rewarded his diligence. Despite some anxiety about a poor performance,[37] his prowess in Mathematics won the rank of 30th Wrangler.[38] A month later in the Classical Tripos, having handed in papers which were said to contain nothing that might fairly be called a mistake,[39] he finished 125 1/2 marks ahead of his nearest rival, J.B. Mayor - subsequently Professor of Classics at King's College, London.[40] To this success he added the title "First Chancellor's Medallist" in the prize examination which followed soon after.[41] Eighteen months of additional study were rewarded late in

---

sacramentalism are not dissimilar to the outlook of "the orthodox" of the early nineteenth century (on whom, see Storr, *English Theology*, ch. V). But both the changes in ecclesiastical opinion following the advent of Tractarianism and the extent of Lightfoot's liberalism make this classification anachronistic, and to that extent unhelpful. On Lightfoot's churchmanship, see further in Chapter 9 below.

[31] DNB XI.1112.

[32] For Lightfoot's failure to win the Craven in 1850, C.B. Hutchinson to Lightfoot, 22 March 1851 (quoting from his private journal for 20 March 1850). On the University and Craven Scholarships, see Tanner, *Historical Register*, 259.

[33] R. Deacon, *The Cambridge Apostles. A History of Cambridge University's Elite Intellectual Secret Society* (London: R. Royce, 1985) esp. ch. 4.

[34] In his Freshman's, Junior and Senior Sophomore years (examination lists in College Notices, vol. 1, TCC). Benson to Lightfoot, 5 July 1848 & 1849 (PLAB 1842-1848 & 1849-1851, TCC).

[35] UP 18, f. 46 (CUA).

[36] E.W. Benson to his mother, 28 April 1849 (PLAB 1849-1851, TCC). DNB XI.1112.

[37] J.T. Pearse to Lightfoot, 7 January 1851.

[38] "List of Honours At the Bachelor of Arts Commencement, January 25, 1851," UP 20, f. 534 (CUA).

[39] C. Bullock, *The Two Bishops. A Welcome and a Memory* (London: "Home Words", 1890) 51, relates that Lightfoot stayed up the night before his Honours Examination "to read through the only extant classical author whose writings he had not mastered". He was rewarded the next day with a piece of unseen translation from this author.

[40] "Marks. Classical Tripos List. 1851. Made out at the time and sent to me by Roberts December 3rd/67." For Mayor, see Venn, *Alumni* II.IV.379.

[41] A prize designed to promote excellence in Classical learning. J. Willis Clark, *Endowments of the University of Cambridge* (Cambridge: University Press, 1904) 370-3. The medal itself is among the Lightfoot artifacts at the Dean and Chapter Library.

1852 when, unexpectedly, he was elected a Fellow of his College.[42] Over the winter of 1852-3 he drew his formal education to a close by competing successfully for the Norrisian Prize, with an essay on the origin of the Gospels.[43]

Thereafter, Lightfoot stayed on at Trinity, settling down to the routine life of a young resident Fellow, coaching private pupils; and, from 1854, delivering College lectures.[44] In the time left over from these duties he pursued his own studies. The combination of diligence and devotion was later described by Handley Moule:

> No man ever loitered so late in the Great Court that he did not see Lightfoot's lamp burning in his study window; though no man either was so regularly present in morning Chapel at seven o'clock that he did not find Lightfoot always there with him.[45]

From this commitment to study came the beginning of his literary career. The most important undertaking was the inauguration of *The Journal of Classical and Sacred Philology* in association with a number of his contemporaries.[46] The prospectus placed the project in the line of two previous Cambridge attempts to bring English philology up to the German standard, the *Museum Criticum* (1814, 1826) and the *Philological Museum* (1832, 1833). It was due to Lightfoot that "Sacred" was included in the title, and Biblical literature incorporated in the programme.[47] Himself an editor, he contributed articles and reviews on both Classical and Biblical subjects which were the first public indication of his characteristic "exactness of scholarship, width of erudition, scientific method, sobriety of judgment, [and] lucidity of style".[48] After several years the periodical failed, but it had laid down what a specialist philological journal should be like, and helped to establish the philological outlook in English Biblical study where the "evidences" approach still prevailed.[49]

---

[42] Lightfoot to Westcott, 20 August & 9 October 1852 (LAC).

[43] Reprinted in full in G.R. Treloar & B.N. Kaye, "J.B. Lightfoot On Strauss and Christian Origins: An Unpublished Manuscript," *Durham University Journal* LXXIX (1987) 165-200. See further in Chapter 10 below.

[44] DNB XI.1112 says he took private pupils only until 1855. *The Cambridge University Calendar 1854,* 327 & 329 lists him as a Fellow & Assistant Tutor.

[45] H.C.G. Moule, *My Cambridge Classical Teachers* (Durham & Newcastle-on-Tyne: Andrews & Co./W.E. Franklin, 1913) 13.

[46] "The Journal of Classical and Sacred Philology" (Camb. Uni. Papers MR1, CUL). H. Aarsleff, *The Study of Language in England 1780-1860* (Princeton: University Press, 1967) 219-222.

[47] LD 174-5.

[48] W. Sanday, "Bishop Lightfoot," *The Expositor* IV (1886) 13-29, esp. 14, 14-17, 21, 26. For instances of Lightfoot's work in connection with the journal, see Westcott to Lightfoot, 29 November 1853; & Lightfoot to Westcott, 10 April & 17 May 1854 (LAC).

[49] In 1868 the advertisement of its successor, "The Journal of Philology", claimed continuity as "a Second Series of the Journal of Classical and Sacred Philology" (Camb. Uni. Papers MR1, CUL).

It was an article in the *Journal* in 1856 that drew attention to Lightfoot outside Cambridge for the first time. A review of recent English work on St Paul consisted mainly of a stinging critique of editions by A.P. Stanley and Benjamin Jowett, both soon to be professors at Oxford.[50] At a time of considerable *odium theologicum,* the absence of malignity was as impressive as the manifest competence of the analysis.[51] When consulted, John Conington, Professor of Latin at Oxford, advised Stanley to surrender at discretion. Stanley did better than this. He put forward Lightfoot's name to the Bishop of London as a likely Cambridge chaplain.[52]

As his reputation grew Lightfoot was subsequently invited to contribute to a dictionary of the Bible and a commentary to be compiled by the distinguished editor William Smith (1813-93).[53] Also in the field of early Christian literature he undertook projected editions of St Paul,[54] the Muratorian Fragment,[55] and the Apostolic Fathers.[56] In Classics he planned to edit Aristotle and Aeschylus,[57] and took part in arrangements for a Cambridge Plato.[58] Compared with the seed sown, little fruit was harvested — at least in the short term — but a conception of Cambridge as a place for energetic study, and literary output, had already taken shape when many dons were still sunk in their more leisurely Georgian ways.[59]

Following the discipline of the two triposes, Lightfoot indulged in a new diversity of activity in his pursuit of knowledge and understanding. At Cam-

[50] J.B. Lightfoot, "Recent Editions of St Paul's Epistles," *Journal of Classical and Sacred Philology* III.vii (1856) 81-121.

[51] R.E. Prothero & G.G. Bradley, *The Life and Correspondence of Arthur Penrhyn Stanley* (2 vols; London: John Murray, 1893) I.475-6. The author of this part of the biography actually quotes (without acknowledgement) Lightfoot's review for his description of the two editions. *Ibid.*, 473-4.

[52] Stanley to A.C. Tait, 12 October 1856, in Prothero & Bradley, *Life of Stanley,* I.207.

[53] Lightfoot to Westcott, 23 & 26 February 1857, & 15 February 1858 (LAC); W. Smith to Lightfoot, 8 April & 28 October 1861. See "Romans," "Thessalonians, First Epistle to the," & "Thessalonians, Second Epistle to the," *A Dictionary of The Bible* (3 vols; W. Smith ed.; London: John Murray, 1863) III.1053-8, 1477-84. On Smith, see DNB XVIII.561-2.

[54] Lightfoot to Westcott, 4 December 1859 (LAC). See 312-3 below.

[55] S.P. Tregelles to Lightfoot, 25 June 1859.

[56] LD 8-9 (probably an inference from AF II.I².ix). See further 336-8 below.

[57] Lightfoot to Westcott, 12 March 1852 (LAC). "The Aeschylean Tetralogy," unpublished manuscript among the Lightfoot Papers.

[58] H. Montagu Butler to Lightfoot, 2 April 1860; F. Vaughan Hawkins to Lightfoot, 13 October 1860. LH I.349, 361, 416, 424. The plan ran into Jowett's Oxford scheme and was abandoned. Jowett to Lightfoot, 14 May 1860.

[59] J.W. Clark, "Social Life at Cambridge - 'Tis Sixty Years Since," in *Cambridge. Brief Historical and Descriptive Notes* (London: Seeley, Jackson & Haliday, 1881) ch. XI. See also Walter Besant's memories of the dons at Christ's College in the 1850s in *Autobiography* (1902) 81, quoted in W. Houghton, *The Victorian Frame of Mind 1830-1870* (New Haven & London: Yale University Press, 1957) 144 n. 23.

bridge he took an interest in attempts to study the mind-body relationship.[60] He displayed a similar openness to phenomena, by joining the much maligned "Ghostly Guild", a society established by Westcott "for the investigation of all supernatural appearances and effects".[61] Beyond Cambridge, the physical world was explored through long walks and through the interest in geology he shared with Westcott.[62]

Lightfoot was also drawn increasingly into the domain of practical affairs. Friends noted an increasing interest in politics, in which he was an active Conservative.[63] As the work of the Royal Commissions into Cambridge proceeded he became involved in the reform of his College.[64] From 1855 he took an increasing part in the educational and administrative work of the University, serving often as an examiner and on numerous committees, syndicates and boards.[65] His activities beyond reached an ever widening circle. He lectured for a term in German in the Cambridge Working Man's College,[66] and he was regularly invited to examine in Classics in a number of public schools such as Harrow, Rugby and Sherbourne.

With the benefit of his income as a College Fellow and 'coach', Lightfoot also at this time began a life-long habit of foreign travel. Mostly the trips were devoted to acquiring a first-hand knowledge of art treasures and classical and ecclesiastical antiquities, while the visit to Rome in the winter of 1854-5 brought the additional gratification of an audience with the Pope.[67] In the summers he also liked to escape the heat of Cambridge for the cool of highland areas in Scotland or Northern Europe. Even here his efforts were marked by deep seriousness of purpose, as when in the summer of 1856 he

---

[60] Lightfoot to Westcott, 12 March 1852 (LAC). See also the remark in LS 176.

[61] For the prospectus, see Camb. Uni. Papers MR 101 (CUL). See also LW I.117-20; LH I.171-2, 211, 219-20; A.S. & E.M.S., *Henry Sidgwick: A Memoir* (London: Macmillan, 1906) 43. For Lightfoot's membership, LB I.98, & J.T. Pearse to Lightfoot, 8 April 1852.

[62] On Lightfoot's propensity for walking, see E.A. Lightfoot to J.R. Harmer, 3 April n.y. [1893?]. Westcott to Lightfoot, 1 September 1855 (partly printed in LW I.232-3) & 27 April 1856. Also "Geological notes with coloured sections of strata" (MS 274.208.L5, DUL).

[63] R. Livingstone to Lightfoot, 9 May 1853. For Lightfoot's activities as a Conservative, Cam.b.1.1.4.74, 85, 91 & Cam.a.500.6[18c] (CUL).

[64] For an example of this involvement, see E. Graham, *The Harrow Life of Henry Montagu Butler* (London: Longmans, 1920) 82. See further 174-77 below.

[65] His first task was to examine for the Le Bas Prize in 1855 (Collecteana UP 23, CUA). He first examined in Theology in 1857 (*ibid.*, UP 25). His first syndicate was the Library Syndicate, in 1855 (*ibid.*, UP 25).

[66] Letter of thanks from members of the class dated 15 December 1855. For the College, H.D. Rawnsley, *Harvey Goodwin, Bishop of Carlyle. A Biographical Memoir* (London: John Murray, 1896) 80-3; & LH I.300, 315, 317-19.

[67] Lightfoot recorded the events of the tour in two pocket notebooks which are now preserved among the Lightfoot papers. Also LB I.122-3.

spent two months mountaineering in Switzerland.[68] The world was the scene
of God's activity, past and present, and not a moment was to be lost in learning his ways from it and in rising to the challenges it presented.

Amid all these changes, Lightfoot's friendships entered a new phase as
his close acquaintances, all of whom wanted to marry, moved on to posts
away from the University. In 1852 Benson and Westcott accepted teaching
appointments at Rugby and Harrow respectively. Five years later Hort accepted the College living of St Ippolyt's near Hitchin. In the years to come
there developed between them something of a network which was held together by common concerns, regular correspondence, periodic visits to one
another and occasional shared holidays. The continuing link with Benson
was marked by the dedication of the 1876 edition of *Galatians,* "In affectionate and grateful recognition of a long, close, and unbroken friendship".[69]
What this meant was revealed in 1883 when Benson became Archbishop of
Canterbury. From their schooldays, Lightfoot reminisced, "I do not believe
there has been a thought or wish in the mind or heart of either which he has
not shared with the other".[70] The youthful A.C. Benson found the gravity of
a mid-Victorian clerical friendship rather strange.[71] It is true that not much
of a personal nature seemed to pass between them, and Lightfoot was evidently unaware of his friend's disposition to depression.[72] But, concerned
mainly with ecclesiastical affairs and theology, their mutual support and criticism was a source of great help to both of them, and therefore became a
force in the life of the Church.[73]

Of yet greater significance, however, was the continuing connection with
Westcott. For the time being Lightfoot kept him in touch with events in
Cambridge. They consulted on career choices — already they were contriv-
ing to get Westcott back to the University.[74] They encouraged one another
in their literary work, acted as mutual sources of bibliographic and factual
information, and worked together on a number of joint literary projects. At

---

[68] Hort to Lightfoot, 3 & 10 July 1856. LH I.306-7, 326-45. See F. Vaughan Hawkins,
Peaks, Passes and Glaciers (London, 1859) 58-74.

[69] LB I.408.

[70] LB II.8-9. Benson responded in Benson to Lightfoot, 14 May 1883, in LB II.10.

[71] A.C. Benson, *The Trefoil. Wellington College, Lincoln and Truro* (London: John
Murray, 1923) 160.

[72] On Benson & his family, see D. Williams, *Genesis and Exodus. A Portrait of the
Benson Family* (London: Hamish Hamilton, 1979).

[73] When Benson was proposed for the See of Calcutta, Lightfoot said that he did not
know what he would do without his friend close at hand. Lightfoot to Westcott, 22 May
1876 (LAC). For Benson's irritation with Lightfoot at a later point, see 225 & 374 below.

[74] Lightfoot to Westcott, 23 February 1857; 3 June, 15 August & 5, 11, 12, 13 October
1861. Westcott to Lightfoot, 26 February 1857 (LW I.202); 3 January 1859 (LW I.203); 26
& 27 September, 3, 12 & 14 October 1861.

one point Westcott asked Lightfoot to report on his orthodoxy, a request that was renewed at least once subsequently.[75] In return he consulted Westcott on points of interpretation.[76] Lightfoot memorialized his indebtedness in the dedication of *Colossians* to Westcott:

In Affectionate Remembrance

of

MANY VALUABLE LESSONS LEARNT

From

An Intimate Private Friendship

And From

Association In a Common Work

Westcott in turn passed judgment on his friend's career on three landmark occasions and found in it a fulfilment of the law of the Christian life, "from strength to strength".[77] The inscription he subsequently composed for Lightfoot's monument in Durham Cathedral — *Antiquitatis investigator, evangelii interpres, ecclesiae rector* — applied equally to himself, and summed up the importance of their close association for the Church and theology of Victorian England.[78]

Amid this activity Lightfoot worried increasingly about his career. There was no question about becoming a clergyman. This had been his unaltered intention at least from the beginning of his undergraduateship. Accordingly, he was ordained deacon by Prince Lee in 1857 and priest in 1859.[79] But he was uncertain about which branch of ministry to pursue. His preference was for parochial work, but school teaching was an alternative he could not quite dismiss. Before ordination, Prince Lee had written:

> I can easily understand your uncertainty as to your future course. If you decide on taking orders I most earnestly beseech you at once to decide, and act on the decision, as to what branch of ministry you will follow up. If pastoral teaching, at once, take a Curacy; if teaching in general education, at once seek a school; if theology, at once begin to read, and edit, or write. *Virtus in agendo constat.*[80]

But Lightfoot could not decide.[81] At one stage he thought of following in Prince Lee's footsteps, and sought the Headmastership of Repton School in

---

[75] Westcott to Lightfoot, 3 November 1859, in LW I.208. Westcott to Lightfoot, 13 January & 21 February 1865. Lightfoot to Westcott, 26 September 1865 (LAC). Lightfoot deprecated publication of a paper on Our Lady of La Salette. Lightfoot to Westcott, 3 November n.y. [1865] (LAC). Cf. LW I.253-6.

[76] Eg. Lightfoot to Westcott, 25 March 1862 & 15 April n.y. (LAC).

[77] B.F. Westcott, *From Strength to Strength. Three Sermons on Stages in a Conse-crated Life* (London: Macmillan, 1890).

[78] See further on the Lightfoot-Westcott relationship on 125 below.

[79] His Letters of Orders are among the Lightfoot Papers at Durham Cathedral.

[80] Prince Lee to Lightfoot, 19 February 1853. The emphases are Prince Lee's.

[81] His indecision is reflected in letters by C.B. Scott, 21 July 1854; A.E. Ellis, 15 July 1854; J.T. Pearse, 3 August 1854; P.R. Atkinson, 17 August & 6 September 1854, & 8 February 1857; & J.S. Purton, 28 September 1855.

Derby, withdrawing only at the last minute.[82] Under the influence of Professor Blunt,[83] he then reverted to the earlier notion that a parish might be the place to realize his service ethic, an ideal invigorated by the visit to Cambridge of Bishop Selwyn of New Zealand.[84] But he went no further than serving as a *locum tenens* in the Warwickshire village of Harborough Magna in the summer of 1854.[85]

Nor did he necessarily want to remain at Cambridge. This was partly because the University did not yet offer an established career structure for promising young scholars.[86] But Lightfoot had also long had reservations about "the easy and insidious life" which election to a Fellowship had done nothing to resolve.[87] But two events indicated that Cambridge might be his post of duty after all. The article in the *Journal of Classical and Sacred Philology* in 1856 that reviewed recent English work on St Paul demonstrated his prowess as a scholar. Benson advised:

> It is indeed the best thing you ever have done yet, and I hope and trust the *worst* of all that you are going to do. Depend upon it scholarship and not parochialism is your field.[88]

More important, early in 1857 Lightfoot was appointed unexpectedly as one of the three Tutors of Trinity.[89] He regarded the position as "a noble one" and the work as "hopeful".[90] Handley Moule recorded the prayer with which he embarked on his new role:

---

[82] Lightfoot to Westcott, 17, 20, 26 May 1854 (LAC). Westcott to Lightfoot, 13, 22, 30 May 1854. Testimonials of B.F. Westcott, H.A.J. Munro & W.H. Bateson. The appointment went to the highly successful S.A. Pears. See A. MacDonald, *A Short History of Repton* (London: Ernest Benn, 1929) esp. ch. VII.

[83] LB I.103. Blunt was Lady Margaret Professor of Divinity. His lectures on 'The Duties of a Parish Priest' delivered in the Lent term of 1852 (Cam.a.500.1.32, CUL) were published as J.J. Blunt, *The Acquirements and Principal Obligations and Duties of the Parish Priest.* I have used the second edition of 1857.

[84] Lightfoot to Westcott, 31 May 1854 (LAC). Together with the Indian Mutiny of 1857, the visit seems also to have stimulated his interest in Christian missions. Eg. 4th Group, 1858, 21 & 23.

[85] His first three sermons were preached there, between 16 July & 27 August 1854. See 398 in the Bibliography below.

[86] Rothblatt, *Revolution of the Dons*, 180, 198-202.

[87] Lightfoot to Benson, 8 March 1848 (LB I.56). Lightfoot to Westcott, 17 October 1856. There is a hint that Lightfoot thought of matrimony in H.B. Purton to Lightfoot, 1 November 1853, but the evidence that he seriously considered an act which would have taken him from Cambridge does not amount to very much.

[88] LB I.127.

[89] "Tutors of Trinity College, Cambridge, From the Commencement of Regular Sides About A.D. 1750," Cam.a.500.2.21 (CUL). "... it appears that he [E.M. Cope] took in dudgeon being passed over for Lightfoot." Diary of Joseph Romilly, vol. 30, entry of 4 November 1861 (Add 6840², CUL). LD 4 wrongly assigns the appointment to 1859.

[90] Lightfoot to Westcott, 23 February 1857 (LAC).

Since it hath pleased thee, O Lord, that I should be called to take my part in the teaching of this College ... grant that neither by word or [sic] deed I may do aught that may weaken the faith or slacken the practice of those committed to my charge; but rather grant me such a measure of Thy Holy Spirit that my duties may be discharged to Thy honour and glory, and to the welfare of both the teacher and the taught.[91]

This recognition of the possibilities of the position accounts for Lightfoot's being at Trinity the first of the new breed of tutors just beginning to appear in Cambridge.[92] These were men who rejected the donnish aloofness that had characterized tutors in recent times.[93] Instead they took the teaching and pastoral responsibilities of the position seriously, and sought to get alongside the undergraduates in their interests and pursuits. While not going so far as Leslie Stephen,[94] Lightfoot took an interest in the College boats and in its cricket teams.[95] Awkward disciplinary functions were exercized in a gentlemanly and considerate manner — although he could be firm when necessary.[96] He supported a proposal to obviate the abuse of undergraduates not hearing a single sermon in their time at College and took his share of the additional preaching in the chapel this required.[97] His teaching of Classics and Theology was of the highest order. In addition to his routine classes he gave evening readings in his rooms on Aeschylus at which attendance was voluntary.[98] Occasionally in the long vacations he took groups to the Lakes District as reading parties.[99] He seems to have known the men on his side and their individual requirements,[100] and in the case of one man at least who was not well off provided occasional private tuition.[101] Predictably, the un-

---

[91] "From a Prayer by J.B. Lightfoot upon entering on the Tutorship," 1857, in H.C.G. Moule, *"Wise Men and Scribes." A Commemoration Sermon Preached in the Chapel of Trinity College Cambridge, December 10th, 1907* (Cambridge: Bowes & Bowes, 1907) 12.

[92] Henry Jackson to A.O. Pritchard, 11 June 1916, in R. St John Parry, *Henry Jackson, O.M.* (Cambridge: University Press, 1926) 243. Jackson cursed his luck that he was not on Lightfoot's side.

[93] Rothblatt, *Revolution of the Dons*, ch. 6.

[94] *Ibid.*, 188-9. Annan, *Godless Victorian*, 28-39.

[95] LD 6; Collecteana UP 31, f. 525 (CUA) records that Lightfoot gave fifty pounds towards a new cricket ground for the College. The context suggests 1861 as the date. "You will be glad to hear that First Trinity kept its place on the river." Lightfoot to Jenny Barber, 1 June 1869 (Malden Gift, DCL).

[96] LD 7.

[97] Letters to Seniors (Chapel) (Add. Ms.a.6$^{32-3}$, TCC).

[98] Moule, *"Wise Men,"* 10; & *My Cambridge Classical Teachers,* 14-15.

[99] H. Montagu Butler to Lightfoot, 2 April & 4 May 1860; A. Sidgwick to Lightfoot, 19 September 1860.

[100] C. Jebb, *Life and Letters of Sir Richard Claverhouse Jebb* (Cambridge: University Press, 1907) 25, 32-3.

[101] Moule, *"Wise Men,"* 10. J.B. Harford & F.C. MacDonald, *Handley Carr Glyn Moule Bishop of Durham,* (London: Hodder & Stoughton, n.d.) 16, 19.

dergraduates were mixed in their responses. The indolent no doubt found him priggish, while others found his shyness and reserve a barrier to their progress.[102] But there were some — Handley Moule, Richard Jebb, and the American William Everett — who found in Lightfoot a friend and model for their own formation.[103] Being Tutor of Trinity satisfied Lightfoot's pastoral ambitions, at least for the time being.

But this did not mean that he was finally committed to life at the University. Four years later he confided to Westcott:

> I am happy enough in my present position, but my tutorship will cease in the natural course of things in a few years and, if I know my own mind, will cease much earlier by my own act. Whether it is good for me to remain at Cambridge or not, I cannot make up my mind. And in this perplexity I hope it is not acting an ungodly part to be led by circumstances- Therefore as at present advised I shall accept either University office or parochial work as it falls my way.[104]

In this state of uncertainty Lightfoot had become a candidate (in 1860) for the newly created Hulsean Professorship of Divinity, though he did not consider himself a theologian.[105] When C.J. Ellicott was elected, he decided that Classics would be his field of scholarship, and Aeschylus his special subject.[106] But this resolve was put aside a year later when Ellicott was appointed to the Deanery of Exeter.[107] Suspicion of his opinions notwithstanding,[108] Lightfoot was chosen as his successor though still only 33 years of age. The election was to be the turning point in his career in two respects. "Circumstances" had determined that the vocation he had long sought was to be at Cambridge as a clerical don, and also that Theology would be his discipline. A further result was that Trinity College remained his home, as it had been already for fifteen years.

II

Apart from noting the fact of his academic success, almost no attention has been given to the effect on his formation of Lightfoot's time at Trinity. Indeed, one impression created by Newsome's account of his school is that, after Prince Lee, the University contributed little to the thinking of King

---

[102] Farrar, "Bishop Lightfoot," 174, 180.

[103] Moule, '*Wise Men*," 9-11; Jebb, *Jebb*, 20, 119; H. Montagu Butler to Lightfoot, 4 May 1860.

[104] Lightfoot to Westcott, 5 October 1861 (LAC).

[105] Lightfoot to Westcott, 15 August & 25 October 1861 (LAC). He wanted the post because it would afford greater leisure for reading.

[106] BL 20. On Ellicott (1819-1905), see DNB Supplement January 1901 - December 1911, I.618-19.

[107] Ellicott to the Vice Chancellor, 19 June 1861 (CUR 39.25.3.11a, CUA).

[108] "I am told that when some one mentioned my name to Ellicott as his probable successor, he declared that we must have a safer man." Lightfoot to Westcott, 16 October n.y. [1861] (LAC).

Edward's alumni.[109] Superficially, at least, there appear to be some grounds for the inference. Lee's teaching had been intended partly as a preparation for Cambridge,[110] while the subjects taught at College were largely the same, except that Mathematics became more prominent.[111] As an undergraduate, moreover, Lightfoot continued in the Birmingham "set", while in his determination to be a "reading man",[112] he displayed the same intensely moral attitude to knowledge inculcated at school. But although his University education was continuous in content and spirit with his schooling, it would be strange if somebody of Lightfoot's wide ranging intellect and capacity for work, at such an impressionable time of life, were not significantly affected by the environment of Trinity College.

A fundamental influence was the curriculum itself. At mid-century, College instruction was governed by the idea of a liberal education, according to which the object of undergraduate study was mental training.[113] Notwithstanding the introduction of Natural and Moral Sciences Triposes in 1848, Mathematics and Classics were still seen as the supreme means of attaining this end. Lightfoot was an ornament of the system. Apart from his success in both subjects, the qualities which the regimen was said to engender — speed, accuracy, thoroughness, comprehensiveness, method and objectivity —[114] were the very qualities contemporaries noted as characteristic of his work.[115] In time, he showed himself capable of mastering new disciplines, as the "ideal" required. Not only did Lightfoot reflect the rationale of the system in his intellectual development; he also adopted it when he himself became a College teacher. The specified ends of mental training and character-formation were important to him, as subsequent attitudes to Cambridge indicate.[116] The basic principle, the doctrine of final causes, was affirmed frequently,[117] while its correlate, the unity of knowledge, underlay his conception of a university.[118]

---

[109] This is partly corrected in D. Newsome, *Two Classes of Men. Platonism and English Romantic Thought* (London: John Murray, 1974) ch. 5.
[110] E.W. Benson to William Jackson, 30 November 1844 (PLAB 1842-1848, TCC).
[111] The subjects for College examinations are listed in College Notices, vol. I, TCC.
[112] C.B. Hutchinson to Lightfoot, Feast of St Michael [29 September], 1847.
[113] On which, see Garland, *Cambridge Before Darwin*; R.G. McPherson, *Theory of Higher Education in Nineteenth-Century England* (Athens: University of Georgia Press, 1959); & S. Rothblatt, *"Tradition and Change" in English Liberal Education: An Essay in History and Culture* (London: Faber & Faber, 1976).
[114] Bristed, *Five Years in an English University*, 15ff., 123.
[115] Moule, *My Cambridge Classical Teachers*, 12-15. W. Sanday, "Bishop Lightfoot," *The Expositor* IV (July 1886) 13-29, & "Bishop Lightfoot," *The Academy* no. 922 (4 January 1890) 9-10. B.F. Westcott, "Prefatory Note," in A.F. I.1.vii.
[116] See 169-70, 176-7 & 181-2 below.
[117] NTI 172; BE 225-6; CS 16-17; SSO 115; & OA 299-300.
[118] CS 188.

While noting, in passing, that Cambridge was still a virtual clerical monopoly, writers on the subject have undervalued the character of the Christianity which stood behind its educational ideology. This was a "natural theology" — no longer strictly Paleyan —[119] which stressed the spiritual nature of all reality, and which justified formal study, in its diversity, as a unified quest for knowledge of God's ways. This was the outlook which Lightfoot, prepared at school by his reading of Butler, readily embraced at the University and carried into manhood.[120]

The leading exponents of this outlook in contemporary Cambridge were William Whewell and Adam Sedgwick, Master and Vice-Master of Lightfoot's College, both of whom had an important bearing on his formation.[121] In a letter to Lightfoot, Benson remembered Sedgwick as one of "the great stimulating powers of healthful study in our undergraduateship".[122] When Lightfoot became a Fellow, this influence ripened into personal friendship — the experience of which, because of Sedgwick's longevity, confirmed in him that faith in the capacity of the human mind to remember over long periods of time that functioned as one of his assumptions in dealing with early Christian traditions.[123] He was also helpful to a young clerical don as one who combined "the spirit of scientific discovery" with "the spirit of hopefulness, of devout trust in an Eternal Purpose".[124]

The more aloof Whewell, too, was known from undergraduate days, but mainly by means of his books, which had to be studied for College exams.[125] Subsequently, Lightfoot came to such an appreciation of Whewell's academic career that he was pressed to become the official biographer.[126] When

---

[119] On the modifications to eighteenth century natural theology in early Victorian scientific thought, R. Young, "The Impact of Darwin on Conventional Thought," in *The Victorian Crisis of Faith* (ed. A. Symondson; London: S.P.C.K., 1970) 13-35.

[120] Eg. OA 221, 299-300.

[121] William Whewell (1794-1866), Professor of Mineralogy (1828-32) & of Moral Philosophy (1838-55); Master of Trinity College (1841-1866). Venn, *Alumni* II.VI.425. Adam Sedgwick (1785-1873), Woodwardian Professor of Geology (1818-73); Vice Master of Trinity College (1844-62). *Ibid.*, II.V.456. See G.M. Trevelyan, *Trinity College. An Historical Sketch* (Cambridge: University Press, 1943) ch. IX; & Robson, "Trinity College," 332ff.

[122] Benson to Lightfoot, 8 June 1875 (PLAB 1873 to 1877, TCC).

[123] EWSR 99. CS 222.

[124] *Cambridge University Reporter* (27 March 1873) 125. Lightfoot subscribed 200 pounds to the Sedgwick memorial fund (Camb. Uni. Papers FA 7799, CUL).

[125] Whewell introduced Philosophy into the Trinity Fellowship Examination, and his *Elements of Morality* had been prescribed for Trinity undergraduates as an introduction to the subject. Lightfoot also read his studies in Natural Theology. Tanner, *Historical Register*, 84 n. 6; A.S. & E.M.S., *Henry Sidgwick*, 42 n. 1; & Appendix 1 below.

[126] Lightfoot to J.L. Hammond, 16, 27, 29 October 1874; 11, 16, 30 April & 22 August 1875 (Ad. Ms.a.17[217-223], TCC). J. Stair-Douglas to Lightfoot, n.d. & 21 May & 12 October 1875.

Whewell died, Lightfoot regarded him as irreplaceable;[127] and the commemorative sermon he preached put aside acknowledged character flaws, and instead extolled his "range and vigour of intellect".[128]

Apart from providing a general scholarly ideal, Whewell and Sedgwick helped Lightfoot to an understanding of the phenomenon of man and mind, which was basic to his whole outlook. Beginning with Sedgwick's *Discourse* in 1832,[129] and continuing in a series of educational, and scientific and philosophical treatises by Whewell, they developed a metaphysical epistemology, opposed to the Lockean philosophy of mind dominant in Georgian Cambridge.[130] With Whewell the more sophisticated, both men stressed the creative contribution of the mind itself in the generation of knowledge. While certainly not innate, it was the outcome of the interaction between divinely planted mental faculties, and the external world of stimuli. In Whewell's scheme, the native powers of mind, or fundamental truths, were dynamic, in that, as they are acted upon by experience, they lead on to the creation of new truths in a never ending series. Thus knowledge, he claimed, consists of "thought and things", and cannot exist where there is not a practical union of the two. Lightfoot never considered the philosophy of mind formally, since it was never in his interest to do so, but the elements of the Trinity perspective are present throughout his works. There was a similar belief in inherent mental powers, spoken of as "intellectual endowments",[131] "faculties of mind",[132] and"intuitions".[133] Lightfoot also claimed the necessary reciprocity between these capacities and the phenomena of sense in cognition: "... on the one hand our intuitions are developed by contact with the external world, while on the other no accumulation of facts can call forth an idea, the germ of which is not implanted in our soul".[134]

The interrelation of the two sources of knowledge was clarified by the use of Whewell's distinction between the subjective and objective as Idea and Fact. The Idea is the informing principle which imparts meaning to the

---

[127] Lightfoot to Westcott, 6 March 1866 (LAC).

[128] J.B. Lightfoot, *In Memory of William Whewell. A Sermon Preached in the College Chapel on Sunday, March 18, 1866* (London & Cambridge: Macmillan, 1866). Reprinted in CS, 109-25, to which reference is made. See esp. 115-17.

[129] A. Sedgwick, *A Discourse on the Studies of the University of Cambridge. The Fifth Edition, With Additions, and a Preliminary Dissertation* (Cambridge & London: John Deighton/John Parker, 1850).

[130] The best account in a growing body of scholarship is Yeo, "British Natural Theology," ch. 4.

[131] CS 53.

[132] Eg. CS 55, 58-9.

[133] LS 178.

[134] LS 178.

Facts, while reception of the Facts as such is the condition of properly understanding the Idea.[135]

Finally, Lightfoot allowed a like scope for the progressive realization of mental conceptions — "Education *does* develope [*sic*]; experience *does* ripen" — an understanding applied not only to "the intellectual reason" but also to "the moral consciousness".[136] Although too rudimentary and inchoate to be called a theory of mind, Lightfoot's understanding of knowledge, like that of his Cambridge mentors, was idealist, and the concomitant ethical theory, likewise intuitionist.[137]

This epistemology provided the rationale of Lightfoot's own homiletical and scholarly efforts. Preaching became the presentation of the facts established by the intellect to the religious consciousness for its existential deliverances. Experience and reason were thus held together in the apprehension and interpretation of religious truth. In formal study, Lightfoot was attracted to the working Baconianism which underpinned the achievement of his mentors.[138] He himself had read the *Novum Organum* of Francis Bacon,[139] while he also lauded the thirteenth century Roger Bacon whose persistence in the establishment of facts in the face of ecclesiastical opposition entitled him to rank as one of the founders of modern England.[140] Confidence in the same method underlay his understanding of how knowledge advances. Using the pendulum as a model for what appears to happen to disputed subjects in history and theology, he maintained that:

> those who watch its motion narrowly will see that its arc is each time shorter than before, and that in spite of the impulse given to it by perverted ingenuity, it is being brought gradually to a position of equilibrium, under the gravitation of common sense. This is an obvious, and probably a trite, comparison, but it is worthy the attention of those who see in the shoals of treatises and articles on minute critical subjects with which the modern press teems, only the multiplying of books without any corresponding increase of knowledge.[141]

---

[135] LS 187. The distinction occurs in W. Whewell, *The Elements of Morality, Including Polity* (2 vols; London: J.W. Parker, 1845) I.2-3.

[136] CS 168. The emphases are Lightfoot's.

[137] On the nature of Cambridge thought in the period, R.O. Preyer, "The Romantic Tide Reaches Trinity: Notes on the Transmission and Diffusion of New Approaches to Traditional Studies at Cambridge," in *Victorian Science and Victorian Values: Literary Perspectives* (J. Paradis & T. Postlewait eds; New York: New York Academy of Sciences, 1981) 39-68; & J.B. Schneewind, *Sidgwick's Ethics and Victorian Moral Philosophy* (Oxford: Clarendon Press, 1977).

[138] R. Yeo, "An Idol of the Market-Place: Baconianism in Nineteenth Century Britain," *History of Science* XXIII (1985) 251-98, esp. 267-77. More generally M. Gauvreau, "Baconianism, Darwinism, Fundamentalism: A Transatlantic Crisis of Faith," *Journal of Religious History* 13.4 (December 1985) 434-44.

[139] His notes are written in the back of a Latin prose notebook filed in "Miscellaneous Cambridge Papers" in the Lightfoot Papers.

[140] HE 174-81.

[141] OSCG 289.

Lightfoot's own early writings were conceived as a contribution towards this gradual advance. They also displayed a consciousness of method, and his occasional admissions of the limitations of the induction were an implicit invitation to study further along these lines.[142] Even though vigorously empirical in execution, his studies were conducted on the assumption that they were simultaneously extending understanding of the underlying metaphysical reality, and that no conflict between the two could arise. Like Whewell and Sedgwick — although on a narrower front — Lightfoot became a researcher, Baconian in method within an idealist framework, rather than a systematizer of existing knowledge, which the Common Sense Philosophy required.

Lightfoot's general intellectual outlook also illuminates his religious development. Sedgwick and Whewell were both liberal Anglicans (though only Sedgwick was a liberal in politics). In this, they carried forward the theological tradition created at Trinity in the 1820s when they were resident Fellows.[143] Particularly important in its formation were Julius Hare and Connop Thirlwall, who were similarly committed to the complementarity of faith and reason, and who promoted Platonic philosophy, German historical scholarship and the poetry of Wordsworth and Coleridge. One pupil who came under their influence and then in turn gave much back to his mentors (without necessarily securing their agreement) was F.D. Maurice.[144] He, too, was a follower of Coleridge.[145] Both Hare and Thirlwall were still powerful influences on the religious thinking of the College almost twenty years later when Lightfoot became a part of its society.

In the past the influence of Coleridge and Maurice on Lightfoot has been assumed by scholars — no doubt because it was probable in itself, and also because it could be clearly traced for the Cambridge Triumvirate in the experience of Hort.[146] If the connection is not so easily exhibited in Lightfoot's case, it can still be shown. Certainly he read Maurice's more important

---

[142] Eg. *ibid.,* 303 n. 2, 305 n. 1, 306-7, 308, 321 n. 1.

[143] See 9-10 above. Brent, *Liberal Anglican Politics,* 163-6; Cannon, *Science in Culture,* ch. 2; Distad, *Guesses at Truth,* ch. 4.

[144] Maurice became Hare's brother-in-law. For Maurice, see A. Vidler, *F.D. Maurice and Company* (London: S.C.M., 1966); & T. Christensen, *The Divine Order. A Study of F.D. Maurice's Theology* (Leiden: Brill, 1973).

[145] For Coleridge, C.R. Sanders, *Coleridge and the Broad Church Movement* (North Carolina: Duke University Press, 1942); & D. Pym, *The Religious Thought of Samuel Taylor Coleridge* (Gerrard's Cross: C. Smythe, 1978).

[146] Newsome, *Godliness,* 11-12, 241 n. 25; C. Welch, *Protestant Thought in the Nineteenth Century* (2 vols; New Haven & London: Yale University Press, 1972-1985) 1.123-4; & I.M. Bubb, "The Theology of F.J.A. Hort, In Relation to Nineteenth Century Thought" (unpublished Ph.D. thesis; Manchester, 1956).

books,[147] and there are Mauricean resonances throughout his early work. He joined with Maurice, for example, in insisting upon the interpenetration of the human order by the kingdom of God.[148] He rejected the orthodox objective view of the atonement as a penal substitution for the sins of mankind,[149] and advanced a similar notion of the day of judgment as a full manifestation of that righteousness which is ever present in the universe as the pre-existent Christ.[150] Further, he came to share the view that the use of theology as a "living stem" is to interpret all the thoughts and aspirations of the age.[151] Lightfoot's participation in the Cambridge Working Men's College is also interesting in this respect. Later he welcomed Maurice's election to the Knightbridge Chair, and maintained a close personal friendship when he returned to Cambridge.[152]

The connection with Coleridge was probably more important. Lightfoot had read the *Aids to Reflection* by 1853,[153] and subsequently at least the *Table Talk*[154] and *Confessions of an Inquiring Spirit*.[155] From the last he accepted the possibility of the miraculous in the communication of revelation, while he echoed frequently the protest of the first against "evidences" theology.[156] Although he conceived of much of his writing as belonging to this genre as he understood it,[157] Lightfoot gave the primacy as a reason for faith to the capacity of Christianity to meet the individual's needs at the point of experience.[158] This crucial Coleridgean distinction, between the inward and the external, corresponded to the duality inherent in his epistemology as Idea and Fact, something which Lightfoot regarded as "the fun-

---

[147] Lightfoot had read *Moral and Metaphysical Philosophy* by 1853 (LS 187 n. 72). His own copy was the edition of 1872. He also possessed *The Conscience. Lectures on Casuistry* (1868) & *Social Morality* (1869). See *Catalogue of Books Bequeathed to the University of Durham, by Joseph Barber Lightfoot, D.D., Late Lord Bishop* (Durham, 1891) 55.

[148] Lightfoot preached three separate sermons under the title, "The Kingdom of God," on 5 August 1855, 6 March 1859, & 23 June 1861. Between them, they were preached on 14 occasions between 1855 and 1876.

[149] CS 289-96.

[150] For Lightfoot's eschatology, see 66 & 113 below.

[151] RCC (1873) 231.

[152] LH II.78. Maurice to Lightfoot 26 October & 12 November 1866. Lightfoot also subscribed to the Maurice Memorial Fund ("Professor J.F.D. Maurice Memorial Fund [1872]," Camb. Uni. Papers BP 552, CUL).

[153] LS 194 n. 114. Cf. Notes on the Epistles of James, f. 5.

[154] BE 400 n. 2.

[155] Lightfoot to Westcott, 7 November 1871 (LAC).

[156] Eg. RCC (1871) 83.

[157] "We discuss much in these days, as we are compelled to discuss, the evidences of Christianity." Charity, 1874, 20. Lightfoot to Liddon, 19 February 1878, speaking of his work on Ignatius (Envelope 27, LPO).

[158] LS 198.

damental anthithesis of our faith".[159] While taken from Whewell, the antithesis stemmed from Coleridge's differentiation between the reason and the understanding. Similarly Lightfoot's insistence that spiritual things are discerned by the spiritual faculty was no pious platitude but an epistemological position that recalls the creative contribution of mind to knowledge. Whether the influence was direct or mediated by Lightfoot's mentors and peers who were drinking from the same well,[160] many of Lightfoot's most basic notions have affinities with Coleridge's thinking on the same matters.[161] Theologically Lightfoot takes his place among the Germano-Coleridgeans (as they have come to be known).[162]

Against this background, Lightfoot began to articulate the incarnational understanding of Christianity that became characteristic. In the Norrisian Prize essay he defended the orthodox explanation of the origins of the Gospels from the mythological interpretation of Strauss.[163] His early sermons directed attention to the historical Jesus described in these Gospels as a revelation of God the Father.[164] Christian living consisted in the imitation of the example thus provided, for it furnished a way for human nature to be sanctified by the indwelling of the divine and aroused to a life of practical goodness. The culmination of this development allowed Lightfoot to answer the perennial question of how it was possible "to hold communion with God, to conform ourselves to Him, to become one with Him" as the "end and aim of our lives":

> Christ is this link between God and man being the Eternal Word God manifested unto men [sic]. By Him we have knowledge of the Father. Through Him we have access to the Father. In Him we are united with the Father. Thus this central doctrine of Christianity is the very soul of Christian practice also.[165]

Moreover, Lightfoot now openly identified himself with the theological tradition of the College. He served as collector in Cambridge for the Hare Memorial Committee,[166] and as secretary of the committee formed to secure a portrait for the University of the liberal Henry Philpott, Master of St Catherine's College, when he became Bishop of Worcester in 1858.[167] Early in 1861, Lightfoot became a chaplain to the Prince Consort, who was known

---

[159] LS 187.
[160] Newsome, *Godliness*, 14-16.
[161] An outline for a sermon many years later includes the note, "The great English thinker of this century — Coleridge". Advent, 1879, 12.
[162] See 123-4 below for Lightfoot's interest in German thought.
[163] See Chapter 10 below.
[164] Esp. Veil & Christ in 1855.
[165] Life, 1860, 9-10.
[166] R.C. Trench to Lightfoot, 29 May 1858. The Hare Prize was founded in 1861 by his friends to "testify their admiration". Venn, *Alumni* II.III.241. "Hare Memorial" (Collecteana UP 27, 440, CUA).
[167] Camb. Uni. Papers BP 481 (1858), CUL. Cf. Collecteana UP 28, 1056 (CUA).

to favour liberal views.[168] The following year he became the Examining
Chaplain to another liberal, the Bishop of London, A.C. Tait,[169] a task he
shared with A.P. Stanley, possibly the most notorious Broad Churchman of
the day.[170] Later he subscribed to memorial funds for H.H. Milman[171] and
Thirlwall.[172] This affiliation did not involve any reduction in personal religiosity. Nor did it imply participation in the factional rivalry which was so
marked a feature of contemporary Church life. For devotion was readily
compatible with the tradition of liberal Anglican Christianity to which he
belonged while comprehension and tolerance were required by it.

By late 1861, when Lightfoot embarked on his life's work, he had emerged
as a promising young scholar and Christian moralist, occupying a position
on the right wing of the liberal strand of Anglicanism, committed to the idea
that through his own striving and activity at some strategic point in society
the world could be made a better place. The Liverpool background had
instilled the typical middle class values of hard work and self reliance. Birmingham spiritualized and directed these values by the addition of an
Arnoldian moral earnestness and sense of mission grounded in deep Christian conviction. It also provided an expansive Classical training based on
an exacting linguistic discipline. Trinity College built on the foundation
laid by its representative at King Edward's the intellectual framework for
Lightfoot's subsequent thought, by establishing fundamental, liberal Anglican dispositions about the nature of God, the world, man and his reason.
Bound up with this tissue of influences was the Romantic temper, which, in
its belief in an immanent God, maintained the unity of the sacred and secular, and of the reason and imagination.[173] The resultant outlook recognized
the existence of both metaphysical and empirical truths, and thereby affirmed
the simultaneous reality of the spiritual and the rational. No dichotomy

---

[168] Lightfoot was recommended by Philpott (Correspondence of H.R.H. Prince Albert,
The Prince Consort, As Chancellor of Cambridge University, microfilm copy at CUL).
See also A. Grey to Lightfoot, 9 February 1861.

[169] For a recommendation of Lightfoot to Tait as one whose views are "tolerant and
liberal", see Jeremie to Tait, 2 April 1862. Tait insisted on theological agreement as the
condition of accepting the position. Tait to Lightfoot, 5 April 1862. For Lightfoot's approval of Tait's churchmanship and theology, Lightfoot to Westcott, 5 December 1862
(LAC).

[170] Prothero & Bradley, *Life of Stanley,* esp. II.ch. XXI.

[171] Lightfoot agreed to serve on the Committee to secure a Memorial in St Paul's for
Milman. *The Guardian* (20 March 1872) 397. This gesture indicates loyalty to St Paul's
as well as theological affinity.

[172] "Bishop Connop Thirlwall Memorial (1875)" (Camb. Uni. Papers BP 567, CUL).
Cf. EWSR 1-2.

[173] On the influence of romanticism and its results in Lightfoot's historical thinking,
see further on 120 below.

resulted, however, as the doctrine of final causes held the two together in an essential unity.

It is the influence of his University that bears most on the question of Lightfoot's intellectual character. It connects him with that intellectual group, centred on Cambridge and deriving from the seventeenth-century Platonists, which in the last 25 years has emerged from the shadow cast over Victorian religious history by Oxford and the Tractarians. This means that, following on from his intellectual antecedents, Lightfoot's epistemology was not empiricist but idealist; his psychology, not sensationalist, but intuitionist; and his theology, not Lockean, but Coleridgean. If there is any utility in reducing his position to that of an intellectual label, Lightfoot, at this point in his life at least, was not a "common sense empiricist", but a Cambridge Christian idealist. It was with this perspective that he addressed the question of the meaning and purpose of history when it was raised for fresh consideration by the English Church on the publication of *Essays and Reviews*.

Part II
History as Theology: The Nature of History

At its broadest 'history' refers to the whole of space-time reality, the totality of events. Attempts to render this continuum intelligible through the discernment of pattern and purpose are loosely called 'philosophies of history'. Whether sophisticated or simple, they will be historicist or theological as meaning is found either in history itself or beyond by faith in God or the gods. Themselves having a long history, philosophies of history arise out of the social-psychological need to make life meaningful, purposive, and to some extent manageable.[1]

While such 'philosophies' were common in Victorian England, whether Lightfoot subscribed to one has become a matter of some scholarly controversy. According to one recent pundit, an important difference between Lightfoot and the Hegelian idealist F.C. Baur was that he "showed no interest in a theory of history".[2] On this view, Lightfoot had no general idea of history, and no use for one. This contemporary view reflects what was thought in Lightfoot's own day. In 1885 the first Dixie Professor of Ecclesiastical History stated in his Inaugural Lecture that the Cambridge theologians had made theology historical without at the same time making history theological.[3] New to Cambridge and taking up a new chair, Mandell Creighton claimed Lightfoot, Westcott and Hort as his antecedents in the practice of historical method. He saw as their particular merit an empirical approach to Christian ideas and institutions as strictly historical phenomena. Himself in the grip of an "unmetaphysical" reaction to the Hegelianism of his youth, Creighton implied as a further merit that in their work the supernatural had

---

[1] See K. Löwith, *Meaning in History* (Chicago & New York: University of Chicago Press, 1949). For some 'philosophies' of history, see H. Meyerhoff (ed.), *The Philosophy of History in Our Time* (New York: Anchor Books, 1959); & P. Gardiner (ed.), *Theories of History* (New York: Free Press, 1959) esp. 7-8.

[2] Barrett, "Quomodo," 316.

[3] M. Creighton, "The Teaching of Ecclesiastical History," in *Historical Lectures and Addresses* (ed. L. Creighton; London: Longmans, Green and Co., 1903) 1-28, esp. 2. The lecture was delivered on 23 January 1885.

not encroached upon the natural.[4] In avoiding this pitfall, the metahistorical had been excluded from the historical.[5] Thus Creighton too denied Lightfoot (along with Westcott and Hort) an interest in a substantive interpretation of history, not even "the historical conception of progress" in which he himself was interested.[6] Or, if Lightfoot had such an interest, it had had no effect on his application of the historical method.

This, however, is a view that has been opposed. Not only is a definite understanding of history ascribed to Lightfoot: it is also said to have had a polemical edge. On the publication of the second edition of *The Apostolic Fathers,* the Irish Benedictine E.C. Butler discerned in Lightfoot's treatment of the Petrine texts the influence of a view of Church history as "from the beginning a strong grave and ever accelerated declension; it is ... the wrong ever overcoming the right".[7] It was a view calculated to discredit the development of the Papacy, and thereby to undermine Roman Catholic claims. Not dissimilar to this 'degenerationist' perspective is the 'preservationist' view advanced by B.N. Kaye against that of Barrett. He assigns to Lightfoot an understanding of Church history as "a continuing struggle ... with what we may call the lower nature in mankind" to maintain the truth given in the Incarnation — a static view of history in fact as opposed to the "dynamic and developmental terms" of Baur's reconstructions.[8] Who in this conflict of opinion is correct? Did Lightfoot have "a theory of history"? And, if so, what was it like?

The suggestion that Lightfoot was a "common sense empiricist" is also pertinent to this debate. For the commitment to empirical method that Barrett wished to highlight has often been regarded as incompatible or unconcerned with an holistic perspective on history.[9] In Lightfoot's day, however, this did not necessarily follow. The nineteenth century saw the emergence of two broad historiographical traditions associated with the names of Jeremy Bentham and S.T. Coleridge. The Benthamite tradition was rationalist in spirit, empiricist in basic epistemology and utilitarian in outlook. It was represented by writers like George Grote. The Germano-Coleridgeans, on

---

[4] Cf. *ibid.*, 9. On Creighton, see L. Creighton, *Life and Letters of Mandell Creighton* (London: Longmans, Green, and Co., 1904) I. ch. II, III & IX; & O. Chadwick, *Creighton on Luther* (Cambridge: University Press, 1959) 21 ff.

[5] It is of course Creighton whose epitaph reads, "He tried to write true history". W.G. Fallows, *Mandell Creighton and the English Church* (London: Oxford University Press, 1964) 110-11.

[6] Creighton, "Teaching," 7. Parker, *English Historical Tradition,* 57, makes the point that there was a residual Idealism in Creighton's outlook.

[7] E.C. Butler, "Bishop Lightfoot and the Early Roman See," *Dublin Review* 4th series 4 (July 1893) 213. On Butler, subsequently abbot of Downside, see DNB 1931-40, 126-7.

[8] Kaye, "Lightfoot and Baur," 217-23 (quotations on 221 & 223).

[9] Parker, *English Historical Tradition,* 79-80.

the other hand, were idealist, intuitionist and Christian, even Anglican. Its representatives were men like H.H. Milman and Connop Thirlwall. In the course of the century the two traditions converged in two important respects. Both accepted progress as the general meaning of what happens in history, although they came up with two versions — a continuous, linear and an episodic, cyclic model — of how this actually occurs. Both also accepted the new methods for handling the evidence out of which histories are written. A trend to separate philosophy and history resulted, so that it became increasingly difficult to ascertain allegiance to a tradition unless it was specifically avowed. This means that a positivist complexion in an historical work does not necessarily signify an empiricist epistemology or a rationalist philosophy. Of the progenitors of the two traditions Robert Preyer has written:

> Looking back we can see that Bentham and Coleridge substantially strengthened the "common sense" and "intuitive" modes of thought to which they were directed.[10]

If Barrett is right, then it is to the Benthamite tradition of historiography that Lightfoot belongs. This, of course, is again inherently unlikely, and it is also inconsistent with his general intellectual position which aligns him with the Germano-Coleridgeans. The question, therefore, is whether Lightfoot, in fact, followed in the right wing liberal Anglican line of historiography. It is answered by an examination of the sources of his historical outlook and the purposes it was meant to serve.

Interestingly, existing judgments on these matters have been formed on a limited basis. They arise from the desire to understand better Lightfoot's treatment of early Christianity and use only his formal theological writings as evidence. For the most part these exhibit him pursuing strictly scholarly purposes in relation to informed audiences. But scholarship was only one part of his life, and its processes only one of the ways in which he took part in Victorian society. As an Anglican clergyman, Lightfoot had a broader range of concerns and made use of the institutions of the national Church and platforms of other organizations to purvey his ideas. Both the content and institutional basis of these are reflected in the sermons and addresses he delivered over the full span of his career before a variety of audiences in many different centres. The way they exhibit Lightfoot explaining Christian belief and seeking to apply it in the life of the Church and the nation makes them the proper primary evidence for addressing the questions raised by the broader issue of his interest in a theory of history. Indeed, it was in one such sermon that he considered the nature and meaning of history in the immediate aftermath of *Essays and Reviews*.

---

[10] R. Preyer, *Bentham, Coleridge, and the Science of History* (Bochum-Langendreer: Heinrich Poppinghaus, 1958) 78. See also P.J. Bowler, *The Invention of Progress. The Victorians and the Past* (Oxford: Blackwell, 1989).

Chapter Four

"The Increasing Purpose of God": Lightfoot's Theology of History

In 1860, the year prior to Lightfoot's appointment to the Hulsean Chair, a group of liberal Anglican scholars, six of whom were clergyman, published *Essays and Reviews*.[1] An attempt at restatement, it sought to establish free inquiry inside the Church, and bring its thought up to the knowledge of the day, as the only viable method for maintaining the hold of Christianity on contemporary English society.[2] In the eyes of many, clergy and laity alike, the authors were held to have exceeded the limits of acceptable opinion for a clergyman. A vigorous literary debate ensued, the bishops condemned the book early in 1861, and over the next couple of years two of the writers came before Church and secular courts charged with having taught what was inconsistent with the formularies of the Church of England. As a result the controversy smouldered for the remainder of the decade, flaring up again in 1869 when one of the contributors was raised to the episcopate.[3] Though the writers of *Essays and Reviews* either died or gave up theology, this kept up the pressure on the Church to adjust its teaching to known truth while maintaining its own institutional interests and respecting the religious sensibilities of the people.[4]

---

[1] *Essays and Reviews* (8th ed; London: Longman, Green, Longman & Roberts, 1861) has been used in the present investigation.

[2] See the preface, "To the Reader," in *Essays and Reviews*; & R.B. Kennard, *"Essays and Reviews". Their Origin, History, General Character and Significance, Persecution, Prosecution, The Judgment of the Arches Court, - Review of Judgment* (London: Robert Hardwicke, 1863) ch. I & II. See also M. Francis, "The Origins of *Essays and Reviews*. An Interpretation of Mark Pattison in the 1850s," *The Historical Journal* XVII.4 (1974) 797-811.

[3] For all aspects of the controversy, see Chadwick, *Victorian Church,* II.75-90; M.A. Crowther, *Church Embattled: Religious Controversy in Mid-Victorian England* (Newton Abbot, Devon & Hamden, Connecticut: Archon Books, 1970); I. Ellis, *Seven Against Christ. A Study of "Essays and Reviews"* (Leiden: Brill, 1980); & J.L. Altholz, *Anatomy of a Controversy. The Debate Over "Essays and Reviews"* (Aldershot: Scolar Press, 1994).

[4] See, for example, the letter of Hort to Benson, 23 October 1869, quoted in *Memoirs of Archbishop Temple by Seven Friends* (2 vols; ed. E.G. Sandford; London: Macmillan, 1906) I.288-9.

While there was nothing like the stir that occurred elsewhere, *Essays and Reviews* did not go unnoticed at Cambridge.[5] Certainly it attracted the attention of the Fellows of Trinity College,[6] and there seems to be some allusion to it (together with Darwin's *The Origin of Species*) in the Commemoration Sermon Lightfoot preached late in 1860.[7] But within his circle of friends it was Westcott who was most disturbed.[8] Five days after Lightfoot's Commemoration Sermon, he wrote to Lightfoot from Harrow suggesting a volume of essays to "make good a position equally removed from sceptical dogmatism and unbelief".[9] However, the reaction, particularly the episcopal condemnation, also distressed Hort and Lightfoot.[10] By mid-February 1861 the three had agreed to publish *Revelation and History* as a joint statement of their position on the key issues pending the appearance of their New Testament commentary.[11] It was intended as a mediating volume, "to show that there is a mean between *Essays and Reviews* and Traditionalism".[12] Not a refutation so much as a qualification, its centre was to be the Incarnation with the historical preparation for it on one side and its apprehension on the other. For his part Lightfoot undertook the account of "'the preparation of the Gospel,' i.e. the stages of Jewish history, the work of the different nations of antiquity and the special calling of Israel".[13]

This prospectus suggests that Lightfoot's contribution was to be directed mainly at the essay of Frederick Temple.[14] In "The Education of the World" the Headmaster of Rugby explicitly canvassed the progressive scheme of world history endorsed by the volume as a whole. In line with its general purpose, Temple attempted to integrate modern understandings of history into the Christian synthesis. Influenced by the liberal Bishop Tait of London, the bishops found nothing directly unorthodox in it. But the essay suffered because of its association with the other six, and it was widely felt to be unbiblical and rationalistic.

---

[5] For example, Charles Kingsley to A.P. Stanley, 19 February 1861, in *Charles Kingsley. His Letters and Memories of his Life. Edited by his Wife* (2 vols; London: Henry S. King & Co., 1877) II.129-30.

[6] Romilly's Diary, vol. 30, entries for 16 & 18 March, 14 April, 2 August, 1861 (CUL, Add. 6840[2]). Also the letter in *The Times* (20 February 1861) 12, by Henry Sidgwick and signed 'A Cambridge Graduate'.

[7] CP 15, 23, 24-5.

[8] LW I.212.

[9] Westcott to Lightfoot, 20 December 1860, in LW I.214-15.

[10] See the correspondence in LW I.213-15; & LH I.428-9, 434-9. Also the two letters by Lightfoot to Westcott written on 7 February 1861 (LAC).

[11] For the Lightfoot-Westcott-Hort commentary scheme, see 312-13 below.

[12] Westcott to Hort, 6 August 1860, in LW I.213.

[13] Hort to Ellerton, 15 February 1861, in LH I.442.

[14] F. Temple, "The Education of the World," in *Essays and Reviews*, 1-49.

In his own treatment of the essay it is not likely that Lightfoot would have been critical to any great extent. Of Temple himself he was supportive. When the controversy threatened repercussions at Rugby, Lightfoot was "unable to conceive a greater calamity ... not only to Rugby, but to the English Church generally, than the resignation of Dr Temple",[15] and proposed to A.P. Stanley that a statement expressing confidence in Temple be circularized.[16] Perhaps this was one reason for finding the task of writing his own essay burdensome. Two months after its inception Lightfoot seceded from the scheme, thereby causing its abandonment.[17] Constructive critical work, without the fanfare or dangers of polemical statement, seemed a better course. The newly conceived edition of St Paul was to be his reply.[18] Yet the preparation for *Revelation and History* was not entirely without result. In May, in his capacity as Chaplain to the Prince Consort, Lightfoot preached a sermon before the Corporation of Trinity House in which his thinking for the essay was evidently put to some use.[19] An integral part of an annual service, the sermon was chiefly concerned with the spiritual and moral significance of the passage of the last year. But the immediate pastoral interest raised the larger question of the meaning and direction of what happens in time. Although a summary and hortatory statement, Lightfoot's answer embodied the elements of an understanding of history.

I

Lightfoot, like Temple, meant to advance a conception of universal history. He did not employ the same analogy between history and the life of the individual on which Temple had based his essay, although he could when appropriate.[20] Instead, on this occasion he equated history with the tide, a metaphor which implied unitary and holistic motion. It was not only by implication that the oneness of history was affirmed. The sermon took in

---

[15] Undated letter to A.P. Stanley in R.E. Prothero & G.G. Bradley, *The Life and Correspondence of Arthur Penrhyn Stanley* (2 vols; London: John Murray, 1893) II.39. See *The Times* (19 March 1861) 12 e for the suggestion that Temple should resign. His headmastership of Rugby was something of a refrain in the early reaction. See Altholz, *Anatomy of a Controversy*, ch. 5 & 54-5.

[16] A copy of such a statement has not been traced. Stanley's letters at Durham do not indicate how the matter finished. Cf. LW I.212.

[17] Lightfoot to Westcott, 7 February & 25 March 1861 (LAC). Cf. Hort to Ellerton, 9 April 1861, in LH I.444.

[18] There has been a tendency to speculate about Lightfoot's reasons for withdrawing from *Revelation and History*. Eg. Patrick, *Hort*, 47; Altholz, *Anatomy of a Controversy*, 73. Ellis, *Seven Against Christ*, 124, implies a failure of nerve on Lightfoot's part.

[19] J.B. Lightfoot, *The Increasing Purpose of God* (London: Rivingtons, 1861). On Trinity House, see *Encyclopaedia Britannica* (9th ed.; Edinburgh: Adam & Charles Black, 1875-1903) 14.831-2 & 23.574.

[20] See 72 below on Lightfoot's organicism.

the whole sweep of human experience. It assumed the beginning, and it foreshadowed the end. It referred to incidents ancient, mediaeval, modern and contemporary. For the latter its perspective was global. Developments in Russia, America, and Asia as well as Britain were included.[21] Events public and private, sacred and profane, came within its ambit. For Lightfoot everything that happens in time belonged to a single course held together and directed by the accomplishment of the divine purpose.

This purpose was furnished by history's goal, the *parousia* of classical Christian theology. The Trinity House sermon was filled with references to the advent of the Lord, the coming of the Redeemer, the day of redemption, and the heavenly destination of the world as the end product and goal of the historical process.[22] Lightfoot expected this to be a time of manifestation when the divine purpose would be disclosed in its fullness and with all of its consequences.[23] Shortly afterwards his attempts to interpret some of the Biblical data on this matter got him into trouble with E.B. Elliott, the evangelical Vicar of Brighton, a noted premillennialist and interpreter of prophecy.[24] Lightfoot characteristically refused to be drawn into controversy,[25] and, although appearing to hold to a futurist and amillennial perspective, in fact never enunciated a clear view on this matter. Such speculation was pointless.[26] It was sufficient to know that history was occurring within a framework of a beginning and movement towards a definite end which determined the meaning of the whole. Antiquity revealed how all events worked together for the achievement of the divine purpose.[27] The contemporary alliance between Christianity and commerce was read as suggesting the same conviction.[28] For Lightfoot, all events — even the outwardly fortuitous and accidental — had a place in this teleological scheme that firmly located human time in its eternal setting.

---

[21] IP 7-8.

[22] IP 9, 10, 10-11, 12 & 16.

[23] IP 13.

[24] Edward Bishop Elliott (1793-1875); Fellow of Trinity College, Cambridge (1817-24); incumbent of St Mark's, Kemptown, Brighton (1853-75); and author of *Horae Apocalypticae* (1844), which he urged Lightfoot to read. DNB VI.686. Lewis (ed.), *Dictionary of Evangelical Biography*, I.354-5. Elliott took exception to Lightfoot's interpreting the 'Man of Sin' in St Paul's Thessalonian correspondence in the light of contemporary history. J.B. Lightfoot, "Thessalonians, Second Epistle to," in Smith (ed.), *Dictionary of the Bible*, III.1482-4. E.B. Elliott, "Prophetic Articles in Smith's Bible Dictionary," *The Christian Observer* (March 1864) 217-18.

[25] Lightfoot remonstrated with Elliott, but in the end gave him up as a hopeless case. Lightfoot to Elliott, 16, 20 March & 3 May 1864. Elliott to Lightfoot, 18 March & 19 May 1864.

[26] See further 113 below.

[27] IP 15.

[28] IP 15, 16.

The emphasis on the divine purpose also involved the doctrine of providence. That history is a divine dispensation, that God has dealings with men, and that a higher hand was at work to guide the course of events, were elements of a conviction well settled and repeatedly expressed before Lightfoot addressed the Trinity House.[29] When now his sermon began with the hope,

> God grant that we may part this afternoon with a livelier sense of the fatherly tenderness and guiding providence of Him who created and sustains us,[30]

he was assuming that the way God operates in the world could be discerned by observing cause and effect in the ordinary course of events, and that his congregation would benefit by the knowledge. Accordingly he exhorted them to

> listen to catch the notes of heavenly music, sounding above the clatter of war and the turmoil of faction ... recognize the presence of God in the sorest trials of the human race, trace an overruling power eliciting good from evil ... see even in the ruin and overthrow of nations a preparation for the coming of the promised Redeemer.[31]

This view lacked the stridency of Lightfoot's Cambridge contemporary, Charles Kingsley, whose Inaugural Lecture the year before won great popularity among the undergraduates because of the moralizing it permitted.[32] This was because Lightfoot's view, while definite, was "general" rather than "special".[33] Direct and apparently arbitrary divine intervention was not excluded, but it was unnecessary for the retention of the idea of purpose in the Christian perspective on history.[34] In this he was similar (at least outwardly) to *Essays and Reviews* which also represented Providence as working neutrally through the natural regularities of the physical and social world.

The outstanding exception to this was the Incarnation, the chief means by which the Divine Purpose was achieved.[35] By this point in his career Lightfoot had already shown that there was nothing in history that could explain Jesus Christ.[36] He went on repeatedly to claim that His coming into

---

[29] St Thomas, 1855, 50-2; Acts I-VIII, 84r., 85r.; I. St Paul's Teaching, 1858, 24-5 ("man proposes and God disposes"); 3rd Group, 1858, 20; & 4th Group, 1858, 24-5. The idea of randomness in God's dealings with people was rejected in Jael, 1855, 8-13.

[30] IP 5.

[31] IP 10-11.

[32] C. Kingsley, "The Limits of Exact Science as Applied to History," in *The Roman and the Teuton* (ed. F.M. Müller; London: Macmillan, 1875) 307-43. See also O. Chadwick, "Charles Kingsley at Cambridge," *Historical Journal* VIII.2 (1975) 303-25.

[33] See further 107-8 below.

[34] For the background of contemporary providentialism, see B. Hilton, "The Role of Providence in Evangelical Social Thought," in *History, Society and the Churches. Essays in Honour of Owen Chadwick* (eds D. Beales & G. Best; Cambridge: University Press, 1985) 215-33. For changes later in the century, Chadwick, *Secularization*, ch. 10.

[35] For Lightfoot's view of miracles, see 116 below.

[36] Principally in his Norrisian Prize Essay of 1853, for which, see Chapter 10 below.

the world was an event altogether without analogy. But, although discontinuous with history in these senses, the Incarnation might also be seen as continuous with it. The plan under which Lightfoot had originally ordered his thoughts for the response to *Essays and Reviews* put the Incarnation at the centre of history.[37] All that preceded led up to it: what followed was its apprehension.[38] This more explicit Christocentric formulation was what had been intended to set the perspective of Lightfoot, Westcott and Hort apart from that of *Essays and Reviews*, the weakest point of which was its inattention to christology. It also took much further Temple's view of the life of Christ as the great example, an outlook which, as far as it went, Lightfoot could happily endorse.[39] But Christ was "the image of God", who entered history not only to show how life should be lived by his example as the pattern man, but also to reveal the nature of the Father and to bridge the gulf between heaven and earth.[40] All life, Lightfoot taught on this basis, was part of the one great purpose which found its meaning primarily in the advent of the Son of God, the realization of which continued through subsequent time. The challenge to the men of Trinity House, as to all men and women at all times, was to make their work an *Imitatio Christi*.[41]

The assurance of God's purpose apart, Lightfoot acknowledged that it was natural for men to wonder in which direction history was heading.[42] His text[43] — the "earth shall be full of the knowledge of the Lord as the waters cover the sea" — furnished the answer. Unlike the Evangelicals,[44] Lightfoot did not see this primarily as a reference to the salvation of souls through the preaching of the Gospel. Instead he used it to identify the providential purpose of God in history with progress. Its nature as such was illustrated by the analogy with the tide implicit in the text. Lightfoot thus affirmed what was a matter of some controversy among Churchmen. In 1858 H.L. Mansel had warned against too easy an acceptance of progress,[45] and Temple's advocacy of the idea in *Essays and Reviews* had incurred criti-

---

[37] Westcott to Hort, 13 December 1860, LW I.214.
[38] For the content and development of Lightfoot's incarnational interpretation of history, see 81-9, 111-12 & 124-8 below.
[39] Eg. NTI 191.
[40] Esp. Christ, 1855, *passim*.
[41] IP 14.
[42] IP 8-9.
[43] Isaiah 11:9.
[44] Eg. B. Stanley, " 'Commerce and Christianity': Providence Theory, the Missionary Movement, and the Imperialism of Free Trade, 1842-1860," *The Historical Journal* 26.1 (1983) 71-94, esp. 72-3.
[45] H.L. Mansel, *The Limits of Religious Thought Examined in Eight Lectures Before the University of Oxford, in the Year MDCCCLVIII* (Oxford: John Murray, 1858) 258.

cism.[46] But Lightfoot was sure that history was characterized by "advancement towards completion",[47] "movement from lower to higher",[48] and "enlarged life ... ever increasing light".[49] It could therefore be read as a divinely intended "gradual progress".[50] Lightfoot used a phrase also employed by another Essayist, the notorious Benjamin Jowett, to sum up his meaning.[51] History was the realization of "the increasing purpose of God".

Lightfoot's description of the tide implied that this progressive movement would not always be apparent.[52] This was partly because the gains made by the component parts tended to be small like the waves. It was also because the shape of progress was neither uniform nor rectilinear. It came in ebbs and flows of uneven dimensions.[53] In its provision for cross and back currents, and even inertia, the image also allowed for the diversity of oblique and counter forces. Thus in history every age was drawn into the plan of God, but each age did not contribute equally to his "increasing purpose". In some indeed progress was more manifest as the development of centuries took place in only a few years.[54] Conversely no age was excluded from the course of progress, and certainly none could hinder its eventual realization. This was a view of change more complex than that offered by Temple, but the emphasis was still on the certain accumulation of progressive forces.

There was of course a problem with this. The action of the tide is cyclical, and taken as a whole the sequence of cycles does not seem to lead to either quantitative or qualitative advancement. Lightfoot characteristically recognized how metaphors could mislead and was no doubt aware of the limitations of this one. Clearly he intended only that phase of the cycle in which the tide moves from its low to its high point with its seemingly inexorable flow. However, this use of the tide analogy was accompanied by an apparent denial that history moves in cycles.[55] In fact Lightfoot's denial referred to that model familiar to him in Classical authors in which the cycle of history returns more or less to the same point. In contrast the linearity of

---

[46] Eg. C.S. Absolom, *Dr Temple's Essay* (London: Wertheim, Macintosh & Hunt, 1861); & R. Blakelock, *Observations on the Rev. Dr Temple's Essay on the Education of the World* (London: Nisbet & Co., n.d.).

[47] Edifying, 1869, 18. Cf. CP 9, 10.

[48] CP 14-15.

[49] CS 144.

[50] IP 9.

[51] B. Jowett, "On the Interpretation of Scripture," in *Essays and Reviews*, 375, uses the expression "increasing purpose" in relation to revelation.

[52] IP 8-9.

[53] Eg. HE 72-3.

[54] SSO 140.

[55] IP 8.

universal history was capable of incorporating a cyclic pattern of rise and fall which advanced the purpose of providence.[56] A race or civilization would emerge and make its contribution before declining and being succeeded by another. Even in ages characterized as effete another era could be seen taking shape, a point Lightfoot made in relation to the breakup of the Roman Empire and the emergence of the mediaeval order. This was the pattern discernible throughout history:

> All the great conjunctures in the history of the world read the same lesson. The advent of a noble era has ever been preceded by a period of deeper gloom. Through the grave and gate of death nations have risen to a higher life.[57]

In doing so they carried forward and upward the line of development, so that the "increasing purpose" transcends the individual experience of the units of history without stultifying them. In this integration of distinct episodes into the larger continuity, Lightfoot's outlook may be characterized as cyclical progressionism.[58]

The progress intended by Providence was seen as wide ranging. Lightfoot endorsed the progress of evolutionists when he acknowledged its occurence in the changes in the face of the earth, which had arisen from confusion and disorder to a condition habitable by man,[59] and in the history of life on earth in the movement "from the lower types of animal life, through the immediate steps, to the creation of man".[60] He was at one with his society in also celebrating greater material comfort and power over nature through science, technology, and the spread of commerce, of which the Trinity House was representative.[61] In the more specifically human domain, although he could not agree with secular thinkers who extended progress to human nature itself,[62] he joined in acknowledging progress in culture and enlightenment, and politically in the extension of liberty. There was much in the secular interpretation of progress that Lightfoot felt able to accept.

Important as these secular manifestations of providence undoubtedly were, they did not constitute the essence of progress. Lightfoot was more unusual for the time when he (like Temple) claimed for progress a religious side, and indeed that "secular progress" sprang from spiritual causes. For him progress was primarily intellectual and moral. He glossed "a gradual progress" with

---

[56] IP 11-12. CS 65-9.

[57] IP 11. Cf. CS 63-79, esp 68-9.

[58] Bowler, *Invention of Progress*, 8-9 for the background.

[59] IP 12. Cf. SSP 310; & [What?] IV, 1877, 8-9.

[60] CP 14-15.

[61] IP 11, 12. Cf. SSP 138-40; All Things, 1872, 15-17; SSO 110.

[62] CP 8-9, where Lightfoot made the point that Scripture does not teach the perfectibility of man. See also M. Mandelbaum, *History, Man and Reason* (Baltimore & London: Johns Hopkins Press, 1971) esp. Pt III.

"a steadily advancing tide of knowledge".[63] A range of metaphors characterized the true nature of historical advance. Light came from darkness; good, from evil; order, from confusion; strength, from weakness; energy, from lethargy; and life, from death.[64] Of course others of a different frame of mind thought of progress as intellectual and moral, and would not have demurred at these metaphors. But for Lightfoot progress was intellectual and moral because it was first spiritual. The truth-seeking spirit had been refined and properly directed by Christianity. Moreover, "the progressive development of God's scheme for our redemption, and for the regeneration of the world" had brought the benefits which constituted the real progress of the world.[65] Increasingly evident through the ages, its chief embodiment was the birth and growth of Christianity with its "seeds of new spiritual life".[66] In Lightfoot's understanding the world was a spiritual and moral order characterized by advancement as the divine purpose moved towards fulfilment.

The nature of progress reflected its cause at both a secular and spiritual level. Progress occurred as "a steadily advancing tide of knowledge".[67] In other words, the melioration intended by Providence resulted from increasing enlightenment. This was not the "March of Mind" of the individual rationalist tradition reflected in Temple, according to which progress occurred through the application of reason to society to find the underlying principles of human behaviour and the consequent removal of the obstacles to freedom bequeathed by the past.[68] Rather than "progress as freedom", it was — to use Robert Nisbet's dichotomy — "progress as power",[69] and came about through acceptance and appropriation of the facts of existence understood not so much as constraints on action as guidelines to it. To be sure this might still mean that artificial or unwarranted constraints might have to be removed as part of truthful existence. More importantly, it involved release from the thraldom of sin and ignorance as the truth in Christ becomes better known.[70] This process of increasing moral and spiritual freedom was open-ended as it would continue to history's end and beyond.[71] Viewed in this framework the world was a school and history a process of divine education

---

[63] IP 9.
[64] IP 11-12.
[65] Jael, 1855, 21. Cf. Acts I-VIII, 1855, 84 r.; True, 1860, 4-6: & Truth, 1864, 8-9.
[66] IP 15. Cf. LS 177, 177-8, 187; & I. St Paul's Teaching, 1858, 5-6.
[67] IP 9.
[68] Ellis, *Seven Against Christ*, 288, 289.
[69] The titles of ch 6 & 7 in R. Nisbet, *History of the Idea of Progress* (London: Heinemann, 1980).
[70] Eg. Christ, 1855, 1-5.
[71] Will He, 1869, 10-12.

preparing men and women for heavenly citizenship.[72] The "increasing purpose of God" echoed Temple's "Education of the World".

Progress, Lightfoot made clear, would be "gradual" and quantitative.[73] For the action of the tide is slow and cumulative. Other — mainly biological and botanical — images extended this sense of steady natural increase. Lightfoot likened the mental and moral growth of societies to the unfolding of the day, from "the first dawn of intellect and conscience" to the "full noontide blaze of ... heightened faculties".[74] He particularly favoured the notion of a "germ" which will grow and become fruitful.[75] This disposition led to the frequent use of arborial metaphors to convey the connection between origins deep in the past and ramified, open ended development in the future.[76] The same cluster of ideas — change in stages within a continuous process leading to a higher end inherent in the beginning — was also involved in the comparison of the life course of the individual human being with that of other historical entities, such as a heresy,[77] the Church,[78] a nation (Israel),[79] humankind,[80] or the world itself.[81] Lightfoot's developmentalism was based on a view of the interrelatedness and organic connection of life.

This understanding of change was diffusionist as well as cumulative. Again this was implicit in Lightfoot's leading image: the rising tide fills the available space. How this happens in history was clarified a few years later in a sermon for the Society for the Propagation of the Gospel.[82] The principal forces for historical change were seen as the growth of the Church and the spread of the Gospel. Their impact was best described in terms of the twin parables of the mustard seed and the leaven. As an external society the Church emerged from insignificant beginnings, "gradually expanding from a small nucleus, growing ever silently and steadily, spreading its branches

---

[72] Kingdom, 1855, 22-4; G 167-8, 172-3; Saving, 1873, 13-15; Glory, 1877, 26; He Shall Take, 1877, 25; & CS 134, 318-19.

[73] IP 9.

[74] CS 130.

[75] LS 186, 187, 193; P 276. The possibility of blighting was acknowledged as something that had to be prevented. Cf. CS 75, 168; SSP 61-2; HE 22-3; England Six Hundred Years Ago, 1874, 4.

[76] 1st Group, 1858, 1-2; 3rd Group, 1858, 20; IP 12.

[77] BE 416.

[78] DAA 139, 159.

[79] G 172. Cf. Valley, 1873, 2-3.

[80] CS 78.

[81] Life, 1860, 29-30; IP 12; G 167, 168. Cf. Light, 1872, 22-3; Vision, 1873, 14.

[82] J.B. Lightfoot, 'The Mustard Seed and the Leaven': A Sermon Preached on Tuesday, September 18, at St Paul's Church, Bedford, On Behalf of the Society for the Propagation of the Gospel in Foreign Parts (London & Cambridge: Macmillan, 1866).

far and wide," to shelter and support the ignorant, oppressed and sin-laden.[83] Similarly the teaching of the Gospel "works its way into every outlying portion of society" and incorporates and ennobles all that it touches.[84] The two together commended ideal change:

> The greatest results arise from the smallest beginnings. The growth, which is most gradual, is also the strongest. The diffusion, which is least perceptible, is likely to prove the most complete.[85]

While this is where the emphasis fell, Lightfoot's understanding did not exclude other patterns of change. Rapid and cataclysmic turnabouts also had a place, as was necessary for the full range of historical events to be included. The lives of individuals could change suddenly and dramatically. The first Christians had experienced a conversion from darkness to light such as was now scarcely possible in a country like England where Christianity had leavened the mass of society.[86] St Paul, Augustine and St Francis of Assisi were favourite examples of this same possibility.[87] Sudden episodic change with transforming effects also occurred at the level of societies and whole civilisations. The Trinity House sermon mentioned the French Revolution, "that thunder-cloud which burst over Europe at the close of the last century".[88] But even this "outburst of revolutionary fury" was to be understood as the result of a build up of forces over more than a century.[89] The exceptions to the usual mode of historical development only served to make clear the norm.[90]

Finally, Lightfoot's understanding of history at this point was optimistic, as such views tended to be. God's purposes are ultimately irresistible and work for the well-being of humanity here and hereafter. Clearly this was a liberal disposition which was broadly shared with the writers of *Essays and Reviews*. Of Temple it was said that he underestimated sin, and thereby reduced the need for the Atonement and revelation in the Bible.[91] The same basic criticism might well have been made of Lightfoot. Sin was not omitted from his perspective, but it was not represented as a fatal flaw in man's spiritual condition or barrier to progress. While it was proper to speak of "this desert of ignorance, and sin, and misery", it was also necessary to re-

---

[83] MSL 4-6.

[84] MSL 6-7. Cf. LS 177; Truth, 1864, 8-9; Will He, 1869, 9-12, 21.

[85] MSL 8.

[86] Christian Priesthood, 1862, 13-15. Cf. Sheep, 1873, 2-8.

[87] BE 211; SSP 246-52; SSO 103-4; OA 127-8.

[88] IP 12.

[89] Sins, 1872, 12-16.

[90] For an example of the effect of Lightfoot's expectation in his New Testament studies, see BE 403-10.

[91] Eg. W.H. Parker, *Brief Remarks on the Rev. Dr Temple's Essay, on the "Education of the World"* (London: Wertheim & Hunt, n.d.).

member that "a highway has at length been prepared for our God".[92] Lightfoot understood sin as disloyalty to the Father and the Son, and to other men.[93] It would remain a part of life until history's end, but it would be resolved on the "day of redemption, when sorrow shall cease to trouble and sin shall be no more, when death shall be swallowed up in victory, and the tear shall be wiped from every eye".[94] Prospects of hell did not figure largely in his construction. Thus sin did not have the destructive effect upon humanity which adherents of the Evangelical and High Church interpretation of Christianity were more inclined to see.[95] It was a problem because it limited the power of Christianity to transform life and achieve God's "increasing purpose".

A view of history which assigned this importance to the divine purpose was plainly idealist. The image of the incoming tide as the manifestation of an inbuilt mechanism leading to its own fulfilment reflected a view of the world of outward appearance as suffused with the absolute, eternal idea inherent in the divine intention for creation.[96] History similarly evinced a duality of outward events embodying and giving expession to God's all encompassing plan. All the differentiated phenomena of the contingent order belonged to a single unitary process of movement towards the fuller realization of the directing divine ideal. "In the terror and perplexity of events," Lightfoot reminded the men of Trinity House, "the divine purpose is working itself out."[97]

This perspective had plainly moved the transcendent God of traditional Christian thought inside the historical process as immanent presence. The "Eternal, Invincible Will" that had expressed itself in the creation also maintained and took part in the world order from which *a posteriori* it was knowable. From the men of Trinity House Lightfoot sought the proper response:

> We must look above and beyond the excitement of the present. We must listen to catch the notes of heavenly music, sounding above the clatter of war and turmoil of faction. We must recognize the presence of God in the sorest trials of the human race.[98]

In the years to come congregations were similarly reminded that God "is about and around us always".[99] He not only created, but was also present in, the processes of human history.

---

[92] IP 9.

[93] P 290, 321; C 119; & SSP 23-4.

[94] IP 13.

[95] The underlying similarities between the two schools of thought within Anglicanism is a theme of D. Voll, *Catholic Evangelicalism. The Acceptance of Evangelical Traditions by the Oxford Movement During the Second Half of the Nineteenth Century* (London: Faith Press, 1963). See also Altholz, "Mind of Victorian Orthodoxy," 186-97.

[96] For which, see CP 14.

[97] IP 12, 16. Cf. 1st Group, 1858, 24-5; & 3rd Group, 1858, 20.

[98] IP 10.

[99] TTT 7.

This transcendence-immanence duality is important for understanding the character of Lightfoot's historical standpoint. Several times he drew on the patristic distinction between the θεολογία and the οἰκονομία — the "contemplation of Christ's Eternal Being — His relation to the Father and the Holy Spirit before the worlds were made", and "the plan by which God rules his household" —[100] to differentiate the essential and existential aspects of the one God. Characteristically this was no more than a simple juxtaposition of the two orders of Divine Being. For Lightfoot it was sufficient to erect the framework of the God-world relation. Transcendence provided for divine sovereignty over the world, while appreciating God's triune nature allowed for his continuous activity within it. But Lightfoot's emphasis was always on divine immanence. The practical corollaries rather than the speculative implications were what mattered.

Although only an occasional address, Lightfoot's Trinity House sermon indicates that on the threshold of his professorial career his outlook included the rudiments of a genuine "theory" of history. Brought forward as an assertion that human time occurs in an eternal setting which establishes its meaning and direction, the "increasing purpose of God" stood for a perspective that was universal in scope and teleological, providential, incarnational, organicist, gradualist, diffusionist, cumulative, optimistic and idealist in its leading characteristics. Together they warranted the claim that the contemporary doctrine of progress owed its existence ultimately to Christianity. Read against the background of the controversy sparked by *Essays and Reviews*, the inclusiveness of this view was a defence of the principle of the essential oneness between faith and life which was intended to present a mediating perspective between the more clear-cut alternatives available within contemporary Anglicanism. The parallels with Temple's unpopular essay and a similarity of terminology point to an affinity with the aim of *Essays and Reviews* to be modern which might have been controversial had it become better known at the time. On the other hand, the elaboration of this perspective evinces an intention to stick closer to the Christian tradition, particularly in relation to Trinitarian orthodoxy. In its wish to be traditional and yet modern, Lightfoot's understanding of history held out a principle of cohesion capable of comprehending Churchmen of all outlooks in a unity that paralleled the unity of history itself.

II

Even as it was being formulated this was a view which was becoming increasingly difficult to maintain. In the eyes of its first critics in the major periodicals, *Essays and Reviews* represented an accommodation of theology

---

[100] BE 229-30. Cf. 3rd Group, 1858, 20; & St John's Gospel. Introduction. I.1-I.28, f. 20, on v. 18.

to the increasingly positivist tendency in the English empirical tradition.[101] Frederic Harrison — still only on the verge of his positivist phase, but already urging the incompatability of effete Christianity and modernity — precipitated the crisis by rejecting this enterprise as unviable and dishonest.[102] From the opposite perspective Bishop Samuel Wilberforce — intent upon securing the retention of Christianity as the religious foundation of English life — agreed.[103] Either the Essayists must believe more, give up their dangerous flirtation with secular thought, and continue in the Church; or they must believe less, follow the logic of their present position, and leave the Church. Over the next decade there was a vogue for this either-or thinking, with the conservatives seeming to get the upper hand inside the Church. Contemporary society appeared to have come to a parting of the ways.

Lightfoot was among those who refused to accept this dilemma. The years following his appointment as Hulsean Professor were a time of some reconsideration in his thinking as he turned to the intellectual work of the Church as his vocation and to Theology as his subject specialism.[104] Like the writers of *Essays and Reviews*, he recognized the need for the Church to restate its position on the relation of theology to contemporary knowledge if it was actually to hold the position of spiritual and cultural leadership in contemporary society to which it aspired.[105] As he adjusted to the work of his new office against a background of intense controversy in the wider Church, Lightfoot settled on what was to become his life-purpose. This was promoting "the great cause" of "truth in theology".[106] For the moment it seemed to require three things. The first was a programme for developing a fresh perspective on Christian theology, the main element of which was a broader view of revelation centring on the Incarnation as the leading doctrine of Christianity.[107] The second was life at Cambridge, and to this end

---

[101] See the accounts in Ellis, *Seven Against Christ*, ch. 3; & Altholz, *Anatomy of a Controversy*, ch. 6.

[102] F. Harrison, "Neo-Christianity," *The Westminster and Foreign Review* LXXIV (October 1860) 293-332.

[103] [S. Wilberforce], "Essays and Reviews," *The Quarterly Review* 109 (January 1861) 248-305; & *Replies to 'Essays and Reviews'... With a Preface by the Lord Bishop of Oxford* (Oxford & London: John Henry & James Parker, 1862) iii-x.

[104] This was done largely in consultation with Westcott still absent at Harrow. See further 125 below.

[105] On the place of the Church of England in English society, see further Chapter 9 below.

[106] Westcott to Lightfoot, 26 January 1864 (in LW I.246-7) speaks of "the cause *we* hold to be true" and wanting "to represent what I hold most firmly to be truth in theology" [my emphasis].

[107] Their commitment to it was signified by the legend on the monogram adopted for the commentary scheme — πολυμερῶς καὶ πολυτρόπως ["by divers portions and in divers manners" (trans. of Hebrews I:1, R.V.)]. "It would, I think, exactly express the combination of ideas, which *we* wish to express." Lightfoot to Westcott, 19 October n.y. [1863]

Lightfoot turned down the See of Lichfield in 1867.[108] The third was "a common work" with Westcott,[109] a commitment which in turn called for getting him back to the University, sustained personal literary output, establishing a theological review,[110] and editing a dictionary of Christian biography and antiquities.[111] The task of propagating the intellectual basis of this position was begun in 1868, incidentally in the important commentary on 'Philippians', but chiefly in 'Shew Us the Father', a sermon before the University later in the year.[112] Recognizing a similarity between the present and the challenge to the Church in the second and third centuries, Lightfoot reproduced the response of the Alexandrian Fathers by reviving the Johannine doctrine of the Logos.

Provided that the extreme of pantheism was avoided, the answer to the intellectual and cultural questions of the day seemed to lie in the elaboration of the world as an extension of God's mind. The Logos, Lightfoot now claimed, was the link between the Infinite and the Finite:[113]

> He is the Divine Reason, for He is the expression of God's will in the creation and government of the Universe ... This Word of God is His Agent in all His words and works, howsoever and whensoever He manifests Himself. This is no less true of the natural world, than of the spiritual world. All things were created, all things are sustained, through Him.[114]

The life of creation and the world, then, springs from, and is upheld by, the divine life. Its phenomena exhibit the harmony, unity and teleology of the Logos structure, of which they are the expression. All acquisition of truth, it followed, is discovery of this truth. Openness to science and culture, and incorporation of their teachings into the Christian synthesis was but due reverence for the God who, in His triune Being, was the master of the universe, and expressed Himself in creation and history.[115] Christology thus contained the resources for reconciling traditional Christian belief and modern knowl-

---

(my emphasis). Lightfoot in fact saw revelation as a process, ongoing and still occurring, "wheresoever and howsoever [God] speaks". Westcott also asserted the ongoing nature of this revelation in a letter to Benson of 17 November 1865 (in LW I.251-2). The idea was explored in B.F. Westcott, *Essays in the History of Religious Thought in the West* (London: Macmillan, 1891) a number of the essays of which were written in mid 1860s in consultation with Lightfoot.

[108] For Lightfoot's commitment to Cambridge, see Chapter 7 below.

[109] See 46-7 above.

[110] Lightfoot to Westcott, 21 February 1864, contains a prospectus of the proposed review.

[111] Lightfoot to Westcott, 9 July 1863 (LAC), indicates the need for a dictionary of Christian antiquity, which eventually appeared as the *Dictionary of Christian Biography*.

[112] See CS 129-49.

[113] See also LS 184-5.

[114] CS 129-30.

[115] SSP 300-2.

edge. For Lightfoot had fallen back on the θεολογία in order to retain his understanding of the οἰκονομία. To the problems posed for Churchmen by *Essays and Reviews* Lightfoot found his solution in the main aspect of theology his liberal Anglican contemporaries at Oxford had overlooked.

The application of the Logos doctrine proved to be the one significant development in Lightfoot's historical thinking. For he soon realized that, in the face of naturalistic conceptions, it provided fresh warrants for the interpretation of history as God's "increasing purpose". Very early in his time of reassessment, Lightfoot noted:

> [the Word of God] speaks to us in the records of history bearing witness to "one increasing purpose" which runs through the ages, visible in the earliest dawn of time countless centuries before the history of the earth became the history of man, ever advancing, ever gathering force, a yearning and a striving after the realization of some higher type, a going on unto perfection.[116]

This was because of four particular benefits the Logos structure of thought conferred on Christian historical understanding.

First, it allowed Lightfoot as a Churchman to present history to both sides of the contemporary debate. On the one hand, the Logos warranted the way in which he wanted to read history, as part of the πολυμερῶς καὶ πολυτρόπως. For it sustained a distinction between two types of divine self-disclosure.[117] It could be "Revelation natural". This revelation was a function of the Logos as the "Word Impersonal": it was "the operation or the agency", "the speech not the speaker". As such it was typical and incomplete. With nature, persons and the inward witness of the human heart, history was part of it. The other category was "Revelation special". This was the "agent" and the "speaker", the "Word Personal". This was a better revelation, and occurred when the "Word Personal" made Himself known directly by coming into the world as the man Jesus. Combining the two types widened the general phenomenon from direct intervention to speak to include continuous divine activity in the whole of life. While he did not say how the revelatory component was to be discerned, Lightfoot insisted that it was so. In varying degrees, all events were religious events.

While in this way the Logos allowed Lightfoot to keep history within the Christian framework of understanding, it also enabled him to use the idiom current in contemporary discussion in presenting a Christian interpretation of history to the wider society. The general positivism of the day gave rise to a wish to speak in terms of the operation of law in history, although there was considerable difference as to what this might mean.[118] Lightfoot similarly invoked the laws of history, nominating the laws of progress and of

---

[116] Truth, 1864, 33. Also Sword, 1864, 14 [= CS 160].

[117] For what follows, see CS 155-8.

[118] See C. Parker, "English Historians and the Opposition to Positivism," *History and Theory* XXII.2 (1983) 120-45.

continuity as chief among them.[119] What he said of nature was true also of history:

A larger knowledge of nature's laws — which are God's laws — may change the point of view, but it may not hide the object of view. The modes of operation may be other than we thought, but it is still God our Father, who worketh all in all, God our Father, who was revealed in the Word made flesh, who is still revealed in the Word working through nature, in the Word working in his Church.[120]

But Lightfoot's view of law was evidently more metaphorical than prescriptive. A "law" described apparent natural regularities and orderly sequences, and defined the conditions under which men live.[121] As a mental construct it allowed for apparent exceptions and variations necessitated by the complexity of phenomena and increases in knowledge. However, while the tendency of observation was to "multiplicity of phenomena", the tendency of induction was to "unity of origin [in] the Hand of God", which was identified with the Logos.[122] Moving God inside the historical process therefore allowed Lightfoot to retain Providence in harmony with the naturalistic modes of understanding coming increasingly into vogue. Law was the mode of Providence, not its negation, as some contemporaries maintained.[123]

As a second benefit, this perspective resolved the question of historical causation under the rule of law for Lightfoot's Christian standpoint. Numerous intramundane causes were allowed throughout his *oeuvre*. They fall easily into his own classification of political, social and intellectual forces, which work silently and invisibly for the most part but occasionally burst to the surface leaving devastation and ruin.[124] Two sorts were singled out as the key to explaining what happens in history. The law and institutions, by their protection of the material and moral condition of people from the operations of chance and caprice, constituted one of the two main influences by which society is moulded.[125] The other was "its ideas, sentiments and beliefs" which are the determinants of character, guides to behaviour, and stimuli to action.[126] Of the two, ideas were the more important. Law sets a

---

[119] IP 12, 13; CS 68; & SSP 310.

[120] Will He, 1869, 18-19.

[121] Divided, 1866, 20-2; Teaching, 1871, 15-17, 19-20; Sins, 1872, 16, 25-6, 28-9; War, 1877, 23-4; Hunger, 1877, 30-2; CS 49, 54-5, 66-8, 169-70; SSO 9, 106; & SSP 13-14, 169, 313.

[122] I. St Paul's Teaching, 1858, 16-18; Teaching, 1871, 17; Eagles, 1873, 18-20; & [What?] IV, 1877, 7-10.

[123] Eg. H.T. Buckle, *History of Civilization in England* (2 vols; new ed.; London: Longmans, Green & Co.,1882 [originally published in 1857]) I.7-8.

[124] SSO 78-9. Interestingly economic forces do not occupy any special place in Lightfoot's calculation of causes. Economic causation had not yet come into its own among English historians. On the development of economic history, see Parker, *English Historical Tradition*, 59-66.

[125] SSP 97-8, 297-8.

[126] SSP 292-5.

standard of morality and thereby creates an ideal which becomes the basis of conduct. Behind the influence of institutions and persons stands a living spirit actuated by some idea or ideal. Not only are they fundamental, but ideas transcend the limitations of space and time, so that they linger and spread until they have their effect.[127] In a manner reflecting his Christian idealism, Lightfoot gave the primacy to intellectual factors in history.

But none of these causes in themselves was a sufficient explanation for what happens in history. For Lightfoot it was important that naturalistic explanation be seen in its relation to the First Cause. This need was demonstrated in relation to the challenge to Christian understanding posed by Gibbon. Lightfoot was not insensible to the merits of the historian of the fall of the Roman Empire, and made use of his work when it suited his own purpose.[128] Indeed the five causes for the triumph of Christianity assigned by Gibbon could all be allowed. But the deficiency in his explanation was that these were "secondary causes" and missed the essential point. The reason for the impact of Christianity on the world was "the incarnation of the Divine Word, the realization of God's love and God's presence through the human life and death of Christ".[129] Thus Gibbon's explanation was incomplete and lacking in the very cause that gave the phenomenon its grandeur. Similar reference to the divine First Cause gave other historical causes their true status. Of the law, for example, Lightfoot said:

> it looks up to those eternal principles of deity and order and self-restraint, whch are the expression of the Mind of God, as the Great Original, of which it is only a partial shadowy image, the Fountain-Head from which it derives its truest inspiration.[130]

The mundane causes of the triumph of Christianity, like all mundane causes and the laws according to which they operated, could all be accepted, but they were secondary causes working under the sovereignty of God and the creative energy of the Logos.

Third, the Logos provided the principle of unity necessary for the maintenance of the conception of universal history. By His indwelling, Lightfoot maintained, the Divine Word effectively causes, directs and sustains history as a unitary whole:[131]

> We men have our distinctions of nature, of history, of revelation, and the like. In themselves, they are only parts of one vast plan, only manifestations of one boundless Providence — expressions of one Mind, one Reason, one Word of God.[132]

Commitment to a transcendent personal God prevented total identification of God and history in the manner of Absolute Idealism. But the theological

---

[127] Christ, 1876, 4, 31-3; CS 245, 266, 287-8.
[128] P 324, 326-7; HE 7-8, 74.
[129] HE 8.
[130] SSP 298.
[131] CS 103, 130-45, 155, 182; SSO 18; RCC (1873) 233; [What?] IV, 1877, 11.
[132] [What?] IV, 1877, 6.

monism inherent in the Logos doctrine permitted retention of the view that all history belonged to a single providential order.

At the same time as showing how all history was one, the Logos also accommodated the differences to be discerned within it. The Word of God, Lightfoot now said,

> has indeed illumined and quickened all men and all races in their several degrees. He has been present in universal history, as He has been present in every individual soul of man. But nevertheless He has specially visited one family, one race.[133]

With this in mind he characteristically differentiated between "sacred" and "ordinary" history. "Sacred" history encompassed "the progressive development of God's scheme for our redemption, & for the regeneration of the world".[134] It was (more or less) equivalent with the history of Israel and of the new Israel, the Church. "Ordinary" history referred to all that was outside the domain of the specific history of redemption. Conceptually difference within a unity was difficult, and Lightfoot evidently struggled with it. Two images were employed to clarify the relation. The first was a plane traversed by "one conspicuous bright line".[135] "Sacred" history was this mainline running across the surface of "ordinary" history which supported it and provided its setting. The other image was a river fed by smaller streams. "Sacred" history was "the main stream of religious history", while the tributaries swelling its flow came from "ordinary" history.[136] From this point the river image became the principal means by which Lightfoot drew out not only the centrality of redemptive history to all history, but the dependence of history on it for the achievement of progress.[137]

Within this framework of diversity within unity, fourth and perhaps most importantly, the Logos provided the basis of the incarnational interpretation of history which became more prominent from this point in Lightfoot's career.[138] He now insisted that the Incarnation was "not an isolated event, not the only operation of the Divine Word", and needed to be seen in its wider relations:

> It is the explanation of the past, the culminating point of human history, the consummation of God's revelation to man. For now first the Divine and the human are united in immediate and inalienable contact. But it does not stand alone nor does it profess an

---

[133] CS 131.

[134] This is to be distinguished from Lightfoot's use of "sacred history" to refer to the Bible. This usage is treated on 104-5 below.

[135] CS 132.

[136] CS 131. RCC (1871) 81.

[137] See esp. SSO 146-59.

[138] This greater prominence was partly due simply to the increased opportunities to speak that followed soon after the 1868 sermon before the University (and in turn generated more evidence for the historian to examine). But he also now had more to say as his understanding of the contemporary situation and how to address it had clarified.

affinity only with the Jewish dispensation. God has revealed Himself also in nature
and in history, in the workings of the individual conscience and in the education of the
whole race.[139]

In its intimate connection with all that had preceded and all that followed a
three-fold relationship was posited for the Incarnation. As the explanation
of the past it made sense of "the religious development of nations" and "the
spiritual yearnings of individual souls" by offering "a sanction and a basis
for what was vague and uncertain before".[140] As the culmination of human
history it was the high point up to which history had led, and away from
which everything came.[141] Thus the Incarnation was both the realization of
"the shadowy surmises of the rational mind of man" and the fulfilment of
the messianic hopes of the Jews.[142] It was also an anticipation of the future:
the Incarnate Word was to be seen "in the long lapse of those eighteen centuries of Christian History, in which He has lived again in the lives of His
saints, and died again in the sufferings of His heroes".[143]

In commending this view Lightfoot grasped at Pascal's idea that all history leads up to, and then away from, the life of Christ, and called upon his
contemporaries for a fuller exploration of the idea.[144] In the event he himself did not contribute much towards the task. Nevertheless, such an account of history was well established in Lightfoot's mind and came to expression piecemeal over the final twenty years of his life as the situation in
hand required. The outline of this incarnational interpretation of history is
recoverable from these occasional indications.

Somewhat surprisingly Lightfoot said very little about the beginning of
history in the Creation and the Fall.[145] But in the postlapsarian era he divided history into two according to the modes of revelation. The first was
distinguished by God's "revelation of Himself to the conscience of mankind
generally".[146] Corresponding to "ordinary" history, it lasted until the Incarnation itself. The principal outward developments — the spread of races,
the development of languages, the rise of social and political institutions,
and the growth of intellectual and religious ideas — were represented as
agencies of the Word.[147] Spiritually the response to the general revelation
was not the worship of the Creator but the development of polytheistic reli-

---

[139] CS 134.

[140] Mystery, 1876, 7-9, 16-17.

[141] RCC (1871) 81. Sudden, 1881, 6-7.

[142] CS 86-7. Sheep, 1873, 7-8.

[143] CS 145-6. Cf. SSO 4-5; & Philip's, 1880, 23.

[144] RCC (1871) 81-2.

[145] Cf. Westcott in this respect. See Olofsson, *Christus Redemptor et Consummator*,
ch. 4 & 5.

[146] For the eras of revelation, see "I. St John's Gospel. Introduction. I.1-I.28," f. 11 in
the box file marked "St John. Notes".

[147] CS 130-1. P 327-8. [What?] IV, 1877, 10-11. OA 305-6.

gions and pagan philosophies, while morally humankind was given over to sensuality, sin and shame. The other side of history was defined by God's "revelation of Himself to the Hebrew race especially". This side corresponded to "sacred" history and was constituted by the history of Israel. With few exceptions Lightfoot showed only a limited interest in discrete episodes and personalities. In line with its telic purpose, it was the function of the whole that counted.[148] Through its successive stages Israel taught the human race a strict monotheism, its dependence on revelation, the power of hope in a divine calling and messianic expectation. This general understanding was not disturbed by the researches of archaeologists, ethnologers and antiquaries, which were doing so much to change received historical perspectives.[149] Instead Lightfoot welcomed them as showing how through long ages God schooled man to an ever fuller knowledge of himself.[150] What others wanted to assign to material causes could be explained as the work of the Logos. The incarnational understanding of history — filled out and enriched by the work of philosophical historians and social evolutionists — remained the framework Lightfoot drew on as he had need.

This meant that for him the starting point for understanding history was its centre, not (as was more usual in both theology and social evolutionary perspectives) its beginning.[151] As the completion and "the central point of God's manifest revelation of Himself around which all phenomena of spiritual life revolve", the Incarnation was the reference point for understanding all else. In practice this led to the exaltation of the first century. Lightfoot explained why to his students:

> as the Life of Christ and the foundation of the Church are the turning points of the world's history — the events of this epoch being of incalculably greater importance than those of any other — so we may consider them as the antitype to which all the minor repetitions of similar circumstances stand in the relation of types-[152]

This was preeminently so because this historical era furnished the life of Christ, the pattern man, of whom the lives of men and women were to be an imitation.[153] In St Paul it also furnished a model of how to follow the pattern.[154] The lives of the leading Apostles were also a prefiguring of what was to come in history. By its capacity to frame a true understanding of life the age of the Incarnation was a destination of continual return.

---

[148] Esp. S 29-43. Also LS 177-80; CS 131-2; SSP 213; & SSO 204-10, 234-5, 254-6.
[149] CS 243. See Bowler, *Invention of Progress*, esp. ch. II & III.
[150] The "succession of epochs, the divergences of races" they had discovered evinced "the lines of progress running through the ages" and "the stream of knowledge and civilization broadening slowly down". CS 144.
[151] Bowler, *Invention of Progress*, Pt II. Olofsson, *Christus Redemptor et Consummator*, ch. 4 & 5.
[152] Acts I-VIII, 1855, 85r.
[153] LS 191; 2nd Group, 1858, 23-6; Life, 1862, 20-1.
[154] Christ, 1855, 16-20, 28-30.

It also meant that at the heart of Lightfoot's thinking about history there was a tension which was never really resolved. In its relations to history the Incarnation at one level of understanding was continuous with the past. Quantitatively it came as the end term in a process of growth and fulfilment:

> All previous revelations — and they were manifold — revelations to heathen[,] revelations to Jew — revelations through the wonders of nature, revelations through the history of nations, revelations through the workings of individual hearts — revelations natural and revelations supernatural — all these were partial, fragmentary, typical, shadowy. Now at length the great mystery — hidden from the foundation of the world — was disclosed. This was the explanation, the sum, the substance, of all that had gone before.[155]

The Incarnation was the culmination and completion of the history of revelation.

At another level of understanding the Incarnation was in a category of its own. While ever since the docetic heresy it had been necessary to insist upon its historicity, now in response to the naturalistic explanations emanating from the *Aufklärung* (which interpreted faith in Christ as the product of the religious consciousness of the first Christians),[156] Lightfoot had to qualify its status as an event by emphasizing its uniqueness and radical discontinuity with the past.[157] Christ, he asserted,

> was not the product of time. His person and character cannot be derived from any historical elements then existing in the world ... the spark which alone could fire it came immediately from heaven.[158]

Neither fully constituted nor entirely conditioned historically, the Incarnation defied normal historical explanation. Nor was it susceptible of analogy.[159] Nothing recorded in history afforded a remote parallel to the condescension, sacrifice and humiliation involved in the humanity of Christ.[160] Thus the Incarnation was the point at which Providence became decisive in Lightfoot's historical outlook, since God was held to have worked on, rather than through, history, albeit in the form of an historical life. But it introduced a striking element of discontinuity into a perspective otherwise distinguished by its emphasis on continuity.

It is not surprising that Lightfoot should have left this tension unresolved. For his interest in the Incarnation was practical rather than metaphysical. Questions about how the divine Word could become human flesh or how the integrity of humankind could be maintained in the presence of the divine did

---

[155] Will He, 1869, 15.

[156] See C. Brown, *Jesus in European Protestant Thought 1778-1860* (Durham, N.C.: Labrynth Press, 1985).

[157] See 287 below.

[158] RCC (1871) 81.

[159] [What?] I, 1877, 8-9; Delhi Mission, 1878, 12-15; CS 301.

[160] "No reiteration of the finite can compass the infinite." CS 326-7. Cf. [What?] III, 1877, 6-9.

not engage him. The historical factuality of the Incarnation was the crucial point: the difference it had made was the important issue. It was a revelation of God as the loving Father of all humankind with whom a filial relationship was possible.[161] God becoming man engendered a new estimate of human life which endorsed and directed the innate aspirations of humanity as well as establishing the "universal brotherhood of man".[162] The Atonement broke the power of sin and redeemed the world from judgment.[163] The resurrection and ascension broke the power of death and established the doctrine of immortality.[164] Together they introduced a new point of view into the world, and with it a new era in religion and ethics was inaugurated.[165] So powerful were its effects that the Incarnation, while continuous with the past in some respects, also achieved a significant break with it and lifted history on to a new plane.

The adoption of this continuity-discontinuity structure of historical understanding brings into relief a further difficulty inherent in Lightfoot's outlook, the place of progress after the Incarnation. If the Incarnation represented the culmination of the "increasing purpose", it might reasonably be asked on what basis was he able to maintain that progress continued after its end. Lightfoot's general response was that, while it was true that the Incarnation completed the history of revelation, the Christ-episode was only the beginning of the realization of what this final instalment meant. Although the revelation given in Christ was itself full and complete, it remained to be apprehended and appropriated fully. Subsequent history was the sphere for this increasing apprehension and appropriation at the level of the individual and society of the principles of life given in Christ. Lightfoot had two main explanations for how this happened.

Part of his resolution of the problem was to point out that the Ascension inaugurated the dispensation of the Holy Spirit. In its weakness Lightfoot's pneumatology was typical of the age.[166] Not only is it not an important theme in his *oeuvre*, but he failed to clarify the relation between the operations of the Word and those of the Spirit. But he did insist on the phenomenal reality and practical effect of the Spirit.[167] Although the Word was flesh no longer, the divine was still active in the world as Spirit. For Lightfoot's purposes it was sufficient to identify the difference made by "the

---

[161] Eg. CS 93-4, 104, 291-3; SSP 116, 149; OA 22-4, 174, 314-15.

[162] RCC (1873) 233; CS 280-1.

[163] Vision, 1873, 17-19; War, 1877, 28-30; SSP 214.

[164] CS 63-79.

[165] CS 27-8, 102; Divided Allegiance, 1866, 1-2.

[166] Elliott-Binns *English Thought,* 236.

[167] Eg. Through a Glass, 1875, 26-30. Cf. II. St John II. I.29-IV.5, f. 56. "Of the operations of the Spirit we are conscious. But with this consciousness our knowledge ends. The before & after — the mode & sequence of the operation — are unknown to us."

reign of God the Spirit" after Pentecost. It represented an advance because the restrictions of the carnal presence of Christ had been removed. In their place was a spiritual presence subject to no conditions of time or place.[168] In its "ordinary operations", the noiseless and unseen (yet powerful) influence symbolized by the breeze,[169] the Spirit guides the minds and moulds the hearts of men, giving them access to new powers of wisdom and understanding, strength and courage, and holiness and godliness.[170] The outcome for history was anticipated in the effect on the Twelve.[171] For the first time they apprehended the true character of the Gospel as a spiritual dispensation and were transformed into its devoted advocates as a result. This experience had been repeated many times since.[172] As intellectual force and moral power, the Spirit had gone on teaching the lesson of the Word becoming man, the Passion and the Resurrection for the transformation of thought and life.[173] For He is

> the Universal Teacher Who takes of all those things which the Father has wrought through the Son, and shows them to us, Who exhibits, interprets, brings home to us, the external workings of the Son, translating them, as it were, from the world of the senses to the world of the understanding, speaking as Spirit to spirits.[174]

The age of the Spirit was for the fulfilment of the Incarnation, a process which continued the progressive realization of God's "increasing purpose".[175] After the Incarnation the world had more of Christ, because He was now the Christ of all times and places.[176] His going away was necessary for the next stage in the realization of God's plan, the universalization of Christianity.

The second component of Lightfoot's solution to the problem of progress after the Incarnation was the Church. Like the Incarnation itself, it evinced a duality in its historical relations. On the one hand, it had enjoyed a continuous existence since its founder Abraham,[177] and actually succeeded "Israel after the flesh" as "Israel after the spirit".[178] On the other hand, the Church had been especially constituted by Jesus, and his death, though a devastating ending, was at the same time "the great beginning of a heavenly kingdom, the beginning of a rescue of souls from sin and death, the begin-

---

[168] Veil, 1855, 13-14; Worship, 1871, 15; OA 296-302.

[169] Worship, 1871, 13-15; SSP 208; OA 49.

[170] DDC (1881) 95-6. Cf. OA 57, 63-5.

[171] Another Paraclete, 1875, 18-20; OA 294-9.

[172] Three Notes, 1873, 24-6.

[173] He Shall Take, 1877, 27-30.

[174] SSO 99-100.

[175] The need for this translation of the words and works of Christ "into modern language, and adapt them to modern life" was as strong in the present as ever. SSP 216-17. He Shall Take, 1877, 21-4.

[176] Veil, 1855, 13-14; Worship, 1871, 13-17; & SSP 209.

[177] RCC (1871) 81; Attracting Power, 1874, 3-7; Vision, 1878, 1-2; & SSO 148-9.

[178] SSO 194, 196-7.

ning of an ingathering of a holy people of God, the foundation of a second and spiritual temple, the Church of Christ".[179] From this dominical beginning it had continued as a practical necessity of Christian living.[180] The utilitarianism of this view has caused some scholars to think Lightfoot regarded the Church as a mere external society, 'a sociological necessity'.[181] In fact he was not free of the high theorizing characteristic of nineteenth century Anglican ecclesiology. The Church, he asserted, "is Christ, nothing less than Christ Himself" and "the Church of Christ, is the body of Christ".[182] On occasions he also affirmed that the Divine Word is at work in the Church as its Head to give it life and power.[183] No attempt was made to bring these elements into due relation, but they indicate that for Lightfoot the body of Christ, although no longer present in the flesh, was still present as the Church.

While insisting on the "absolute entire identity" between the founder and the members, Lightfoot usually assumed this dimension, and concentrated on that which the Church is in its outward life, its *historical* existence, in which its essential character is increasingly realized.[184] This occurs as the Church carries out its task of witness, which involves, as its highest form, worship and thanksgiving, but also expectant waiting for the *parousia*, the enunciation of truth in creeds and articles, preservation and interpretation of the Bible, administration of the sacrament, evangelism and missionary labour, opposition to injustice, and protection of the weak and oppressed.[185] As it does so in its passage from being the "church militant" to the "church triumphant", the Church itself progresses and leads the world in its progress. After the life of Christ, the Church "as the depository of the Word" is the leading agent in the movement of history towards its "goal, perfection in Christ".[186]

Of course Lightfoot was too familiar with the details of the church's history to suggest uniformity in its outward life. Periods of backwardness and its conflicts and atrocities had to be acknowledged.[187] But rather than

---

[179] LNC 98.

[180] P 181-4.

[181] The term "sociological" is used by S. Sykes, *The Identity of Christianity. Theologians and the Essence of Christianity From Schleiermacher to Barth* (London: S.P.C.K.,1984) 48.

[182] SSO 180-1, 190. Cf. Members, 1855, 7; II. St John II. I.29-IV.5, f. 48; Edifying, 1869, 4; SSO 213.

[183] Edifying, 1869, 4; Will He, 1869, 19; C 117-18; & LNC 76.

[184] P 326-8; & OA 35-6.

[185] 4th Group, 1858, 20-1.

[186] MSL 7-8; P 326; CS 141, 145-6, 179; & LNC 75-7.

[187] Eg. SSP 141-2. Also, Not Peace, 1875, 16-20; CS 254-7; SSO 183-4, 210-11; & OA 210-11.

focussing on specific episodes, Lightfoot preferred taking the larger view.[188] In one of his favourite and most potent images, the Church was likened to a river, small in its beginnings, uneven but ever swelling in its flow and issuing finally in due time into the sea.[189] This made clear that the conditions in which the Church has its life and exercises its influence arise from the world setting.[190] As it meets the dangers and rises to the opportunities presented by its changing environment, the Church manifests the power of modification and adaptation that enables it to become more at any one time what it is essentially at all times.[191] In this way its witness to Christ is maintained in successively intelligible forms and its continuity extended for the further religious and moral transformation of the world. On this basis Lightfoot emphasized the succession of states in the history of the Church which constituted a cycle of intense spiritual life, decline and torpor, and then revival and new life.[192] The early Church was not to be idealized, but it was still "without parallel in the history of the world — a sublime example of faith triumphant over death[,] of strength made perfect in weakness, of joy abounding in tribulation, of faith triumphant over death — a glorious spectacle for men and angels".[193] The contemporary mediaeval revival notwithstanding, the Middle Ages were characterized by "gathering corruptions", "ignorance", "superstition", and increasing papal pretensions.[194] Much of this was corrected during the Reformation, when the Church was brought "into harmony with the intellectual and social acquisitions of a more enlightened age" and its corruptions were reformed.[195] Since then the cycle had been repeated once more as the Church had emerged from the "spiritual deadness" of the eighteenth century into the vigorous life and activity of the nineteenth.[196] Lightfoot interpreted its history in typically Protestant terms to subsume the ambivalent and regrettable in the life of the Church.

A growing problem for Lightfoot was how to sustain historically the view that Christianity and the Church are the progressive forces in history.[197] In response he frequently drew attention to the results of the gradual triumph

---

[188] Eg. CS 249: "I know no stronger evidence of the inherent power and vitality of Christianity, than that it should have triumphed over the scandals of Christendom."

[189] See esp. SSO 146-59.

[190] MSL 5. The importance of the environment was implicit in the identification of the Church militant with Israel in the wilderness. Acts I-VIII, 1855, 90-1.

[191] RCC (1871) 81; Attracting Power, 1874, 7; LNC 76.

[192] Revival, 1881, 15-17; & LNC 75-6, 77.

[193] Christian Priesthood, 1862, 7; & What Advantageth It?, 1876, 1-8.

[194] SSO 243; Christ's Little Ones, 1867, 1-2; & LNC 51.

[195] CS 187; SSO 59, 140, 157; LNC 115, 127-9.

[196] SSO 16-17, 152-3, 214, 243.

[197] Lightfoot's response to the appropriation of history by the opponents of Christianity is treated more fully on 157-62 below.

of Christianity over its rivals for the religious and ethical allegiance of humankind.[198] Received values had been transformed; forgiveness, glorified; weakness, apotheosized; and purity, exalted.[199] As a result society had been amended, with the emancipation of the slave and the woman, the ending of infanticide, the ennoblement of children, and establishment of charities for the poor and destitute, and hospitals for the ill.[200] Of course the spiritual and moral transformation of the world was not complete, but this was because the freedom of people to choose had meant that the principles and transforming power made available in the Incarnation had never been universally or fully accepted.[201] It was not the case (as Bruce Kaye suggested) that Lightfoot thought the given in the Incarnation has continually struggled with the lower nature of mankind for its maintenance. Rather the given in the Incarnation has continually overcome the resistance of men and women for the ongoing realization of God's "increasing purpose", and would continue to do so. The Incarnation created Christianity, and Christianity created, and was still creating, Christendom.[202] In this the continuation of progress to the end of the world was assured.

While this view of the Spirit and the Church sustained the optimism of Lightfoot's idea of history as God's "increasing purpose" for the post-Incarnation era, the underlying continuity-discontinuity structure is decisive for evaluating Lightfoot's progressive Christian historiography. The centrality and importance of the Incarnation means that the progress expressive of the "increasing purpose" depended on the unique and miraculous irruption into time and space of a divine being. As Lightfoot well understood, this was to draw on the θεολογία to understand the meaning and purpose of the mundane happenings of human history. The final consummation of history would also require a second coming of Christ, an event which remained in the mind and gift of God alone.[203] On the eve of Lightfoot's professional career, his adversary in early Christian studies, F.C. Baur, had made the point:

> If Christianity is an absolutely supernatural miracle, shattering the continuity of history, then history has nothing further to do with it, it can only stand before the miracle and see in it the end of its research and understanding. As miracle the origin of Christianity is an absolutely incomprehensible beginning.[204]

---

[198] True, 1860, 4-6; Christ, 1876, 17-20; Glory, 1877, 12-15; CS 86-7, 276, 279-80.

[199] Weakness, 1875, 27-31; Hunger, 1877, 8-9; [What?] III, 1877, 17-20; CS 272, 280-1; SSO 239, 241-2.

[200] Christ's, 1867, 2-11, 18-19; Will He, 1869, 21; Pure, 1880, 26; C 323-9; WCA 3-6; SSO 222-3.

[201] Scene, 1874, 17. Cf. SSP 252-3.

[202] I. St Paul's Teaching, 1858, 5-6; Will He, 1869, 10-12.

[203] For the details of Lightfoot's eschatological thinking, see 113 below.

[204] F.C. Baur, "The Epochs of Church Historiography," in *Ferdinand Christian Baur: On the Writings of Church History* (ed. & trans. P.C. Hodgson; New York: Oxford Univer-

There is no evidence that Lightfoot ever faced this problem in quite the same terms, but the emphasis on continuity certainly minimized its effect and averted the need for such a radically agnostic assessment. On the other hand, his reliance on the supernatural for making sense of the course of historical events retained an unhistorical element in his outlook. Lightfoot not only had a theory of history: it was also a genuine theology of history in its recourse to an ultimately transcendent God for its meaning, means and purpose.

The same point follows from Lightfoot's use of the Logos as a device for reconciling a Christian interpretation of history with the intramundane approaches coming increasingly into vogue in a kind of 'supernatural naturalism'.[205] Its significance for the understanding of history in general, but especially for the Incarnation and progress, was purportedly a recognition of something *in* the facts themselves. To his University congregation Lightfoot addressed the question:

> Have you spent hour after hour on the literature of the two greatest nations of antiquity? And have you listened as though only Greeks and Romans are speaking to you? Have you heard no echo of the Divine Word, sounding above and through the din of human voices; seen no impress of the Divine Mind — blurred and partial though it was — in the philosophic penetration of the one and the legal precision of the other. Have you pored over the long roll of human history ...? And has all this opened out no revelation of the Word, though the scroll is written over with His name within and without?[206]

That this might in fact be the imposition of meaning is suggested by the admission that the Logos is a spiritual perception available only to those with eyes to see:

> I would not be mistaken. Neither philosophy, nor mathematics, nor nature, nor history will of themselves teach this lesson. But the Spirit will speak through these studies to the spiritually-minded: will quicken them with a higher life; will impart through them a revelation of God.[207]

Reflecting the Platonic mysticism typical of right wing liberal Anglicanism, the true meaning of history was discerned by the spiritual faculties. In other words it was known by a mechanism which was not part of the means by which knowledge about the past was generated. Evidently himself unaware that it was so, the Logos as the principle of interpretation was a preconception introduced into Lightfoot's historical understanding from the realm of private belief.

---

sity Press, 1968) 213. Baur made the point as part of an analysis of the Christian historiography of J.A.W. Neander. For Neander's influence on Lightfoot, see 123-4 below.

[205] The phrase is of course adapted from the influential M.H. Abrams, *Natural Supernaturalism: Tradition and Revolution in Romantic Literature* (New York: Norton, 1971).

[206] CS 144.

[207] CS 145.

The *a priori* quality of Lightfoot's theology of history points to the weakness of its rationale for contemporaries. The Logos was so highly abstract that it could be dismissed as meaningless with the same ease that it could be accepted as the true solution. This perhaps explains in part why, against the background of the Victorian 'crisis of faith', Lightfoot's influence was so strong among his followers but did not become wider than it was. His solution to the difficulties was attractive to those who wanted a solution but not compelling to others. The youthful V.H. Stanton, son of a clerical home and present as an undergraduate when Lightfoot preached "Shew Us the Father" before the University in 1868, was impressed;[208] but Lightfoot's friend, Henry Sidgwick, at that time struggling with his doubt and its institutional consequences, was not.[209] To the Christians Lightfoot spoke words of reassurance.[210] From the doubters he commanded respect but not assent. A theology of history grounded on the Logos offered much to contemporaries, but not as much as Lightfoot believed.

These shortcomings notwithstanding, the Logos sustained Lightfoot's perspective on history as the "increasing purpose of God" for the remainder of his career. On occasion he used the expression itself, but the incarnational interpretation of history it stood for was never far away in his teaching and practice. In the year of his death much of what Lightfoot had been saying about history for some thirty years was enshrined in *Lux Mundi*, the volume usually celebrated as heralding the beginning of liberal Catholicism in England.[211] Thus the gradualism and evolutionism of the incarnational understanding which Lightfoot had long advocated as the answer to the problems raised for discussion by *Essays and Reviews* was in the process of being absorbed into a new Anglican orthodoxy. However, its development, par-

---

[208] Vincent Henry Stanton (1846-1924), son of the Rector of Halesworth, Suffolk; entered Trinity College 1866; BA 1870; Ely Professor of Divinity 1916-22; Regius Professor of Divinity 1922-1927. Venn, *Alumni* II.VI.14. Stanton recalled the effect of the sermon at the meeting for procuring a memorial of Lightfoot in Cambridge. *Reporter* (8 February 1890) 416-17.

[209] Henry Sidgwick (1838-1900); Fellow of Trinity College (1859-1869); Knightbridge Professor of Moral Philosophy (1883-1900), author of *The Methods of Ethics* (1874). For Lightfoot's part in his deliberations, see A.S. & E.M.S., *Henry Sidgwick: A Memoir*, 198.

[210] A.J. Mason, afterwards Lady Margaret Professor of Divinity (1895-1903) and Master of Pembroke College (1903-12) said that he owed Lightfoot his life. Mason to Lightfoot, 16 December 1887. Another who was greatly helped was W.P. Turnbull, Assistant Tutor at Trinity (1865-70) and an Inspector of Schools from 1871. H.W. Turnbull, *Some Memories of William Peverill Turnbull* (London: G. Bell & Sons, 1919) 60, 142-5. Lightfoot wrote him "a letter of apostolic length" in answer to his difficulties. Turnbull to Lightfoot, 8 & 22 August 1870; & n.d.

[211] C. Gore (ed.), *Lux Mundi. A Series of Studies in the Religion of the Incarnation* (4th ed.; London: John Murray, 1890 [originally published in 1889]). On the emergence of liberal Catholicism, see 270-1 below.

ticularly by E.S. Talbot and J.R. Illingworth, brings into relief the limitations of Lightfoot's outlook.[212] As a "theory" of history it was incomplete,
unsystematic, and even unsophisticated. Nevertheless it was definite and a
part of Lightfoot's perspective for the whole of his career, with important
consequences for his thought and conduct as both Churchman and scholar.
Thus Mandell Creighton was wrong about the Cambridge school and history, in Lightfoot's case at least. While he was able to write apparently
objective record history, he did have that metahistorical interest that Creighton
denied him. Moreover, the supernatural was the key factor in his thinking.
With the divine Logos for its rationale, the miracle of the Incarnation for its
centre, and the *parousia* for its *telos*, history for Lightfoot *was* theological:
in fact, the domain of "the increasing purpose of God".

---

[212] E.S. Talbot, "The Preparation in History for Christ" & J.R. Illingworth, "The Incarnation in Relation to Development," in *Lux Mundi*, 127-214. For an analysis of their own
shortcomings, see Hinchliff, *God and History*, ch. 5.

Chapter Five

The "Intensification of History": The Bible and History

The fundamental problem for all interpreters of history is epistemological. How they, who are inescapably a part of history, can know the meaning of the whole which they cannot see, is a question of which they must give some account.[1] The difficulty of upholding such claims to independent knowledge means that comprehensive views of the historical process are invariably reducible to a moment of encounter between the past and the present in the experience of the interpreter. While thus conditioned and contingent, these formulations are by no means meaningless. For they represent a synthesis of what one individual thinks is worthwhile in the past and significant in the present. To the extent that it affects the thought and conduct of himself and others, it also becomes a force in history itself. Tracing the elements of the synthesis to their sources in both past and present is therefore a useful way of explaining the interpreter, his interpretation and his influence. In an historical consideration of Lightfoot's life and thought, this approach further clarifies the nature of his understanding of history as "the increasing purpose of God" and points to its intended social and cultural function.

Despite the importance of the epistemological question, so far as extant writings enable us to tell, how the meaning of history is known is not a matter that ever seriously engaged Lightfoot's attention. This in itself reflects his confidence in his principal source. At every turn it is clear that his views were based chiefly on the Bible. This was no more than the fulfilment of his own declared principles. The same sermon that identified "the increasing purpose of God" as the meaning of history also indicated that the Bible was intended to be a guide in the interpretation of history. It prescribed the spirit in which history should be read, and furnished a "sure word of prophecy to guide us".[2]

However, what this meant was not at all straightforward in England in the 1860s and 1870s. How the Bible was to be understood as an authority, and

---

[1] Eg. R.F. Atkinson, *Knowledge and Explanation in History. An Introduction to the Philosophy of History* (Ithaca, New York: Cornell University Press, 1978).

[2] IP 12-13.

how it was to be read, were matters of considerable debate.[3] According to the orthodoxy of the day, the Bible was of supernatural origin furnishing infallible information, a status that automatically brought with it a role in the determination of moral thought and social arrangements in addition to religious beliefs.[4] An alternative to this 'oracular view' of the conservatives was furnished by the 'Illuminist' understanding of revelation taught by Coleridge.[5] He maintained that the Bible promoted revelation in the immediacy of personal experience, and was therefore not so much an external standard as an 'aid to faith'. This was attractive to many of those interested in finding the proper relation between the Bible's teaching and the findings of empirical research. Again it was the publication of *Essays and Reviews* that brought into relief a debate that had been simmering for many years.[6] The bitterness of the controversy is understandable. Bound up with the nature and authority of the Biblical revelation was the social order and the meaning and value of life itself. It was against this background that Lightfoot became the incumbent of the recently established Hulsean Chair of Divinity.[7]

I

Lightfoot himself did not ever consider systematically the question of Biblical authority. This was not for want of requests that he do so. Prince Lee urged him to tackle the subject of inspiration when he became Hulsean Professor.[8] No more than the publication of *Essays and Reviews* itself did his appointment to a Divinity chair move him to pronounce on a general issue of importance. As late as December 1889 Lightfoot was still refusing to write a paper on the Church's teaching on this subject, deprecating "the desire to make everything right and tight", and counselling patience.[9] As the requests of Prince Lee and Archbishop Benson indicate, however, there were many who would have welcomed a statement from Lightfoot on the basis upon which the Bible warranted retention as an authority for belief and action. In this respect too Lightfoot did not take the lead that might have been expected of him.

---

[3]   The debate is expounded in H.D. MacDonald, *Ideas of Revelation. An Historical Study A.D. 1700 to A.D. 1860* (London: Macmillan, 1959); & *Theories of Revelation. An Historical Study 1860-1960* (London: Allen & Unwin, 1963).

[4]   Cf. Chadwick, *Victorian Church*, II.73. See further, n. 24 below.

[5]   I owe the term 'oracular view' to R.P.C. Hanson, *The Bible as a Norm of Faith* (Durham: Durham University, 1963).

[6]   The immediately preceding debate between Mansel and Maurice was more a theological dispute than a major public debate. See Chadwick, *Victorian Church*, I.556-8.

[7]   See above 50. Also Willis Clark, *Endowments*, 117-21; & Tanner, *Historical Register*, 97.

[8]   Prince Lee to Lightfoot, 28 October 1861.

[9]   Lightfoot to Benson, 14 December 1889, in LB II.289. Lightfoot died a week later.

Although he did not write systematically on the subject, Lightfoot evinced a high view of the Bible throughout his career. He referred to it frequently as the "inspired" or "sacred" volume",[10] "the book of revelation",[11] "the oracles of God",[12] "the voice of the Holy Spirit Himself",[13] "God's Holy Word",[14] and "the book of books".[15] He also maintained that the Bible was the "record of God's judgments" and "the fullest expression of His divine will & purpose".[16] Lightfoot insisted further that "all Holy Scripture was written for our learning",[17] and that the Bible teaches deep theological truths and inculcates penetrating moral lessons.[18] He was able to speak too of "the authoritative message of an accredited prophet or apostle",[19] and to assert that "The doctrine of Paul is the doctrine of our own time, because the doctrine for all times".[20] In relation to the Church, "the Scriptures of the New Testament" were "the title deeds of its inheritance & the charter of its corporate life",[21] while taken as a whole, the Bible was "the charter of Christendom".[22] In its wider public importance it ranked at least with the Church:

> No mere abstract philosophy has influenced or can influence permanently large masses of men. A Bible and a Church — a sacred record and a religious community — are primary conditions of extensive and abiding success.[23]

Such sentiments clearly envisage a constitutive role and teaching authority in the life of both the Church and English society at large, but Lightfoot never in the manner of more conservative thinkers asserted the preeminence of the Bible over other sources of truth and understanding, or humankind's dependence on it for a knowledge of God and salvation.[24] Although the rhetoric was appropriate, for the times his view of the nature and authority of the Bible was undefined and relatively vague.

---

[10] I. St Paul's Teaching, 1858, 8, 9.

[11] I. St Paul's Teaching, 1858, 18; People, 1867, 29.

[12] 4th Group, 1858, 21.

[13] The Right, 1874, 16.

[14] LNC 97.

[15] LNC 97.

[16] Truth, 1864, 34.

[17] CS 3.

[18] Moral Freedom, 1873, 2. Cf. CS 163-4, S 20 & SSP 275-6.

[19] [What?] IV, 1877, 4.

[20] OA 103. Cf. SSO 58.

[21] Temple, 1880, 16.

[22] OA 154. Cf. Temple, 1880, 16.

[23] P 376.

[24] Two contemporary examples of this position were J.W. Burgon, *Inspiration and Interpretation: Seven Sermons Preached Before the University of Oxford ... Being an Answer to a Volume Entitled "Essays and Reviews"* (Oxford & London: J.H. & J. Parker, 1861); & E. Garbett, *The Bible and its Critics: An Enquiry Into the Objective Reality of Revealed Truths* (London: Seeley & Griffiths, 1861).

Although Lightfoot had regularly addressed the twin issues of the status and interpretation of Scripture in lectures since 1855,[25] he was more reticent before the wider public. A position on the Biblical question does not seem to have been declared beyond Cambridge until 1864. In that year Pusey and his High Church supporters issued the Oxford Declaration in response to the rejection by the Judicial Committee of the Privy Council of charges that Roland Williams and H.B. Wilson denied in *Essays and Reviews* that the Bible is properly the "Word of God". Their purpose was to reassure the English people that the clergy "maintains without reserve or qualification the Inspiration and Divine Authority of the whole Canonical Scriptures as not only containing but being the Word of God".[26] Lightfoot refused to sign the Declaration.[27]

Several months later he travelled to Oxford itself where, despite the delicacy of the occasion, he boldly declared before a conference of local clergymen that identification of the Bible with the Word of God was not a Biblical usage of the term, and in fact placed a limitation on it.[28] Characteristically Lightfoot did not go on exactly to define his attitude. This was due partly to the caution required by the situation; partly to his reluctance to be precise in doctrinal matters; and partly to the true bearings of the question. Neither ministerial activity nor Christianity itself depended on the outcome of the controversy, so that by implication current attempts to enforce specific propositions were misguided. But Lightfoot did attempt to direct opinion. The 'Word of God' could be taken in either a restricted sense — as "a special message communicated by the lips of prophet or Apostle or Evangelist", or as a reference to Christ — or in a comprehensive sense — "to denote the revelation of the power, the will & attributes of God in whatever way to the

---

[25] See B.N. Kaye & G.R. Treloar, "J.B. Lightfoot and New Testament Interpretation. An Unpublished Manuscript of 1855," *Durham University Journal* LXXXII.2 (July 1990) 161-75.

[26] H.P. Liddon, *Life of Edward Bouverie Pusey* (4 vols; London: Longmans, Green & Co., 1897) IV.38-62, 67-8. The Declaration is on 54. For Williams and Wilson, see Crowther, *Church Embattled*, ch. 4, 5, esp. 102-3, 111-12, 118-19, 121-3. The question was also raised by Jowett.

[27] A copy of the Oxford Declaration is still included with E.B. Pusey to Lightfoot, 1 March, 1864. It is possible that a letter to Pusey by Lightfoot, catalogued among the Pusey manuscripts at Pusey House, Oxford, but no longer traceable, was Lightfoot's reply. Cf. Benson to Lightfoot, 4 March 1864, agreeing with the judgment, but predicting trouble in the Church. LB I.229.

[28] "The Sword of the Word," 8 August 1864, annotated "before a conference of the clergy", esp. 7-12. The conservatism of the Oxfordshire clery at the time was notorious. See D. McClatchey, *Oxfordshire Clergy 1777-1869. A Study of the Established Church and of the Role of its Clergy in Local Society* (Oxford: Clarendon Press, 1960).

human heart and understanding".[29] It was in this latter sense, Lightfoot
maintained, that the Bible should be regarded as the Word of God. For this
is how it functions. Moral and religious experience was the domain in which
the question of Biblical authority should be decided.

This was a very different kind of authority from that envisaged in the
Oxford Declaration. For the orthodox the Bible was directly from God, a
status authenticated by miracle and the fulfilment of prophecy.[30] However,
Lightfoot rejected, or at least minimized, the 'evidences' approach. Instead
he maintained that, by its congruence with human experience and capacity
to meet human need, the Bible was self-authenticating. On other occasions
indeed he endorsed Coleridge's dictum in the *Confessions*, "whatever finds
me, bears witness for itself that it has proceeded from a Holy Spirit".[31] Biblical authority was not a matter of 'evidences' but of religious function and
efficacy. Moreover, the shift of attention to the personal and inward, and the
proposition that the divine power is known in personal encounter, had a strong
affinity with the "subjectivist" approach which said that divine revelation is
known at the point of individual experience.[32] Thus Lightfoot's view, a clear
attempt to adjust Biblical authority to the πολυμερῶς καὶ πολυτρόπως framework, involved the very perspective which the Oxford Declaration opposed.
In the charged post *Essays and Reviews* atmosphere, he seems to have judged
that it would be divisive to take a definite stand with those who directly or
indirectly were seeking a revision of the received oracular perspective. Directing attention to the moral power in the inner life of each individual as a
sufficient evidence of the Bible's divine origin was a point which secured
what was important and on which all could agree. Even so, though he did
not declare it, Lightfoot had moved away from the orthodox position of the
day.

Lightfoot's constructive position turned on the Coleridgean distinction
between the outward and inward sides of the Bible. These corresponded
more or less to its human and divine aspects.[33] At a time when many denied
or struggled to accept the implications of the former, Lightfoot attached great
value to it. For him it meant two things. On the one hand, there was the
"outward form & history of the Bible", its existence as a collection of writ-

---

[29] Sword, 1864, 9. Much of this sermon was repeated six years later before the University of Cambridge. See CS 150-71. On this occasion "human heart" was changed to
"human conscience".

[30] Cf. the statement of Christopher Wordsworth in *Replies to 'Essays and Reviews'*,
456: "the Bible must be interpreted as a book written by a Being to whom all things are
present, and who contemplates all things at once in the panoramic view of his own Omnis-
cience."

[31] Eg. RCC (1871) 83.

[32] For the "subjectivist" approach, see MacDonald, *Ideas of Revelation,* ch. I & II.

[33] Right, 1874, 15-18

ings.[34] At this level of understanding it could be said to be the accidental
growth of many centuries.[35] On the other hand, the Bible was "the history
and literature of a nation".[36] At this level it needed to be read as the national
literature of Israel. In both respects the Bible evinced "exceptional diversity".[37] On the literary side there was great variety of form, content and
character. As a national literature it incorporated writings by different authors, in different languages, from different countries, and relating to incidents spread over several thousands of years at different stages of the development of human society, involving all the circumstances and vicissitudes
of human life.[38] Read in this way the meaning was what the writers had
intended to convey to their own day and generation.[39]

The inward side of the Bible was its "principle of life" or "animating
soul".[40] It consisted in the Eternal Word "speaking through lawgiver and
captain, through priest and prophet and king, speaking in the continuous
history of a nation and in the chequered but unbroken life of a Church, till at
length He became incarnate in the Man Jesus Christ".[41] Throughout the
chief concern was "the idea of a rescue, the hope of a redemption", from
"earthly trouble", and from "the more intolerable thraldom of sin".[42] Again
there were two aspects. On the divine side the Bible recorded the light given
through successive revelations, the development of a dispensation from all
eternity. On the human side it was "the Pilgrim's Progress of humanity",
recording the responses of men and women to these revelations and the
effort of a world — alienated by sin — to reunite itself with God. Read in
this way its meaning was what it said to the religious and moral sensibilities
of people in the present.

At first sight inherent in this approach was a dualism at variance with
Lightfoot's understanding of how God works in the world. It was avoided
by his characteristic incarnational understanding of the God-world relation
to which the Bible conformed. The combination of the outward and the
inward reflected the condescension of God for the exaltation of humankind:

---

[34] Light, 1872, 8-9.

[35] RCC (1871) 81.

[36] Right, 1874, 15-18; OA 77.

[37] Sudden Coming, 1881, 8.

[38] Light, 1872, 8-10; Right, 1874, 15-18; OA 32-3, 77; Sudden Coming, 1881, 3-5; &
LO 3.

[39] On Lightfoot's approach to the meaning and interpretation of the Bible, see further
below in Part IV.

[40] LO 4.

[41] *Ibid.*

[42] Vision, 1878, 2-4. The emphases are Lightfoot's.

The hands may be the hands of history, but the voice is the voice of God ... May we not say that ... God took of the dust of the earth, of the strivings of men and the turmoils of nations, and breathed into it the breath of life, thoughts that thrill and words that speak — speak to all time and through all time to eternity.[43]

Thus the humanity of the Bible was the channel for the divine teaching. Lightfoot did not explain how the two were to be distinguished,[44] but he proceeded in the belief that God came to the men and women of the Bible and revealed Himself in their mundane human experience. Through the written account of these experiences He revealed Himself to the men and women of the present.

This approach to the Bible required some adjustment of the basic categories of Biblical authority. On the specific question of inspiration, Lightfoot also differed from the strictly orthodox position reflected in the responses to *Essays and Reviews*. In early lectures, taking up the interest in the question generated by such recent developments as the *Vestiges of Creation*, Coleridge's *Confessions of an Inquiring Spirit*, and German Biblical criticism, he discerned in the plethora of available opinions three main divisions according to how the necessary constituent elements — the human and the divine — were apportioned.[45] The irrational or mechanical view was unacceptable because it virtually excluded human agency. For the opposite reason the rationalistic view was no better: it so emphasized the human agency that the divine was virtually denied. The true view recognized both elements and harmoniously combined them. Inspiration was

not a mechanical power or a magical agency. It does not use men merely as its instruments. It is a moral and spiritual power. It does not transmute its agents: it moulds them. Hence, as a natural result arising from the varied circumstances and training of the inspired writers, it is not uniform.[46]

Its locus was therefore as much in the writers as in their writings. It referred to that providential ordering of circumstances and character which fitted the writers for their allotted task.[47] With the Spirit seen to be "acting upon and through the natural faculties of man rather than apart from them, and availing itself of the influences and associations of outward things to win its way", and then "overruling the writers for the fulfilment of a great design",[48] 'in-

---

[43] OA 32-3.

[44] The difficulties of this approach are pointed out by P. Addinall, *Philosophy and Biblical Interpretation. A Study in Nineteenth Century Conflict* (Cambridge: University Press, 1991) 211-14, in relation to one of its later exponents, the Old Testament scholar, S.R. Driver.

[45] NTI 171-5; & BE 224-7.

[46] BE 226.

[47] I. St Paul's Teaching, 1858, 10-11, 15-16, 24-5; 1st Group, 1858, 1-3; Life Hidden, 1860, 5-6; & BE 206-7

[48] Light, 1872, 9-10. Also Right, 1874, 15-18; & OA 32-3.

spiration' pointed as much to the underlying historical process as to the textual result.

Similarly Lightfoot rejected orthodoxy's identification of revelation with the record. Instead he claimed the Biblical documents professed only to "contain the revelation".[49] The "history of the communication of the revelation", the Old and New Testaments embodied "successive revelations", so that the Bible was "the record of the revelation", not the revelation itself. As such it was speech, not the speaker, and evidently belongs to the category of "Revelation natural".[50] At first sight this is awkward. For Lightfoot also held that there were "special" revelations in the Bible. Moreover, the "truths of revelation" were not only contrasted with natural theology but put in authority over it. In fact the Bible reported natural revelations — as in David's response to the physical creation and his sense of sin in the Psalms.[51] But it also reported "supernatural revelations", "revelations from heaven" — to Adam, Abraham, Jacob, Moses, Isaiah, Ezekiel, Stephen and Paul — while the Incarnate Word Himself made "the supreme revelations of His purposes, as in those private discourses concerning the Second Advent on Olivet".[52] The Bible therefore exhibited revelation in its complexity as a record of both "Revelation natural" and "Revelation special". At both levels it described religious experience in which additional truth about God was disclosed. For Lightfoot the locus of revelation had shifted from the written word to the words, events and processes it reports. In other words the revelation was in the history, not in the letter. The Bible gave access to it.

Lightfoot's approach left considerable scope for the use of reason in Biblical interpretation without necessarily (as some contemporaries supposed) derogating from its authority.[53] For Lightfoot this extended beyond the more usual defence of the Bible's credentials and systematization of its teaching to the evaluation of its content. Thus he happily embraced in principle the application of the new critical procedures in Biblical study, observing to his students:

> If the Scriptures are indeed true they must be in accord with every true principle of whatever kind ... From the full light of science and criticism we have nothing to fear.[54]

Nor was he committed to the "absolute infallibility" of the New Testament, as Hort at one stage feared.[55] Empirical criticism and the discovery of error

---

[49]   CS 155-8. RCC (1871) 81.

[50]   For Lightfoot's understanding of revelation in general, see 78 above.

[51]   CS 229-30. SSP 19-23.

[52]   OA 152-3.

[53]   G xi-xii.

[54]   NTI 174.

[55]   Hort to Lightfoot, 1 May 1860, in LH I.418-21.

were allowed to be compatible with "belief in Providence", one of the two
elements in Lightfoot's exegetical creed.[56] The inaccuracies in Stephen's
account of the history of Israel, though slight and unimportant for his argument, were telling:

> He, who was filled with the Holy Ghost — He who saw the heavens opened and Jesus
> standing at the right hand of God, even he was not allowed at that moment of his great-
> est exhaltation, and his deepest insight into spiritual things, to speak perfect truth-[57]

Moreover, Lightfoot allowed some of the moral obscurities and deficiencies
which so concerned contemporaries.[58] The general point was that

> We do not find that the prophet always speaks the words of prophecy — always speaks
> by the Inspiration of God — ... and ... [the Bible] gives us no assurance that in any
> special case, we are to accept the words of one of God's prophets, as the words of God
> Himself — unless it is clearly stated that they are such.[59]

In these matters where an unacceptable standard of duty was proffered readers should place themselves "freely and unreservedly" under the guidance
of their consciences.[60] The Bible was subject to the historical and moral
reason.

On the other hand, in his encounter with the radical criticism of the Con-
tinent Lightfoot largely upheld traditional positions. But this was the result
of open and rigorous application of an historical method characterized by
comprehensiveness and attention to detail.[61] If this justified faith, then it
was as it should be. Faith was "the sequel, the supplement, the crown of
reason".[62] This reversed the usual sequence, but Lightfoot insisted that God
gave revelation to explain, not obscure, the truth. It was absurd to regard it
as in any way a trial to human reason.[63] Its use in reading the Bible was an
affirmation, not a denial, of faith.

Although Lightfoot's emphasis was on personal response, this was an
understanding of Biblical authority which left the Bible some part to play in
understanding the external world. Knowledge of the natural world was a
case in point. Lightfoot exalted the progress of science as one of the glories
of the age, and continued to speak of that other Bible, "the Bible of na-

---

[56] Referred to in Westcott to Lightfoot, 28 April 1860.

[57] Jael, 1855, 19-20. Cf. Acts I-VIII, 73r. & 74r.; & "St Stephen's Speech. Acts VII.
Its Authenticity," (in the box file marked "Acts") 11 & 37.

[58] H.R. Murphy, "The Ethical Revolt Against Christian Orthodoxy in Early Victorian
England," *American Historical Review* LX.4 (1955) 800-17.

[59] Jael, 1855, 17-18. Apart from the well-known case of the treacherous murder of
Sisera by Jael, the wife of Heber, Lightfoot referred frequently in the same manner to the
episode of Balaam and Balaak. Eg. SSP 1-15.

[60] Jael, 1855, 13-15.

[61] Described and analyzed in Part IV below.

[62] Trisagion, 1874, 10-11.

[63] G xi-xii.

102

102 *II. History as Theology*

ture".[64] Again he allowed no dualism and insisted on the harmony of natural and revealed theology in a unitary order. At the same time he differentiated between them, to keep science in its proper place, and to insist on the primacy of "the Bible of revelation". For the Bible showed the way in those areas of knowledge and experience inaccessible to scientific method, directing attention away from the laws of science to the lawgiver. How to understand waste and suffering, and how to interpret the process of time as applied to nature, were also indicated.[65] Most importantly, the Bible taught that all the works of creation and all the processes come into being, are sustained and governed by the divine Logos.[66] While the Bible did not explain or present every reality about the natural world, it did identify the ultimate reality.

This helps to define and delimit the function and authority of the Bible in Lightfoot's thought. In the troubled post-*Essays and Reviews* situation, he did not directly oppose the orthodox view. Instead, as occasion permitted, he carefully advanced the elements of a liberal alternative in the Coleridgean tradition which again might have been controversial if better known.[67] On this understanding the Bible remained an inspired revelation, not as a body of infallible propositions, but as a record of experience directed principally to the religious and moral sensiblities to produce true self knowledge and moral response. It also provided instruction in the spiritual dimension of the facets of life knowable from the intuition and the reason. At both levels the Bible (in terms of Lightfoot's general epistemology) belonged to the domain of Fact, given to educate the Idea: that is, it instructed and directed innate faculties and aspirations. Accepting that both the divine and human nature do not change, this function remained contemporary because spiritually and morally the Biblical world was the same as the present. Though distant in time, the experiences depicted were still able to instruct and challenge, and thereby continue the revelation with all of its demands. Lightfoot's was therefore a dynamic and open-ended conception aimed at extending the process of which it was the record, divine disclosure and human response. The Bible was a living book,[68] not so much a rule as an influence intended to shape the present and the future.

---

[64] This and the next expression occurs in God's Witness, 1875, 15-17. Cf. I. St Paul's Teaching, 1858, 18.

[65] Eg. Trisagion, 1874, 18-22; God's Witness, 1875, 14-30.

[66] Eg. Teaching, 1871, 17-19; God's Witness, 1875, 27-8; He Shall Take, 1877, 18-21; SSO 18-19; SSP 289-91, 301.

[67] See 333 below for the reaction to his first commentary.

[68] See esp. J.B. Lightfoot, *"Living Oracles." A Sermon Preached in St Paul's Cathedral at the Anniversary of the British and Foreign Bible Society, By the Right Rev. The Lord Bishop of Durham, Vice President of the Society, On Tuesday, May 2, 1882* (London: The Bible House, 1882).

Clearly this approach represented an adjustment of Biblical authority to the incarnational perspective with its emphasis on life and process. It was also in accord with the broader view of revelation Lightfoot promoted as the means to "truth in theology". But it meant too that the Bible was not necessarily or absolutely normative. For Lightfoot allowed that the intuitions and reason act reflexively on it to bring Biblical teaching into line with the deliverances of conscience and the findings of the intellect. While he regarded this as a function of the incarnational nature of life, it was a structure that left considerable scope for the individual to shape interpretation in line with personal intellectual preferences and practical requirements. To a large extent this is the dynamic evident in Lightfoot's use of the Bible as the principal source for his theology of history, although, to the extent that he was aware of it, he believed that this enhanced rather than reduced its social and cultural authority.

II

What does the Bible teach about history? In Lightfoot's understanding, this was one of its main concerns. His conception of Biblical authority was clearly in itself historical, and in fact a three-fold relation between the Bible and history was implicit in it. With the inspiration in the experience of the writers, and the revelation in and through the events reported, the Bible was *of* history. Given that it was intended to shape the thinking and conduct of the men and women to whom the revelation came, the Bible was at the same time *for* history. Its part in understanding the natural world suggested that it would also indicate what to think about what happens in human time. The Bible was also *over* history.

Two letters in the Lightfoot corpus delineate this third aspect of the relation of the Bible to history. In 1863, reporting on the prospect of participating in a commentary scheme sponsored by the evangelical, F.C. Cook, he wrote to Westcott:

> He is not deterred by my plain statement that I did not consider the Bible was intended to teach history (except so far as is necessary for the purpose of revelation).[69]

The response to Cook appears to be another example of the canniness Lightfoot evinced on the subject of the Bible in the post *Essays and Reviews* situation. Amid the rush to write commentaries, his intention was to assert his unsuitability for a scheme which he took to be conservative and traditionalist in purpose by suggesting the Bible did not dictate what was to be believed about history. In fact Lightfoot's claim was a long way from his stated position on other occasions, as well as being inconsistent with his regular practice in both preaching and exegesis. He did allow that the Bible (or parts of it) was a history, and certainly provided the materials out of

---

[69] Lightfoot to Westcott, 1 July 1863 (LAC).

which history could be written.[70] Nevertheless, while somewhat disingenu-
ous, Lightfoot's statement to Cook did reflect his purpose and priority at the
time. Concerned both to avoid controversy and to lead people to "truth in
theology", he was anxious not to be associated with a general perspective he
regarded as erroneous in its narrowness. At the same time it was the Bible's
revelatory significance that was most important for the historical understanding he wished to promote.

What this meant was adumbrated in another letter to Westcott commenting on a D.D. dissertation by F.W. Farrar.[71] Lightfoot suggested that the
conclusion required expansion, "so as to give prominence to some facts passed
over". These included the "special truths, of which it is the record, which
appeal to History and Nature and Conscience, but which these alone do not
and cannot reveal, and which therefore may be said to constitute a difference in kind from those channels of inspiration". History was ranked with
nature and conscience as a source of knowledge and understanding in need
of the Biblical revelation for insight which unaided human observation and
reflection could not achieve. In relation to history the Bible was at some
point a necessary supplement to the natural reason.

On several occasions Lightfoot stated directly what he saw as the manner
in which the Bible assisted human reason as a revelation of history:

> Sacred history is an intensification of secular history. All the conditions, modes of
> operation, processes, consequences, appear in stronger forms & sharper outline in the
> course of Revelation, than in the career of common life. The same lessons, which in
> the latter are confused & blurred, stand out in the former in distinct & legible charac-
> ters, so that one may run who reads.[72]

In the context "sacred history" and "the course of Revelation" are equated
with the Bible, while "secular history" was identified with "the career of
common life". The striking feature of Lightfoot's claim is the essential same-
ness between the two entities. This of course was predicated upon the unity
of the natural and supernatural integral to his understanding of the God-
world relation and warranted by the theology of the Logos. It meant both
were regarded as revelatory, with the qualification that while secular history
was "confused & blurred", sacred history was "distinct & legible". Thus the
Bible was a better expression of what is and had always been evidently true
rather than a radically different disclosure of what is actually true appearances notwithstanding.[73]

---

[70] See 97-8, and Part IV below.

[71] Lightfoot to Westcott, 7 November 1871 (on which see further NTI 166).

[72] Christ, 1876, 5-6. Cf. Acts I-VIII, 1855, 85r.; S 20; CS 267 & f. 4 in the MS; & OA
228-9.

[73] Lightfoot anticipates by a generation the approach taken by F.W. Farrar. See
Addinall, *Philosophy*, 188-91.

It followed from this that the Bible enjoyed a comparative rather than an absolute advantage, so that the priority in the interpretation of history properly belonged with it. In other words, "intensification" involved the idea that secular history depended on sacred history for its proper understanding. The basis of this dependency was twofold. The Biblical record was qualitatively superior to secular history because of its greater clarity and subtlety. The Bible said the same things better.[74] It was also quantitatively superior because it was at the same time fuller and stronger; and also more definite and concentrated.[75] The Bible said more of the same thing. Together these advantages meant that the Bible was more direct, powerful and appropriate as a means of revelation than secular history, and therefore capable of reaching and moving more people.[76] They also invested the events and personalities of the Bible with a typical or symbolic bearing. These were "the substance": the repetitions in secular history were "the shadow".[77] While men and women might by themselves discern the meaning of events in outline, in its proper sphere the Bible was required to delineate and confirm the reality.[78]

What this meant in detail depends upon Lightfoot's use of the Bible to interpret "the conditions, modes of operation, processes, [&] consequences" of history. Characteristically he gave no indication of how he distinguished between each of these elements of historical understanding. It may be that the accumulation of terms was no more than a tautology designed to bring out the continued importance of the Bible for making sense of the world. However, Lightfoot's usage and practice as he went about providing a practical alternative to propositional revelation permit some differentiation of the terms in which the Bible was "the intensification of history", and thereby show how it functioned as "a sure word of prophecy to guide us".

The "conditions" seem to have been the basic entities, on which all that happens in history is contingent, and which form the absolute presuppositions of Lightfoot's historical outlook. The Bible gave him three. First, while recognizing the difficulties experienced by finite minds trying to understand the infinite, and also the inability of language to describe deity fully and accurately, Lightfoot was content to draw on the Bible for what could be known in detail about God. He did not rely on it for "the Idea of God" itself: in line with his basic epistemology, that was known primarily

---

[74] Eg. Disobedient, 1855, 6-10. Cf. BE 225-6. This was why the sacred writers could be called "inspired" whereas "heathen writers" could not.

[75] CS 131-2.

[76] Disobedient, 1855, 6-10; All, 1861, 14-15; Truth, 1864, 33-34; MSL 3; SSP 274-7.

[77] Acts I-VIII, 1855, 85r. Cf. SSP 13-15.

[78] Cf. "The common needs of life, the inward feelings of our heart are here our teachers, but in Holy Scripture alone does this truth find its full and perfect expression." Members, 1854, 2. Also Christ, 1876, 1-2.

by intuition, and also as an inference from the natural world.[79] But the Bible filled in the lines of the portrait. For "in no other book," Lightfoot averred, "are fuller revelations of the divine nature".[80] On the one hand, it furnished passages which enforced the truth of divine transcendence.[81] But alongside these had to be ranged those which taught the complementary truth of divine immanence.[82] The prayer arising out of consideration of one such passage epitomized the perspective and its importance for history:

> Lord ... Teach us to find thee everywhere — to find thee in all the processes of nature & all the lessons of science & all the developments of history.[83]

It was the Bible that warranted the crucial move of bringing God inside history as a distinct and active presence.

The Bible was also Lightfoot's chief source for understanding humanity. There was no other book that provided "subtler analyses of the human spirit".[84] With this penetration went range of understanding. "In no other book that ever was written," he claimed, "is humanity so fully exhibited."[85] Of course Lightfoot accepted the universal sinfulness of Biblical teaching. Throughout his writings the Fall was assumed, and Romans 1 — "where the degradation and decay of the heathen is traced to the wilful perversion of their aims and darkening of their hearts, which refused to listen to the oracle of conscience speaking within them, and to the voices of nature responding to it from without" — was taken to be "the earliest and most truthful sketch of the philosophy of religious history".[86] On the other hand, man was shown to be interested in God and seeking reconciliation with him. The two sides coexist in human being which does not change substantially.[87] The tension between them was a perennial dynamic in history. As "the great storehouse" not only of precept but also of example,[88] the Bible illustrated the dynamic

---

[79]   LS 178.

[80]   MSL 3.

[81]   For example, in relation to Isaiah 57:15, 'The high and holy One that inhabiteth eternity', Lightfoot said, "let us adopt the prophet's description ... Language cannot go beyond this". Similarly, I Timothy 6:15-16 "serves as an image of the eternal perfection".

[82]   Lightfoot's favourite passage in this regard was undoubtedly the description of the prophet's call in Isaiah 6. The cry, 'Holy, holy, holy, is the Lord God of Hosts. Heaven and earth are full of thy Glory", indicated that "He is present in all the works of creation & all the facts of history & that He makes this presence known to the souls of men". Trisagion, 1874, 3-4.

[83]   Vision, 1877, 41.

[84]   MSL 3.

[85]   OA 30-3.

[86]   CS 50.

[87]   Though he liked to quote Thucydides to make his point — πολὺ διαφέρειν οὐ δεῖ νομίζειν ἄνθρωπον ἀνθρώπου — Lightfoot's was essentially a Biblical understanding. See Acts I-VIII, 1855, 85r.; & RE 118.

[88]   Truth, 1864, 33-4.

but also provided the types by which the resulting dilemma was to be understood and managed.

Third, the Bible established the character of the order in which life is lived. As a corollary of the unity and orderliness of creation, it extended the law of cause and effect to the domain of the moral and the theological from which Lightfoot observed a tendency to exclude it.[89] Its importance was seen in two frequently quoted verses. The first — "whatsoever a man soweth, that shall he also reap" —[90] declared that "certain courses of action, certain modes of life, entail certain inevitable consequences".[91] The other — "the fathers have eaten sour grapes and the children's teeth are set on edge" —[92] affirmed the persistence of the consequences over time, and explained how the innocent sometimes suffer in place of the guilty.[93] The Bible's view of the world as a moral order in which reward and retribution are tied to specific actions prescribed the ethical determinism characteristic of Lightfoot's historical understanding.

On the whole Lightfoot's theology of history was an attempt to understand the course history takes in terms of these three "conditions". By the "modes of operation" he seems to have envisaged the ways of acting effectively in history in the light of them. The first of these was Providence. The Bible more than anything else provided the warrants for what at the time was seen to be increasingly problematic, the belief that God is actively involved in history, and that its movement is determined to meet His ends. As "the history of God's dealings and not man's",[94] this was reflected in the whole. It was seen more particularly in the Old Testament, which established the immediate and direct control of the Supreme Lord over the material world and over the affairs of humankind, a principle that was assumed in the New.[95] In addition to this general Providence,[96] the Bible also taught the reality of special Providence, that God intervenes directly to achieve His purposes.[97] Thus the monotheism of the Old Testament was complemented by the theanthropism of the New — which pointed out how God acts to hold communion with humanity and enable people to become one with Him — to complete "the economy of revelation".[98] Lightfoot made full use of the doc-

---

[89] Teaching, 1871, 15-20; CS 49.

[90] Galatians 6:7.

[91] CS 49, 54-5 & ff. 17-20 of the MS. Cf. G 219; SSP 104, 169; Hunger, 1877, 30-2; & Eagles, 1873, 18-20.

[92] Ezekiel 18:2.

[93] Divided Allegiance, 1866, 20-2; Sins, 1872, 14-16, 25-26; & Pure, 1880, 19-20.

[94] Jael, 1855, 2-5; & Acts I-VIII, 1855, 84r., 85r. Cf. BE 416.

[95] BE 415.

[96] For which, see 3rd Group, 1858, 8-11; 4th Group, 1858, 10-12, 22, 23-4; Life, 1860, 1-2; BE 232-3; & Vision, 1878, 8.

[97] BE 237-8.

[98] C 119. Cf. I. St John's Gospel. Introduction. I.1-1.28, 1.

trine of the Trinity — which, while acknowledging that it was recognized much later than other Christian doctrines, he insisted was present in the Scriptures — to show the means by which God works in the world.[99] Indeed, the christological and pneumatological aspects were the "special truths" made available by the Bible to assist the mind in understanding the God-world relation. But a preference for the Second Person of the Godhead acting as the Logos meant that the emphasis was not on special interventions but on the orderliness and regularities of the Divine dispensation.

Although people were "the governed" in the providential order,[100] Lightfoot insisted that the Bible also assigned considerable importance to human agency in history. Such was this importance that the spiritual and ethical choices of people were the second mode of operation. The case of Jesus Himself demonstrated that the greatest triumphs of humanity are triumphs of personal influence.[101] This was admittedly a unique case of which it might be said that it had no relevance beyond itself. But a series of Biblical examples from Moses to Paul demonstrated the difference the individual could make when working in harmony with Providence. These were "signal illustrations" of the paradox of Providence, of strength made perfect in weakness when people appropriate God's Spirit by faith and self-devotion.[102] Of course it was possible for persons also to mar, but not defeat, the divine purpose. All individuals, the Bible confirmed, are "appreciable factors in the history of humanity" for good or ill.[103] It followed that in the ethical order of God's world all are bound to choose a side in the battle of life, between flesh and spirit, darkness and light, life and death.[104] Real effectiveness and greatness was achieved only by those who were willing to be an instrument of Providence. For one congregation at least the point was made explicit:

> You are part of a Divine Order; and, so far only as your life is in harmony with this order, will it give you any true and lasting satisfaction.[105]

The Bible assigned men and women a key role in the making of history, but it was more cooperative than creative.

Although the individual was the decisive unit of human historical agency,[106] Lightfoot understood the Bible also to affirm the historical im-

---

[99] SSP 288-91.

[100] Acts I-VIII, 1855, 85r.

[101] SSO 4-5. Cf. CS 28-9, 301-2. He was "the example of examples" even of the triumph of failure. SSP 133-4.

[102] SMPW 4-8, 13-15. Cf. Three Notes, 1873, 24-6; & SSP 198-9, 312-14.

[103] OA 288.

[104] CS 52.

[105] Vanity, 1878, 22.

[106] HE 10; War, 1877, 12.

portance of collectives. This followed primarily from its teaching about the Church. The body image secured the importance of corporate identity under Christ and called for mutual tolerance, cooperation and interdependence.[107] 'They of Caesar's household' suggested the importance of the lowly and unknown in changing the world from the bottom up, an effect which was seen again in the historical experience of the Church.[108] In this it was not unique. As the "intensification of the moral world",[109] it demonstrated what men and women achieve in the groups, organizations, institutions and classes they form within society as they acted in accordance with the divine purpose. The case of Israel secured the nation as an instrument of this purpose.[110] Although it also showed that Providence was not dependent on the efforts of humans either as individuals or in collectives, the knowledge that individual and group effort made a difference was both responsibility and incentive to strive and labour. The Bible ensured that Lightfoot's historical outlook was morally activist.

The "processes" of history appear to have been the larger movements in time that result from the action of the "conditions" and "modes of operation". Part of Lightfoot's claim for the Bible as "the intensification of history" was its provision of a unique basis for understanding these wider movements. Only the Bible spanned the whole from beginning to end, so that "in no other book are ... more comprehensive views of the world's past history and its future destination".[111] This singular range and perspective provided the standpoint from which the pattern of all history could be determined.

For example, the Bible was the guarantee of the oneness of history implicit in the understanding of the world as the divine order. The completeness of its coverage (from creation to the *eschaton*), its symmetry,[112] and the structural and thematic unity arising from the unfolding of one eternal purpose from beginning to end,[113] identified the single life course which encompasses all individual and organized being. The inward side of the Bible showed how the history of nations exhibited in its outward side in fact belonged to a single unitive process of redemption and justified (among other things) a belief in world historical peoples who for a time take history for-

---

[107] CS 184-7. Cf. IACC 3-4.

[108] J.B. Lightfoot, "They That Are of Caesar's Household," *Journal of Classical and Sacred Philology* IV.x (March 1857) 57-79; P 171-8; HE 10-11; Delhi, 1878, 28-9. See MSL 19 for what could be achieved by small nameless groups.

[109] SSO 188.

[110] SSO 254-6.

[111] MSL 3.

[112] RCC (1871) 81; & Light, 1872, 6-8.

[113] CS 160; Light, 1872, 8-10; & OA 30-3.

ward.[114] Its specific teaching showed the way in the application of the analogy of a single human life to the life of nations and of humanity.[115] The "unrivalled unity" of the Bible stood for the unity of history.

Similarly the Bible testified to the continuity of history. The manifest diversity of its parts did not obscure the underlying connectedness.[116] As the history of the communication of God's revelation and part of "the history of its reception and results" in the life of the Church, it documented "the very mainstream of history: the one which alone has a continuous existence from the first dawn of the historical epoch to the present day".[117] The Bible also set forth the "continuous course" of the dispensation of God "from first to last",[118] and furnished the water images — the tide and the river — which assisted the apprehension of the idea. While they accommodated unevenness and periods of apparent aimlessness or retrogression, they enforced the unbrokenness and inexorability of the flow of all history.[119]

Lightfoot further maintained that the Bible construed this continuity as progressive. As "the progressive history" of God's dealings with humankind,[120] it exhibits "the same increasing purpose throughout, manifesting it under various forms and in diverse ages".[121] 'Genesis' recorded how, as a result of the Fall, a progressive order of existence was substituted for a stationary.[122] Thereafter the Bible recorded the widening of God's dispensation, from a family, through a nation, to the whole of humanity.[123] At the same time it was the record of the education of the church, and through it of humankind.[124] It established that "the natural order of things", from flesh to spirit and from law to faith, is "the divine order of progress".[125] In the twin parables of the mustard seed and the leaven the Bible supplied the images which vivified the gradualism and diffusionism of progressive change.[126] By establishing that death is the condition of higher life in mundane things the Bible also made clear that the destructive effects of time did not defeat

---

[114] This inner unity amid great outer diversity was signified by a frequently repeated metaphor of Jerome: the Bible was a divine library contained within the covers of a single book. CS 160; RCC (1871) 81; Light, 1872, 8-10; Sudden Coming, 1881, 4; & LO 3.

[115] G 165-8, 172-3.

[116] Vision, 1878, 1-4; SSP 22-5.

[117] RCC (1871) 80-1.

[118] Light, 1872, 6-8.

[119] SSO 76-8 & 146-8. Cf. RCC (1871) 81.

[120] Acts I-VIII, 1855, 84r.; Truth, 1864, 33-4; BE 416.

[121] CS 160. Cf. Good Shepherd, 1868, 1-2; & OA 32-3.

[122] Curse, 1860, 11-15.

[123] Vision, 1877, 11-13. Cf. CS 212-14.

[124] RCC (1871) 81; G 165; Right, 1874, 15-18.

[125] G 134-5.

[126] MSL, *passim.*

"the law of progress".[127] While history itself might suggest as much, it was the Biblical writers who confirmed progress as the purpose of providence. As the hopes of 1851 faded, Lightfoot stressed that the Bible, not observable improvement, furnished the ultimate grounds for hope and optimism.[128]

Progress was also implicit in the declaration that Christ had come "in the fullness of time".[129] A New Testament reflection on what had gone before, it involved three key ideas about the process of history. One was divine preparation.[130] This followed from the notion that God withheld the Gospel "until the world had arrived at mature age".[131] Negatively this meant that the point had been reached at which it was clear that existing systems were unable to bring men near to God.[132] Positively it meant that its moral and spiritual development was such that the world was now capable of apprehending the Gospel. The second was the fulfilment rather than the abolition of all that had gone before. Within the Bible itself the whole of the history represented in the Old Testament was messianic and looked forward to what was proclaimed in the New.[133] The last was the aptness of the timing. Πλήρωμα signified completeness and totality, "the full measure of time".[134] It indicated that the optimum moment ordained from the beginning by God had arrived.[135] All that was necessary had occurred: the Incarnation was history's culmination. In each respect the Bible called for the quantitative notions of change characteristic of Lightfoot's approach to history.

Lightfoot went one step further and maintained that the Bible placed the achievement of this fullness in the centre of history, and thereby determined how it should be structured. This was not so much a matter of direct teaching as the Bible's overall effect. Lightfoot found an instructive analogy

---

[127] CS 63-9.

[128] CP 14-15; IP 8-9; RCC (1871) 81; Vision, 1878, 1-4; SSP 306-12, esp. 306. "Forward, not backward, is the keynote of the Bible." For the importance of 1851, see A. Briggs, *Victorian People. A Reassessment of Persons and Themes 1851-1867* (Harmondsworth: Penguin, 1965) 21-2 & ch. 2.

[129] Note that this was Temple's text for the sermon that became "The Education of the World" in *Essays and Reviews*.

[130] Lightfoot acknowledged his indebtedness to Augustine in this matter. Will He, 1869, 2-6; HE 21-2. The Graeco-Roman *praeparatio evangelica* was something of a commonplace in Christian apologetics.

[131] G 167-8; & CS 50-1, 85-6.

[132] Paul's claim in 1 Corinthians 1.21 that 'the world by wisdom knew not God' was taken to point to the failure of humankind to provide for its needs by its own efforts. CS 276-8; Christ, 1876, 17-20; NEP 161. The picture of Athens in Acts 17 was interpreted as a type of the world at the time. CS 85-8.

[133] Thus the Incarnation came as the culmination of the ever clearer views of Messiah's Person and Office reflected in the Old Testament. Cf. St John IV.4 - VI end, ff. 72-3.

[134] C 257-73, esp. 260.

[135] G 167.

with its incarnational shape in the layout of St Paul's Cathedral in which he was working at the time:

> [The] centre is the Gospel revelation, the record of the Incarnation & Passion & Resurrection of the Son of God. Thither leads up, like the long-drawn nave of our Cathedral, the Old Testament ... thence diverge right & left, as adjuncts, like the transepts, the Apostolical Epistles; thence starts, as the choir, the prophetic vision of the Revelation, which sums up the future history of the Church.[136]

Similarly in history all that precedes leads up to the Incarnation, while all that follows flows from it.[137] While this was obviously in line with the received Christian tradition, it was the Bible which finally determined that history be divided into the age before Christ, and the age of the Spirit which would last to the end, with the middle term, the Incarnation, the key to the whole.

Finally, because of its "comprehensive views" of the world's "future destination" the Bible made clear the "consequences" of history.[138] At one level this referred to the time after Christ. The results of the Incarnation were adumbrated in the 'Acts of the Apostles' through its demonstration of the work of Christ as influencing the future to the end of the world.[139] It did so first by indicating what happened in the "progressive career" of the Church in the Apostolic period, not only in the narrative as a whole, but in the presentation of "representative facts". Beyond that it looked forward to "the great and terrible day, the consummation of all things, when this history shall be wound up". The interval was spanned potentially, so that 'Acts' provided an "anticipatory abstract of the history of the Christian Church".[140] As such it anticipated the continuing conflict between good and evil, and the steady spread and penetration of Christianity, as the true meaning and end of history.[141] For the Apostles this perspective meant that the age of the present transitory world and of eternity overlapped.[142] Contemporary events were therefore properly regarded as belonging to this larger scheme. This entailed in turn that national histories and individual lives were a part of "the great battle of Armageddon" that "is even now raging".[143] The trials of life as comings of Christ were anticipations of "the Great Coming".[144] Thus the Bible provided the framework in which to view the present: it directed men and women to regard their time as belonging to the end time.[145]

---

[136] Light, 1872, 14-15. Cf. Will He, 1869, 4; Sudden Coming, 1881, 5-8.

[137] RCC (1871) 81-2; CS 212-14, 225-8.

[138] MSL 3.

[139] Acts I-VIII, 1855, 27v. Worship, 1871, 9-11.

[140] Acts I-VIII, 1855, 30r.

[141] Acts I-VIII, 1855 27v.-30r.; 1st Group, 1858, 19-22.

[142] G 74, on τοῦ αἰῶνος τοῦ ἐνεστῶτος. Cf. 3rd Group, 1858, 20; Mystery, 1876, 20-5.

[143] Eagles, 1873, 16-18.

[144] SSP 109-14.

[145] 1st Group, 1858, 24-5; CS 113; SSP 304-7.

The idea of the "world's future destination" also referred to history's chronological end. Despite the apparent emphasis on eschatology, Lightfoot ignored 'Daniel' and the teachings of Jesus on the end times, texts which fed the millennial excitement of earlier in the century.[146] He in fact reacted strongly against this preoccupation with the 'end things'.[147] In so far as he was prepared to consider the subject, he relied (at different stages of his career) on Paul's Thessalonian correspondence and 'Revelation'.[148] But he did not press the texts hard. The language was metaphorical, intended to provide broad teaching only.[149] The conflict between good and evil would come to a final showdown, and bring on the Second Coming which would be a day of manifestation and recompense.[150] Then would come "the new heaven and the new earth", and the end of sorrow, pain, sin and death.[151] Beyond this Lightfoot was not prepared to go. Instead he urged men and women to look forward to and prepare for this end time, but they should not dissipate their energies speculating about when it was to happen.[152] "Earth is the scene of your labours now," Lightfoot urged as the true Biblical perspective, "earth must be the centre of your interests."[153] Paradoxically the eschatological teaching of the Bible directed attention to the present rather than the future.

Although clearly very important to Lightfoot and advanced with some confidence, this view of the Bible as the 'intensification of history' was not without its shortcomings. Although clarity was said to be an advantage of "intensification", one difficulty Lightfoot faced was that the teaching of the Bible was not always clear. It was especially in relation to the moral order and the place of the individual in it that obscurities seemed to arise. Indeed it was difficult passages of this order that incurred some of the moral criticisms of the Bible and Christianity that were current.[154] Lightfoot acknowl-

---

[146] On which see E.R. Sandeen, *The Roots of Fundamentalism: British and American Millenarianism, 1800-1930* (Chicago: University Press, 1970); W.H. Oliver, *Prophets and Millennialists. The Uses of Biblical Prophecy in England From the 1790s to the 1840s* ([Auckland] Auckland University Press, 1978); & D.W. Bebbington, *Evangelicalism in Modern Britain. A History From the 1730s to the 1980s* (London: Unwin Hyman, 1989) ch. 3.

[147] Secrets, 1870, 9-11; SSP 153-7.

[148] 1st Group, 1858, 23-4; Light, 1872, 6-7; SSP 305 ff.

[149] Secrets, 1870, 9-11; Glory, 1877, 26-7.

[150] Acts I-VIII, 1855, 53r.; Disobedient, 1855, 9; Kingdom, 1855, 22-4; 1st Group, 1858, 19-20; Life, 1860, 29-30; Our Heavenly, 1862, 25; Sonship, 1864, 2-4; CS 141-2; Sins, 1872, 26, 28-9; [What?] I, 1877, 16-17, 18-20.

[151] SSP 306, 311-12; CS 244; & SSO 233.

[152] Kingdom, 1855, 22-4; 1st Group, 1858, 24-5; Sonship, 1864, 23-4; Eagles, 1873, 16-18; Saving, 1874 ; SSP 153-7, 161-3, 172, 267-8; What?, 1878, 163-4.

[153] SSP 153.

[154] Murphy, "Ethical Revolt," 800-17.

edged that there were "parts of Holy Scripture which appear to us very per-
plexing and unintelligible, which we are disposed perhaps to give up in despair".[155] But he responded with the claim that these difficult passages required extra work. The reward was a perception of the finer lines in the
portraiture of how God deals with humankind. Moral obscurities were an
opportunity to test the Bible as "the intensification of history".

However, not every perplexity could be resolved in this way, and in relation to the cherished role of the individual in history Lightfoot did not even
try. On the important question of sin in its relations to the divine will and
human freedom, Lightfoot held that the "final inevitable law of God's justice" was "individual responsibility, individual retribution for individual sin".
In this he admitted enigma:

> Offences are a necessity, and yet offences must not be. Scandals are permitted, and yet
> they are forbidden ... God hates sin, and yet God allows sin.[156]

On the other hand, divine necessity appeared to overwhelm individual freedom. The same authority (the Bible) which asserted man's free choice also
related how God hardened men's hearts. Lightfoot escaped this dilemma by
analyzing the sequence of the sin event.[157] The point at which God became
causally active was "not the first but the last term in the series, not the opening but the close of God's dealings with His creatures".[158] This made Divine necessity the consequence, not the cause, of human choice. Yet the
analysis was inexact. The point at which God's action took over and human
freedom was lost remained unclear.[159] Nor was it complete. Was God forced
by the choices of men to take the sequence to its sinful outcome, in which
case grave questions about His sovereignty and benevolence would be raised?
The *locus classicus* furnished by Judas' betrayal of Christ forced the larger
speculative question on his attention:

> We cannot say how God's foreknowledge and our free-will should coexist. We cannot
> explain why God should call human beings into life and give them capacities which, if
> they will, they may use to their ruin. But we know it is so. The Bible teaches us this;
> our own experience confirms it. The case of Judas introduces no new difficulty. It is
> only one more example of the great insoluble problem, the world-wide enigma of God's
> omnipotence & man's sinfulness.[160]

With a frustrating irresolution Lightfoot asserted that Christianity did not
create the difficulty, and Christianity did not have to solve it.[161] It was suf-

---

[155] CS 3-4.
[156] CS 248-9.
[157] SSP 62-3; & Moral Freedom, 1873, 23-5.
[158] Moral Freedom, 1873, 23.
[159] CS 16; & Moral Freedom, 1873, 26-7.
[160] SSP 63-4 & the MS of "The Fall of Judas," 3 September 1871, f. 9. The bulk of this
quotation was omitted from the published version.
[161] Acts I-VIII, 1855, 53r. CS 249.

ficient to present the Biblical data and draw the moral.[162] On this hard question Lightfoot was characteristically unwilling to go beyond it.

A second difficulty, as was perhaps to be expected, was that the '*a priorism*' resulting from his virtual subordination of the Bible to the critical and moral reason manifested itself in a highly selective use of its materials, so that in practice he did not do justice to the Bible itself, and thus to history. When Lightfoot came to think about the movement and meaning of history as a whole he looked to the prophets of the Captivity in the Old Testament, and to 'Luke-Acts' in the New. The appeal of these prophets was the way in which they showed that the religion of Israel was destined to become the religion of humankind, and that the source of progress was the vision of God. Significantly they also supplied the water images which figure so prominently in his construction of history. Their perspective enabled Lightfoot to ignore or minimize discordant teaching. 'Ecclesiastes', the despair of which was out of step with the message of hope perceived in the rest of the Bible, was dismissed as the exception that proved the rule:

> It shows us what human life is ... without a reliance on an overruling providence, without a present sense of a Divine order and government, without a looking forward to the great hereafter which shall straighten the irregularities and satisfy the cravings of the present.[163]

The ambiguities and regressions of Israel's history were subordinated to the triumphalist perspective of the "increasing purpose". Lightfoot's reading of the Bible permitted a simplified and overly schematic reading of history.

The other important element in his 'canon within the canon' was the exaltation of the teaching of 'John', the later Paul and 'Hebrews' on the 'Word made flesh'. Although this might have been a valuable corrective to the Biblical preoccupations of his Church, it again led to the neglect or minimization of other perspectives present in the New Testament. Most seriously the soteriology of the early Paul was not given due weight. Consequently, while Lightfoot spoke often about sin, the radical and structural evil of the 'Epistle to the Romans' is absent from his perspective. Similarly the dark side of his favourite water images goes unappreciated.[164] The absence of any discussion of the Fall in his *oeuvre* is also highly revealing. While there was much both in his learning and personal experience to draw attention to it,[165] Lightfoot's reading of the Bible blocked a full appreciation of the depth and extent of evil in history.

---

[162] CS 17.

[163] Vanity, 1878, 20-1.

[164] See C.A. Simpson, "An Inquiry into the Biblical Theology of History," *Journal of Theological Studies* n.s. 12 (1961) 1-13.

[165] See, for example, his comments on slavery, C 323-9; his advocacy of the White Cross Army following exposure in the *Pall Mall Gazette* of the "white slave traffic" and child prostitution in "The White Cross," *Contemporary Review* 48 (August 1885) 262-8;

A third effect of the 'intensification' perspective was a tendency to concentrate on the ordinary experience of the men and women of the Bible. In fact, Lightfoot showed a distinct preference for the incidents exhibiting God working through the conscience rather than through supernatural intervention into the normal course of events. This is partly why the Biblical miracles do not figure prominently in his writings.[166] Even the miracles of the Gospels were more interesting in their moral rather than their physical aspect. It was better to treat them, not as manifestations of divine power, but as parables.[167] This was a preference well suited to a view of the world as a place of religious and moral education. In line with the purpose of the broader view of revelation, the effect of Lightfoot's approach was to raise in importance the general experience of humankind.

This levelling effect, which lowered the "sacred" but elevated its "ordinary" component, did not allow to history the impact on his Biblical understanding that might have been expected. Certainly Lightfoot's view of revelation allowed for some benefit to the Biblical perspective from history. But in fact distinctly historical study had little effect on his outlook. The new ways of construing the Biblical history itself made available by contemporary criticism made only a limited impact.[168] In regard to both Old and New Testaments historical viewpoints were conformed to his own ostensibly Biblically based expectations.[169] In other contexts Lightfoot was able to draw on history as needed on the basis of his wide reading. But history functioned only as commentary, clarifying already revealed truth, but not creating any fresh point of view. With the reciprocal benefit to the Bible so limited, Lightfoot's was a decidedly Biblical theology of history.

But, as both the preferences and shortcomings it embodied indicate, it was a Biblical theology of a type determined by his own moral and intellectual predispositions. Reacting against the eschatologically driven perspectives that had been influential earlier in the century, Lightfoot presented to the religious consciousness of his contemporaries a reading that was characterized by divine immanence and human responsibility, continuity and orderly process, and progress and purpose. It secured an eternal framework for terrestrial existence at the same time as exalting the value of what happens in human time. It also established the life of Christ as the pattern life for all men and women, and accordingly presented an exemplarist rather

---

and his awareness of the problems of the urban masses in SMPW 11-13 & RCC (1881) 15-15, 17.

[166] The Incarnation is, of course, the outstanding exception.

[167] S 20.

[168] For the Old Testament, see J. Rogerson, *Old Testament Criticism in the Nineteenth Century. England and Germany* (London: S.P.C.K., 1984).

[169] This statement anticipates one finding of Part IV of the present investigation.

than a forensic interpretation of the Atonement.[170] At every point as he presented the Bible's teaching on the conditions, modes, processes and consequences of history, Lightfoot's emphasis was on what could be done instead
of on what had to be overcome. The reassurance of such a view helped men
and women to see where they fitted in and what they could do to contribute
to the realization of "the increasing purpose". As Fact working on Idea,
Lightfoot's Biblical theology of history was a vehicle of the cherished cause
of "truth in theology" intended to correct and redirect English Christianity
to an incarnational standpoint. In seeking this change Lightfoot had two
interrelated objectives before him.

As a revelation of history, the Bible offered a kind of cosmic paradigm,
presenting to the reason and intuition a vision of history centred on Christ as
an integrated whole that explained the past, defined the present and anticipated the future. In this there was much to reassure the orthodox. Its clear
importance in the matter upheld the authority of the Bible. Its perspective
retained supernatural involvement and affirmed redemption as the essential
concern of history. In doing so it justified adherence to the doctrine of the
Trinity, while also emphasizing the importance of the Incarnation and Atonement (if not Creation and the Fall) and the special role of Israel. At every
point, moreover, the religious and moral correlates were drawn out, so that
it was a guide to Christian life with eternal outcomes. But there was also
much that challenged the radical supernaturalist to broaden his understanding. The importance of the key elements in the Christian outlook was due
more to their place in the process than their status as specific propositional
truths. Similarly, the Bible seemingly endorsed the developmental perspective which many had said was incompatible with revelation. It also required
taking account of the whole of humanity and its achievements. Lightfoot's
Biblical theology of history offered a basis for Church people to be recon-
ciled with modern viewpoints.

Second, it provided a basis for incorporating new historical knowledge
into the Christian synthesis. No matter what was discovered, it was assimilable to the framework the Bible provided. This was an important principle,
because it countered the likely claim that, since there was no essential difference between sacred and secular history, there was in fact no real difference at all. Such an inference would have led to the loss of the Bible's status
as a revelation and elimination of the need to look for God in the common
experiences of humanity, consequences which would have justified the abandonment of Christianity. But the notion of 'intensification' retained the authority of the Bible in relation to history in a general perspective urging
greater attention to divine immanence. An inclusive perspective of this kind

---

[170] The classic example is "Bought With a Price", his farewell sermon when he left
Cambridge in 1879. See CS 283-99.

held out to society a greater identity between Christianity and life as experienced by contemporary English people. Certainly it catered to much in the general Victorian consciousness and endorsed it as Christian. For it answered the desire for meaning and order in the temporal domain as an alternative to the view of life as chance encounter with circumstance; it tamed the spectre of change by presenting it as fulfilment of a higher purpose; and both the promise of progress and the possibility of regress held out the certainty of individual effectiveness as choice between contributing to improvement or bearing responsibility for opposition. In spite of great recent intellectual advances, the Bible and the religion it sustained were still needed to make sense of things. Lightfoot's Biblical theology of history also provided a basis for modern society to remain Christian.

These mediatory purposes and the content of Lightfoot's views were particularly well suited to the prevailing intellectual climate and help to explain his appeal, particularly as the reaction against *Essays and Reviews* waned in the 1870s and 1880s. There were many who, like V.H. Stanton,[171] appreciated the way in which he was able to hold together a Christian outlook and modern ideas.[172] To a large extent he had deliberately responded to what he perceived as the contemporary conditions of thought. But their effect on his outlook cut much deeper than he knew. For Lightfoot had applied an historically conceived reading of the Bible to history for his understanding of what history is like.[173] His 'supernatural naturalism' was less a Biblical, and more a contemporary, outlook than he seems to have realized. But this was no barrier to his effectiveness with the many who shared the same dis-

---

[171] On whom, see 91 above.

[172] See esp. the remarkable monument to the influence of Lightfoot, Westcott and Hort furnished in 1902 by an old pupil, John Battersby Harford, in his statement of the rationale for Lightfoot Hall (the renamed Midland Clergy College in Birmingham) quoted in A.M.G. Stephenson, *The Rise and Decline of English Modernism* (London: S.P.C.K., 1984) 81-2. Also J.E.C. Welldon, *Recollections and Reflections* (London: Cassell, 1915) 55; & H.W. Turnbull, *Some Memories of William Peveril Turnbull* (London: S. Bell & Sons, 1919) 142-5. Lightfoot is listed with those who adjusted theology to "the advance of the times" in the Hazeltine MS 'Life of H.M. Gwatkin' among the Gwatkin Papers at Emmanuel College, Cambridge. Similarly, in the Epilogue of his *Cambridge University. An Episodic History* (Cambridge: W. Heffer & Sons, 1926), A. Gray includes Lightfoot among those who incorporated the doctrines of evolution and ordered progress into the articles of the Christian religion.

[173] A review of the English translation of Johannes Bleek's *Introduction to the Old Testament* is particularly revealing in this respect. Apart from rejecting many of his critical theories, Lightfoot condemned Bleek's failure to provide "a sketch of the progressive development of the revelation as connected with and arising out of the continuous history of the people". The expectation of development and organic connection behind this criticism points to dispositions that he brought to the Biblical text rather than read out of it. See J.B. Lightfoot, Review of J. Bleek, *An Introduction to the Old Testament*, *Cambridge University Gazette* 23 (2 June 1869) 184-5.

positions and welcomed the way he had constructed them. Identifying the contemporary sources that enabled him to hold together religion and life, therefore, suggests part of the reason for his influence. It also further clarifies the nature of Lightfoot's Biblical theology of history, and indicates something more of its projected cultural function.

III

The very desire for an understanding of history reflects the wider tendency among mid-Victorians to all inclusive philosophies of life. It has itself been traced to a need to live with reference to a larger identity, a wish for self-sacrifice, and an uneasiness about worldly success which was rooted in the kind of evangelical consciousness Lightfoot had met at home and school.[174] His response was only one of many arising from a protean force in contemporary culture. The combination of this religious impulse with the role assigned to reason and the preference for a broader, more inclusive view of revelation reflects two other influences that shaped more advanced mid-Victorian minds, liberalism and immanentism.[175] The desire for intellectual freedom and openness to modern knowledge had slowly been gaining ground in England since the seventeenth century. In Victorian thought it had spawned a powerful tendency to consider processes taking place within the world itself as the key to its meaning and value. In the 1850s and 1860s these forces were still restricted in their direct impact to the less conservative members of the society. As a Christian nurtured in the traditions of Cambridge liberal Anglicanism, Lightfoot was among those affected.

Immanentism did not come to Lightfoot through Hegel, as has been recently suggested.[176] He did not read overtly Hegelian texts, and he was justly suspicious of the German church historians whose work embodied Hegelian perspectives and agendas, most notably the left wing Hegelian D.F. Strauss and his teacher Baur.[177] With them and their followers in mind, Lightfoot complained continually about the influence of speculative ideas on the criticism of early Christian literature. Evidently to some extent aware of the influence of Hegel on their work, he seems to have found it no more appealing than the theories which resulted. It is possible that the 'underlying metaphysic' of Lightfoot's Biblical historical standpoint was an

---

[174] M. Richter, *The Politics of Conscience. T.H. Green and his Age* (London: Weidenfeld & Nicolson, 1964) 33-6.

[175] Still important on this theme is C.C.J. Webb, *A Study of Religious Thought in England From 1850* (Oxford: Clarendon Press, 1933).

[176] K. Willis, "The Introduction and Critical Reception of Hegelian Thought in Britain 1830-1900," *Victorian Studies* 32.1 (Autumn 1988) 85-111, esp. 96-7.

[177] Lightfoot's interaction with them is examined in Part IV below.

Hegelianism already generalized in European culture,[178] but there are sufficient — largely English — influences ready to hand to explain his willingness to participate in the wider movements of mid-Victorian thought.

The romanticism which pervaded English culture during Lightfoot's
formative years was fundamental.[179] With its emotionalism and emphasis
on the spiritual significance of the everyday world, and thus the importance
of nature, individual experience and history, it came to him largely through
the reading of imaginative literature in which he had been encouraged at
school. Certainly he was in touch with the "romantic recollection of the
past", perhaps through Sir Walter Scott, the fountainhead of this stream in
English writing.[180] But the poetry in which he delighted appears to have had
the deepest effect on his historical consciousness.[181] Particularly important
was the organicism of Wordsworth. No poetic utterance was more often
quoted than his "The child is father to the man and all his days are bound
each to each by natural piety" to secure the fundamental notion of continuity and essential harmony amidst organic growth.[182] John Keble's "Two
worlds are ours" evinced the correspondence of the outer world to inner
spiritual truth and movement, a perception which required divine immanence
alongside transcendence.[183] Of the poets of mid-century, Tennyson — "our
great living poet" — and Browning — "the Christian poet" —[184] contributed most to his time sense and historical understanding. Tennyson directed
attention to the end of the age and the transience of everything before then.
The dramatic assertion of the destructive, yet recreative, effects of time in
"The Passing of Arthur" struck a keynote, especially as Lightfoot himself
faced death.[185] Furthermore, *In Memoriam* applied the organic understanding of change to the growth of knowledge, and asserted its compatibility
with faith.[186] Most importantly, in "I doubt not thro' the ages one increasing

---

[178] This is the suggestion of Burrow, *A Liberal Descent*, 147-8, in relation to the
organicism of Stubbs.

[179] G.S.R. Kitson Clark, "The Romantic Element 1830-50," *Studies in Social History:
A Tribute to G.M. Trevelyan* (ed. J.H. Plumb; London, New York, Toronto: Longmans,
Green & Co., 1955) 209-39.

[180] RE 87. For the impact of Scott on historical thinking, see H.R. Trevor-Roper, *The
Romantic Movement and the Study of History* (London: Athlone Press, 1969).

[181] For Lightfoot's assessment of English poetry, see LNC 67. For the background, see
S. Prickett, *Romanticism and Religion. The Tradition of Coleridge and Wordsworth in the
Victorian Church* (Cambridge: University Press, 1976).

[182] CS 116; RCC (1871) 81; HE 129; Vision, 1878, 2-3; SSO 103-4; LO 4; & LNC 4.

[183] SSP 147; S 161; SSO 250; & OA 187.

[184] SSP 126-7. Cf. RCC (1873) 228 & AF II.1^2.38-9.

[185] See the verse quoted on 139 below.

[186] LS 175; Acts I-VIII, 1855, 9 v.; RCC (1871) 83; C 116-17; & Healthy, 1879, 19.

purpose runs", Tennyson furnished the phrase which epitomized Lightfoot's progressive theology of history.[187]

Natural theology was another source of the immanentist tendency in his thought. More particularly the radical natural theology in which Lightfoot was nurtured — with its "grander view of the creator" —[188] inculcated the monistic principle in its insistence at once on (for the most part) invariable sequence and the ultimate unity of the physical and moral worlds. Here astronomy — with its capacity to explain "the intricate mazes and apparently capricious wanderings of the stars" with "one simple all pervading law" — was the model science.[189] What it did was represented in Lightfoot's thinking by the need — to which the Logos was the answer — to find the unifying ground principle underlying the diverse phenomena of life.

Immanentist natural theology also did much to shape Lightfoot's expectations about how things happen in the world. This was suggested at once by the image of the tide, which not only suggested the operation of constant laws but also led away from the static and cyclic conceptions of time and change typical of more established approaches.[190] Geology and Biology both indicated the wide time frame necessary to accommodate natural history, and also emphasized the importance of continuity for growth and change. These sciences suggested further that the process was directional and meaningful. In relation to Geology, Lightfoot asserted:

> Nowhere else do we find more vivid and striking illustrations of the increasing purpose which runs through the ages.[191]

The "principle of natural selection" in Darwinian biology was a further sign of "God's law of progressive improvement".[192] Furthermore, Geology provided the models — uniformitarianism and catastrophism — by which Lightfoot understood the nature of change.[193] The compromise position of the Cambridge scientists showed how the two could be combined. Occasional "catastrophist" intervention by God took place within a uniformitarian framework.[194] In a similar way, the work of the Word impersonal intensified when the Word became flesh in the Incarnation. The same force which

---

[187] From the 69th stanza of *Locksley Hall*.

[188] See 52 above.

[189] I. St Paul's Teaching, 1858, 16-17.

[190] For which, see Hilton, *Age of Atonement*, 153-4, 299-300.

[191] RCC (1881) 16.

[192] OFR 13.

[193] SSO 105.

[194] This was why, against the background of the so-called "Prayer Gauge Debate", Lightfoot could insist on the efficacy of prayer at the same time as calling for "frank and reverential sympathy" for scientific discovery. RCC (1873) 229-30, 233. For the background, see F.M. Turner, "Rainfall, Plagues, and the Prince of Wales: A Chapter in the Conflict of Science and Religion," *Journal of British Studies* XIII.2 (May 1974) 46-65.

called for a generally 'Newtonian' or 'natural law' conception of Providence,[195] also allowed the particular interventions the viability of Lightfoot's Biblical view of history required.

Philology, Lightfoot's primary intellectual preoccupation, was a further basic influence on his emerging historical outlook. *Altertumswissenschaft* — to which Lightfoot was introduced by his teachers, and which he experienced for himself in the works of some of its leading German representatives —[196] employed a comprehensive mode of investigation that considered antiquity in all its aspects and evinced an interest in ancient literatures as expressions of life experience. His adherence to what has been called its "universal historical-philological perspective on antiquity"[197] is reflected in the prospectus of *The Journal of Classical and Sacred Philology* which announced that its subject matter would be approached "in its wider signification, comprising not only the criticism of language, but every topic connected with the Literature and History of Antiquity".[198] Although only minor or preliminary studies, Lightfoot's own (predominantly textual) Classical writings also reflect the holism of the 'new philology'. The determination of readings took account of the individuality of the writer at hand and the life situation presupposed by the text. Subsequently Lightfoot read with approval the works of his pupil Farrar and Max Müller which drew out the implications of the growth of language for a providential theory of history.[199] An interest in the total effect of Classical societies within a providential framework is evident in frequent judgments on the contribution of the Greeks and Romans both to civilization and the spread of the Gospel.[200] Language study itself pointed to the structure of the theology of history Lightfoot claimed to find in the Bible.

The basic dispositions resulting from these contemporary influences were given historical content and definition by contemporary historiography. As was to be expected, the liberal Anglican historians, in whom Lightfoot was well read, made their contribution. In the previous generation they had led the way in applying the idea of progress to the Bible and provided an alternative to the rationalism of the secular historiographical tradition. Arnold

---

[195] The terms are Hilton's. See Hilton, "Role of Providence," 228.

[196] Such as B.G. Niebuhr, C.C. Bunsen & August Böckh, to name only three.

[197] W. Unte, "Karl Otfied Müller," *Classical Scholarship. A Biographical Encyclopedia* (eds W.W. Briggs & W.M. Calder III; New York & London: Garland, 1990) 314. Lightfoot admired Müller's *Denkmäler der Alten Kunst, nach der Auswahl und Anordnung* in a review in *The Journal of Classical and Sacred Philology* II.v (1855) 240-1.

[198] "The Journal of Classical and Sacred Philology" (Camb. Uni. Papers MR1, CUL).

[199] Eg. G 77, 243 n. 1. On Farrar & Müller, see Burrow, "Uses of Philology in Victorian England," *passim*.

[200] Eg. IP 15; Triumph, 1874, 15-16; Christ, 1876, 6-9, 17-20; SSO 156-7; & LNC 80-1.

was read early, and as an undergraduate preferred to Thirlwall.[201] As Lightfoot's attention turned to the history of the Church, H.H. Milman, Stanley and Herman Merivale were used extensively. Disentangling specific influences from the general Romantic heritage they shared is difficult. The metaphor of the individual life, for example, as important to Lightfoot as to them, was common enough in liberal circles. Nevertheless it is clear that they provided an idealist and developmental pattern of historical thought which contained many of the features that reappeared in Lightfoot's historiography.[202] Most important were the insistence on the unity and continuity of history, concern for the inward side of history understood as the spiritual and moral condition of life over time, belief in the universality and irreducibility of the religious impulse in human nature, understanding of progress as the education of the human race in Christian morality, and retention of a role for Providence as the decisive historical cause. In the liberal Anglican historians there was every encouragement to develop a specifically Christian version of the contemporary doctrine of historical progress.[203]

Like the earlier generation of liberal Anglican historians, Lightfoot was deeply influenced by German historiography. Whereas they had been most interested in the Roman historian B.G. Niebuhr, the German scholar from whom Lightfoot's view of history and the history of the Church drew most was the converted Jew and mediating theologian, J.A.W. Neander.[204] This would appear to be the correct inference from his own acknowledgement of Neander as the writer to whom he owed his greatest debt.[205] Unfortunately the acknowledgement went unelaborated, and references to Neander are not so frequent as it might suggest would be the case. Significantly they are

---

[201] Lightfoot to Wescott, n.d. 1850.

[202] Forbes, *Liberal Anglican Historians, passim.*; Parker, *English Historical Tradition*, ch. 1; & Turner, *Greek Heritage,* esp. 11-12, 25-8, 84-5, 209-13, & 358.

[203] With development so important in Lightfoot's thinking, it might have been expected that, of English writers, Newman may have been influential. A comparison was ventured in G.H. Curteis, "Cardinal Newman and Bishop Lightfoot," *Edinburgh Review* 178 (July 1893) 248-65, but, as the anonymous reply, 'The "Edinburgh Review" On Newman,' *The Spectator* (5 August 1893) 172-3, makes clear, the original article was conceived mainly as an opportunity to attack Newman and sheds little light on the relationship. The contact between the two was in fact slight, but Lightfoot used Newman's books in his patristics research.

[204] On whom see "Neander, Johann August Wilhelm," *A Religious Encyclopedia* (ed. P. Schaff; 3rd ed.; New York: Funk & Wagnalls, 1891) III.1612-14; & P. Schaff, *Germany; Its Universities, Theology and Religion* (Edinburgh: T. & T. Clark, 1857) 261-77.

[205] "If there is any recent theologian from whom I have learnt more than another, it is the German Neander." EWSR 141. Lightfoot was also familiar with the work of the German-American Phillip Schaff who claimed also to have been influenced by Neander. See esp. J.B. Lightfoot, Review of P. Schaff, *History of the Apostolic Church, With a General Introduction to Church History, Journal of Classical and Sacred Philology* II.iv (March 1855) 119-20.

concentrated in the period when he began to write on the New Testament at a serious level;[206] that is, at that point in his career when he needed conceptual guidance and methodological aid in maintaining a traditional but scholarly supernaturalistic interpretation of Christian history, especially in the period of its origins.[207]

Although in time Lightfoot achieved a certain critical independence from Neander, "notwithstanding his great name",[208] two important hermeneutic principles appear to have come from, or at least been reinforced and sharpened by, him. First, Neander exemplified in church historiography the organological method descending from Herder and Humboldt. According to this perspective, every individual historical phenomenon needed to be assigned to its place in a unitive evolutionary pattern of development. More specifically, Neander showed the way in exhibiting the history of the Church as a progressive development and, beyond that, in placing it in the totality of the historical process. If not expounded in the same way in large works of historical narrative, the "increasing purpose" was still an expression of the same approach.

Second, in Neander's outlook Christianity is a principle of life which adapts itself to all individualities in order to transform and regenerate them. It is reflected in the various types of doctrine or Christian testimony in the New Testament. Certainly Lightfoot adopted this perspective on the New Testament writings, but also accepted in a qualified way Neander's extension of these types — the Petrine, the Pauline and the Johannine — as typifying the three main ages of Church History.[209] Neander's attitude to Christianity as a force in life, rather than only a dogma, was readily taken over as well.[210] Its corollary, history as the interpenetration of man's life with the divine life, also became Lightfoot's standpoint on the meaning of history. As a result the parable of the mustard seed and the leaven, which furnished the central metaphor of Neander's *Church History*, was readily adopted to describe the process by which Christianity permeates and transforms society; while the image of a tree implicit in the title of *A History of the Planting of Christianity* became a symbol for the nature of the Church's expansion.[211]

The religious side of these influences was incarnationalism. This was the tendency to look as much to the life of Christ as to his death. It was accom-

---

[206] LS 180 n. 23; 181 n. 24, 30; 182 n. 38; 184 n. 44, 46; 186 n. 67; 187 n. 70; 190 n. 95; & 195 n. 116, 118.

[207] It was therfore prior to, and possibly more formative than, the influence of Albrecht Ritschl which Lightfoot also acknowledged. P 187 n. 1. Cf. *ibid.,* 188 n. 3 for important differences between the two scholars.

[208] P 250 n. 1; AF I.1.363.

[209] RE 81-2.

[210] Eg. LS 182.

[211] See 72-3 above.

panied generally by a preference for immanence over transcendence, confidence that the divine purpose was working itself out in the terrestrial order, morality as a principle of life in cooperation with the divine will rather than restraint, gentleness and compassion in place of the retributiveness of earlier decades, and theologically by a retreat from hell, the eternity of future punishment and literal interpretations of the Atonement. As the recent analysis of Boyd Hilton has shown, it was far more than a theological movement.[212] It stemmed from literary and scientific sources of the very kind which influenced Lightfoot. The result was the disposition to respond to the theological conceptions he found in Coleridge and especially Maurice, the first significant incarnational theologian of the day.

The writer who in turn educated and nurtured this basic orientation was, of course, Westcott.[213] Most important in this respect was *The Gospel of the Resurrection,* published in response to Newman's *Apologia* in the mid 60s when Lightfoot was still finding his way theologically. Westcott objected to Newman's tendency to concentrate on God and the individual and to leave out of consideration the crucial element of the world in theological presentation. Consequently, when he took up the subject of the resurrection he presented it "in its manifold relations" — historically and socially as well as theologically and soteriologically. In the process he also directed attention to the unity and progress observable in history which was attributed in the New Testament to the existence of Christianity from the beginning in the divine counsel.[214] From this it followed that "the true conception of the World and of Humanity becomes first possible when they are thus regarded in their essential relation to the Word, the Son". He added:

> We do not at present demand more for this statement than a recognition of its significance. At least it places before us what the first exponents of Christianity believed Christianity to be. It was according to their interpretation eternal in its essence, as well as universal in its application. It was in itself beyond time though it was wrought out in time.[215]

Of course this was the very perspective Lightfoot sought to revive shortly afterwards. He was aware of it beforehand,[216] but it seems to have been at least with the encouragement of Westcott that he took it up as the basis of the synthesis between Christianity and secular life and knowledge, and as the explanation of progressive history.

---

[212] Hilton, *Age of Atonement*, ch. 8.

[213] That Westcott generally confirmed and educated Lightfoot's incarnationalism is evident from a response to a lecture on Benjamin Whichcote: 'It is a pleasant surprise to me ... to find that I have been a disciple of Whichcote without knowing it.' Lightfoot to Westcott, 5 July 1877 (LAC).

[214] B.F. Westcott, *The Gospel of the Resurrection* (London & Cambridge: Macmillan, 1866, 1879⁴) 61-2.

[215] *Ibid.* Cf. 88-90.

[216] See 3rd Group, 1858, 5-6; & Life, 1860, 5-10.

Incarnationalism also had a negative side which required correction.[217] Inside the church there was a tendency to concentrate on dogma, as in H.P. Liddon's *Life of Christ*.[218] Outside the Church an understandable reaction against excess of dogma engendered a tendency to concentrate on ethical precepts, as in John Seeley's *Ecce Homo*,[219] while there were others whose unbelieving criticisms were more trenchant, though they might respect Christ.[220] In relation to these currents of thought Lightfoot observed, "We may need to be reminded that it is one thing to know Christ, and another to know him aright".[221] Providing the necessary guidance was one purpose of *Philippians*:

> To all ages of the Church — to our own especially — this epistle reads a great lesson. While we are expending our strength on theological definitions or ecclesiastical rules, it recalls us from these distractions to the very heart and centre of the Gospel — the life of Christ and the life in Christ. Here is the meeting-point of all our differences, the healing of all our feuds, the true life alike of individuals and sects and churches: here doctrine and practice are wedded together; for here is the 'Creed of creeds" involved in and arising out of the Work of works.[222]

Apart from bringing the dogmatic and ethical aspects into due relation, knowing Christ aright included correctly understanding His life in its historical dimension, as the Incarnate One who revealed the Father by His life and redeemed humanity by His death, and thereby transformed history iself. Promoting such an understanding assumed greater prominence in Lightfoot's teaching from this point, but not only because of the way in which incarnationalism had been misconceived.

If Seeley presented Christ without dogma, other liberals were presenting dogma without Christ. In a striking sermon of 1871, Lightfoot recognized in the contemporary ferment of ideas four "modern idolatries" as the foes of Christianity.[223] Two were perverted theisms: two were forms of atheism. All four were theologically and morally mischievous in their corollaries. "Philosophical deism" postulated a metaphysical conception of God which at least satisfied the intellect. Yet the denial of His involvement in the world

---

[217] P ix. In reading other contemporary works I have benefited from P.H. Sedgwick, "'The Character of Christ': The Correlation of Moral Theology and Christology in Anglican Theology, 1830-1870 (unpublished Ph.D. dissertation; Durham University, 1983).

[218] H.P. Liddon, *The Divinity of Our Lord and Saviour Jesus Christ. Eight Lectures Preached Before the University of Oxford in the Year 1866* (London: Rivingtons, 1867, 1878[8]).

[219] [J.R. Seeley], *Ecce Homo: A Survey of the Life and Work of Jesus Christ* (London: Macmillan, 1865, 1868[9]).

[220] Scene, 1874, 14-20; Clerical Office, 1874, 8-11.

[221] Right, 1874, 1-2.

[222] P 73. Cf. P ix.

[223] CS 88-92. The printed version is assigned to 1873. However, the sermon was preached first in the Temple Church on 6 December 1871. Cf. OA 31.

as a Father meant there could be no special revelation, and thus an end of personal religion and the assurances of Christianity.[224] "Pantheism" equated God with nature, and thereby made man, including his vices, a part of God, reducing the distinction between right and wrong to meaninglessness.[225] "Positivism" offered Humanity itself for the worship of men, an absurdity in the prospect.[226] "How can we prostrate ourselves before a mere abstract conception, a comprehensive name for the aggregate of beings like ourselves, with our own capricious passions, our own manifold imperfections — some higher and some viler, much viler, than we are?" England was now a varied moral and theological market place in which Christianity had to compete.

Lightfoot's estimate of the seriousness of the situation is evident in his attitude to the fourth modern idolatry, "materialism". Its denial of individual freedom and responsibility, and the reduction of morality to mere convention, made it the most threatening of Christianty's contemporary foes.[227] Nor was its social agenda acceptable. Since God is unknowable (if He exists), it was deemed "best to devote all energies to perfecting our machinery and tilling our lands, to increasing our material comforts and diminishing our natural wants".[228] This limited vision of life was compounded by its futile representation of death as the end of life and individual annihilation.[229] So radical were its implications that Lightfoot believed the increasing appeal of materialism as the basis of social organization had brought society to a parting of the ways:

> Brethren, we cannot disguise it from ourselves. A great conflict is raging in the world now, in which we, all of us, great or humble, ignorant or learned alike, are called to take a side — an internecine conflict, a conflict between two directly antagonistic, irreconcilable views of human life and human destiny.[230]

Thus his fears of the early 1860s were being realized. The unitary vision of life presupposed in the slogan πολυμερῶς καὶ πολυτρόπως was being lost and other outlooks unfavourable to Christianity were pressing their claims for the intellectual and ethical allegiance of contemporary society. At this point in his career Lightfoot believed himself to be facing the crisis of Christian civilization in England.

That Lightfoot's theology of history aimed to oppose these other approaches to life is evident in the dissertation "St Paul and Seneca" which appeared in 1868 as a component of the important commentary on

---

[224] Cf. LNC 99.

[225] Cf. C 118-19; SSP 300-1; Through a Glass, 1875, 27-8.

[226] CS 82.

[227] See in particular Lightfoot's characterization of materialism in SSP 312-14. Cf. SSP 24-5 & 265-7; CS 235-9 & 278-80; & Moral Freedom, 1873, 17-22.

[228] Vision, 1873, 10.

[229] SSP 312-13; CS 78-9; & S 26.

[230] SSP 312.

'Philippians'. Part of a larger scheme to show the relevance of the Pauline literature to present day needs,[231] it traced the historical connections of early Christianity and Stoicism before expanding into a comparision of the two systems of thought which Lightfoot expected "not to be uninstructive".[232] As such it was part of a more extensive reading back of present day debates into the contest between Christianity and the major pagan philosophies in the early Christian centuries. John Tyndall's claim that the materialistic or non-religious theory of the universe had not yet had a fair trial was attacked as a new Epicureanism.[233] But the demise of Epicureanism in antiquity showed that it had nothing further to offer mankind, and its part in the decline of the ancient world foreshadowed its danger to modern England. Stoicism was *rededivus* in the philosophical theism of the day.[234] For those attracted by its possibilities Lightfoot used his essay to discredit the pantheism it represented.[235] Fundamentally it was "gross materialism".[236] It was also shockingly blasphemous and evinced no consciousness of sin. In ethics it was shown to be indifferent to the sufferings of others and to aim at control of human nature rather than at guiding and training it. The similarities with the teaching and language of Christianity were dissolved into conformity with nature. Logically Stoicism was "the most incongruous, the most self-contradictory, of all philosophical systems",[237] while historically it had produced only transient and limited effects.[238] At its best Stoicism was not quite Christian.[239] It was certainly not good enough in its ancient or modern form to be an alternative to Christianity.

The triumphalism of this interpretation of the Christian past indicates that Lightfoot's Biblical theology of history was developed and articulated increasingly as a means of maintaining Christianity as a major cultural alternative.[240] He recognized that the age was concerned with law, development and continuity; and that the consonance of the alternative theologies and

---

[231] For which, see 331-2 below.

[232] P 271.

[233] See the discussion in "Mill On Religion," 19-25. Cf. RCC (1873) 230: "The materialism of today has an exact counterpart in the Epicureanism of that age." Lightfoot was answering J. Tyndall, "Address by the President," *Report of the Forty-Fourth Meeting of the British Association for the Advancement of Science; Held at Belfast in August 1874*, 1875, lxvi-xcvii.

[234] RCC (1873) 230.

[235] P 293-8. Stoicism is equated with pantheism twice at P 295.

[236] P 294-5.

[237] P 298.

[238] P 308-19.

[239] P 316-18. Cf. 293-4.

[240] The notion of competition for cultural dominance informs the essays collected in Turner, *Contesting Cultural Authority*. It does much to capture the dynamism and contingency of the situation Lightfoot confronted.

philosophies of life with these concerns was part of their appeal. The Christian idea of history, he countered, was well able to meet these same demands. Indeed it showed that Christianity was the true expression of all such phenomena.

Lightfoot also recognized that the advocates of rival approaches to social organization were interested in much the same thing as he was, the moral condition of English society. But he wanted to show that they were seriously misguided in their willingness to separate society from its religion. In particular he concentrated on their depreciation of belief itself.[241] Increasingly it was being said that it did not matter what a person thought, only what s/he did. This claim carried with it a severence of religion from conduct, and became in turn a warrant for dispensing with Christianity. Both the proposition and its corollary, Lightfoot insisted, were contrary to common sense and experience.[242] As conduct originated in thought, there must be a connection between belief and action, and thus between religion and morality.[243] History showed, moreover, that cutting off morality from its roots resulted in the loss of its substance. It also foreshadowed that it would take a good deal of time before the effects of abandoning the Christian basis of English society would be felt.[244] Much therefore was at stake. Before it was too late, the theology of history was necessary as a demonstration of the truth of the importance and power of Christian belief for civil society in a community more and more inclined to dispense with it. This indeed was the final significance of the "increasing purpose" perspective. In the broadest sense,[245] it was a social theology directed to retaining Christianity as the fundamental "public doctrine" of contemporary England.[246]

In bringing forward his understanding of history as the "increasing purpose of God" Lightfoot took his stand on Biblical authority. His aim was to present men and women with the truth about history, which the unassisted mind was incapable of discerning, for their personal appropriation and response. However his reading of the Bible was based on the disposition and choices resulting from intellectual conditions and perceived cultural needs of the time. It reflected Lightfoot's conviction that Christianity incorporated these influences and directed them to proper outcomes for society. The

---

[241] SSP 292-7; RCC (1873) 231-2; CS 287-8; Pure, 1880, 2-4.

[242] To think otherwise was "a direct contradiction of common experience and of universal history". SSP 293. Cf. CS 287-8. "There is hardly a page of history which does not give the lie to it." RCC (1873) 231.

[243] Lightfoot's assumption of human rationality is taken up on 142-5 below.

[244] EWSR 29-31.

[245] It is not meant to suggest that Lightfoot was using the historical argument in favour of a 'social gospel'. For Lightfoot the social mission of the Church was subordinate to its spiritual mission. Eg. Lightfoot to Gladstone, 5 July 1884 (GBL, 44 487, f. 47).

[246] For the notion of "public doctrine", see 19 above.

historical standpoint that followed was intended to show the way inside the Church to a *rapprochement* with contemporary culture by providing an alternative to other constructions of Christianity, particularly the radical supernaturalism of orthodoxy. It was also intended to demonstrate before the wider society that it would be a great mistake to surrender Biblical Christianity as the basis of belief and social organization in the face of the claims of strident liberal intellectualism. Of course the belief the theology of history represented was not intended to be just one of a number of cultural alternatives. The theology of history was also an argument for its necessity and superiority over its rivals. In line with its Biblical provenance, Lightfoot's purpose was for it to be a religious and ethical force, affecting thought and conduct in the present for the benefit of the intellectual, spiritual and moral life of the nation. It was therefore the product of a moment in the perennial struggle of Christianity to win over the world in which it exists. As such it testified to another belief Lightfoot wished to promote. As it was being articulated, the "increasing purpose" reflected the underlying conviction that the Christian understanding of history was inherently useful and necessary for the continuation of the "increasing purpose of God" in and through England.

Chapter Six

"All Things Are Yours":
The Usefulness of History

What is the point of historical understanding? Is it possible for knowledge of the movement and purpose of history to lead to action that affects its course? In the nineteenth century these questions gave less trouble than they do today because people more readily assigned a didactic role to their metahistorical constructs.[1] The English in particular saw such value in its results "that they made the historical method the preeminent paradigm of their age".[2] Caught up in the changes generated by the Industrial and French Revolutions, they lived self-consciously in an age of transition and experienced the conflicts of "hope and dismay, optimism and anxiety".[3] The result was a widespread, if highly differentiated, turning to history for self understanding and for orientation towards contemporary problems, particularly between about 1825 and 1875.[4] The underlying belief in the usefulness of history was a significant component of early- and mid-Victorian social and cultural life.

Such a belief was certainly a part of the liberal Anglican sub-culture in which Lightfoot was nurtured. It was present in the thought of the Cambridge scientists as a first principle of their method.[5] It was also part of the outlook of the liberal Anglican historians themselves. Indeed, Duncan Forbes shows that they were men of their times when he demonstrates how their history was "essentially practical".[6] The need for an understanding of history that could be applied to the present was what had partly driven their historical enterprise. To this end they devised a science of history which, they believed, furnished a sound basis on which to bring the past into a meaningful relation with the present.

---

[1] J.H. Plumb, *The Death of the Past* (London: Macmillan, 1969).

[2] Jann, *Art and Science of Victorian History*, xi-xii.

[3] The thesis of W. Houghton, *The Victorian Frame of Mind 1830-1870* (New Haven & London: Yale University Press, 1957).

[4] J. Clive, "The Use of the Past in Victorian England," *Salmagundi* 68-9 (Fall 1985 - Winter 1986) 48-65; & J.W. Burrow, "The Sense of the Past," in *The Victorians* (L. Lerner ed.; New York: Holmes & Meier, 1978) 120-38.

[5] Yeo, "Natural Theology," 273-8.

[6] Forbes, *Liberal Anglican Idea of History, passim* & viii for the quotation.

Lightfoot signified his own participation in this larger cultural phenomenon by his use of the idiom common to its representatives. For him, as for
them, the past was a "mirror" in which to see the true nature of things.[7] The
fact that most of his utterance on the pattern and purpose of history occurred
in sermons is revealing. It indicates, first, that he shared the liberal Anglican aspiration. That is, Lightfoot pursued his interest in history in the belief
that it is in the nature of historical understanding for it to be a guide to
thought and conduct. At the same time, however, he did not make use of
their science of history as the means to that understanding. Given that he
responded to his society's interest in history on a different basis, it is necessary next to show on what grounds Lightfoot carried forward into the next
generation the conviction that the providential scheme of history is inherently useful.

Second, it is a reminder that his thinking in this area occurred within the
Church and was intended primarily for the Church. More particularly, in
this setting Lightfoot sought to influence individual thought and motivation,
and thus action. But his concern was not limited to the Church. The ultimate point of Lightfoot's concern was the nation. His hope was that through
the thought and conduct of individuals nurtured in the Church English society as a whole would benefit. But how, and to what end? It therefore needs
to be shown as well what general uses of history Lightfoot aimed to secure
and what he thought was at stake.

                                    I

For Lightfoot the usefulness of history was again the clear teaching of the
Bible. At numerous points the need to proceed historically was either directed or modelled. He noted the tendency of Israel to look back to the point
of its origins as a reminder of the continuity of the national life.[8] The speech
of Stephen in 'Acts' encouraged tracing the gradual development of God's
purpose in His dealings with men and women.[9] The provision of typical
stories and characters was intended to provide spiritual and moral guidance.
Most important, the idea of the person of Christ was communicated through
the life of Christ.[10] Having exhibited "all moral perfections", Jesus also
became the pattern man held up for imitation.[11] An example of how to follow this pattern, and what would result, was furnished in the life of Paul.[12]

---

[7]   RCC (1871) 79; (1873) 230-1. A.D. Culler, *The Victorian Mirror of History* (New
Haven & London: Yale University Press, 1985).
[8]   LNC 3.
[9]   Acts I-VIII, 84 r.
[10]   RCC (1871) 82.
[11]   Christ, 1855, 5.
[12]   *Ibid.*, 28-30.

In these ways the Bible pointed to the place of history in the ethical structure of Christian living. At the beginning of his career Lightfoot observed:

> Christianity is not merely a collection of moral precepts however lofty and unexceptionable; It enforces its precepts by its sanctions and its truths by its history.[13]

The use of history was a component of the kind of Biblical Christianity he endeavoured to promote.

At the same time his commitment to the usefulness of history was another response to the major cultural influences of the day. Like many of his contemporaries who grew up in Christian homes in the 1830s and 1840s, Lightfoot took seriously the life of the Church and its theological foundations. This means that he is to be seen as a part of the movement recalling the Church of England to doctrine and religious duty by connecting faith and conduct.[14] But Lightfoot also felt the impact of the utilitarianism that was equally widespread in early Victorian society. Recognizing his own as an age of utility, he reckoned that its demands were reasonable:

> When it pays respect [he observed] its rule is payment by results. It is unable to appreciate and therefore slow to recognize, anything of which it does not see the use.[15]

Even Christian doctrine was subject to this determination of significance by usefulness, and Lightfoot believed it was well able to meet the test:

> with Christianity doctrine and practice are not independent ... Every doctrine of the Faith entails some consequent duty, every duty receives its sanction and its explanation in some corresponding doctrine.[16]

Thus the theology of history came within what might be called his system of Christian doctrine. As well as teaching it, the Church had to make clear its practical benefits. While it has the appearance of self-fulfilment, Lightfoot's seeking the uses of the theology of history was in fact driven by pervasive Victorian values. This was why, from the beginning, it occupied a strategic place in his commitment to adapting Christianity to the needs and wants of the age.

Early in 1872 Lightfoot indicated the specific grounds for using history. Twice within a few months he preached on the text πάντα ὑμῶν, ὑμεῖς δὲ Χριστοῦ, Χριστὸς δὲ θεοῦ.[17] Among the deductions he made from "all things", Lightfoot specified that:

---

[13] LS 182.

[14] On this, see F.M. Turner and J. von Arx, "Victorian Ethics of Belief: A Reconsideration," in *The Secular Mind* (W. Wagar ed.; New York: Holmes & Meier, 1982) 83-101, esp. 86-9.

[15] RCC (1873) 231.

[16] Life, 1860, 8. Cf. Christ, 1855, 8-9; 4th Group, 1858, 18; Truth, 1864, 36; & Passed, 1866, 28.

[17] 1 Corinthians 3:22-3: "... all are yours, and ye are Christ's, and Christ is God's" (RV).

> All history is yours. Whatever of heroism, whatever of philanthropic self-devotion,
> whatever of prudent foresight, whatever of adventurous daring stands recorded in the
> annals of the past — these are yours.[18]

On such an understanding history was among the resources given providentially for interpreting and directing life. At this point in Lightfoot's career
this was something of an *ex post facto* justification for an outlook and practice in which he had long engaged. But it was now integrated into the basic
structure of his thought as it came to maturity and was commended to others. For it was made to depend on the fundamental theological relation.[19]
Being ἐν Χριστῷ was the key to correct understanding and constructive use
of the means of life in the divine economy. Like the theology of history
itself, practical history was a natural extension of Lightfoot's characteristic
incarnational theology.

In this perspective history was a possession. Its meaning as such was
signified by the point at issue in the text, the role of human teachers.[20] As a
partial reflection of Christ, each had something to contribute towards an
understanding of God's will. Together they incorporated all the elements of
His message at that time and place.[21] For those people wanting to understand and act on that message, they imparted form and substance to their
aspiration. It was the same with history. To the members of the Cambridge
University Church Society, Lightfoot observed:

> You are the heirs of eighteen Christian centuries. The long role of history is unfolded
> before you. The achievements of your spiritual ancestry are the heirloom of you, the
> latest sons of the Church. Not in vain have martyrs suffered, and fathers taught, and
> saints prayed, and philanthropists laboured, and reformers preached. All these too are
> yours.[22]

The past furnished countless such instances of endeavour and achievement
of a kind to give direction to similar aspirations in the present. Regarded as
a substantive resource, history was intended to be a help to thought and
action.

Consciousness of these things was presented as true wisdom. Again this
was a theme of the passage from which Lightfoot drew. In the background
was the recent discussion in *Philippians* of the wise man in both Christianity and Stoicism. Both systems promised "universal dominion to him", but
they differed in how it was to be achieved:

---

[18] All Things, 1872, 28. Also SSO 15-18. Cf. He Shall Take, 1877, 18-21.
[19] For the importance of being ἐν Χριστῷ for St Paul, greater even than justification
by faith, see BE 231. Cf. P ix.
[20] Note that on the first occasion this was 1 Corinthians 3:21-3. The teachers are
mentioned in v. 22. NEP 195-6. All Things, 1872, 23-6. SSO 9-13.
[21] SSO 12-13.
[22] SSO 16.

the one must attain it by self-isolation, the other by incorporation. The essential requisite in the former case is a proud independence; in the latter an entire reliance on, and intimate union with, an unseen power.[23]

It was this condition of being ἐν Χριστῷ that accounted for the end of "a mere human philosophy" and the continuing effectiveness of the "Divine revelation". The continuing usefulness of history was part of this superiority.

Two lines of reasoning converged on this result. The first began in the fundamental relations of the universe. The expression Χριστὸς δὲ θεοῦ directed the mundane order in which humans live to the Godhead for the ultimate source of its meaning.[24] Such a setting reflects, if it was not caused by, the increasing cosmological interest evident elsewhere in Lightfoot's development. Behind the πάντα ὑμῶν formula was the theological conception of the Person of Christ which he was in the process of working out for his *Colossians*. Indeed it reversed the sequence of relations evident in the key statement in Colossians 1:15-20. Whereas it worked up from the world to the Godhead, the 'Colossians' passage worked down from the relations between the Father and the Son to the creation and the Church. Common to both was Christ as the link between heaven and earth. This was the point on which Lightfoot insisted both for the understanding of the 'Colossians' text and for presenting Christianity in the present day.[25] It envisaged Christ as both the Logos and the incarnate one. The former referred to His agency in the universe; the latter, to his work in the Church. Πάντα ὑμῶν encompassed both, but it was the relation of the Logos to the universe that most concerned the teaching office of history:

> All the laws and purposes which guide the creation and government of the Universe reside in Him, the Eternal Word, as their meeting point. The Apostolic doctrine of the Logos teaches us to regard the Eternal Word as holding the same relation to the Universe which the Incarnate Christ holds to the Church. He is the source of its life, the centre of all its developments, the mainspring of all its motions.[26]

In this teaching Lightfoot saw the principle of religious comprehension which required of Christians wide and varied intellectual sympathies. An interest in history as a sphere of the operation of the Divine Logos was a proper and necessary component of the Christian outlook.

Bound up with this was the notion of history as an integrated whole centring in Christ. This line of thinking was informed by the body image of the Church in addition to the relations in the Godhead. As all parts were organically connected with its head, so they were also organically connected with one other. Christ was God's: therefore all things were Christ's. Churchmen

---

[23] P 305.
[24] NEP 194.
[25] See esp. C 116-17, 118.
[26] C 150, note on ἐν αὐτῷ.

were Christ's: therefore all things were theirs. This was the vital connection:

> For Christ is the bond of union. You have no interest in that with which you have no connection. You receive no advantage from it; you exercise no control over it.[27]

In a mysterious way,[28] therefore, being ἐν Χριστῷ brought men and women into the same set of relations involved in the Χριστὸς δὲ θεοῦ formula. This put them into connection with the entire universe, and thus into a position to enjoy all the advantages of that relation. A certain mastery over the universe results.[29] History was among its aspects placed at the disposal of believers to minister to their good.

In the second line of reasoning, historical usefulness also followed from the immanentist model of understanding Lightfoot put forward as the best way of dealing with the modern world. With God involved in its processes — as Logos and Incarnate Son — and therefore manifest in it, history was of interest and value as a disclosure of His purpose and ways. In its "ordinary" as well as its "sacred" mode, it needed to be taken seriously and appropriated as a practical application of the πολυμερῶς καὶ πολυτρόπως perspective.

On history in this revelatory mode, Lightfoot commented:

> All history is a parable of God's dealings, and we must learn the interpretation of the parable.[30]

There was an ambiguity in this programmatic statement that was perhaps intentional. "All history" could apply to the whole of history taken as a single unity, or it could apply to history in all its parts. Whether corporately or severally, Lightfoot believed that the changing circumstances of time and place mediated eternal truths and values to guide the thought and conduct of men and women.[31] Discovering the interpretation not only achieved a more complete picture of the truth, but also broadened the horizon of Christian hope and put a new instrument into the hands of interpreters and gave direction to their energies.[32]

The cosmological and immanentist sides of Lightfoot's historical thought provided the link between his understanding of the nature of history and its practical application. The usefulness of history was implicit in the theology of history itself and followed along these lines as a natural extension from

---

[27] SSO 15.

[28] "Mystery" bears the technical sense of something which could only be known by revelation. See Mystery, 1876, 14-15.

[29] The sermon material is supplemented by NEP 194-6; G 74, note on τοῦ αἰῶνος τοῦ ἐνεστῶτος; P 92, note on τὸ ἀποθανεῖν κέρδος.

[30] CS 310. Cf. OA 77-8.

[31] Lightfoot commented on another occasion: "the parable is for the sake of the lesson; not the lesson for the sake of the parable". Sheep, 1873, 13.

[32] SSO 3, 12-13.

it. Taken as a specimen of liberal Anglican thinking on the matter, it is clear that in Lightfoot's system theology had replaced science as the basis of practical history. Against the backdrop of contemporary cultural development, this was an important shift. At a time when it was being given up by many, Lightfoot insisted that history as a basis of thought and conduct be understood within the framework of eternal purpose.[33]

The grounds of history's usefulness also set the conditions of its proper usage. The emphasis on "all history" referred to the whole process, not just the past.

> Christ is not of one age, or of one communion only. He is the Head of the Universal Church through all time.[34]

Past, present and future were of equal significance in the perspective of the "increasing purpose of God". This meant that the present was but a moment in the realization of the Incarnation, the inner dynamic of all history. While it was in order to view its personages and events discretely and in relation to one another, their true significance derived from their place in the ongoing process. "Take all, combine all, use all", Lightfoot urged in a call for inclusiveness and synthesis.[35] In relation to the past every age, as a manifestation of the Logos, had something to offer and could not be ignored without loss. The present and each age to come would make their own distinctive contribution. All that history had to offer should therefore be appropriated. Both "sacred" and "ordinary" history could be drawn on. No period, civilization or aspect of human culture should be put outside its ambit. Each component needed to be viewed in relation to the whole. The promised result was fullness in the apprehension of the benefit.

That the theology of history was intended to have an effect of a certain kind is evident in the progamme of optimum historical usage that followed from these axioms. "All history is yours," Lightfoot averred: "Yours to interpret, yours to assimilate, yours to reproduce." This was a power as well as a requirement:

> In Christ you have the key of discernment; in Christ you have the faculty of assimilation; in Christ you have the power of reproduction.[36]

The primary theological relationship not only suggested the usefulness of history, but furnished the resources to use it effectively.

Interpretation, then, was "discernment" "in Christ". Above all this required recognizing the hand of God in history as the Logos and equating progress and providence:

---

[33] See Turner, *Contesting Cultural Authority*, esp. ch. 4.
[34] SSO 16.
[35] All Things, 1872, 25.
[36] All Things, 1872, 28.

to you is given to follow the great lines of history, & to trace the increasing purpose which runs through all the ages, because to you is granted to see God's will and to mark His working in all things.[37]

Everything that happens in history needed to be viewed in relation to what was known of its central dynamic. Lightfoot chided Philo for not making "the proper use of history as illustrating the progressive development of the relations of man to his fellow and to his God".[38] Even great crises such as the fall of the Roman Empire and the French Revolution — the staples of Victorian historical moralizing — offered empirical guarantees of how all the phenomena of history followed its inner progressive tendency.[39] In this reminder of the true setting and destiny of life, the "increasing purpose" perspective was its own use.

This same impulse is transparent in the allied directive to "test the spirits" and choose the good and reject the bad.[40] In relation to three of his heroes, Martin Luther, Francis Xavier, and John Wesley, Lightfoot observed:

> There will be some marring imperfection in all, an impatience of authority in one, a savour of pride in another, a taint of superstition in a third; but as these defects will not blind you to what is noble, so neither will they mislead you into what is false. Brilliant though their lives may have been, they are after all only broken lights of Him Who is the full and perfect light.[41]

The Christ-like in these men was what had promoted the "increasing purpose", but it had been limited by their personal failings. It was important to distinguish between these two factors in character formation, lest the lives and example of such luminaries be misused. The task of interpretation required moral evaluation and identification of what contributed to the advance of the Church and, through it, of history itself.

That "all things are yours" was always true for the believer, but only potentially. It became true actually only as the position was realized.[42] For historical understanding to make a practical difference it was necessary to take the next step after "interpretation" and assimilate "every type of good, & every element of truth".[43] Assimilation was in part a Coleridgean idea which called for past and present to be put into proper relation instead of being opposed to one another.[44] In taking it up, Lightfoot was claiming that Churchmen needed to cultivate the habit of finding the links and similarities

---

[37] All Things, 1872, 28-9.

[38] LS 187.

[39] IP 11-12.

[40] LNC 30.

[41] SSO 17-18.

[42] Lightfoot's characteristic teaching was that "facts ... must be realized and appropriated". WCA 9.

[43] All Things, 1872, 26-7.

[44] Sanders, *Coleridge*, 53-5.

between the events and developments of their own with former and coming ages. Christ as the cause of the interconnectedness of all things was the warrant for doing so. No doubt this was why Lightfoot thought it the role of the historian to trace the connections of things.[45] Churchmen likewise needed to think historically, as he himself understood the term.

About the third stage in the sequence of historical usage Lightfoot was more guarded. At first sight, "reproduction" suggested that simple restoration of the past which he continually criticized.[46] When the use of the past involved no more than the wish to return to some previous period, or imitate the life of some past luminary, it had been misconceived as mere traditionalism, or worse, nostalgia. Lightfoot did not idealize the past in either way. Correctly understood, the present was not the slave, but the child, of the past, growing out of, and then beyond it into the next stage of development in God's "increasing purpose".[47] This model justified those occasions when it was necessary for the present to be set free from its historical incubus for its needs to be met. Lightfoot would not allow that this kind of break repudiated the past. Organically conceived, such change was its fulfilment, a view which he stamped with the Tennysonian imprimatur:

And God fulfils himself in many ways,

Lest one good custom should corrupt the world.[48]

In every way the past was the point of departure for the future.

The restoration model of historical usage was also theologically inappropriate. God had ordained, not that religion be the same in every age and place, but that it grow towards fullness through interaction with its surroundings. Simple imitation of the past, even if it were possible, was a denial of God and His way.[49] Because His revelation is progressive, it was a mistake to identify the nineteenth century "with the sixteenth, or with the thirteenth, or with the fourth and fifth, or even with the first".[50] It was also a mistake to think that God would speak in anything other than the language of the nineteenth century. Expecting His message in the terms delivered to an Augustine, a Luther, or even a Wesley, meant it would probably pass unheard.[51] Lightfoot made a shrewd appeal to the sensibilities of Churchmen when he said, "The school of human history ... is a school of the Holy Spirit, for it is

---

[45] "The historian strives to detect hidden resemblances: he traces the thread of connection between different ages, and shews how the days of the world's history are 'bound each to each by natural piety'." RE 118.

[46] CS 186-8; SSO 9-10, 59-61, 153-4; SSP 216.

[47] Eg. LNC 3; SSO 15-18.

[48] Edifying, 1869, 19.

[49] Edifying, 1869, 14-5, 19-21.

[50] SSO 12-13.

[51] Vision, 1877, 18-19.

a setting forth of Christ".[52]   Accordingly they needed to seek the Spirit's guidance in finding the manner in which Christ's self-disclosure was taking place in their own day.[53] If they preferred to stick with some outdated mode of revelation, they would block the "increasing purpose", albeit unwittingly or for the noblest reasons, and Christ, the chief object of their devotion, would be not so much realized as diminished.[54]

Behind both tendencies Lightfoot saw a static mode of thinking about the past. Correction of this error was the purpose of the 'anti-history' passages in numerous addresses.[55] While they appear to preclude any historical interest, in fact they point to the importance of a controlled use of the past.[56] Always there was a need for a proper historical sense, the simple recognition that times change, and that any character, institution or episode should be viewed in relation to its own time.[57] Otherwise there was the perennial practical danger of the anachronism of bygone arrangements or dispositions introduced into an alien state of society which, without a total return to past conditions, would only create distortions.[58] Even though committed to the unity and continuity of history, Lightfoot's own historic sense was strong. His programme of historical usage affirmed a unique present and anticipated a different future.

Although not seeking exact copying, reproduction did involve a measure of recurrence. When looking to the lessons of the past, present day characters in the ongoing drama of history should follow the spirit but not the practices of those who had gone before. In relation to the all important first century, it should be the endeavour of Churchmen "not to stereotype the processes, but to revive the mind, of their Apostolic masters".[59] The same was true for other periods. For example, the unselfishness of the religious movement of the thirteenth century was to be valued "as a protest against the selfishness of all times".[60] Churchmen would "imitate the spirit — the love, the tenderness, the absolute self-sacrifice — but they would not copy the methods, of a Francis of Assisi".[61] Clearly, effective reproduction depended on the discernment of the interpretation. It also meant seeking methods and arrangements that were appropriate to the present. Adaptation and innovation were as much a part of it as imitation. In negotiating the circum-

---

[52]   He Shall Take, [1877], 25.
[53]   For the working of the Spirit in the time after the Incarnation, see 85-6 above.
[54]   All Things, 1872, 26-7.
[55]   Eg. CP 13-14, 19-21.
[56]   All Things, 1872, 24-6.
[57]   Jael, 1855, 21-2; CS 4, 153-4; SSO 61-2; SSP 148-9, 216; PC 38-40.
[58]   SSO 59; PC 65-6.
[59]   SSO 60.
[60]   SSO 59.
[61]   SSO 59-60. Cf. SSO 15-18, 61-2; SSP 216; Vision, 1877, 18-20.

stances, and dealing with the problems, of everyday life, the need was to be ever mindful that the present moment was the link between the past and the future; to take account of the law of progress; and to grasp the opportunity to contribute to the realization of God's "increasing purpose". As the end point in the programme of optimum historical usage, reproduction meant taking part in history by identifying with and promoting its progressive forces.

The ethical interest of Lightfoot's perspective is palpable. While the ideal called for an interest in "all things", the programme of optimum usage was concerned with the moral and spiritual aspects of life. It was in "whatever is noble, whatever is truthful, whatever is self-denying, whatever is enlightened" that Church people should take an active interest.[62] This preference did not necessarily narrow Lightfoot's ambit, but it did determine the perspective. The case of George Stephenson was typical. It was the patience and perseverence behind it rather than his technological achievement that Lightfoot lauded. Such religious and moral victories contributed to "the increasing purpose of God" more than "ordinary" accomplishment. In turning to history Lightfoot intended to promote progressive thought and action of this order.

This perspective was applicable to all the varied pursuits and activities of life. In antiquity Cyrus, Alexander and Caesar were equally God's instruments with prophets and apostles, Lightfoot insisted, as he declared the interdependence of the "ordinary" and the "sacred". In 1861 the men of Trinity House were encouraged to think of themselves as doing the work of Christ. Men and women from many walks of life were similarly encouraged to regard their own activity in this light as Lightfoot spoke from pulpits at various points around the country. While he acknowledged the importance of high politics and culture, he was prepared to assert the superiority of the many anonymous individuals who rise to the religious and ethical challenges of their mundane circumstances.[63] The "increasing purpose" was a framework for appreciating the dignity of all people in all places and situations. Every man and woman at their own level could contribute to its realization.

Historical knowledge, it followed, was neither antiquarian, ornamental nor traditionalist, as it was with some of Lightfoot's contemporaries. Rather his understanding of history might be described as existential. The approach Lightfoot advocated was not about returning to some ideal past, but was necessarily concerned with securing the action that would shape the present and the future. The rationale for this aspiration, and the priorities it set, were embedded in the theology of history itself. Viewed in its practical aspect, the "increasing purpose" constituted a strong affirmation of what

---

[62] Edifying, 1869, 20.
[63] Eg. CS 265-7.

life in an eternal setting required. History as a resource for living that life entailed seeing all of its moments as part of a single spiritual and moral growth which led up to and included the present, and would continue beyond. These connections imposed a heavy responsibility on the present for the shape of subsequent developments. Similarly, representing the past as the record of spiritual and moral achievement was an ongoing call to progressive action of the same order. The underlying hope reflects a confidence in the capacity of those who saw that history was 'theirs' to function as 'historians' at the level of history lived and made. Such a confidence assumed that the precise conditions of life as they exist in the structure of historical reality are knowable, and that human beings are more or less fitted to receiving this knowledge. This was precisely Lightfoot's position, as the anthropological and epistemological aspects of his outlook indicate.

II

Lightfoot's assigning history to its place in the incarnational scheme of life was a development of its function in the purpose summed up in the slogan πολυμερῶς καὶ πολυτρόπως. The usefulness of history was therefore a way of promoting the larger theological task he had set himself, the cultivation of a broader view of revelation with all that this entailed for thought and practice. But the exhortation to the use of history in the "all things" formula was largely hortatory and gave no indication of specific means and its more immediate benefits. In fact, Lightfoot's basis for using history did go beyond the broad rationale to what it offered as a form of knowledge and understanding. What might be called the instrumental side of the theology of history showed how its broad directions could be carried into effect. The anticipated result was for the intentions it formed to be realized in the domain of conduct for the furtherance of the "increasing purpose" in their ultimate impact. The capacity of history to teach and sustain its lessons within this framework rested on two primary conditions in Lightfoot's thought.

The first was the inherently historical nature of people. A striking feature of Lightfoot's anthropological statements is recognition of human capacity to deal with historical knowledge in all of its aspects. This was in line with the principle that revelation is always an accommodation to human capacity.[64] In this case it meant, first, that men and women are creatures given to questioning and seeking to provide for the relation of their personal time to time itself.[65] Lightfoot further assigned to them a "power of memory and imagination which annihilates time and space, penetrating into the prehistoric past and projecting itself into a boundless future"; a "capacity of progress

---

[64] LS 186.
[65] All, 1861, 22-4; CS 76-7, 240; S 26; & OA 163-4.

... which urges ... ever forward eager and restless"; and an "anxiety about the hereafter, this desire of posthumous fame, this interest in descendants yet unborn".[66] People also had the ability to deal with the data of history by using their cognitive faculties — those intellectual powers which enabled them to collect, organize and assess the facts of time and place —[67] while the faculty of experience created the possibility of learning from it.[68] Through the conscience the native propensity to the truth addresses the eternal struggle between good and evil transparent in events.[69] By means of the will, it took a side.[70] Human beings were well fitted to the requirement that they interpret, assimilate and reproduce the history that was theirs.

The second primary condition of this perspective was the ready accessibility of history in the present. The meaning of the whole as "the increasing purpose of God" was made known and brought to bear by the Bible.[71] This provided the framework for understanding the significance of the parts. Practically this was important mainly for the past, in which the revelation was available *a posteriori*. Recent advances in knowledge about the past meant that the position in this respect was continually improving. Indeed, Lightfoot considered the abundance and fecundity of the resources left by the past to be one of the blessings of contemporary society:

> reflect on the privileges which you, as a child of this nineteenth century, you as the heir of all the ages, enjoy. Only think of the fruits of knowledge & learning which have ripened for you to gather; all these magnificent acquisitions of science, all these rich treasures of archaeology & language & history, all these accumulated stores of poetry & art & philosophy — of imagination & thought — the intellectual capital amassed by untold generations of men.[72]

Several characteristic ideas — organic connection and development, and the filial sense of inheritance — were involved as history took its place alongside the other forms of knowledge and culture that engendered the favoured position of the present. All in turn presupposed that the present takes place in the same way as the past, an axiom Lightfoot was happy to affirm:

> "Wherever certain conditions exist, there certain consequences will follow." ... It is a perfectly natural consequence in many cases; you can trace the results to their causes: you can almost establish a law by induction; the dissipated life brings the shattered health; the decline of patriotism and the corruption of morals brings a nation's ruin.[73]

At both the individual and the national level certain lines of conduct gave rise to predictable results. As the past revealed ethical patterns and enforced

---

[66] SSP 56.
[67] SSP 287-8.
[68] CS 241.
[69] Jael, 1855, 13-15. RCC (1871) 76. SSP 293.
[70] IP 13. SSP 312-14.
[71] See Chapter Five above.
[72] Harvest, 1874, 4-5.
[73] Eagles, 1873, 18-19.

their implications — whether as "sacred" or "ordinary" history — it could function as one of the religious, intellectual and cultural means of the day.

The grounds of this second condition were the two modes in which Lightfoot saw history as being available to the present. Each involved a form of historical knowledge, catered for some need in humanity, and offered specific advantages. While separated for analysis, in fact the two modes often coincided and together furnished additional advantages and led to a desired end.

The first mode was history as the source and repository of facts. History, Lightfoot averred, is "the foundation of existing facts".[74] By implication it was also the deposit from which new facts would be established.

This understanding assumed the efficacy of historical enquiry. Lightfoot was well aware that what was sometimes alleged to be factual was not properly grounded. He also understood that new facts could change the point of view.[75] But he did not doubt that, when properly carried out, the appropriate methods of investigation furnished "accredited history",[76] firm and reliable facts. It was, of course, in this conviction that he carried out his investigations into the history of earliest Christianity.[77] The widespread historical positivism of the day found in Lightfoot a significant representative.

History as fact met the interest of men and women in the truth about the world in which they live.[78] Its specific advantage was provision of a large body of principles by which life could be directed. Lightfoot's writings abound with such principles and propositions made clear by history. Not all had a religious referent. Thus the improvements brought by railways and machinery were invoked to calm fears arising from the emergence of the cooperative movement.[79] But the facts of history were mainly adduced for apologetical purposes. It was "the lesson of all history", for example, that Christ's cross can never fail.[80] Other facts provided reassurance: in particular, times of apparent setback were often shown to have been in reality times of preparation for greater spiritual achievement.[81] Still others were a "terrible satire on the prevision and judgment of mankind",[82] and showed repeatedly how people prefer the letter to the spirit.[83] At this level history was also a guide to Church policy, as when it commended compromise in rela-

---

[74] "England Six Hundred Years Ago," 2.
[75] PC 84.
[76] Moral Freedom, 1873, 1.
[77] See Part IV below.
[78] RCC (1871) 76. See 249 below.
[79] IACC 15-16.
[80] OA 14-16.
[81] SSP 132-3; Hidden, 1875, 4-5; LNC 84-5.
[82] Vision, 1878, 23-5.
[83] SSP 210-11.

tion to a Burials Bill in 1880 by showing what had been achieved previously by a policy of "thoroughness" on points of principle in dealing with Nonconformists.[84] Similarly, at the national level historical fact showed that it was folly to get rid of religion in order to eliminate the excesses of religious zeal.[85] A resevoir of "common experience and universal history", history indicated what can and cannot happen, in time and over time. As a source of regulative principles bringing life and thought into closer conformity with fact, the historical perspective was among the means of truthful existence.[86] The basic consideration in any important matter was, 'what are the facts?'

Lightfoot well understood that knowing the truth was not sufficient reason for people to behave in accordance with it. Something else was needed to stimulate the motivating forces latent in the human imagination. He believed that this requirement was furnished by the second, perhaps more important, mode in which the past was available to the present. As the source of examples or types, history satisfied the propensity in men and women to see and feel as well as understand. For, in addition to being "the foundation of existing facts", history was "the storehouse of past experience".[87] This standing was behind Lightfoot's frequent observation that "history teems with examples" and "all history teaches by example".[88]

While speaking often of 'types' and 'antitypes', he preferred to call this use of prefigurement the "symbolical" mode of interpretation.[89] It was an approach to the past familiar from and commended by the Bible.[90] Like his contemporaries, Lightfoot extended it beyond Scripture to secular subjects:[91]

> For we may view any person or event not only with regard to his or its place in history, i.e. in the progressive development of God's dealing with man, as one link in a chain — but also as a symbol or type, of that which will recur again and again. Such an application may be made with more or less exactness in ordinary history. History, it is said, repeats itself ... and therefore analogous situations will be repeated.[92]

He recognized that this involved significant hermeneutical difficulties, but

---

[84] YJC (1880) 50-1.
[85] SSP 142-3. History showed that censorship of English drama had not worked either: it was better to try to influence those responsible for it. SSO 24-7.
[86] "History corrects many errors and dispels many illusions." PC 83.
[87] "England 600 Years Ago," 2.
[88] S 20.
[89] Acts I-VIII, 1855, 86r.
[90] For an example of Lightfoot wrestling with the interpretation of a Biblical type, see Lightfoot to Westcott, 25 & 29 March 1862; Westcott to Lightfoot, 28 March 1862; and the result in G 180-4.
[91] For the background, see P.J. Korshin, *Typologies in England 1650-1820* (Princeton: University Press, 1982); & for contemporary typological practice, G.P. Landow, *Victorian Types, Victorian Shadows: Biblical Typology in Victorian Literature, Art and Thought* (Boston: Routledge and Kegan Paul, 1980).
[92] Acts I-VIII, 1855, 85r.

on the occasion he revealed his method he felt able to skirt them:

> It would be beyond our purpose to enter into the question of analogies here — to exam-
> ine what is their exact value and what their limits — This is a question θειας και μακρας
> διηγησεως [*sic*] .[93]

It was sufficient to acknowledge that this was one application of the great
principle of analogy learned from Butler, according to which likeness between events could be taken as the warrant for believing they had the same
inner meaning.

This minimization of the difficulties was typical. Lightfoot was rarely
self-conscious about these analogies, but the one important exception be-
trays some awareness of the problems raised by applying an earlier to a later
situation.[94] Nevertheless his practice was simply to relate events or characters from different times on the basis of some similarity. As occasion required, history was surveyed for instances which anticipated current needs
and problems. Clearly this was eclectic,[95] but Lightfoot saw no reason to
think it inappropriate. While different and belonging to their own era, historical occurrences still had common properties which connected them in a
recurrence relationship. Linkage on the basis of resemblances meant that
Lightfoot's analogies were rooted in a sense of filiation. They arose from an
affinity or common belonging, principally to the Church, but also to nation,
place or institution, and thus of hope and aspiration. Confident of the line-
ages he established, Lightfoot proceeded to draw out the lessons.

The need to be met was principally moral. "We measure ourselves with
others," Lightfoot observed, "we see our defects mirrored in their excellen-
cies." This was a stimulus to the will by a kind of moral quantification:

> our ideal is heightened by the comparison. Thus there gathers and ferments in us a
> *discontent* with ourselves ... with the conduct of that personality which is free to disci-
> pline, to mould, to direct, to develop our endowments. This dissatisfaction with self is
> the mainspring of all high enterprise and all moral achievement.[96]

So conceived the past was a standard, measuring out for the present its true
character and setting the ideals which become the basis of conduct.

The specific advantage of history as typology was the provision of a seemingly limitless number of anticipations of the present day. In Lightfoot's
own case the majority were Biblical. But they could be extra-Biblical too.
Often they involved individuals. But they could also involve institutions
and places, attitudes and systems of thought, patterns of behaviour and development, and even whole ages. Thus figures like Abraham, Joseph, Moses, and Esau are ranged alongside Girolamo Savonarola, George Stephenson

---

[93] "of divine and lengthy account" [translation].
[94] SSO 15-18.
[95] For the way in which Lightfoot's use of history served the present, see section III of
the present chapter.
[96] CS 321-2.

and Francis of Assisi. The Franciscan Order and the S.P.G. represented organizations of different kinds, those for which everything is on a grand scale, and those which have a steady unobtrusive growth.[97] Athens was a type of the state of the whole civilized world when Paul preached there.[98] Formalism and speculation have counterparts throughout the ages.[99] Alongside the Pharisees and Sadducees stood Stoicism and Epicureanism. Party spirit in Corinth was paralleled by Donatism in northern Africa.[100] Ages of scepticism and over-busyness have their characteristic results. Whatever the nature of the type, it could be used to provide a heritage or create an identity, suggest misgivings or issue a warning, and provide a standard of measurement or lay down the pattern development. In this way present day activity was guided and effort encouraged. Such prefigurements defied reduction to formulae, and so the specification of rules of conduct was superfluous. The will, aroused by the imagination and moved by sympathy, becomes the basis of conduct. It was at this kind of response that Lightfoot usually aimed.

The modes in which Lightfoot saw history as readily available to the human intellect and imagination meant that the guidance needed by humanity was embedded in existing reality. There was no need for any theologian or philosopher to prescribe norms of behaviour and perhaps oppose an 'is' with an 'ought'.[101] Individuals themselves could read out of history rather than into it what should be in terms of thought and conduct. The function of teachers like Lightfoot was to alert others to the possibility and provide guidance in how to do it. For the reality of history itself, he believed, clarifies and articulates the norms and standards of belief and behaviour. Direction in what a person should think and do awaited discovery or disclosure from the facts and types of historical existence.

Although separated for purposes of analysis the two modes in which the past is available to the present tended to overlap. While the facts of history did not necessarily function typically, the use of types assumed a factual picture of the past. Lightfoot juxtaposed the two modes in the comment:

> The human race has grown older in experience since then. Vast accumulations of thought and knowledge have been amassed.[102]

Together they constituted an ever growing resource, and, in their capacity to adumbrate how things happen in history, they enabled Lightfoot to ask rhetorically, "Will not history repeat itself?"[103] It was not that he expected

---

[97] SSO 105.
[98] CS 85.
[99] SSP 156-7, 210.
[100] UC 5-6.
[101] For Lightfoot's view of the Christian ministry, see 200-9 below.
[102] CS 270.
[103] RCC (1881) 16.

identical recurrence. But situations similar in character could be expected to follow a corresponding pattern according to the principles and qualities they embodied. Although by no means prescriptive, the knowledge that they would do so was an invitation to confident, informed action.

Two further advantages were conferred by the combined action of history as fact and type. Perspective permitted an appreciation of the true proportions of men and events:

> Only when we take up a position aloof from the field of action can we duly appreciate the relations of all the parts of the great battles of history.[104]

A twofold advantage of past over present followed. There was exemption from the tendency in the study of contemporary religion and politics to "approach the subject with the blind partiality of men who have taken a distinct side in the conflicts which they are reviewing".[105] The passage of time also reversed the effect of nearness of view, which was unduly to magnify the proportion of events.[106] Both points were elucidated from the narrative of Josephus. By including the meeting of Festus with Agrippa and ignoring that with St Paul known from 'Acts', "His account illustrates the false estimate of the relative proportions of events, which men inevitably take who are mixed up in them". Seen in retrospect it was clear that St Paul was the more important figure: "time has wholly reversed the verdict of contemporary history".[107] The detachment of the historical stance permitted seeing things as they really had been.

The corollary for Lightfoot was that history permitted seeing things as they really are. In turn, when applied to the future this generated a certain power of prediction:

> You cannot understand aright the state of things in which you live unless you know something about the state of things out of which it arose; You cannot forecast the consequences of your actions, & so guide your measures aright, unless you have learnt what results have ensued from similar processes in previous cases, to what ends this social movement or that intellectual tendency has led mankind in former times.[108]

He seems to have meant by this no more than a very general indication of the lines along which the future would unfold. How men react to truths of great importance, for example, was made clear by the past.[109] If "great results had evolved from small beginnings" once, it could happen again.[110] It was also probable that aspirations which had already led to significant moral

---

[104] HE 2.
[105] HE 1-2.
[106] *Ibid.* & SSO 78.
[107] SSP 257-8.
[108] "England Six Hundred Years Ago," 2.
[109] SSP 140-2.
[110] MSL 19.

achievement would continue to do so.[111] Because of its generally positive effect in adumbrating the future Lightfoot could say, "History is an excellent cordial for the drooping courage".[112] The experience of the past was meant to inspire hope for the time to come.[113]

The total benefit for those who drew on historical understanding as a resource for living was a certain independence of the age in which they found themselves. Placement of the present against the larger historical canvas relativized its leading concerns and interests.[114] This was the necessary obverse of the historic sense. Whereas that was a perspective on past events in terms of the conditions under which they actually occurred, this meant seeing the present both as the product of its own constitutive influences and forces and also as the soil out of which the future would grow. In turn a power of choice was engendered, between acceptance and resistance, according to the satisfactoriness of what was discerned. It was important to do so given the tendency of people to accept as final the current taken by intellectual and social life in their own day.[115] Historical consciousness enabled men and women instead to detach themselves from these currents, and to make the choices that would take — or block — "the increasing purpose of God" into the next stage of its progress. Its liberating effect made history the necessary basis of effective, progressive action in the present.

The power of choice assigned to historically conscious people in Lightfoot's scheme clarified the nature of the role the individual was called upon to play in history.[116] As people become conscious of their place in the pattern, they feel obligation to the process. From each one this requires subordination of the self to the ruling tendency and overall purpose of the world. This is achieved primarily in orientation to Christ. Beyond that self-denial and performance of duty follow as the proper way of life for an historically conceived identity. For such persons there is no need to worry about results, because their actions are caught up in the dynamic of the "increasing purpose". This is a point of some importance for explaining Lightfoot's own praxis and personal style. While it no doubt suited a man of such a shy and taciturn temperament, there was no need for him to promote himself or to become a propagandist for his point of view. It was sufficient for him to embody and patiently disseminate his ideals as he went about his normal work. In due course they would be taken up by those other individuals who would bring about the historic effects. In the manner that he urged

---

[111] Only, 1872, 24-5; Vision of Isaiah, 1877, 9-10; Teach, 1878, 11-17.
[112] HE 72-3.
[113] SSO 79; PC 52-4.
[114] RCC (1873) 230-1.
[115] RCC (1871) 76.
[116] On this, see 106-7 & 108 above.

upon others, Lightfoot stuck to the tasks which he believed were properly his, and relied on the process of history to secure the benefits.[117]

Locating human existence within a progressive continuum in this manner brought people into the ethical structure of universal history. Perceiving the tendency of things imposed the duty to advance rather than retard. At Whewell's funeral in 1866, Lightfoot dramatized the point by likening life to the contests of the amphitheatre.[118] Even its mundane struggles were exalted as warfare against "the fierce monsters of ignorance and sin".[119] They were, moreover, part of the same fight that had raged throughout Christian history. Participation at any one moment took place in the company of "a vast concourse from all ages and climes".[120] Their presence raised a standard to surpass and a tradition to pass on, enriched and further ennobled. As well as looking around himself, the present day-gladiator needed to look behind and forward. Knowing where they fitted in was the key to knowing what action to take for any individual, group, or even a whole age. In this process perspective they were confronted with the question of their relation to the whole course — did they help or hinder? — and the knowledge that they were in a position to make a difference was sufficient encouragement to choosing the option which promoted the most healthful future. In this way metahistory led to metaethics.

This outcome conforms the notion of history as possession or cultural resource to Lightfoot's general intellectual outlook. Like the Biblical revelation of history, historical knowledge as such — whether as fact or type, or the two together — acted on what is given in human nature intellectually to give it form and content. As it did so the innate spiritual and moral sense was continually confronted by spiritual and moral realities greater than itself. In this way history was seen to press the claims of duty and affirmed compliance as the way to happiness and satisfaction. Faith and morality were therefore a response to the conditions of life rather than enlightened self-interest. The intuitionism of his view of how and why history is useful further set the idealist-empiricalist Lightfoot against the utilitarian-empiricists.

There was some tension in this between freedom and responsibility. The notion that "all things are yours" posited a morally autonomous individual as the decisive historical agent. On the one hand, historical understanding confronted those elements of human identity — the will, motive, desire —

---

[117] For the irritation this single mindedness brought about in Benson, see 225 & 374 below.
[118] CS 109-14; Cf. What Advantageth It?, 1876, 10-14, 33-4.
[119] CS 110.
[120] CS 109.

that contributed to the moral action through which Christian commitment is expressed. Yet, on the other, it was also a call for the self to be immersed in the wider relations of society in and across time that made morality meaningful. Thus history — in the overall pattern, and in the facts and types it furnishes — placed before people an ideal of what they might be and do. The claim that this was the only way to a satisfying, purposive existence suggested further that this was a necessity for success in a world that required adaptation to the conditions in which life is lived. This meant that, while the individual remains free to choose whether to rise to the possibilities and responsibilities of historical existence, there was no real alternative to his doing so.

But in Lightfoot's mind history viewed instrumentally left the individual extremely well placed to make use of his privileges and meet his obligations. It provided the motivation and the resources for effective action together with the reassurance that individual effort would make a difference. So conceived, the efficacy of historical knowledge brought Lightfoot to the point presupposed in the "all things are yours" perspective, history as a potentially powerful existential force as immanent presence. As well as a way to look at the world, it furnished a way to act in the world. The challenge he faced was securing historically informed thought and action in his own day.

III

In Lightfoot's thought, both the obligation to use "all history" as the basis of progressive action and the empowering advantages of historical understanding were perennial. They laid down what could be done at any time and should be done at all times. It is clear, however, that his real concern was with his own times. As a teacher promoting this outlook, Lightfoot was seeking to guide the contemporary Church into sound thought and practice, while the very point of the notion of history as possession was its function as a resource for living in the present. The persistence with which he urged the usefulness of history indicates that for him it was a serious matter. For a number of reasons Lightfoot considered that what should be done at all times was especially needed at the present time.

One reason for pressing the usefulness of history was his assessment of the age. Although well aware that nearness of view unduly magnifies the proportion of events, when he applied his comparative perspective to his own lifetime, Lightfoot rated his own times as one of the great epochs of history.[121] It was "an age of exceptional energy, rapid in its movements and manifold in its developments", ranking with fifth century Athens and the

---

[121] Vision, 1877, 3-4; SSO 78-9.

Reformation "as one of those exceptional periods of intensified human life, when the work of centuries is compressed into decades".[122] This assessment was based on the convergence of several developments of revolutionary proportions. In the political domain, the emphasis on individual freedom and the brotherhood of man had given rise to electoral and other related reforms that had enabled England to avoid problems faced in Europe and achieve a smoothe flow of social and political life.[123] Changes in the industrial world, of which the railway was the symbol, had transformed the material conditions of life, annihilating space, accelerating travel, promoting rapid interchange of ideas, and multiplying mechanical appliances.[124] Commercially there had been such outward growth and prosperity that England not only evinced unprecedented vitality but stood out as the first commercial and maritime nation in the world.[125] In the sphere of intellect there had been an unprecedented expansion of human knowledge, thought and interest.[126] Lightfoot rejoiced to live at such a time.[127] He, with his contemporaries, was an heir to the accomplishments of the ages, which made life fuller, more varied and more energetic.

But Lightfoot was not one-sided or complacent in his assessment of the age. Its strengths had brought corresponding faults and dangers. Intensity of life had made it an over-busy and distracted age.[128] In politics the assertion of individual liberty had caused "self discipline" and "self renunciation", "without which the liberty of the individual becomes intolerable to himself and society", to be ignored.[129] Changed material conditions of life had created large cities with their slums and massive social problems. The prosperity achieved by commerce had been inequitably shared, and brought on industrial conflict, the "self-indulgence of the rich" and "the restlessness and intemperance of the poor", while the promise of peace held out by international exhibitions had never been realized.[130] Most serious for Lightfoot was the intellectual and religious component of contemporary life. The vogue for science had led to an exaggeration of its claims and a one-sidedness in the mental development of the age.[131] Moreover, the rapid growth of knowledge was not an unmixed blessing. As he told the Select Committee of the

---

[122] RCC (1881) 458; LNC 145. SSO 140-1.
[123] RCC (1873) 231, 232; SSP 282-3; SSO 140-1; CS 287-8.
[124] RCC (1881) 14-15; Harvest, 1874, 3-5.
[125] MSL 13-14; SSO 242-3.
[126] CS 189-90; C 116-17; SSO 78-9.
[127] HE 161-2.
[128] Veil, 1854, 16-18; DDC (1880) 98-9; RCC (1881) 458.
[129] CS 41-2.
[130] What Advantageth It?, 1876, 1-8; SSO 60; IACC 10.
[131] Eg. Only, 1872, 3-5.

House of Lords on University Tests:

> It is impossible to shut our eyes to the fact that a flood of new ideas has been poured in upon the world, and that at present they have not found their proper level; minds are unsettled in consequence.[132]

Worst of all was the danger that the acquisitions of eighteen Christian centuries could be discarded.[133] An age of great achievement, Lightfoot's was also an age of anxiety with something of the contingent about it.

Of the responses required at such a time, Lightfoot judged that the wider use of history as an instrument for educating national self-consciousness was among them. This was because it was now well understood that the welfare of, and course taken by, a society was governed by its appropriation of the results of rational enquiry:

> The well-being and the progress of society depend on its recognizing *truths*. The physical health of a community is secured by the standard of sanitary conditions. The advance of a people in civilization and in the appliances of art and manufacture is proportionate to the attention which it bestows on the facts of mechanics, of chemistry, of political economy, and the like.[134]

The analogy with sanitary reform was telling. Only recently had it been realized that the health of the community required systematic application of the scientific findings in this area of public concern. No less important was knowledge about history. Especially by helping men to realize their relations to coming time, it facilitated that providence which was the measure of progress in the scale of humanity.[135] To this extent history as a cultural resource was a condition of civilization and its advancement.

An age like his own, Lightfoot believed, confronted Church and society at large with the need to manage the change that caused its unsettlement. At such a time his second reason for seeking the use of history was what it had to offer in this respect. While Lightfoot's historical outlook focused on the present, it was by no means an endorsement of the *status quo*. Drawing on existing reality for belief and conduct might be taken to mean that true belief and morality would be aligned with prevailing views and established custom. There were two reasons inherent in the theology of history that would make the inference mistaken. One was the dynamic of history itself. However satisfactory the present might be, it was not yet the full realization of the given in the Incarnation. In the time before history's end, much remained to be done in a growth "from more to more". Second, the Incarnation itself functioned as a criterion of change. If experience does not correspond with what is given in Christ, there is a powerful impulse to alter things until they do. This might mean correcting what is wrong, developing what

---

[132] PP IX (1871) 183.
[133] Sheep, 1873, 2-5.
[134] Moral Freedom, 1873, 16-17.
[135] IACC 7-8; SSO 237-8.

is incomplete, or commencing what does not yet exist. For both reasons the
"increasing purpose" itself was an imperative for change.

However, it was change of a type that Lightfoot urged. Such change as
the times required should be gradual and cumulative. There was need to
incorporate the novel by building on the old to produce a new synthesis.
Indeed, in the very sermon before the University of Cambridge in which he
first proposed the Logos as the basis of the Church's response to the age,
Lightfoot asserted:

> The great work, it would seem, of your generation is to reconcile the present and the
> past. Study therefore the present in the light of the past, and the past in the light of the
> present.[136]

Lightfoot was well aware of the advocates of radical social change among
his contemporaries.[137] The pressure for change they represented needed to
be allowed but also controlled. His own outlook held together belief in
continuity with faith in progress. History itself seemed to commend managing change by confining it within tradition.

The approach prescribed for the historically conscious was encapsulated
for Lightfoot in the Gospel parable of the householder who continually brings
forth out of his stores things new and old.[138] This was an image of the scribe
who, expert in the Jewish law, was able to preserve past understandings and
build on them as a disciple of Jesus. Adopted early in his career, Lightfoot
continually held it up as a model of the ideal Churchman-theologian.[139] It
provided a paradigm in which the starting point for thought and action would
be what had been received, but also an assurance that what has been received would not be an absolute constraint. By bringing this theoretical
need to balance change and continuity to his own spheres of direct influence
in the mid-Victorian Church, Lightfoot emerged ideologically as a liberal
conservative.[140]

Both of Lightfoot's reasons for seeking a greater use of history were
spurred on by a third. This was the tendency to neglect or misuse history
that he saw as widespread. He saw it first in his own immediate sphere of
interest, the Church. Here neglect was a serious matter, since it disregarded
the nature of the Church in the scheme of the "increasing purpose". Its need
of history was an inference from the main images — a building,[141] the body,[142]

---

[136] CS 148. Cf. SSP 238, for the same idea, slightly modified.
[137] See 126-30 above.
[138] See Matthew 13: 52.
[139] Introduction to Greek Testament Lectures, 1855, 1 ; Charity, 1874, 6; SSO 68.
[140] This is the argument of Part III below.
[141] Edifying, 1869, 21; LNC 29-30.
[142] CS 172-92; OA 192-3.

a household,[143] a tree[144] and a river[145] — the Bible used to delineate its character. Involved in each was the notion of continuity, inter-connection, mutual dependence and support, and cumulation towards completeness. A model for the whole Church in realizing its historical nature was furnished by the genuine missionary spirit:

> like everything else that is godlike in man, [it] presses forward, acts for the future, hopes for the future, lives in the future. But it draws strength and refreshment from the experience, the examples, the accumulated power and wisdom of the past. Nay, just in proportion as we are animated by this reverence for the past, as we acknowledge our obligations to it, as we feel our connexion with it; in short as we realise this idea of continuity in the Church of Christ, in the same degree will be the truest missionary spirit — wise, zealous, humble, self-denying, enlightened, enterprising, innovating in the best sense, because conservative in the best sense.[146]

Because of its constitution the Church in the present was intended to work towards the future by drawing from the past instruction, assurance, encouragement and hope, and to feel an obligation to vigorous self-denying action, as the basis of its encounter with the world. This would bring change, but it would be gradual and cumulative as the Church realized more and more of its inherent nature. The result to be expected was a "far more glorious destiny ... than ever attended the Church of the past".[147]

It was also simply a matter of the Church making the most of its natural advantages. As it was a privilege to belong to an ancient institution — "Antiquity [having] gathered together a mass of precedents, of examples, of ideas, of rules, & the like, which form an inexhaustible storehouse of wealth" —[148] members of the oldest and most widespread institution were, *a fortiori*, the most privileged of all. Their responsibility to make use of the privilege was correspondingly greater.[149] It was also in the general interest of Churchmen to do so:

> The prosperity of a Church ... depends largely on its connexion with the past. Progress is not severence. A healthy Church is not indeed the slave, but it is essentially the child and the pupil, of the past. The accumulated lessons of its bygone history are its rich inheritance, lessons learnt alike from its failures and successes.[150]

These lessons gave depth and range of vision in place of the blinding self-centredness of preoccupation of the present. As with society at large, the Church's success in the world depended to a great extent on how it used its own rich store of gathered wealth.

---

[143] 4th Group, 1858, 19-20.
[144] SSO 148.
[145] *Ibid.*
[146] SSO 149.
[147] SSO 80.
[148] Bearing Fruit, 1877, 1.
[149] "Where there is a privilege, there must also be a responsibility." Christ, 1866, 19.
[150] LNC 3.

In one sense, exhortations to Church people to mobilize their history in this way was unnecessary. It was already a well established part of their praxis. But the variety of modes and ends signalled the existence of confusion and error about how to deal with the apparently conflicting claims of the old and the new. The great need, therefore, was to secure the right use of history, and Lightfoot's advocacy of the "all things are yours" perspective was directed primarily to this end.[151] For contemporary Church people taking all that history had to offer into the Christian synthesis as a basis for thought and conduct was a double challenge. It required openness to the whole range and variety of the past, not just favoured periods or phases, such as the age of the Fathers or the Reformation. It also required willingness to accept the novel. Whether it was new facts, the extended vistas made available by archaeologists and prehistorians, or the perspectives made available by new philosophical conceptions,[152] whatever was found to be true needed to be incorporated into the working outlook and teaching of Church people. At this level Lightfoot aimed at correction and redirection of a well established practice.

Beyond it in the nation at large, he saw the same tendency to neglect and misuse history. Lightfoot thought progressivists, who wanted to break free from the past, undervalued it. He answered them by invoking the twelfth century *topos* of the dwarf on the giant's shoulders.[153] Outwardly equating the present with a dwarf was a direct challenge to those who exalted its superiority. But the *topos* simply asserted that such advantages as the present offered were built upon the past. With this qualification the giant-dwarf parallel actually validated the present by emphasizing the broader vision resulting from the vantage point raised by lateness in time. A clearer perception of the lead-up was meant to make plain the next steps in the ongoing ascent. Failure to recognize the dependence of the present on the past was tantamount to physical blindness, and blocked off an important avenue into the future.

Lightfoot also feared that history was being overshadowed by developments in other fields. Its manifest benefits meant that science was clamouring for attention, and he could well understand the appeal of political subjects at a time of franchise extension. But, as he explained to a working class audience at Rochdale in 1874, the need to make use of history required some reordering of priorities:

> Politics necessarily force themselves upon our attention, because in some form or other we are brought across political questions every day of our lives. Scientific subjects again are brought more or less prominently before all at the present time; & the obvi-

---

[151]   His efforts in this area constitute the principal theme of Part III below.
[152]   SSO 78-9; RCC (1871) 82-3.
[153]   "England 600 Years Ago," 5; LNC 68.

ous & immediate advantage which working men derive in their respective crafts from some scientific knowledge is a security that science will not be altogether forgotten in a place like this. But this is not the case with history. And, unless history is brought definitely before our notice, unless we make a distinct *effort* to master its lessons, it will fail to receive the attention which it deserves.[154]

In an age of science and great practical affairs it was important that all Englishmen, irrespective of social class, give history due attention, lest it be eclipsed as an instrument for influencing the course taken by English society.

At the same time Lightfoot discerned a tendency for history to be misused. Jeffrey von Arx has shown how in the second half of the nineteenth century "dissident intellectuals" sought to legitimate their reformist programmes by making them a function of the progressive movement of history.[155] Lightfoot opposed this strategy by taking on John Stuart Mill, the dissident intellectual in whom he was evidently most interested. From 1864, he recurred repeatedly to the view that morality is neither a function of utility nor a mere growth of education.[156] The chronology alone suggests that the allusion was to Mill's *Utilitarianism*, published in 1863. But Lightfoot had taken up what for him was plainly one of its main points. While this concern was something of a preoccupation, his most substantial response to Mill occurred over ten years later in the Eranus, a Cambridge discussion club said to have been formed by Henry Sidgwick for the very purpose of discovering what the taciturn Lightfoot really thought.[157] On at least one occasion Lightfoot was canny, claiming that he had been too busy to prepare the promised paper and blandly reading instead an essay on Edward I. However, the publication of *Three Essays On Religion* in 1874 was a sufficient cause to make Lightfoot speak his mind on a subject that mattered.[158]

Lightfoot happily concurred with Mill's shifting the issue from the truth to the usefulness of religion. For this was a criterion which he himself used to test and measure the truth claims of Christianity. At this level of argument there was a difference on the fundamental question of character formation. According to Lightfoot the "Utility of Religion" had missed the importance of religion as a real cause of moral behaviour because of a failure

---

[154] "England 600 Years Ago," 2-3.
[155] J. von Arx, *Progress and Pessimism. Religion, Politics, and History in Late Nineteenth Century Britain* (Cambridge, Massachusetts & London: Harvard University Press, 1985). The expression "dissident intellectuals" is that of J.R. Moore, "The Crisis of Faith: Reformation Versus Revolution," in *Religion in Victorian Britain. Vol II. Controversies* (G. Parsons ed.; Manchester: University Press, 1988) 220-37.
[156] Sword, 1864, 23-4. The opinion was repeated with only verbal alterations in a subsequent version of the same sermon. See CS 165.
[157] J. Stuart, *Reminiscences* (London: Chiswick Press, 1911) 195-6. Also LH II.184-6.
[158] "Mill On Religion". The date of the manuscript is inconclusive.

to understand the true nature and modality of religious influences. Mill had resolved them into a fear of, and hope for, future consequences, and argued that authority, early education and public opinion were the efficient cause of moral behaviour.[159] These were important, Lightfoot conceded, but secondary. Experience showed that moral aspirations and the sense of obligation and shame originate within, independently of external causes. Religious motivation was to be understood as the operation of five influences: a sense of living in the presence of a perfectly righteous power; the inspiration arising from the opportunity to cooperate with this power; the sense that actions have an eternal value; the conviction of shame and degradation which results from disloyalty to this power; and the stimulus to gratitude and affection from the assurance that the righteous power is boundless love.[160] Thus the religious consciousness was irreducible, producing, not produced by, moral utility. Lightfoot concluded:

> I know that even though I am not as good as my neighbour Z, I shall be very far worse than I am without religion. And this is to me a gauge of its moral utility. Assuming that I represent the average of men, I have only to multiply its influence so many times over to form a rough estimate of what its value is or might be to mankind.[161]

It was this power of elevating society, and for transforming history, that would be discarded if Mill had his way. Intuitionist ethics, not the utilitarian alternative, remained the condition of historical progress.

While this first point was fundamental, a second was no less important. From Coleridge, Mill had learned the importance of the concrete, and thus the value of the testimony of history.[162] But his contact with Lightfoot's own tradition produced a result he could not accept. When the "Utility of Religion" argued that the power of Greek and Roman morality was not religious, it propounded an ambiguity that had no place in Lightfoot's unitary conception of ancient religious history. At stake was not only the propaedeutic role assigned to Greece and Rome in the theology of history, but the theology itself, with its corollary that the connection between religion and morality was a universal truth. This was why Lightfoot felt impelled to say, "His appeals to history are unsatisfactory, and may in many cases be turned against himself".[163] In neither the Greek popular religion nor that of philosophy was social and individual morality independent of religion, as Mill had argued. Certainly the power of the idea of Rome in the years down to the Late

---

[159] J.S. Mill, "Utility of Religion," *Essays on Ethics, Religion and Society* (The Collected Works of John Stuart Mill X; J.M. Robson ed.; Toronto: University Press, 1969) 403 ff.

[160] "Mill On Religion," 7-11.

[161] *Ibid.*, 11.

[162] M. Mandelbaum, *History, Man and Reason. A Study in Nineteenth Century Thought* (Baltimore & London: Johns Hopkins Press, 1971) 164-7, 430 n. 10.

[163] "Mill On Religion," 2. Cf. *ibid.*, 12-19.

Republic was undeniable, but this was entirely due to its theological character. In both Greek and Roman history, Lightfoot added as a matter of his
own observation, a decline in religious belief was accompanied by a decline
in the highest forms of political and social morality. There was little to be
gained, too, by ranging Marcus Aurelius against Christ as an instance of a
non-theological morality since in his own way Aurelius was a decidedly
religious man. With the religious dimensions of Greek and Roman morality
restored, secular ethics had failed to establish the case for severing the connection between religion and morality. The theology of history had demonstrated its importance.

Although more accurate, Lightfoot's reading of the history of morality
was clearly no less tendentious than Mill's. The inference from history of
the "Utility of Religion", that supernatural religion was unnecessary for social purposes, implied that Christianity was no longer important in the making of English society, and thereby denied the social role of the Church of
England and rendered otiose the function Lightfoot assigned to himself as a
clergyman.[164] Behind this challenge were the Saint-Simonian historical stages
which identified the present as a "critical" age and set Mill on his course as
a reformer in the world, attempting at this point (albeit posthumously) to
establish the religion of humanity as a sufficient moral framework for human life.[165] His own Christian developmentalism vindicated by the appeal
to history, Lightfoot contended that Mill confronted society with a dilemma
in which the wrong choice would mean the voluntary relinquishment of the
principle of social progress. While in common with liberal Anglicans generally Lightfoot urged adjustments to Christianity in England, he stood against
Mill the reformer as a religious conservative. Taking his stand on history as
the "increasing purpose of God", he insisted that English society needed not
to be set free from Christianity, but brought more under its influence. Progress
would continue, not with the demise of Christianity and its morality, but
with its continued realization. The battle for the past was the battle for England's future.

The background to Lightfoot's concern to secure the use of history in
contemporary England was the place assigned to his own country in the
scheme of "the increasing purpose". He was, as Sanday observed, "English
to the backbone",[166] and proud of England's achievement.[167] He also knew

---

[164] Mill, "Utility of Religion," 417.
[165] J.S. Mill, *Autobiography* (with an Introduction by C.V. Shields; New York: Liberal
Arts Press, 1957) 105-7.
[166] Sanday, "Lightfoot as an Historian," 214.
[167] S 157-8; OA 183-4; SSO 248-50.

its history well and could work it up as occasion required.[168] National pride was instructed by the contemporary historians of England, most notably Macaulay,[169] but also Stubbs and Freeman. From their narratives he obtained not only the outline of the English story, but also a conception of English history as the realization of national genius and the evolution of freedom through the development of the constitution.[170] Such a view was easily harmonized with the organic framework of the "increasing purpose", as the underlying Burkean traditionalism had also been absorbed into the Coleridgean tradition of which Lightfoot was a part. His own assimilation of it is indicated by his use of the expression "from precedent to precedent" to describe both the continuity of the growth of English freedom and the pattern of revelation.[171] It was also evident in the exaltation of the thirteenth century as the time when "we have the germ of the England of our own age" and to which "we trace the beginning alike of our parliamentary institutions & the beginning of our scientific conquests, the beginnings of the Reformation in the Church & of the Revival of Learning which we generally connect with the age of the Reformation".[172] But it was not only a fresh illustration and reinforcement of Lightfoot's larger historical viewpoint. In that it held together belief in continuity with faith in progress, and thereby simultaneously allowed and controlled change by confining it within tradition, it commended a strategy for the management of pressure for reform. The continuity of English history was a weapon for use in the debate with the advocates of radical social change.

This is clear from the important adaptation Lightfoot made to the Whig view. In the Whig understanding, it was the constitution that caused the progress of the English nation. In Lightfoot's, it was not the constitution but Christianity and the Church. For he insisted that the moral and spiritual life of England was interpenetrated by the Christian tradition, so that, as he told one group of the English people, "All that is highest & best in you is shaped & coloured by its lessons".[173] The decisive time for this seminal influence was the period of Christian beginnings in England when the Church made two important contributions to the life of the nation.[174] One was the spirit of

---

[168] Eg. HE 93-181 & "England Six Hundred Years Ago". Cf. SSO 25-6, 30-2, 106-10; SSP 35 (with f. 9 of the MS); LNC *passim*; Inaugural Address,' 1886, *passim*.

[169] "our brilliant historian and essayist": SSO 26.

[170] IP 15; MSL 11-18; Attracting Power, 1874, 1-3; "England Six Hundred Years Ago," 4; SSO 212-13, 244-5, 249.

[171] Attracting Power, 1874, 3; S 157; SSO 106.

[172] England Six Hundred Years Ago, 4.

[173] Attracting Power, 1874, 5-7, esp. 6.

[174] On this period in general, see G.W. Bonner, "Religion in Anglo-Saxon England," in *Religion in England* (S. Gilley & W.J. Sheils eds; Oxford & Cambridge, Massachusetts: Blackwell, 1994) 24-44.

independence received from the Celtic missionaries which became the hallmark of the English people.[175] The other was the achievement of the unity of the Church out of which the unity of the state arose.[176] The tension between them — at the Synod of Whitby in 664 the Church had come under the authority of Rome — was mitigated by the Church of England's being "the least enslaved of all the Churches" during the period of the Roman domination.[177] In any case, this was but an opportunity for English independence to assert itself at the Reformation.[178] Since then the Church had grown with the growth of the English people, but this was not to conceal the fact that the longevity of the nation was due "in no slight measure to the forward, hopeful gaze of Christianity, the optimism of the Gospel".[179] History suggested that the national well-being and mission required Christianity and the Church at the heart of its corporate life.[180]

This is ultimately what was at stake for Lightfoot in urging the theology of history as a major cultural resource in contemporary England. On one front, he pressed the efficacy of history in the incarnational scheme upon Churchmen to equip them to realize in their own day the Church's true nature and to achieve its proper spiritual and moral leadership in society. On a broader front, he was concerned that the English people were in danger of squandering the inheritance of many centuries of Christian commitment. His concern for the nation's place in God's "increasing purpose", and his prescription for securing it, show finally that Lightfoot does not belong to the 'common sense' paradigm of historical thinking, despite his commitment to the value of facts and the outwardly positivist nature of his scholarly writing. Mill's teaching about religion and ethics indicates the direction in which that mode of thought was heading, and others who had been inspired by him — men such as Leslie Stephen and John Morley — were hard at work taking the utilitarian-empiricist tradition where it could go.[181] Against their relegation of Christianity to the status of a relic left over from an earlier phase of human development, Lightfoot held up a theory of history that enabled him to defend the viability of Christianity and its fundamental place in English society without rejecting any of the legitimate elements of contemporary culture. He took his stand in this 'contest for cultural authority' as a Christian idealist with a theology of history that used the notions of progress and

---

[175] SSO 212-14. LNC 11-14.

[176] LNC 15, 61.

[177] LNC 52.

[178] "... though the strong will of the reigning sovereign was the active agent, yet it was the independent spirit of the clergy and people which rendered the change possible." LNC 52-3.

[179] SSO 243, 244.

[180] See on this point in detail in Chapter 9 below.

[181] See von Arx, *Progress and Pessimism*, ch. 2 & 4.

organic growth according to law to affirm the necessity of his religion as the condition of national well-being and advancement. While Oxford trained liberal Anglicans such as Matthew Arnold and T.H. Green endeavoured to develop an ethic no longer tied to revelation, Lightfoot stuck much closer to the received Christian tradition in the belief that the programme of action required by its incarnational structure would enable Christianity to emerge the victor in the present crisis of Christian civilization in England, as it had emerged the victor in earlier struggles. The part he assigned himself in this process is the measure of the importance of denying he had a theory of history. Without it, how Lightfoot understood his life purpose and the means of achieving it remains hidden and his work as a Churchman and scholar goes unexplained. For, in both spheres, with the model of the Gospel householder before him, Lightfoot took up the "great work" of the age, the reconciliation of past and present, as his own contribution towards realizing the "increasing purpose of God" in contemporary England.

Part III

History as Ideology:
The Use of History as a Churchman

Lightfoot's thinking about history, it emerges, was rooted in national consciousness. While its bases were theological, it came to expression out of a concern to secure the well being of the English community and the effectiveness of the Church. In its embodiment of ideas that involved a broad plan for society and furnished means for putting it into effect, the interest of the theology of history was, therefore, practical rather than speculative. In promoting it, Lightfoot aimed to engender progressive action that would secure the future of Christian England and realize her place in God's "increasing purpose". Along this front where belief passed into social action in the interests of the Church and nation, 'history' as theology became ideology.[1]

Although he never used the word, it was always Lightfoot's intention that the theology of history should be ideological in this sense. While largely abstracted for purposes of identification and analysis, it was developed and came to expression in particular localities and situations for specific ends as he played his part on "the stage of this world's history" through an active career in the Church. Its summons to action was directed to the men and women who, he believed, were intended to be the means by which God would achieve His purpose in Lightfoot's own day. For himself this was a natural extension of his life's work of purveying "truth in theology" as a recognized Church scholar and teacher. As an historically conscious individual, he was bound to bring the theology of history as God's "increasing purpose" before the people of England to enable them to rise to their historic responsibility. In doing so, Lightfoot rose to his.

The way in which his theorising about history influenced him at the level of history lived and made is not a matter that has previously engaged the attention of scholars. Apart from anything else, this is due to the general neglect of his career in the Church in favour of his work on the history and literature of incipient Christianity. However, it is being recognized increasingly that a proper critical appreciation even of this scholarship requires

---

[1] On which, see the helpful account of M. Goldie, "Ideology," *Political Innovation and Conceptual Change* (ed. T. Ball *et. al.*; Cambridge: University Press, 1989) 266-91.

reference to the context of the contemporary Church.[2] Certainly it is a reasonable expectation that the affairs of the Church had some effect on the scholarship, and that (reciprocally) the scholarship had some bearing on the affairs of the Church.[3] The fact is that for some thirty years Lightfoot occupied key ecclesiastical positions and was close to the main sources of power and influence in the Church. This took him into the domain of social action with its perennial competition for power, influence and scarce resources. This, moreover, was as a leading representative of an institution older than the nation itself which had always to reckon with tradition and the continuing effects of the past. While a full account of Lightfoot's career as a Churchman must await a proper biography, his use of history in this sphere is the second trajectory through his life taken by the investigation.

The means of doing so is an examination of his life and work at those points where Lightfoot engaged in the "great work" of the day, at Cambridge University and St Paul's Cathedral in London, in the diocese of Durham, and before the wider Church of England. In all of these settings the way in which history functioned ideologically needs to be exhibited. This will require considering in turn what use Lightfoot made of both his general framework of interpretation and specific historical knowledge in each sphere of his involvement, and what he hoped to achieve by it. On this basis, larger questions about Lightfoot's life and thought can be answered. What was the precise nature of the ideology he followed? In his commitment to both change and continuity, was he in practice more conservative or liberal? What kind of a Churchman did this make him? Establishing the applications of his historical understanding in relation to specific situations explains much about Lightfoot's own aspirations and praxis in his career as a clergyman of the Church of England, and also furnishes something of the explanation for the remarkable influence he exercised among his contemporaries.

---

[2] One of the strengths of the recent Lightfoot Centenary Lectures is this recognition of the importance of "Lightfoot as Victorian Churchman" (the title of David Thompson's contribution). While there is only a minimal attempt to integrate the ecclesiastical and scholarly careers, this confirms the change in the direction of interpretation anticipated by Barrett and Kaye in the early 1980s. See Chapter 1 above.

[3] It is this reciprocal effect that is in view in Part III. The role of the Church in Lightfoot's scholarship is considered in Part IV below.

Chapter Seven

"The Spiritual Power of the Nineteenth Century": The University and History

After early hesitation Lightfoot decided to stay at Cambridge where he remained for all but the final ten years of his life.[1] The thirty years of his residence coincided with the most significant period in the history of the University since Newton as its curriculum and governing regulations underwent extensive modification and the research ideal first came into prominence.[2] The full extent of Lightfoot's participation in these developments is concealed by a political style which preferred to disguise individual influence in the corporate responsibility of committees.[3] Yet such was his role that Westcott once remarked, "I wish there was some adequate record of his part in University affairs".[4] Wilson's thesis attempted to fill this gap, but it is vitiated by a failure to place Lightfoot's efforts in the twin contexts of his general idea of the University, and of contemporary debate about the function of the ancient universities in the life of the Church and English society at large.[5] Only within this wider framework is it possible to understand his Cambridge career and appreciate the way in which he balanced the claims of the University's past and the needs of its present in contributing to the "great work" of the day. It also brings into clear focus the function assigned to specifically historical thinking and training at the University.

---

[1] For his indecision, see 48-50 above.

[2] Roach, "University of Cambridge," 136. For Lightfoot's own awareness, see CS 319-20.

[3] G.F. Browne, *Recollections of a Bishop* (London: Smith, Elder and Co., 1915) 132.

[4] B.F. Westcott, "Preface," in BL ix. Hort too commented on Lightfoot's influence at Cambridge following a visit in 1867. LH II.88-9. See also the enthusiasm in passing of O. Chadwick, *Westcott and the University* (Cambridge: University Press, 1963).

[5] Wilson, "Life," ch. II.

For the whole of Lightfoot's time at Cambridge the traditional idea of the university was under attack.[6] In his first year, the long-standing condemnation of narrow and allegedly useless curricula, which had called forth the theory of a liberal education as an *ex post facto* justification of existing educational practice, led to the introduction of a few new subjects.[7] But this was not enough. Continued allegations of failure to provide intellectual leadership and of misdirection of resources engendered the Royal Commissions of the 1850s which asked unsettling questions about whose interests the Universities were meant to serve. The resultant reforms initiated a change to the *status quo*, but did not dislodge the received view according to which the Universities were part of the Church, with the function of educating the clergy and the nation's social elite in Christian discipline and morality.[8] As the nation continued to call Oxbridge to account in the 1860s and 1870s, it was asked increasingly whether the remaining arrangements that supported the Anglican monopoly should be allowed to continue. Attempts to find the answer to this question provided the background against which Lightfoot's Cambridge career unfolded.

I

Implicit in his conduct as one of the "new breed" of tutors, and his continuing unwillingness on moral grounds to seek a career at the University, was not only a dissatisfaction with Cambridge as it was, but also an incipient vision of what it might be — a place "where fresh accessions of knowledge are gathered ... by the renewed importunity and incessant zeal of the student"; and, through work, "forming habits in a man ... bracing him and nerving him for the serious business of life".[9] This combination of an intellectual and moral function identified Lightfoot from the first with the wider community aspiration for the ancient Universities — that they be useful to the whole of English society — and the dilemmas about how to achieve it within the framework of the Anglican monopoly and the theory of a general

---

[6] See the older accounts of L. Campbell, *On the Nationalization of the Old English Universities* (London: Chapman & Hall, 1901); & A.I. Tillyard, *A History of University Reform From 1800 to the Present* (Cambridge: W. Heffer & Sons, 1913); Winstanley, *Early Victorian Cambridge* and *Late Victorian Cambridge*. More recently, see M. Sanderson (ed.), *The Universities in the Nineteenth Century* (London and Boston: Routledge & Kegan Paul, 1975); & Heyck, *Transformation*, ch. 3, 6.

[7] See Chapter 3 above & P.R.H. Slee, *Learning and a Liberal Education. The Study of Modern History in the Universities of Oxford, Cambridge and Manchester 1800-1914* (Manchester: University Press, 1986) ch. 1.

[8] For their role in educating the clergy, see Haig, *Victorian Clergy*, ch. 2.

[9] Curse, 1860, 9, 21. Cf. f. 20. "The hard workers are the few, the idle and the listless are the many. It does not require a long term of residence here to learn this sad truth."

liberal education.[10] Within a few years of his appointment as a professor he had responded with an idea of the University which assigned it a place of real importance in the life of the nation, and, by balancing the pressure for change with the need for continuity, had overcome his earlier reluctance to remain there.

Apart from the Royal Commissions of the 1850s, Lightfoot's understanding of what Cambridge might achieve for the Church and English society was sharpened in the first instance by increasing involvement in the administrative side of University life.[11] Throughout the 1860s and 1870s he continued to serve on the Council of the Senate and numerous syndicates and boards of studies. From this vantage point Lightfoot not only saw the full range of University business, but was also aware of the occasional requests coming in from beyond Cambridge that indicated how the country thought the University might serve its educational needs. In this strategic position, Hort recalled, Lightfoot supported whatever promoted the usefulness of the University.[12]

The decisive influence on Lightfoot's hopes for Cambridge, however, was appointment to the Hulsean Chair. A few months afterwards he was still critical of the general tone of the University, but from 1864 lack of moral purpose and commitment to study were seen more as dangers to be avoided.[13] The brighter outlook also showed in correspondence to Westcott.[14] On one occasion Lightfoot defended the quality of the "best men" at the Universities; and on another, protested against allegations of "Cambridge degeneracy", claiming that it was "much more active and stirring in most respects, than I have ever known it before".[15] The outcome of this new estimate was "a passionate devotion" to the University, which impelled him to turn down Lord Derby's offer of the See of Lichfield in 1867.[16] Defending the decision to Bishop Tait, who had strongly urged him to accept, Lightfoot confessed:

---

[10] *Report of the Commissioners appointed to inquire into the state, discipline, studies and revenues of the University and colleges of Cambridge; together with the evidence, and an appendix and index (Graham Commission).* 1852-3, xliv, esp. 24-7, 31-7, 153-5, & 209-11. See also Heyck, *Transformation*, ch. 6; & Slee, *Learning*, ch. 1.

[11] See 45 above.

[12] DNB XI.1113. In 1866 he himself extolled Whewell's "keen interest in University progress". CS 119. Cf. 120-1.

[13] Priesthood, 1862, 29-32. Morning, 1864, 17-18.

[14] Westcott was reliant on Lightfoot for University intelligence. "You know the state of Cambridge now far better than I do." Westcott to Lightfoot, 20 November 1867.

[15] Lightfoot to Westcott, 12 May 1863; & 7 June 1865 (LAC). He seems to have made a similar defence to Hort. Hort to Lightfoot, 24 June 1865, in LH II.36-7.

[16] The quotation is from Lightfoot to Cooke, 5 May 1875 ("Lady Margaret Professorship. 1875," Box 2).

my ideal of life has been to spend my best energies in the service of Cambridge, which
I love dearly, thinking that in so doing I might in my own way be serving my Master ...
I can hardly explain how very strongly I feel the importance of working at Cambridge
at the present time. I have a certain belief in the capabilities of Cambridge, which I can
scarcely expect Oxford men to enter into. I want to see it great and strong and energetic, as it ought to be and as it might be.[17]

It was this sense that the ends he had earlier wished to serve, first as a schoolmaster, and then as a parochial clergyman, could be realized at Cambridge,
that caused Lightfoot in the early 1860s to transfer to the University his
career aspirations, with all that this implied about its wider social function.

Although he came to this high estimate of Cambridge life independently,
it was transmuted into a specific ideal through his association with Westcott,
who, by Lightfoot's remonstrances and achievement, was converted from
an earlier diffidence.[18] After supporting his friend's rejection of Lichfield
to Tait, Westcott added:

This conviction is further strengthened by the belief which is forced upon me more
strongly every day, that the only effectual organization of a spiritual power for the
immediate future is at the University. I do not think that the Clergy as a corporation
can organize it. Therefore I believe that the success which Dr Lightfoot has achieved
is a vantage ground which ought not to be abandoned.[19]

Westcott proceeded to proselytize:

Benson spent Sunday with us ... I tried to make him see the true relative positions of
Cambridge and Lichfield. He had not realized that the former must be the seat of the
spiritual power of the nineteenth century.[20]

Although others away from Cambridge came to share the vision in this way,
they looked to Lightfoot to lead the effort to make the ideal a reality because
of the position he already occupied. Almost a year later, Westcott wrote:

I am longing to think uninterruptedly about the "spiritual power" which is to be organized at Cambridge. You must come to Langland to be made pontiff.[21]

---

[17] Lightfoot to Tait, 22 November 1867 (TPL, vol. 83, f. 266). For an account of
Lightfoot's refusal of the offer, and an assessment of his position in Cambridge at the
time, see LH II.88-9. Lightfoot's view was not unqualified. He regretted decline in moral
earnestness. Lightfoot to Westcott, 15 February 1868 (LAC).
[18] Westcott sounded like Lightfoot himself when he said, "I have unbounded faith in
& love for Cambridge". Westcott to R. Payne Smith, 2 December 1870 (BLO,
MS.Eng.lett.d.171, f. 211).
[19] Westcott to Tait, 23 November 1867 (TPL, vol. 83, f. 247).
[20] Westcott to Lightfoot, 22 January 1868. Cf. Benson to Lightfoot, 23 November
1867.
[21] Westcott to Lightfoot, 1 August 1868, in LW I.294. When thinking about the possibility of his returning to Cambridge, Westcott wrote: "whatever the result, may it only be
for the furtherance of the one great cause which *we* have at heart. To serve this is all *we*
must ask, and what *we* shall surely gain - ἐπεκτεινόμενοι." [trans.: "stretching forward to",
probably an allusion to Philippians 3:13. The emphases in the quotation are mine]. Westcott
to Lightfoot, 3 October 1870. Cf. Westcott to Lightfoot, 1 November 1870, in LW I.366.

The results of this thinking were expounded publicly soon afterwards by Westcott in characteristically rarefied prose.[22] By implication the opposite and complement of the state, or "temporal power", the Church existed as "the spiritual power" to bring to the transient wants of the day the abiding concerns of religion and morality. It did so by presenting religion in its human and divine bearings, for the concentration and guidance of the desires and aspirations of men and women.[23] Cambridge, as an arm of the Church, was uniquely fitted by its social organization and studies to lead opinion and conduct in this way. Three attitudes — "the relativity of all human developments", "the catholicity of study", and "the spiritual destination of every personal effort" — needed to be taught in order to mediate the meaning of revelation for every day life.[24] The immediate object of this teaching was the elite, briefly gathered together at Cambridge as students during the most impressionable period of their lives.[25] From this teaching and the social influences of the University they stood to gain "a lofty ideal of duty", "an enthusiasm for right and truth", and "a vital sense of a Divine Spirit animating all labour".[26] As graduates they would go forth to their place in society, transmitting these beliefs and values to the rest of the community by teaching and example, while their influence would secure the embodiment of the faith in conceptions of national and religious policy. In this way the work of the University would reach its ultimate object, the nation, and education in the true meaning of revelation pass into life.[27]

This was no fully blown theory of the University: certainly it was vague about specific means and secondary ends. But, as a general conception, it drew together the main elements of the outlook Lightfoot espoused but never expressed systematically. This is signified at once by his like understanding of the University as a Church within the Church.[28] Westcott's three cardinal truths were repeated in the obligation of the fleeting individual to contribute to the progress of the wider society;[29] the connection between faith and all

---

[22] Primarily in B.F. Westcott, "The Universities as a Spiritual Power," a Sermon Preached on 15 December 1868, at the Commemoration of Benefactors in the Chapel of Trinity College, Cambridge, in *On Some Points in the Religious Office of the Universities* (London: Macmillan, 1873) 45-76. Cf. vi-vii. The title suggests a general treatment, but both the occasion and the content indicate that Westcott had Cambridge in mind. See also Chadwick, *Westcott and the University, passim.*

[23] Westcott, *Religious Office*, 80, 128-9.

[24] *Ibid.*, 56.

[25] *Ibid.*, 69-70.

[26] *Ibid.*, 73.

[27] *Ibid.*

[28] Eg. CS 260.

[29] CP 19-20. Sonship, 1864, 27. CS 113-21.

branches of human thought established by the Logos;[30] and the emphasis
upon personal devotion, moral purpose, and self-sacrifice.[31] A similarly high
estimate of the intellectual and moral formation of the nation's rising leadership elite was conveyed through an almost mystical attitude towards the
possibilities for the future of the period of early adulthood at Cambridge.[32]
Westcott's evaluation of the importance of this elite for society was reproduced in the claim that,

> you, the students of this University are missionaries by force of circumstances, mis-
> sionaries despite yourself. Year by year, as you go hence, you carry into all depart-
> ments of life, the traditions and habits of this place.[33]

Through them the educational work of Cambridge would be a continuing
force for the renewal of the inner life of the community from which its outward actions flowed. While neither he nor Westcott appreciated (Jowett-
like) the opportunities created by the opening of the civil service,[34] Lightfoot
also looked for the transformation of undergraduates into responsible leaders in public life.[35] Even in the one area of divergence there was substantial
agreement. According to Westcott the work of the University for national
unity was done through its social arrangements.[36] Lightfoot looked more to
its intellectual activity which, holding together religion and life, and faith
and knowledge, promised to avert the fissure between the Church and society evident elsewhere in Europe.[37] In its pervasive emphasis upon commit-
ting the self to the common good, and the institution to the nation, Westcott
and Lightfoot's was still not only a service ideal, as opposed to the commitment to research coming into vogue, but one grounded in the ideology of the
"increasing purpose" perspective.

Apart from the influence of Westcott, there were two main impulses to
this outlook in Lightfoot's thinking. One was university history, of which
he appears to have had an intimate knowledge.[38] The university as an "intellectual light" was anticipated by ancient Athens and Alexandria, and by
Renaissance Florence.[39] In the thirteenth century the British universities

---

[30] I. St Paul's Teaching, 1858, 31-2. CP 23.
[31] CP 19-20. Priesthood, 1862, 29-32.
[32] I. St Paul's Teaching, 1858, 33-4. CS 148-9. SSO 6, 19-20. Vision, 1877, 38-40.
[33] I Ascend, 1880, 33.
[34] See E. Abbott and L. Campbell, *The Life and Letters of Benjamin Jowett* (2 vols; 2nd ed.; 2 vols; London: John Murray, 1897) II.ch. 5; & Hinchliff, *Jowett*, 36, 193.
[35] Stir Up, 1863, 9-10. CS 30-1. Divided Allegiance, 1866, 24-5.
[36] Westcott, *Religious Office*, viii-ix, 10-13.
[37] SSO 143-4.
[38] Lightfoot's *Address On the Distribution of Scholarships and Prizes ... in ... Liver-pool* in 1879 evinces a knowledge of the Universities of Leyden, Athens, Florence, Paris, Oxford and Cambridge. Also HE 155-69 & LNC 109-19.
[39] LA 18.

had been in the vanguard of intellectual progress, and also provided education to all comers, irrespective of station in life.[40] During the Reformation
Cambridge had guided England through a crisis of intellectual and religious
change similar to that of the present.[41] The relation of faith and thought had
already been developed by the "many bright examples" of a combination of
the "highest scientific intellect" with "absolute childlike faith",[42] while the
task of co-ordinating the different branches of knowledge was illustrated
recently by the history of King's College, London.[43] Models of the influence of alumni on English society were furnished not only by the many who
had risen to positions of political, social and intellectual eminence, but also
by lives of devotion and self-sacrifice, such as those of recent missionaries,
Henry Martyn, Charles MacKenzie and John Coleridge Patteson.[44] The call
of Ignatius Loyola to Francis Xavier at the University of Paris provided data
for answering the question, "Where else but in a famous university should
the keenest and best instruments for a great religious movement be found?"[45]
Closer to home, and nearer in time, Lightfoot pointed to Wesleyanism and
Tractarianism at Oxford, and the Evangelical movement at Cambridge, "all
of them incalculably important factors in the spiritual history of the Eng-
lish-speaking race, all of them cradled in our great Universities as their nurs-
ery".[46] The possibilities suggested by the idea of "the spiritual power" received their warrants and impetus partly from what had been achieved typically in the past.

Second, this notion of "the spiritual power" itself was neither new nor
without currency. A mediaeval concept, it was now resurgent in a secularized
form in the thought of the French positivists whom Westcott was reading at
the time of his correspondence with Lightfoot about the state of Cambridge.[47]
There was also ample English precedent in talk about the Universities as the
home of a spiritual power against a background of social and ecclesiastical
strife in the 1830s and 1840s, and more particularly in Coleridge's concept
of the clerisy.[48] Taking the Church as his model, he had conceived of an
intellectual establishment which would purify and revivify the nation by

[40] HE 159-60, 161, 166-9. LA 19-21.
[41] HE 156.
[42] CS 305.
[43] SSO 138-45. Cf. LNC 110-16.
[44] CP 22. SSO 47-9.
[45] OA 273-4, 275-6. Cf. SSO 48; I Ascend, 1880, 32-3.
[46] OA 275. Cf. 48-9.
[47] B.F. Westcott, "Comte on the Philosophy of the History of Christianity," *Contem-porary Review* VI (1867) 399-421, esp. 406-7, 412, 415-16; "Aspects of Positivism in Relation to Christianity," *ibid.* VIII (1868) 371-86; and *Religious Office*, 54. H.B. Acton, *The Idea of a Spiritual Power* (London: Athlone Press, 1974) 8-9.
[48] See B. Knights, *The Idea of the Clerisy in the Nineteenth Century* (Cambridge: University Press, 1978) ch. 2, esp. 63-71 & 181-4.

presenting its findings in terms of morality and religion. While developed quite specifically by some, the clerisy ideal was more influential in the generalized missionary function assigned to the educated by the liberal Anglicans, and in the idea of a liberal education at the Universities, notions which were often held together in the thinking of the same men. According to the latter, the University sent out young men especially trained to serve society. The view frequently expressed before the Royal Commission of 1850-2 as an alternative to the ultra-conservative idea that the role of the University was to transmit the doctrines of Christianity, it provided the rationale of those more liberal-minded conservatives who sought to maintain the relation between Cambridge and the Church at the same time as strengthening the relation between the Church and the nation.[49]

Although well read in Coleridge and the liberal Anglicans, it was in this latter mode that the idea was likely to have made its deepest impact on Lightfoot. His Trinity mentors were among its leading theorists, while the consequences of the 1850 Royal Commission dominated the life of Trinity College for the remainder of the decade.[50] This accounts for the somewhat conventional appearance of his outlook. Indeed, neither he nor Westcott made any claim to novelty. The task as they saw it was, through adaptation and variation, to make the present day reality correspond more closely to an old ideal. For understanding Lightfoot's Cambridge career this is the important point. A significant contemporary cultural and educational ideal was merged with his moral aspiration to provide personal reassurance and sense of direction. Through its work of education and research properly conducted, the University would be a key influence in the making of England's future. Its special responsibility was to ensure that nothing of value from the past was lost, that no unreasonable conservatism block desirable innovation, and that past, present and future be bound together in a oneness characterized by stablility and growth.[51] Thus the historical relations assigned to Cambridge placed the University, and Lightfoot himself, at a stategic point in English society for carrying out the great work of the age.[52] In a successful outcome he saw the answer to the spiritual crisis of England. For it provided the hope, justified historically by the case of Francis Xavier, of rekindling that power and influence which, in the future, "might change the face of society, might revive a Church or regenerate a nation".[53] In what it gave him to work towards, Cambridge as "the spiritual power" justified Lightfoot's decision

---

[49] Knights, *Clerisy*, ch. 6.
[50] See College Notices, vol. I (TCC).
[51] CS 148.
[52] For which, see 154 above.
[53] CS 61-2. Cf. Vision, 1877, 39.

to remain at the University, and defined the social significance of his activity as a clerical don.

During the 1860s participation in University affairs, discussion with Westcott, and consideration of historical precedent, directed Lightfoot's moral aspiration to an idealized view of Cambridge as a centre from which national leadership might emanate. As a result he shared in a larger movement to make the ancient Universities a force in English life, providing (with other members of the so-called Cambridge School) a specifically Christian rationale for the hope which, in line with the need of the day, was at once conservative and reformist. In effect it was a much needed programme for not only retaining but also revitalizing the traditional role of the University. As "the spiritual power of the nineteenth century", Cambridge would maintain its historic relation with the Church and, through it, the nation in a new age under changing circumstances to continue its contribution to the realization of God's "increasing purpose" in and for England. How this was to be done at a time of pressure for change can be traced best, in accordance with the Cambridge power structure, at the level of both the colleges and the University.

II

"Cambridge life," one contemporary observed, "is ... mainly college life; the University has not the corporate wealth, nor does it take the same constant energetic action, as the University of Oxford."[54] While this was a situation he hoped to modify, Lightfoot's first loyalty at Cambridge was to his College. Having continued as a resident Fellow and member of the Seniority after resigning the Tutorship in 1862,[55] it was not until he had done all that he could for Trinity that he finally accepted major ecclesiastical preferment elsewhere, with its unavoidable concomitant of loss of his Fellowship.[56] Lightfoot's devotion to the College was matched by its high estimate of him. As soon as he resigned new statutes were invoked to make him an honorary Fellow.[57] In this capacity Lightfoot remained a resident of Trinity until the end of his Cambridge days, promoting and protecting the College ideal.[58]

---

[54] F. Arnold, *Oxford and Cambridge* (London: R.T.S., 1873) 176. Cf. A.S. & E.M.S., *Henry Sidgwick*, 217 for the effect of college feeling in University matters.

[55] See the staff lists for Trinity in *The Cambridge University Calendar*, 1862-71.

[56] B.F. Westcott, "Prefatory Note," in BL x-xi. The same consideration influenced his decision not to seek the Regius Professorship of Divinity in 1870.

[57] W.H. Thompson to Lightfoot, 22 May 1872, reporting Lightfoot's unanimous election 'as a "Professor of the University" & a "person distinguished for literary merit".'

[58] For a general account of the idea of the college in contemporary Cambridge, see Rothblatt, *Revolution of the Dons*, ch. 7.

Although content to remain a junior member of a society dominated by
the Master, Vice Master and Bursar,[59] Lightfoot's own efforts to maintain
the college ideal began when he was still a Fellow. Change, he thought, was
unavoidable and "might avoid some of the scandals (real or imaginary) of
the present".[60] The real problem, however, was explained to Westcott:

> Our failings, it appears to me, are just those which no constitution will rectify. We
> want good men, not good machinery. Our present machinery, if it is a little rusty, is at
> least strong and goes well enough. Our grievance is that we lose our best men so fast,
> and I am afraid no change can be devised which will keep them up.[61]

It was on the all important matter of College personnel that Lightfoot made
his one significant contribution to the debates of the 1850s.[62]

When the reformers were given the opportunity to air their views, the
abolition of the requirement of celibacy on College Fellows was among the
proposals.[63] For a time it looked like they might succeed, for the Master
agreed that this could be a way of halting the admitted loss of teaching
power.[64] But when he retracted, David Vaughan accused him of vacilla-
tion.[65] With feelings running high on the eve of the next meeting of the
Governing Body, there was a need for a calm reconsideration of the matter
which Lightfoot sought to provide.[66]

At first sight exactly the kind of measure he might have been expected to
support, Lightfoot nevertheless upheld the *status quo*. No principle was

---

[59] See the accounts of Governing Body meetings in the diary of J. Romilly, University
Registrary (1832-1861) and a Fellow of Trinity (Add 6838-9, CUL). The Bursar was
Francis Martin (1802-1868).

[60] Lightfoot to Westcott, 6 November n.y. [1857 or 1858?] (LAC).

[61] Lightfoot to Westcott, 17 October 1856 (LAC).

[62] Wilson, "Life," 25, exaggerates Lightfoot's involvement by ascribing to him an
anonymous pamphlet of 1854 entitled *Notes on the Oxford University Bill in Reference to
the Colleges at Cambridge*. The author was Whewell, under whose name the pamphlet is
listed in the catalogues of the Wren and University Libraries at Cambridge. The mistaken
ascription is probably due to the occurrence of Lightfoot's name at the top of the front
page of one of the three copies at Trinity where Wilson claims to have read the pamphlet.
But Lightfoot's name, written in Whewell's distinctive hand, is followed by, "With the
Master's compliments". Winstanley, *Early Victorian Cambridge*, 50 n. 1, notes Lightfoot's
signature on a petition presented to the House of Lords in May 1855. This seems to have
been his earliest declaration of opinion.

[63] Report of the Committee, 9 June 1857, 4-6, 8-9 (Adv.c.16.57[10], TCC).

[64] W. Whewell, *Remarks on Proposed Changes in the College Statutes*, 23 September
1857, 4-5.

[65] W. Whewell, *Further Remarks on Proposed Changes in the College Statutes*, 18
October 1857, 1-2. D. Vaughan, *Remarks on the Master of Trinity's Second Paper*, 20
October 1857, 3-4.

[66] J.B. Lightfoot, *On the Celibacy Question*, 26 October [1857]. Whewell was grateful for Lightfoot's support and requested additional copies of the pamphlet. Whewell to
Lightfoot, 27 October 1857.

involved, since the prohibition on marriage was not absolute, and there were advantages in either state. Reduced to a question of expediency, no social benefit was guaranteed by the change. Rather, since married Fellows were to live outside, a conflict would arise between the College and family life from which one or other must suffer. Moreover, no successful precedent could be cited in favour of an innovation which would be irrevocable. Contrary to appearances, Lightfoot maintained, the end of celibacy would not secure the best teachers.

But his main contribution to the debate was the abandonment of the "family" analogy as representing the theory of the College. Instead, he claimed, it would be better to speak of a society in which the authority of the teacher as one of its members is exercised through continuous residence. Only on this basis was the special feature of the collegiate system — the close relations between Fellows and students — possible. It provided for the close supervision, example, and guidance through which the moral influence of the older men came to bear upon the undergraduates. This traditional disciplinary role, with its outcomes in character formation and educational efficiency, was now at stake, and while Lightfoot conceded the disparity between the ideal and the reality,[67] he asserted in its favour that "no one can deny that for some reason or other the system has worked well for many centuries".[68] Although Lightfoot might agree with the reformers about the cause of College ills, he could not accept a remedy of doubtful effectiveness purchased at the expense of the theory of the College bequeathed and endorsed by its history.[69]

But adherence to the received theory did not preclude reform. Possibly taking up a suggestion of the Royal Commissioners, or even looking to the model provided by University and King's Colleges, London, Lightfoot suggested as a corollary to his argument the creation of "a kind of college professoriate" not subject to restrictions of tenure.[70] The career structure thus provided was an alternative method of securing the alleged benefits of abolishing celibacy without at the same time weakening College discipline. Such a scheme not only promised the retention of the abler men, but the accompa-

---

[67] Pointed out by J. Ll. Davies, *The Proposed Conditions of Tenure of Fellowships in Trinity College*, 12 October 1857.

[68] Lightfoot, *Celibacy*, 8.

[69] On the traditional idea of the University, to which the role of the college was central, see Chadwick, *Westcott and the University*, 3-4. A similar blend of traditionalism and innovation is evident in the second cause Lightfoot championed, an increase in the number and value of Minor Scholarships. Untitled circulars of 17 & 31 March 1859 (College Notices, vol. I, TCC). He carried the point about the number, but not the value. Conclusion Book, 24 April 1860 (TCC).

[70] Lightfoot, *Celibacy*, 9-10. Rothblatt, *Revolution of the Dons*, 235, 321.

nying proposal that lecturers be appointed from inside and outside the circle of Fellows meant that a larger pool of men, some possibly of proven capacity, would be made available for "the higher teaching of the College".[71] It also had the advantage of neutralizing some proposals on the tenure of fellowships which threatened "to pour in upon the College a crowd of indolent or indifferent men".[72] Making Trinity a "mini-university" in this way was a change within the framework provided by the theory of the College which would promote further the all important consideration, "the reputation and prosperity of Trinity".[73]

In the following decade, by a similar willingness to allow some variation to the established approach, Lightfoot maintained this commitment to making the received idea of the College effective in his own day. Although no longer directly involved in the teaching, he continued to promote Trinity as a place of education by supporting the move to modernize the curriculum.[74] On the other hand, his contribution to the College as a place of moral formation — by word and example — was undiminished. Recognizing the need to recreate continually the College culture because of the annual flow of student arrivals and departures, Lightfoot repeatedly exalted its social organization as the means by which friendship and rivalry were brought to bear as the stimuli to loftier aspirations and greater moral exertion.[75] But central to his efforts to influence the character of other men at Trinity was the College chapel.

While Lightfoot expected larger views of human life and personal discipline to result from the formal studies of the College, direct Christian teaching and worship were required to fire the spirits of the undergraduates.[76] This was why he frequently urged the advantages of regular chapel attendance and stressed the value of daily early morning worship as an opportunity to dedicate each day to God.[77] Indifference in this matter jeopardized Trinity's larger work: "if this College is ever to rise to a sense of its highest

---

[71] Carried at a meeting of the Governing Body in November, 1857. Circular to Fellows, 28 October, & 6, 12, 20 & 26 November 1857 (College Notices, vol. I, TCC). Minutes of the Governing Body 1857-60, f. 39v. (TCC).

[72] Lightfoot to Westcott, 6 November [1858 ?] (LAC) where the two matters are juxtaposed.

[73] Trinity introduced a reform along these lines in 1870. Rothblatt, *Revolution of the Dons*, 235.

[74] In 1867 he supported the introduction of Natural Science teaching at Trinity (Letter to Fellows, 20 November 1867, in College Notices, vol. I, TCC).

[75] Stir Up, 1863 12, 14-16. Will He, 1869, 25-8. CS 190-2, 249-51, 260-3, 297-8, 307-8, 312-14, 319-26.

[76] Curse, 1860, 26-8. All, 1861, 20-2. Stir Up, 1863, 12. CS 60, 297-8, 307-8.

[77] CS 60-1, 208. Also Moule, *My Cambridge Classical Teachers*, 13.

mission, it must shake off this spiritual lethargy, and throw itself earnestly into this divine life".[78]

The Sunday sermon — still a rarity in the College chapels early in Lightfoot's Cambridge period —[79] was seen as a strategic opportunity to place their religious duties before the undergraduates. This was why in 1858 he (with 15 others) requisitioned the Trinity Seniority for a sermon every Sunday to obviate the abuse of undergraduates passing through the University without hearing a single sermon.[80] In addition to securing this important continuity in the life of the College, Lightfoot also took his place in a preaching roster for this purpose, so that the pulpit of the Trinity Chapel became the main platform from which he taught his characteristic incarnational version of Christianity.[81] It was important to establish this understanding locally, lest the men to whom Lightfoot looked to leaven English society left "the spiritual power" without an initiation into the true nature and practice of Christianity.

If the College Chapel was the place for transmitting right beliefs, Lightfoot ensured that sensitivity to the historical dimension of life was among them. Viewed Christianly, the all-important, organically conceived, idea of community was capable of chronological extension. It was this added perspective that permitted appreciation of its full meaning and implications for conduct, and inculcated in the undergraduates a true perspective on the self as part of the larger whole in time as well as space. At the Commemoration of Benefactors in 1860, Lightfoot reminded its members of the antiquity and nobility of the College, and of the progress that was the principle of its life.[82] The point was enforced by "historizing" the present and the future:

> Let us only carry our thoughts forward through a period of three or four centuries, and ask ourselves whether anything we have done in our generation, whether anything we are likely to do hereafter, may be expected to exert such important influence for good on this College, and through the College on the country at large, as the efforts made by those whom we this day commemorate are producing in our own age.[83]

By thus localizing the "increasing purpose", Lightfoot drew the College and its members into the larger movement of history. From identification with

---

[78] CS 61.

[79] Roach, "University of Cambridge," 250.

[80] Lightfoot (and nine, then fifteen others) to the Master and Seniors, n.d., Add.Ms.a.63[32-3], Bursar's Minutes. From 10 October, 1857 to 7 December, 1861, 43-6 (TCC).

[81] Lightfoot also preached regularly in Great St Mary's, the University Church, and in the numerous parish churches around Cambridge.

[82] CP, *passim*.

[83] *Ibid.*, 21.

this process would come a sense of personal importance, and a sharper understanding of duty to the College, and the society it was meant to serve.[84]

The traditional idea of the College was one of the influences leading to the definition of Cambridge as "the spiritual power of the nineteenth century", and in due course, adjusted to the circumstances of the day, it became a fundamental component of Lightfoot's developed university-ideal. Almost immediately, however, it was challenged by the attack on the Anglican monopoly of University and college government perpetuated by religious tests for fellowships and membership of the Senate. After dragging on for most of the 1860s, the controversy ended with the removal of these restrictions by the Universities Tests Act of 1871.[85]

Lightfoot's response to this matter is an interesting indication of how he responded to strong pressure for change which he himself did not like. While he favoured opening the University to non-Anglicans, initially he was unable to agree that the proposed change did not endanger the role of the colleges as the moral component of a Cambridge education.[86] With its capacity to promote "the spiritual power" thus under threat, he sided with the large body of opinion still in favour of the Tests, promoting in 1868 a petition to Parliament against their abolition.[87] One year later he was more sympathetic to the reform, although careful to distance himself from "the revolutionary party".[88] Lightfoot now conceded the unanswerable claim that the Tests deprived colleges of the services of able Nonconformists, to the detri-

---

[84] The same perspective was brought forward in the sermon preached at Whewell's funeral. For its general significance, see Chapter 6 above.

[85] For disputes over subscription earlier in the century, see Roach, "University of Cambridge," 239-40; & Brent, *Liberal Anglican Politics*, ch. 4. The episode of the 1860s & 1870s is chronicled by Campbell, *Nationalization*, ch. VIII; Winstanley, *Late Victorian Cambridge*, ch. III; Harvie, *Lights of Liberalism*, ch. 4; & C.N.L. Brooke, *A History of the University of Cambridge. Volume IV. 1870-1990* (Cambridge: University Press, 1993) 99-106.

[86] On Lightfoot's response to the Tests agitation, see Wilson, "Life," 83-5. The case against the Tests was summarized by G. Young, *University Tests*, 1868 (copy at Cam.c.868.6, CUL).

[87] See the flysheets in support of the Tests in the Cambridge University Papers C1 (1869-1889) (CUL). Winstanley, *Late Victorian Cambridge*, 42 notes Lightfoot's early opinion, but it is clearly dependent on his own statement in PP IX [1871] 163. However, see the letters of 1868 to Lightfoot by H. Alford (14 March); G.B. Airy (18 March); B.F. Westcott, H.W. Moss,. A.M. Harvey, J.P. Norris (19 March); & A. Barry (23 March). Lightfoot is not among the signatories of the petition of 13 May 1868 in favour of abolition reproduced in Young, *University Tests*, 42-7. Christopher Brooke's supposition that Lightfoot signed the 1868 petition in favour of abolition is unlikely to be correct. Brooke, *History*, 100.

[88] Lightfoot to Westcott, 9 March 1869 (LAC).

ment of their educational efficiency.[89] The close relation between educational and moral power gave some appeal to Westcott's somewhat unrealistic compromise proposal of a two-tiered system, only one tier of which should require Church membership and admit to college government.[90] Lightfoot was also prepared to acquiesce in Roundell Palmer's amendment to J.D. Coleridge's bill — that professors and other teachers declare that they would not express opinions contrary to the teaching of the Bible and Anglican Church (a negative test, in fact) — as something that might be achieved.[91] More flexible now as to method, Lightfoot still saw Cambridge as an arm of the Church of England.

It was about this time that Henry Sidgwick resigned his Trinity Fellowship, an act which evidently made a big impact on the University.[92] The class of action it represented brought Lightfoot to see that the Tests, while protecting the Church of England, were actually damaging the cause of Christianity itself. This in turn enabled him to appreciate the wisdom of Hort's line, that judicious concession would "keep our position as the standard 'denomination', though not as the exclusive one".[93] By the time Lightfoot appeared before the Parliamentary Select Committee in 1870, he was ready to acquiesce in the abolition of the Tests:

> it is not that my own religious opinions are at all changed, or that my opinions as to what is advisable in the abstract are changed, but having regard to the change of opinion around me, and seeing the dangers that attend the maintenance of the present state of things, I have arrived at the conclusion I have stated.[94]

Lightfoot's liberality in this matter has been praised,[95] but it did not come easily, and then only when something greater was at stake.

Yet, while allowing that the Tests should be abolished, he urged that adequate safeguards be incorporated into the legislation to retain the denominational character of the colleges. As the centre of the religious system, the College Head had to be a member of the Church of England, while the Anglican character and resources for chapel services had to be maintained. A limited reform of this kind, it was anticipated, would remove the causes for prejudice against Christianity, while retaining "the imperceptible every day influences" Lightfoot felt contributed most to the moral and religious for-

---

[89]   PP IX [1871] 183.

[90]   Westcott to Lightfoot, 9 March 1869.

[91]   Campbell, *Nationalization*, 155-6, 164. Winstanley, *Late Victorian Cambridge*, 63-5.

[92]   A.S. & E.M.S., *Henry Sidgwick*, 196-202, esp. 198 for Lightfoot's part in his deliberations. W.E. Heitland, *After Many Years. A Tale of Experiences & Impressions Gathered in the Course of an Obscure Life* (Cambridge: University Press, 1926) 145-6, 176-9.

[93]   LH II.94-5.

[94]   PP IX [1871] 168.

[95]   Chadwick, *Westcott and the University*, 14-15.

mation of undergraduate minds, and which produced an uninterrupted flow of Churchmen from Cambridge. Having conceded much to the reformers, he was not yet prepared for totally undenominational colleges.[96]

The problems stemming from the Cambridge power structure came to a head soon after the resolution of the Tests agitation. Increasingly among reformers the power and wealth of the colleges were seen as impediments to the further educational development of the University. Teaching and research would advance, it was argued, only if the colleges contributed to the expense, a suggestion from which they continually recoiled.[97] Their internal arrangements were also a problem. Celibacy was still a powerful disincentive to those who might otherwise aspire to a teaching career at Cambridge, while permanent fellowships and non-residence meant that resources were deflected from educational purposes. In 1877 doubt that the Universities could adequately reform themselves led the Government to establish a Statutory Commission, charged to secure improvements to learning and teaching by making provision for the colleges to contribute to University purposes, and requiring that fellowships and other college emoluments be attached to University offices, and that the tenure of fellowships not attached to such offices be reviewed.[98]

Appointment to the Commission presented Lightfoot with a dilemma.[99] Aspects of the collegiate system which he had previously supported now clashed with another ideal objective, the growing educational importance of the University.[100] According to its Secretary, Lightfoot was among those sympathetic to the needs which had called the Commission into being.[101] No doubt this attitude was continuous with the change evoked by the Tests agitation. Whatever he himself felt, Lightfoot was prepared to bow to the necessity imposed by change of circumstance and shifts of opinion at Cambridge and beyond. Certainly this was the case with the abolition of celi-

---

[96] For an observation on the deleterious effect on chapel attendance in the long term, see T.G. Bonney, *Memories of a Long Life* (Cambridge: Metcalfe and Co., 1921) 34-5.

[97] Roach, "University of Cambridge," 247-8, 254-5. Winstanley, *Early Victorian Cambridge*, 280.

[98] For the text of the "Universities of Oxford and Cambridge Act 1877 (40 & 41 Vict. c. 48)", and "Preliminary Statement of the Commissioners [20 February 1878]," see *Statutes for the University of Cambridge and for the Colleges Within It, Made, Published, and Approved (1878-1882) Under the Universities of Oxford and Cambridge Act, 1877* (H. Bradshaw ed.; Cambridge: University Press, 1883).

[99] A detailed account is made difficult by the failure of the Cambridge Commission to publish. Cf. the analysis of its Oxford counterpart in A.J. Engel, *From Clergyman to Don. The Rise of the Academic Profession in Nineteenth Century Oxford* (New York: Oxford University Press, 1983) ch. IV. Lightfoot's elevation to the episcopal bench meant that his later attendance was much disrupted. DNB XI.1113-14.

[100] See sect. III of the present chapter, 183-91 below.

[101] Browne, *Recollections*, 161.

bacy, which the Chairman, Lord Cockburn, opposed. His appeal to Lightfoot following Browne's summary of the objections to the change met with the reply: "There is a great deal in what our Secretary says. But we are here to do it, and do it we must".[102]

Possibly the same resignation did not apply to financial exactions from the colleges. Lightfoot drew up the questionnaire sent out in December 1877, to elicit information about the main needs of the University and the revenues to meet them, sources from which the money was to be raised, and methods by which college contributions were to be assessed.[103] If he felt any discomfort in these activities, he seems to have pressed on in the conviction that they were necessary in order to achieve an important reality in a time of change.[104]

As circumstances changed, Lightfoot had plainly judged — however reluctantly — that it was better for Cambridge to be Christian and national rather than Anglican and parochial. Yet, while moving with the times and accepting nationalization, his continued personal adherence to the older college ideal amid change was indicated by his enthusiastic support for the unpopular move to create Selwyn College.[105] When the project was initiated, he donated 500 pounds, not only to honour the hero of his early manhood, but also to retain a denominational college at Cambridge.[106] Although Selwyn was widely seen as an attempt to counter the effects of the Tests Act of 1871, this commitment owed nothing to regret at the enforced retreat of Christianity in the other colleges after the lifting of the legal barriers around the Church of England. In fact Lightfoot believed that Christianity at the University was stronger for the reform. Moreover, he maintained that it was important for the health of the faith of young Christians to interact with other opinions.[107] Yet Selwyn College would provide a place "where the principles of the Church of England might have free course; where the rule

---

[102] *Ibid.*

[103] Winstanley, *Late Victorian Cambridge*, 307-8. There are copies of the Commission's questionnaires dated 6 December 1877 & 28 February 1878 in the Cambridge University Papers C1 (1869-1889) (CUL).

[104] Brooke, *History*, 85-6, implies that by this time Lightfoot was also willing to give up the idea that heads of houses should have to be clergymen. But it is not clear whether Lightfoot was still attending meetings when the matter was decided. See Winstanley, *Late Victorian Cambridge*, 356-7, & DNB XI.1113-14.

[105] On the foundation of Selwyn College, see Roach, "University of Cambridge," 266; Rothblatt, *Revolution*, 240-1; & Brooke, *History*, 93-5. On the importance of Lightfoot for the venture, see W.R. Brock and P.H.M. Cooper, *Selwyn College. A History* (Edinburgh, Cambridge & Durham: Pentland Press, 1994) ch. 4, esp. 56. I owe this reference to Dr Brian Dickey of the Flinders University of South Australia.

[106] Speeches Delivered at Selwyn College, June 1, 1881 (Cam.a.500.6.116, CUL).

[107] LA 26.

of the students would be plain living and high thinking, and if God will, of high praying too".[108] It therefore preserved within reformed Cambridge the union of Anglicanism and learning — Lightfoot's preferred formula for moral education — alongside the voluntaryism which now characterized the collegiate system. A continuing link between the Church of England and the University, Selwyn College retained a remnant of what he had helped to dismantle.

Of course by this point Lightfoot had left the University. Following his departure, Christianity remained a strong force at Cambridge, and optimism about its prospects was possible.[109] However, the situation was changing rapidly, as the teaching force and ethos of the colleges were increasingly secularized.[110] Westcott and Hort kept Lightfoot informed, as he had earlier kept them in touch with Cambridge developments.[111] When he addressed the Oxbridge clerical dons in 1885 and 1887, the change in college life was practically the framework of his thinking.[112] Nevertheless, he still insisted that the college tutor was doing God's work, and that his was a pastoral duty ideally characterized by sympathy and self-giving.[113] Thus Lightfoot remained wedded to his essential outlook. For teacher and taught alike the college was still a place for promoting a better self, with all that this meant for the society beyond. But the emphasis was not on preserving, but on invigorating by adaptation to new circumstances, the idea of the college received over thirty years previously.[114] Lightfoot's abiding confidence in the contribution of the colleges to "the spiritual power of the nineteenth century" after nationalization was signified by his continuing to look to Oxbridge for graduates to staff the parishes of his own diocese. These men

---

[108] Speeches Delivered at Selwyn College, June 1, 1881 (Cam.a.500.6.116, CUL).

[109] "The Position and Prospects of the Church in Cambridge," *Church Quarterly Review* XIII (Oct. 1881-Jan. 1882) 180-204. Chadwick, *Victorian Church*, II.448-50.

[110] A. Haig, "The Church, the Universities and Learning in Later Victorian England," *The Historical Journal* 29.1 (1986) 187-201 (with the caveats of Brooke, *History*, 143-6). D. Newsome, *On the Edge of Paradise. A.C. Benson the Diarist* (Chicago: University Press, 1980). Roach, "University of Cambridge," 266-8. W. Jesse, "Cambridge in the 80s," *Cornhill Magazine* CLV (March 1937) 340-56 makes no mention of the religious side of college life in his recollections. A.E. Shipley & H.A. Roberts, "A Plea For Cambridge," *The Quarterly Review* CCV (April 1906) 499-525 overlooked both Theology and Christianity.

[111] Hort to Lightfoot, 29 October 1879; 12 December 1879; 3 February 1880; 1 March 1884. Westcott to Lightfoot, 24 November 1879; 19 & 29 January 1880; 28 July 1883; 20 & 29 November 1884.

[112] OA 223-4, 263-4, 276, 278.

[113] OA 221-4, 248, 254-7, 286-93, 311-12. See Engel, *Clergyman*, 262-3 for the attitude of the clerical don at the end of the century.

[114] OA 276-7, 279-80, 282, 312-13.

would now help to make the English community, as the college community had already helped to make them.[115]

III

The vision of Cambridge as "the spiritual power of the nineteenth century" required also that it be a specifically educational power. As with the college ideal, this was part of the theory Lightfoot had received as a young man. Sustained criticism over a generation had heightened awareness of the shortcomings of Cambridge in this respect, so that again the challenge he inherited was to make the everyday reality continuous with the theory. Already established as Hulsean Professor, Lightfoot pursued this aspect of his ideal at the level of the University. His efforts were complicated by changes to the theory itself under the impact of the vogue for research. On the other hand, they were greatly stimulated by the growing attack on the intellectual integrity of Christianity.

At one level Lightfoot's aspiration for Cambridge led to his continued support for efforts to widen its circle of influence, indirect as well as direct. Early in his career he took part in the scheme to stage examinations for middle class schools and advocated — unsuccessfully in the event — awarding a title as a way of binding English society more closely to Cambridge.[116] Subsequently he became an admirer of the university extension movement pioneered by James Stuart because it brought the University into contact with the commercial classes.[117] He also served on the 'University Expences [sic] Syndicate' set up in November 1867 to find ways "to cheapen the University education of poor students" and on the resultant Non-Collegiate Students' Syndicate because it promised to "open out quite a new field of University extension", particularly among middle class schools.[118] For the same

---

[115] OA 377-8.

[116] "Local Examinations and Local Lectures," CUR 57.1.1-4 (CUA). On the origins of the scheme, see E.G. Sandford (ed.), *Memoirs of Archbishop Temple. By Seven Friends* (2 vols; London: Macmillan, 1906) I.129-32. The University had received a deputation requesting that the two systems be standardized. See CUR 57.1.17 for the resultant report. Lightfoot wrote two flysheets on the question dated 6 and 8 March 1860. Copies are included among the Cambridge University Papers ET 61 (CUL). The proposal for awarding a title was rejected by the Senate on 8 March 1860 by 69 votes to 33. Romilly's Diary, vol. 29, 106 (Add 6840, CUL).

[117] See J. Stuart, *Reminiscences* (London: Chiswick Press, 1911) 182. On Stuart's work, see E. Welch, *The Peripatetic University. Cambridge Local Lectures 1873-1973* (Cambridge: University Press, 1973) ch. 2-4. CUR 57.1.48 (CUA). Lightfoot signed only the interim, and not the final, report because he was absent (at St Paul's) on the day. *Reporter* (18 March 1873) 151-2; & (27 May 1873) 83-103.

[118] Appointed 11 November 1867. "Non-Collegiate Students," CUR 60.1 (CUA). "Minutes of the University Expences [Sic] Syndicate," Min.VI.60, and CUR 60.2, 4 (CUA).

reason he was prepared to support the (as it proved) short-lived Cavendish College, which, as a hostel, aimed to permit cheaper university residence.[119]

But there was a limit to those Lightfoot would countenance as direct beneficiaries. For a number of years he aided attempts to bring women into the sphere of Cambridge influence, recommending (as a Syndicate member) a departure from the Oxford model by allowing schoolgirls to make use of Cambridge Local Examinations,[120] and by helping to create in 1868 a special examination whose object was to set a standard for women teachers.[121] Emily Davies' attempt to found a women's college at nearby Hitchin also secured his active support.[122] But when she tried to incorporate her women's college into the University, he withdrew it.[123] The purposes of Cambridge as "the spiritual power" would be achieved, it seems, only if it remained a University for men, an attitude which divided Lightfoot from the radical reformers like John Seeley and Henry Sidgwick.[124]

Apart from extending its influence, Lightfoot saw Cambridge's general educational capacity to depend upon two further changes. One was curriculum reform. Ostensibly the monopoly of Mathematics and Classics was broken in 1848 when the Natural and Moral Science Triposes were introduced.[125] But little actually changed since, as Lightfoot reported to Prince Albert, they remained unpopular into the 1860s.[126] As late as 1865, he could still complain of "the narrowness of our classical and mathematical training, as the heritage of a past generation (academically speaking)".[127] This was why Lightfoot took part in attempts to nurture the new degree subjects by serving on the Board of Moral Science Studies for most of the 1860s.[128] His advocacy of a Professorship of Zoology reflects as well a wish to strengthen the position of natural science.[129] He sought also to broaden further the

---

[119] Lightfoot to F.W. Farrar, 18 May 1876 (FC, Bundle 27). Rothblatt, *Revolution of the Dons*, 71.

[120] Report dated 16 February 1865, CUR 57.1.31 (CUA). See also R. McWilliams-Tullberg, *Women at Cambridge* (London: Gollancz, 1975) 26-35.

[121] CUR 57.1.40, 42 (CUA). Tullberg, *Women at Cambridge*, 53-6.

[122] Lightfoot is listed as a member of the "Cambridge Committee For Women, at Hitchin, Hertfordshire," and contributed twenty pounds. Cam.c.154.12 (CUL). See also B. Stephen, *Emily Davies and Girton College* (London: Constable and Co., 1927) 159, 172, 206-7.

[123] Lightfoot to Emily Davies, 12 December 1872 (DGC, ED XVII/GC/5/8).

[124] Wormell, *Seeley*, 58-60; & A.S. & E.M.S., *Henry Sidgwick*, 204-12.

[125] Garland, *Cambridge Before Darwin*, 3-4, 28.

[126] Lightfoot to H.R.H. Prince Albert, 17 February & 9 April 1861 (CUL, RA F35 116, 118).

[127] Lightfoot to Westcott, 7 June 1865 (LAC).

[128] See Min.V.10 (CUA).

[129] J.B. Lightfoot, *The New Professorship*, 6 February 1866. Privately printed (CUL, Cam.b.8.65.20). Note as well Lightfoot's donation of ten pounds to the improvement of the Museum of Zoology (CUL, Cam.a.863.1.6).

curriculum, as his support for an Oriental Languages Tripos indicates.[130] At the same time his resistence to excessive reforming zeal expressed itself as opposition to the abolition of Compulsory Greek.[131] Without discarding what was sound in the received system, diversification of curriculum and specialization of study were essential if Cambridge was adequately to reflect the vast expansion of human interest and understanding which he noted as a special feature of the age.[132]

In addition to seeking the right subjects, Lightfoot also made considerable exertions to obtain the right teachers. In 1867 he observed to Bishop Tait that he was a single unit, while the strength of Cambridge "consists in the number of such units; and each withdrawn is so far a diminution of power".[133] The converse was also true for each unit added, so that he took a strong interest in the composition of the professoriate. The vacancy in the Professorship of Modern History in 1869 provided an occasion to call for the kind of man needed to help bring about the desired transformation of the University.[134] He must be an able and energetic man, with a made historical reputation, who would devote himself to the work of his chair (which had languished during the occupation of James Stephen and Charles Kingsley) rather than treating it as "a mere ornament or appendage to some other pursuit".[135] Efforts to obtain men of such scholarly devotion and achievement had already been made. In 1863 Lightfoot voted for J.E.B. Mayor against Henry Fawcett for the Chair of Political Economy, perhaps an error of judgment.[136] Three years later he strongly encouraged the reluctant Hort to become a candidate for the Knightbridge Chair of Moral Philosophy, relenting only when it became known that F.D. Maurice was to stand.[137] He also recalled with satisfaction that university connections had not prevented the election of E.B. Cowell to the new Sanskrit Chair.[138] As an extension of this activity Lightfoot sought to ensure exposure of undergraduates to the teaching of these men by stoutly defending compulsory attendance of professors'

---

[130] *Reporter* (22 March 1872) 199-204; (24 April 1872) 260-1; (8 May 1872) 275.

[131] Successfully resisted in 1873. "Compulsory Greek" Syndicate June 1870-April 1871 (CUA, V.C. Corr. V.8[1-16]).

[132] OFR 208-10. OA 300-1. PP IX [1871] 183.

[133] Lightfoot to Tait, 22 November 1867 (TPL, vol. 83, f. 266).

[134] Lightfoot to Stanley, 3 July 1869 (GBL, 44 318, f. 83).

[135] For the fortunes of history under Stephen and Kingsley, see J.M. Ward, "The Retirement of a Titan: James Stephen 1847-50," *Journal of Modern History* XXXI.3 (September 1959) 189-205, esp. 205; Chadwick, "Charles Kingsley at Cambridge," 308, 311, 316-17; & Slee, *Learning,* 23-36.

[136] Poll for the Chair of Political Economy (CUL, Cam.a.500.68).

[137] LH II.79. His attempts to control the outcome of the election nettled John Mayor who accused Lightfoot of telling him what to do. J.B. Mayor to Lightfoot, 13 October 1866.

[138] Lightfoot to Stanley, 3 July 1869 (GBL, 44 318, f. 83).

lectures when it came under fire in the mid 1870s.[139] For the example of such men taken separately would lead to the efficacy of their several subjects, while corporately they would give to Cambridge that intellectual and moral energy that he wished to see.

Understandably it was within his own faculty that Lightfoot's concern for the professoriate was as its most intense. Apart from Professor Jeremie,[140] whose long standing indolence was compounded in the 1860s by ill health and plurality, he was generally satisfied with the men already holding the Divinity Chairs. For their successors he looked to men with made reputations as theological authors as a guarantee that the Divinity Professors would be a learned body, a criterion, interestingly, Lightfoot himself would barely have met in 1861.[141] The man who, for character and accomplishments, came closest to his ideal was, of course, Westcott. The prospect of work together in a common cause induced Lightfoot to connive at his return to Cambridge for more than a decade before achieving success in 1870. Thereafter, as vacancies occurred, Lightfoot sought the appointments that would most conduce to the theological and religious interests of the University. In 1875 this meant acquiescence in the election of J.J.S. Perowne as Hulsean Professor — though he had wanted Hort or Benson — because of the manifest need for an Old Testament specialist.[142] Three years later, however, Hort was finally added to the Divinity professoriate when Perowne went to the deanery of Peterborough. Although these attempts to influence elections caused irritation in the University, Lightfoot remained committed to the principle that, for important appointments, those who know should lead those who don't.[143] If Lightfoot, Westcott and Hort ever constituted a Cambridge School of Theology, the germ idea of men of like mind and scholarly achievement occupying the key teaching and administrative posts in the Divinity Faculty was Lightfoot's. The design, together with the earliest efforts to bring it about, entitle him to be regarded as its architect and first builder.

---

[139] J.B. Lightfoot, *On the Proposed Grace For Abolishing Compulsory Attendance at Professors' Lectures* (Cambridge: University Press, 1877). Cf. *Memorial to the Council of the Senate Opposing Compulsory Attendance at Professors' Lectures* (CUL, Cam.a.500.6.73**).

[140] James Amiraux Jeremie (1802-1872) was Regius Professor of Divinity, 1850-70, and Dean of Lincoln, 1864-72. See DNB X.775-6; & Venn, *Alumni* II.III.569.

[141] He did not regard himself as a theologian prior to his election to the Hulsean Professorship. "... I know no theology." Lightfoot to Westcott, 15 August 1861 (LAC).

[142] Lightfoot to Westcott, 7 June 1875 (LAC). Wesctcott to Lightfoot, 12 June 1875.

[143] See the correspondence in two boxes labelled 'Lady Margaret Professorship' in the Lightfoot Papers, esp. draft of Lightfoot to Swainson, n.d.; to Cooke, 5 May 1875; & to the Master of Clare, 5 May 1875.

Lightfoot's especial concern for the Divinity Professoriate was due to its importance as a direct spiritual influence on the country. Whatever doubts flowed from the ideal of a liberal education about the appropriateness of vocational training at the University, the Divinity Faculty had long been seen as responsible for preparing candidates for Holy Orders. Its shortcomings in this role had been caught up in the reform movement of the 1850s, and led to the institution of the Voluntary Theological Examination in 1856.[144] However, dissatisfaction did not abate, and reform was taken much further during the period of Lightfoot's professorships when theological education at Cambridge underwent a major overhaul. The credit is often given to Westcott, but he did not return to the University until the process was virtually concluded.[145] In fact the move for improvement was led from about 1858 by E.H. Browne.[146] By the time of his departure for the See of Ely in 1864, changes had been set in train which led in 1865 to Theology becoming a "Special Subject" for the third year of the Poll degree. From this point Lightfoot took over as the leading spokesman for the Faculty and sponsor of new schemes. He was well placed to respond when the opportunity presented itself to bring the arrangements for Theology into line with other major subjects and set it on a footing from which it developed into a modern academic discipline.

In February 1870, T.G. Bonney remarked in passing that a Theological Tripos ought to be established.[147] This suggestion led to a full review of the University's theological examinations by an especially appointed Theological Examinations Syndicate on which Lightfoot served. But he had not waited for it to initiate change. Just prior to its appointment he proposed to the Board of Theological Studies:

> That it would be desirable for the Board to hold a conference with the Colleges in order to consider the possibility of arranging a concerted system of Theological teaching in the University to be carried on by the College Lecturers in connection with the Divinity Professors.[148]

The suggestion "was very favourably received", and led in due course to the Intercollegiate Lecture Scheme by which all the resources for teaching Theology within the University were made available to the undergraduates. Theological teaching at Cambridge had been rationalized.

When the Theological Examinations Syndicate met later in the year, Lightfoot successfully moved that classes and exams in another subject area

---

[144] Tanner, *Register*, 802 ff. Lightfoot first examined for the Voluntary in 1857.

[145] Chadwick, *Westcott and the University*, 14-15, 21-5.

[146] For Browne's Cambridge career, see G.W. Kitchen, *Edward Harold Browne. A Memoir* (London: John Murray, 1895) ch. 3.

[147] Winstanley, *Late Victorian Cambridge*, 158-9.

[148] Minutes of the Board of Theological Studies, 2 March 1870 (SDS).

cease to be required in the last stage of the Ordinary degree, as the extra work interfered with the preparation for the Special Examination in Theology without securing the broader knowledge that had been hoped for.[149] The effect was to complete the reform of 1865. As a result reading began in the so-called liberal arts, but then concentrated on Theology in the third year. Pass degree candidates for the ministry could now effectively prepare for their careers while undergraduates.

At the postgraduate level, Lightfoot added a scheme for replacing B.D. and D.D. Exercises with a dissertation on an approved subject.[150] The reason for this concern came out in his opposition to granting an honorary Divinity degree to E.A. Abbott of the City of London School, on the grounds of his having achieved no distinction in the field.[151] To do so would set a precedent whereby Cambridge would "no longer be able to require any evidence of knowledge or to exact any results of study from candidates for Theological degrees". However, under the plan Lightfoot now proposed, they would be a reward for substantive scholarly achievement, and theological learning at Cambridge was to benefit as "the University would obtain from time to time valuable monographs, like the theses produced in Germany".[152] Hort's *Two Dissertations* were at once among the first fruits of the scheme and its vindication.[153]

For the new Tripos Lightfoot was the only Divinity Professor on the Subsyndicate which established the course content by means of the draft schedule it prepared.[154] In the ensuing deliberations of the full Syndicate Professor Selwyn attempted to include more traditional subjects, and the absence of Systematic Theology and Christian Evidences was felt.[155] Yet

---

[149] Minutes of the Theological Examinations Syndicate, 10 February 1871 (CUA, Min.VI.11).

[150] *Ibid.*, 16 May 1870. The motion was proposed by Professor Swainson, and seconded by Lightfoot who then volunteered to prepare the draft scheme, which is included in the Minutes for 23 May 1870. Although modified in detail, Lightfoot's scheme was accepted in substance.

[151] Lightfoot to the Vice Chancellor, 14 October [1872] (CUA, CUR 28.2.28a). The year is supplied from the Vice Chancellor's reply.

[152] *Reporter* (15 March 1871) 248.

[153] F.J.A. Hort, *Two Dissertations. I On ΜΟΝΟΓΕΝΗΣ ΘΕΟΣ in Scripture and Tradition. II On the "Constantinopolitan" Creed and Other Eastern Creeds of the Fourth Century* (Cambridge & London: Macmillan, 1876) for which he earned the B.D. and D.D. degrees.

[154] Minutes of the Theological Examinations Syndicate, 9–23 May 1870 (CUA, Min.VI.11). Westcott and Swainson joined Lightfoot as three of the four members of the subsyndicate set up on 21 February 1871 to prepare the Regulations for the actual Tripos Examination.

[155] The report of the Subsyndicate was not considered until February 1871. Selwyn and the traditionalists attempted to introduce Natural Theology, Butler's *Analogy*, and Messianic Prophecy. *Ibid.* 7, 14 & 21 March 1871.

only two important alterations were made to the proposed schedule, which means it is not unreasonable to attribute to Lightfoot the principal influence in the making of the new Honours Degree course.[156]

With its acceptance each level of theological examination had been reformed. Thinking that English theology generally was below the mark,[157] and well aware of the deficiencies in the preparation of clergy at Cambridge, Lightfoot made a more comprehensive and creative contribution to the changes of 1870-71 than any other Divinity Professor or Syndicate member, so that as a body they are quite properly to be regarded as his reform. His success owed something to changes within the dominant educational ideal at Cambridge which accommodated his aspiration for vocational preparation of the clergy. Much too flowed from the German model of the university providing a discipline leading to substantive theological achievement and literary production. Underlying both, however, was Lightfoot's own ideal of the place of theology in the University which was symbolized by efforts to obtain a new Divinity school.[158] From 1858 he supported Selwyn's attempt to secure a comely building as close as possible to the living centre of the University,[159] eventually guiding the scheme to completion as the only surviving member of the Trust set up in 1864.[160] Although named after its benefactor, and not opened until after Lightfoot's departure from Cambridge, the Selwyn Divinity School was a monument to what Lightfoot had attempted during the apogee of his administrative endeavour between 1864 and 1871.[161] Theology, the queen of sciences, needed to be at the centre of the University as a productive and life giving force.

The importance of History in the new Theology Tripos was noted thirty years ago by Owen Chadwick.[162] In fact the need for History was both in part the aspiration and achievement of the entire reform of theological education in which Lightfoot was involved, for Chadwick's analysis of the Tripos syllabus can be matched by similar analyses of the other courses in Theol-

---

[156] *Ibid.*

[157] See 342 below.

[158] Willis Clark, *Architectural History*, III.229-40. G. Rupp, "A Cambridge Centenary. The Selwyn Divinity School, 1879-1979," *Historical Journal* 24.2 (1981) 417-28.

[159] Report of the Board of Theological Studies, 30 December 1858 (CUL, Cambridge University Papers DC 8550). Correspondence Between the Museums and Lecture Rooms Syndicate and the Professors of Divinity [issued March 27, 1862], *ibid.*, F 51. Minutes of the Council of the Senate, 30 January & 27 March 1871 (CUA, Min.I.6); 27 January & 28 April 1873; 25 May, 1 & 8 June 1874 (CUA, Min.I.7).

[160] See esp. Selwyn Benefaction Trust: Vouchers for Erection of Divinity Schools (Correspondence, etc. Prem.V.4, CUA).

[161] The stature of his contribution to theological education at Cambridge is recognized more particularly by the inclusion of a statuette of Lightfoot among those of the 'greats' over the entrance to the Divinity School.

[162] Chadwick, *Westcott and the University*, 22-5, 30-1.

ogy. Even more was wanted. When the Syndicate appointed in 1875 "to consider the requirements of the University in different departments of Study" asked the Board of Theological Studies to outline the amount of teaching needed in its department, two of the additional professorships requested were in History.[163] This emphasis on History was partly due to intellectual fashion. As Chadwick suggests, it seemed the way to make Theology, like other bodies of knowledge, properly critical. For Lightfoot's part, critical historical method also offered assured facts for use in theological formulations and apologetics which were beyond the reach of the religious iconoclast or atheistic propagandist.[164] His theology of history too was involved. History's status as the sphere of divine disclosure principally in and through the Church meant that the teaching of the Church in every age should be found in the unbroken life of the Church through the ages. This was a high office for History, and no doubt overrated — if it did not misconceive — the utility of historical knowledge, but, in Lightfoot's judgment, its provision in such a key area of the University's social function brought it closer to realizing its role as "the spiritual power of the nineteenth century".

From this point, with the leading theological chair so capably filled by the appointment of Westcott, Lightfoot was content for his influence to become less direct.[165] Ecclesiastical preferment, which required his absence from Cambridge for a quarter of the year, was also accepted.[166] Nevertheless, the final innovation in Cambridge theological education during Lightfoot's professorship was a joint effort with Westcott, now fully established as Regius Professor. When the "Voluntary" came to an end in 1873, the University refused to supply an examination for its students who had not read Theology, even though intending to be ordained.[167] To meet this need, Lightfoot and Westcott devised the "Preliminary Examination for Candidates for Holy Orders" which the latter described with a misleading optimism as "Not a University Examination" but "instituted by members of the Theological Faculty, in co-operation with a considerable number of bishops".[168] Lightfoot was more anxious, for only 14 of the 30 English bishops

---

[163] *Reporter* (12 December 1877) 196.

[164] See Part IV below. Cf. Westcott's observation in the Arts School discussion of 9 March 1871 in *Reporter* (15 March 1871) 248.

[165] "As I learned more of the ways of the Council [of the Senate], I learned that the whispers of Professor Lightfoot to Dr Westcott, to whom he sat next, not infrequently neutralized Dr Westcott's vote without — one may feel quite sure — altering his opinion." Browne, *Recollections*, 132.

[166] See 209-12 below. In 1877 he withdrew further from direct involvement because of his appointment as a University Commissioner.

[167] Winstanley, *Late Victorian Cambridge*, 162-3.

[168] B.F. Westcott, "On Preparation for the Theological Exams," in *The Students's Guide to the University of Cambridge*, 1874, 298, 304.

had consented to giving the Examination a trial, and some of them only because of personal loyalty.[169] By the time he left Cambridge, however, it had become established, and its objectives were secured in 1884 when all but two of the bishops agreed that diocesan examinations should harmonize with the Cambridge Preliminary.[170] In one important respect Lightfoot and Westcott had miscalculated. Instead of appealing to graduates who had not read Theology, it was used mainly by students of the numerous theological colleges.[171] This unexpected outcome had the effect of making the "Preliminary" into a species of "Local Examination" with the highly desirable effect of lifting the general level of attainments among candidates for the ministry. As a new connection between the University and the Church at the very time when traditional links were being eroded, it was a fitting if unexpected climax to Lightfoot's sustained attempt to make Cambridge a centre of theological learning and influence.

In the mid-Victorian debate about the Universitites two clear positions emerged. They were either higher schools, preparing men for a role in the leadership of society, or institutes for research and higher culture of the mind.[172] A moderate, influencing both the conservatives and the radical reformers, Lightfoot tended to the former, viewing Cambridge as a place of education, although his own scholarship showed how the cultivation of higher learning was readily assimilable to the educational function. This, together with lack of high college office, was possibly why he did not work out the insight in a manner similar to Benjamin Jowett at Oxford. He preferred to create the conditions under which the University might better carry out its educational work, particularly in his own faculty. At this level of the Cambridge system, where religious and moral formation was not so much at stake, Lightfoot showed a greater willingness to change. A sound intellectual training for men otherwise nurtured in the Cambridge environment would promote its wider social function as "the spiritual power of the nineteenth century". The historical perspective and method of knowing occupied a key place in this approach — so much so in fact, that, at a time when the place of History at Cambridge was precarious, Lightfoot felt the necessity to consolidate its presence.

---

[169] Lightfoot to Westcott, 21 January 1874 (LAC).

[170] F.W.B. Bullock, *A History of Training for the Ministry of the Church of England 1875-1974* (London: Home Words, 1976) 21-2.

[171] F.W.B. Bullock, *A History of Training for the Ministry of the Church of England 1800-1874* (St. Leonard's-On-Sea: Budd and Gillatt, 1955) 123-5. Wilson, "Life," 88-9.

[172] Roach, "Intelligentsia," 147-8.

IV

The efficacy of Lightfoot's vision for the University required more than historically trained clergyman. It was also important that English society be
provided with an adequate quota of properly trained historians. As a step
towards securing this objective, Lightfoot made his one direct contribution
towards the study of History at Cambridge. On May 18 1870, at the height
of his reforming activity, he indicated privately to the Vice-Chancellor his
intention of founding a History scholarship.[173] Since the Easter term was
drawing to its close, the matter was deferred until the new academic year in
order to avoid "inconvenient haste" in bringing it before the Senate.[174] Accordingly, he presented his matured scheme in October.[175] When it was accepted by the Senate in November, almost 5,000 pounds worth of stocks
were given to fund three scholarships, each tenable for three years, and
awarded successively in a three year cycle from the results of a competitive
examination.[176]

Noting the apparent coincidence of the Scholarship with Westcott's return to Cambridge, Wilson inferred that the offer sprang from Lightfoot's
gratitude for the recall of his friend to his proper sphere of labour.[177] However, with negotiations having opened six months previously and the Scholarship having been accepted by the Senate the day before Westcott's election, it cannot be explained as an act of personal piety.[178] It arose instead out
of more strictly academic considerations transparent in the plan itself.

Lightfoot intended that, once the scheme was fully operational, two levels of study in Ecclesiastical History take place in every year. In the first
phase, all the candidates would be exposed to the subject through the course
of reading leading up to the examination. The successful candidate then had
the opportunity to pass on to the second phase of three years during which
he was to engage in a piece of original historical research. The Scholarship
thereby provided an opportunity for students to discover whether they had a
capacity for historical study, and then for those of proven ability to develop
it. At the level of the University, its function was to create conditions under
which the amount of historical study taking place might increase, and to
raise the level of specific historical cultivation.

---

[173] Lightfoot to E.A. Atkinson, 18 May 1870 (CUA, CUR 38.38.A).

[174] Lightfoot to E.A. Atkinson, 3 June 1870 (CUA, CUR 38.38.B).

[175] Reconsidered after evaluation by Seeley & Westcott. Westcott & Seeley to Lightfoot,
16 & 20 May 1870.

[176] *Reporter* (2 & 23 November 1870) 58-9, 112-14.

[177] Wilson, "Life," 82-3.

[178] Minutes of the Council of the Senate, 31 October 1870 (CUA, Min.I.6). Lightfoot
to Westcott, 1 November 1870 (CUL, Add 8317, letter 57).

Behind this intention were the two dissatisfactions expressed in the formal letter of offer. "I have long felt," Lightfoot complained,

> that the study of history does not receive proper encouragement in this University, and at the present time, when the just demands of Natural Science are so eagerly urged, there is a great danger that an instrument of education, which I venture to consider even more important, may be forgotten.[179]

In 1861 he had pointed out to the Chancellor that the new Moral Sciences Tripos, of which Modern History was a part, had failed to attract students, a position which improved little over the remainder of the decade.[180] One reason for this poor state of affairs was the inadequate lead furnished by the only representative of the subject in the University, the Regius Professor of Modern History.[181] Nor was Lightfoot likely to have been happy with the appointment of John Seeley as Kingsley's successor, since he was unproven in the field, his scholarship having lacked a specific historical content.[182]

If no improvement in the representation of the subject seemed imminent, the position of History in the Cambridge curriculum was still worse. This was a situation which Lightfoot had been well placed to follow as a member of the Moral Sciences Board. He was present at its Meeting in November 1866 when the problems experienced by History in the Moral Sciences Tripos were reviewed, and again in the following year when it was finally ejected. At this point Lightfoot took the lead of those who feared the entire disappearance of History from Cambridge studies. In November 1867, he successfully proposed the appointment of a Syndicate "to consider how the study of Modern History ... may be encouraged in the University".[183] The outcome was the unfortunate coupling of History with Law in a new Tripos. By 1870 the barrenness of the union had become apparent.[184] Despairing of any immediate improvement to the bleak outlook for History, particularly when contrasted with the rising popularity of Natural Science, which had also entered the Cambridge curriculum in 1848, Lightfoot invoked the other method traditionally employed to foster the study of a subject at the University, the institution of a prize.

---

[179] *Reporter* (2 November 1870) 60.

[180] Lightfoot to Prince Albert, 17 February 1861 (CUL, RA F35.16).

[181] See above. The failings of Stephen & Kingsley are further canvassed in G. Kitson Clark, "A Hundred Years of the Teaching of History at Cambridge, 1873-1973," *The Historical Journal* XVI.3 (1973) 535-53; & J.O. McLachlan, "The Origin and Early Development of the Cambridge Historical Tripos," *Cambridge Historical Journal* IX (1947-9) 78-105.

[182] Lightfoot specifically dismissed Seeley from consideration in Lightfoot to Stanley, 3 July 1869 (GBL, 44 318, f. 83).

[183] Minute Book of the Council of the Senate, 11 November 1867 (CUA, Min.I.5).

[184] Slee, *Learning*, 56-64.

The outcome Lightfoot was trying to produce is evident from the regulations.[185] The chronological range of the required reading — from the "accession of Marcus Aurelius (AD 161)" to "the Fall of the Holy Roman Empire (AD 1806)" — was vast. This explains the most traditional aspect of the scheme, the use of set books for one part of the examination. They were not for "getting up" in the customary manner as ends in themselves. Rather they were intended as the means to the extended factual knowledge necessary as the setting for that particularity at which Lightfoot also aimed by devoting one third of the examination to a "selected portion of History",[186] and another to Essays in which the Examiners were at liberty to require a single response. Such concentration made possible a fourth feature, the encouragement of work "as far as possible" from original authorities. Finally, the study of Ecclesiastical History was to be carried out "in connexion with General History", so that it would be taken not as a unique or insulated line of development but in relation to its social and political matrix. When these five ideals of scholarship operated together according to the intended dynamic of the scheme, they were to inculcate an approach to any subject in Ecclesiastical History on the basis of original authorities over against the background of almost the whole continuous life of the Church considered as a social phenomenon. As a conception of historical study the scheme was sounder than that developed in the History School under Seeley who aimed at a similar breadth of view, but remained unconcerned to provide the same scope for original study on specific subjects by individual students. These practices appeared in the History Tripos only in the mid 1880s, so that for method the Lightfoot Scholarship was 15 years ahead of its time at Cambridge. It seems therefore to have been part of Lightfoot's intention to provide a training in modern historical method — known from German and outside English sources — such as was otherwise unobtainable in the University.

But it was not part of Lightfoot's aim that the benefits be confined to Cambridge. To one early winner he wrote:

> I have been more than rewarded for any sacrifice I may have made in the establishment of the Scholarships by seeing the good work which they have stimulated. I trust that you will take up some portion of history and make it your own that you may give it in due time to others.[187]

---

[185] *Reporter* (23 November 1870) 112-14.

[186] F. Foakes-Jackson recalled the value of the books to himself in "Books Recommended By Bishop Lightfoot," in *History of Church History* (Cambridge: Heffer, 1939) 171-82. The design behind the assortment of titles, he thought (182), was "to lay the foundation of a knowledge of human history as an aid to the study of all Christian learning".

[187] Lightfoot to Foakes-Jackson, 5 June 1880, reprinted in *History of Church History*, v.

Thus the Scholarship was intended to lead eventually to the provision of the English public with learned works of historical scholarship. Lightfoot's objective in this was not narrowly academic. In the letter of offer he had written:

> I have ventured to stipulate that especial, though not exclusive attention shall be paid to Ecclesiastical History, not only because my connection with the Theological faculty gives it a direct claim upon me, but also because I regard it when properly treated, as the most important and instructive branch of historical study.[188]

Clearly Lightfoot expected that the works called into being by the scheme would, through their scholarship, teach valuable historical lessons, and above all vindicate his own providentialist outlook by placing it on a sounder factual basis. Cambridge University would better serve English society by including History in the construction of a strong Christian consensus.

Almost 100 years after Lightfoot's death, the failure of the Lightfoot Scholarships to achieve its grand social object is obvious. Neither the increasing educational efficiency of Cambridge University nor the teaching activity of the Divinity School, nor the provision of a clerisy of historians, has been able to prevent English society changing in the manner Lightfoot feared. Indeed History has actually aided the process, first by secularizing the meliorism essential to his providentialist outlook, and then by questioning whether the historical continuum is meaningful at all.[189] It is unlikely that History could have ever performed the office Lightfoot posited for it. His view of the educational use of History was based on intellectualist assumptions, which were understandable in a university environment, and common enough in his day.[190] But even as he wrote men were at work who would show how limited a perspective this was as an account of the full reality of a modern industrial society.[191] Materialist conceptions of history have certainly not been able to command universal assent, but the limitations they expose in an alternative such as Lightfoot's points to the fatuousness of his hopes for historical training at the University.

In the limited sphere of the historical education provided by Cambridge, the Lightfoot Scholarship was far more successful. Its effect in stimulating

---

[188] *Reporter* (2 November 1870) 60.

[189] Of the numerous works treating this theme, see F.L. Baumer, *Modern European Thought. Continuity and Change in Ideas, 1600-1950* (New York: Macmillan, 1977); A.D. Gilbert, *The Making of Post-Christian Britain. A History of the Secularization of Modern Society* (London & New York: Longman, 1980); & H. Stuart Hughes, *Consciousness and Society. The Reorientation of European Social Thought, 1890-1930* (London: MacGibbon & Kee, 1959).

[190] Eg. R. Soffa, "Nation, Duty, Character and Confidence: History at Oxford, 1850-1914," *The Historical Journal* 30.1 (1987) 77-104.

[191] For the impact of Marxism on English historical writing, see Parker, *English Historical Tradition*, ch. 8.

historical study and contributing to the formation of historians is acknowledged by those who benefited directly.[192] Objective evidence supports these
impressions. Of the 36 winners before the disruption caused by the Great
War, 23 went on to write or edit an historical work, of which 11 were connected with ecclesiastical history.[193] Included in the list are such
historiographically noteworthy names as F.J. Foakes-Jackson, J.P. Whitney,
J.N. Figgis, G.P. Gooch, J.H. Clapham, D.A. Winstanley, H.G. Wood, Z.N.
Brooke and B.L. Manning. A failure as an instrument for constituting English society, the Lightfoot Scholarship was a notable success as a medium
for training historians.

Although not as successful in what he attempted as he would have liked,
Cambridge University was for Lightfoot one of the key points in contemporary English society for carrying out the work of the age. His experience at
Cambridge, which was almost exactly coterminous with the decisive stage
of what J.P. Roach called "The Age of Reforms", interacted with his theology of history to produce a perspective on the University as "the spiritual
power of the nineteenth century". Personally important for Lightfoot's sense
of vocation, this was at once a reforming and restraining image, enabling
him — working usually with and through others in committees, but coming
forward to take the lead when necessary — to embrace and promote those
changes which in his judgment tended to make the received idea of the University as a place of moral and intellectual formation a reality in his own
day, and oppose those which did not. It also favoured the educational, rather
than the research, ideal, although Lightfoot would have seen the antithesis
as overdrawn. Moreover, the Janus-like openness to the proposals of the
reformers at the same time as adhering to the traditional doctrine of the conservatives gave him considerable influence among both groups which curbed
the zeal of one and softened the opposition of the other. The outcome was a
significant contribution to the nationalization and modernization of the University and colleges, the overhaul of theological education, and provision
for historical training more in line with newly emergent professional standards. Commenting on the completion of the process of reform begun in
1850 by the Statutory Commission of which Lightfoot was a member, J.P.
Roach has written:

---

[192] Apart from Foakes-Jackson above, see J.P. Whitney, "The Lightfoot Scholarships
for Ecclesiastical History," in LD 142-6.

[193] i.e. 1874-1916. Tanner, *Register*, 274. *The Historical Register of the University of
Cambridge. Supplement 1911-20*, Cambridge, 1922, 34. Bibliographical calculations are
based on the *British Library Catalogue to 1975*.

The great problem of the age was to keep alive the ancient spirit and to infuse it into the new forms, to modernize the University without shattering its historic continuity, its self respect, or its independence. That this difficult task was successfully accomplished is due to many individuals, to favourable external circumstances, perhaps even to luck, but, among the whole complex of causes, the restraint of two Statutory Commissions should not be forgotten.[194]

As one who appreciated this need and tried to balance the often competing claims of the past and the future (giving up cherished notions in the process) Lightfoot was among those individuals entitled to a share in the credit.

On the other hand, the larger result for English Society to which Lightfoot aspired did not materialize. Cambridge University did not regenerate the nation. Fundamental to this failure was the declining hold of Christianity on the life of the country, which Lightfoot perceived and resisted, but also underestimated. The future belonged more to those who had secularized the function of Cambridge which has gone on to be a major educational power, not only in England but well beyond. Ironically this was a process to which Lightfoot himself contributed in some measure through changes in which he acquiesced or actively promoted. For revivifying Cambridge as a place of learning changed the University and both consolidated and accelerated the secularization that was already under way. But if revivifying the tradition did not always produce the results envisaged, nevertheless the process was relatively straightforward in a place where the traditions were palpably available and symbolic constructions of the past a part of everyday life. It was not so in London and Durham, the other main localities of Lightfoot's life and work.

---

[194] Roach, "Cambridge," 265.

Chapter Eight

"Representatives of God to Men and Men to God": The Ministry and History

While for most of his life Cambridge University was the primary centre of his activity, fundamentally Lightfoot's involvement in the life of the nation was as a clergyman of the established Church. From very early in life he had wanted to become a minister, an aspiration he quickly realized by ordination to his Fellowship at Trinity College.[1] Thereafter he did not follow the usual pattern of going to a College living upon getting married, but instead remained at Cambridge as a clerical don and went on to a part time cathedral canonry and eventually to a bishopric. Apart from the brief period at Harborough Magna in the summer of 1854, Lightfoot never served in a parish. Yet, as his preaching records show,[2] he visited many parishes all over the country on an occasional basis. As a University lecturer and examining chaplain he also prepared men for the parish ministry over many years, and as a bishop supervised the work of ministry in a large and difficult diocese. While his personal experience of parish ministry was perhaps limited, the subject was a major interest on which Lightfoot thought and wrote a great deal. As a result his idea of the Christian ministry is the most accessible of his understandings of the key institutions in which he worked.

Partly for this reason, and partly because of the perennial interest in the subject for those involved in ministry, it has also been the most studied. However, the interest has tended to be hermeneutical and phenomenological rather than historical. New Testament scholars have looked chiefly to Lightfoot's treatment of the ancient evidence,[3] while theologians and church people of various denominations look to his writings for the light shed on their own present day concerns.[4] Even Wilson, whose biographical study

---

[1] See 47-50 above.

[2] See the Bibliography, 397-403 below.

[3] See esp. Kaye, "Lightfoot and Baur," 206-14. Kaye suggestively touches on wider issues on 218-20 of the same paper.

[4] Philip Hughes, for example, considers the bearing of Lightfoot's views on the validity and significance of apostolic succession against the background of ecumenical dialogue and the ordination of women debate. He also regrets the unavailability of Lightfoot's

took as its focus Lightfoot's interest in the ministry, does not clearly relate it to the nineteenth century setting. In particular, ideological influences on Lightfoot's views on the ministry have not been considered. Not the least of these was his idea of history which in this matter, as elsewhere, is likely to have been fundamental to his thinking.

Lightfoot's interest, and the response to it, are a reflection of the importance of the ministry in the nineteenth century Church. As a number of studies has shown, it was a resurgent profession, an earlier tradition of professionalism and moral earnestness being revived because of a changing political, social and religious environment.[5] The state provided the structural conditions for improvement of ministerial practice by the reforms of the 1830s, particularly the creation of the Ecclesiastical Commission. This was accompanied by a clerical renaissance from within the profession itself as it responded to both the Evangelical Revival and the Oxford Movement, and to the broader pressure for a distinct and useful role in society. But within this general movement there was great variety which generated considerable difference of opinion. Apart from the problem of the relationship between Church and State, seemingly perennial issues were the authority, status and role of the clergy. Lightfoot's contribution is often regarded as the beginning of a debate.[6] In fact it picked up and extended a discussion that had begun at least a generation earlier with Newman's publication of *Tract I*. While Dissenters continued to doubt the validity of Anglican orders,[7] the Tractarians exalted their divine origin by means of the doctrine of apostolic succession.[8] Together with the responsibility of the ministerial office, the importance they assigned to the eucharist also led to a revival of

---

judgment on the charismatic movement "in the light of various movements in the patristic period". See his contribution to J.B. Lightfoot, *The Christian Ministry* (edited with an introduction by P.E. Hughes; Wilton, Connecticut: Morehouse-Barlow, 1983) 7-25, esp. 24-5. See also Dunn, "Lightfoot in Retrospect," 90-1.

[5] In addition to Haig, *Victorian Clergy*, see B. Heeney, *A Different Kind of Gentleman. Parish Clergy as Professional Men in Early and Mid-Victorian England* (Hamden, Connecticut: Archon Books, 1976); R. O'Day, "The Clerical Renaissance in Victorian England and Wales," *Religion in Victorian Britain. Volume I. Traditions* (ed. G. Parsons; Manchester: University Press, 1988) 184-212; & R. O'Day, "The Men From the Ministry," *Religion in Victorian Britain. Volume II. Controversies* (ed. G. Parsons; Manchester: University Press, 1988) 258-79.

[6] S. Mayor, "Discussion of the Ministry in Late Nineteenth-Century Anglicanism," *The Church Quarterly* 2.1 (July 1969) 54-62. See also his "The Anglo-Catholic Understanding of the Ministry: Some Protestant Comments," *The Church Quarterly* 2.2 (October 1969) 152-9.

[7] It was not the pressing issue it had been in the past, but, as the sequel showed, the disagreement remained. D.M. Thompson, *Nonconformity in the Nineteenth Century* (London & Boston: Routledge & Kegan Paul, 1972) 8-9.

[8] J.B. Webster, "Ministry and Priesthood," *The Study of Anglicanism* (eds S. Sykes & J. Booty; London & Philadelphia: S.P.C.K., 1988) 285-96, esp. 291-2.

a sacerdotal concept of the priesthood.[9] These were matters Lightfoot felt the need to address.

I

Lightfoot's understanding of the ministry was another area where his scholarship contributed directly to his work as a Churchman.[10] In 1868 he included in the important commentary on 'Philippians' a dissertation on 'The Christian Ministry'.[11] Ostensibly this was to clear space for the difficult matters that would have to be discussed in relation to the 'Pastoral Epistles' in a later commentary.[12] It also arose from a belief that Church people needed to know the history of the ministry, particularly in the early period of the Church's corporate life.[13] Confronted by "a clamour of antagonistic opinions" about the origin and authority of the three-fold ministry, discovering what the ministry had been in the earliest age of the Church seemed to provide the key to what it is by nature.[14] This in turn would set the norm for what the ministry ought to be in the present. "The doctrine," Lightfoot asserted, "is involved in the history."[15] Accordingly, as he later recalled, "The object of the Essay was an investigation into the origin of the Christian Ministry".[16] Its method was to trace "the progressive growth and development of the ministry, until it arrived at its mature and normal state",[17] with a view to settling disagreement over the status and roles of the contemporary Christian minister.

On the basis of a review of the tradition of the ministry in the first three centuries of its existence, Lightfoot allowed that the ministry was dominical at the beginning. Certainly the apostolate was created by Jesus,[18] but this was a temporary office devoted to the conversion of souls and the creation of new churches. Given the physical limitations of the Apostles, its very success necessitated the creation of a permanent ministry. This began at

---

[9]   See A. Härdelin, *The Tractarian Understanding of the Eucharist* (Studia historico-ecclesiastica upsaliensia no. 8; Uppsala: Boktryckeri Aktiebolag, 1965) esp. Part 2.1 & Part 3.3a.

[10]   See 127-30 above.

[11]   P 181-269. On the place of dissertations in Lightfoot's commentaries, see 330-1 below.

[12]   P viii.

[13]   P 186-7.

[14]   Lightfoot freely admitted in answer to his critics that the essay was grounded in historical study. "Preface to the Sixth Edition," dated 9 September 1881, P x.

[15]   P 187.

[16]   "Preface to the Sixth Edition," 9 September 1881, P x. This accords with the dissertation itself, which claims "to investigate the historical development of this divine institution". P 182.

[17]   P 186.

[18]   P 184-7.

Jerusalem with the creation of the diaconate, an arrangement which was soon adopted elsewhere.[19] Originally an office for the distribution of alms, it continued to develop and in time acquired a teaching component and came to include women.

The next order of ministry, the presbyterate, developed in imitation of the organization of the synagogue.[20] Again the development spread from Jerusalem. The catalyst was the persecution of James and the dispersion of the Apostles on a wider mission. To provide for the permanent direction of the Jerusalem Church, a body of elders was appointed. As the Church spread, this form of organization was reproduced, particularly as Jewish presbyterates already existed in the cities of the dispersion. Over time the teaching side of the role increased as visits from Apostles and evangelists became less frequent. By the close of the apostolic age the presbyterate had emerged as a second order of ministry.

Episcopacy, the third order, developed out of the second.[21] On the timing and cause Lightfoot was not precise. He assigned it to the last thirty years of the first century following the fall of Jerusalem and the dispersion of the surviving Apostles to Asia Minor. The many irregularities and threats of disruption they encountered seemed to call for the system of church government suggested by the superintendance of the Apostles and their delegates of churches elsewhere and commended by the effectiveness of the ascendancy of St James in the Jerusalem Church. Accordingly the elevation of one of the elders to the superintendancy of the congregation was widely encouraged in the Gentile Churches. Its spread was uneven, but the manifest utility of the office under the circumstances combined with the sanction of St John's name to secure a wide if gradual acceptance. By about 120 A.D. episcopacy was the system of government in the Catholic Church.[22]

To Lightfoot's mind, historical investigation along these lines settled at least two of the issues debated by the Victorians in relation to the ministry. The first was the legitimacy of Anglican orders. To the criticisms of Dissent, Lightfoot replied:

> If the preceding investigation be substantially correct, the three-fold ministry can be traced to Apostolic direction, and short of an express statement we can possess no better assurance of a Divine appointment or at least a Divine sanction. If the facts do not allow us to unchurch other Christian communities differently organized, they may at least justify our jealous adhesion to a polity derived from this source.[23]

---

[19] P 187-91.

[20] P 191-5.

[21] P 195-244, esp. 196, 206-7, 227-8, 234.

[22] Cf. RRH 4-5; AF II.1².39-40, 389-99, 594.

[23] P 267. This was taken to be confirmation of the three orders of the Anglican Ordinal. P x.

This statement also contained his response to the Tractarian revival of apostolic succession. Episcopacy was only derived from the apostolate through St John: it had not come from the Apostles laying their hands on those who should succeed them as a matter of policy. In affirming only a limited apostolic succession which had been occasioned in any case by historical circumstance, Lightfoot claimed that history endorsed the standard Anglican position, that bishops are of the *bene esse* of the Church, but not of its *esse*.[24]

But there was more to Lightfoot's essay than this. As at least one contemporary writer noted, Lightfoot's contribution to a long running discussion was his "strikingly original ... philosophical presentation of his case".[25] By this he meant the introduction of the evolutionary perspective as a means of organizing and interpreting already well studied evidence. Whether this was true in any scientific sense is debatable, but certainly Lightfoot's idea of history was influential in both respects. The early history of the ministry was presented as "a progressive growth and development".[26] It was also described as the result of ordinary natural causes. Various internal and external difficulties interacted with national characteristics and temper to produce different patterns of advance in different places.[27] Although part of the one "progressive development", the emergence of the three orders of ministry did not occur at a uniform rate throughout the Church. Lightfoot's was an environmental as well as a circumstantial interpretation.

At first sight this was something of a problem for his "increasing purpose" perspective, for the emergence of a permanent ministry was seemingly a departure from what was given as the ideal of the Church.[28] The principle of universality meant that, at one level, the Church had no need of practical arrangements which differentiated time, place and persons. At another level, however, their appearance was rather a means to achieving the Church's purposes than a move away from its ideal. In particular, Lightfoot held, "the Church could not fulfil the purposes for which she exists ... without an order of men who may in some sense be designated a priesthood".[29] The ministry therefore reflected the "universal law" that, in reality, organization is needed to make ideals attainable. Provided that the principles of the ideal were not set aside, both the ministry itself and its subsequent mutations were proper developments. Even the rise of the absolute supremacy of

---

[24] See the brief account of the development of Anglican thinking about episcopacy in S. Gilley, *Newman and his Age* (London: Darton, Longman & Todd, 1990) 114-16.

[25] J.L. Parks, "Bishop Lightfoot's Theory of Episcopate," *Sewanee Review* 2 (August 1894) 425-48, esp. 425 (for the quotation) & 430-1.

[26] P 186.

[27] P 198, 205-6, 227-8, 234.

[28] P 181-3.

[29] P 182. Cf. P 183, 183-4, 184-5.

the bishop in the second and third centuries was progressive, because it enabled the Church to survive and function amid threatening circumstances.[30]
To the consternation of many, Lightfoot maintained that the Christian ministry was legitimately a function of social rather than theological necessity.

That this demythologization of the tradition of the ministry should apply
to the present seems to have been readily understood. On one occasion it
was suggested that Lightfoot had intended in part to rebut the claims of the
ritualists.[31] The remark was probably a projection from the circumstances
of the time at which it was made,[32] but in any case Lightfoot denied that he
would use a commentary on St Paul indirectly to attack a section of his
brother clergy. Something of the true contemporary purpose of "The Christian Ministry" is reflected in a letter to Westcott shortly before *Philippians*
appeared. The well being of the Church, Lightfoot told his friend, required
a return to the apostolic ideal:

> The Pauline idea of the Church seems to me so important — almost exclusively impor-
> tant — in these days, when raw sacerdotalism is alienating the Church sympathies of
> so many.[33]

This connects the essay with Lightfoot's broader wish to serve the needs of
the contemporary Church. It also identifies its specific target as the sacerdotal conceptions of priesthood that had revived in the wake of Tractarianism.

This required in turn the lengthy account of the origin, development and
reception of the sacerdotal idea in the early Church.[34] Some scholars have
been inclined to see this component of the essay as a digression. But this is
mistaken. Given history's role as "umpire", the "progress of the sacerdotal
view of the ministry" as "one of the most striking and important phenomena
in the history of the Church" could hardly be ignored. More importantly, as
an aspect of a progressive history, it had to be decided whether the rise of
sacerdotalism was a true development. Historical analysis showed that in
fact sacerdotalism was not a New Testament idea. Rather, it was "a new
principle" introduced in the third century because of the pagan inclinations
of Gentile converts. Moreover, the advent of a priestly caste violated the
radical new tenet introduced by Christianity, the direct relations between
God and people. As the perpetuation of a false development in the life of
the Church, sacerdotal conceptions of priesthood had no valid place in the
contemporary ministry.

With the regressive import of sacerdotalism revealed, the way had been
cleared for the reintroduction to the discussion of a distinction made by F.D.

---

[30] P 234-44.
[31] YJC (1879) 113-14.
[32] For the problem of ritualism in the late 1870s, see Chapter 9 below.
[33] Lightfoot to Westcott, 15 February n.y. [1868 ?] (LAC).
[34] P 244-64.

Maurice thirty years previously. The office of the Christian minister was "representative" rather than "vicarial".[35] He was a priest only "as one who represents God to man and man to God". On the one hand, "he unfolds the will of heaven; he declares in God's name the terms on which pardon is offered; and he pronounces in God's name the absolution of the penitent". On the other, the "alms, the prayers, the thanksgivings of the community are offered through him". In neither role was he absolutely essential. In an emergency a "layman" could adequately and acceptably carry out both. None of this detracted from the spirituality of the office, or weakened the claim "that the form of the ministry has been handed down from Apostolic times and may well be presumed to have a Divine sanction". Paul Avis has recently called the Tractarian approach to ministry the "Apostolic paradigm".[36] To the extent that Lightfoot opposed what they stood for in order to restore the Pauline idea of the Church, with this "representative" view he had endeavoured to recover the true apostolic paradigm.[37]

Where so much was at stake, it is not surprising that Lightfoot's attempt at clarifying the doctrinal bearings of the early history of the ministry proved controversial. Perhaps most vexatious was the insistence of Dissenters that an Anglican had proved that there were only two orders of ministry in apostolic times, and that the first bishops were congregational rather than diocesan.[38] To this he simply reaffirmed that the result of his investigation had been to confirm the statement in the Ordinal that the evidence of Scripture and antiquity indicated "that from the Apostles' time there have been these orders of Ministers in Christ's Church, Bishops, Priests, and Deacons".[39] Lightfoot insisted the tradition was against the view of Dissent.

More serious for Lightfoot himself was the retort from within his own Church that he had weakened the basis of its orders. Even his friends with High Church leanings taxed him about his findings.[40] But the main lines of the High Church critique were laid down by Charles Wordsworth, Bishop of St Andrews.[41] He objected, first, to the apparent indifference to forms and

---

[35] For the distinction and the quotations that follow, P 267-8.

[36] Avis, *Anglicanism and the Christian Church*, esp. Pt III.

[37] See also Christian Priesthood, 1862, 27-9; Christ, 1866, 16-22; OA 57-8; & SSO 196-7. For his diffidence in using the primitive Church as a model, see SSO 60-1, PC 65-6 & YJC (1883) 55-6.

[38] For a late statement of this viewpoint, see R.W. Dale, *A Manual of Congregational Principles* (London: Hodder & Stoughton, 1884) 97 & Art. III of the Appendix, 216-39.

[39] P x.

[40] Hort to Lightfoot, 26 October 1867, in LH II.86, responding to a pre-publication version. Also the recollection of H.P. Liddon to G. Marshall, 10 January 1890, in Johnston, *Life of Liddon*, 369-70.

[41] C. Wordsworth, *Some Remarks on Bishop Lightfoot's Dissertation on the Christian Ministry* (Edinburgh & London: W. Blackwood & Sons, 1879, 1884²).

means implicit in Lightfoot's historical explanation.[42] It attributed far too much to secondary causes and left no room for Divine provision. Wordsworth also opposed Lightfoot's dismissal of sacerdotalism on the grounds that it meant no special grace was conferred at ordination and confirmation by the episcopal laying on of hands. He then furnished an alternative account of some of the evidence to show that Lightfoot's interpretation was less than the evidence demands. Soon afterwards Wordsworth's case was supplemented by the young Charles Gore.[43] Alerted more fully to the implications of the historical method by Edwin Hatch's Bampton Lectures,[44] he protested against the expediency implicit in the claim, "it became necessary to appoint special officers". Instead, Gore derived the ministry from the divine appointment by Christ of an apostolic succession of bishops. At each point he opposed devolution from above to Lightfoot's evolution from below. If Dissenters accepted his history but drew different inferences, High Church Anglicans refused even to accept his history.

Although history did not establish the doctrine in the manner expected, Lightfoot did not resile from his position. His only response was to reaffirm his findings,[45] and to publish catenae of passages from his own writings in their support.[46] Despite continuing criticism, Lightfoot's insistence on his standpoint was not without effect.[47] Within the diversity of Anglicanism, the critical-historical approach which he introduced became the basis for subsequent Anglican reflection on the ministry.[48] Among liberal Anglicans

---

[42] This was taken up in a notable discussion of form and essence by R.C. Moberly, *Ministerial Priesthood* (reprinted with a new introduction by A.T. Hanson; London: S.P.C.K., 1969 [= reprint of 2nd ed. of 1910]). See also S.W. Sykes, *The Essence of Christianity* (London: S.P.C.K., 1984) 47-50; & W.L. Sachs, *The Transformation of Anglicanism. From State Church to Global Communion* (Cambridge: University Press, 1993) 161-2.

[43] Wilson, "Life," 253-4, summarizing C. Gore, *The Church and the Ministry, a Review of the Rev'd E. Hatch's Bampton Lectures*, 1882, which I have not seen. But see also C. Gore, *The Ministry of the Christian Church* (London: Longmans, Green, & Co., 1888, 1893³) esp. Appended Note A. Cf. the letter of 1896 by William Bright in *Selected Letters of William Bright. With an Introductory Memoir by the Rev. P.G. Medd* (ed. B.J. Kidd; London: Wells Gardner, Darton & Co., 1903) 120-2.

[44] The controversial *The Organization of the Early Christian Churches*, 1881 (the Bampton Lectures for 1880). For a Dissenter's appreciation of Hatch's work *vis-a-vis* that of Lightfoot, see A.M. Fairbairn, "Some Recent English Theologians: Lightfoot, Wescott, Hort, Jowett, Hatch," *Contemporary Review* 71 (March 1897) 342-65.

[45] P x.

[46] P xi-xiv, & *The Threefold Ministry. From the Writings of the Bishop of Durham* (privately printed, 1888) & reprinted in DAA 241-6 & BL 129-39. It may be more than coincidental that the use of catenae was an important Tractarian strategy.

[47] His influence in this matter is touched on in T. Langford, *In Search of Foundations. English Theology 1900-1920* (Nashville: Abingdon, 1969) 148-62.

[48] Though some had difficulty in being free of the principle of authority. The dilemma for men of a different frame of mind is caught in Gore's comment:

his substantive view of the ministry found a following because of a willingness to accept his underlying principles, the instrumental view of the Church
and history as the vehicle of the divine intention.[49] Even among High Churchmen the idea of priesthood as representative was taken into the liberal catholic
consensus. If apostolic succession and sacerdotalism were not displaced
from the Anglican theology of the ministry, they were at least significantly
qualified.[50] To the extent that his work facilitated these changes, Lightfoot
might be reckoned to have succeeded in his contemporary purpose.

At the level of history lived and made, his essay provided the framework
within which he viewed the ministry of the contemporary Church of England. That Lightfoot claimed continuity with the true apostolic paradigm is
evident in the Biblical concepts he used as his basic categories in numerous
addresses and meditations to ordinands and clergy. From the range available, two were emphasized.[51]

"Shepherd" encapsulated the pastoral role, "the very heart and kernel" of
the ministry.[52] All those tasks involving service — public ministrations,
administering the sacraments, preaching, teaching the Bible, visitation, consolation of the sick and dispirited, parochial organization and schooling —
were now gathered under this rubric.[53] The ministry in general, but particularly the cure of souls,[54] was "a work of infinite moment for good or evil,
fraught with the issues of eternity".[55] Nothing less than going to work as a
"Son of man" in the manner of Christ Himself was involved.[56]

> We, the ministers of Christ, are invested with the most magnificent of all functions. No
> office can compare with ours for its far reaching issues. No subject of human speech is
> so lofty, so potent, so impressive, as our message.[57]

In the pastoral duties of his office, the Christian minister was a truly significant individual in history.[58]

The principles which find expression in church history are at least as important as the facts in
which they are expressed. It is fatal to neglect either one or the other. Dr Lightfoot's facts may
be pefectly true, but he may still err by ignoring the spirit at work in them.
Gore, *Ministry of the Christian Church*, 354.

[49]   Eg. W. Sanday, *The Conception of Priesthood in the Early Church and in the Church
of England* (London: Longmans, Green, & Co., 1898).

[50]   Sachs, *Transformation*, 162.

[51]   Others were 'servant', 'steward', 'watchman' and 'physician'.

[52]   Good Shepherd, 1868; Advent 1879, 3-4 (f. 4 for the quotation); OA 45; & Advent
1882, 22-5.

[53]   Clerical Office, 1874; & throughout OA 3-213.

[54]   Advent, 1879, 5. Advent, 1882, 12. OA 97-9.

[55]   June, 1879, 1.

[56]   Revival, 1881, 23-4.

[57]   OA 111-12. Cf. OA 80-1.

[58]   For Lightfoot's exaltation of the individual in history, see 108, 141-2 & 149-50
above.

'Ambassador' was the title to which Lightfoot recurred most often.[59] No doubt this was because it encapsulated the understanding for which he was contending. As an 'ambassador', the minister was an accredited representative and agent, entrusted with God's glory[60] and bearing His "transferred personality"[61] as he presents the Gospel message. In this role, Lightfoot asserted, "he is charged with the ministry of reconciliation; he unfolds the will of heaven; he declares in God's name the terms on which pardon is offered; and he pronounces in God's name the absolution of the penitent".[62] In purely temporal terms, his commission was to improve the moral and material condition of life by bringing to bear on society the Christian idea,[63] and to fight vice and misery in all its forms.[64] As the "guardians of morality", the clergy, not social and political reformers, were the true architects of human progress.[65]

Clearly Lightfoot's rejection of sacerdotalism involved no loss of status for the Christian minister. But while the clergyman possessed this dignity in virtue of his function, he was not automatically a maker of history. He, more than anybody else, was obliged to look to his responsibility. As Lightfoot observed to one group, "humanly speaking the destiny of the Church will be decided by the character of the clergy".[66] This was why he always gave so much attention to the conditions of ministerial effectiveness. Often he stated the obvious — the need for industry, regularity, system, thoroughness — lest the great freedom enjoyed by the clergyman dissipate his potential for good.[67] But in this area character mattered most.[68] In common with the pastoral theologians, Lightfoot was keenly aware of the power for good or ill of the clergyman's example.[69] At stake was his credibility. Repeatedly Lightfoot exhorted clergy to avoid debt, follow stricter notions of honour, and avoid amusements and levities allowable to others, since these were the tests of sincerity which parishioners would apply.[70] A ministry unhampered by offence in these areas, and characterized by sympathy, humility and self-

---

[59] June 1879, 2. OA 14-16, 24, 27-8, 45-50 & 58.

[60] OA 99-100.

[61] Untitled ordination address, 1885, 8-9.

[62] P 267.

[63] OA 61-2.

[64] Curse, 1860, 6-7. Sword, 1864, 27-32. SMPW 7-8.

[65] J.B. Lightfoot, "The White Cross," *Contemporary Review* 48 (August 1885) 264, 267-8.

[66] OA 222.

[67] Good Shepherd, 1868, 21-2. OA 85-6.

[68] OA 52.

[69] Sword, 1864, 29-32. Clerical Office, 1874, 29-30. OA 87-8. Heeney, *Different Kind of Gentleman*, ch. II.

[70] Clerical Office, 1874, 24-5. June 1879, 4-6. Advent 1879, 11. OA 24-8, 51-2, 100-2. Untitled ordination address, 1885, 9-23.

denial, was the kind that "would win a way for the Gospel to the hearts of men",[71] and thereby contribute to the realization of "the increasing purpose of God".[72]

But this was not all. Much had changed within the broad representative function of the minister since apostolic times. Certainly it was now more complex than the relatively straightforward roles of the first deacons, presbyters and bishops. Because of their education and status as gentlemen, the English clergy had long been called upon to engage in a range of secular activities in addition to their specifically religious functions. In the nineteenth century such tasks as developing local schools, running charitable and self-help agencies, and even organizing recreational activities for parishioners, were seen as a normal part of the minister's role.[73] Lightfoot accepted all these accretions provided they facilitated the better realization of the basic ideal and did not conflict with it.[74] Indeed such activities were in line with those that had made the Church a progressive force in history.[75] Lightfoot also urged continued adaptation to contemporary conditions. No social class and no problem or manifestation of sin or vice was to be left outside its scope.[76] The same flexibility was required of episcopal superintendency within the English diocesan structure. As Lightfoot reminded Benson at his consecration as first Bishop of Truro in 1877, it was the bishop's task to lead his Church towards that fuller development of organization and more comprehensive study of means required by the times.[77] At all levels, the evolution evident from the beginning needed to continue as the condition of ministerial effectiveness.

In his consideration of the ministry, Lightfoot encountered a dynamic tradition. As contemporaries debated the meaning of the original deposit for the present, it was an area where the "great work" of the day pressed with some urgency. The historical perspective upheld Anglican arrangements against the criticisms of Dissenters but countered the extravagant claims for the ministry within Anglicanism. The role of deacon, presbyter and bishop legitimated by history was merely representative and concerned with spiritual and pastoral effectiveness. Achieving this end in a changing

---

[71]   Good Shepherd, 1868, 19-25, & 31-2 for the quotation. OA 40-1, 52-4, 78-80, 111-16.

[72]   Lightfoot assigned to the right-spirited clergyman a "distinct place and ... proper function in God's vast and varied economy". SMPW 15

[73]   These activities are described in Heeney, *Different Kind of Gentleman*, ch. IV; & G.S.R. Kitson Clark, *Churchmen and the Condition of England 1832-1885* (London: Methuen, 1973).

[74]   PC 65-6 & YJC (1883) 54-6, opposing the permanent diaconate.

[75]   See 86-9 above.

[76]   SMPW 7-8, 11-13; SSO 59-64, 197-8.

[77]   SSO 67-8. Cf. DDC (1881) 100-1.

society also called for innovativeness. This was the role and ideal that guided Lightfoot when he came to face the challenge of ministry away from the familiar conditions of the University, at St Paul's Cathedral in London and in the diocese of Durham.

II

Early in 1871, there came from the Prime Minister an offer of the stall at St Paul's Cathedral vacated by the death of the celebrated Evangelical preacher, Henry Melvill.[78] Confident that this new office could be held concurrently with his Cambridge professorship, Lightfoot took a night to consider but accepted "without hesitation".[79] Prizing the opportunity Mr Gladstone had presented, he "threw himself with his wonted energy into the new work".[80] Three months in each year were now spent in residence, engaged in the day-to-day administration of the Cathedral, conduct of services, weekly preaching, and dealing with private enquiries, an aspect of the work in which he was said to excel. Lightfoot was also rarely absent from Chapter meetings, even during University terms.[81]

One reason for this commitment was an earnest desire of "some ecclesiastical position for its own sake".[82] Since he despised absenteeism,[83] only a part time cathedral position would allow Lightfoot to participate regularly in the wider life of the Church while still at the University. Westcott and Benson had already shown how two offices could be combined,[84] as well as

---

[78] Henry Melvill (1798-1871); Canon of St Paul's (1858-1871) & Rector of Barnes (1863-1871). Lewis (ed.), *Dictionary of Evangelical Biography*, II.764. According to Landow, *Victorian Types*, 15-16, he was considered by good judges to be the greatest preacher of the day.

[79] Lightfoot to Gladstone, 11 February 1871 (GBL, 44 424, f. 281). Watkins, BL 59, speaks of "much hesitation", with a final decision being postponed until it was determined that the period of London residence would not interfere with Cambridge terms. Apart from Lightfoot's eagerness to accept, "taking a night to consider" hardly constitutes "much hesitation". In any case it was still unclear at the time of acceptance whether it would be possible for residence in London not to encroach upon academic duties. Further, the true cause of Lightfoot's concern was the necessity of severing his formal link with Trinity College.

[80] DNB XI.1113.

[81] See the Chapter Minute Books (SPL).

[82] Lightfoot to Gladstone, 10 February 1871 (GBL, 44 424, f. 275).

[83] Lightfoot to Stanley, 3 July 1869 (GBL, 44 318, f. 83).

[84] Benson was Prebendary at Lincoln while still Headmaster at Wellington College. LB I.266-72. When Westcott became Regius Professor the year before, he retained his stall at Peterborough. Lightfoot's three months of residence were usually January, May and September, the vacations or less busy periods of the University year.

nurturing an interest in cathedral reform.[85] Consequently Lightfoot was glad
to join those who were anxious that St Paul's occupy its proper place in the
life of the diocese and nation.[86] His role in schemes for reform and reconstruction was distinctly secondary to that of Robert Gregory, and even of
Liddon, but he was supportive of "anything that made for the effective utili-
zation of the great church",[87] an end for which he was prepared to compromise on non-essentials with his High Church colleagues — though great
awkwardness sometimes resulted.[88] In fact his contribution to the revival of
St Paul's went beyond support of the fundamental principle of usefulness.
His reputation for scholarship and moderation gave respectability to changes
which might otherwise have been opposed on "party" grounds.[89] In this
unique way he helped to place St Paul's at the head of the movement for
cathedral reform throughout England in the period of his canonry.[90]

Lightfoot was especially glad to come to St Paul's. The position was, he
said, "exactly what I should have chosen, if the choice had been left to myself".[91] This was due in part to the coincidence of his appointment with a
move to complete the Cathedral. In September of the previous year, Dean
Mansel had announced a scheme "to render the Cathedral worthy of its unrivalled exterior, and to carry out the intentions of its great architect".[92] When
R.W. Church succeeded to the Deanery, Lightfoot wrote:

---

[85] Eg. Benson to Lightfoot, 10 July 1869, on the duties of prebendaries in cathedral churches following his own appointment as Prebendary at Lincoln. LB I.266-7. Cf. Benson to Lightfoot, December 1869 [sic], in *ibid.,* I.326. Westcott spoke of the ideals and enthusiasms he shared in this respect with Benson and Lightfoot. LB II.691. See B.F. Westcott, "Cathedral Work," *Macmillan's Magazine* 21 (January 1870) 246-51; & 21 (February 1870) 308-14. Lightfoot was on holiday with Benson and Westcott in the Lakes District when Benson sent off his "Cathedral Life and Cathedral Work," *Quarterly Review* 130 (January 1871) 225-55. Entry for 6 January 1871 (TCC, Benson Diaries).

[86] Reform had begun under Dean Milman. It surged ahead with the appointment of Robert Gregory in 1868. He found an ally in H.P. Liddon, appointed in 1870. See G.L. Prestige, *St Paul's in its Glory: A Candid History of the Cathedral 1831-1911* (London: S.P.C.K., 1955); W.M. Atkins, "The Age of Reform 1831-1934," *A History of St Paul's Cathedral and the Men Associated With It* (eds W.R. Matthews & W.M. Atkins; London: Phoenix, 1957) 250-99. For the larger setting, see now P. Barrett, *Barchester. English Cathedral Life in the Nineteenth Century* (London: S.P.C.K., 1993).

[87] M.C. Church, *Life and Letters of Dean Church* (London: Macmillan, 1897) 262.

[88] W. Russell, *St Paul's Under Dean Church and His Associates* (London, 1922) 28.

[89] *Ibid.,* 25. A.O. Charles, "The Ministry at St Paul's Under Dean Church as Guide to a Contemporary Pastoral Challenge" (unpublished Diploma thesis; St Augustine's College, Canterbury, 1965 [copy at St Paul's Cathedral Library, press mark 52.c.22a]).

[90] Prestige, *St Paul's*, esp. ch. 6ff. Chadwick, *Victorian Church* II.366-95. Barrett, *Barchester*, 71.

[91] Lightfoot to Tait, 15 March 1871 (TPL, vol. 89, f. 161).

[92] Prestige, *St Paul's*, 133. For Lightfoot's initial reaction to the grandeur of St Paul's, see Lightfoot to Westcott, 8 May 1871 (LAC). Cf. HE 143.

I seem to see very great grounds for hope. If the work of decoration is undertaken with energy, there seems no reason why it should not be completed within our generation. The means are there, if only the enthusiasm can be fired.[93]

He himself had lost no time in appealing for help.[94] But in this respect his canonry was less successful. The matter soon became controversial,[95] and in the discussions which followed Lightfoot himself took an independent line.[96] By the time he left eight years later nothing had been achieved.[97]

Lightfoot also had a keen sense of the importance of the Cathedral's location, as the dedication of the second edition of *Ignatius and Polycarp* suggests:

To Henry Parry Liddon, D.D., to whom God has given special gifts as a Christian Preacher and matched the gifts with the opportunities assigning him to his place, beneath the great dome of St Paul's, the centre of the world's concourse.[98]

Despite this great opportunity, or perhaps because of it, when it was Lightfoot's turn to preach under the dome there was "much sinking of heart".[99] The congregations he drew were never so large as Liddon's. Indeed, Lightfoot was the one in the contemporary skit "who could write but not preach", his sermons being marred by poor delivery, though "full of good matter".[100] Nevertheless, he attracted a following among those who could appreciate what he offered. "We have made Lightfoot a preacher;" Tait once remarked, "and, when asked to explain the process by which such preachers were made, added, 'We have given the finest pulpit in the world to a man to whom God has given the power to use it,' and expressed his conviction that better use of it had never been made."[101] If Cambridge had to be made into the spiritual power of the nineteenth century, the voice to the world at St Paul's had only to be sounded For the second time in his career Lightfoot found himself at a centre of strategic importance for contemporary Christianity.

His understanding of what it meant to work there was further defined by the history of St Paul's.[102] Two features in particular contributed to his vi-

---

[93] Lightfoot to Church, 19 August 1871 (CPO, Red Filing Box C, no. 15 of 35 miscellaneous letters).

[94] Worship, 1871, 23-4.

[95] Eg. *The Guardian* (22 May 1872) 680-1; J.T. Emmet, "The Completion of St Paul's," *Quarterly Review* 133 (October 1872) 342-86; & J. Fergusson, "St Paul's Cathedral," *Contemporary Review* 24 (October 1874) 750-71.

[96] Atkins, "Age of Reform," 275. Eg. Lightfoot to Westcott, 27 June 1874 (LAC) with Chapter Minute Book 1860-74, 27 June 1874 (SPL).

[97] Russell, *St Paul's,* 69.

[98] AF II.1^2.v.

[99] Lightfoot to Westcott, 31 August, 12 & 15 September 1871 (LAC).

[100] Russell, *St Paul's,* 26-7.

[101] BL 56.

[102] He read Milman's *Annals of St Paul's Cathedral.* HE 231 n. 2, 233-4 For a detailed knowledge of one period, see the sermon on John Donne, "the first of our classic preachers", in HE 221-45 (quotation on 241). His very first sermon included an illustration from the history. Likeness, 1871, 28-9.

sion.[103] One was the sixth century dedication in the name of St Paul, at a time when it was rarely given to any church. The inheritence of the name of "the Apostle of the Gentiles" delimited the sphere of its ministry as all the world, and prescribed "union with God in Christ" as the doctrine that was to be taught.[104] The other impressive feature was "the long continuity of this history, which connects the site with the name of St Paul". With all of its power to animate and direct, this name had been before those who used the location for more than a thousand years. Lightfoot willingly placed himself under the obligation to maintain this tradition. It provided a chance to match his aspirations for England's leading cathedral with the view of Christianity he purveyed from his Cambridge chair.

The missionary challenge arising out of this identification with St Paul was in part realized by reforms intended to secure the complete and more general use of the building. Services were improved and made regular. On Sunday they were brought out of the choir into the more commodious nave. New services were introduced to attract different groups and types of worshipper, while changes in the music under the new organist, Dr John Stainer, made St Paul's a centre of interest. The church was also opened for private prayer on week days, and additional chapels were provided to increase the facilities available to diocesan organizations.[105] On Saturday afternoons, large parties were conducted over the Cathedral free of the normal charges, with Lightfoot taking his turn as guide.[106] Some restrictions were also required. One was the stipulation that the annual charity children's service, which caused normal services to be suspended for a month, could continue only if the promoters met certain conditions. Lightfoot defended the decision:

> with our increased number of services and very largely increased attendances, we feel that we should incur a grave responsibility if we interrupted them even for a single week ... I may add, also, that after expending a very large sum in cleaning the Cathedral, the Dean and Chapter would not be justified in giving over the building for several weeks annually to the confusion and dirt which are the necessary consequences of turning it into a carpenter's shop.[107]

If it was to reach out to the community, the Cathedral had to be available at all times for the purposes for which it was consecrated.

---

[103] SSP 218-29. Cf. God's Witness, 1875, 14.

[104] SSP 223-4, 227, 228. P ix.

[105] Russell, *St Paul's, passim.* Charles, "Ministry," ch. 2. Prestige, *St Paul's,* 106, 121-2. W.M. Sinclair, *Memorials of St Paul's Cathedral* (London: Chapman & Hall, 1909) 307-11.

[106] *Ibid.,* 322.

[107] Lightfoot to the Editor, *The Times* (23 May 1873) 12. See also Chapter Minute Book 1860-1874, 22 March & 14 June 1873; 3 March 1874; & 20 April & 11 June 1877 (SPL).

As St Paul's "was waking up to practical realities and learning the greatness of its opportunities,"[108] it was realized that this missionary ideal had one important local application. Within its precincts was a significant working population which the Dean and Chapter were anxious to attract into the Cathedral.[109] Employed in the business houses of the neighbourhood, and boarded by their firms, these men had no natural connection with any parochial organization, a deficiency aggravated by the absenteeism of inner city incumbents, who seldom did more than conduct a Sunday service in their churches.[110] Advised that anything like an ordinary service would not overcome the fear of being ridiculed, Gregory, drawing on his extensive experience at St Mary's, Lambeth, sought to tap the vogue for adult education by proposing a series of mid-week lectures of a semi-secular character.[111] Commenced in November, 1871, with well over a thousand in attendance, the response so exceeded expectations that the lectures were not only continued, but also supplemented by Wednesday night soirees to enable the Cathedral staff to become acquainted personally with the men attending.[112] On one occasion Lightfoot offered his own collection of photographs as the entertainment,[113] a gesture which reflected his support for a scheme which "made St Paul's at that period a sort of parish church for the City".[114]

When Lightfoot's turn to lecture came round in 1872, he selected an historical subject, a preference maintained the following year in his second course.[115] The choice involved turning away from the immediate concerns of Gregory's "the conditions of present and recent ages".[116] In justification,

---

[108] From the diary of Verger Green, quoted in Charles, "Ministry," 15.

[109] Prestige, *St Paul's*, 168. Russell, *St Paul's*, 40-1, 57-9. B.A. Smith, *Dean Church. The Anglican Response to Newman* (London: Oxford University Press, 1958) 162.

[110] For Lightfoot's sense of the pastoral problems in London parishes, see SMPW 11-13.

[111] R. Gregory, *Robert Gregory, 1819-1911: Being the Autobiography of Robert Gregory, Dean of St Paul's* (ed. W.H. Hutton; London: Longmans, 1912) 197; & his letter to *The Times* (10 November 1871) 6. Heeney, *Different Kind of Gentleman*, 82-5. For Lightfoot's understanding of the same problem, see Leaven, 1877, 26-8.

[112] Gregory's lectures, "Are We Better Than Our Fathers?", were reported in *The Times* (8, 16, & 23 November, & 1 December 1871). Prestige, *St Paul's*, 106-7. Liddon on one occasion addressed up to 1700 men. Smith, *Dean Church*, 160. For the soirees, see *The Times* (5 January & 22 October 1872). For the continuation of the lectures, see Chapter Minute Book 1860-1874, 22 December 1871 & 14 June 1873 (SPL). The Chapter also hoped to establish a library for the workingmen attached to the Cathedral. *Ibid.*, 16 October 1873.

[113] *The Times* (5 January 1872) 4.

[114] Smith, *Dean Church*, 162. Atkins, "Age of Reform," 276.

[115] "Christian Life in the Second and Third Centuries," in HE 1-71; & "Christianity and Paganism," in S 65-116.

[116] R. Gregory, "Some of the Bonds of Society, Past and Present, Material, Social, and Moral," reported in *The Times,* (30 October, & 7 & 13 November 1872).

Lightfoot cited the didacticism of historical knowledge. "If only we can read them aright, the records of the difficulties, the sufferings, the triumphs of early Christianity are replete with lessons of immediate interest."[117] Contrary to what members of the congregation might have thought, an historical topic, because of its capacity to instruct the concerns of the present in the regulative truths of life, had an importance at least equal to that of Gregory's more contemporary subject matter.

The choice of early Christianity as the topic was also significant. Clearly Lightfoot will have felt at home in the area of his scholarly expertise. But there was more to it than that. Apart from the association with St Paul, there was not much of a local tradition ready to hand for Lightfoot to work with. He responded by invoking the generalized tradition of the early Church. It readily permitted connecting his working class audience with the educational function he took to be the point of historical understanding.

The first lesson discerned by Lightfoot suggests adaptation to the social standing of his congregation. Christianity's record in the early centuries endorsed its teaching, that it is a religion for all classes of men.[118] Perhaps with an eye to the contrast offered by the present day, particularly at a fashionable church like the city cathedral, he pointed out that converts were at first drawn mainly from the less influential and educated classes in society.[119] Seizing the opportunity to emphasize their achievement, he averred that it was to them that the Church owed its success in commending Christianity to the world. Of course, this was characteristic of Lightfoot's interpretation of early church history;[120] but he went further on this occasion, suggesting that it was almost as though only the lower classes could have done it:

> There was nothing in the social experiences of the high-born and wealthy, or in the technical education of the philosopher or the rhetorician, which peculiarly qualified them for appraising the worth of Christianity. Nay, just so far as the higher classes were removed from the hardest trials of their fellow men, just so far as convention had dulled and stiffened in them the common instincts of humanity, they were absolutely incapacitated as judges.[121]

The inference which followed was clear enough, although, possibly in order to avoid condescension, Lightfoot did not make it explicit. The labouring classes were still as important as ever to the well being of the Church. At the very least there was a place for them at St Paul's.

---

[117] HE 1.

[118] HE 9-15; cf. 23-4.

[119] For Lightfoot's consciousness of the problem of class in the contemporary church, see RCC (1873) 233.

[120] J.B. Lightfoot, "They That Are of Caesar's Household," *Journal of Classical and Sacred Philology* IV.x (March 1857) 57-79; & P 171-8.

[121] HE 11.

The second lesson was complementary to the first. If he had shown what the lower classes had done for the Church, it could also be shown what the Church had done for them. Indeed this was part of Lightfoot's reason for selecting the early period in church history for presentation on these occasions.[122] In the first century, Christianity was aided by "the special influence and extraordinary inspiration of the Apostles".[123] In the fourth century, it was first supported by the state, and then laboured under the strong disadvantage occasioned by Julian's restoration of paganism.[124] By contrast, the second and third centuries exhibited Christianity "as an independent force, working in and by itself". During this phase of church history its capacity as a morally transforming power was disclosed, both at the level of society and also of the individual.[125] Again, it followed that what had happened then could happen now. Just as history taught that the Church needed the labouring classes, it also taught that they needed the Church as a morally regenerating and sustaining force in their lives.

By creating these images Lightfoot drew on the Christian past as an agent in the missionary endeavour of the Cathedral ministry. His adaptation of the material was calculated to counter working class resistance to the Christian message. In taking this approach, Lightfoot assumed a moral outlook in the working men of London similar to his own. The strategic consequences of building on this moral aspiration were disclosed at the end of the 1872 series, when he summed up the objectives he had been pursuing. In the first instance Lightfoot had aimed simply at the creation of an interest in the past itself. His task had been achieved, he said, "If I have succeeded in exciting in any one member of this congregation a desire for a more familiar acquaintance with the records of his spiritual ancestry in primitive times".[126] To this end Lightfoot had brought before them the great achievements of Christianity in history, measured, of course, by "their moral significance and their moral results".[127]

Beyond interest in the Christian past lay an enthusiasm for Christianity based on its moral greatness. This was why Lightfoot focussed on the men and women who had made possible its historic achievements.[128] Of the two groups in the early church who had represented Christianity before a hostile State, it was not the apologists, but rather the martyrs — by their apprecia-

---

[122] HE 14-15 for Lightfoot's other reason.
[123] HE 2-3.
[124] S 65-9.
[125] HE 14-15.
[126] HE 70.
[127] HE 41.
[128] HE 40-2.

tion of the moral significance of the conflict, and the courage and the ardour of belief that sustained a willingness to die — who secured the victory in the conflict between heaven and earth, between Christ and Anti-Christ.[129] This preference for the mainly anonymous martyrs was important for its effect of bringing the influence of Christianity upon western society down to the level of ordinary individual achievement. In turn, this reduced the remoteness of the heroes of history, arising from their distance in time and the exaltation of their sacrifice, making similar deeds accessible to men and women in the present. For in the Christianity which Lightfoot urged there was still great moral opportunity. A meaningful share in its struggles, and thus a contribution to the progress of history, was something to which the members of the congregation might themselves aspire, despite their lowly social status.[130] The memories Lightfoot provided were intended to motivate and energize to secure participation in the "increasing purpose".

Having exposed them to its challenge, Lightfoot sought also to lead these workingmen further, into a direct engagement with the history of the Church. His job was done, he reflected, "if I have struck out in one intelligent heart a fresh spark of sympathy with the grand historic past".[131] To the meaning and value of this sympathy Lightfoot was directed by the early Christians themselves, in their practice of repairing to the catacombs as places of assembly and worship.[132] As it had for them, sympathy still meant a conscious oneness with those who had gone before, in their emotions and feelings, struggles and hopes. It arises from understanding all experience as a continuum suffused by "the Eternal Presence". With the past, present and future thus held together in unity, the individual's sense of isolation in a boundless world is replaced by a sense of association which produces for him a "strength of purpose" and "an assurance of hope". As a mode of appreciating the value of individual existence, strongly under challenge from modern science, and especially contemporary industrial organization, Lightfoot commended the early history of the Church for personal appropriation. Amid the social dislocation enforced by the conditions of their material existence, incorporation into this history offered the warehousemen an awareness of individual significance through corporate identity. Creating a sense of identity with other members of the Church in the past was the means of building a sense of Church membership in the present.

The final aim in Lightfoot's introduction to the early history of Christianity, up to which all else had led, was the release of its power into the lives of

---

[129] HE 26-48, esp. 31. Cf. CS 252-3.
[130] HE 24.
[131] HE 70-1.
[132] HE 69-70.

the men to prepare and equip them for present day challenges and struggles as church members. The lectures were a success if "only a single hearer has carried away ... into the fretting cares and distractions and trials of daily life, one cheering memory or one heroic resolve or one ennobling thought".[133] This objective was at work in the use of the material to illustrate what identification with Christianity might mean, particularly in relation to the demands of the dominical saying recorded in Matthew 22:21.[134] Given the composition of the congregation, Lightfoot's application was somewhat forced. He himself admitted the question of the competing claims of Church and State was not so urgent in their own day. Yet, its relevance was pressed:

> the great problem which must engage the attention of every conscientious man is how he can harmonize these claims ... in some form or other it must always press for solution. It is as fresh to you and to me today as it was to any member of this small and persecuted sect more than seventeen hundred years ago.[135]

Their example was an incentive to maintain the struggle to satisfy the claims of the State without compromising personal belief. How to be good citizens and good Churchmen at the same time was arguably still the dilemma.

More appropriate to St Paul's perhaps was the much vexed question of worship. Lightfoot compared the primitive form "with its latest developments as we witness them ourselves", and the "contrast between them and the past is drawn out". Moreover, the subject was meant to suggest "important reflections" to the congregation.[136] That external emblems and imposing rites were not intrinsic to Christianity was one of them. Appearing later as mere historical accretions, they were in no way normative for the Church in the present.[137] It followed from this that contemporary proponents of elaborate worship, whatever else they might say, could not appeal to the sanction of antiquity to uphold their position. More seriously, Lightfoot warned that there was great danger to a Church troubled by ritualists who forgot that their excessive practices in the past had provoked the reaction of the "iconoclast and the puritan" to the great detriment of its corporate spiritual life.[138] However, historial precedent, properly understood, cut two ways. Appeal to the simple worship of the early church as prescriptive for the nineteenth century was equally facile.[139] Primitive simplicity was not a principle of the faith either, but merely a necessity occasioned by the legal position of the first Christian congregations.[140]

---

[133] HE 71.

[134] "Render ... to Caesar the things that are Caesar's, and to God the things that are God's." Cf. Mark 12:17. HE 36-8.

[135] HE 8.

[136] HE 54-5, 59.

[137] HE 52-4.

[138] HE 56-7.

[139] HE 54-6.

[140] HE 52-4, 60-1.

Further, Lightfoot ventured the suggestion that enforced abstention from more elaborate forms of worship fulfilled a recognizable function within the divine plan by creating the conditions for a decisive break with the spirit of paganism.[141] But what had then been potentially injurious — special buildings for worship, music, paintings, sculpture — could now be defended as useful, even indispensable, an important point to make at a church attempting not only to attract workingmen but also to provide services consonant with the magnificent architectural setting.[142] Neither side in the controversy could therefore effectively buttress its position by precedent. Historical consideration showed that what mattered was not any phase or dislocation in the worship of the church, but its continuity, which meant that the development from simple to elaborate worship was legitimate, provided always that the spirituality of the Gospel is maintained.[143] The only practical approach to the problem of worship suggested by reference to early Christian history was toleration from the Church for ritualism, and moderation from ritualists within the Church.

While Lightfoot's examples were probably remote from the lives of the warehousemen, so employed the past guided them away from what Christianity is not, and redirected them to what it is, and might become, consistently with the maintenance of its essential character. The scope allowed to development also pointed to the place of the future in the Christian life. In language recalling what was said to Cambridge undergraduates, Lightfoot noted that, with the privilege of holding the past as a possession for use in the present, there existed a responsibility to generations still to come. As the latest representatives of the Church, in its ongoing struggle with the world around, they must see to it that, in their contribution under the conditions of their own society, there was no loss of purity or weakening of resolve.[144] Accordingly Lightfoot's invitation to make use of the past carried the condition of being willing to bear this burden. He wanted the men who heard him to go away with the understanding that, in making the history of the Church their own possession, they themselves became the possession of the Church. If they would be Churchmen, there was much for them to receive, but much also they must pass on.

Lightfoot's presentation of the second and third Christian centuries not only extended the missionary concern of St Paul, but also continued his characteristic teaching as well. This was achieved by quoting from the Epistle of Diognetus at the beginning of the first lecture, where it served as the text

---

[141] HE 55-6.
[142] Worship, 1871, 19-20.
[143] HE 57-9.
[144] HE 24.

for both series.[145] The superiority of its picture of the "struggles and the aspirations and victories of Christianity in the early ages", over the utterance of contemporary heathen writers, was "a Person and a Fact":

> the incarnation of the Divine Word, the realization of God's presence through the human life and death of Christ. Here is the mainspring of this energy, the hidden source of this new and vigorous life.[146]

Thus the Church in this period exhibited both the moral achievement of Christianity and the "vital energy" that produced it. Its history, therefore, served as a commentary on Paul's conception of the Gospel, "a Person and a Life" working within the Christian society.[147] As the means of bringing forward the operation of the Logos, past and potential, the history was theologically conceived, and expressed Lightfoot's faith in the pastoral efficacy of his most fundamental theological principle. As such it was the instrument at the local level of the wider programme he set himself for reviving the Logos theology in the life of the contemporary English Church.

The lectures delivered by Lightfoot at St Paul's in 1872 and 1873 constitute a specimen of him in action as a minister before an ordinary "parish" congregation. Bringing the working men of London into contact with their history so that they might feel its uplifting effects in their lives was in line with the task of representing God to humanity. Similarly, leading them in their response as Church members was part of representing humanity to God. It also fulfilled the historically strategic function of the Christian minister. On the assumption that what was achieved in London would be felt far beyond, geographically and chronologically, Lightfoot had sought the maintenance of the continuity of church life which was the essence of all history. His immediate object was to tap the power of the lower orders working upwards from below in the life of his Church and society. By adumbrating problems and possible responses, the Christian past was also an instrument for instructing these workingmen in the responsibilities of membership in both the Church and the wider society. History in the setting of St Paul's was both the missionary and educative device intended for it in the framework of "the increasing purpose of God".

Lightfoot's participation in this congenial ministry was short lived. The success of the outreach to the warehousemen was such that the work was turned over to the Minor Canons to continue on a regular basis.[148] This left Lightfoot free for other aspects of the work. By the time he left St Paul's he had made his mark. The historian of contemporary English cathedral life includes Lightfoot among those deans and canons "who cared deeply, not

---

[145] HE 3-7.

[146] HE 8.

[147] P ix.

[148] Russell, *St Paul's*, 58.

only for the cathedral and its services, but also for its impact on the life of the city and diocese and on the general public", and thereby transformed the mission of cathedrals to English society.[149] The means by which this had been achieved were not forgotten, and something similar in the use of history was attempted in a more sustained fashion over a wider area when Lightfoot became a bishop six years later. There the situation was somewhat different. If at St Paul's his ministry had required the invention of a tradition, in Durham the need was for an existing tradition to be revived and enhanced.

III

On January 18, 1879, after advice and encouragement from Archbishop Tait,[150] Lord Beaconsfield offered Lightfoot the Bishopric of Durham left vacant by the retirement of Charles Baring.[151] Despite being urged strenuously to accept by many of those whose counsel he sought, Lightfoot demurred, as he had done twelve years previously when offered Lichfield.[152] Intervention by Dean Vaughan from a sickbed caused him to reconsider,[153] while the final advice of Benson at last produced a change of mind.[154] Putting aside his own personal inclinations, Lightfoot accepted Durham nine days after the offer.[155]

Lightfoot viewed his unexpected accession to the bishop's role as "the most momentous crisis of his life".[156] His dismay also arose out of the overturning of the ideal of life formed almost twenty years previously, when he settled on Cambridge as his home, and the interpretation of earliest Christianity as his work. What it cost to leave Cambridge for Durham was reflected in his valedictory sermon. Lightfoot spoke as much to himself as to the undergraduates when he said in characteristic tones of heavy gravitas:

---

[149] Barrett, *Barchester*, 270-1.

[150] J. Hassard to Lightfoot, 31 January 1879, quoting the advice sent to the Prime Minister on 13 January 1879.

[151] Lord Beaconsfield to Lightfoot, 18 January 1879.

[152] A draft of the reply intended for the Prime Minister survives among the Lightfoot Papers. The extent of correction and recasting points to the struggle of his deliberations. See also Lightfoot to Benson, 24 January 1879 (PLAB 1878-1882, TCC).

[153] A.P. Stanley to Lightfoot, 24 January 1879; & C.J. Vaughan to Lightfoot, 25 January 1879.

[154] Lightfoot to Benson, 24 January 1879 (PLAB 1878-1882, TCC); & Benson to Lightfoot, 26 January 1879. For Benson's recollection of the events leading to the change, see LB I.471-3. See also Lightfoot to H. Sidgwick, 28 January [1879] (TCC, Add Ms.c.94[86]); & Lightfoot to Tait, 29 January 1879 (TLP, vol. 99, f. 38).

[155] M. Corry to Lightfoot, 27 January 1879. Lightfoot to Westcott, 27 January 1879 (LAC).

[156] LNC 164. Cf. "the great trial of my life", in Lightfoot to Henry Sidgwick, 8 January 1879 (TCC, Add Ms.c.94[86]).

Be slaves, and accept frankly the consequences of your slavery ... the grip of a Divine necessity will fasten upon you. Another will gird you and carry you whither you would not — far away from the home that you have cherished, from the friends that you have loved, from the work that has been a pleasure to you. Your ideal of life is shattered in a moment. Your hopes and projects for the future crumble into dust at the touch of God. Nay, do not repine. Follow him cheerfully, whithersoever He may take you. Your cross will be your consolation; your trial will be your glory.[157]

Looking back, he remembered the time as a great venture of faith, which warranted the same identification with Abraham he had already made for others who had had to face the unknown.[158]

Yet, while so acutely aware of the magnitude of the change, Lightfoot also sought the elements of continuity. At the luncheon following the enthronement, he compared the Cambridge and Durham coats of arms.[159] Four lions were present in both, but in the Durham shield they were no longer rampant, but passant, and the book in the Cambridge shield was gone. In prospect, the move from student and university teacher to the bishopric of a large and important diocese did not mean that his theology and characteristic thinking would have to change, only the sphere of its application. This was why he was able to throw himself into the studies and duties required by the new circumstances of his life.[160] From this day he spoke of "my own Durham",[161] and, to the people of the diocese, of "our own Durham".[162] It was not long before he convinced himself that his diocese was where the work of the Church of England would be done.[163] Once more, Lightfoot had found a grand historic function for his ministry.

The history of the Church in Durham played a key part in Lightfoot's adjustment to his new work. This association of himself with the previous life of the diocese began at least as early as the choice of Butler as the subject for his enthronement sermon. By turning to the only previous "Joseph Dunelm", he established publicly at the very outset his personal contact with the See's past. The continuity Lightfoot wanted to see in his career went beyond a similarity of names. The sermon also recalled Butler's judgment

---

[157] CS 296-7.

[158] OA 195-6. Cf. J.B. Lightfoot, *The Father of Missionaries. A Sermon Preached on S. Andrew's Day, 1876, Before Members of the University, In S. Michael's Church, Cambridge* (Cambridge: privately printed, 1877). Reprinted in SSO 38-54, to which reference is made.

[159] DDC (1880) 91. LD 56-7.

[160] OA 195-6. B.F. Westcott, "Prefatory Note," in HE vi-vii.

[161] LNC 169.

[162] LNC 63, 157. In the words of his chaplain, Henry Savage, "he had given himself wholly for better or worse" to the diocese. LD 113.

[163] RCC (1881) 17. Lightfoot to G.H. Wilkinson, 24 November 1882, in A.J. Mason, *Memoir of George Howard Wilkinson* (2 vols; London: Longmans, Green, & Co., 1909) II.5-6. Cf. 3.

on the prospect of death, "as an awful thing to appear before the moral governor of the world".[164] Although expressed at the last, this idea — the "consciousness of an Eternal Presence, this sense of a Supreme Righteousness, this conviction of a Divine Order" — had dominated Butler's entire life, as it had already dominated his own.[165] In this understanding, Lightfoot recognized a mode of his favourite Logos theology, for "this Presence, this Order, this Righteousness" is "in the language of Holy Scripture this Word of the Lord".[166] His own characteristic way of thinking had not only been represented in the diocese before, but by "the greatest of the bishops of Durham".[167] It was personally reassuring that the past showed that the conception of the Christian life, and the approach to Church problems, that he had first formed in the study at Cambridge and applied already at St Paul's could operate equally well in this new area of action.

This personal identification with the history of the diocese continued throughout Lightfoot's episcopate. Against attempts to have the Bishop's residence transferred to Durham, Lightfoot preferred to live at Bishop Auckland, in "the home of my fathers".[168] Westcott regarded the unfinished essay on Auckland Castle as "a remarkable example of that enthusiasm with which the Bishop threw himself into inquiries, foreign to the general line of his studies, which were suggested by the circumstances of his life".[169] Indeed, the request once sent from Lambeth for Low's *Durham Diocesan History* suggests that the history of the Church in Durham was never far from his thoughts.[170] He was continually impressed by the personal qualities of the men and women whose lives adorned the history of the diocese.[171] He was also moved by the achievement of the northern Church, not only for the English Church and nation, but also for western Europe, and, as he later realized, the wider world.[172] In every age there was cause for satisfaction at what had been done inside and outside the diocese by the Durham Church.

[164] LNC 161.
[165] Eg. CS 225-8, 244-7.
[166] LNC 162.
[167] LNC 161.
[168] DDC (1880) 96-7.
[169] B.F. Westcott, "Prefatory Note," in HE vi-vii, referring to "The Chapel of St Peter and the Manor House of Auckland," 182-220. Further evidence of these studies is the memorandum on previous Bishops of Durham in the Lightfoot Papers which an assistant was commissioned to prepare.
[170] Lightfoot to J. Armitage Robinson, 19 May 1884, quoted in LD 161. Cf. AF I.1².54 n. 3.
[171] The windows in the restored St Peter's Chapel were especially important in this respect, as Benson recalled after Lightfoot's death: "... the last time I was here he went round dwelling on the force and teaching and art of each window." LB II.291. For Lightfoot's conception of the windows, see LNC 200 n. 99.
[172] See esp. "The Celtic Mission of Iona and Lindisfarne" and "John Cosin" in LNC 1-17 & 137-57, in which Lightfoot presented his understanding of the diocesan history.

It was an historical 'bequest' into which Lightfoot entered gladly. Contemporaries marvelled that he made the transition from university to bishopric so easily and so completely; and, looking back, Westcott thought the decade at Durham the happiest of Lightfoot's life.[173] What they saw was illusory. There had had to be a sustained identification of himself with the processes of diocesan Church life. The great crisis of his life had produced Lightfoot's greatest personal use of history.

The continuity Lightfoot was inclined to see in his own career was also transferred to the diocese. It was again significant that he chose the example of Butler as the ideal to realize in the course of his episcopate. Sharing a community of ideas, he would be actuated by the same view of the life of an individual and holder of high office as his illustrious predecessor.

> And what more seasonable prayer can you offer for him who addresses you now, at this most momentous crisis of his life, than that he — the latest successor of Butler — may enter upon the duties of his high and responsible office in the same spirit; that the realization of this great fact, may be the constant effort of his life; that glimpses of the invisible Righteousness, of the Invisible Grace, of the Invisible Glory, may be vouchsafed to him; and that the Eternal Presence, thus haunting him night and day, may rebuke, may deter, may guide, may strengthen, may comfort, may illumine, may consecrate and subdue the feeble and wayward impulses of his own heart to God's holy will and purpose.[174]

While he sought the personal resources for the episcopate in this ideal,[175] the implied hope was that, in this sense, his own career as bishop would be as fortunate for Durham as Butler's and thereby maintain the great tradition to which he was heir. This wish for continuity made it a prayer as much for the diocese as for himself.[176] It too was brought within the structure of his theology of history as he made the transfer from Cambridge to Durham.

The diocese to which Lightfoot came ran from the River Tees in the south to the Scottish border in the north, and embraced the counties of Durham and Northumberland. It was approaching the end of a century of industrial expansion that had been at its most intense from 1850.[177] Exceptional growth in the mining and metal industries had stimulated ship-building and engineering, developments which added a large migrant labour force to an already growing population. Mining settlements too continually mushroomed

---

[173] Entry for 30 April 1879 (seeing what he wanted to see), Diary of E.W. Benson 1871-1881, 304 (TCC). LD 15 (Dean Welldon). B.F. Westcott, *From Strength to Strength* (London: Macmillan, 1890) 46.

[174] LNC 164-5.

[175] LNC 167-71.

[176] LNC 165.

[177] For statistics and demographic trends, see J.W. House, *North Eastern England. Population Movements and the Landscape Since the Early Nineteenth Century* (University of Durham, King's College Dept of Geography, Research Series no. 1; Newcastle-Upon-Tyne, [1959]).

throughout the southern half of the diocese. Each of its three tidal rivers became closely settled industrial regions, spawning monotonous streets of uniformly dull housing. The squalor and ill-health of these towns was notorious.[178]

Already the Durham ecclesiastical establishment had made a strong effort to meet the challenges posed by rapid industrial expansion, albeit reluctantly at first under the pressure of public opinion and the legislation of the 1830s.[179] In the following twenty five years church accommodation was substantially increased — although not at a rate to keep pace with population growth, or even regain lost ground — and clerical supervision improved, as pluralism, and non-residence were sharply reduced by means of augmentation of benefices and provision of habitable parsonages.[180] These initiatives were continued by Lightfoot's immediate predecessor, the Evangelical Charles Baring.[181] Aided by the recent Local Claims Act, he added the creation of new ecclesiastical districts to the range of Church responses. During his episcopate 102 new parishes were created, 110 churches built, and 138 additional clergy recruited. Finding Durham too much for one man, he also secured provision for a new see of Newcastle in the 1878 Act extending the episcopate. By such measures Baring laid a strong foundation for Lightfoot to build on. He deserved more credit for the revival of the diocese than Lightfoot's followers allowed.[182]

Notwithstanding Baring's judgment on the eve of his retirement, that the work of church extension was virtually complete, much remained to be done at Lightfoot's appointment. Even before leaving Cambridge, he had turned his attention to the new responsibilities. Over the next decade, in order to be free for the work of the diocese, he generally held aloof from the wider

---

[178] N. McCord, *North East England. The Region's Development 1760-1960. An Economic and Social History* (London: Batsford Academic, 1979).

[179] E.A. Varley, *The Last of the Prince Bishops: The Episcopate of William Van Mildert (1826-1836)* (Durham: Dean & Chapter of Durham, 1986) & *The Last of the Prince Bishops. William Van Mildert and the High Church Movement of the Early Nineteenth Century* (Cambridge: University Press, 1992); & esp. the meticulous study of W.B. Maynard, "The Ecclesiastical Administration of the Archdeaconry of Durham 1774-1856" (unpublished Ph.D. thesis; Durham University, 1973).

[180] H. Gee, "Ecclesiastical History," *The Victoria History of the County of Durham* (ed. W. Page; London: Archibald Constable, 1907) 2.1-77, esp. 74-5; & W.B. Maynard, "The Response of the Church of England to Economic and Demographic Change: The Archdeaconry of Durham, 1800-1851," *Journal of Ecclesiastical History* 42.3 (July 1991) 437-62.

[181] Charles Baring (1807-1879), Bishop of Gloucester (1857-61) and Bishop of Durham (1861-79). Lewis (ed.), *Dictionary of Evangelical Biography*, I.59.

[182] G.T. Willett, "The Durham Episcopate of Charles Baring (1807-1879)" (unpublished M.A. thesis; Durham University, 1982). For Lightfoot's estimate of Baring's administration, see DDC (1881) 93. See also the perceptive assessment in J. Gray to Lightfoot, 29 October, 1889.

counsels of the Church, and took only a limited role in the House of Lords. He also went for months without adding a sentence to unfinished literary projects.[183] So committed to Durham was he that Benson accused him of being selfish in his unselfishness.[184]

This is not the place to write the history of Lightfoot's episcopate.[185] But it is important to note that, apart from the general intention of promoting the life of the Church in Durham, the main objective of his 'charge' was the improvement of the closeness and quality of clerical supervision over the rapidly growing population. The principal means to this end was a comprehensive restructuring of the diocese, so pressing that he began almost immediately. Indeed, one reason for accepting the See was the possibility of realizing his ideal of episcopal oversight through the division of the diocese, a reform finally secured in 1882.[186] In the meantime Lightfoot had commenced reorganizing what would be the residual diocese. The Rural Deaneries were increased in number and their boundaries redrawn, in 1880,[187] while the creation of the diocese of Newcastle afforded an opportunity to divide what had been the Archdeaconry of Durham.[188] To maintain the efficiency of the parochial system a further 27 parishes were created under Lightfoot's direction.[189] Extensive church building was required in order to overcome chronic accommodation shortages, an initiative supported by the Special Church Building Fund established in 1884.[190]

This tendency towards smaller administrative units created a need for additional personnel. Lightfoot sought not only to increase the number, but also to raise the quality, of the Durham clergy. His main innovation to this end was the formation of a quasi-theological college at Auckland Castle, the aim of which was to attract Oxbridge men to the diocese.[191] The outcome

---

[183] AF II.1^2.xii.

[184] G.K. Bell, *Randal Davidson Archbishop of Canterbury* (London: Oxford University Press, 1938) 169.

[185] See Wilson, "Life," ch. IV. How much further the matter can be taken is suggested by N. McCord, *The Days of Visitation: An Examination of Some Durham Records 1857-1936* (Durham: Dean & Chapter of Durham, 1987) 7-9.

[186] For Lightfoot's account of the matter in prospect, see DDC (1881) 99-100; and in retrospect, PC 4-15. Also P. Jagger, "The Formation of the Diocese of Newcastle," *A Social History of the Diocese of Newcastle* (ed. W.S.F. Pickering; Stocksfield, Northumberland: Oriel Press, 1981) 24-52.

[187] DDC (1881) 93-5. PC 19-21.

[188] DDM II (1882) 82.

[189] DDC (1890) 182-3.

[190] DDM III (1883) 148; & IV (1884) 14-16. Ch 10-11. Five years later 45 buildings had been constructed at a cost of 104 636 pounds by means of the Fund. DDC (1890) 135-8.

[191] DNB XI.1114-15. The model Lightfoot followed was that of C.J. Vaughan who had been personally preparing ordinands for the work of the ministry since 1860, first as Vicar of Doncaster, and then as Master of the Temple.

was 'the Auckland Brotherhood', a coterie of young clergymen who completed their training under Lightfoot.[192] They remained intensely loyal to their Bishop, who used them as "shock troops" in an 'assault' on the most difficult areas in the diocese.[193] Lightfoot otherwise extended his influence over deployment of the clergy by increasing the livings in his gift,[194] and by making recommendations when the patronage lay elsewhere.[195] A tight discipline was also maintained: "...honest work honestly done" was the ideal to be met, and episcopal intervention occurred when the prospect of scandal or controversy threatened the work of the Church.[196]

For all his success in these initiatives, Lightfoot still recognized their inadequacy. Accordingly, he promoted several supplements to parochial organization. First, he endeavoured to bring to Durham the success enjoyed by mission preaching elsewhere by the appointment of George Body as Canon Missioner in 1883.[197] Second, branches of the Church Army were permitted in several parishes, to do inside the Church the less conventional work done outside by the Salvation Army.[198] Third, while he deprecated the permanent diaconate, he actively encouraged the female diaconate, so that the Church in Durham was no longer "one handed".[199] But, in line with the main need of the day, Lightfoot's greatest faith was placed in lay agency. In 1882 an order of Lay Readers was created as supernumerary church workers.[200] A second order of Lay Evangelists was established in 1886 as a partial solu-

---

[192] The main source is LD. See also "Bishop Lightfoot's Influence: His Trust in Young Men," A Paper by the Very Rev. H.E. Savage (Dean of Lichfield, 1909-39), edited with an introductory note by B.S. Benedikz, *Durham University Journal* LXXVII.1 (December 1984) 1-6. There are also numerous letters from members of the 'Brotherhood' among the Lightfoot Papers.

[193] See, for example, A.F. Sim, *The Life and Letters of Arthur Fraser Sim. With a Preface by ... Canon Body* (London: Universities Mission, 1896).

[194] The patronage lists in the annual *Durham Diocesan Calendar* exhibit a steady increase.

[195] Eg. Lightfoot to Gladstone, 27 March 1882; 3 January, n.d.; August & 15 December 1883; 7 January 1884 (GBL, 44 474, f. 323; 44 479, f. 52; 44 482, f. 286; 44 484, f. 232; & 44 485, f. 46). Lightfoot to Mary Gladstone, 1 October 1883; 24 January & 28 October 1884; & 15 February 1885 (GBL, 44 483, f. 181; 44 485, f. 119; 44 487, f. 345; & 44 489, f. 227).

[196] Two files of correspondence at Auckland Castle are concerned with Lightfoot's relations with errant diocesan clergy. "Bishop Lightfoot 1879-1886" and "Bishop Lightfoot 1887-1889" (LAC).

[197] PC 39-40. Ch 20-2.

[198] Ch 27-9. For Lightfoot's attitude to the Salvatian Army, see PC 67-77.

[199] PC 61-7 & 33-5. Ch 21. Also *The Society of Christ and the Blessed Mary the Virgin (Durham Diocesan Church Workers) Jubilee Book 1887-1937*, n.y. [copy in the Durham University Library].

[200] PC 31-2.

tion to the problem that the parishes most in need of lay help were least able to furnish it themselves.[201]

With the creation of smaller units, and the multiplication of spiritual agencies and Church organizations, it was necessary to find some way to give the Church in Durham greater cohesiveness and unity of purpose. Accordingly, Lightfoot promoted the idea of the Church as involving the conception of a corporate life. "To extend the sympathies and motives of common membership beyond the limits of the parish to the limits of the diocese is to make an important stride in the realization of this idea ..."[202] That interchange of ideas which gave coherence to the work was facilitated by conferences of clergy and laity at ruridecanal and diocesan levels.[203] Similarly meetings for devotional purposes at centres like Durham Cathedral and Auckland Castle were intended to promote "the unity of the body of which we severally are members".[204] Less successful in this respect was the *Durham Diocesan Magazine* which, for lack of support, was collapsed into the more modest *Durham Diocesan Gazette* as an authoritative Agenda and Acta of the diocese.[205]

Lightfoot's reforms take their place among other efforts to adapt the parochial system of the English Church to an urban and industrial society. None of his measures was novel; but, implemented with characteristic thoroughness and efficiency, they enabled the diocese of Durham to catch up with what had been attempted elsewhere. He was criticized subsequently for placing too much emphasis on administration.[206] It might well have appeared so to a young curate at a time of such extensive change. In fact, in Lightfoot's own mind structures were a mere framework within which the work of the Church was done, and the extent of reform was only the extent of the need.[207] He has been criticized, too, for looking to buildings as the answer to the Church's problems.[208] But Lightfoot always claimed the work of building a church was only a prelude to the building of the life of faith in individuals.[209] In this more important work of edification, he thought the history of the diocese had an important part to play.

---

[201] DDM VI (1886) 25, 37. Ch 23-7.

[202] DDC (1881) 93.

[203] *Ibid.* PC 21, 23-4, 29-30. DDM III (1883) 147-8.

[204] PC 29-30, 42, 205 n. 16. J.B. Lightfoot, *An Address. On the Reopening of the Chapel, Auckland Castle, August 1, 1888, By the Bishop of Durham* (Bishop Auckland: Cummins, n.d.). Reprinted in LNC 139-57, to which reference is made.

[205] DDM I (1881) 4; VI (1886) 49-50. PC 46-7. DDG I (1887) 1.

[206] A.V. Baillie, *My First Eighty Years* (London: John Murray, 1951) 70.

[207] SSO 4-7. PC 52-3.

[208] Henson, *More Letters*, 71.

[209] J.B. Lightfoot, *The Three Temples. An Address Delivered in the Temporary Church of S. Luke's, New Chesterton, Cambridge, On S. Luke's Day, October 18th, 1873* (Cambridge: n.p., 1873). LNC 42-3. SSO 172-3.

The public use a bishop might make of the diocesan history was foreshadowed at Benson's consecration. Lightfoot seized upon Cornwall's unique
past as one of the local peculiarities it would be necessary to study in organizing a new see in the conditions of the nineteenth century.[210] For a bishop,
too, "as a scribe instructed unto the kingdom of heaven ... is compelled to
bring forth out of his treasure things new and old".[211] The potential of Durham in this respect was similarly highlighted by Westcott at Lightfoot's consecration.[212] The reminder was unnecessary. What the history of the northern church had come to mean for him, it could be made to mean for others.
From the outset Lightfoot determined to make the inspiration of a great heritage one of the principles of his administration.[213]

Accordingly Lightfoot promoted awareness of the diocesan past as a matter
of policy. Significant occurrences in the life of the diocese were used to
celebrate, with the people, the great events and personalities of the history
of their Church.[214] The sermon expected from the Bishop provided an ideal
opportunity to summon the thronging memories suggested by the occasion,
place or dedication;[215] to recall the lives and achievements of the "saints and
heroes" of the Northumbrian Church; and to evoke some of its more poign-
ant moments, such as the deaths of Cuthbert and Bede, and the wanderings
of the Lindisfarne monks.[216] The standpoint from which he worked was
declared to the people of Blackhill: "We English Churchmen have a spiritual ancestry great and glorious, such as few churches can boast".[217] No
chance to impress others with the historic greatness of the See was missed,
as the recollection of one of the Castle choir boys indicates.[218]

Making its abiding presence more manifest was a corollary of this determination. The intention to publish the sermons is to be seen in this light.[219]
In this form they could be expected to follow the life course of any book:

---

[210] For the role of the past in the creation of the Cornish bishopric, see P.S. Morrish,
"History, Celticism and Propaganda in the Formation of the Diocese of Truro," *Southern
History* 5 (1983) 238-66.

[211] SSO 68-9.

[212] Westcott, *Strength*, 4-7.

[213] LD 98-9.

[214] Lightfoot seems to have initiated something of importance. His sermon for the
10th centenary of the Church in Chester-le-Street was revived for the occasion of the 11th
by a former rector of the parish, The Rev. P. Blair. I. Bunting & J. Brewster, *1883-1983.
The Eleventh Century of the Parish Church in Chester-le-Street* (Chester-le-Street: The
Parish Church of St Mary & St Cuthbert, Chester-le-Street, [1983]) 85-6.

[215] LNC Sermons II-VI, VIII.

[216] LNC 77-9 (Cuthbert); 87 ff. (Bede); 84-5 (the Lindisfarne monks).

[217] LNC 52.

[218] LD 69.

[219] LNC ix, for Lightfoot's intention to publish.

Like the corn of wheat, it is sown in the ground. If it is a fertile book, it springs up, and blossoms, and bears fruit a hundred or a thousand fold. Generations come and go, but still it blossoms, still it fructifies.[220]

Thus the riches of the diocesan history could be shared, not only with immediate congregations, but also with those beyond, temporally and spatially. For the same reason, Lightfoot wanted church dedications to rescue the memory of Aidan from the neglect into which it had fallen because of the victory of the Roman usage at the Council of Whitby.[221] When the deanieres were reorganized, they were given historic names.[222] At Auckland Castle, artifacts reflecting the diocesan past were collected.[223] Much trouble was taken to ensure that there was a portrait of all previous bishops of Durham in the collection;[224] and, towards the end of the episcopate, the presentation of a pastoral staff was welcomed as the addition of a valuable heirloom to the diocese.[225] Lightfoot himself contributed to the material record by the installation in St Peter's Chapel of windows depicting the Celtic and Roman periods of Northumbrian history, so that, as he said, "the saints and heroes of this Church ... look down upon us".[226] When his chaplain, H.R. Banton, died, another window was installed as a memorial to a member of the Auckland Brotherhood, thereby including the present in this material record.[227] Augmenting the tangible evidence in this way kept vividly alive the achievements and lessons of the past.[228]

Bringing the past into focus when not self-evident was the other side of this approach. At the Jubilee of the University of Durham, when its lack of years contrasted unfavourably with the venerable antiquity of Oxford and Cambridge, Lightfoot responded by exposing the true depth of its roots.[229] In fact, the history of the University began with Aidan and his pupils on

---

[220] LNC 96.

[221] LNC 31-2, 49. Later it was gratifying to Lightfoot that Aidan's name had reappeared in modern dedications. LNC 51-2.

[222] DDC (1881) 94.

[223] LD 111.

[224] There is considerable correspondence on this matter among the Lightfoot Papers.

[225] LD 96. Also *Presentation of a Pastoral Staff to the Bishop of Durham (With Description and Plate)* (Durham: Andrews & Co., 1890).

[226] LNC 154. OA 211. See the unpublished pamphlet *The Chapel of St Peter, Auckland Castle. The Windows*, of which there is a copy at the Dean and Chapter Library; & F.C. MacDonald, *The Story of St Peter's Chapel, Auckland Castle, with an Appreciation Describing the Windows and Other Features of Interest* (revised and completed by H.F. MacDonald; West Hartlepool: G.R. Todd, 1937).

[227] On Banton (1859-86), see OA 157-8; & Venn, *Alumni* II.I.143.

[228] On the value of artifacts, see "Re-opening of the Saxon Church at Escombe. Sermon By the Bishop," *Durham County Advertiser* (8 October 1880). Filed with "Newspaper Cuttings. 1880 B".

[229] LNC 107-119.

Lindisfarne. It continued in the foundations of Benedict Biscop and Alcuin, and in the learning of Bede. Not only was Durham University older than Oxbridge, but it actually gave the collegiate system to English education, and provided the basis of the country's first significant university or college library. And, although the University only materialized in the age of the Great Reform Bill, the idea could be traced as far back as the Reformation.[230] The practical inference of Lightfoot's apology was expressed as a rhetorical question:

> Here is your historical inheritence; and what fairer estate could you desire? Here is
> your ancient lineage; and what more illustrious ancestry could any student boast?[231]

At Durham, too, the past bequeathed a great ideal with the power to "make the world wiser and better".[232]

Similarly, Lightfoot created a past where it might be thought that no past existed. In the church of St Ignatius' which he had built in the Sunderland working class district, Hendon Docks, the dedication, and the reredos and windows, put the new parish in touch with its deepest roots.[233] Westcott appreciated what Lightfoot had intended:

> It teaches you to look beyond England in order that you may feel your debt and your
> duty. It reminds you of the wide-spread glory of your spiritual ancestry, in which you
> reckon side by side an apostle of the far East and an apostle of the far West - Ignatius of
> Antioch and Columba of Hy.[234]

The spiritual ancestry which the Durham Church could claim as its own need not be limited to the diocese.

Lightfoot also sought to promote an appreciation of its significance in the history of the Church, not only in England, but also in Europe and beyond.[235] This was why events and characters from the diocesan past were represented as the recurrence of Biblical antecedents.[236] It was also why, when the Bishops of the Third Lambeth Conference gathered at Auckland Castle in 1888,

---

[230] For a very different account of the University's origins one hundred years later, see A. Heesom, *The Foundation of the University of Durham* (Durham: Dean & Chapter of Durham, 1982).

[231] LNC 109.

[232] Bearing Fruit, 1877, 1-7. SSO 186-7. CP 24, 26.

[233] "St. Ignatius' Church, Hendon. The Foundation Stone Ceremony. Address By the Bishop of Durham." Newspaper Cuttings 1887. Lightfoot also requested that a gift from Archdeacon and Mrs Watkins be spent on communion plate for St Ignatius', which was to be inscribed with pertinent expressions from the letters of Ignatius. Lightfoot to Mrs Watkins, 9 May 1889 (DUL, Ad'l MS 132).

[234] Westcott, *Strength*, 33-4.

[235] LNC 6-8, 13, 16-17, 41-2, 47, 61-2, 64, 67, 93-4, 109, 111-12, 114-15, 132. Cf. IACC 4-6; LO 6; SSO 159, 212; J.B. Lightfoot, "Inaugural Address," *Journal of the British Archaeological Association* XLIII (March 1887) 1-12.

[236] Columba was a second Abraham; Oswald recalled Josiah; Hilda was another Deborah; and the wandering of the Lindisfarne monks was equivalent to Israel's period in the wilderness. LNC 5, 25-7, 60-3, 84-5.

Lightfoot made the peroration of his sermon a short review of the "twelve centuries of history" represented in the restored chapel.[237] The leaders of the wider Anglican communion were reminded that the Church of the north had borne "the chief part in the making of the English Church".[238] This was particularly true of its earliest phase, the Celtic. As an age of 'saintliness' it was unequalled.[239] It was important to realize, too, that the evangelization of England proceeded from Lindisfarne, not Kent.[240] Moreover, Aidan, not Augustine, was "the true Apostle of England", and the evangelist to whom the English speaking people "owe their very selves".[241] As a scholar himself, it was a matter of no little pride to Lightfoot that the concern of the monks for learning made Iona "the focus of intellectual life to Western Christendom", so that it was at the same time its "spiritual and intellectual metropolis".[242] As "the English speaking peoples," he told the other Bishops, they were a unit, hewn from the same rock, and enjoying together the "continuity of our Church". Accordingly, he spoke of the distinguished men and women of Durham's past as "our spiritual ancestors," and then, more emphatically, as "your spiritual ancestors". Inside and outside the diocese, he wanted it understood that the northern Church had contributed to the Church at large. Not the people of Durham only, but all Churchmen, had been its beneficiaries. This was the measure of its importance.

Of course, this heightened sense of the past was meant to react upon Church life in the present, among the laity as well as the clergy.[243] Its value as a spiritual resource was conveyed by the characteristic metaphor of a "rich" and "undeserved inheritance".[244] With the privilege, as always, went responsibility.[245] At the same time as providing inspiring associations, it conferred obligation to honour, emulate, and even surpass previous achievement. At Jarrow, the people were reminded that they were "the trustees of [Bede's] good deeds, and heirs of his fame".[246] The men of the University were told, "On you a necessity, a strong necessity, is laid".[247] By its capacity to motivate, encourage, and instruct, the unique Durham past could continually prepare and equip the people of the diocese for their role in the life

---

[237] LNC 154-7.

[238] Cf. LNC 5.

[239] LNC 14, 16.

[240] LNC 9-11, 16, 17, 31, 41, & 42.

[241] Cf. LNC 9, 11.

[242] Cf. LNC 47, 109.

[243] Six of the sermons reproduced in LNC (II-VI, VIII) were preached before ordinary parish congregations, and another (VII) before the staff and members of its university.

[244] LNC 49, 130.

[245] Eg. Harvest, 1874, 15-17; Teach, 1878, 18.

[246] LNC 94. For a reflection on the significance of Bede, AF I.2.436.

[247] LNC 109.

and mission of their Church, as it did for the Bishop. The use of history itself was the chief object of Lightfoot's invocation of the diocesan history.

This, of course, was as a means and not an end. As a bishop in his pastoral role, Lightfoot promoted history to enforce the theological truths he believed structured and sustained life. The most important lesson for Churchmen was the immanence of God. At Durham this in itself was a use of the past. From the day of his enthronement, Lightfoot followed Butler's directive to the clergy in his charge of 1751 to " 'endeavour to raise up in the hearts' of their people 'such a sense of God as shall be an habitual, ready principle of reverence, love, gratitude, hope, trust, resignation and obedience'."[248] The processes of the diocesan past gave an opening to this vision of God, with all of its consecrating and actuating force.[249] By giving this sense of the surpassing value of life, and a glimpse amid the mundane of the grandeur of their lives,[250] it complemented the administrative reforms, as a way to promote hopeful Christian living.[251]

Along with pointing to the interest and involvement of God in their affairs, the past could also teach the people about His ways. Against a background of a modern community, with the anxieties generated by strained industrial relations,[252] and periodic coal mining disasters,[253] Lightfoot pointed out how the premature death of Oswald showed the perplexities of life could only find their meaning in the infinitude of eternity;[254] and how the wanderings of the Lindisfarne monks reflected "the discipline of a period of disaster", which God uses "to chastise with a fatherly chastisement, to amend, to purify, to strengthen, to train for a greater future".[255] It was salutary for Durham Churchmen to be reminded that the measure of present life was its place in the eternal setting of God's increasing purpose.[256]

As at St Paul's, this sense of the eternal setting of life was meant to direct them to the corporate life of the Church as the source of individual significance. The abiding presence of God gave to the long spans of time in north-

---

[248] LNC 163, 165-6.

[249] LNC 161-2, 171.

[250] LNC 168-9.

[251] See Three Notes, 1873, 24-6 for the conception of the spiritual life he wanted for the diocese.

[252] LNC 166-7. Though aware of the mediatorial role the clergy might play in industrial relations (SSO 61), he never became involved in the same way as Westcott. See G.F. Best, *Westcott and the Miners* (Cambridge: University Press, 1967).

[253] For Lightfoot's reaction to coal mining disasters at Seaham, Trimdon, Tudhoe and Stanley in 1882, see "Newspaper Cuttings. 1882". Also PC 50.

[254] LNC 34-5.

[255] LNC 84-5. J.B. Lightfoot, "Inaugural Address," *Journal of the British Archaeological Association* XLIII (March 1887) 10.

[256] Cf. OA 189-90.

ern church history an organic unity, which incorporated the present and the future. 'New beginnings,' in particular, were interpreted in this way. They were not really starting points at all, but the extension of the goals of the past, albeit with a change in direction.[257] The end of the Palatinate had begun a new era, with the Durham Episcopate "delivered from a great clog to its usefulness".[258] The opening of St Paul's Church, West Hartlepool, represented "the latest fruit of a mighty tree planted by Hilda between twelve and thirteen centuries ago".[259] Similarly, the dedication of the cathedral of the new diocese of Newcastle — "the latest development" in the history of the Northumbrian Church — was the proper time to bring its "latest sons and daughters" into direct contact with the first, to "link together the last days with the first in the bonds of a natural piety".[260] This use of the past was an assertion of the continuity of the diocesan history, which indicated that the effects of present day effort would continue to be felt in the future. Not only of Bede could it be said, "The good work which he did, the good cause which he advocated, the good example which he left, these remain, these blossom and bear fruit".[261] The men and women addressed were also the immediately effective agents in the history of the Durham Church.

Still more than this was intended. Lightfoot wanted his people to see that the well-being and progress of the diocese was actually in their hands. Again, the lesson followed from the immanence of God. For it also involved His direction and control over their lives. At the Millenary Festival of the Parish Church at Chester-le-Street in 1883, "God's purposes in the chain of cause and consequence" were traced from before the Incarnation in order to bring into relief His "manifest and great mercies to the Church in this place during the thousand years past".[262] Knowing that in their own history "some constant thread of a divine purpose runs", was incentive to parishioners to go on in their own efforts to the next stage, giving their best towards achieving God's purposes as they were discerned.[263] Later the same day, after congratulating the parish on the restoration of the church building in the context of its history, Lightfoot expressed the wish that "this history of the outward fabric [would] be a type and a symbol of the future of the Church in this parish and in this diocese; may it grow ever larger and larger in its aims, in its activities: may it ever throw out fresh developments."[264]

---

[257] LNC 95-6, 98-9.

[258] Cf. DDG I (1887) 3.

[259] LNC 61, 68-9.

[260] LNC 3-4.

[261] LNC 97.

[262] LNC 80-1, 85. Cf. 75-6.

[263] LNC 76.

[264] "Chester-le-Street Church. Thousandth Anniversary. The Luncheon," *Newcastle Chronicle* (19 July 1883). "Newspaper Cuttings. 1883."

III. History as Ideology

Confronting the people of the diocese with the eternal truths expressed in the particularities of their local history was seen by Lightfoot as a key to the present day success of the Church in Durham. He intended it to form again that Christian character which explained the greatness of the past:

> If we desire to know the secret of their success [the Celtic missionaries], it is soon told. It was the power of earnest, simple, self-denying lives, pleading with a force which no eloquence of words can command.[265]

At the consecration of the Church of St Aidan at Blackhill he asked rhetorically:

> With your larger opportunities, and your wider intellectual range, what may you not achieve, if you reproduce in your lives the humility, the holiness, the unbounded self-devotion, the unfailing sympathy and love, of this ancient servant of God?[266]

Lightfoot hoped for such achievement "that some future Bede will again trace in words of tender and regretful sympathy the undying record of a Christ-like life and work".[267]

Similarly, the diocesan past was used to help the Church in Durham realize its vocation:

> Thanksgiving is the crown of Christian worship; thanksgiving is the purpose for which the Church exists. The glory, which redounds to God through the thanksgiving of his people, is the ultimate end and aim of their being. The thankful heart, the thankful lips, the thankful life, these alone can fulfil the purpose for which they were created.[268]

Accordingly, for their work and example, the lives of Oswald, Aidan, Hilda, Bede and Bernard Gilpin were all held up at some stage as spurs to corporate thanksgiving.[269] Indeed the lives of the diocesan luminaries were ranked with the foundation of the Church and the Reformation itself, as reasons for thankfulness.[270] God was also seen as the giver of "the traditions of Iona and Lindisfarne, of Jarrow and Wearmouth".[271] Lightfoot's predecessor had been troubled by controversy with High Churchmen, whose practices he sought to suppress.[272] Because he minimized matters so important to such individuals as G.H. Wilkinson and J.B. Dykes,[273] his own administration

---

[265] LNC 9-10. Cf. 46-7.

[266] LNC 53-4.

[267] LNC 17.

[268] LNC 129. Cf. OA 200, 316-18.

[269] LNC 32-4, 53, 60, 94, 129-30, 135.

[270] LNC 30-4, 85-6, 99-100, 106-7, 125-7, 129-35.

[271] LNC 117-18.

[272] *Correspondence Between the Right Rev. The Lord Bishop of Durham and The Rev. and Hon. F.R. Gray, Rector of Morpeth* (London: E. Longhurst, 1873); J.B. Dykes, *Eucharistic Truth and Ritual. A Letter to the ... Lord Bishop of Durham, occasioned by his Lordship's reply to an address from certain laymen in the diocese* (2nd ed;London, 1874); Mason, *Wilkinson*, I.ch. III & IV ; Willett, "Baring," ch. V. He attracted the nickname, "Over-Baring". Lewis (ed.), *Dictionary of Evangelical Biography*, I.59.

[273] Wilkinson (1833-1907), Vicar of Bishop Auckland (1863-7), left the diocese because of strained relations with Baring. Dykes (1823-76) was Vicar of St Oswald's, Durham, and a noted writer of hymn tunes.

was peaceful in this respect.[274] While other dioceses were troubled by the forms of worship during the eighties,[275] in Durham Lightfoot was more concerned to advance through the history of his See the grounds of worship.

Lightfoot's enthusiasm for diocesan history was accompanied by a characteristic concern that the use made of the past be the right one.[276] The guidance tendered in this respect before coming to Durham was frequently given local expression.[277] But the danger of allowing the past to enslave the present called for special comment in the case of the Newcastle Bishopric. One objection to the division was the severence of Newcastle from the historic associations of Durham.[278] Lightfoot claimed to feel the regret himself. The loss, in fact, would be mutual. If Newcastle lost Durham Cathedral and nine centuries of tradition, Durham stood to lose the birthplace of Christianity in northern England. Even so, the efficiency of the diocese demanded the measure, historic sentiment notwithstanding. This was not inconsistent with the general historical outlook Lightfoot urged upon the diocese, which absorbed major change into the continuity of its life. No real severence was involved. Instead, the mother-daughter relationship implied organic extension, which actually added to the dignity of Durham. Further, the mother see could continue to draw from the spiritual resources of the period of her origins. Such changes, moreoever, were required:

> Historic associations and local attachments were intended to be stepping-stones: we must not convert them into barriers. When once historic sentiment flings itself across the path of an urgent practical need, then away with it in the name of God ... The voice of a higher authority is heard summoning us forward on the path of a larger future; "Let the dead bury their dead" — dead traditions, dead historic associations, the dead past in all its forms "and follow thou Me".[279]

If historic sentiment were allowed to stand in the way, it would cease to be the life-giving force Lightfoot intended.

In dealing with the early history of the diocese, he encountered the difficulties of hagiography highlighted earlier in the century by the Tractarian work, *The Lives of the English Saints*.[280] In Lightfoot's case, they were augmented by the need to fit the material for pulpit presentation. Despite the difficulties, he evidently tried to present the diocese with true history, a

---

[274] PC 82-5. Ch 67-9.

[275] Bowen, *Idea*, ch. III.

[276] See 155-6 & 157-9 above.

[277] Eg. LNC 17, 29-30, 39-40, 53-4, & 145.

[278] DDC (1881) 100-1. PC 4-6. DDG (1887) 2-3.

[279] DDC (1881) 101.

[280] Reconsidered by J. Derek Holmes, "Newman's Reputation and *The Lives of the English Saints*," *Catholic Historical Review* LI.4 (1966) 528-38; & "John Henry Newman's Attitude Towards History and Hagiography," *Downside Review* 92 (1974) 248-64.

fact which accounts for the abiding scholarly value of his work.[281] Although sermons are not the place for expatiating upon the problems presented by historical sources, Lightfoot occasionally commented on their origins and leanings, their strengths and weaknesses, and the caution required in using them.[282] The problem was sharpest in treating the miracles with which his sources abounded. In general, they were avoided. When miracles did come up for comment, Lightfoot was guarded, without being openly sceptical.[283] He could see how they had arisen, and credited them to that extent. With the story of the Lindisfarne Gospels, he concentrated on its symbolic truth.[284]

For all his care, there remained a tension between Lightfoot's scholarly instincts and pastoral objectives. This was especially true of his assessment of the importance of the northern church for English Christianity. He avoided the appearance of special pleading by invoking the authority of the French Roman Catholic scholar, Charles Montalambert.[285] Exaggeration, too, was deprecated. Yet, not even within his own tradition, has the claim that England owed its conversion to Iona been upheld.[286] Before going to Durham he held the received view, which attributed the conversion to Gregory and Augustine, although the *volte face* may have been due as much to closer study, as his stronger stake in what happened.[287] Of greater interest is the more temperate tone adopted before less partial audiences.[288] Inside the diocese enthusiasm for its historic importance, coupled with the desire to edify, caused some suspension of Lightfoot's usual scholarly reserve.

His judgments also reflected a tendency to protestantize its history.[289] The conversion of the English was simplified into a contest between Rome and Iona.[290] There was no mitigation of the withdrawal of Paulinus, and the

---

[281] Mr G. Bonner, formerly of Durham University, claimed in a lecture entitled "St Cuthbert in Chester-le-Street" and delivered in 1983 in the parish church at Chester-le-Street that Lightfoot's "S. Cuthbert" would be the starting point for all subsequent discussion of the subject. This observation is omitted from the published version in *St Cuthbert, His Cult and Community to A.D. 1200* (eds G. Bonner, D. Rollason, C. Stancliffe; Woodbridge, Suffolk & Wolfeboro, N.H.: Boydell Press/Boydell & Brewer, 1989) 387-95.

[282] LNC 46, 48-9, 64-6, 79, 83.

[283] Eg. LNC 28-30 (Oswald); 67-8 (Hilda); 83, 85 (Cuthbert). For Lightfoot's attitude to miracles, see 116 above.

[284] LNC 76-7.

[285] LNC 10-11, 244. J.B. Lightfoot, "Inaugural Address," *Journal of the British Archaeological Association* XLIII (March 1887) 9.

[286] N.P. Williams, *The Durham Tradition* (London & Oxford: A.R. Mowbray, 1932) 5.

[287] Teach, 1878, 11-22.

[288] SSO 157-9, 181-2, 212.

[289] First noticed by P.W.D., a correspondent to the *Newcastle Chronicle* (23 & 28 July 1883) [the second letter was incorrectly annotated "June 28" by Lightfoot]. Lightfoot replied in the edition of 25 July 1883. Newspaper Cuttings 1883.

[290] Eg. LNC 41-2, 63.

interesting figure of James the Deacon was overlooked.[291] The benefits of the Synod of Whitby were conceded, but they were placed in the context of papal pretension.[292] Bernard Gilpin was exalted as the true representative of the English Reformation,[293] and John Cosin lauded for his resistance to the strong temptation to go over to Rome.[294] Throughout, Lightfoot was able to detect that spirit of freedom which he regarded as the hallmark of the Church of England.[295] To this extent, he read back into the diocesan history his own ecclesiastical position and his own conception of English history.

Similarly, the wish to edify affected Lightfoot's treatment of 'character'. On occasions he was prepared to be critical.[296] Indeed, his heroes were not expected to be perfect,[297] and the need for discernment in scanning the lives of the saints was pointed out.[298] But alongside this concession to historical reality was the ethical interest. Because of a shared concern for the example of good men, Bede's portraits of Aidan and Cuthbert were accepted, though not without a pang of conscience in the case of the former.[299] This wishfulness was pervasive. Other received encomia went unchallenged, as with the post-Tractarian estimate of Bernard Gilpin.[300] Lightfoot hoped too that John Cosin was not involved in the worst excesses of the Restoration.[301] When the possibility of fault was acknowledged, he often excused,[302] minimized,[303] ignored,[304] or rebutted.[305] There was also idealization, which Lightfoot virtually admitted when he claimed the value of saintly lives actually increases as they become more distant — since after death all that they had stood for and done are no longer restricted by personal faults, or the petty feuds and jealousies of contemporaries.[306] While the sanctifying effect of time might

---

[291] On Paulinus, see LNC 8, 25-6, 41, 43. Cf. the more balanced account of the Oxford High Churchman, W. Bright, *Chapters of Early English Church History* (2nd ed.; Oxford: Clarendon Press, 1888) 134-7.

[292] LNC 50-1.

[293] LNC 130.

[294] LNC 146-7. For the modulations of his position, see G. Cuming, *The Anglicanism of John Cosin* (Durham: Dean & Chapter of Durham, 1975).

[295] For Lightfoot's anti-Roman outlook, see LNC 6-7, 11-15, 41-2, 50-1, 52-3, 64-5.

[296] OA 211. The faults of Columba are given, though perhaps they could hardly be denied. LNC 5-6, 8-9, 44. Cf. DCB I.604. LNC 84 for criticism of Cuthbert's seclusion.

[297] LNC 31-3.

[298] LNC 29-30, 84.

[299] LNC 44-6, 48-9. DCB I.66 is similarly enthusiastic for Aidan.

[300] The ambiguities of Gilpin's career are brought out by D. Marcombe, "Bernard Gilpin: Anatomy of an Elizabethan Legend," *Northern History* XVI (1980) 20-39.

[301] LNC 149.

[302] LNC 84. Cuthbert's faults were "more of the age than of the man".

[303] LNC 151-2.

[304] LNC 5-6, 8-9. It was inappropriate to focus on Columba's faults.

[305] LNC 146-7. Cosin was defended from the charge of leaning to Rome.

[306] LNC 14-15, 97-8, 107. Cf. Bearing Fruit, 1877, 2.

permit greater access to what is timeless and can be reproduced in any age, it also meant Lightfoot was able to find in his heroes what he sought.

Given that the application was marked by these limitations, Lightfoot acted throughout the length of his episcopate in the conviction that it was part of the Bishop's historic role to secure within his diocese a functional attitude towards the past, as a means of promoting spiritual life within the Church structures required by the age. No previous nineteenth century Bishop of Durham had the same awareness of the pastoral efficacy of the history of his diocese.[307] Few since have been altogether free of it.[308] Together with his organizational reforms, which lasted well into the twentieth century, the usefulness of the diocesan past was Lightfoot's distinctive contribution to Church life in Durham.

At Durham, as at St Paul's, Lightfoot made a sustained attempt to bring the people under his ministry into vital connection with history. He invoked various images, artifacts, persons and events to make their history available and intelligible. The aim of such 'assimilation' was to enable these people to 'interpret' their lives as part of the large movement of history under God's direction, and thereby empower them to 'reproduce' effective Church membership and active Christian citizenship. Success promised the maintenance of the progressive continuity of Church life, an important end for a minister to pursue. Lightfoot's inclusion of the program of optimum historical usage within the range of activities proper to the Christian ministry was therefore part of an attempt to make his own clerical career effective in historic terms. It was also personally significant, in that it achieved in his own case what was intended for the projected beneficiaries, a sense of individual importance and purpose. Thus the use of history was a means of combining in practice the twin roles of "shepherd" and "ambassador" as Lightfoot sought to represent God to man and present man to God. To this extent, history was in part both agent and substance of Lightfoot's ministry at St Paul's and Durham.

The history he taught in these spheres was the record of the triumph of Christian character over paganism. It was intended as an illustration of the qualities required of all present day Churchmen in order to extend past success. In all of this, there was little that in principle was new. However, the historical outlook applied to the prospective national leadership elite at Cambridge had to be adapted to another segment of the population, and a different element of the Church's constituency. The change involved the localiza-

---

[307] LD 58, 111, 145.

[308] Eg. B.F. Westcott, "S. Columba," in LNC 175-89; H.H. Henson, *Bishoprick Papers* (London: Oxford University Press, 1946); A.M. Ramsey, *Durham Essays and Addresses* (London: S.P.C.K., 1956); I. Ramsey, *Joseph Butler 1692-1752. Author of "The Analogy of Religion". Some Features of his Life and Thought* (London: Dr Williams Trust, 1969).

tion of Lightfoot's ideas about history, as the circumstances of his life became bound up with specific regions of England. At St Paul's, where there
was no past with which the working class 'parish' might readily identify, a
tradition had to be invented. In contrast, at Durham a uniquely rich diocesan past lay ready to hand. But it had fallen into desuetude and had to be
revived for Lightfoot's purposes. In both places the manoeuvre seemed to
energize and enable lay people to take part in the life of the Church. Along
with the organizational and administrative reforms to which he had contributed or engineered, Lightfoot's use of history contributed to a quickening of
Church life that linked both St Paul's and the diocese of Durham with the
recovery achieved by the Church of England nationally as it neared the end
of the century. On this larger front too Lightfoot had had a part to play.

Chapter Nine

"An Ensign for the Nations": History and the Church of England.

While Cambridge, St Paul's and the diocese of Durham provided the imme-diate settings for Lightfoot's career to 1879, the ultimate point of institu-tional loyalty was the Church of England. Following ordination in 1854 to a College Fellowship, he enjoyed a slowly burgeoning career in the wider Church. Minor preferment came early with his selection as Chaplain to the Prince Consort in 1861. After Albert's death, he was retained as Chaplain to the Queen, rising in 1875 to the post of Deputy Clerk of the Closet. Direct participation in the wider work of the Church began in 1862 with the ap-pointment as Examining Chaplain to the Bishop of London, a connection and role that was retained when Tait went to Canterbury six years later. A regular ministry opened up at Whitehall in 1866, where he was Preacher for two years. In 1871 a cathedral canonry was accepted, but at least three additional offers of higher preferment were turned down.[1] Lightfoot's com-mitment to the Church finally took him away from the University when he accepted a place on the episcopal bench early in 1879. With Tait and then Benson at Canterbury, he was close to the highest counsels of the Church continuously from 1868 until the end of his life. For much of his career Lightfoot had a significant role in the Church of England well beyond the point of his local involvement.

What kind of a Churchman was he? The ideals evinced in Lightfoot's career in the Church of England have been examined recently by David Thompson in his contribution to the centenary lectures.[2] He ascribes to Lightfoot a comprehensive churchmanship at once typical of the Cambridge spirit and catholic both in seeking a synthesis of different outlooks in the one Church and a relation of faith to the whole of life. As the first serious published attempt to probe the issue, this is a valuable contribution to

---

[1]   Apart from the Bishopric of Lichfield, Lightfoot also declined the Deaneries of Lincoln & Ripon. Lightfoot to Gladstone, 16 June 1872 (GBL, 44 434, f. 194); & draft of Lightfoot to Disraeli, 7 December 1875.

[2]   D.M. Thompson, "Lightfoot as Victorian Churchman," in Dunn (ed.), *Lightfoot Centenary Lectures*, 3-21, esp. 4, 8-9, 13-15, 17, 19. The only other significant discussion is in Wilson, "Life," 236-40. I am very grateful to Dr Thompson for sending me a copy of his paper prior to its publication.

Lightfoot studies. However, the confines of a commemorative lecture did not afford Dr Thompson an opportunity to pursue the issues raised by his ascription. It remains, for example, to furnish the reasons for this comprehensive churchmanship; to examine its application and effectiveness; to enquire whether it changed or developed; and to establish its significance, particularly in relation to the contemporary debate on the question. These matters also impinge on the larger issues raised by this investigation. For they assist in the discovery Lightfoot's understanding of the nature and role of the Church of England, particularly in its relation to his doctrine of the Church,[3] a relation which establishes the place and significance of history in his thinking about Anglican ecclesiology.

For much of the nineteenth century debate about the nature and mission of the Church of England had been a recurring feature of Church life.[4] Reforms of the late 1820s and 1830s dissipated what was left of the identity between Church and State posited in the "Erastian paradigm" enunciated by Richard Hooker in the sixteenth century. As the Church of England was being effectively denominationalized, two broad approaches to its place in English society emerged.[5] The Oxford High Churchmen put forward the "Apostolic paradigm", according to which the integrity of the Church depends not on its location but on its connection with incipient Christiantity, a relation validated by the controverted doctrine of the apostolic succession of her ministers.[6] This outlook survived the shocks of Newman's defection and the Gorham Judgment and, under the leadership of Keble, Pusey and Liddon, held a large following in the mid-Victorian years.[7] Alongside of it the "Erastian paradigm" had been carried forward in a modified form by the Germano-Coleridgeans (most notably by Thomas Arnold) as the idea of the national Church. Aimed at making the role of the Church in the life of the nation effective, and embracing as many points of view as possible, it was constituted by several key elements: liberality and comprehension of doctrine; tolerance and inclusiveness in the formularies; the exaltation of morality as an expression of spirituality and the importance of duty as a social principle; the immanence of divinity in everyday life, and thus the Church as the spiritual image of the State; and the closest possible identification between Church and State. Very important too was the view of the Church as rooted in the nation's past and expressive of its historic continuity.

---

[3]   For which, see 86-7 above.

[4]   Bowen, *Idea of the Victorian Church*, is a narrative history written around this theme.

[5]   On this, see most recently Sachs, *Transformation of Anglicanism*; & Avis, *Anglicanism and the Christian Church*, esp. Pt III.

[6]   See 199-200 & 204-5 above.

[7]   See K. Hylson-Smith, *High Churchmanship in the Church of England. From the Sixteenth Century to the Late Twentieth Century* (Edinburgh: T. & T. Clark, 1993).

Repristination of the national church idea by H.B. Wilson in his contribution to *Essays and Reviews* stirred the ecclesiological debate to new life.[8] The measures he was prepared to take to achieve comprehension gave offence, and evoked a strong reaction from within the Church. Such arguments about how the Church of England related to the church itself and to the life of the nation furnished the context for the expression of Lightfoot's ideas about its nature and role.[9]

I

Lightfoot's idea of the Church of England and its mission is more difficult to make out than his ideas of the University and the ministry. Notwithstanding the contemporary debate, it seems that this was something he never had to work out for his own benefit. Nor was he ever called upon to speak or write on the matter as such at any length. It was more an assumption or precondition of remarks on other subjects. However, something of this understanding of the nature and role of the Church of England can be gleaned from these indirect indications. The speeches Lightfoot delivered to the Church Congress are particularly helpful in this respect.

The Church Congress was part of the organizational response to the 'problem' of the Church of England at mid-century. It sprang from the movement for Church defence which saw the formation of numerous local 'Church defence' committees and associations and of the Church Defence Institution at the national level in 1859.[10] Two years later the Cambridge Church Defence Association initiated the Church Congress as an attempt to utilize internal resources and otherwise scattered energies as the best way of dealing with threats to Church interests. A kind of annual synod with membership open to almost everyone, it soon developed into an unofficial but influential national forum of clergy and laity for the constructive discussion of Church administration and activity.[11]

---

[8]   H.B. Wilson, "Seances Historiques De Geneve - The National Church," in *Essays and Reviews*, 145-206. Wilson had earlier (in 1851) delivered a controversial series of Bampton Lectures along the same lines entitled *The Communion of the Saints*.

[9]   The national church idea was developed further in Lightfoot's lifetime by (among others) J.R. Seeley, W.H. Fremantle and Westcott. P.T. Phillips, "The Concept of a National Church in Late Nineteenth-Century England and America," *Journal of Religious History* 14.1 (June 1986) 26-37.

[10] Crowther, *Church Embattled*, ch. 8; Gilbert, *Religion*, 166-7; & M.J.D. Roberts, "Pressure-Group Politics and the Church of England: the Church Defence Institution 1859-1896," *Journal of Ecclesiastical History* 35.4 (October 1985) 560-82, esp. 560-5.

[11] On its origins, see K.A. Thompson, *Bureaucracy and Church Reform. The Organizational Response of the Church of England to Social Change 1800-1965* (Oxford: Clarendon Press, 1970) 101-3. Its *raison d'être* was lost when the laity were included in the convocations at the end of the century.

This was an innovation Lightfoot was happy to support. Still a College tutor, he was among those attending the inaugural session. Subsequently he defended the Congress on the grounds that it provided much needed machinery for the exchange of opinion in an increasingly pluralist Church.[12] But his defence of the Congress went much further than that. When it was accused of being a mere talk shop, he replied that its discussions contributed to the formation of opinion, and thereby stimulated individual and collective action.[13] Invitations to speak were therefore readily accepted as an opportunity to carry out the role Lightfoot had set himself early in his career. Indeed, for somebody committed to purveying "truth in theology", it was a strategic point from which to guide the thinking of, and thus to influence the course taken by, the Church as it pursued its mission to English society. The Church Congress was ideally suited to Lightfoot's intellectualist understanding of how change is secured in history, and he took advantage of it.

The speeches that resulted are important as the point at which Lightfoot faced on the widest front the problem of the Church of England and the challenges to its traditional role in the life of the nation. They are, moreover, an attempt to influence those — clerical and lay — who were similarly committed to its work.[14] At Cambridge he prepared young men for Christian citizenship, and in both London and Durham he sought to help different sections of the Church's constituency to see the possibilities of Christian living in their immediate settings. Now he could assume a devotion to Christ in a more mature audience already committed to the well being of the Church. Before such a group his objective was to shape the consciousness of Church identity and mission that would engender the decisions taken at the various levels of its corporate life. Structural change would have undoubted value, but it was this educative process that would have the biggest bearing on the Church's capacity to fulfil its mission. Because of their purpose, Lightfoot's speeches to the Church Congress reflect his view of the relation of the Church to the life of the nation, and the nature of its role in English society in relation to his idea of history.

General ecclesiological matters were given greatest attention in the Sermon of 1877. Free to choose his own subject for the first time, and seeking to provide a keynote for the Congress as a whole, Lightfoot addressed the question of the present condition of the Church of England and how it should respond to its situation. Against a background that caused him great anxi-

---

[12] RCC (1881) 13.

[13] RCC (1881) 18-19. Cf. SSO 86-7. Lightfoot will have had in mind the likes of the Duke of Northumberland (28 January 1881) and Bishop Magee of Peterborough (29 January 1881), both of whom expressed their opposition to Church Congresses in declining to come to Newcastle for the Congress of 1881.

[14] Eg. SSO 87.

ety, but which he ventured to interpret as a great opportunity,[15] Lightfoot
followed his own prescription for those times when the Church is in jeop-
ardy from "powerful and well-directed attacks from without aided by errors
and dissenssions [sic] within" and turned to history.[16] Three typical perspectives were developed, not only for reassurance, but also to establish the
legitimacy of the Church and delineate its mission.

Lightfoot opened by drawing on the initial chapter of Ezekiel for its picture of the whirlwind sweeping down from the north as a representative description of the contemporary Church.[17] This advanced his claims in two
ways.

First, it was an expression of a characteristic identification of the Church
of England with ancient Israel.[18] The significance of this follows from the
connection Lightfoot made with the prophet's vision of the river of God as
an ever expanding life giving force among the nations of the world.[19] In his
mind the Church of England was in its identity and function an extension of
the historic Church that had had an unbroken existence since the call of
Abraham. Apostolicity was implicit in this, but for Lightfoot the important
thing was its place in the larger continuity. This meant in turn that, whatever else, it was an integral part of the pattern and mode of God's "increasing purpose" in history.[20]

Second, the prophecy of Ezekiel located the place of the contemporary
Church in the providential scheme of history. For the whirlwind was the
measure of the seriousness of its situation, ranking it with the fall of the
Roman Empire and the Reformation as episodes anticipated by the
Babylonian exile. What was about to happen was also foreshadowed by the
paradigm:

> the vision of Ezekiel is not a dead or dying story, which has served its turn and may
> now pass out of mind. It lives still as the very charter of the Church of the future.[21]

As in the history of Israel after the Restoration, the whirlwind would be
followed by a cloud of confusion and disarray, and then by the flame of new
and larger life. But realization in the present was not automatic. The insight
into the future allowed by the pattern of the past required that the life of the
Church be brought within the framework of the paradigm. Three broad responses were adumbrated: "mobility" in its processes; "spirituality" as the

---

[15] From the same year, see SSO 62-6 & Vision, 1877, 36-8.

[16] LS 175.

[17] The text was in fact selected by Westcott when Lightfoot was at a loss for a subject.
Lightfoot to Westcott, 24, 28 August 1877 (LAC).

[18] See further on this on 268-9 below.

[19] SSO 76-7, 85.

[20] For the river image, see 88 above.

[21] SSO 85.

motive power of its efforts; and "universality" as the goal.[22] The outcome
Lightfoot expected from following this pattern was "a larger, freer Church",
able to encompass the whole of humanity.[23] He was confident that, in a
manner similar to the Jews in antiquity, the Church of England would be the
instrument for the realization of the next stage in God's plan for the Church
and history;[24] indeed, "that for the Church of the future a far more glorious
destiny is in store than ever attended the Church of the past".[25]

Lightfoot further enforced the credentials of the Church of England by
reminding the Congress of its relation to the people and culture of England
in and over time. In meeting at Croydon, he pointed out, "the Congress may
be said to have stormed the citadel of the English Church".[26] By this he
meant that the gathering was taking place "under the shadow of that great
see, which even under papal domination was regarded as second only to
Rome in Latin Christendom, and which, liberated from that yoke, has certainly not lost in importance by the world-wide diffusion of the English race
and language — a see which in its first beginnings was ennobled by an Augustine and a Theodore, and in after ages by the saintly scholar Anselm, by
the patriot statesman Stephen Langton, by a long line of famous names which
it would be difficult to match elsewhere".[27] It was an observation incorporating the three points Lightfoot liked to make about the history of the English Church. The reference to Augustine and Theodore reminded that it was
older than the English nation itself. Mention of liberation from the Roman
yoke pointed to Lightfoot's qualified acceptance of the Reformation as a
'negative revolution' opening the way to freedom and enlightenment.[28] Its
continuing importance in the wider world, thirdly, commended the Church
not only for its capacity to survive through times of setback and declension
but also for the power of revival evinced by Church life in the nineteenth
century.[29] Together these facts meant that the Church of England was "in its
essential character" the true Church of Christ in England,[30] rather than an

---

[22] SSO 81-4.

[23] SSO 85.

[24] SSO 84-5, with 71-2 & 76-8.

[25] SSO 80.

[26] SSO 87.

[27] *Ibid.*

[28] Cf. SSO 140, 212-13; LNC 127-9. L.O. Frappell, "The Reformation as Negative
Revolution or Obscurantist Reaction: The Liberal Debate on the Reformation in Nineteenth Century Britain," *Journal of Religious History* 11.2 (December 1980) 289-307.

[29] Cf. SSO 143-4, 152-3, 153, 213-14, 243; LNC 152-4.

[30] Eg. at Benson's consecration as Bishop of Truro in 1877: "He succeeds to the im-
memorial institutions of an ancient faith and an ancient church". SSO 68. Cf. *ibid.*,148-
52, 171-2; CDI 7.

establishment imposed by the State,[31] and had been able to hand on the constitution and creeds of the ancient Church free of the corruptions and accretions which had grown up around practice and doctrine.[32] The continuity and progress of its longer course, and the manifest presence of the Holy Spirit in its recent history, indicated further that the Church of England was God's instrument for building and maintaining a Christian nation, and for leading the English people to the achievement of their destiny in the divine plan. The basis of his own personal confidence, this was the strong point from which it conducted its mission.

Finally Lightfoot invoked English church history again in the peroration as a way of dramatizing the function and duty of the Church Congress itself at the present time. Recognizing the intensity of feeling in the Church in the aftermath of the Public Worship Regulation Act of 1874, he furnished a warning of the destructive consequences of an "unlovely spirit" from the very beginning of the history of the See of Canterbury when the British Church was alienated from Augustine by his failure to rise on the approach of the native bishops.[33] Was not this, Lightfoot asked, "a type, an analogue, a parable of the disastrous spirit in which from age to age Churches have fostered animosities and created schisms by stiffness, by discourtesy, by severity and unfairness to opponents, thus engendering an exasperation which blinds to the real points at issue"?[34] Even more was at stake. Lightfoot noted that, as an ecclesiastical council, the Congress was the latest instalment in a long history which highlighted the dangers of such gatherings:

> From Julian to Gibbon the strifes of Churchmen have been a fertile theme of scorn to the enemies of the faith. They have neutralized the sufferings of many a martyr, and drowned the eloquence of many an apologist.[35]

Viewed in the light of this paradigm, the Congress represented the Church before the watching world. Upon the manner of its proceedings not only the efficacy of the Congress, but also the integrity and credibility of the Church itself, in part depended. This recognition signified Lightfoot's acceptance of its *de facto* denominationalization. In spite of its historic connections, the Church of England had now to win the respect and support of the English people.

---

[31] MSL 11-15. LNC 75-6. For Lightfoot's thinking on the establishment question, see 255 below.

[32] Cf. SSO 64-5, 213, 259-60.

[33] SSO 88-90.

[34] SSO 89. Again in 1881, when he presided over the Congress at Newcastle, Lightfoot stressed the need for a right spirit as a condition of its success, and on several occasions intervened in the debates to secure it. RCC (1881) 18-19, 130.

[35] SSO 86-8 (88 for the quotation). Again this was characteristic of his warnings to such gatherings. Cf. DDC (1881) 95-6.

The provisional nature of its standing in contemporary society drew the Church into the "great work" of the day. Part of its mission was to adapt the privileged position received from the past to a new and rapidly changing situation. Lightfoot indicated that a negative and a positive response was called for:

> Not to cling obstinately to the decayed anachronisms of the past, not to linger wistfully over the death stricken forms of the past, not to stunt our moral sympathies; but to adapt and to enlarge, to absorb new truths, to gather new ideas, to develope new institutions, to follow always the teaching of the Spirit ...[36]

He elaborated on what he meant shortly afterwards by combining two Biblical injunctions in a sermon preached for the Society For Promoting Christian Knowledge.[37] One was to "lengthen thy cords". This referred to the Church's duty to take into its outlook "new ideas and modes of thought, new branches of learning, [and] new developments of life" and allow them to effect "a new treatment of old truths".[38] As stated on another occasion, incorporating these novelties should be carried out boldly and confidently,[39] in line with the principle behind the "broader view of revelation":

> Be sure that every one of these has its true and proper relation to the 'faith once delivered to the saints' that in the end this faith will be more deeply apprehended, will be driven more directly home to the hearts and intellects of men, if the Church gives a cheerful welcome to whatever is noble, whatever is truthful, whatever is self-denying, whatever is enlightened, though the light seems to flash from without and not from within ...[40]

Approached with this confidence, modern experience was actually a condition of appreciating the full meaning and value of Christian belief. The true policy of the Church, therefore, was to expand its sympathies and change its institutions to remain in step with all the social and intellectual movements of the present.

The other injunction was to "strengthen thy stakes". As the Church engaged with modern thought and life it was necessary to hold firmly to old truths. For in the same way that the Church could not afford to be reckless of the future, it could not afford to neglect the past.[41] In particular this meant holding to the doctrine of the Incarnation:

> this is the central fact of all history; this is the converging point of all knowledge; this is your hope, your comfort, your strength, your joy, your peace; this is the light of the individual soul, and this is the life of the universal Church.[42]

---

[36] SSO 86.
[37] At St Martin's-in-the-Fields on 3 November 1879, taking Isaiah 54:2-3 as his text.
[38] SSO 115.
[39] SSO 117.
[40] Edifying, 1869, 19-20.
[41] Edifying, 1869, 20-1.
[42] SSO 116.

Not even science and technology could meet all the needs of humanity. Men and women still needed the spiritual help handed down from the Church's ancient past.[43] Old and fundamental truths remained the condition of constructive advance. A balance between change and continuity was required to achieve that comprehension of legitimate diversity which would lead to fullness in the Church's own life and the maintenance of its rightful place in English society.[44]

Together these perspectives embody the rudiments of a recognizable Anglican ecclesiology. It is clear at once that Lightfoot identified the Church of England with the historic church viewed against the entire panorama of God's "increasing purpose". More particularly, he regarded it as the local manifestation of the true church of Christ, continuing the work begun with Abraham, carried forward decisively by the Apostles, brought to England by Augustine and Aidan, and repristinated by the Reformation. There was much in this to mollify the descendants of the Tractarians, but Lightfoot's thinking also had manifest links with the national Church idea. Indeed, his ecclesiology was something of a synthesis of the 'apostolic' and 'erastian' paradigms.[45] As such it was bound to effect that inclusiveness of ideas and interests which distinguished incarnational Christianity, and would make the Church of England truly national without losing its identity as a Church.[46] According to Lightfoot, this integration of faith and life constituted true catholicity, and offered the hope of recovery amid loss of power and influence in a society increasingly bearing the marks of weakening Christian belief. Lightfoot's "comprehensive churchmanship" was the practical expression of this construct shaped out of the historical sources of Anglican identity and sharpened by the demands of the day. The specific matters on which he spoke on other occasions furnished three opportunities to demonstrate what it meant in practice.

II

No doubt because of his standing as Hulsean Professor and interpreter of St Paul, Lightfoot's first addresses to the Church Congress dealt with the intellectual side of Church life.[47] His remarks assumed that the Church had an intellectual mission to the English community. The challenge was to establish its precise nature at the present time and find ways in which it might be carried out effectively.

---

[43] Triumph, 1874, 25-6.

[44] Cf. CS 186-7.

[45] Lightfoot exulted in the idea of the *via media*. SSO 106-7.

[46] UC 9.

[47] See J.B. Lightfoot, "The Evidences of Christianity in Relation to the Current Forms of Scepticism," RCC (1871) 76-84; & "The Present Need and the Best Means of Quickening Interest in Theological Thought," RCC (1873) 227-33.

While for Lightfoot the Church's intellectual mission was not a proposition to defend, there appear to have been two grounds for it in his thinking. One — the status of Christianity as "the absolute religion" — was theological. By this he meant that "Christianity is intimately bound up with science, with history, with all the developments of life and thought in the past [and] with all the ... intellectual movements of the present". Always, however, it remained to make good this title "by embracing, combining, reconciling all that is true in the sphere of mind".[48] In Lightfoot's day, as his two addresses on these matters make clear, this meant coming to terms with new historical perspectives, Biblical criticism, science, new religions and the social aspirations involved in the doctrine of universal brotherhood.[49]

The other ground was anthropological. For Lightfoot it was axiomatic that human beings have a desire and capacity for apprehending the truth. As "the absolute truth", Christianity was in principle the satisfaction of this truth disposition.[50] The task of theology, therefore, was the presentation of the essential content of Christianity in terms of the intellectual interests, moral aspirations, and social enthusiasms of the age in order to satisfy the aspiration for truth underlying these phenomena.[51] On the other hand, there was a tendency for this faculty to be misdirected by the *Zeitgeist* which had to be corrected. Accordingly, while always seeking to speak in contemporary terms, the Church needed to remain uncommitted to the spirit of the age, accepting or resisting, qualifying or redirecting, whenever necessary.

These two grounds meant that, for Lightfoot, the Church's intellectual mission was the incorporation into the Christian outlook as far as possible the cultural and intellectual developments occurring in contemporary English society. While an accommodation to the age, this interpretation did not require fully sanctioning it. A double linkage with society was therefore involved.. It was the Church's function to provide intellectual leadership by directing people in what to think. But it needed also to follow the lead of society, by taking account of all that concerns its constituency. In other words, for the Church to teach effectively, it must also be willing to learn. When able to do so, the Church would achieve the optimum integration of human thought into its theological synthesis, and thereby achieve a proper comprehension and maintain its place in the vanguard of cultural progress. Wide intellectual sympathies were the condition of success in this side of its work.

While this was Lightfoot's ideal of the Church's relation to society intellectually, his two addresses on the matter arose out of its perceived short-

---

[48] RCC (1871) 76-7.
[49] RCC (1871) 79-83. RCC (1873) 231-3.
[50] RCC (1871) 76.
[51] RCC (1873) 231.

comings in this area. Theology, he noted, had once been the 'Queen of Sciences', but in both addresses he recognized that the Church was struggling to provide the intellectual leadership that followed from this status. He also conceded that it had been unable even to maintain interest in specifically Christian theology. The very considerable contemporary concern with theological issues had become "preoccupied with the more elementary problems of theology", such as the existence of God and the efficacy of prayer.[52] The wider society was witholding the right to direct its thought which the Church claimed for itself. To regain the initiative was the intellectual mission of the Church at the present time.

In devising a strategy to overcome this alienation, Lightfoot indicated the importance of history in his approach to theological matters. Identifying the basic cause as the widespread unbelief that was such a concern to him, in line with his preferred method of analysis, he looked into the mirror of history and gathered precedents to create a paradigm which defined what was happening and prescribed what should be done. The procedure revealed that the fundamental cause of unbelief at any time was the proper insistence of Christianity as "the absolute religion" on maintaining its independence of the times. The effect was to alienate those who were committed to the spirit of the age, producing in turn distrust and scepticism.[53] This was why, in different ages, as social and intellectual tendencies changed, the declared reasons for unbelief also changed. The practical corollary was that there could be no presentation of Christianity valid for every age. Instead theology in general, and apologetics in particular, must be progressive, in the sense of shifting their ground to meet the distinctive needs and interests of the age to which they were directed.[54] The tradition of defence would be maintained by changing the defences.

Clearly this reflexiveness required that the theologian be a keen observer of current thought. But the maintenance of an historical outlook was fundamental to his effectiveness. By placing the distinctive intellectual concerns of his day in this longer context, the theologian would be better able to assess their importance, and also perceive changes of interest and need, adjusting his presentation accordingly. That is, an historical perspective created the independence of the age necessary to understand and correctly address it. As a weapon in the theologian's armoury, history did not furnish an assured solution to the Church's intellectual problems waiting to be reactivated, but it did mark out a method and spirit of response, and justified hope in responding. To the extent that Lightfoot was promoting his own approach

---

[52] RCC (1873) 229-30.
[53] RCC (1871) 76-7.
[54] RCC (1871) 79.

in this, part of the Church's intellectual mission was the adoption of his theological method.

As a result of himself applying this method to his own age, Lightfoot urged two specific intellectual tasks upon the mid-Victorian Church. One was the development of a new apologetics. His dissatisfaction with contemporary practice in this respect was due in part to the belief that it was misguided. The true grounds of Christian belief were found more in religious experience than in intellectual conviction.[55] More pressing was the view that the "Evidences" theology received from the eighteenth century was now outmoded, despite the refinements of H.L. Mansel and J.B. Mozley in recent Bampton Lectures.[56] One line of attack on Christianity, the criticism of the genuineness of the Biblical documents, was quite new, and Lightfoot had already devoted much of his scholarly life to dealing with it.[57] The other, "attacks made on the revelation itself", were not new, but "the arms of the assailants had changed".[58] Apart from raising a bulwark against the new assault, a fresh strategy to combat an old attack revivified by the discovery of new methods was needed.

The defence of revelation at the present time, Lightfoot contended, required two main adjustments. The first was direction of attention to "the history of revelation", by which he understood "not only the history of its communication, but also the history of its reception and results ... not only the narratives of the Old and New Testaments, but also the progress of the Christian Church". Its unity and progress, he expected, would command respect at a time when law, development and continuity were "watchwords".[59] More particularly, it permitted a revamping of the argument from prophecy. Again with the *Zeitgeist* in mind, Lightfoot suggested that it must be impressive to note that the whole history of Israel was prophetic, looking hopefully to the future and the advent of the Messiah. This in turn put the Incarnation at the centre of history and opened the way to presenting post Christian history as the impact on the world of Christian ideas propagated through the Church.[60] Second, the "Substance of the Revelation" needed now to

---

[55] Lightfoot quoted approvingly Coleridge's well known outburst: "Evidences of Christianity ... I am weary of the word. Make the man feel the want of it. Rouse him, if you can, to the self-knowledge of his need of it; and you may safely trust to its own evidence." RCC (1871) 82.

[56] Mansel, *Limits of Religious Thought*; & J.B. Mozley, *Eight Lectures on Miracles* (2nd ed.; London: Rivingtons, 1867).

[57] RCC (1871) 79, 80. Lightfoot's recommendations to the Church regarding Higher Criticism were no more than the rationale of his own characteristic procedures. See Part IV below. His work as a member of the translation team for the Revised Version of the New Testament was also in part to rebut this criticism. See OFR 22-5.

[58] RCC (1871) 79, 80.

[59] RCC (1871) 80. Cf. OA 32-3.

[60] See 88-9, 108-9 & 111-12 above for Lightfoot's interpretation of this.

concentrate on "the idea of the Person of Christ" as the satisfaction of man's spiritual needs and the practical solution of many of the perplexities that arise. Together these lines of argument meant that present day apologetics should now be concerned with the progress and divine immanence evident in the providential and progressive history of the Church. It was Lightfoot's own theology of history based on "a broader view of revelation" that he commended to the Church of England as the content of a new "Christian Evidences".

Not essentially different, but more fundamental, was the second task. In 1873 Lightfoot urged the revivification of Christian dogmatics for the rechristianization of English theological interest. He rejected the attempt of more extreme liberals to have a Christianity without theology, but in a utilitarian age, when men rightly looked for the application of the Church's teaching, the task of Churchmen was to show forth the results for life of Christian dogma. In the "Substance of the Revelation" it possessed the means of doing so.

On the basis of the Logos doctrine — now put directly before the wider Church as the basis of the divine governance of the world — Lightfoot believed it was possible to present theology in a form acceptable to the age. It required from Churchmen "a frank and reverential sympathy" towards the advances of science. Indeed it provided a challenge to "really believe the teaching of St John and St Paul", whose christologies showed "that all the works of creation and all the processes of nature use the direct agency of the same Divine Word, Who was made flesh, and became man for us. Thus our scientific interests are intimately linked with our religious aspirations."[61] Similarly it provided the means of responding to "the lately acquired knowledge of Eastern religions" which had resulted from more intimate contact with the religions of the world in "an age of travel".[62] By regarding these religions as "a series of historical manifestations, wherein the Word has spoken to man, has associated with man, has wrought with man", what they taught could be placed in a proper relation to the main doctrines of Christianity in a wider exposition of the Faith than had hitherto been possible. If Churchmen could do it, "they would find not only that numberless objections to Christianity founded on the partial resemblances, the imperfect gropings after truth, in other religious systems, would melt away in the process, but that a flood of new light would at the same time be shed upon the significance and power of the Gospel".[63] In the same way that the first task

---

[61] RCC (1873) 233. Cf. SSO 115-17 & OA 304-6.
[62] RCC (1873) 232.
[63] CS 134-5. For the background, see T. Thomas, "The Impact of Other Religions," *Religion in Victorian Britain. Volume II. Controversies* (ed. G. Parsons; Manchester: University Press, 1988) 280-98.

required the Church to adopt Lightfoot's own theology of history, the second required that it take up its basis in his characteristic incarnational theology.

That Christian theology could in fact be restored to its proper regnancy, and the Church to a position of cultural and intellectual leadership, Lightfoot seems hardly to have doubted. This was in deep contrast to people of the temperament of Hort.[64] In 1882 he wrote to their mutual friend Benson, who had just been appointed Archbishop of Canterbury:

> the convulsions of our English Church itself, grievous as they are, seem to be as nothing beside the danger of its calm and unobtrusive alienation in thought and spirit from the great silent multitude of Englishmen, and again of alienation from fact and love of fact — mutual alienations both.[65]

Apart from the temporary misgivings of 1877, Lightfoot on the other hand continued to exult in the Logos as the basis for just this reconciliation of fact and faith for the maintenance of the oneness between the Church and English society.[66] History, moreover, warranted confidence in its success. The prevalent scientism was anticipated as an example of intellectual one-sidedness producing unbelief by the revival of Classical learning during the Renaissance, and suggested that the unfavourable climate for revelation was only temporary. Lightfoot also reminded the Church that in the passage from the fifteenth to the nineteenth century both Astronomy and Geology had been transformed from enemies into allies of Christian faith. "Will not history repeat itself?", he asked, as the Church confronted the challenge of Darwinian Biology. In 1884 he also enthused over the strengthening of the Church's position owing to the recent progress of knowledge in the field of New Testament archaeology and history.[67] For Lightfoot the maintenance of an historically sustained optimism was just as much a part of the Church's intellectual mission as the content and approach of his method.

This hopefulness minimized the difficulties by which Hort at least was overwhelmed. In commending his own historically conceived and executed scholarly programme and theological method as the way the Church should approach the intellectual side of its work, Lightfoot seemed to offer a way around one of the principal barriers to its effectiveness in its mission to English society, loss of confidence or interest in its teaching. Adaptation of Christian tradition to the circumstances of the day suggested a way of real-

---

[64] Lightfoot regarded Hort as of a naturally critical turn of mind. Lightfoot to Hammond, 30 April 1875 (TCC, Add Ms.a.77²²³).

[65] Hort to Benson, S. Stephen's Day, 1882, in LH II.290. The incident is discussed in Edwards, *Leaders*, 184-5.

[66] RCC (1881) 15-16. The classic expression of his viewpoint was the sermon entitled "Both One" preached at the Jubilee of King's College, London, in 1881. See SSO 131-45.

[67] RRH 1-6.

izing the vision of the Church as independent of the age but in vital contact with it as its interpreter and teacher. Moreover, the idea of the Logos as the source of all that is good and true in thought provided a way of realizing that unified conception of life which it was the Church's role to model to its host society. However, as Lightfoot was keenly aware, the success that the Church might achieve in this respect was likely to be undermined by the manifest outward disunity among Churchmen. Promoting a genuine unity among them was the next specific, and not unrelated, matter on which he addressed the Congress.

III

As early as 1872 Lightfoot placed alongside the need "to reconcile antagonisms without" the further need of "a remedy for divisions within" as one "of the two most serious difficulties which beset this Church of England".[68] The difficulty of the problem was not underestimated. To some extent, Lightfoot conceded, factionalism was inevitable. Because of man's religious nature, both genuine zeal and the preference for externals led to loss of perspective and fault finding partisanship.[69] Nor could the Church expect to escape the excessive individualism and conflict characteristic of the age itself.[70] Yet internal disunity, while readily explicable, discredited the Church before the watching world,[71] and led to dissipation of vital energy and force as well as lost opportunity.[72] If it was even to approximate to its mission as the national Church, it needed to solve the problem of division within and realize more the corporate dimensions of Church life, with its necessary concomitants of toleration, co-operation and mutual dependence in a common cause.

The background to the problem Lightfoot addressed was the increasing pluralism inside the Church of England itself. The situation had become complex and dangerous owing to the increasing institutionalization of disputation as a result of the theological legitimation of conflict in defence of the Church by the Tractarians and the Evangelicals.[73] Matters came to a head when Archbishop Tait and Prime Minister Disraeli tried to "put down

---

[68] SSO 2. Cf. 4th Group, 1858, 19-20.

[69] Stir Up, 1863, 18-19; True Blessedness, 1864, 13-14, 23-8; Lord, 1865, 27-9; Grieve Not, 1869, 12-13, 25-7; SSP 54-5, 142, 181-2; Christ, 1876, 27-9; Hunger, 1877, 30-2; YJC (1880) 49-50; I Ascend, 1880, 39-40; OA 65, 111-12, 265-6; SSO 177.

[70] Members, 1854, 1-2; Christian Fellowship, 1882, 7-9; OA 263, 312.

[71] Veil, 1855, 15-16; Life, 1862, 20-1; SSP 141-2; CS 258-9; SSO 88-90, 210-11; DDC (1881) 95-6; DJCS 7-8; OA 268.

[72] Sins, 1872, 3-9; SSO 2-3, 177, 186, 189; CS 53; PC 52, 93-4; SSO 218.

[73] Crowther, *Church Embattled*, ch. 8. Gilley & Sykes, " 'No Bishop, No Church!'," 120-39. Roberts, "Pressure Group Politics," 560-82.

ritualism" by means of the Public Worship Regulation Act of 1874.[74] The upshot was a parlous state of discipline within the Church, the virtual impotence of its courts, and eventually the scandal of four clergymen gaoled on grounds of conscience between 1877 and 1882. With schism threatening, and disestablishment advocated from inside, the situation was critical. If the Church did not achieve peace within, Lightfoot warned, it would hardly facilitate peace without. As matters stood, the Church of England could not promote that social integration which was part of its *raison d'être* as the national Church.[75]

Having touched on it at Croydon in 1877,[76] Lightfoot tackled the subject directly and at greatest length at the Leicester Congress of 1880.[77] On this occasion, Lightfoot regarded the problem of "outward relations with the state" as the lesser of the two main threats to the unity of the Church. But such a ranking only demonstrates how seriously he viewed the other, "the state of opinion within the Church itself", for he dreaded the prospect of disestablishment. As he explained to R.W. Church, Dean of St Paul's, this was for three reasons: it would mean the withdrawal from a large number of parishes "the present means of spiritual and moral education which the Church affords"; the terms of communion within the Church would be narrowed "in the interests of the dominant party for the time being"; and the likely secession of a party or parties would be "followed by a still further narrowing of the terms of Communion".[78] Lightfoot also looked to "the ultimate control of Parliament and the Crown" as the guarantor of liberty and justice in and for the Church. At the same time he deprecated making the Church of England in any way dependent on its connection with the state. For Lightfoot the establishment was principally a matter of expediency, and he continued to defend it on these grounds for the rest of the decade.[79]

---

[74] P.T. Marsh, *The Victorian Church in Decline: Archbishop Tait and the Church of England 1868-1882* (London: Routledge & Kegan Paul, 1969) esp. ch. 5, 7 & 9; & J. Bentley, *Ritualism and Politics in Victorian Britain. The Attempt to Legislate for Belief* (Oxford: University Press, 1978).

[75] SSO 13-14, 185.

[76] See 243-6 above.

[77] J.B. Lightfoot, *The Unity of the Church. A Paper Read at the Leicester Church Congress, September 29, 1880* (Durham: Andrews & Co., 1880).

[78] Draft of Lightfoot to R.W. Church, n.d. [but subsequent to the Public Worship Regulation Bill, to which reference is made].

[79] "I am driven ... to the conclusion that, viewed from the side of the Church, the relations between Church and State, so far at least as regards existing complications resolve themselves ultimately into a question of expediency." PC 85-9, esp. 87 for the quotation; Ch 67-9; LNC 21, 32; WDWI 4, 8; DDG (1887) 7-8; & especially in the lead up to a General Election in 1885, WDWI 1-8, & *Durham Diocesan Church Conference. Manifesto On Disestablishment. Inaugural Address By the Right Rev. The Lord Bishop of Durham* (Newcastle-Upon-Tyne: Andrew Reid, 1885). For the revival of the disestablishment

At Leicester it was almost enough simply to invoke the appropriate historical paradigm. Of the previous instances of schism arising from the same cause, the clearest was the formation of the separatist Church in fourth century Africa, when the "unworldly zeal and courage and intensity" of the Donatists led ultimately to the destruction of the African Church.[80] In the same vein, but more recently, the Scottish Disruption had engendered a self-perpetuating schism, even though the causes were no longer effective.[81] The magnitude of the present situation thus defined, and the likely outcome anticipated as the destruction of national churches, history also suggested how such situations should be dealt with. Augustine's application of the parable of the tares suggested that the worldly and the unworldly should be allowed to go on together, in order to preserve the integrity of the Church. With the alternatives so clearly adumbrated, Lightfoot urged dominically, "He that hath ears to hear, let him hear".[82]

But he did not leave Church people to draw their own conclusions. At a time when a repetition of the "magnificent unworldliness" of the Donatists threatened, "with all its fatal consequences", Lightfoot warned against extreme measures.[83] With great tact he recognized the difficulties of the position and acknowledged the appeal of the sacrifice to "zealous and chivalrous natures". Nevertheless, he also urged that the advocates did not see what great advantages for the Church in years to come they were prepared to squander. In the background he set himself to do what he could to ease the situation. Privately he identified the extremists as the ritualists, classified them as "irreconcilables" and advocated weakening their support by removing the grievances that drove men and women into their arms. In effect this meant finding a way to make the law conform to accepted practice within the Church of England.[84] On this matter Lightfoot set himself to oppose the repetition of history.

A similar attitude governed the line Lightfoot took towards the other side of the push for disestablishment. Since the 1850s Dissenters had agitated for the abolition of the Church's privileged status. Lightfoot did not think the New Testament evidence so clear as to warrant unchurching bodies with

---

question in 1885, see A. Simon, "Church Disestablishment as a Factor in the General Election of 1885," *Historical Journal* XVIII.4 (1975) 791-820; &, for the Durham background, J.S. Newton, "Edward Miall and the Diocese of Durham: The Disestablishment Question in the North-East in the Nineteenth Century," *Durham University Journal* LXXII.2 (June 1980) 157-68.

[80] UC 4.

[81] UC 4-5. Cf. SSO 181-6, for similar remarks to the Representative Council of the Scottish Episcopal Church.

[82] UC 4, 5.

[83] UC 5.

[84] Draft of Lightfoot to R.W. Church, n.d.

a non-episcopal polity.[85] For this reason he regretted rather than opposed Dissent. He always remembered that the existence of dissenting churches was due in part to the faults of the Church of England itself.[86] He also readily acknowledged their work and achievement, and even allowed the stimulation of an honourable rivalry.[87] Such concessions amounted to recognition of the legitimacy of Dissent, and Lightfoot deprecated narrowness and irritability in dealing with it. On this basis he urged compromise wherever possible and minimization of offence. While he subscribed to the national church ideal, Lightfoot had abandoned the monopolistic pretensions of the establishment. The integrity of the Church of England now depended on the effectiveness with which it conducted its mission in a competitive situation.

Of greater immediate importance to Lightfoot at Leicester was "the state of opinion within the Church itself".[88] In addressing this issue he again brought his Biblical scholarship into play. Lightfoot had long accepted the conflict in the early Church rediscovered in the nineteenth century by F.C. Baur.[89] Applying the view that conflict was far worse in the first than in the nineteenth century, he drew for a prototype of the contemporary situation on the same materials Baur had used to make his case.[90] He now maintained that each of the main Church "parties" of the day — or "schools of thought", as he preferred to call them — was anticipated at Corinth in the first century. Those who said they were "of Cephas", "of Paul", and "of Apollos" corresponded to High Churchmen, Evangelicals and Broad Churchmen respectively.[91] Far from being abnormal, the present situation, it followed, was legitimated by a pattern established at the very beginning of church history. Since St Paul had allowed the coexistence of the three different groups within one church, contemporaries under similar circumstances could hardly respond differently.

Lightfoot's prototype was ironic in two respects. First, the very passage in which Baur had found the fundamental cleavage of incipient Christianity had been turned into the grounds for promoting an apostolically inspired conception of unity. Second, the exclusivism which some advocated as the means of achieving the purity of the ideal church was precluded by the very period to which they looked for its historic existence. While perhaps neglecting the complexity of the evidence on this difficult subject, this was

---

[85] P 267.
[86] RCC (1881) 16-17. Cf. OA 264, 267; SSO 263.
[87] YJC (1880) 48-51. MD 13-14.
[88] UC 5.
[89] G 374.
[90] That is, 1 Corinthians 1-3.
[91] UC 5-6, 8.

shrewd. If his presentation of the matter was accepted, there could be no appeal to the apostolic age to justify the removal of the adherents of any outlook from the Church. Instead it required acceptance of parties and toleration of different shades of opinion.[92] Diversity in unity was the tradition of the Church from the very beginning, and thus a line of continuity to be maintained in the present day.

Lightfoot further enforced the 'lessons' of history for the internal unity of the Church by assimilating its experience in the nineteenth century to the cumulative perspective of the "increasing purpose of God".[93] First had come the Evangelicals, with their emphasis "on personal religion, the relation of the individual soul to God". A wider vision had been made possible by the Tractarian concentration on the "history, the constitution, the ritual, the laws, the continuous corporate life of the Christian body". Finally, a cosmopolitan outlook was introduced to the Church by the Broad Churchmen, who had confronted the question of the relation of the Church to "All these problems of social and political life, all these unconverted heathen throughout the world, all these past ages of human history, all these manifold processes of nature". Lightfoot presented the order of their appearance as progressive and providential: "... these three schools have followed each other in the order which was most conducive to the well being of the Church." Moreover, the benefit of their coexistence to each party and to the Church as a whole was that "they moderate, and are moderated by, contact with one another".[94] Mere acquiescence in the existence of the different schools of thought within the Church was therefore not enough. Working with Providence required a warm acceptance of the presence of all three 'parties' and active co-operation between Churchmen as the condition of fullness of life within and an effective mission to the society without. Unity, as Lightfoot liked to say, did not require uniformity.[95]

The rationale for Lightfoot's position in this respect was laid down eight years earlier at the inauguration of the Cambridge Church Society. In its aim "to unite a wide comprehension of men and ideas with concentration of unity of purpose and unity of spirit", and in its dependence on the efforts of its individual members, this new organization was seen as a microcosm of the wider Church.[96] Because it had need of all perspectives "if there is to be anything like fulness in the final result", the responsibility of the individual member was clear. On each

---

[92]　UC 5-6.
[93]　For what follows, UC 7-10.
[94]　UC 9.
[95]　SSO 8-14, 19, 174-90. OA 258-70.
[96]　SSO 8-9. Cf. 9-12, 12-13.

it is incumbent not to addict himself to this party or that, but to endeavour to learn of all. He will reject the exaggerations of each; but he will seek to appropriate the truths of each.[97]

The principle of the desired cohesion in the life of the Church, as in all things, was Christ, a point to which Lightfoot continually tried to recall his contemporaries.

Neither Church nor creeds must be our starting point, but the history of the Saviour. If we begin with this, all other questions will settle themselves in time. The claims of the Church will be adjusted. The value of a creed will find its proper estimate. Only lay the foundation aright.[98]

A part of the larger *Imitatio Christi* pattern, this necessarily involved taking seriously the ἐπιείκεια which Jesus taught and practised,[99] and which Lightfoot himself attempted through his scholarship and teaching to restore to its proper place in the thinking of Churchmen.[100] This cooperative ecclesiology was an extension of his characteristic incarnational theology.

Of course the attitude prescribed by the theology of history did not preclude criticism of each outlook. Though he eschewed doing so in public,[101] Lightfoot's critique of contemporary Churchmen and Church parties was occasionally expressed in general terms, albeit allusively. He pinpointed a tendency to base a position on loyalty to the Church, its creeds and sacraments; or on slogans, such as "justification by faith" — transparent references to High Churchmen and Evangelicals respectively.[102] Similarly, he warned the Broad Churchmen against making a religion out of critical enquiry and theological speculation.[103] His harshest words were reserved for those committed to an excess of formalism — a perhaps not altogether fair allusion to the ritualists —[104] which he regarded as a recurrence of that "heartless formalism, tied down to ritual observances" anticipated in the conflict of incipient Christianity with Judaism.[105] The characteristic emphases of each group could be right in themselves, but their historic effect had been to divert them from the cultivation of genuine personal religion. It was to the true Gospel of Christ that he exhorted each to aspire.

---

[97] SSO 12.

[98] Life, 1862, 16-17. Cf. Morning, 1864, 25-6; CS 179-80, 185.

[99] Lightfoot's own translation is best: "...moderation, ... sobriety of temper and reasonableness of conduct". See AF I.1.97.

[100] Eg. SSO 218, 263. DJCS 7-8. OA 265, 268-9. AF I.1.97; 2.169-70. Cf. CS 106 & NEP 185-6.

[101] YJC (1879) 113-14.

[102] Life, 1862, 16-17; True Blessedness, 1864, 23-8; Life's Pilgrimage, 1864, 26-7; Morning, 1864, 25-6; The Lord, 1865, 27-9; SSP 190-2, 296-7; SSO 9-10; Hunger, 1877, 31; OA 103, 113-14.

[103] Morning, 1864, 25-6, 30-2.

[104] For the ardour and sincerity of one of the best ritualists, see L.E. Ellsworth, *Charles Lowder and the Ritualist Movement* (London: Darton, 1982).

[105] Acts VIII-XIV, f. 3r.

Lightfoot's eirenicism determined his attitude on the difficult question of discipline. Although to some extent critical of all the factions in the contemporary Church, he sought even-handed treatment for all, particularly for those with whom he was least in sympathy. Certainly the reaction to the Purchas Judgment of 1870 had been excessive. He hoped, not merely from expediency, but as a matter of justice, that the formularies, which had been "interpreted with the greatest liberality — not to say, laxity — to include the Low Churchmen in the Gorham Case, and the Broad Churchmen in the *Essays and Reviews* case", would be applied to the ritualists with due latitude.[106] In this way a proper comprehension would be maintained, and the contribution of each "school" retained for the Church of England.[107]

This did not mean that Lightfoot was incapable of taking a firm stand on matters dividing the Church. Indeed, on the question of vestments he came to see that "the rule should be plain and distinct so that we may know exactly what is our position".[108] Similarly, on the vexed question of creeds, he insisted on their place in the Church as a help to personal religion and bond of union.[109] On the other hand, Lightfoot would not countenance additional tests, as his refusal to become Visitor of Ridley Hall in Cambridge indicates.[110] While they needed to be as broad as possible,[111] the Church of England had to be clear on the terms of membership.

At the same time he was prepared to modify the tradition of the Church in the interests of facilitating its proper comprehensiveness. This was the basis of his response to the controversy over the Athanasian Creed.[112] Shortly before he left Cambridge a petition with some 200 signatures — "not only men of very considerable intellectual standing, a large number of Junior Fellows and Scholars of the Colleges, but the very men ... on whom I should have laid my finger as the hope of the Church in years to come" — served as a reminder that what were seen as its immoral components debarred people from the Church, distressed its members, and deterred young men from Orders.[113] Its removal not being practical, Lightfoot wanted its use made op-

---

[106] Lightfoot to Tait, 15 March 1871; & to Sandford, 15 March 1871 (TPL, vol. 89, f. 161, 163). On the Purchas Judgment, see LT II.92-100.

[107] Cf. Lightfoot's appreciation of the lives of A.P. Stanley and E.B. Pusey in PC 91-2.

[108] YJC (1881) 24. Cf. his hesitation over the issue two years previously. YJC (1879) 113-14.

[109] 4th Group, 1858, 20-1. Life, 1860, 8-9. SSP 296-7. Ch 40-51.

[110] Wilson, "Life," 115-19. F.W. Bullock, *A History of Ridley Hall* (2 vols; Cambridge: University Press, 1941-1953) I.185.

[111] Eg. "It is to a larger comprehension, rather than a stricter exclusion, that I have always looked as the hope of our Church." Lightfoot to the Editor, 30 June 1877, in *The Guardian* (4 July 1877).

[112] On which, see LT II.ch. XXII; & Marsh, *Victorian Church*, 40-51.

[113] A copy of the petition is included among the Lightfoot papers. The 159 signatures include such names as G.H. Rendall, E.C. Selwyn, J.E.C. Welldon & G.W. Prothero.

tional in public services. This was because historical criticism showed it to a canticle rather than a creed.[114] Moreover, its form was a product of its history, the original text having been added to, and the damnatory clauses strengthened.[115] With the other Cambridge Divinity Professors, Lightfoot agreed "that the admonitory clauses may be treated as separate from the Exposition itself, and may be modified without in any way touching what is declared therein to be the Catholic Faith," and that such changes could be made by the Church "for the right understanding of her own meaning".[116] It was this last point that provided the stumbling block when, at Archbishop Tait's suggestion, Lightfoot tried to win over — unsuccessfully — the belli-cose Liddon to a more flexible attitude.[117] When the evidence allowed, and when the welfare of the Church was endangered, Lightfoot held out for change, tradition and the loyalties of Churchmen notwithstanding.[118]

This commitment to inclusiveness and toleration won for Lightfoot a de-served reputation for moderation and wisdom which gave him considerable influence in the life of the contemporary Church.[119] Its basis in history prob-ably oversimplified the contemporary situation but it did not invalidate the prescription derived from it. Comprehension based on what each held in common, irrespective of the number of "schools" to be accommodated, was essential to the Church's integrity and a precondition of success in its mis-sion to English society. It was a line of thinking that also had implications for the new situation created by the world wide spread of Anglicanism.

IV

Lightfoot's confidence in the Church of England attained a new height in his final address to the Congress. In a fresh wave of optimism, the earlier con-cern about its capacity to perform its mission within English society gave way to the hope that it would achieve something similar beyond. "To our-selves," Lightfoot had proclaimed repeatedly before 1887, "all men are fel-

---

[114] Draft letter to an unnamed bishop [probably C.J. Ellicott of Gloucester and Bristol who, shortly afterwards, referred to a "short paper on the Creed by Professor Lightfoot": see n. 116 below], 30 November 1871. Also Lightfoot to Westcott, 28, 28, 30 December 1871; 1, 2, 17 January 1872; March 1872; 4 November 1878 (LAC).

[115] Lightfoot cited the Nicene Creed as an historical precedent for reducing its status.

[116] "The Cambridge Report," dated 3 February 1872, and signed by Lightfoot, Westcott & C.A. Swainson, in *Report of the Committee of Bishops on the Revision of the Text and Translation of the Athanasian Creed with an Introduction and Notes by Charles John, Lord Bishop of Gloucester* (ed. C.J. Ellicott; London: Rivingtons, 1872) 34-6.

[117] Johnston, *Life of Liddon*, 164-5. Liddon had threatened to resign his orders if the Creed was in any way downgraded.

[118] Cf. "My motive is the promotion of God's glory and the welfare of this our dear Church of England." YJC (1880) 48.

[119] Eg. Johnston, *Life of Liddon*, 265-6.

low-countrymen, are brothers in Christ."[120] Now he appropriated the principle as a viable object for the mission of the English Church. Not all Englishmen, but all men, were the proper objects of its evangelistic, pastoral and pedagogical functions. Universality, not nationality, must be its aim. This was the climax of Lightfoot's aspiration. The idea of the Church of England as a denomination was not so much bypassed as transcended in the hope that it would become a "universal" church.

Ultimately Lightfoot's aspiration was a response to the growth of the British Empire from the late sixteenth to the nineteenth centuries. Only during his lifetime, as another aspect of the Anglican revival of the 1830s and 40s, had the Church awakened to the opportunity presented by this development.[121]

At first Lightfoot's response manifested itself as support for the missionary movement.[122] Missionary zeal, he insisted, "is on the whole the surest test of the vitality of the Church".[123] But Lightfoot also believed that vigorous missionary effort was necessary to realize the historic inheritance received by the English Church from Pope Gregory, Augustine and the early Celtic missionaries.[124] Obvious failures and shortcomings notwithstanding, its achievement in this respect made the modern missionary movement "the glory of the present day".[125] But the success of the Society for the Propagation of the Gospel (S.P.G.) and the other associations it had inspired only showed that there was a greater work yet to be done. History beckoned the Church forward.

This was why Lightfoot defended the modern missionary movement with such vigour when it seemed to falter in the 1860s and early 1870s.[126] Lest disappointment lead to a slackening of effort, at the annual meeting of the S.P.G. in 1873, he rebutted the charge that missions had failed.[127] To this

---

[120] Members, 1854, 2-6, 13-17. Will He, 1869, 19-23. CS 27. RCC (1873) 233.

[121] G. Rowell, *The Vision Glorious. Themes and Personalities of the Catholic Revival in Anglicanism* (Oxford: University Press, 1983) ch. VIII. For an account of the dilemmas raised by the extension of the Church of England, see P.H.E. Thomas, "The Lambeth Conferences and the Development of Anglican Ecclesiology 1867-1978" (unpublished Ph.D. thesis; Durham University, 1982) ch. 2.

[122] For his early interest in missions, see 48 n.84 above. In the 1850s Lightfoot was a member of the Cambridge committee of the Oxford and Cambridge Mission to Central Africa. UP 28, f. 573 & 1046 (CUA).

[123] MSL 15. Cf. Philip's Life, 1880, 11-12.

[124] MSL 15-16, 18. Teach All, 1878, 7-17, 20-2. SSO 158, 159. LNC 44-6.

[125] 4th Group, 1858, 21.

[126] The real income of missionary societies had either decreased or flattened out, while the number of missionary candidates was down on the peak of 1858. B. Stanley, "Home Support For Overseas Missions in Early Victorian England, ca. 1838-1873" (unpublished Ph.D. thesis; Cambridge University, 1979) 58-9, 64, 71.

[127] Originally published in *Missions: Their Temporal Utility, Rate of Progress, and Spiritual Foundation, Stated in the Addresses of Lord Napier, Canon Lightfoot, and Bishop Kelly, at the Annual Meeting of the Society for the Propagation of the Gospel, on the 29th*

end he cited the counter claims of the colonial statesman, Sir Bartle Frere, which were based on first hand experience. The real basis of his case, however, was the past. "History," Lightfoot promised, would be "a cordial for the drooping courage."[128]

Close analysis of the evidence revealed an increase in the ratio of Christians to the world population in the mid-third and nineteenth centuries from 1/150 to 1/5.[129] Two purposes were served by the comparison. It forced a realistic appraisal of the missionary achievement of the early Church, which there was a tendency to idealize. This in turn permitted seeing its modern counterpart in its true historical relations. With a touch of the irony Lightfoot reserved for controversy, the moral was drawn out:

> I am quite aware that the relative strengths of Christendom at the two epochs is determined by other considerations as well as the numbers. But, after all deductions on this account, shall we suffer ourselves to be overwhelmed with dismay because, as we pass from the third century to the nineteenth, the proportion of one in a hundred and fifty is only exchanged to one in five?[130]

Quantitatively the facts did not sustain the charge that modern missions had failed.[131]

The comparison between ancient and modern missions also produced five analogies which had "their lessons of consolation and encouragement".[132] First, the early centuries revealed different rates of progress among different religions and races. This suggested that it was best to labour and wait where the culture required it, and look elsewhere for rapid results. Second, the historical paradigm laid down stages in missionary progress to which resistant cultures were subject. A heuristic tool of this kind permitted identification of the point reached as an encouragement to hopeful effort. It suggested, third, that periods of slow progress were really a preparation for periods of rapid expansion, so that the great need in missions (as in other aspects of Church work) was energetic and patient labour in the present without thought about the results. The sectarian divisions between Christians, fourth, were shown not to be such a great hindrance to success. Alleged obstacles, finally, were reduced to their proper dimensions. In this perspective recent setbacks did not seem so serious. *"Nos passi graviora,"* Lightfoot concluded, "We have survived worse calamities than these."[133]

April, 1873 (London: Macmillan, 1873); & separately as J.B. Lightfoot, *Comparative Progress of Ancient and Modern Missions* (London: Clay, 1874). Reprinted in HE 72-92, to which reference is made.

[128] HE 73.
[129] HE 73-82.
[130] HE 80 n. 2.
[131] HE 81.
[132] HE 82-91 (83 for the quotation).
[133] HE 91.

Lightfoot's analysis portended "the advent of a more glorious future, if we will only nerve ourselves to renewed efforts".[134] However, his answer to the critics turned on his assimilation of the story of missions to the theology of history. He even employed the characteristic water image to describe the pattern of their progress. Both ancient and modern missions had

the same alternations of success and failure, periods of acceleration followed by periods of retardation, when the surging wave has been sucked back in the retiring current, while yet the flood has been rising steadily all along, though the unobservant eye might fail to mark it, advancing towards that final consummation when the earth shall be covered with the knowledge of the Lord as the waters cover the sea.[135]

Viewed in this perspective, history sustained that hope in certain victory which was the true missionary spirit. The detractors had not seen that in this special way the English Church had become the instrument of God's "increasing purpose".

While presented as a general defence of contemporary missions, Lightfoot's principal concern was for the Indian mission, "our special charge, as a Christian nation; ... our hardest problem as a missionary Church".[136] In this special case he was again concerned to establish the facts, pointing out that the number of Indian Christians had more than doubled in the twenty years since 1851.[137] Moreover, the progress of Christianity in India far exceeded what had been achieved in the infancy of the British Church itself.[138] Three of the five analogies were referred specifically to the Indian situation. There was further cause for confidence in the growing recognition of the need to develop missionary methods appropriate to the Indian context.[139] Lightfoot did something to capitalize on the hopefulness of the situation by taking a leading part in setting up and directing the Cambridge Mission to Delhi.[140]

Lightfoot remained an active supporter of missions for the rest of his life, usually drawing on the same historical arguments and types.[141] He continu-

---

[134] HE 91.

[135] HE 72-3.

[136] HE 91.

[137] HE 88.

[138] HE 82.

[139] HE 91-2. Lightfoot also supported entrusting the work of ministry to natives. Necessity, 1873, 28-31. Cf. SSO 59; & DDG I (1887) 9.

[140] See A Brief Account of the Cambridge Mission to North India (Delhi), dated 'January, 1881'. J.B. Dunelm, The Cambridge Mission to Delhi. Repr. from The Cambridge Review (23 November 1881). (Both pamphlets are among the Camb. Uni. Papers MD5, CUL). Lightfoot to Westcott, 1 July 1876; 27 September 1877 (LAC). SSO 38-54. Delhi Mission, 1878. See also S. Bickersteth, Life and Letters of Edward Bickersteth Bishop of South Tokyo (2nd ed.; London: Sampson Low & Co., 1905) 34-7, 60-3.

[141] Usually on behalf of the C.M.S. and S.P.G.. See Stockton, n.d., where he updated the argument and figures of "Comparative Progress". See the file of Lightfoot's missionary speeches as Bishop of Durham labelled 'Missions: S.P.G. & C.M.S.'.

ally extolled the "more definite interest in foreign missionary work" in both Church and nation.[142] He was optimistic too about prospects on the mission field itself, and remained especially hopeful of success among the prime resistant cultures, the Hindus and the Chinese.[143] Indeed he insisted that progress hitherto exceeded what the English people had a right to expect. Always quick to criticize, they had not so readily given thanks for undoubted progress, and their outlay on missions in men and money continued to be paltry.[144] The argument from progressive history reached its highest point in the implication that, if England could only rise to the call of God, the best days of her missionary enterprise still lay in the future.

This bright prospect notwithstanding, Lightfoot began to think during the 1870s that the Empire offered more than the challenge to be a missionary church of historic achievement. It is not simply that he was now speaking more on Church affairs away from the University. There had been earlier opportunities — such as the address to Trinity House — for dwelling on the possibilities for the Church of England opened by the extent of British power. Rather Lightfoot was feeling his way towards a new understanding of his Church's role in the world. In 1872 he was already thinking in ecumenical terms when he anticipated that by healing its internal divisions the Church of England might do something to promote that unity of Christendom for which men were hoping.[145] Five years later at the Church Congress he averred that the influence of the Church of England was second only to that of Rome.[146] But this was in the context of a general summons to the Church to recover amidst adversity. The possibility of some kind of ecumenical mission for it was not yet more than an aspiration.

Two wider events seem to have encouraged the conception of this hope. One was the succession of the "Little England era" by the renewal of discussion about the importance of the Empire in the 1870s and early 1880s.[147] The increased frequency of references to it in his writings of this period suggest that Lightfoot was affected by this heightened consciousness. Moreover, the reproduction of imperial rhetoric indicates that he agreed with those who — however reluctantly — were beginning to accept exalted notions of imperial mission. Although not altogether blind to its faults,[148] Lightfoot's

---

[142] Eg. OA 277-8.

[143] SSO 158-9.

[144] Necessity, 1873, 8-11, 22. Vision, 1877, 37, 38. Teach, 1878, 6-7, 20-2.

[145] SSO 13-14.

[146] SSO 87. Cf. 64-5.

[147] On which see C.C. Eldridge, *England's Mission. The Imperial Idea in the Age of Gladstone and Disraeli 1868-1880* (London: Macmillan, 1973).

[148] Eg. Sunderland, 1887, 4, in the file 'Missions: SPG & CMS', where Lightfoot acknowledged English lawlessness, moral excesses, etc. Cf. CS 259.

was the sanitized view of the Empire which concentrated on the benefits of English rule. But his perspective went beyond the more common notions of trusteeship and humanitarian obligation. Nationalism was consecrated when Lightfoot welcomed "the position of England as the mother of so many colonies and dependencies, the heart and centre of the world's commerce and manufacture", as evidence of a divine call.[149]

Giving shape to his aspiration, secondly, were developments within Roman Catholicism. Lightfoot deplored the declaration of Papal Infallibility at the First Vatican Council as an unconscionable affront to man's mind and independence.[150] So serious was it that, under the circumstances, he regarded the unjustifiable — schism, in the form of the Old Catholic Movement — as justified.[151] Rome had abdicated the claim to be the centre of Church unity by claiming too much. The succession of the Church of England to this role might be the meaning of the "larger and truer ideal of the external commission of the Church" implicit in the spread of the Anglican Communion.[152] Lightfoot seized on the point made more than fifty years previously by the French Ultramontane writer, Joseph De Maistre, that "this our English Church seemed destined by her position to give the impulse to a great movement which should result in the union of the divided Churches and sects".[153]

By 1887 this idea had firmed. In his final Church Congress address Lightfoot announced the emergence of this larger, freer Church of England. "Catholic indeed she was potentially before in her doctrine and polity; but now she is catholic in fact, catholic in her interests and sympathies, catholic in her responsibilities and duties."[154] Significantly the transformation in Lightfoot's outlook between the Sermons of 1877 and 1887 involved a switch from 'Ezekiel' to 'Isaiah' as his Scriptural source. This was a change from the prophet of the Captivity to "the evangelic prophet", whose calling had opened a new era in the religious history of the world.[155] In effect he proclaimed the fulfilment of the prophecy of Ezekiel, which he had invoked ten years previously. Whereas universality was regarded in 1877 as an ideal to pursue, now it was regarded as an accomplished fact to service.[156] The Church of England stood on the threshold of a new phase, not only of its own history, but of the history of the Church.

---

[149] SSO 117. Cf. 215.
[150] Eg. Sins, 1872, 3-9; LNC 128-9.
[151] Sins, 1872, 3-9.
[152] Delhi Mission, alternate ending written as an appeal for the S.P.G., and preached 30 November 1879, 5.
[153] SSO 64. Cf. ibid., 258.
[154] SSO 262.
[155] Vision, 1877, 11-13.
[156] Eg. DDG I (1887) 7.

Lightfoot's change of attitude was partly due to the success of the Lambeth Conferences. In 1887 the meeting of the Church Congress at Wolverhampton, which had also been the venue in the inaugural year of the Lambeth Conference, forged a link with the "first visible presentation of the catholicity of the English Church".[157] Ten years previously this new development within the burgeoning Anglican Communion could hardly be regarded as established. The first Lambeth Conference had been an object of deep suspicion, and it was too early to estimate the success of the second. In this respect Lightfoot could make no capital in 1877 out of the meeting of the Congress at Croydon. But on the eve of the third Lambeth Conference greater confidence was warranted. Its meeting was a symbol of the position that had been reached.

> The successor of S. Augustine is coming to be regarded as the Patriarch in substance, if not in name, of the Anglican Churches throughout the world. The proud title, *papa alterius orbis*, has a far more real meaning now than when it was conferred many centuries ago.[158]

More immediately important was "the imperial destiny of England — her world wide interests and responsibilities" recently symbolized in the triumphant Jubilee of Queen Victoria.[159] The meaning of the event had been emphasized by contemporary historians and publicists, most notably Seeley and Froude, and also in various commemorative acts, such as the Imperial Institute.[160] While others sought to find how the occasion might be turned to commercial advantage, Lightfoot looked for how the Church might benefit.[161] If the Holy Roman Empire had suggested the idea of the Holy Roman Church, was it not legitimate, he asked, to see the spiritual counterpart of the age of Victoria as "the catholicity of the English Church, with all the responsibilities which it involves — the world wide opportunities — the unique destiny which in God's providence seems to be reserved for the Anglican community in shaping the future of Christendom"?[162]

In a note superficially reminiscent of the 1830s, Lightfoot criticized the Church for holding its catholicity lightly, and challenged it to grasp its opportunity. When the notion was revived fifty years earlier by the Tractarians, the focus had been on the catholicity of the Church's commission. Among High Churchmen generally this led to enthusiastic support for the concept of missionary bishop as the proper founder of churches overseas.[163] After

---

[157] SSO 257-8. Cf. SSO 217-18.
[158] SSO 261-2. Cf. PC 93.
[159] SSO 248-9. Cf. OA 181-2; S 157-8.
[160] SSO 249-50, 251-3.
[161] SSO 250-1. For the impact of the Jubilee, see T. Richards, "The Image of Victoria in the Year of Jubilee," *Victorian Studies* 31.1 (Autumn 1987) 7-32.
[162] SSO 251. Cf. SSO 260.
[163] Rowell, *Vision Glorious*, 161-2.

1845 it also led to an emphasis on the catholicity of the Church's mission to English society.[164] Without denying the validity of either conception, Lightfoot now urged that the identity of the English Church be adapted to the reality of England's empire. Her mission was not limited to the nation: the proper sphere of her activity was Christendom and the world.[165] While always inherent in both its doctrine and polity, the catholicity of the Church of England was now manifestly a catholicity of extent, a development which meant that the responsibility to work was not diminished but intensified. The national Church had become an international Church.

Once more history formed and directed the aspiration it had created. Lightfoot evoked the high destiny of his Church in the plan of Providence by again identifying it with ancient Israel. In the religious history of the world, the Jews had been the "ensign for the Lord", around which the nations had gathered at the call of the Divine voice. The power of this idea of a providentially ordained mission in the world was evident in their history:

> It was a centre of unity and a fountain of strength to the nation, when all the external organizations failed. It taught them a deep self-respect, and it inspired them with a boundless hope ... Ever and again, when disasters crowded upon them, and their doom seemed inevitable, this triumphant note was sounded from the abyss of the nation's despair. Ever and again they awakened to the consciousness of their magnificent destiny.[166]

The function of the typology was first pressed upon the alumni of Wells Theological College:

> Try and individualize this idea — the destiny of your Church; take it distinctively to yourself as an object to labour for, to pray for, to live for; strive to work, as fellow-workers of God, in His great purpose.[167]

The same end was in view when Lightfoot brought it to the attention of the Church Congress. Through the aggregated efforts of its constituent individuals dealing with its practical demands in this light he hoped that the English Church would rise to its opportunity and responsibility as God's elect.[168]

In order to realize this role as the "Ensign of the Nations", Lightfoot set as the precondition of success the vigorous prosecution of its mission at home in all its aspects.[169] Beyond that he called on the Church to continue its efforts to evangelize the heathen world, with a view to creating inde-

---

[164] Bowen, *Idea of the Victorian Church*, esp. Part II.

[165] DDG I (1887) 7.

[166] SSO 208.

[167] SSO 218-19. Cf. SSO 211-12.

[168] SSO 257. Cf. Teach All, 1878, 30-2. For an indication of the effect of Lightfoot's speech within the Anglican Communion, see J. Frederickton [Metropolitan of Canada] & the Bishop of Edinburgh to Lightfoot, 7 December 1887 & 2 January 1888.

[169] SSO 263.

pendent native churches.[170] He urged it to see to the religious needs of British emigrants all around the globe, so that the "practical heathenism of Englishmen abroad" would be no "stumbling block in the way of the conversion of the nation".[171] He also looked for cultivation of more intimate relations with the ancient Churches of the East, in the manner made possible by the Archbishop's Mission to the Assyrian Church.[172] Finally, he expected the Church of England to do a mother's duty to her offspring, the American and colonial churches — "promoting their increase and fostering their growth" — since it was through the Anglican communion that the Church of England would appeal to Christendom.[173] In terms of contemporary imperial thought, Lightfoot envisaged an informal hegemony for the Church of England over the churches which submitted to her influence. A paramountcy had been thrust upon her which it remained to consolidate and develop through its good offices. That which he regarded as the greatest Church in Christendom should be the leader of the Church in Christendom.[174]

The high point of Lightfoot's own commitment to this ideal came at the third Lambeth Conference in the following year. Although dangerously ill,[175] he took a full and energetic part, contributing in two main ways.[176] First, he was substantially involved in the preliminary discussions, vigorously defending his essay on "The Christian Ministry"[177] from the misconstruction of the Bishop of St Andrews in the debate on home reunion,[178] and leading the debate on "Polygamy and Heathen Converts". He subsequently chaired the committees appointed to deal with that subject and "The Church's Practical Work in Relation to the Subject of Purity", as well as serving on the committee considering divorce.[179] Second, towards the end Lightfoot was joint author of the Encyclical Letter sent out by the Conference. With Randall

---

[170] SSO 263-4. Cf. SSO 65-6; Teach All, 1878, 17-20, 28-30; Sunderland, 1887, 5.

[171] CS 259. S.P.G. Address. Sunderland & Darlington 1883, 4-5, in the file 'Missions: S.P.G. & C.M.S.'.

[172] SSO 262, 264. Cf. SSO 216-17. For an account of the mission, see LB II.175-6.

[173] Philip's Life, 1880, 11-12.

[174] Cf. PC 92-3; SSO 207-19; DDG I (1887) 9-10.

[175] One participant observed that the hand of death was already upon him. Stephenson, *Anglicanism*, 87.

[176] LD 73-4. For the procedures of the Conference, see LB II.215.

[177] For which, see 200-6 above.

[178] Stephenson, *Anglicanism*, 87. Earlier in the year the Bishop of St Andrews had sought Lightfoot's reassurance that he held the Ignatian bishops to be diocesan, not congregational, bishops. C. Wordsworth to Lightfoot, 7 February 1888. For his opposition to Lightfoot's views, see 204-5 above.

[179] Stephenson, *Anglicanism*, 80. For the reports of the committees, see *Conference of Bishops of the Anglican Communion. Holden at Lambeth Palace, in July 1888. Encyclical Letter From the Bishops, With the Resolutions and Reports* (London: S.P.C.K., 1888) 45-7, 39-42. LD 74.

Davidson and Bishop Stubbs, he stayed up for most of two nights in Lollard's Tower to finish it in time.[180] The strain of such efforts broke Lightfoot's health and hastened his death, but the opportunity to provide the lead to thinking about the well-being and work of the Church around the globe was sufficient justification.[181] The willing sacrifice of his life to the Lambeth Conference was the measure of Lightfoot's personal devotion to the cause of world-wide Anglicanism as a part of the providential scheme of history.[182]

It was also the measure of both the scope and importance his "comprehensive churchmanship". Basically this was an ideal that stood for inclusiveness along the lines laid down by the national church idea. In practice it led to the desire for a theology that incorporated the interests and served the needs of the people, a membership that willingly embraced all points of view and the entire Anglican communion as the sphere of the Church's mission. Within this framework there had been clear development, for the conviction that the Church of England was becoming a genuinely universal church only settled late in Lightfoot's career. A combination of practical and theological reasons underlay this aspiration. Each element in its own way was a condition of success in the mission to the nation and the world. To this extent Lightfoot's comprehensive churchmanship was a response to the denominationalization over the previous half century, but fundamentally it was the ecclesiological expression of the incarnational theology which interpreted the world as a unity centred upon Christ. With this as its true rationale, Lightfoot clung to the "whig-liberal" hope that the Church of England, while a "denomination", might function as a "church", at home and abroad.

The significance of this may be gauged from the recent suggestion of William Sachs that a new Anglican consensus — which he (not altogether felicitously)[183] calls Liberal Catholicism — emerged after 1871 in the wake of the ecclesiological confusion of the mid-century years.[184] It was the result of a melding of liberal Anglican and High Church concerns that provided Churchmen with a basis for encountering the modern world together without agreement on every point. From the liberals came a Biblically derived belief in progress towards final unity, the conviction that the Church

---

[180] LD 74-5.

[181] Significantly, Lightfoot urged the reading of the Encyclical Letter in his own diocese. Lightfoot to Benson, 11 September 1888 (BLL, vol. 57, f. 197).

[182] See Lightfoot's speech to the Durham Diocesan Conference in October 1889, quoted in BL 102 & LD 75.

[183] The difficulty is the easy confusion with the segment of the Anglo-Catholic subculture led by Charles Gore. Something of what is intended is reflected in Owen Chadwick's meditation on "Catholicism" for the Gore Memorial Lecture for 1972 reproduced in *Theology* LXXVI.634 (April 1973) 171-80, esp. 177.

[184] Sachs, *Transformation*, 147-63, esp. 148.

realizes its nature and purpose by absorbing social trends, and the confidence that the truth of Christianity is vindicated by the Church's ability to overcome challenges to its existence. The High Churchmen anchored this sense of history as movement in a commitment to the Scripture as the standard of doctrine, the historic creeds and the sacraments of baptism and the eucharist mediated by the ministry of bishops, priests and deacons.[185] Lightfoot was among those who showed the way toward this *de facto* merging of the national church idea with the apostolic paradigm to bring together tradition and modernity. Although he may have sat more loosely to the catholic elements than Hort and Benson,[186] he regarded the Church's work of teaching the meaning of God's essence assuming human form as continuous with apostolic Christianity. The liberal component, of course, followed from the theology of divine immanence Lightfoot had made it his life's work to propagate. As he had hoped, in combination they offered that faithfulness to antiquity urged by Pusey and Liddon with the openness to the contemporary advocated by Stanley. While the emergence of the new Anglican consensus was clearly a complex phenomenon,[187] the conservative liberalism of Lightfoot's comprehensive churchmanship was a part of it.

Clearly underlying what Lightfoot contributed to *fin de siècle* Anglicanism was his thinking about history and tradition. In a manner typical of the idealist disposition to see the whole in the part, the place of the church in the "increasing purpose" furnished the connections that determined the identity and function of the Church of England. Similarly, the theology of history furnished the framework to which Lightfoot referred the different aspects of its mission for their true proportions and meaning. This procedure brought the Church's work into line with the great task of the day and set in motion the moral momentum necessary to see it through. Each dimension of the historical continuum was involved. The Church's past provided the starting point and basis for action as well as engendering the obligation to act. Forming the aspiration it had created drew out its typological potential more than

---

[185] Cf. Hylson-Smith, *High Churchmanship in the Church of England*, 189-95.

[186] See Chapter 8 above for Lightfoot's devotion to Holy Communion and commitment to the three-fold ministry (though not apostolic succession). For his attitude towards the creeds, see 260 above.

[187] It certainly involved more than the marrying of T.H. Green's neo-Hegelian idealism and Tractarianism as many scholars (following Benjamin Jowett) suggest. W.R. Ward offers a more complex explanation in "Oxford and the Origins of Liberal Catholicism in the Church of England," *Studies in Church History* I (1964) 233-52. But he still imputes Liberal Catholicism to Oxford sources. A full study of the subject would probably prove rewarding. Sachs takes a step in this direction, but while he includes Hort and Westcott, he omits Lightfoot. Yet Lightfoot had connections with the *Lux Mundi* group, especially with R.L. Ottley. He is a forgotten contributor to the Liberal Catholic consensus of the late nineteenth century Church of England.

in any other area of Lightfoot's formal involvement. For each aspect of the Church's work there was a paradigm that justified and adumbrated its course. In this way the historical vision generated confidence, hope, and a measure of prescience in confronting the future. In promoting the proper relation between past, present and future Lightfoot was seeking to find the full meaning of the Anglican tradition through adaptation. All that he called on Church people (himself included) to do to this end was an appeal for the release of the moral and spiritual energy necessary for the Church of England to fulfill its mission for the greater realization of the "increasing purpose of God".

Part IV
History as Method:
The Use of History as a Scholar

While Lightfoot had this career as a Church leader, it is chiefly as a student of earliest Christianity that he is best known and continues to attract interest. Despite his acknowledged significance, his scholarly work has yet to be studied historically — in its chronological sequence and biographical and contemporary setting. Single works and specific aspects have been examined, but not his scholarship as a living whole in its religious historical context. While it is not possible in the present study to give as full an account as might be desired, it is in order to provide an outline, identifying its principal concerns and tracing its development. In particular the place and importance of the Tübingen School — the subject of recent scholarly controversy —[1] may be considered. Such an account of Lightfoot's scholarship is the third trajectory through his career taken by the investigation.

In the setting of Lightfoot's career in scholarship the meaning of "history" again changes. It shifts to the sense bequeathed by the German Enlightenment, a discipline or systematic method of achieving verifiable knowledge about the past. Applied to the study of the Bible, this historical-critical method affected the long practised procedures of textual criticism and basic philological research. But it also became the basis of the relatively new discipline of 'higher criticism' — the attempt to ascertain the origins, authorship, character and teaching of the Biblical books in relation to their historical contexts.[2] Over the course of the nineteenth century, although understood and applied in different ways — and often with disturbing results — the historical-critical method became the principal means by which advanced Biblical study took place.[3]

---

[1]   See 6-8 above.

[2]   From a large literature, see the brief accounts of F. Gerald Downing, "Historical Critical Method," *A Dictionary of Biblical Interpretation* (eds R.J. Coggins & J.L. Houlden; London & Philadelphia: S.C.M./Trinity Press, 1990) 284-5; & J. Barton & F. Watson, "Biblical Criticism and Interpretation," *The Blackwell Encyclopedia of Modern Christian Thought* (ed. A.E. McGrath; Oxford & Cambridge, Massachusetts: Blackwell, 1993) 35-50; & the more substantial studies of E. Krentz, *The Historical Critical Method* (Philadelphia: Fortress Press, 1975); & R. Morgan with J. Barton, *Biblical Interpretation* (Oxford: University Press, 1988).

[3]   W. Baird, *History of New Testament Research. Volume One: From Deism to Tübingen* (Minneapolis: Fortress Press, 1992).

Despite its progress elsewhere, in England the adoption of the historical-critical method was delayed until after about 1860.[4] To this point critical study of the Bible along continental lines was known more by its notorious reputation than by direct acquaintance. This situation was challenged by *Essays and Reviews,* and an intense debate on the Biblical question took place in the quarter of a century that followed. Opinion is said to have polarized with conservatives and critics contending for their respective positions without ever bringing their arguments into meaningful contact.[5] Among the intelligentsia, the right of Christians, particularly clergymen, to hold and articulate advanced critical positions as conscience and scholarship required became one of the leading questions of the day. But by about 1890 much of the heat had gone out of the controversy as a measure of acceptance of critical procedures in Biblical study was secured.[6] An important change in the outlook of Victorian Christianity was more or less coincident with Lightfoot's career as a Biblical scholar.

While Lightfoot is often given much credit for it, his place in this development is more often asserted than studied. In his important treatment of the subject, N.M. de S. Cameron found Lightfoot difficult to classify and assigned to him a *de facto* infallibilism which effectively aligned him with the conservatives.[7] This unlikely result points to a fundamental problem with Cameron's study. Controlled by a philosophical model,[8] it has predictable trouble with somebody who does not fit its expectations. A proper historical examination is required to locate Lightfoot's place in the contemporary debate and define his contribution to the improved standing of Biblical criticism in the English Church.

Against this background numerous questions arise for the present investigation.[9] Given its general rejection by the English Church, why did

---

[4]   Chadwick, *Victorian Church*, II.ch. II. G. Parsons, "Reform, Revival and Realignment," 14-66, esp. 38-47; & "Biblical Criticism in Victorian Britain: From Controversy to Acceptance?" in *Religion in Victorian Britain. II. Controversies* (Manchester: University Press, 1988) 238-57.

[5]   The argument of N.M. de S. Cameron, *Biblical Higher Criticism and the Defense of Infallibilism in 19th Century Britian* (Lewiston, Queenstown: Edwin Mellor, 1987).

[6]   Eg. "The critical study of the Bible by competent scholars is essential to the maintenance in the Church of a healthy faith." From the Encyclical Letter of the 1897 Lambeth Conference, quoted in *The Anglican Tradition. A Handbook of Sources* (eds G.R. Evans & J.R. Wright; London & Minneapolis: S.P.C.K., 1991) 359.

[7]   Cameron, *Biblical Higher Criticism*, 39-42.

[8]   For which, see esp N.M. de S. Cameron, "Inspiration and Criticism: The Nineteenth Century Crisis," *Tyndale Bulletin* 35 (1984) 129-59.

[9]   While recent scholarship has shown considerable interest in Lightfoot's method of study, a distinct lack of contextualization warrants the approach taken in what follows. Even the historian Stephen Pointer pays little attention to the mid-Victorian setting in his otherwise illuminating discussion of Lightfoot as an historian. See S. Pointer, "J.B.

Lightfoot embrace the historical-critical method of Biblical study from the first? What was the understanding of it that he brought to the sources of incipient Christianity, and how did it develop? In what ways did he apply it, and with what results? What were the values and assumptions underlying his practice? In particular, what was its relation to the "increasing purpose" perspective of the theology of history? What was its relation to the life of the Church, and what did he contribute to the 'acceptance' of the method by the end of his lifetime?

Lightfoot as a Christian Historian of Early Christian Literature," *Christian Scholars Review* XXIII.4 (June 1994) 426-44.

Chapter 10

"The Image of the Invisible God": History and Jesus

In 1850, on the eve of Lightfoot's career as a Biblical scholar, the possibilities for historical-critical study in England were very limited. While there was awareness of the phenomenon, it was not widely understood. Worse than that, it was the object of suspicion and hostility.[1] Few ventured into the area, and, as several notorious cases show, some of these resiled from the practice, while others paid a price for persisting in it.[2] In consequence, as Lightfoot embarked upon his studies of the New Testament, there was no real native critical tradition for him to draw on, and very little encouragement for him to create one. This environment set the parameters for his work as a historical-critical Biblical scholar. If he was interested in pursuing such a method of New Testament study within the Church, he would have largely to devise it for himself, and then secure acceptance for it. Although barely a graduate, Lightfoot was not in the least deterred by the prospect.

I

Right at the close of his formal education, and like Westcott before him, Lightfoot chose as the final instalment of the programme he had set himself the Norrisian Prize, a competition established in 1777 for an essay on a sacred subject.[3] The proposition set for 1853 was that "The Gospels could not have originated in any or all those forms of religious opinion which pre-

---

[1]   Parsons, "Biblical Criticism," offers the best summary account. R. Whitehouse, "Biblical and Historical Criticism in Anglican Theology, 1800-1860. A Study in Authority and Reason in Religion" (unpublished M.Litt. thesis; Bristol University, n.y.) offers a mass of helpful information but draws no conclusions. Against his opening claim (2) that "there was a far larger body of critical literature available between 1800 and 1860 than is generally realized," it needs to be said that, while there was substantial discussion of criticism, there was very little actual practice of it.

[2]   Pusey is the outstanding case of the first category, while the dismissals of Maurice and Samuel Davidson from their respective posts in the 1850s are notable cases of the second.

[3]   Willis Clark, *Endowments*, 112-13; Tanner, *Historical Register*, 312-13.

vailed among the Jews at the time of our Saviour's incarnation".[4] Over the winter of 1852-3, fresh from his success in the Trinity Fellowship examination, Lightfoot worked on his entry in the time left over from "coaching" and other commitments.[5] Although not quite complete at the point of submission, and despite the lacunae in the conclusion, it was still sufficient to win the competition. The prize, however, was never collected, for the condition of publication within one year went unfulfilled. In fact Lightfoot maintained the intention to publish for two years, but there is no evidence that he ever returned to the essay in earnest.[6] It remains as it was left in the spring of 1853, a hasty and immature production to be sure, but a reflection of his mind and method at the beginning of his serious study of the New Testament, though he still did not regard himself as a specialist.[7] As the earliest piece of considered writing in the Lightfoot corpus, it is the proper starting point for an examination of his scholarship.

Although his reading of modern theological literature to this point will have been limited by the demands of College and University examinations, Lightfoot evidently soon recognized that the proposition stemmed from *Das Leben Jesu* by D.F. Strauss of Tübingen.[8] First published in 1835, it had been a reaction against "the crudity of supernaturalism" and "the emptiness of rationalism".[9] Over the whole range of the Gospel narratives the contradictions and difficulties of the supernatural view of Christian origins were exposed by opposition to the rationalistic alternatives of the eighteenth and nineteenth centuries in a process of mutual cancellation. Out of this dialectic came the need for a new explanation. Strauss furnished this need by the

---

[4]   Cambridge University Papers GF 113, Norrisian Prize (CUL). The announcement is dated 6 November 1852.

[5]   Lightfoot to Westcott, 9 October [1852 ?] (LAC). Westcott to Lightfoot, 10 October 1852; 3, 7, 12 March 1853. Prince Lee wrote, "I am glad you are writing for some of the prizes. They are of no great import but a good and wholesome exercise for future efforts." Prince Lee to Lightfoot, 19 February 1853.

[6]   Allusions in letters to Lightfoot by Westcott, 13 May 1854, & 1 September 1855; H.B. Purton, 20 February & 28 September 1855; & J.T. Pearse, 17 September 1855. See also LS 167 n. 16.

[7]   Hort, to whom the Lightfoot Trustees assigned the task of looking over Lightfoot's papers with a view to ordering the unpublished New Testament materials, states that it is no longer extant. *DNB* XI.1112. However he appears to have overlooked it. See the memorandum in Hort's hand entitled "Dr Lightfoot's notes for lectures on books of the New Testament". For the identification of the manuscript, see the present writer's contribution to G.R. Treloar & B.N. Kaye, "J.B. Lightfoot On Strauss and Christian Origins: An Unpublished Manuscript," *Durham University Journal* LXXIX.2 (June 1987) 165-200, where the text is also reproduced.

[8]   D.F. Strauss, *The Life of Jesus Critically Examined* (3rd ed. of 1840; translated by George Eliot; edited & with an introduction by P.C. Hodgson; London: S.C.M., 1973).

[9]   Strauss to C. Märklin, 6 February 1832, quoted in H. Harris, *David Friedrich Strauss and his Theology* (Cambridge: University Press, 1973) 32-5.

mythological principle, according to which the messianic expectation of the Jews, nourished by the Old Testament and tradition, acted on the facts of the actual life of Jesus to create the ideal Christ figure among the earliest Christians.[10] An unconscious process, the stories in the Gospel narratives were written down quite ingenuously in order to convince of the very belief which had created them in the first place, that Jesus was the Messiah. This approach had the advantage of dissolving the discrepancies between the Gospel accounts, and defined the object of criticism as the explanation of the narrative through disclosure of this process in action. What would be left as the ultimate datum of the Gospels was not Jesus but the national consciousness of the Jews. That such a programme involved the dismantling of the historical basis of Christianity was obvious. Somewhat naïvely, Strauss hastened to avert a hostile reaction in a concluding section with the assurance that what had been destroyed critically could be restored speculatively.[11] Christianity should continue as the institutionalized expression of Hegelian philosophy.[12]

In Germany the divergence of Strauss' views from the traditional church teaching caused a theological sensation which destroyed his academic career, and in Zurich even contributed to the downfall of a government.[13] There was no parallel to this excitement in Britain where the reaction was slight.[14] None of the major periodicals noticed the *Leben*, and only a small group of working-class radicals and Unitarians seemed to grasp what was at stake.[15] In so far as there was any scholarly counterattack, the argument ran along traditional lines.[16] H.H. Milman called for a new harmony of the Gospels, the consistency of which would vindicate the writers as observers. Others, alarmed by the non-acceptance of miracles on philosophical grounds, fell back on the eighteenth century argument from miracles in vindication of Christianity. It was not until a decade after the book's first appearance that the reaction acquired any momentum, and it was strengthened in 1846 by

---

[10] For the mythical principle, an account of its functioning, and its application to the case of miracles, see Strauss, *Life*, sect. 8, 56-7; sect. 15, 86-7; & sect. 91, 413.

[11] *Ibid.*, "Concluding Dissertation," esp. sect. 152.

[12] See the reading of Strauss in A. Brazill, *The Young Hegelians* (New Haven & London: Yale University Press, 1970) ch. 3, esp. 110-13.

[13] Harris, *Strauss*, ch. 8-11. B.N. Kaye, "D.F. Strauss and the European Theological Tradition: '*Der Ischariotismus unsere Tag*'," *Journal of Religious History* 17.2 (December 1992) 172-93.

[14] On which, see D. Pals, *The Victorian "Lives" of Jesus* (San Antonio, Texas: Trinity University Press, 1982) 25-9.

[15] V. Dodds, "Strauss' English Propagandists and the Politics of Unitarianism, 1841-1845," *Church History* 50 (December 1981) 425-9.

[16] Pals, *Victorian "Lives"*, 28, 30. The reaction of Thomas Arnold, who criticized the work without having read it, was probably not uncommon. *Ibid.*, 52 n. 26.

the lifting of the language barrier by George Eliot's translation.[17] More notice was now taken in the popular press, and the faith of a few intellectuals was shaken. But generally the *Leben Jesu* was notorious more by reputation than direct acquaintance.

At Cambridge Strauss was noticed quite early. W.H. Mill, the Christian Advocate, lectured on Strauss for four years, from 1841, and transmitted the arguments of the previous century to a new generation.[18] Otherwise the *Leben* caused no great stir. At the time of the Essay competition there seems to have been (as in the wider community) little more than a general awareness of Strauss and his work.[19] For the Norrisian Professor who set the proposition in 1852, assent was probably the only conceivable response.[20]

In this situation Lightfoot evinced a remarkable receptiveness to Strauss, at least in principle. The keynote of his response was struck by the invocation of Tennyson in the epigraph of the essay:

Let knowledge grow from more to more,
But more of reverence in us dwell,
That mind and soul, according well,
May make one music as before.
But vaster.[21]

Similarly the essay opened with the claim that "real and substantial knowledge ... accumulates from age to age" and leads to a fuller view of the truth. Thus Christianity and the Church stood to gain by openness to challenging works of Biblical criticism. Knowledge, even about the Bible, was subject to Lightfoot's doctrine of progress.

---

[17] According to the *British Library Catalogue to 1975,* vol. 315, 291-7, three responses to Strauss appeared in 1844 and 1845. Three more came out between 1850 and 1856. The aggregate doubled after the publication of Strauss' *New Life of Jesus* in 1865.

[18] W.H. Mill, *Observations on the Attempted Application of Pantheistic Principles to the Theory and Historic Criticism of the Gospel* (2nd ed.; Cambridge: Deighton, Bell & Co., 1861). On Mill, see Chadwick, *Victorian Church,* I.532.

[19] Significantly, Westcott referred in passing to Strauss in his own Norrisian Prize Essay. B.F. Westcott, *The Elements of the Gospel Harmony* (Cambridge: Macmillan, 1851) 3-4, 128 n. 1.

[20] Corrie was described as "an English Churchman" who found the satisfaction of his faith in "the doctrines of the Reformed Protestant Church of England". E.H.P. in M. Holroyd, *Memorials of the Life of George Elwes Corrie* (Cambridge: University Press, 1890) viii. Note also the competition's penalty of disqualification for any opinion "contrary to the National Church's articles, with respect to our Saviour's Divinity, and the personality of the Holy Spirit". Willis Clark, *Endowments,* 113.

[21] From the sixth and seventh stanzas of the Prologue to *In Memoriam.* LS 175. This was characteristic. See also NTI 174; Acts I-VIII, f. 9 v.; RCC (1871) 83; & Healthy, 1879, 19. Cf. C 116-17 & SSO 131-2.

Nor could Strauss be dismissed (as it was still not unfashionable to do) simply because he was a German.[22] As Lightfoot told his first Greek Testament students two years later:

> A sweeping condemnation of everything that is German is not honest, it is not Christian. There is as much diversity among German writers, as there is among ourselves. Then and only then shall we — as a nation — have a right to inflict this undiscriminating censure, when we have spent as much time & pains over the Sacred Writings as they have, & produced results as considerable. If the amount of evil in modern German criticism is to be deplored, the amount of good is at least greater, than anything which we have to show on our parts.[23]

This was a protest entered "in the name of charity and of truth".[24] The manifest learning behind the volume at least created a presumption of benefit from taking it seriously. In any case the diversity of German theological opinion stood to provide the resources out of which a proper response could be fashioned. On moral grounds alone the *Leben* was entitled to a hearing.

The set proposition apart, Lightfoot's openness to the *Leben* required that he face the problem of the origin of the Gospels. Moreover, the twin questions of where the Gospels had come from and what had caused them to exist in their current form were reasonable on Lightfoot's own view of inspiration.[25] However, there were two problems with Strauss' solution that needed to be opposed.

First, Lightfoot objected to the underlying rationalism of the *Leben*. In the draft he wrote, "His fundamental philosophical assumption against the truth of the miraculous is with him everything, and the historical investigation merely an appendage avowedly ... The documents must yield/give way before this treatment".[26] Thus the *Leben* was interpreted as a philosophically conceived programme for disposing of the received records of the life of Jesus as genuine history. No doubt Lightfoot (in common with most contemporaries) exaggerated the extent of Strauss' historical scepticism.[27] But he rightly urged that Strauss had come to the evidence having already decided what must have taken place. Lightfoot therefore set out to abandon theory. A straightforward Baconian induction, uninfluenced (as he thought) by philosophical norms, was a better basis for solving the problem of the origin of the Gospels. If after rigorous scholarship in the sources, free from

---

[22] For the background see J.S. Andrews, "German Influence on English Religious Life in the Victorian Era," *Evangelical Quarterly* 44 (Oct.-Dec. 1972) 218-33.

[23] NTI 174

[24] NTI 174.

[25] See 99-100 above.

[26] LS 176 note.

[27] The cumulative force of the separate historical components of the *Leben* is uged by V.A. Harvey, "D.F. Strauss' *Life of Jesus* Revisited," *Church History* 30 (1961) 191-211. See also Hodgson's introduction to Strauss, *Life of Jesus*, xxviii; & Kaye, "Strauss," 186-7.

preconceived ideas of what can and cannot happen, the evidence called for a miracle as the explanation, this was a finding that would have to be accepted, not explained away as myth.

Second, Strauss' Hegelian axiom, that the forms of consciousness of one age are radically different from those of another, meant that the Gospels could not be explained in terms of modern thought, and caused him systematically to apply to the earliest Christians the concept of myth as the mode of thought appropriate to an ancient people. A metaphysically conceived historicism was the peculiar challenge that he presented.[28] Again a proper historical investigation along strict inductive lines was called for by way of response.

This required no major adjustment in Lightfoot's thinking, for he was already committed to taking an historical view of things. Reports of his youthful reading are replete with references to historical works, and evince a desire for a fair and balanced account of important matters. Moreover, he was able to find some good German studies on which to build as he worked out his response to Strauss. The notes include references to Ewald, Dorner, Gieseler, Bunsen and especially Neander. Most were writers of the 'mediating school' with which he had a strong affinity. Lightfoot's work would similarly allow the presence of the supernatural in the natural and seek to combine the insights of the religious instinct and empirical method.[29]

While Strauss had asked how the mythological process had taken place, Lightfoot now asked whether it took place at all. Taking his cue from the set proposition, he furnished the necessary historical treatment by examining the context out of which Christianity emerged. Lightfoot sought to fix the limits of the creative potential of Judaism by a consideration of its history.

In a manner that was to become characteristic of his method, his induction moved through two main stages. First he considered the antecedent historical probability of the mythicizing process. This was done by passing in review the history of Israel down to the Christian era. Initially he traced the relations of the Jews to the Gentile world.[30] Against polytheism and pantheism they had maintained the knowledge of monotheism and divine transcendence. Amid attempts to realize a more perfect union between the human and the divine, their history indicated that it would be by revelation rather than human speculation. This historic function was facilitated by a fitness of national character. Because the Hebrews "belonged to that family of the human race which is receptive rather than originative," they were

---

[28] Harvey, "Strauss' *Life of Jesus* Revisited," 196-8.

[29] On the mediating school, see F. Lichtenberger, *History of German Theology in the Nineteenth Century* (trans. and ed. by W. Hastie; Edinburgh: T. & T. Clark, 1889) ch. V, esp. 467-72.

[30] LS 177-80.

appropriately "the appointed guardians of the 'oracles of God'". Moreover, their recent history confirmed this role. The Babylonish Captivity restored fidelity to "the God of their forefathers", a sense of national identity strengthened in turn from the period of the Maccabaean revolt onwards by the presence of foreign oppressors. This progressive history gave grounds to "pause ere we attribute any highly religious system to the unaided efforts of the Jewish mind".[31] The function of Israel in the religious history of the world was not such as to suggest the corporate Jewish mind could have generated out of itself a new religious system.

The history of Israel also established the framework for the decisive question:

> there was a peculiar fitness in the time, which was selected for the reconciliation of Messiah to His people. But can we venture a step beyond, and say that we see in the popular mind of the day a germ of a natural development of the Christian scheme?[32]

Lightfoot answered the question by aligning the main groups in contemporary Judaism with incipient Christianity.[33] The most recent development had been the rise of the Sadducees, but they were directly opposed to Christianity, particularly in their denial of the resurrection from the dead. The Pharisees presented only one point of contact, by affirming that which the Sadducees denied. The doctrines and way of life of the more attractive Essenes were also in marked contrast with those of the New Testament. But criticism had placed its emphasis on the theosophy of the Alexandrian School, and so Lightfoot turned to its most typical representative and asked how far Philo was a precursor of the Gospel. There were significant contrasts between his doctrine and that of Christian teaching, but, as coming closest to anticipating the idea of the Incarnation, he actually showed how far short of the Christian idea human speculation had fallen. Thus the religious history of man was different to what Strauss had supposed. The fundamental discontinuity between Judaism and Christianity meant that revelation was still its only adequate explanation.

The messianic idea, the lynch pin of Strauss' mythological principle, provided the crucial case study in testing the capacity of Judaism to have created Christianity.[34] Lightfoot's examination of contemporary thinking on the subject showed that Old Testament prophecy had been misconceived. It was a political victory, not a spiritual and moral freedom, to which the Jews looked forward. This was especially true of the Pharisees who could have had no motive for inventing the stories in the Gospels. Even the more spiritually minded minority constituted by the Essenes did not anticipate the

---

[31] LS 179.
[32] LS 180.
[33] LS 180-8.
[34] LS 188-92.

idea of God manifest in the flesh. When it had taken place, the ideas clustering about the Fact of the Incarnation were disappointing, even repugnant to the Jews. Messianic expectation was incapable of the result Strauss had predicated upon it.

Having shown the antecedent incredibility of Strauss' theory, Lightfoot took the second step in his argument by considering what had actually happened. He did this by reviewing the post-resurrection period when by reflection the Church was alleged to have made the Christ of faith out of the Jesus of history.[35] By doing so he pinpointed a further grave weakness of the *Leben*. Strauss' work was unhistorical in that he had confidently developed a theory of Christian origins without a systematic study of the apostolic and sub-apostolic periods in which the Gospels were supposed to have been written. The deficiency had already been identified in Germany. Throughout the 1840s an attempt had been made to repair it by Strauss' successors at Tübingen.[36] The outcome of their work, according to Lightfoot, was a view of the development of Christianity which intercalated a "stage of transition between the old aera of Judaism and the new aera of Christianity".[37] The implications were serious, for it meant that historic Christianity was "not the same with that of the primitive Church, least of all the Church of the circumcision".[38] His inductive method required that he "investigate its claim to truth on historical grounds".[39] The encounter with Strauss led on to the first encounter with the Tübingen School proper.

Ebionitism, the alleged transitional stage between Judaism and Christianity, in fact provided the test of how Judaism did develop when it came into contact with Christianity.[40] Lightfoot discerned two distinct sects in its history. One differed from Jewish christology only in that its members accepted the humble and earthly life and crucifixion of Jesus. In other respects they were "strictly Jews of the Pharisaic School". On the other hand, Gnostic Ebionitism, a natural outgrowth of Essenism, regarded Christianity as a return to primitive Judaism stripped of the excrescences of a later age. Lightfoot pressed the inference:

---

[35] LS 192-8.

[36] H. Harris, *The Tübingen School* (Oxford: Clarendon Press, 1975) 186-216.

[37] LS 192. Cf. Kaye, *ibid.*, 171-2. How, and to what extent, Lightfoot had come into contact with the writers of the Tübingen School is not immediately clear, since none is explicitly cited in the course of the essay. The draft, however, suggests that he owed some of his knowledge at least to Baur's opponent H.W.I. Thiersch, *Einige Wate über die Aechtheit N.T. Schriften*, 1846. LS 200 n. 136. For Thiersch, see Lichtenberger, *History*, 415-16; and Harris, *Tübingen School*, 51, 238. No doubt he had collected additional information from other German writers (such as Neander who interacted extensively with the writings of his contemporaries).

[38] LS 193.

[39] LS 192.

[40] LS 192-3.

it confirms our opinion, derived from other sources, of the direction which Jewish speculation would, if unaided, naturally take; it explains where existing prejudices and feelings found vent; in their resemblance to Jewish theosophy, and contrast to Christianity, it affords a strong proof of the divine origins of the latter.[41]

Lightfoot completed his argument by subjecting the claim that Ebionitism was the true parent of Christianity to an "historical examination" consisting of four tests.[42] First, it was unlikely that the doctrine of the Gentile Church could ever have been Ebionite, since St Paul was regarded by the Ebionites as a heretic and impostor. But, as the critics had evaded the implication of this fact by either minimizing Paul's influence or rejecting the authenticity of the Epistles bearing his name, Lightfoot surveyed the writings of the Apostolic Fathers — Gentiles all, and writing at the end of the first, or early in the second century — but found only orthodox christology and no trace of Ebionitism. Nor, secondly, was there any such trace in the evidence extant from the teaching Church at Jerusalem, and such differences with Gentile Christianity as appeared were not due to an antipathy between them, but to viewing the Gospel in different perspectives. Third, a more detailed study of the history of the relations between the two groups indicated that the continued observance of the law in the Jerusalem Church was a matter of preference and policy under local circumstances, and not a matter of principle. It was, moreover, a matter on which compromise could be reached. Finally, the attitude of the Church towards Ebionitism, from the second century to Eusebius, was one of direct antagonism. The sect itself was probably a Judaizing splinter from the Jewish Church (which remained orthodox) caused by the influx of adherents of the spirit of both Essenism and Pharisaism. In each respect the continuity from primitive historic Christianity was vindicated. The development of Strauss' idea by the Tübingen School commanded the support of the facts of history no more than Strauss' idea itself.

This critique arose out of a different understanding of what an historical approach to the problem of Gospel origins required. Lightfoot accepted that the issue was how the life of Jesus was to be understood in relation to its Jewish background. He found that the extensive analysis of sources in the *Leben* — after the manner pioneered by B.G. Niebuhr in his groundbreaking *History of Rome* — was something of a facade. Instead of establishing the connection by the account of how it actually happened, Strauss' claim that the Church had created the Gospels out of the Old Testament was based on a description of a hypothetical literary process. Believing in the creative capacity of the mythological consciousness, he simply showed how the vari-

---

[41] LS 193.
[42] LS 193-8.

ous *logiae* might have arisen from Old Testament antecedents.[43] Lightfoot, by contrast, sought for greater empirical control over the effects of critical theory. He did not follow W.H. Mill with a counter-analysis of specific texts. Instead he furnished the delineation of the precise relation of the Gospels to contemporary religious opinion seen to be missing from Strauss. He looked primarily, not to the Old Testament, completed 500 years previously, but — using mainly Philo and Josephus as sources — to the Judaism of the time, and brought out something of its complexity and limited creative potential. This gave him the necessary standard by which to judge what had happened in the making of the Gospels outside the Gospels themselves. None of the strands discernible within contemporary Judaism was capable of the achievement Strauss propounded.

Lightfoot's insistence on historical context as a control on the critical reading of documents led to two further objections to Strauss' handling of the evidence. First, to find parallels to the Christian scheme, Strauss and his principal follower, G.F. Gfrörer, had had to draw from a wide range of Jewish materials. The point was not developed, but, although even at this early stage of his career (with the example of his seventeenth century namesake before him)[44] Lightfoot appreciated the value of Jewish sources for interpreting the New Testament, it is clear that he thought this too was haphazard and ineffective. It had not been shown that the distinctive teachings of Christianity had analogues in Judaism.

Similarly, Strauss' use of patristic writings was misleading. He had drawn mainly on the Fathers of the third century — and concentrated on Origen, the main exponent of the allegorizing method — for his evidence of what the Church had done with the life of Jesus. Lightfoot by contrast looked to the more prosaic writers of the immediate sub-apostolic period who did not reflect the alleged development. Again this was more rigorous historically, since his sources were nearer in time to the episode in question. Its empirical shortcomings further exposed the nature of the mythical principle as an untested hypothesis applied *a priori* to the Biblical data.

This is not to say that Lightfoot saw no value in the Tübingen, and especially Strauss', analysis. Indeed he conceded the existence of difference within the New Testament witness, and allowed its importance at a time when such a concession was rare in England. It was possible because of his conception of the Biblical writings as human testimony. In the case of the life of Christ, the Gospel writers (or their sources) were not representatives

---

[43] The *Leben* was in fact only the critical section of the original plan. It had been mistitled in that it was not so much about the life of Jesus as the sources for that life. Harris, *Strauss*, ch. 7. Hodgson, editor's introduction to Strauss, *Life of Jesus*, xxiii.

[44] LS 199 n. 133.

of the national consciousness, but observers of a phenomenon which they appreciated more or less, but always in part only. In ascribing to them this "scientific" stance — they witnessed to fact —[45] Lightfoot assumed that observation then was the same as in his own day. Instead of going behind the record to the history by Strauss' *Verstehen*, the imaginative effort required to understand "ideas of possibility and actuality" radically different from his own,[46] a scientifically conceived induction of the credentials of the Gospels to be reliable history in themselves was the appropriate method for their study. By establishing the veracity of the records, Lightfoot presumed he had established *ipso facto* the history.

The fact that the Christian tradition as perceived in Victorian England survived virtually intact following the application of the historical method to the question of Gospel origins reflects the values and assumptions Lightfoot brought to the task. More rigorous in method than Strauss, he was less radical in historical perception. Whereas Strauss had a profound sense of the differences separating past and present, Lightfoot was impressed with their continuity. The task of the historian in his eyes was to see the similarities between periods and to trace the connections. This was a function of the view that all the differentiated phenomena of history are an expression of the same underlying metaphysical reality. They could be approached through historical study which allowed their richness, diversity and complexity understood as reflections of the Logos. In this way his Christian idealism differed from the Hegelian idealism of Strauss which reduced historical phenomena to the one central panlogistic concept. It was not his method that prevented Lightfoot from taking a more radical approach to the New Testament. It was his view of the nature of reality.

This positivist conception of evidence was important to the intended function of the essay. It needs to be remembered that it was not merely an academic exercise performed in order to add another distinction to an already impressive list. The contest itself was apologetical in aim, and publication of the winning entry the projected outcome. Simply by participating Lightfoot was encouraged to see himself as a defendant of the Church in a matter of some importance to the Christian public.[47] Had he completed and published the essay his use of the historical method of investigation would have delivered several results.

First, he seemed to have demonstrated that the Gospels are what they purport to be, accounts of the life and teaching of Jesus by eye-witnesses and contemporaries. This meant they gave direct access to the life of the

---

[45] SSO 119-30, esp. 121-6.

[46] Harris, *Strauss*, ch. 7.

[47] Cf. the awareness of Westcott in the published version of his successful essay of 1851. Westcott, *Elements*, vii.

historical Jesus rather than it being refracted through the perspective of the Church. In turn this gave Lightfoot the use of the life of Christ as the basis of Christian faith and practice. Outward conditions might change, but Christian experience as the *Imitatio Christi* remained what it was at the beginning:

> Christ is to us the pattern-man. It has been said "be ye holy, even as I am holy"; but the Christian teacher could enforce this by reference to Him, whose human nature was perfectly sanctified by the "indwelling of the Godhead bodily".[48]

The importance of this result becomes clear when Lightfoot is seen soon afterwards inviting congregations to know Jesus as his contemporaries knew him, to live in his presence as they had done, and to allow the same impact on their own lives as he had had then.[49] Despite appearances to the contrary, when properly conceived, modern historical criticism vindicated the traditional use of the life of Christ.

Yet it is obvious that Lightfoot's argument encompassed more than the origin of the Gospels. Indeed there is some confusion throughout as to whether this or the origin of Christianity itself was the question. It arose because for Lightfoot — and no doubt the whole Church establishment — the two were not separate issues. This was why his second main complaint against Strauss was the inadequacy of the *Leben* as an historical explanation. Several times he repeated the charge that the mythical interpretation did not account for the historical effects of the life of Jesus, including the Gospel records. The only cause that provided sufficient explanation was the irruption into history of the divine. However, Lightfoot came to this result indirectly. The purpose and method of the essay were to apply the norms of history to the study of Christian origins, but the outcome was the disclosure of a phenomenon unaccountable in normal historical terms.[50] History could know but not explain Jesus Christ. As there was nothing in Judaism that could have created the Christ figure, so there was nothing in Judaism for Jesus to impersonate to become a leader of this character and stature. It therefore appeared from historical analysis that he had transcended his own historical conditions, introduced a new factor into history, and thereby constituted history's great turning point. But this could only be understood by some other mode of knowledge than history. Without revelation there would be that in history which could not be explained. Almost by default historical investigation had vindicated incarnational Christianity.

Despite these favourable results Lightfoot was anxious not to overstate his achievement. He was already too much the Coleridgean to think the viability of Christianity depended upon the results of criticism:

---

[48] LS 191.

[49] Veil, 1855, 9-12; Christ, 1855, 5, 9, 12-15; 2nd Group, 1858, 23-6; & Life, 1862, 13-14, 20-2.

[50] LS 177, 180, 186, 188, & 191-2.

there is a testimony, which it is not in the power of historical criticism to grasp: the testimony of the heart, which finds in Christianity its deepest aspirations realized and its fondest hopes fulfilled — the testimony of the conscience smitten and pierced, as by a sharp two-edged sword, by the record of His words, who spake as never man spake — the testimony of experience which reminds the Christian that in proportion as he has cultivated the best faculties and highest feelings of his nature, the clouds of doubt and difficulty have been dispersed before the light of the "spirit witnessing to his spirit", and have only gathered again when he has been betrayed into spiritual careless-ness or moral obliquity.[51]

On the other hand Lightfoot did not think with Strauss that Christianity was independent of critical investigation. He found an exemplar of his position on the relations between faith and reason in Pascal, who had endorsed the most rigorous scientific method, while engaging in the fullest faith.[52] Yet, while affirming their complementarity, Lightfoot assigned the priority to religious experience. In practice this did not so much limit historical method as the instrument of reason as challenge its sufficiency. Strauss could not destroy orthodox Christianity, as God is known primarily in the heart, a do-main beyond the reach of critical scrutiny. Nor, however, could the kind of rebuttal embodied in Lightfoot's essay suffice. In its support of orthodoxy, historical method was only one source of knowledge. In accordance with his dualistic epistemology, Lightfoot maintained that history known from the Gospels needed to interact with the spiritual faculty to have its fullest effect in the apprehension of truth. His defence of their origins safeguarded this possibility.

Finally, therefore, Lightfoot had maintained the viability of Christianity in the modern world. The problem posed by Straussian criticism was an apparent contradiction between the spirit of the age, of which it was an ex-pression, and the intuitions of the religious consciousness. In his endorse-ment of the historical method, Lightfoot was at one with this spirit. But in his conception of it, and the result of its application, the conflict was re-moved. The Gospels remained what the world of sense furnishes to meet the needs of the religious consciousness. In a typically liberal Anglican ma-noeuvre,[53] the historical investigation of the essay made available a duly certified body of knowledge from the external world for interaction with the impulses of intuition in the generation of religious knowledge. This dis-posed of the fear that the Church "would, when exposed to the light and air of modern criticism and science, crumble away instantly and leave but a handful of dust in place of its once imposing form".[54]

---

[51] LS 198.

[52] LS 198.

[53] See A.J. Harding, "Sterling, Carlyle, and German Higher Criticism: A Reassess-ment," *Victorian Studies* 26.3 (1983) 269-85.

[54] LS 175.

But of course Lightfoot did not publish the Essay. Perceiving the enormity of the subject, and with other matters clamouring for attention following the institution of the *Journal of Classical and Sacred Philology* and appointment to an assistant lectureship at Trinity College, enough had been achieved for his present purpose. With the shock of Strauss having been withstood and the received view of Christian origins and practice upheld in the face of the most serious attack to date, Lightfoot moderated his intentions for the Essay and delayed publication.[55] Its benefit therefore remained largely private where, however, it was of lasting importance for the course of his career in both Biblical scholarship and the Church.

For one thing, it involved him at the outset of his career in the major theological enterprise of the nineteenth century, the attempt to see the life of Jesus as a part of history, a movement in which, because he did not venture into the field of public literature by writing a "life" of Jesus or Gospel commentary, he has not been thought previously to have taken part. In the process he had engaged with the most advanced New Testament scholarship of the day, though he began with Strauss, not Baur. This alerted him to issues to which he returned again and again, and seemed to lay down a programme of study and writing which was carried out over the next 35 years.

In other ways the encounter with the *Leben* helped to shape Lightfoot's understanding of the role and method of the Christian scholar. Strauss was a reformer, intent upon rebuilding the world on a new metaphysical foundation. His challenge needed to be taken seriously to determine whether it was an ephemeral expression of the age or a genuine addition to the stock of Christian knowledge. In handling the documents left by the early Church, this required the formulation of a method which placed great stress on historical context as a control on critical opinion and interpretation. Lightfoot's insistence on external conditions and a knowledge of the true relations between the documents remained the basis of his scholarly labours. In his mind, he was engaged in the task of delivering the facts with which the Christian consciousness had to work. For almost forty years meeting this need remained the fundamental sense in which the affairs of the contemporary Church were involved in his scholarship.

On the substantive issue Lightfoot had also taken an important stand. Behind the *Leben* was the claim of Enlightenment rationalism that the Jesus of history and the Christ of faith should be separated. Like Strauss, Lightfoot held the two together as cause and effect. However, in his case the link was

---

[55] The appearance of Wescott's books on the New Testament soon afterwards further justified postponing the elaboration of his position. See B.F. Westcott, *A General Survey of the History of the Canon of the New Testament* (London: Macmillan, 1855, 1874[4]); & *An Introduction to the Study of the Gospels* (London: Macmillan, 1860, 1895[8]).

not the mythical principle but the impact upon His contemporaries of Jesus the Son of God. Having disposed of the mythological explanation of the Gospels, Lightfoot was left by historical analysis with the miraculous irruption into history of the incarnate God as the only cause adequate to explain the historical effect. This finding had two further results for his career as a scholar in the Church. It left him with the conviction that, by holding history and dogma together in this way, he was able to furnish historical proofs for cherished theological beliefs, a strategy which he applied on numerous occasions. It also established the basis of the continuity-discontinuity structure of all history. Lightfoot's rebuttal of Strauss was at once the first presentation and defence of the theology of history he took into maturity.

For all of its interaction with critical scholarship, finally, the encounter upheld a precritical attitude to the Gospels that matched confidence in their historical worth with the deep Christian piety that was at the heart of all Lightfoot's scholarly labours. Obviously the whole of Strauss had not been dealt with in so brief a discussion. But the clear implication was that, with the foundation undermined, the whole edifice would crumble. Yet the vast apparatus of inconsistencies and difficulties which Strauss had constructed using the source criticism in vogue in contemporary German historiography was independent of the mythical principle,[56] and the flow of rationalistic accounts of the life of Christ went unstaunched. Whenever the subject came up, Lightfoot fell back on this result and stressed the complementarity of the narratives, with its easy corollary, that they could be harmonized.[57] This was a position from which he never budged. Content to identify the Gospels with the history on the grounds that they were what they purported to be, Lightfoot felt no compelling need to go further and get behind the Gospel texts themselves or to write the life of Jesus as history. Most attempts to do so he regarded as either rationalist or mythicizing.[58] Strauss had dealt with the former, and he had dealt with Strauss. Lightfoot's first solution to the problem of the Gospels was also his last.

II

After an interval of fifteen years Lightfoot returned to the subject of Jesus and the Gospels. During the Michaelmas term of 1867 he lectured on "The Gospel of St John" at Cambridge, and kept it up for three terms. In the

---

[56] For Victorian England possibly the most significant part of the book. See N. Annan, "Introduction" to "Science, Religion, and the Critical Mind," *1859: Entering and Age of Crisis*, (eds P. Appleman, W.A. Madden & M. Wolff; Bloomington: Indiana University Press, 1959) 34.

[57] LS 195; S 17-20; OA 123-6, 225-8. Cf. the harmonization of Paul and James in LS 194-5. Compatibility of the Gospel accounts is assumed at Scene, 1874, 8-9 & CS 103-4. 103-4.

[58] RCC (1871) 78-9.

1872-3 academic year he returned to the subject, narrowing the focus this time to the "Introduction to St John's Gospel", by which he meant the evidence for its genuineness and authenticity.[59] For a time Lightfoot entertained the idea of turning the lectures into a commentary, but this intention was abandoned when Westcott undertook the book for *The Speaker's Commentary*.[60] The lecture notes suggest that, had he proceeded with this project, it will have been along the lines of his work on St Paul by which in the meantime he had developed a method for dealing with the actual text of the New Testament.[61] Much else had changed since Lightfoot last formally dealt with the Gospels. The twin controversies over *The Origin of Species* and *Essays and Reviews* had intensified the problem of the Church's relation to modern culture, while the early phase of the 'lives of Jesus' movement had raised new problems for Christian faith in its relations to criticism.[62] As a result, the question of the place of empirical methods in the life of the Church was more pressing than ever.

On the face of it the switch to teaching on the Fourth Gospel was a significant interruption to the main scholarly tasks Lightfoot had set himself by this point. Explaining it to Westcott, he claimed simply to have drifted into the subject.[63] In the absence of further comment, Lightfoot's statement is difficult to interpret, but no doubt his immediate situation at Cambridge was one factor. At the would-be "spiritual power of the nineteenth century", with men aspiring to a truly historical understanding of Christian origins, the Gospels in general called for attention. Since the publication of Westcott's *Introduction to the Gospels*, E. Renan's *Vie de Jésus* and the non-dogmatic *Ecce Homo* had caused widespread unease through their challenge to an orthodox supernaturalist reading of the Gospel documents.[64] Given that they continued to provide not only the basis, but much of the actual content, of Lightfoot's religion, this was a serious matter.[65] The time was propitious for a series of lectures stressing the primacy and the "truthfulness of St John's narrative" as a source for the life of Jesus.[66]

---

[59] See Appendix 2 below.

[60] That undertaking was made in 1869. B.F. Westcott, *The Gospel According to St John* (with a new introduction by A. Fox; London: James Clarke & Co., 1958 [originally published 1880]) iib.

[61] Outlined in Chapter 11 below.

[62] See Pals, *Victorian "Lives" of Jesus, passim*.

[63] Lightfoot to Westcott, 23 July 1868 (LAC).

[64] D. Pals, "The Reception of *Ecce Homo*," *Historical Magazine of the Protestant Episcopal Church* XLVI.1 (March 1977) 63-84.

[65] Cf. Westcott, "Notice to the Third Edition" (dated Christmas Eve, 1866), in *Introduction*, ix-x.

[66] "II. St John II. I.29-IV.5," 1, 30, 36; "III. St John. IV.4-VI.end," 96; "IV. St John. VII.1-[VIII.9]," first of two unnumbered introductory sheets, 1, 22; in the Box File, "St John. Notes".

Moreover, since his Norrisian Prize Essay the critical bearings of the question of the Gospels had changed. In 1853 Strauss' teacher, F.C. Baur, published an alternative to his pupil's portrayal of the historical Jesus based on the literary and historical criticism he felt the earlier work had lacked.[67] Much more constructive than Strauss, Baur answered the question, "Synoptics or John?" as the source for the life of Jesus in favour of the former. "John" was represented as an idealizing account designed to enhance the divine dignity and glory of Jesus. The operative idea shaping the narrative presentation was the Logos. This theological "tendency" indicated that it belonged to a date late in the second century, about 170 A.D., and served the eirenic needs of the newly emergent Catholic Church. The Fourth Gospel was no longer an eyewitness authority or source for the historical Jesus, although for Baur it remained the "witness of a genuine evangelical spirit".[68] Baur's concession notwithstanding, this development in criticism gave Lightfoot another reason for directing attention to the Fourth Gospel. As he noted at the beginning of the lecture series, "the genuineness of St John's Gospel is the centre of the position of those who uphold the historical truth of our Lord Jesus Christ given us in the New Testament".[69]

It probably also explains his taking action exactly when he did. Although the Tübingen perspective was in eclipse in Germany following Baur's death in 1860,[70] it had recently won a native adherent. In 1867 the Unitarian, J.J. Tayler, made what is said to have been the first full statement by an Englishman of the case for non-apostolic authorship.[71] Lightfoot thought he discerned sectarian motivation, for it was probably to Tayler that he referred by including Unitarians among the traducers of the genuineness of the Gospel, noting that in fact "it enunciates in the most express terms the Divinity, the

---

[67] For Baur's reaction to Strauss, see P.C. Hodgson, *The Formation of Historical Theology. A Study of Ferdinand Christian Baur* (New York: Harper & Row, 1966) 24-5, 29-31, 73-4. Also Harris, *Strauss, & Tübingen School.*

[68] A synopsis based on F.C. Baur, *The Church History of the First Three Centuries* (3rd ed.; trans. & ed. by A. Menzies; London & Edinburgh: Williams & Norgate, 1878) I.153-83; & the passages from Baur's "Die Einleitung in das Neue Testament als theologie Wissenschaft," *Kritische Untersuchungen über die kanonischen Evangelien, ihr Verhaltnis zueinander, ihren Charakter und Ursprung* (1847), & *Vorlesungen über neutestamentliche Theologie* (1864), quoted in Kümmel, *New Testament*, 127-9, 137-8, 141. See also Hengel, "Lightfoot and the Tübingen School," 24-5; Harris, *Tübingen School*, 193-5; & Hodgson, *Formation*, 212-14.

[69] BE 47.

[70] Harris, *Tübingen School*, ch. 13.

[71] J.J. Tayler, *An Attempt to Ascertain the Character of the Fourth Gospel; Especially in its Relation to the First Three* (London & Edinburgh: Williams & Norgate, 1867). See also H. McLachlan, *The Unitarian Movement in the Religious Life of England* (London: Allen & Unwin, 1934) 55-7.

Deity, of our Lord".[72] Tayler made no secret of his indebtedness to German scholarship, and Lightfoot noted that he "reproduced the argument of Baur and others".[73] The book itself was dismissed as inadequately executed,[74] but with critical views somewhat out of date in Germany now being openly purveyed in his own country, it was necessary to head off the challenge.

Appearances notwithstanding, the change from Paul to John was not so abrupt as it might seem. As Lightfoot saw matters, the connection between the two areas of study was in fact close and sequential. For the shift in Lightfoot's attention to the letters of the third group in the Pauline corpus had had two important effects. First, it focused his interest in the development of Christianity in Asia Minor.[75] As Lightfoot traced the results for the recipient churches of their contact with Paul, he directed attention to their links with the Apocalypse of St John, and seized on important continuities in the early Christian history of the area.[76] He also noted how, soon after, it had become the geographical centre of Christianity, because it was here, following the fall of Jerusalem, that a number of the Apostles who survived into the last three decades of the first century, chose to settle.[77] As "the focus of the light and energy of Christendom," it was, Lightfoot observed, "in Asia Minor ... that one may hope to catch the lingering echo of the voice of Apostolic Christianity".[78] The Fourth Gospel, written at Ephesus towards the end of the first century, was the outstanding product and reflection of this development.

It was also Paul who stimulated Lightfoot's interest in the dogmatic import of the Johannine writings. The christological teaching of 'Philippians', 'Ephesians' and 'Colossians' was made explicit in the Fourth Gospel.[79] This was why, when urging Westcott to take 'John' for *The Speaker's Commentary*, he claimed that it was the most important part of the New Testament in relation to the intellectual question of the day.[80] At one level this was a reference to the viability of the doctrine of the Incarnation — the key to the identity and power of Christianity — which pervaded the Fourth Gospel, and was seen largely to depend on its historicity.[81]

---

[72] BE 47. Significantly Tayler demoted the doctrine of the Incarnation of the Eternal Logos in Jesus to the status of a subsequent philosphical interpretation of the purpose of Christianity. Tayler, *Attempt*, 182-4.

[73] BE 10-11. See Tayler, *Attempt*, 70-1, 84, 121, 147-8, 180-1.

[74] BE 50. Westcott thought it "very poor". Westcott to Lightfoot, 22 September 1869.

[75] Three of these letters — Ephesians, Colossians and Philemon — were directed to towns in Asia Minor. For the shift and its significance, see Chapter 11 below.

[76] C 41-4.

[77] C 44-7. Cf. BE 51-3; EWSR 90-2, 217.

[78] PH 398.

[79] P ix, 72-3. C 116-9, 123-4.

[80] Lightfoot to Westcott, 18 May 1869 (LAC).

[81] "II. St John II. I.29-IV.5," 20.

More specifically, the remark to Westcott referred to John's Logos christology, which Lightfoot had come to see provided the Church with the basis for the proper response to a wide range of its problems in the intellectual sphere. Its application and advocacy called for deeper study in, and exposition of, the document in which "the leading conception in the writer's own mind is ... the Word, the Logos," and which "illustrates, and is illustrated by, the teaching of St Paul".[82] In the year after Lightfoot lectured on the later Captivity Epistles, he began to lecture on the Fourth Gospel: in the year after that, he urged the revival of the Logos doctrine upon the Church.[83]

At first Lightfoot's lectures were expository, and clearly resemble those on the Epistles of St Paul. But in time his interest became almost entirely apologetical as he moved on to the controverted question of the Gospel's credentials. Again this interest in the authenticity and genuineness of New Testament documents was anticipated in work on the Pauline writings, but Lightfoot had not pursued it at any length. An opportunity for a public vindication of a matter that was crucial to the viability of his proposed response to the modern world provided an occasion to develop this part of his method.

Towards the end of 1870 Lightfoot was invited to speak for the Christian Evidence Society.[84] This was an organization set up earlier in the year to counter by means of rational argument the scepticism seen to be pervading Victorian society.[85] One of the methods adopted was lectures to educated audiences on controverted topics. The perceived need to address the special difficulties connected with the Bible, and especially the New Testament, provided Lightfoot with an opening to put his findings on the important matter of the authority of the Fourth Gospel before the wider public. He approached the matter with great diffidence, recognizing that a single lecture offered insufficient scope for presenting his case. Yet, while there was the danger that an incomplete presentation might be mistaken for a weak argument, the opportunity to argue this part of the case for incarnational Christianity before an educated audience could not be wasted. In the spring of 1871 Lightfoot defended the authenticity and genuineness of the Fourth Gospel before a large audience in St George's Hall, Langham Place.

Lightfoot's treatment of the subject proceeded on two levels. Outwardly he mounted a critical case. In this he elaborated the method for determining

---

[82] BE 23. C 123-4. Esp. "Doctrine of the Logos" in "St John's Gospel. Introduction. I.1-I.28," 49-56.

[83] See Appendix 2 and 77-8 above.

[84] Lord Harrowby to Lightfoot, 18 November 1870.

[85] On the Society, see C.J. Ellicott, "Explanatory Paper," in *Modern Scepticism. A Course of Lectures Delivered at the Request of the Christian Evidence Society* (4th ed.; London: Hodder & Stoughton, 1871) 505-27, esp. 506, 512-4; & D.A. Johnson, "Popular Apologetics in Late Victorian England: The Work of the Christian Evidence Society," *Journal of Religious History* 11.4 (December 1981) 558-77.

the authorship of a New Testament document adumbrated in the work on Paul. Less conspicuously he presented what might be called an ethical case. Throughout Lightfoot commented on the credibility of his procedures and arguments, while at the end he made clear the implications of his findings for faith and life. The two levels of the argument corresponded to his understanding of the historical method and its uses.

Lightfoot's critical position on the question of the Fourth Gospel held that it was both authentic and genuine. It had been written by "a Jew contemporary with and cognisant of the facts which he relates", and he was "the Apostle St John".[86] The formulation of this position reflects the influence of Baur upon the debate. For it was he who had polarized the issue, insisting that one must hold to the historical inauthenticity and later authorship of the Gospel, or to its historical authenticity and apostolic authorship, but not to a combination.[87] Lightfoot accepted the dilemma, dismissing the compromise proposal of Tayler,[88] and taking the opposite view to Baur's. He retained the Gospel as a product of the direct observation and personal experience of the author in the first century. The idealism, of which Baur had made so much, was not rejected, but the complementary realism, which in Lightfoot's judgment excluded the possibility of an inventive design of the second century, was stressed.[89] Moreover, the theology of the Logos was seen to arise out of the events rather than being the controlling idea behind the generation of the narrative. Thus John's eyewitness status was restored, and his Gospel remained of primary importance as an evangelical witness for research into the life of Jesus and faith in the Christ, the two sides of the one historical figure.[90]

It was also part of Baur's case that the authorship of the Gospel was of secondary concern.[91] Lightfoot differed on this point too: the authorship was the key to the problem. Although he began with the exegesis of the text, in the end he concentrated on the Gospel's authenticity and genuineness.[92] This was an historical question — did John write the Gospel or not? — and therefore Lightfoot accepted (this time agreeing with Baur) that it was a proper subject for historical enquiry. He responded with a critque of the content of Baur's theory, supported by reservations about his method. Both were corrected in an alternative presentation based, in accordance with the

---

[86] BE 16.

[87] Hodgson, *Formation*, 214 n. 55.

[88] BE 34, 42-3.

[89] OA 242-3.

[90] Life, 1862, 10-13; CS 219-23; SSP 91-2 & 2-4 in the MS, omitted in the published version; SSO 124-6; OA 241-5, 168-9, 174; AF II.1².381.

[91] Lichtenberger, *History*, 386.

[92] See above 291; & Appendix 2 below.

rationalist tendencies of contemporary Anglican apologetical theology,[93] on a classical Baconian induction, modified in its expectations by Butlerian standards of probability, to show that John the son of Zebedee really was the author, with its corollary that the Gospel was an authentic apostolic report. Thus the argument was about the results, and the nature and application, of the historical method: it was not about the validity of the method itself.

In keeping with his general strategy,[94] before adducing the positive evidence for the Johannine authorship, Lightfoot sought to discredit the alternate theory by demonstrating its inadequacy as an account of the facts of the matter. In doing so he chose not to undermine the local presentation of Tayler, but to block off the danger to the traditional view at its source in the tendency criticism of Baur. This was because, as "the first to develop and systematize the attack on the genuineness of the Fourth Gospel" — a commitment which had had a major impact on critical scholarship in Europe — [95] and also "its most determined and ablest antagonist", he could be taken to represent the negative case. If it could be defeated here, it might be seen to be overthrown.

This involved, first, application of the historical perspective to Tübingen criticism itself, for the history of the negative-critical approach had now to be regarded as part of the factual data bearing on the Johannine question. Lightfoot was able to show how each successive Tübingen writer had been forced to retreat from the more extreme position of a predecessor under the weight of counter considerations until the date had been brought back to nearly the last years of John's lifetime, a change which he regarded as a virtual surrender to orthodoxy. Lightfoot pointed out the moral:

> This tendency to recede nearer and nearer to the evangelist's own age shows that the pressure of facts has begun to tell on the theories of antagonistic criticism, and we may look forward to the time when it will be held discreditable to the reputation of any critic for sobriety and judgment to assign to this gospel any later date than the end of the first century, or the very beginning of the second.[96]

Half a century of sceptical hypothesizing had actually reinforced the traditional view.

The case against the forgery hypothesis of Baur and his followers extended the method employed against Strauss. Again Lightfoot asked of the critics' case whether it could have happened in this way; that is, whether "a gospel written at such a time would probably have presented the phenomena

---

[93] Altholz, "Mind of Victorian Orthodoxy," 186-97; & Johnson, "Popular Apologetics," 558-77.

[94] RCC (1871) 79-80.

[95] See the review of nineteenth century scholarship in BE 50; & his protégé H.W. Watkins' *Modern Criticism Considered in Relation to the Fourth Gospel. Being the Bampton Lectures For 1890* (London: John Murray, 1890) esp. Lectures IV-VI.

[96] BE 11.

which we actually find in the fourth canonical gospel".[97] What was different now was the way in which he analyzed the actual contents of the Fourth Gospel itself. Taking as the date of composition the middle of the second century — the date "less encumbered with difficulties, and therefore more favourable to the opponents of its genuineness" —[98] he compared what was said and left unsaid with what might have been expected of a gospel written at this time. The omissions were barely credible, for its writer held aloof from the distinctive ecclesiastical controversies of the time, a characteristic which made it hard to find a motive for the alleged forgery. Conversely, the subtlety and accuracy of the Gospel's details were hard to accept as the product of an age disjoined from the period it purported to describe by the destruction of Jerusalem at the hands of the Romans. Moreover, the incapacity of the second century to produce such a "subtle historical romance" was evident from the known forgeries of the period which criticism itself dismissed as uncritical. This was a point to which Lightfoot returned repeatedly.[99] The traditional view of the authorship remained the more conceivable account of "John's" contents.

The positive side of Lightfoot's critical case began with a brief consideration of the external evidence. This was because satisfactory attestation at this point created a strong presumption in favour of the traditional authorship which only the "fullest and most decisive marks of spuriousness" could overturn. Lightfoot argued that the external evidence was early, reaching back virtually to the lifetime of the alleged writer, and was "singularly varied", extensive and almost universal. This "universality of its reception" was especially impressive because of the religious and ethical character of the book. With one exception it was not traduced though the advocates of different viewpoints might have benefited from doing so.[100]

Lightfoot went on subsequently to examine the external evidence to correct "an undue disparagement" which inflicted great harm upon "the cause of revealed truth".[101] But on this occasion — in keeping with the extension of his method to the contents of the Gospel — his emphasis was on the internal evidence. Did it support the strong presumption in favour of authenticity created by external attestation? The argument was constructed in three stages. First, Lightfoot's matchless knowledge of Hellenistic Greek permitted demonstration of the intensely Jewish quality of "John's" language, indicating that its writer was "a Hebrew accustomed to speak the language of his fathers", not a Gentile or Hellenistic Christian as recent critical theo-

---

[97] BE 11.
[98] BE 11.
[99] BE 23-4, 25, 28, 30, 31-2, 34, 34-5, 39-40, 42.
[100] BE 5-10.
[101] BE 45-122.

ries would have it.[102] Second, a "thorough and confident" familiarity with the customs and ideas, together with an accurate knowledge of the geography and history, of the time showed that he was "contemporary with and cognisant of the facts which he relates".[103] Finally, the vividness of the narrative, its inconspicuousness of detail and naturalness in characterization and the progress of events — features often overlooked because of the striking quality of the doctrine — pointed further to an eyewitness as the author.[104] As an alternative to the forgery hypothesis, Lightfoot adduced those qualities manifested by the rigorous philological and contextual study of the text required by the "historical-exegetical" method which made the Gospel "thoroughly in keeping" with a first century date, and led to upholding the Johannine authorship.[105]

Lightfoot consolidated his rebuttal of the Tübingen hypothesis by disputing Baur's version of the facts themselves.[106] More than that, he was actually able to turn the difficulties pinpointed by Baur into arguments in favour of the authenticity. 'John's' knowledge of the office of High Priest was a case in point. Far from being deficient, the thrice repeated remark about Caiaphas being high priest for one year, as an "unguarded, and to us unintelligible, way of speaking," actually "betokens a genuine author, who does not feel the necessity of explaining what to himself is a familiar fact". Nor was the dissimilarity of the Gospel with the Apocalypse (which Baur acknowledged as apostolic) to be exaggerated, since there were clear and important links between the two. Finding the true bearing of the facts removed the need for an alternative view of the Fourth Gospel's authorship.

The positive side of the argument was completed with the claim that the Fourth Gospel was genuine as well as authentic.[107] An "examination of indirect allusions and casual notices, from a comparison of things said and things unsaid" in the Gospel itself tended to support the traditional ascription to John the son of Zebedee.[108] A process of elimination of other possibilities pointed to this John as the anonymous disciple who claimed authorship, while the details of the narrative agreed with this result.[109] It was inconceivable to Lightfoot that any forger would have concealed his identity so completely and used language so natural of John the son of Zebedee

---

[102] BE 16-21, esp. 21.

[103] BE 21-36. Cf. BE 126-79. (See 167 & 16 for the quotations.)

[104] BE 22-3, 36-9. Cf. 125, 180-93.

[105] See esp. the summary at BE 15.

[106] Baur's objections to the authenticity and genuineness of the Fourth Gospel are summarized in Harris, *Tübingen School*, 193-4.

[107] "The genuineness of a document implies that it is what it professes to be ..." AF I.1.362.

[108] BE 39 ff.

[109] BE 39-43. Cf. 125.

with such success.[110] Indeed it was a final point against Baur that this reticence on the apostolic authorship undermined the *raison d'être* of the alleged forgery.

Lightfoot's defence of 'John' established the combination of external and internal evidence that was to be the hallmark of his mature method in judging the authenticity and genuineness of ancient documents. But it did not stand alone. That there was also an ethical side of Lightfoot's argument was evident in the moral terms in which he cast the debate.[111] Second century datings of the Gospel were based on the hypothesis that it was a piece of romance writing or a forgery. Although Lightfoot's allusions to these alternative views of its provenance tend to oscillate between the two, it was more often the latter that he chose.[112] His attitude in this respect was conveyed in the view that he who would forge a whole gospel was "a daring adventurer".[113] Yet it is evident that Lightfoot made no clear distinction between the two alternative hypotheses, and that his attitude towards romance writing was the same. For a romancer was "unrestrained by obligations of fact".[114] Explanations advanced as alternatives to the authenticity and genuineness of the Gospel were attended by serious moral shortcomings.[115]

In contrast Lightfoot gave some emphasis to the moral credentials of his own perspective. Twice he indicated that the standard relevant to the debate was that of the truthful historian who is fettered by the obligations of fact.[116] Not only did the writer of the Gospel meet this standard,[117] but his own advocacy of its authenticity and genuineness attempted to do so as well. This was why Lightfoot reiterated that the case should not go beyond ascertainable fact,[118] and depended for its force not on any of the parts but on the total effect of the entire body of evidence.[119] It was also why he invited verification, expressed diffidence about the incompleteness of his presentation of the argument, and invited others to follow up the lines of investigation he suggested.[120] Educated Englishmen did not have to suspend their

---

[110] BE 40, 42.

[111] Analysis of the ethical side of contemporary debate was pioneered by J.C. Livingston, *The Ethics of Belief: An Essay on the Victorian Religious Conscience* (Tallahassee, Florida: American Academy of Religion, 1974).

[112] A romance at BE 13, 14, 34, 34-5, 36 & 42; a forgery at BE 12-13, 13, 15, 23-4, 32, 34-5 & 40.

[113] BE 13.

[114] BE 13.

[115] Hengel, "Lightfoot and the Tübingen School," 38, makes the point that such moral scruples prevented a proper appreciation of the phenomenon of pseudepigraphy.

[116] BE 13, 15, contrasting the artificiality of romance with "genuine history".

[117] BE 27-8, 30, 34-5, 35-6, 39.

[118] BE 22, 31.

[119] BE 18.

[120] BE 7, 16, 22, 43.

normal standards of judgment to accept the authenticity of the Fourth Gospel.

Indeed Lightfoot invoked those same standards in appealing for what was fair and reasonable in this debate. Its own history was held up both as a warning against the excesses of antagonistic criticism and to teach it a wholesome distrust of itself. Similarly Lightfoot directed attention to the inconsistencies and improbabilities arising from the processes of the negative critical perspective. It was hardly likely that an age touted as "uncritical" could have produced such a masterpiece as 'John'.

> For [he insisted] it requires a much higher flight of critical genius to invent an extremely delicate fiction than to detect it when invented. The age which could not expose a coarse forgery was incapable of constructing a subtle historical romance.[121]

Some of the arguments advanced in support of critical propositions were "extremely unlikely", "hardly conceivable", and "incredible".[122] Finally the absence of comment on the main ecclesiastical issues of the suggested time of composition left the alleged forgery without a motive or function.[123] Criticism was not necessarily worthy of the trust which some were prepared to bestow upon it.

On the other hand, Lightfoot made use of analogy to secure a proper consideration of his own case. The known forgeries of the second century were not only dramatically unlike "John" but showed what forgeries of that time were really like.[124] The grounds for the authorship of other ancient writings showed that the "external testimony in favour of St John's Gospel reaches back much nearer to the writer's own time and is far more extensive than can be produced in the case of most Classical writings of the same antiquity".[125] Lightfoot made clear where the moral responsiblity in the argument lay:

> If then the genuiness of this gospel is supported by greater evidence than in ordinary cases we consider conclusive, we approach the investigation of its internal character with a very strong presumption in its favour. The *onus probandi* rests with those who would impugn its genuineness, and nothing short of the fullest and most decisive marks of its spuriousness can fairly be considered sufficient to counterbalance this evidence.[126]

It was also part of Lightfoot's case that his was the progressive view. One of his principles of criticism was that "if ... any alternative which has been proposed introduces greater perplexities than those which it is intended to remove, we are bound (irrespective of any positive arguments in its favour) to fall back upon the account which is exposed to fewest objections.[127]

---

[121] BE 14-15. Cf. 31-2, 32, 34, 40.
[122] BE 25, 28.
[123] BE 11-13.
[124] BE 14-15, 15.
[125] BE 9.
[126] BE 9-10.
[127] BE 10.

In the debate over the authorship of the Fourth Gospel the traditional view was not free from difficulties, but they were not only fewer but "small indeed compared with the improbablities of the only alternative hypothesis".[128] Moreover, it was getting stronger. Recent discoveries testified to "the extensive circulation and wide reception" of the Fourth Gospel "at a very early date".[129] Recent negative criticism was not necessarily the progressive force its proponents maintained.

Lightfoot concluded his case with the claim that he had taken his stand on the authorship of the Fourth Gospel as "a critical question". This was a clear response to the setting in which he had done his work. At a time when the Church had to address both the irritation felt without because of the special status claimed by the clergy for the documents of revelation, and also the great uncertainty felt within about the new critical approaches to the Bible, Lightfoot recognized that it was not appropriate to bring forward non-empirical arguments. The traditional view of the Fourth Gospel could stand only if the most rigorous sifting of the available evidence by the best available critical methods pointed to this as the most defensible finding. In effect this approach meant that the Church must learn in faith to subject its foundation documents to proper processes of empirical investigation while the critics were morally bound to accept the limitations on speculation which such processes imposed. In meeting the requirements of both interests, Lightfoot pressed a secular hermeneutic into service to maintain the authenticity of the document most crucial for his historical ideology.

Yet it is evident that Lightfoot was not quite so single-mindedly 'critical' as he supposed. His piety intruded when he claimed that the state of the evidence in relation to "John" was what could have been expected. "In all the most important matters which affect our interest in this world and our hopes hereafter," he maintained, "God has left some place for diversity of opinion, because He would not remove all opportunity of self-discipline."[130] The evidence that had been given — "greater ... than in ordinary cases we consider conclusive" —[131] was sufficient to warrant belief. Furthermore, the new discoveries that strengthened the traditional view were represented as the outcome of design:

> having been brought to light so soon after its genuineness was for the first time seriously impugned, they seem providentially destined to furnish an answer to the objections of recent criticism.[132]

Thus experience showed that temperate criticism and faith went hand in hand. This confidence also informed Lightfoot's estimate of what he had achieved.

---

[128] BE 15-16. Cf. 10, 34.

[129] BE 7-8.

[130] BE 9.

[131] BE 9.

[132] BE 8.

He left no doubt about what was at stake in his defence of the traditional authorship of 'John'. His lecture closed with a personal declaration:

> as I could not have you think that I am blind to the theological issues directly or indirectly connected with it, I will close with this brief confession of faith. I believe from my heart that the truth which this Gospel more especially enshrines — the truth that Jesus Christ is the very Word Incarnate, the manifestation of the Father to mankind — is the one lesson which, duly apprehended, will do more than all our feeble efforts to purify and elevate human life here by imparting to it hope and light and strength, the one study which alone can fitly prepare us for a joyful immortality hereafter.[133]

Criticism, as Lightfoot understood it, had served ultimately to entrench the Incarnation. The Christian outlook was upheld by the intellectual processes and standards of the day.

In its fullest presentation,[134] Lightfoot's account of the evidence was thorough and impressive, and, according to the pundits, even a century later can be little improved on.[135] However, while it appeared to give him what he wanted, the method did not yield the full answer to Baur for which Lightfoot had hoped. The confidence that it had done so was based on the assumption that the serious questions Baur had raised about the provenance and contents of the Gospel would practically lapse if the Johannine authorship was established and the second century chronology discredited. In fact the problems which the late date had been meant to solve persisted — in particular the difference from the Synoptics and the presence of the *Logos* doctrine — but in a first century setting. For a satisfactory historical explanation of the Fourth Gospel, a far more radical penetration of the document itself was required. Lightfoot's failure to go on to this was due to the fact that, in countering the effects of Baur's subjectivism, he fell into the opposite error of not allowing at all for the subjective element in 'John'. Instead he identified the history and the record, an attitude which scarcely did justice to the event-reporter-report dynamic evinced by Baur. As he understood it, the historical method presented itself as a source of factuality, and therefore a control over metaphysically conceived interpretations of Christian origins which stood to deepen the crisis of Christian civilization he perceived around him.

In some ways Lightfoot's historical approach to the Gospel records achieved too much. By delivering results of this order it seemed to blind him to the complexities of the Gospel question, not only as reflected in Strauss and Baur and foreshadowed by Hort,[136] but also to some extent as involved in his own position. For Lightfoot recognized that there was a significant

---

[133] BE 43-4.

[134] That is, with the addition of the Cambridge lectures reproduced in BE 45-198.

[135] Eg. Robinson, *Lightfoot*, 16-19.

[136] For which, see above 100-1.

difference between the Synoptics and 'John'.[137] He also admitted a pre-literary history for 'John': in the experience of John, his encounter with Jesus and subsequent reflection upon it at a time of great change in the Church's external circumstances; and of the ideas and words used.[138] He spoke too of "theological purpose", the influence of "historical reasons", and a target audience and function for the Gospel within the Church.[139] But the bearing of none of these characteristics was pursued in any serious fashion. In fact, for all of his objections to "evidences theology", Lightfoot's historical method was still working within its rationalist framework and depended on its main assumption, that verification came through external attestation. But the treatment of 'John' also showed the influence of the idealist epistemology on an outwardly empirical approach. The Idea elaborated in the Fourth Gospel depended on historical evidence, not so much for its validity, but for clearer definition and surer apprehension. Once the historical method had verified the status of the Gospel as Fact, through which the Idea comes to full manifestation, it had done what Lightfoot asked of it. But this outlook in effect cordoned off the Gospels from the more radical historical investigation their characteristics called for. As a result, Lightfoot never proceeded to a thorough historical-critical study of the Gospels themselves, and the documentary basis of incarnational belief went unexamined at a crucial point.

Publication of the lecture was intended, though Lightfoot was evidently unaware of the fact.[140] He caused some irritation by keeping it back on the grounds of the inadequacy of the presentation of an important case. Lightfoot did not give up the idea of bringing his work before a larger audience, but with Westcott just back at Cambridge and at work on the subject, it was not urgent. Apart from a course of lectures to undergraduates, Lightfoot was content to express his views on the matter in other settings as circumstances required.[141] Because of this failure to publish, Lightfoot did not have the influence on English Gospel study in his own lifetime that he might have. But there is evidence that he had some effect in the background. He seems to have provided encouragement to men like Farrar and Alfred Edersheim who were seeking to present a supernatural Christ in a historical setting.[142] He seems also to have provided reassurance by his standing as a reverently

---

[137] LS 195. CS 193. SSP 91-2. OA 123-6, 227-8.

[138] 3rd Group, 1858, 9-10. Life, 1862, 11-13, 16. CS 221-3. SSO 124-6. OA 168-9, 244-5. P 202, 206, 302-3. BE 192-3.

[139] BE 197. Cf. OA 241, 244-5.

[140] BE 3.

[141] See 350-2 below.

[142] On Farrar's *Life of Christ* (1874) and Edersheim's *Life and Times of Jesus the Messiah* (1883), see Pals, *Victorian "Lives"*, 77-85 & 104-8.

critical scholar and member of the establishment.[143]   One concrete result, however, was the series of Bampton lectures for 1890 delivered by the Archdeacon of Auckland. A member of Lightfoot's inner circle,[144] H.W. Watkins took up his method and outlook at great length and transmitted them to the next generation.[145]

Amid the illness that was to cause his death, Lightfoot finally relented and allowed the lecture on 'St John' to be printed more or less as delivered.[146] Recognizing that he would have no further opportunity to upgrade his presentation, he was now prepared to let it come before the wider public as an indication that almost twenty years later he still held to his original argument and its conclusion. The effect was to convey to the next generation the approach to the Gospels and use of the historical method to defend the doctrine of the Incarnation which he had devised for the Norrisian Prize Essay.[147] It is of the highest symbolic importance that Jesus and the Gospels were the subject both of Lightfoot's first serious study of the New Testament and the last paper he sanctioned for publication. As his first and last scholarly word, they were (as will be shown) what his scholarly work was really all about. Jesus and the Gospels were the ultimate data of Lightfoot's scholarship, including that on St Paul.

---

[143] This is why Farrar sought Lightfoot's aid in promoting his *The Life of Jesus* among the clergy and people of England. Farrar to Lightfoot, 12 & 16 February 1874. Lightfoot declined on the grounds of lack of time, but expected to be in sympathy with the book. Lightfoot to Farrar, 16 February 1874 (FCC). Edersheim, who sought and received Lightfoot's scholarly assistance, regarded Lightfoot as "the most learned theologian living". Edersheim to Lightfoot, 28 January 1879.

[144] He had sought and gained Lightfoot's blessing on his proposal. See Lightfoot to Watkins, 25 April 1888 (DUL, Ad'l MS 132).

[145] Watkins, *Modern Criticism Considered in Relation to the Fourth Gospel, passim.*

[146] J.B. Lightfoot, "Internal Evidence For the Authenticity and Genuineness of St John's Gospel," *The Expositor* 4th series I (1890) 1-21, 81-92, 176-88 (= BE 1-44).

[147] Most significant here is A.C. Headlam who grew up in the shadow of Durham Cathedral when Lightfoot was the bishop. LD 136-41. On Headlam's early life, see R. Jasper, *Arthur Cayley Headlam. Life and Letters of a Bishop* (London: Faith Press, 1960) ch. 1.

Chapter 11

"The Apostle to the Gentiles": History and Paul

The requirements of the Norrisian Prize had caused Lightfoot to begin his scholarly career with a study of Jesus and the Gospels. By the end of 1855, however, the Gospels had been superseded by the Pauline Epistles as the main focus of Lightfoot's New Testament interest. Over the following twenty years he maintained a steady flow of articles and commentaries on the subject he came to regard as the work of his life.[1] Stephen Neill, working from the internalist perspective typical of histories of New Testament scholarship, attributed this commitment to Paul to the recognition that his Epistles "must always be the starting point for the historical study of the New Testament".[2] Whatever the truth of the general proposition, the reason for the change in Lightfoot's case was more mundane. But in the process he learned his craft as a New Testament critic and exegete. The work on St Paul was the occasion for developing the historical method to take account of the text itself.[3]

I

In 1854 Lightfoot was appointed Assistant Tutor at Trinity College,[4] a post which required him to lecture on the 'Acts of the Apostles' and the Pauline letters.[5] In line with his high sense of duty, he threw himself into his new teaching commitments. He based his approach on the text and commentary recently produced for English students by Henry Alford, while he also made

---

[1] Lightfoot to Farrar, 16 February 1874 (FCC, Bundle 27).

[2] Neill, *Interpretation*, 24, 38 104.

[3] The main previous studies are P.H. Richards, "J.B. Lightfoot as a Biblical Interpreter," *Interpretation* 8 (1954) 50-62; & C.K. Barrett, "J.B. Lightfoot as Biblical Commentator," in Dunn (ed.), *The Lightfoot Centenary Lectures*, 53-70.

[4] *The Cambridge University Calendar 1854*, 327, 329.

[5] These lectures were required to prepare students for examinations internal to Trinity College and for "Subjects For The B.A. Degree, In Addition to Those Fixed". See College Notices, vol. I (TCC); & *The Cambridge University Calendar 1853-1858*. The lectures themselves were written out longhand in three limp bound volumes marked "Acts I-VIII', 'Acts VIII-XIV' & 'Acts XV-XIX'. Note that f. 11 of 'Acts I-VIII' leads in to lectures on Galatians.

frequent reference to the recent New Testament introduction by Samuel Davidson.[6] To these he added the resources furnished by contemporary German scholarship which he defended to the undergraduates from the abuse to which it was still subject.[7] He himself used the new philological aids, most notably the *Grammatik des neutestamentlichen Sprachidioms* and *Biblisches Realwörterbuch* of G.B. Winer.[8] For the interpretation of the text he turned to the recent commentaries of Michael Baumgarten and H.A.W. Meyer.[9] For the larger historical context he drew on the histories of the apostolic period by H.W.I. Thiersch, J.A.W. Neander, C.C.J. Bunsen and Philip Schaff.[10] Although these were acceptable as (in the main) writers of the "mediating school",[11] Lightfoot did not slavishly follow the German scholars, but critically used them to bring out the meaning and historical bearing of the text. Historical criticism of this order was also used to defend the authenticity and veracity of 'Acts' from its critics, most notably F.C. Baur and Eduard Zeller.[12] Teaching of this order was otherwise unavailable at Cambridge, and it soon caught the attention of the College and the wider University.[13]

Lightfoot's purpose in this was more than academic. In theory, the teaching role at Cambridge in the 1850s was as much pastoral as instructional, and Lightfoot was among those taking the theory more seriously.[14] Fully

---

[6]   H. Alford, *The Greek Testament: with a critically revised text … prolegomena and a critical and exegetical commentary*, 1849 ff. S. Davidson, *An Introduction to the New Testament*, 1848-51. Lightfoot also used older authorities like J.A. Bengel (1687-1752) and William Paley's *Horae Paulinae* (1790).

[7]   See 280 above.

[8]   On Winer, see Lichtenberger, *History*, 417-18. He was "the first to study and expound in a really scientific way the principles of the Hellenistic language of the New Testament".

[9]   M. Baumgarten, *Die Apostelgeschichte; oder der Entwickelungsgang der Kirche von Jerusalem bis Rom* (Halle, 1852). H.A.W. Meyer, *Kritisch exegetisches Handbuch über die Apostelgeschichte* (2nd ed.; Göttingen, 1854). On Baumgarten & Meyer, see W. Ward Gasque, *A History of the Criticism of the Acts of the Apostles* (Grand Rapids: Eerdmans, 1975) 56-60 & 66-7.

[10]   Eg. 'Acts I-VIII,' f. 92r., where it is assumed they are the standard authorities. Lightfoot reviewed Schaff in the *Journal of Classical and Sacred Philology* II.iv (March 1855) 119-20.

[11]   For which, see Lichtenberger, *History*, ch. V.

[12]   'Acts I-VIII,' f. 28v. & f. 46r. For a summary of their views, see Gasque, *History*, ch. II.

[13]   LD 176. Late in 1856 he was appointed Examiner in Greek Testament for the University's theological examinations in 1857 & 1858. Entries for 5 November 1856 & 30 May 1857, Board of Theological Studies Minutes (SDS). C.J. Ellicott to Lightfoot, 31 October 1860, comments on his high reputation in the University.

[14]   See 49-50, 186-7 & 192-3 above. Most of his pupils will have brought the early Victorian 'oracular' view of the Bible with them to College.

aware that he was "speaking to Christians",[15] his lectures sought to combine the tasks in the manner required by the ideal. Because of their hermeneutical implications, he introduced his subject with a discussion of theories of inspiration, recommending his own view which saw inspiration as the interaction of the human with the divine.[16] On the human side, it warranted such intellectual matters as settling the text, deciding historical questions and determining interpretation, which other views were inclined to ignore or exaggerate. Indeed, Lightfoot pressed this point:

> The timidity, which shrinks from the application of modern science or criticism to the interpretation of Holy Scripture, evinces a very unworthy view of its character. If the Scriptures are indeed true, they must be in accordance with every true principle of whatever kind ... From the full light of science or criticism we have nothing to fear ...[17]

At the same time, he urged the character of the Scriptures as "spiritual writings".[18] To understand them as such required that they be approached with prayer. Thus true divinity demanded a combination of the rational and the devotional. From the beginning, Lightfoot set himself the task of presenting and defending traditional Christianity to undergraduates through the texts set for study presented devotionally and by the best and most up to date scholarly materials available.

The demands of College teaching were reinforced by developments in contemporary English New Testament scholarship. The recent editions of the New Testament by Alford and Christopher Wordsworth had been followed by a spate of new books on St Paul. In 1852 W.J. Conybeare and J.S. Howson published a "life and letters", the purpose of which was 'to give a living picture of St Paul himself, and the circumstances by which he was surrounded'.[19] This was exactly the kind of treatment Lightfoot was looking for, both for his students and English Christians generally. He called it "a very instructive book", which had had the salutary effect of creating "an enlarged interest in, and more intelligent study of, the New Testament writings among those who before were satisfied with employing the heart only, to the neglect of the understanding".[20] Moreover, because of its attention to the setting of 'Acts' and the Epistles in Palestine, Asia Minor and Greece, now known better through advances in historical, archaeological, geographi-

---

[15] NTI 175.

[16] For which, see 99-100 above.

[17] NTI 174.

[18] NTI 175.

[19] W.J. Conybeare & J.S. Howson, *The Life and Epistles of St Paul* (London: Longman, Brown, Green, Longmans & Roberts, 1852, 1856²) ix.

[20] Although it was the second edition Lightfoot reviewed, it was the first of which he spoke in the quotation. J.B. Lightfoot, Review of W.J. Conybeare & J.S. Howson, *The Life and Epistles of St Paul*, *Journal of Classical and Sacred Philology* IX.x (March 1857) 107-9.

cal and ethnological research, Conybeare and Howson's *Life* is said to have "marked the beginning of the modern understanding of Paul in the English speaking world".[21] To Lightfoot this was a development to foster and extend.

Lightfoot's concern to see the standard of English Biblical study raised was further gratified by the appearance in 1854 and 1855 of critical and grammatical commentaries on two Pauline Epistles by C.J. Ellicott, Professor of New Testament at King's College, London.[22] They too constituted an important step forward. Minor faults aside, Lightfoot judged, Ellicott's undertaking stood "at the head of the New Testament literature of England for patient and accurate scholarship, and will not suffer from a comparison with the best works of Germany".[23] This was because Ellicott had adapted the linguistic discipline of the Cambridge Classical Tripos to the new philological resources emanating from Germany. The result was 'safe' Biblical scholarship fully acceptable to the orthodox. By restricting himself to grammatical criticism, however, Ellicott's conception of philology was too narrow for Lightfoot, but his relatively unambitious work at least showed how Paul's language should be submitted to "a minute and careful study".[24]

Much more challenging were the innovative commentaries of Benjamin Jowett and A.P. Stanley published in 1855.[25] The partial fulfilment of a plan by Dr Arnold to produce an edition of St Paul, these works incorporated his liberal Anglican principles of scriptural interpretation, with their emphasis upon the need to differentiate between the devotional and scientific understanding of the Bible.[26] This in itself was provocative in a country still dominated by an "oracular" view of Scripture,[27] but Jowett in particular evoked a sharp reaction, mainly because of his disregard of other cherished theological notions.[28] Lightfoot was among the few who did not censure, and to that extent identified himself with the liberals. Stanley's handling of the historical aspect of his subject was commendable, while Jowett's essays

---

[21] Gasque, *History*, 112-13.

[22] C.J. Ellicott, *A Critical and Grammatical Commentary on St Paul's Epistle to the Galatians, with a Revised Translation* (London: John W. Parker & Son, 1854); & *A Critical and Grammatical Commentary on St Paul's Epistle to the Ephesians, with a Revised Translation* (London: J.W. Parker & Son, 1855). On Ellicott, see 'W.A.C.', 'Charles John Ellicott, Bishop of Gloucester' (copy at Cam.c.905.14 in the CUL).

[23] RE 84-5.

[24] G ix.

[25] B. Jowett, *The Epistles of St Paul to the Thessalonians, Galatians, Romans: with Critical Notes and Dissertations* (2 vols; London: John Murray, 1855). A.P. Stanley, *The Epistles of St Paul to the Corinthians* (2 vols; London: John Murray, 1855).

[26] See P. Hinchliff, *Benjamin Jowett and the Christian Religion* (Oxford: Clarendon Press, 1987) ch. 3.

[27] See 93-4 above.

[28] *Ibid.* Also Storr, *Development of English Theology*, 398-403.

had something important to say, even if excessively negative.[29] These features added the historical and metaphysical dimension lacking in Ellicott, but his linguistic soundness was missing.

These writers provided the challenge to which Lightfoot's early writings on Paul were in part a response. Taking Ellicott, Jowett and Stanley together, he judged, "it may fairly be questioned whether the amount of ability, intelligence and learning, brought to bear on a single New Testament writer, and given to the public within so short a time, has any parallels in the annals of theological literature in England".[30] But there were still serious defects of execution and principle in English work on Paul that needed to be corrected.[31] While at this stage Lightfoot underestimated the scale of work necessary to put matters to rights, clearly much remained for him (and others) to do to place formal English New Testament study on a sound basis of scholarship and interpretation.

As a founder and editor of the new Cambridge philological journal Lightfoot had already been working towards this end for several years.[32] From the beginning of his career he had discerned the need for the Biblical writings to be a part of Philology "in its wider signification, comprising not only the criticism of language, but every topic connected with the Literature and History of Antiquity".[33] The association of Biblical study with a secular discipline was justified on the grounds that "whatever promotes the application of sound scholarship to Biblical and patristic criticism must tend to banish thence vague and abstract treatment". This was a need often repeated in the 1850s as definiteness became Lightfoot's ideal of Biblical study.[34] Encouraged by the direction taken by English New Testament scholarship, and extending his own work at Trinity College, he undertook to write on Paul for the new periodical. Four papers were directed to the concerns of "Sacred Philology", two to the "illustration of single passages of the Bible",[35] and two to "the methodical study of its separate books and their history".[36]

---

[29] RE 84-5, 85-6, 90, 102, 117-18, 120-1.

[30] RE 83. Both Jowett and Stanley acknowledged the force of Lightfoot's critique, and without giving in on points of principle, looked to him for corrections for subsequent editions. Jowett to Lightfoot, 20 March & 27 December 1856. Stanley to Lightfoot, 27 March, 5 April, & 10 August 1856.

[31] RE, esp. 101 & 119-20.

[32] For the *Journal of Classical and Sacred Philology*, see 43 above.

[33] For this and the other quotations in the paragraph, 'The Journal of Classical and Sacred Philology' (Camb. Uni. Papers, CUL).

[34] 'Acts I-VIII,' ff. 5-6. RE 102-4.

[35] J.B. Lightfoot, "The Mission of Titus to the Corinthians," *Journal of Classical & Sacred Philology* II.v (May 1855) 194-205 [= BE 271-84]; & "They That Are of Caesar's Household," *ibid.* IV.x (March 1857) 57-79.

[36] RE 81-121; & "On the Style and Character of Galatians," *Journal of Classical & Sacred Philology* III.ix (December 1856) 289-327.

Lightfoot's reasons for turning to St Paul were not only scholarly and apologetical, but also religious. The change of subject coincided with his ordination and earliest clerical practice.[37] His sermons at the time reflect a strong interest in the "history of St Paul" as the source of the true nature and content of Christianity.[38] This was because, in his own relation to the historical Jesus, Paul presented an "exact parallel" with that of the present believer. However Paul acquired the facts,[39] "they are the same facts, which are presented to *us* in the Gospel narrative, the same image is held up for our imitation as was for *his*", so that he "shows us that we need not to have known Christ after the flesh". This was the crucial point for the present-day believer:

> surely among those many ends which the epistles of St Paul were designed to secure, we may reckon this as not the least important, that we have here a picture presented to us with the minutest details, of what human nature may become by the faithful copying, as far as may be, of the person and character of Christ- We have not only the image itself, but we have also a copy of that image.[40]

To a young clergyman, intensely committed to Christian duty and still in his formative period, Paul became the exemplar of Christian experience, holding out the key to a life of devotion and heroic achievement. If, in line with his emerging incarnational theology,[41] the *Imitatio Christi* was the ideal of the Christian life, the *Imitatio Pauli* based on the rigorous study of his writings laid down the way to attain it.

This consideration helps to define the sense in which Lightfoot's early interest in Paul may be described as historical. While the Pauline writings were the earliest in the New Testament, the proper starting point was the anterior event — "the Person and Teaching of Christ" — to which they were a response.[42] Viewed in this light the letters reflected in its most advanced form the Christianity of the second order of believers whose faith and practice was not based on direct experience of the Jesus of history. Their value was that "they can tell us of Christ's power in renewing men's hearts, and His Spirit guiding the Church, and of the restitution of all things in His glorious kingdom".[43] It was to Paul especially that he turned "for larger instruction in the diverse aspects of the Gospel teaching and the manifold

---

[37] See 47-8 & 57 above.

[38] Eg. St Paul, 1854; Disobedient, 1855; Kingdom, 1855.

[39] The question of the origin of Paul's religion was a matter of some interest to Lightfoot. See BE 199-233.

[40] Christ's, 1855, 29.

[41] Eg. "the taking up of humanity into God through the incarnation and resurrection of Christ — the central truth of Christianity." Acts I-VIII, f. 80 v.

[42] G xi.

[43] Jael, 1855, 2-5.

bearings of the Christian life".[44] Clearly the New Testament structure Lightfoot regarded as important was not the order of books produced by historical criticism, but that of the Canon which perpetuated the important historical sequence in which, in its first major internal development, Christianity was changed into what it remained, an encounter with Jesus known only by report. Like the rebuttal of Strauss, Lightfoot's early Pauline studies were a reflection of the incarnational structure of sacred history.

To date Lightfoot's scholarly work on Paul had been (by his own admission) typically English in concentrating on "minute critical subjects" for fellow specialists,[45] while its religious aspect had been directed to individual congregations. In 1857 he sought to bring both sides together by tackling some of the difficult theological questions arising out of the use of the historical-critical method of reading Paul's writings.[46] This was to be before a larger audience in a course of Hulsean Lectures. Unfortunately he sent in his name too late, but as a consolation was offered the Select Preachership instead.[47] As he rose to deliver his five sermons before the University of Cambridge on each of the Sundays in May, 1858, the place of the historical method in the interpretation of the Epistles, particularly in its bearing upon Biblical inspiration, that other contentious issue of the day,[48] was uppermost in his mind.

To Jowett's objection that provision of the historical setting was actually a block to understanding the text, Lightfoot had earlier replied that its absence encouraged the popular view of Paul as some vague abstraction, and not a "real, living, acting" man:

> While we view him as the penman of the Spirit, we are apt to forget that he was also one of ourselves, and our understanding of his writings is seriously impaired by this.[49]

At this point it had been the religious appreciation that Lightfoot had in view. As Select Preacher he turned his attention to the relation of inspiration and the reasonable demand for a natural explanation of the Epistles. Nothing was lost, he contended, by acknowledging the importance of the immediate needs of the Church to which they were addressed, and the circumstances of the inward and outward life of Paul when he wrote them.[50] Viewing the Apostle in relation to his background actually heightened the operation of the Spirit in selecting and shaping the writers of Scripture and

---

[44] On the claims of Paul to be regarded as an 'apostle', Christ, 1855, 16-20. Cf. G 71-2 (on I.1), 92-101; & I. St Paul's Teaching, 1858, 8-9.

[45] OSCG 289. RE 83.

[46] On these questions in general, see Bubb, "Theology of F.J.A. Hort," ch. VII.

[47] H. Philpott to Lightfoot, 23 May 1857.

[48] See 99-100 above.

[49] RE 85-6.

[50] I. St Paul's Teaching, 1858, 15-16, 20-3.

securing Christian teaching for the Church in all ages. In an historical approach to the Pauline literature, Lightfoot wanted it understood, the demands
of natural reason and the claims of inspiration were satisfied, while showing
the Epistles to have been the product of genuine religious experience facilitated their impact on contemporary Christians.[51] The historical method gave
the most effective access to "the Apostle to the Gentiles".[52]

Lightfoot's original projection of these sermons for the Hulsean Lectures
indicates that his larger purpose was to adjust the discussion of the Pauline
literature to the outlook of the critical historical method as a matter of Christian Evidences.[53] The problem being addressed was forcefully illustrated in
the following year when George Rawlinson of Exeter College, Oxford, denied in his Bampton Lectures that the Bible had been affected by the revolution which had taken place in profane history because of the science of historical criticism.[54] This separation of faith and the operations of reason was
the very outlook Lightfoot opposed. Instead he insisted that philology broadly
conceived actually served religious interests. Christians could be both scientific and devout in their approach to the Scriptures. Indeed, the former
was the means to the latter.

To further counter this kind of attitude Lightfoot was planning in 1859 to
consolidate his work on St Paul into a complete edition of the Epistles. The
plan was described to Westcott:

> to begin with a thin volume, or a portion of a volume[,] of introductory matter, explain-
> ing the history, doctrinal connexion & so forth, of the Epistles: & then to take the
> Epistles in chronological order, beginning therefore with the Thessalonians: I proposed
> printing the Greek Text & the English Version side by side, with a *selection* of the most
> important vv.ll. [sic.] of the Greek beneath, & the general commentary below that ... I
> would divide the Epistles not of course into chapters, but into paragraphs and divi-
> sions, & prefix a paraphrase to each division. In rare instances, where a subject could
> not well be treated of in the compass of a note, I could consign it to a dissertation[:]
> e.g. The Man of Sin; but these dissertations should be exceptional.[55]

The plan avowedly owed much to the example of Jowett and Stanley, but it
was not his intention to work on the same scale. Lightfoot had scarcely
begun the project when Alexander Macmillan suggested to Westcott the pos-

---

[51] 4th Group, 1858, 22-3. Cf. 'Acts I-VIII,' f. 6v.

[52] Eg. SSO 227 (in a sermon entitled 'S. Paul Our Example') for this characteristic
usage.

[53] For the importance and history of the Hulsean Lectures as a statement of the 'Evidences of Revealed Religion', see J. Hunt, *Religious Thought in England in the Nineteenth Century* (London: Gibbings & Co., 1896) 332-8; & Stephenson, *Rise and Decline
of English Modernism*, 15-16.

[54] G. Rawlinson, *The Historical Evidences of the Truth of the Scripture Records, Stated
Anew, With Special Reference to the Doubts and Discoveries of Modern Times* (London:
John Murray, 1860). Rawlinson was made Camden Professor of Ancient History in 1861.

[55] Lightfoot to Westcott, 4 December 1859 (LAC).

sibility of a Cambridge commentary on the entire New Testament.[56] Relishing the opportunity to collaborate with his erstwhile 'Coach' and friend, Lightfoot put aside his own edition for the time being. When the scheme was restricted to Lightfoot, Westcott and Hort, the division of labour became more or less obvious, and Lightfoot was enabled to resume his work on Paul, albeit in a different form to that which he first envisaged.[57]

It was not long after this that Lightfoot was appointed Hulsean Professor. This greatly benefited the commentary in that, by freeing him from College duties, it afforded the leisure to write.[58] The professorship also provided its institutional context. Lightfoot was anxious to get part of the commentary into print as soon as possible so that it might contribute to "the spiritual power of the nineteenth century".[59]

Two developments occurred at about this time to give great urgency to the task. First, as Lightfoot worked, he came to appreciate the seriousness of the reconstruction of the origins of Christianity advanced by the scholars of the Tübingen School. References to its representatives in his early writings are few in number and only in passing, but now Lightfoot attributed to them the elaboration and systematization of the critical attack on the New Testament Canon.[60] The implications of this perspective seem to have had a great deal to do with with his abandoning the original intention of treating the Epistles in chronological order and beginning with 'Galatians', a letter from the second group. England in the early 1860s was not at all ready for such critical theories, and so Lightfoot made some attempt to lead the public discussion of Christianity by directing attention to one of the cardinal documents for the new view.

> Though circumstances have for the moment concentrated the attention of Englishmen on the Old Testament Scriptures, the questions which have been raised on this Epistle are intrinsically far more important, because they touch the vital parts of Christianity. If the Primitive Gospel was, as some have represented it, merely one of many phases of Judaism, if those cherished beliefs which have been the light and life of many genera-

---

[56] Westcott to Macmillan & Lightfoot [with the ending supplied from the original], 24 November & 7 December 1859, in LW I.205. *Letters of Alexander Macmillan* (ed. with an Introduction by G.A. Macmillan; Glasgow: privately printed, 1908) 29-30. Olofsson, *Christus Redemptor Et Consummator*, 16 incorrectly attributes the commentary to the *Essays and Reviews* crisis.

[57] Hort to Lightfoot, 29 April 1860, in LH I.417-18.

[58] Apart from his three lectures per week for two terms in each academic year, Lightfoot was free to pursue his research, although administrative and outside ecclesiastical responsibilities occupied an increasing proportion of his time.

[59] For which see Chapter 7 above. For Lightfoot's haste, eg. Lightfoot to Westcott, 19 November 1863 (LAC).

[60] Eg. J.B. Lightfoot, "Thessalonians, First Epistle to," *A Dictionary of the Bible* (ed. W. Smith; London: John Murray, 1863) III.1481. For the Tübingen reconstruction, see Harris, *Tübingen School*, esp. ch. 12.

tions were afterthoughts, progressive accretions, having no foundation in the Person and Teaching of Christ, then indeed St Paul's preaching was vain and our faith is vain also.[61]

Lightfoot had his chances to join in the controversy over the Old Testament,[62] but the Tübingen account of Christian beginnings was potentially more destructive of incarnational Christianity than the views of either Darwin or Bishop Colenso.[63] While there was much in this account that must be allowed proper weight — conflict *was* a significant feature of the life of the early Church and should be incorporated into the received picture — its main thesis needed to be refuted in advance.[64]

The second important development was the *Essays and Reviews* controversy which supervened while the negotiations for the commentary were in progress. It was time for the Church, contended the authors, taking a much more aggressive approach than Lightfoot, to face up to the issue of the literary and historical criticism of the Bible. The point that was more or less involved in each essay was elaborated at length in the most important by Benjamin Jowett. "Read the Bible like any other book," he urged several times, repeating the injunction of Coleridge, and reviving the challenge of his own commentary.[65] Jowett meant no more than that, in the "externals of interpretation", i.e. "the meanings of words, the connexion of sentences, the settlement of the text, the evidence of facts", the same rules apply to Scripture as to other ancient texts. Yet his advocacy of a secular hermeneutic was deeply provocative. The effect was to dredge up the pathology of mid-Victorian orthodoxy.[66] In its denial of plenary inspiration, it was widely claimed, Biblical criticism posed a threat to belief, objective standards of doctrine and morality, and ultimately social stability. The underlying assumption that the Bible was a homogeneous collection of data to be received by faith

---

[61] G xi.

[62] F.C. Cook to Lightfoot, 13 July 1863, offering him the Minor Prophets in a new commentary scheme.

[63] For Lightfoot's view of Darwin, see Chapter 5 above. On Colenso, see Lightfoot to Tait, 19 November 1862, in LT I.338; & LT I.478.

[64] Lightfoot shows no sign of having been aware of R.W. Mackay, *The Tübingen School and its Antecedents: A Review of the History and Present Condition of Modern Theology* (London & Edinburgh: Williams & Norgate, 1863). In its contention that "the new school of Baur, Schwegler, Zeller, etc. ... must be the basis of all future research in relation to the New Testament" (x-xi), it was the kind of development Lightfoot was trying to forestall.

[65] B. Jowett, "On the Interpretation of Scripture," in *Essays and Reviews*, 337-8, 377-8. Cf. Ellis, *Seven Against Christ*, 310.

[66] J.L. Altholz, "The Mind of Victorian Orthodoxy: Anglican Responses to *Essays and Reviews*, 1860-1864," *Church History* 51.2 (June 1982) 186-97. For an example, see the passage from T.R. Birks, a Cambridge contemporary, quoted in *Religion in Victorian Britain. Vol III. Sources* (ed. J.R. Moore; Manchester: University Press, 1988) 174-8.

showed that the "oracular" use of the Bible was being strongly reasserted as Lightfoot, Westcott and Hort contemplated their scheme of a historical-critical approach to the entire New Testament. The best response, Lightfoot decided, was simply to show the results of constructive work, without the fanfare or dangers of polemical statement, and leave time to have its inevitable effect.[67] In so far as it took shape against this background, Lightfoot's commentary on St Paul was his answer to *Essays and Reviews*.

II

The "Preface" of the first instalment, *The Epistle of St Paul to the Galatians*, reflects the controversy stirred up by the writers of *Essays and Reviews*, with its emphasis on the importance of reason for faith.[68] Equally pointed was an expression of gratitude for the debt owed to Jowett.[69] This was a reference to his commentary, not the contribution to *Essays and Reviews*. On this occasion the call to 'read the Bible like any other book' was tactfully avoided. Yet Lightfoot agreed that this was the way to deal with the Biblical text. His challenge was to show how it should be done. The approach Lightfoot himself took in pursuit of this secular hermeneutical ideal was adumbrated in the subtitle to his first edition. *Galatians* would furnish "A Revised Text With Introduction, Notes and Dissertations".

The leading position of the text in Lightfoot's programme signified the priority of recovering the original language event in the commentator's task. This was not an issue on which Jowett had had much to say, although he deprecated an irrational conservatism in textual matters.[70] For Lightfoot, by contrast, finding what had actually been written necessarily preceded establishing the text's meaning. The manifest sense of this procedure conceals the significance of what he was attempting. British theology was still in the grip of the *Textus Receptus*, the sixteenth century text of Erasmus and Theodore Beza, which had been used by the translators of the Authorized Version and by almost every English language commentator since.[71] It was with unwarranted optimism that Lightfoot asserted:

> It is no longer necessary to offer any apology for laying aside the received text. When so much conscientious labour has been expended on textual criticism, it would be unpardonable in an editor to acquiesce in readings which for the most part are recommended neither by intrinsic fitness nor by the sanction of antiquity.[72]

---

[67] See 65 above.

[68] G xi-xii. See 100-1 above.

[69] G ix.

[70] Jowett, "Interpretation," 335, 352, 379. Cf. Jowett, *Epistles,* I.v-ix.

[71] Hinchliff, *Jowett,* 45.

[72] G vi. Only a few years later the move to secure a revised translation of the New Testament drew from Lightfoot the apology he had thought otiose. OFR 21-36.

Jowett and Stanley had made a commendable break with convention.[73] Yet
the so-called radicals had not gone far enough. Karl Lachmann, the editor
on whom they had relied, had sought only to recover the text of the fourth
century, and never pretended his readings were the original.[74] For Lightfoot
the proper objective in an editor of Paul could never be less than 'the restitution of a more ancient and purer text'.[75] His position as the latest in time,
together with a promise of assistance from Westcott and Hort (already well
advanced with their epoch making text),[76] created the possibility that, with
improved tools, an admittedly inferior workman might aspire to come closer
to the autograph of St Paul than the existing text of some well known editor.

Lightfoot's conception of textual study was the history of the text. Though
never producing anything so elaborate as Hort's later formulation,[77] his practice shows that he followed similar principles, based on the same historical
assumptions.[78] At its simplest, appeal to manuscript authority meant finding where the preponderance of evidence lay.[79] Since the most supported
was not always the best reading, it was also necessary to evaluate the MSS.
After differentiation according to type, quality was established by antiquity,
of the MS itself or its source. Implicit in this approach was the organization
of the MSS into families descending from a parent text to find those of independent value, a procedure later made explicit in preparing the edition of the
Apostolic Fathers.[80] Emphasis on "growth" from a germ in finding the earliest attestation, and use of the family metaphor itself, point to the assimilation of Lightfoot's textual criticism to the organic conception of history.[81]

The same developmental outlook was evident in Lightfoot's treatment of
variant readings. When external authority did not establish a *prima facie*
case for one reading over another, the key to restoring the text was the recognition that it had had a history, which, in theory at least, could be read
backwards to the original, by means of the traces left in the MS tradition.
Variants were treated as the result of antecedent causes, usually traceable to
the honesty and care of the scribe. Doctrinal preferences, ascetic bias, litur-
gical usage, the desire to avoid an historical difficulty or emphasize supernatural agency and attempts to bring one Epistle or Gospel into literal con-

---

[73] RE 88-9.
[74] In editions of 1831 & 1842-50.
[75] PC 79.
[76] On which, see Patrick, *Hort*, 9, 21-2, 34, 76-84.
[77] On Hort's "Introduction" to the Westcott-Hort text, see Patrick, "A Study of the Writings of F.J.A. Hort," ch. 4.
[78] Hort's approach is endorsed at BE 373-4. Cf. the example on 380.
[79] Cf. AF II.1².25.
[80] BE 373; AF II.1².xiii.
[81] The eclectic approach of the twentieth century highlights what was done in the nineteenth. See Patrick, "A Study of the Writings of F.J.A. Hort," ch. 4.

formity with another by substitution or correction, were the main distorting influences.[82] Allowance had also to be made for the officiousness of copyists in matters of grammar and style. These considerations gave rise to several rules to guide conjecture about what had happened in the transmission of the text. For example, a more difficult reading should be preferred to a simpler.[83] However, the influence of Lightfoot's understanding of what happens in history was clearest in the principle, "The reading which explains all the rest may safely be adopted as the original".[84]

Lightfoot also attempted to explain the mode of the text. This was because, as Hort appreciated, he accepted the principle that the way to understand a great writer like Paul was by faith in his language.[85] Exact investigation of grammar and vocabulary therefore became the hallmark of Lightfoot's approach to what Jowett had called the "outward body" of Scripture.[86] In the notes the reasons for choosing words, and even forms of words, were set out. Hebraisms, Aramaisms, quotations, grammatical peculiarities, deranged word order, and exceptional and difficult constructions were explained as the product of semantic or stylistic intention, characteristic usage, or response to circumstance. There had not been much of this in Jowett, whose more literary approach did not seek to discover anything behind the text.[87] It did have some counterpart in Ellicott, but the naturalism of Lightfoot's historical conception of language as an event in the past, with identifiable causes in the intention, situation and language experience of the writer, stood out beside his commitment to the literal sense. Ellicott's rigorously grammatical notes were justified on the grounds that no pains should be spared in finding the meaning when the locus of inspiration was the letter of the text.[88] Sustained by the view of the new philology, that language was thought, and the religious interpretation of thought as the vehicle of revelation, Lightfoot invoked no such piety.[89]

---

[82] OFR *passim*; Smith (ed.), *Dictionary of the Bible*, III.1079 col. 2; BE 237 n. 2, 297-8.

[83] Eg. Acts I-VIII, 57 v. "Nothing but the absolute badness of this reading would justify us in disregarding such a mass of authority, as I think Tisch[endorf] has rightly done." Cf. BE 384: "a deviation has far higher value, as evidence, than a coincidence."

[84] Cf. AF II.1².xiii, 546-8.

[85] DNB XI.1116. See further below for Lightfoot's defence of the principle against Jowett.

[86] Jowett, "Interpretation," 389. Edwards, "Lightfoot," 75-81, 137-69.

[87] That Jowett was not an historical critic is the main thesis of James Barr, "Jowett and the Reading of the Bible 'Like Any Other Book'," *Horizons in Biblical Theology* 4 & 5 (December 1982-June 1983) 1-44.

[88] Ellicott, *Galatians*, iii ff.

[89] On these aspects of the 'new philology', see Burrow, "Uses of Philology in Victorian Britain," 192-3.

The same attitude governed his attempts to bring out the meaning of the text. Emphasis upon "context" and "natural meaning" show that the intention was to establish the idea conveyed by words and expressions at the time of writing.[90] The historical aim of finding what the text had meant, rather than what it had come to mean, was the same objective Jowett had set up as the aim of Biblical interpretation.[91] On the other hand, Lightfoot did not idealize the text like Jowett, who thought the words themselves, and hence language study, relatively unimportant.[92] Accordingly there is in Lightfoot's notes a greater semantic intricacy. They explored the range of ideas involved in the language, resolved ambiguities, and differentiated possible senses. The referents of technical terms and allusions, and the background and point of metaphors and obscure expressions were provided. Modulations in tone and shifts of emphasis were also traced. Together these procedures fulfilled Jowett's condition that interpretation should allow "for peculiarities of style and language, and modes of thought and figures of speech", but the greater respect for language brought Lightfoot closer than Jowett to realizing the shared hermeneutic ideal of making the interpretation of the text its original meaning.

Lightfoot's exegesis was also congruent with Jowett's second principle, "interpret Scripture from itself".[93] Paul's sense was established primarily from his own usage and thought. After that Lightfoot referred to the wider fields of New Testament and LXX Greek. This was followed, in a manner that had no parallel in Jowett (who thought the meaning of Biblical words should be ascertained from the Bible only)[94] by a consideration of Jewish and Classical authors. Despite this clear preference for Biblical and Hellenistic Greek, it is often said that Lightoot's method was too Classical.[95] This is the criticism of hindsight, when additional materials had become available and new methods had been pioneered, most notably by Adolf Deissman.[96] In fact Lightfoot appreciated the limitations of his position. He acknowledged that Attic Greek was not the standard by which to judge the Greek of the New Testament,[97] and as early as 1863, in reference to some New Testa-

---

[90] Eg. G 157.

[91] Jowett, "Interpretation," 337-8. Cf. 340-1, 368-9, 377-8, 384, 404. Lightfoot agreed that there was no place for scholastic interpretation in the notes. RE 89-90.

[92] Jowett, "Interpretation," 332, 390-1, 393-4. Cf. Ellis, *Seven Against Christ*, 83-6, 314-15.

[93] Jowett, "Interpretation," 382-3.

[94] Barr, "Jowett," 21-2.

[95] Elliott-Binns, *Religion*, 304-5. Cf. Barr, "Jowett," 22.

[96] See J.H. Moulton, "New Testament Greek in the Light of Modern Discovery," *Essays on Some Biblical Questions of the Day by Members of the University of Cambridge* (ed. H.B. Swete; London: Macmillan, 1909) 461-505.

[97] RE 105-6.

ment word which had its only Classical authority in Herodotus, he is reported to have said:

> You are not to suppose that the word had fallen out of use in the interval, only that it had not been used in the books which remain to us: probably it had been part of the common speech all along.

He went on to predict that:

> if we could only recover letters that ordinary people wrote to each other without any thought of being literary, we shall have the greatest possible help for the understanding of the language of the New Testament generally.[98]

To the extent that he was able at the time, Lightfoot followed the historical procedure of using those sources nearest to the text in time and religious culture to understand Paul's language. It was grounded in the principle that Paul wrote in the religious Greek of the day, which had been formed "partly by traditional influences".[99] Thus to Lightfoot the Bible was not a closed corpus, to "be interpreted from and through itself", as it was to Jowett.[100] The frame of reference allowable in an historical interpretation of the text was defined by the entire semantic network of the period.

The word studies scattered throughout Lightfoot's chapter notes and which occasionally followed at greater length as short essays were an extension of this semantically broader method. Jowett had earlier dismissed such "attempts at nice discrimination as so much lost labour", a sentiment he repeated in *Essays and Reviews*.[101] There was some inconsistency in this, as he also called for *lexilogoi* of key New Testament terms. Lightfoot not only ignored the strictures against excessive attention to words, but actually furnished some of the studies Jowett wanted. These in fact were extended etymologies which showed how Paul's usage was continuous with, or differed from, the received sense, and also the reciprocal effect on the word of Christian usage, providing additional support for Jowett's contention that Christianity could transform contemporary vocabulary.[102] At both levels of study, Lightfoot, encouraged by the success of Archbishop Trench's *New Testament Synonyms*,[103] gave special attention to Paul's use of synonyms as "a protest against the tendency of recent criticism to subtle restrictions of meaning, unsupported either by the context or by complicated usage".[104] Jowett's

---

[98] LD 126 n. 1. Moulton, "New Testament Greek," 465 n. 1 speculates on what Lightfoot would have done had he had access to the materials on *Koine* Greek.

[99] Review of Conybeare & Howson, *Journal of Classical and Sacred Philology* IV.x (1857) 107-8. Lightfoot to E. Hatch, 16 October 1878 (Hatch Correspondence, Lambeth Palace Library, MS 1467, ff. 74-6), welcomed Hatch's project of a concordance to the LXX.

[100] Barr, "Jowett," 34.

[101] RE 112-13. Jowett, "Interpretation," 393-4.

[102] *Ibid.*, 367-8, 404-7.

[103] R.C. Trench, *Synonymns of the New Testament* (Cambridge, 1854). P 127 n. 1.

[104] G 157 n. 1.

agenda, it seems, could be achieved by methods of which he did not altogether approve.

Similarly Lightfoot based interpretation on historical investigation into extratextual facts and circumstances, a procedure that counted little with the literary and philosophical Jowett. In his interest in historical fact and research, Jowett's collaborator Stanley had been right and (up to a point) deserved to be followed.[105] Lightfoot's notes were also genuinely historical in the way they clarified allusions to events and people, and probed the connection between 'Galatians' and 'Acts', the other important primary text, which he used as a framework for the history of the Apostolic period.[106] But Lightfoot went further than the illustration at which Stanley excelled.[107] For him recovering the incident behind the text was sometimes necessary to explain the language. In fact Lightfoot's commentary was quite new in the way history and philology functioned reciprocally. Considerations of language controlled inference as to fact, while circumstantial detail behind the text could be the clue to the language. Historical context as well as the semantic field was required for the determination of meaning.

Though first in order the translations which usually headed a note were the outcome and summary of each investigation. Similarly Lightfoot provided expanded paraphrases of each discrete paragraph in order to trace the sequence of thought as the Epistle unfolded, evidently agreeing with Jowett that justice had to be done to the argument of a sacred writer.[108] In both instances a "greater definiteness" was afforded by a free translation as a medium for explaining Paul's stylistic peculiarities and compensating for the loss incurred by rendering the original into another language.[109] This was an aspect of the commentator's task to which he attached the greatest importance, sometimes spending up to eight hours on a single passage.[110] Such lengths were warranted by the prospect of enabling the Epistle to speak to the present generation as a first century text. The ideal was not at all neglected by retaining the Elizabethan English of the Authorised Version. Paul had written in the more elevated religious Greek of the time rather than the language of everyday life. Its dignity and function were represented better in the English of the sixteenth century than that of the nineteenth. Rhetorically Lightfoot asked: "when we have the choice of two languages

---

[105] RE 84-6.

[106] G 123, 125-6, 128-9, 346-7, 349-50, 355, 358-9.

[107] For a criticism of Stanley's commentary, see Chadwick, *Victorian Church*, I.552.

[108] Jowett, "Interpretation," 400-1.

[109] Review of Conybeare & Howson, 107-8. Principles governing translation in a commentary differed from those proper to an actual version where a stricter fidelity to actual expressions of the text was required. OFR 209-14. LO 1-2.

[110] Lightfoot to Sanday, 17 July 1886 (BLO, MSS Eng.misc.d.124.(i), ff. 165-6).

equally well understood, why refuse to translate into that which is best fitted to represent our original?"[111] By using the more appropriate diction, translation too was intended as a device for restoring the meaning of the text.

In that it began with the phenomena of Scripture and required critical procedures to arrive at its meaning, *Galatians* was the kind of work Jowett had called for in *Essays and Reviews*. Somewhat ironically, this was because it embodied two fundamental principles which Lightfoot had earlier had to defend against Jowett, and which were now reiterated.[112] First, against his devaluation of Paul as a writer of Greek, Lightfoot characteristically adduced the historical probabilities of the case. The circumstances of Paul's life gave him every opportunity and inducement for perfecting his knowledge of contemporary Greek. Indeed, in the final twenty years of his life, it was the only language that could have been his familiar tongue. It was conceded that his writings showed Paul to have been occasionally ungrammatical, but only when, as in Thucydides, the language could not adequately express his thought. Otherwise there was nothing in the data to unsettle the conviction that Paul's Greek was skilled and precise.[113]

More fundamental was a disagreement about the capabilities of New Testament Greek. Jowett thought the exactitude and deference to principle in Lightfoot's approach was a mistake.[114] A language in decline like that of the New Testament almost necessarily became indefinite and arbitrary. Lightfoot brought to bear the history of languages to justify the opposite expectation. He allowed that a degenerating language may lose powers of expression as it becomes more meagre through a growing inflexibility of syntax and inability to evolve new words and forms of words.[115] But it did not follow that such a language was more vague. Instead, as grammar and vocabulary became subjects for discussion, rules and principles of composition were laid down which actually led to greater definiteness. Jowett replied that this was no gain: it only led to the "scholasticism of philology". He remained convinced that not much light could be thrown on to the New Testament by investigations of its language.[116]

The outcome of this debate was a matter of some importance to Lightfoot. He regarded Jowett's views as regressive, portending a disturbing return to eighteenth century attitudes towards New Testament interpretation.[117] The

---

[111] Review of Conybeare & Howson, 108.
[112] RE 104-8. G 157 (esp. n. 1) & 220-1.
[113] Moulton, "New Testament Greek," 481-2 upholds this proposition on the basis of the results of a further generation of scholarship.
[114] RE 103-4.
[115] Again there is evidence in Moulton, "New Testament Greek," to support Lightfoot's case. Eg. 499-500.
[116] Jowett, "Interpretation," 392, 393.
[117] RE 102-3. Cf. 'Acts I-VIII,' ff. 4-6.

work of James MacKnight showed how pernicious this arbitrariness could be.[118] If Jowett's approach prevailed, interpretation would be thrown back from the possibility of order and system into chaos. It was therefore a threat to the spiritual evaluation of the Biblical text as the medium of revelation the content of which was discoverable and intelligible. Linguistic analysis, not some subjective influence like Jowett's verifying faculty, was the proper key to its meaning as a divine revelation.

There was one area in the approach to meaning where Lightfoot did not differ from Jowett and Stanley. They had objected to the convention of filling the notes of commentatries with the authorities on either side of different viewpoints on the grounds that nothing so inhibits finding the original meaning as "the traditions of the Church" or "the opinions of the religious world".[119] Lightfoot agreed.[120] The value of an opinion did not depend on who held it. The utility of this dissent from usual practice became spectacularly clear in the case of Galatians 3.20, where Lightfoot simply gave that which appeared linguistically most probable to him from among some 300 available interpretations.[121] But Jowett had gone too far. Lightfoot did not imitate the omission of primary authorities, a practice he thought undermined the student's independence and relaxed the writer's accountability. Interpretation was justified by evidence rather than authority.

Nor was the history of opinion entirely overlooked. Overwhelmingly this meant referring to the Church Fathers whose proximity in time, language and culture might be thought to bring the interpreter closer to the original sense. Lightfoot's principle was to furnish interpretations which seemed "possibly right, or are generally received, or possess some historical interest". Thus the Fathers were used to illustrate his own view (if they had not suggested it), disclose the sources of erroneous interpretation, explain the beliefs and traditions of the Church, and indeed show how those traditions affect the meaning of the text. Where interpretations were disputed, the authorities for and against were given only if "some interest attaches to individual opinions". The emphasis on the development of opinion from identifiable beginnings suggests that once more it was the organic conception that determined "historical interest".

It was in the matter of introduction, one of the new methods generated by the historical-critical approach to Biblical study, that Lightfoot again went well beyond Jowett as an historical critic of Paul. The Oxford Professor

---

[118] Lightfoot was referring to J. MacKnight, *A New Literal Translation From the Original Greek, Of All the Apostolical Epistles, with a commentary and notes*, 1795.

[119] Jowett, "Interpretation," 337-43 (quotations from 340 & 343) & 384 ("The true use of interpretation is to get rid of interpretation.")

[120] RE 89-90. Cf. P 137. Also LD 124-5, 135.

[121] G 146. Cf. on 2.17, 116; 2.19, 118; & 3.16, 142.

furnished little knowledge of the historical context of 'Galatians', and showed less interest in the historical setting as an aid to interpretation.[122] Background matter he regarded as a dangerous diversion from the subject matter of the text.[123] Lightfoot agreed on understanding as the aim of the enterprise, but he contended that it was precisely by attention to historical context that it was achieved. This was because they were seen to be occasional, written to meet special needs and respond to immediate difficulties. "In all S. Paul's Epistles," Lightfoot claimed, "the subject matter is determined by the destination."[124]

As a result the centre-piece of all Lightfoot's introductions was an essay on the recipient church, which was intended to outline "the progress of the Gospel" in each vicinity.[125] A procedure which appears to have moved through four stages indicates what this meant. The wants and capacities of each church were established by an account of its geographical, political and religious situation. The relations of the churches with Paul up to the composition of the Epistle explained the manner of his approach. Because an apostolic letter was not only an outcome, but also a major influence upon, the life of the churches, he next traced the sequel in each to discover what results it had produced.[126] Finally, he followed the subsequent history of the churches as far as the evidence would allow, since in the organic conception, later history could also shed light on the period of composition, particularly in its moral bearing.[127] By requiring that the elucidation of an apostolic Epistle involve finding its place in the entire life course of the church to which it was directed, Lightfoot reflected the influence of contemporary environmentalism much more strongly than Jowett.

The recognition that an Epistle was the product of a church's immediate needs opened the way to new explanatory categories relating to its own condition and character. One was ethnological. The defection of the Galatians was readily understandable in terms of the characteristic fickleness and religious temperament of the Celtic race.[128] A propensity for religious specula-

---

[122] Lightfoot wrote 68 as opposed to 18 pages by Jowett. Cf. Jowett, 'Interpretation,' 384.

[123] RE 86-8, with the qualification on 87.

[124] CS 175. Cf. Healthy, 1879, 4-5. "The Apostle's language is coloured by the circumstances of the time." Also SSP 48; & AF I.1.6-7, 378. On the relation of context to content, CS 34-5, 48-9. On the relation to the special needs and failings of the churches in Revelation 1-3, SSP 270-2. For 'James', Pure, 1880, 7-9, 15-17. Cf. OA 200-5.

[125] G 18-35. P 47-65. C 1-71. For the quotation, P 50 & C 49-50. Cf. "an account of the first preaching of the Gospel among them", G 33.

[126] For the organization of the material into a sequence interpreted developmentally, SSP 273-5.

[127] Teaching, 1858, 29-31, 34-5.

[128] Lightfoot's argument was based on the now generally unacceptable identification of the letter's recipients with the north Galatians. For the identity of the Galatians with a Celtic provenance on philological grounds, G 239-51.

tion in the local mind was opposed in 'Colossians'.[129] Prejudices against Paul arising from the prepossessions of Greek culture were in view in the Corinthian correspondence.[130] The political status of the city explained much about Paul's argument and language in his letter to the Philippians.[131] Similarly Rome was fitted by its position as the world capital to be the destination of a systematic treatise of Christian belief.[132]

A direct result of this concentration on the recipient churches was also an interest in new forms of evidence. Traditional Classical authors were now used not only for the linguistic insights they yielded but whenever possible for their information about peoples and places. Travellers' accounts, of which there was a growing supply, further helped to meet the need to know about the locations themselves.[133] Lightfoot was also among the first British scholars to appreciate the importance of non-literary sources. Archaelogical evidence was used soon after his initial trip to Rome, when the columbaria discovered by Giovanni de Rossi permitted identifying "They of Caesar's household", a finding which disclosed the true extent at that point of the Christian penetration of the imperial household.[134] The willingness to draw on this evidence was the earliest sign of subjoining English New Testament study to the new scientific historiography.

Lightfoot's emphasis upon the recipient churches was not intended to derogate from the importance of the author in any way. The understanding of Paul required that he be seen as a figure of history rather than as a vague abstraction, an end which was promoted by connecting him with outward scenes and events. His Epistles were to be read as the outcome of "the circumstances and outward life of the Apostle when he wrote them".[135] Surprisingly in view of his interest in the habits of thought of the apostolic age, not even this kind of analysis was prominent in Jowett. But with Lightfoot the addition of this component meant that a Pauline Epistle was interpreted as the intersection of two life courses, both of which were required to provide a sufficient explanation of its occasion and content.

The understanding of Paul was the one important area in which Lightfoot was arguably less historical than Jowett had been in his commentary. Part

---

[129] C 97-8.
[130] Cf. True, 1860, 3-4; True, 1864, 14-16. SSO 125-6.
[131] P 50-2.
[132] See the brief notes in the box file marked "St Paul. Romans". 2nd Group, 1858, 9-10. See also the essays on Romans in BE 287-320 & 352-74.
[133] Lightfoot also applauded the work of orientalists. See Triumph, 1874, 24v., 27-9.
[134] J.B. Lightfoot, "They That Are of Caesar's Household," *Journal of Classical and Sacred Philology* IV.x (March 1857) 57-79. For signs of Lightfoot's general interest in archaeology, see S 25; Harvest, 1874, 4-5; SSO 79; J.B. Lightfoot, "Inaugural Address," *Journal of the British Archaeological Association* XLIII (1887) 1-2, 4.
[135] I. St Paul's Teaching, 1858, 15-16.

of the impulse to that work had been the wish to qualify the blind and undiscriminating admiration of St Paul in the scholarly tradition. Jowett depicted him as a man with undoubted excellences, but also as one "whose appearance and discourse made an appearance of feebleness", "out of harmony with life and nature"; and as a confused thinker, uttering himself "in broken words and hesitating forms of speech, with no beauty or comeliness of style, who changed his views of the Gospel to the point of contradiction.[136] Reviewing the literature in 1863, J. Llewellyn Davies noted that this attitude was unique.[137] For all his emphasis on the importance of the historical Paul, Lightfoot did not follow at all closely in this respect. He presented a liberal Anglican Paul, calmly encountering numerous practical and theological difficulties without foolishness or error, and adapting the Gospel message to devise effective solutions of limitless application.[138] Of his shortcomings there was not a great deal. Similarly, and again in contrast with Jowett, Paul's text was never the occasion for theological reflection of his own in relation to current circumstances. This is part of what Hort had in mind when he said:

> his doctrinal comments are far from satisfying me. They belong far too much to the mere Protestant version of St Paul's thoughts, however Christianized and rationalized. One misses the real attempts to fathom St. Paul's own mind, and to compare it with the facts of life which one finds in Jowett.[139]

In fact, quite apart from the reaction it provoked, the destructiveness and historical discontinuities which resulted from this procedure in Jowett were of some concern to Lightfoot.[140] When he came to write his own commentary he avoided it. The full implications of having an historical Paul cannot be said to have been faced.

Part of the original programme announced in *Galatians* was a "General Introduction". Initially Lightfoot thought of publishing it first, perhaps as a separate volume.[141] In the event it remained unwritten, a casualty of the unfinished edition. Nevertheless, the likely content can be inferred from the sermons as Select Preacher in 1858, lecture notes, and the three volumes which were published. There can be little doubt that its intended function was to synthesize the findings made in respect of each Epistle in answer to the questions raised by the new discipline of "introduction".

---

[136] Quoted in J. Llewellyn Davies, "Paul," *A Dictionary of the Bible* (ed. W. Smith; London: John Murray, 1863) II.762-3.

[137] *Ibid.*

[138] For this part of the tradition, see Brent, *Liberal Anglican Politics*, 169-70.

[139] Hort to J. Ellerton, 21 February 1867, in LH II.79.

[140] RE 117-18. It should be noted that this deficiency was overcome to some extent in *Colossians*, the most mature of Lighfoot's commentaries.

[141] Lightfoot to Westcott, 4 December 1859 (LAC).

The historical-critical method required first that each Epistle be assigned as exactly as possible to its place in the chronology of the early church and in the life of Paul. Lightfoot eschewed any quest for originality in this subject.[142] So exhaustive had been the treatment of previous writers, it remained only "to repeat and sift" their results.[143] Again this was a reference chiefly to German writers, to Gieseler in particular. Of recent English writers only Conybeare and Howson had pursued this method with any rigour.[144] Unlike Jowett, who was diverted from historical exactitude by all this (as he saw it) unproductive detail, Lightfoot gave each letter a date and arranged them into chronological order in order to clarify the historical circumstances of their origin.[145] The achievement of previous scholarship notwithstanding, Lightfoot did venture some suggestions of his own. In the case of 'Galatians' especially, he had an important view to advance, going against recent English opinion at least by placing it third instead of first in its group.[146]

The claims of the Tübingen School now required that some account also be given of the genuineness of the Epistles.[147] While such discussions had no real place in the large scale treatment of Conybeare and Howson, Lightfoot followed Jowett in devoting space to them as an essential part of a modern commentary. 'Galatians', with 'Romans' and the Corinthian correspondence, was not really a problem in this respect.[148] Not only were these letters accepted by the Tübingen School: they were actually part of the basis of its position, a point of which Lightfoot made some use in his own reconstruction.[149] The remaining nine letters were more problematic, but Lightfoot defended their genuineness too, with greater or lesser degrees of confidence, insisting upon a combination of internal and external evidence.[150] He admitted the differences that gave rise to suggestions of inauthenticity, but

---

[142] "An approximation to the truth is the most that we can expect .... " BE 215. Cf. 224.

[143] For the outcome, BE 221-3.

[144] Stanley, *Corinthians*, I.23 offers one brief paragraph only. Ellicott's *Galatians* did not consider the date.

[145] ER 393. Cf. 350. For 'Galatians' Jowett wrote only 3 pages on the date, in contrast with Lightfoot's 20. Jowett, *Epistles of St Paul*, I.190-2. Also Barr, "Jowett," 4-5.

[146] OSCG *passim.*; & G 36-56.

[147] This is not to say that he thought a serious refutation was required. Eg. P 74-5. Cf. Jowett, *Epistles of St Paul* (2nd ed. of 1859) I.18-29.

[148] G 57, 293-4. This, of course, helps to explain the absence of such a discussion from Stanley.

[149] G 294, 347.

[150] The Captivity Epistles were of particular importance to him, and although the discussion of their genuineness was to be furnished in the unwritten commentary on 'Ephesians', there is no doubt of his confident acceptance of them. Eg. P 30-1; C vii-viii; BE 377-96.

historical circumstance was always sufficient explanation.[151] It was one appeal of the method that it furnished new means of solving the problems it had first created.[152]

The impact of the Tübingen views meant also that Lightfoot had to consider the relation of the Epistles to the narrative framework in 'Acts'. Baur and his followers regarded 'Acts' as an apologetically motivated production of the mid second century.[153] Against this Lightfoot always maintained the traditional evaluation of 'Acts' as written in Rome, by Paul's companion Luke, drawing on his own personal observations, Paul himself, and other eyewitnesses of the events recorded.[154] It was "the history" into the framework of which he always tried to relate the Epistles.[155] This was not without its difficulties, but some explanation could always be found. Luke's failure to mention the Galatian Church may have been due to a wish to draw "a veil over the infancy of a Church which swerved so soon and so widely from the purity of the Gospel".[156] When no place could be found for the Pastorals he assigned them to a post-Acts setting.[157] Indeed, the differences between the Epistles and 'Acts' could be accepted without undermining the compatibility between them.[158] The conciliatory purpose of the narrative alleged by the Tübingen critics could also be received without damaging its credentials.[159] They belonged, after all, to different genres.[160] Lightfoot's became 'a modified Tübingen' position on this issue because he accepted the facts uncovered by criticism without accepting the critical and dogmatic inferences sometimes drawn from them.

The influence of Lightfoot's historical conception on his method of study is quite clear in these operations. It was important for 'Acts' to retain its framework status and function because it was the key text for tracking God's "increasing purpose" in the immediate post-Incarnation era. The developmental perspective also provided a device for defending the genuineness of all the letters. Indeed the roof metaphor applied to the Pastorals assumed

---

[151] Eg. C 123-4.

[152] Cf. Jowett, *Epistles of St Paul* (2nd ed. of 1859) I.272-86.

[153] See A.C. McGiffert, "The Historical Criticism of Acts in Germany," *The Beginnings of Christianity. Part I. The Acts of the Apostles* (eds F. Foakes Jackson & K. Lake; London: Macmillan, 1922) II.II.363-95. Gasque, *Acts*, ch. 2.

[154] Lightfoot's views on Acts expressed periodically throughout his career were given systematic expression in *A Dictionary of the Bible* (2nd ed.; eds W. Smith & J.M. Fuller; London: John Murray, 1893) I.1.25-43.

[155] G 21-5, 38-40. P 2, 49-62. C 23-31.

[156] G 21.

[157] BE 399-410 & 421-37.

[158] G 349-50.

[159] G 358-9.

[160] P 39-40.

what it was trying to show. In questions of chronology, however, the effect was most direct.[161]

In dating 'Galatians' Lightfoot placed it third in its group, between '2 Corinthians' and 'Romans'. This was because "the Galatians *has greater affinity to either the Romans or 2 Corinthians than the one has to the other*, and therefore in absence of sufficient proof to the contrary, may be regarded chronologically as a link between the two".[162] Clearly this sequence seemed likely because of its conformity with his own gradualist-evolutionist expectations of how things happen. "I venture to think it will be seen," Lightfoot added, "that this position renders the sequence ... more gradual and regular, and is therefore in some degree more appropriate."[163] The tenuousness of this position was acknowledged, but the results pressed nevertheless. When Lightfoot returned to the subject in 1865 he was less diffident.[164] The same order was maintained specifically to preserve the continuity of thought and expression. 'Galatians', "the rough model", was placed earlier than 'Romans', "the finished statue", because 'The matter, which in the one epistle is personal and fragmentary, elicited by the special needs of an individual church, is in the other generalised and arranged so as to form a comprehensive and systematic treatise".[165] This order supported his diffusionist view of early Christianity, but was also to some extent the outcome of it.

This same gradualist evolutionism affected the way Lightfoot arranged the evidence in presenting his case. Passages were juxtaposed to produce an increasingly elaborate expression of similar lines of thought.[166] It was presumed that Paul profited by experience, with passages being connected as cause and effect.[167] Even when the history of the period was used as a check on the suggested date, the assumptions which produced it became manifest. Paul's sufferings as reflected in 'Galatians' were represented as a natural sequel to what had gone before.[168] In the matter of Judaic opposition Lightfoot was also reassured because in his sequence the heresy combated in 'Galatians' was "much more matured" and there is "a growing fulness in St Paul's exposition of those doctrines with which the errors of the Judaizers were in direct conflict".[169]

---

[161] I. St Paul's Teaching, 1858, 23-4, for Lightfoot's methods of dating.

[162] OSCG 310-11. The emphasis is in the original.

[163] OSCG 297.

[164] G 36-56.

[165] G 49. Cf. OSCG 319-26. See also BE 231-2, on 'Romans' regarding 'Galatians' and 'Corinthians'. The possibility that Galatians was an abbreviated application to local circumstances of the more generalized document was not considered.

[166] OSCG 316-17.

[167] OSCG 317-18.

[168] G 50-2.

[169] G 53-4. Cf. the arguments for finding the place of 'Philippians' in its group. P 30-46.

Nevertheless, this reconstruction is important as the clue to the development of Lightfoot's Pauline scholarship, at least in its published form.[170] The intention to work chronologically was to some extent adhered to. The first group of Epistles, and 'Romans' from the second group, were covered in Smith's *Dictionary of the Bible*. The Corinthian correspondence was skipped as 'Galatians' became the subject of the first commentary, probably because of its relevance to the Tübingen controversy and its shortness, which held out the prospect of imminent publication. Lightfoot then settled down with the Epistles of the first Roman Captivity. Three out of the four letters were brought to a publishable state. They too were short, but they were also the writings of the speculative Paul to whom Lightfoot looked (with St John and 'Hebrews') for guidance in the present state of the Church. With the historical controversy over Christian origins emanating from Germany more or less settled in *Galatians*, the immediate needs of the English Church took over as the main determinant of subject choice. Accordingly *Philippians* and *Colossians* became vehicles of the incarnational Christianity, with its development in the Logos doctrine, in which Lightfoot saw the resources for dealing with the intellectual and ethical challenges of the day. Thus his Pauline studies too were a reflection of the main intellectual development of his career, and a means of promoting its aims.

The same quantitative perspective on change informed Lightfoot's attempt to view the Pauline letters as a whole. The half-title of the commentaries indicates that it was his intention to locate each Epistle within the main phases of the Apostle's career.[171] Beyond that his aim was to establish the history and doctrinal connection of the entire corpus.[172] From the traces of this purpose in subsequent writings on the subject, there is no reason to doubt that he would have reproduced the substance of the 1858 sermons as Select Preacher. Nor is there any reason to think that Lightfoot was any more willing to consider the full historical implications of differentiating the Epistles according to time, circumstance and teaching. Paul's career, as reflected in his letters, was seen, like history itself, as a growth "from more to more". By tracing this organic development, the "General Introduction" would have brought out the essential teleology Lightfoot discerned within the corpus. The changes encompassed were providentially ordered to provide the Church with a full and duly sequenced body of teaching to guide and regulate its historical life.

---

[170] Lightfoot's lectures on Paul do not fit this (or apparently any) pattern. See Appendix 2.

[171] In G, "II. The Third Apostolic Journey. 3. Epistle to the Galatians". P & C share "III. The First Roman Captivity" and are differentiated as "1. Epistle to the Philippians" & "2. Epistle to the Colossians. 3. Epistle to Philemon".

[172] Lightfoot to Westcott, 4 December 1859 (LAC).

This was Lightfoot's answer to the problem of the unity of the Pauline corpus. Attention to historical setting had the effect of differentiating between the components and introducing a degree of diversity uncomfortable for the prevailing 'oracular' view of Scripture. In the face of such contrasts, Jowett had attacked the Paleyan method of harmonizing the scriptural text. "Undesigned coincidences" were not so much in the text waiting to be discovered as in Paley's mind waiting to be imposed. While fully aware of the dangers of forcing the data into a preconceived scheme, Lightfoot was still sufficiently Paleyan to put forward a new basis for the coherence of the letters taken as a whole. Four distinct groups, each with a distinctive doctrinal feature, resulted from arranging them in chronological order. Viewed comprehensively, "a rule of sequence" in the doctrine emerged. This protected his outlook from the full implications of the historical method, from which he recoiled. Paul had not changed. Different circumstances drew out new applications of the basic content of his belief to create "a full and complete exposition of Christian doctrine in all its diverse aspects".[173] The most serious obstacle to the validity of Lightfoot's theory in fact furnished the metaphor which clinched it. The Pastoral Epistles were arguably neither Pauline in authorship nor progressive in doctrine. Lightfoot found a place for them in a post-'Acts' setting where their object was to confirm truths already taught and prepare for their transmission to future ages by making practical arrangements for the Church. This made them acceptable as the roof, sealing and holding together the edifice of the apostolic teaching built up over the previous twenty years. To the Pauline Epistles, Lightfoot concluded, "we must ever turn for larger instruction in the divine aspects of the Gospel teaching and the manifold bearings of the Christian life". The idea of development linked all the parts into an essential unity the full value of which was seen only in its diversity.

The final component of Lightfoot's method were the dissertations appended to each commentary. Their inclusion, again intended from the beginning, was a relatively new feature in English New Testament scholarship. They appear in Jowett,[174] and to some extent in Stanley,[175] but had no place in Ellicott's scheme. Hort indicated their dual importance:

> It seems impossible really to explain either the meaning of the Epistles or their significance for present needs without such essays.[176]

---

[173] I. *St Paul's Teaching*, *passim* for this paragraph, & f. 24 & 9 for this and the following quotation.

[174] In the third edition they were published as a separate volume.

[175] Although the *Corinthians* was subtitled, "With ... Dissertations", Stanley's method was marked more by discursive essays, sometimes preceding, but almost always following, the critical notes on each section. But see "The Epistles to the Corinthians, in Relation to the Gospel History" in II.275-300.

[176] Hort to Westcott, 11 & 12 October 1865, in LH II.49. Cf. 434-7, 452, 470-1, 472.

The introduction, textual notes and essays were insufficient to accommodate the consequences of reading the Bible "like any other book".

Although agreed on the need for their inclusion, the dissertations present a further contrast between Lightfoot and Jowett. Whereas Jowett's were more interested in explaining the significance of the Epistles for present needs,[177] Lightfoot's were more concerned with their meaning. Each of his dissertations arose more or less out of the text and was intended for its illumination. In *Galatians*, "Were the Galatians Celts or Teutons?" determined that the people St Paul addressed in ταῖς ἐκκλησίαις τῆς Γαλατίας were genuine Celts,[178] whereas mention of Ἰάκωβον τὸν ἀδελφὸν τοῦ Κυρίου in Galatians 1:19 gave rise to an attempt to determine the identity of "The Brethren of the Lord" as stepbrothers, children of Joseph by a former wife.[179] In clarifying allusions in, and situations presupposed by, the text, Lightfoot's dissertations extended the close historical work of the preceding notes and essays.[180]

Although less marked than in Jowett, Lightfoot's dissertations, despite their rigorously scholarly and historical character, also performed the second function of explaining the significance of the Epistles for present day needs. Indeed there was something of a system linking the dissertations in each of the three commentaries. The "Preface" to *Philippians* revealed a plan to trace the relations of the Gospel with "the three most important types of dogmatic and systematized religion ... with which St Paul was confronted" — Judaism, Stoicism and Gnosticism.[181] As has already been assumed at several points in the investigation, this strictly historical question involved a reading back into the past of contemporary conflicts and problems, and resulted in a demonstration of the truth and superiority of Christianity, which was intended as a vindication of its viability for the present. "St Paul and the Three" in *Galatians* had shown the way. Lightfoot used it to rebut the Tübingen School's historicist explanation of Christianity as "merely one of many phases of Judaism" before it could become influential in England.[182]

---

[177] Barr, "Jowett," 29-30. This, of course, was the reason for the criticism he incurred.

[178] "To the churches of Galatia" (trans of Galatians 1.2). G 239-41.

[179] The so-called Epiphanian theory. G 84, 252-91.

[180] "The Christian Ministry" was prompted by the phrase σὺν ἐπισκόποις καὶ διακόνοις in Philippians 1:1, but was included in *Philippians* to clear space for the difficult questions that would have to be faced in the (unwritten) *Pastoral Epistles* (P viii). The connection with the text of the three studies of the Essenes in *Colossians* was less obvious, for the term itself did not occur in the Epistle. But the portrait of the heresy combated by Paul required a full delineation of the type of Judaism from which it was seen to have stemmed.

[181] P viii.

[182] G xi, 292-374. I elaborated on this point in an earlier version of this chapter. See G.R. Treloar, "J.B. Lightfoot and St Paul, 1854-65: A Study of Intentions and Method," *Lucas. An Evangelical History Review* 7 (December 1989) 20. The investigations into Essenism in *Colossians* performed much the same function.

Subsequent scholarship has of course found cause to dispute Lightfoot's findings about St Paul, but this belongs to the history of New Testament investigation, not the religious history of Victorian England.[183] The comparison of the commentary on *Galatians* with Jowett's theory and practice suggests that in this context he is to be seen as part of the attempt to persuade the contemporary Church to adjust its approach to Scripture study to the perspectives and methods of modern scholarship as the best means of understanding the text and appreciating its religious value. Between the two men there was a striking agreement about the broad aims and the general methods of interpretation. In the particulars there were equally striking differences, so that when they set out 'to read the Bible like any other book' they did not mean the same thing. Lightfoot was more genuinely historical in his method, and went further actually to make the interpretation of Paul his original meaning than Jowett who thought the text alone would yield it up. Lightfoot's heavy reliance on historical and linguistic techniques of study as the basis upon which the meaning and truth of the Biblical text is determined, was intended as a corrective to the literal-linguistic approach of Ellicott and the literary-philosophical alternative advanced by Jowett. To the extent that *Galatians* commended a method for interpreting Paul by example alone, the medium had been the message.

In devising this method, Lightfoot again had German models to guide him. He singled out for mention Meyer, Gieseler and Ewald, "this truly great biblical scholar".[184] But the important thing to note was that the addition of the historical component was an adaptation of the English Classical humanist tradition with its emphases upon manuscripts, the text and linguistic analysis. James Dunn has acutely summed up the result. Lightfoot insisted on

> the importance of reading a historical text within its historical context, [and] that the meaning of a text does not arise out of the text alone, but out of the text, read in context, and that the original context and intention of the author is a determinative and controlling factor in what may be read or heard from such a text.[185]

Such an approach, which may be characterized as 'historical-exegetical', was what 'reading the Bible like any other book' required. At numerous points in the application of this secular hermeneutic the influence of an organically conceived developmental understanding of history is evident, but this will probably have increased the appeal of the outcome to contemporaries among whom the same basic perspective was widespread. Even in its

---

[183] Eg. R.E. Picirelli, "The Meaning of *Epignosis*," *The Evangelical Quarterly* 47 (April-June 1975) 85-93. N.T. Wright, "ἁρπαγμός and the Meaning of Philippians 2:5-11," *Journal of Theological Studies* n.s. 37.2 (October 1986) 321-52.

[184] G ix-x.

[185] Dunn, "Lightfoot in Retrospect," 75-6.

presuppositions Lightfoot's method fulfilled its intention, which was to provide English Christianity in the post *Essays and Reviews* situation with a
suitable method of Biblical study. On the one hand, this entailed use of the
best philological techniques and openly seeking to present the most up to
date scholarly knowledge available. On the other, it called for the soundest
posssible basis for the religious application of the text. Specific questions
of interpretation, such as those raised by the Tübingen School, were best
considered within this wider framework. Again Lightfoot's approach served
the wider moral demands of contemporary intellectual and cultural life.

The abiding value of Lightfoot's method has obscured the fact that at its
promulgation it was new and by no means universally acceptable.[186] While
he did not incur anything like the opprobrium encountered by Jowett,
Lightfoot did not altogether escape the acrimony of the period.[187] *Galatians*
was the target of a hostile review in *The Churchman*, which considered it "a
very painful instance of the boldness of unbelief in the present day", wildly
associated Lightfoot with Paine, Voltaire and Carlisle, and called on him to
tender "an apology, or explanation, to those whose faith he has so terribly
outraged".[188] Lightfoot was incensed, and sought a legal opinion on the
matter, although he did not prosecute.[189] It is not the libel that is interesting,
but the grounds of the reaction. The infallibilist attitude of the conservatives towards the Bible could not countenance the possibility of the natural
explanation of Scripture implicit in Lightfoot's approach.

Lightfoot was undeterred. He continued to lecture and write on Paul along
the same lines, and in 1874 was still speaking of the commentary as the
work of his life.[190] In the meantime *Philippians* had appeared: *Colossians
and Philemon* came out a year later. The last instalment of the project published in his lifetime, it was Lightfoot's best commentary.[191] In its greater
wrestling with the thought of St Paul, it went some way towards meeting
Hort's earlier reproach. Although capable of development in this respect,
the commentary remained the bearer of an historical-exegetical method of
study still quite new in England and unprecedented in its combination of
erudition and exacting linguistic scholarship. This was conceived by

---

[186] The novelty was appreciated by contemporaries. LD 124, 151-2, 177. Cf. W.F.
Howard, *The Romance of New Testament Scholarship* (London: Epworth, 1949) 57.

[187] See 66 above for his earlier encounter with E.B. Elliott.

[188] *The Churchman* (7 September 1865) 1070-1.

[189] Westcott to Lightfoot, 13, 16, 27 September, & 19, 24 October 1865. Lightfoot to
Westcott, 26 September 1865. R. Gale to Lightfoot, 9 October 1865, indicating that a suit
would not be unreasonable if damages were not sought.

[190] Lightfoot to Farrar, 16 February 1874 (FCC, Bundle 27).

[191] Sanday, "Bishop Lightfoot," 26-7; & the same writer's anonymous obituary in *The
Academy* 922 (4 Jan 1890) 9.

Lightfoot as the best available means of understanding and presenting Christianity in an age increasingly under the power of historical analysis.

In the objectives he had set himself Lightfoot clearly secured a large measure of success. Informed observers were quick to appreciate his achievement. Weary of theological polemics, they welcomed his lack of combativeness, the scale of his work, and the new categories of explanation and evidence his method involved.[192] Just as Hort saw his shortcomings most clearly, so he also summed up Lightfoot's strengths as a commentator on St Paul:

> he is surely always admirable on historical ground, and especially in interpreting passages which afford indirect historical evidence, as also in all matters of grammar and language and such like externalities.[193]

At the same time as evaluating his substantive views, other reviewers noted the same qualities. As Lightfoot intended, the result was to provide reassurance.[194] Traditional Christian belief was apparently under no threat from the historical approach to the Bible, and its position in relation to the age actually strengthened by being brought up to the level of modern scholarship.[195] But, importantly, the difficult hermeneutical questions raised by Jowett had not been faced in the actual commentary, so that the comfortable impression was left that, in the transition from a sacred to a secular hermeneutic, interpretation was merely philological. This remained a serious deficiency in Lightfoot's position, but by avoiding theoretical statement, which at the time unavoidably amounted to theological polemic, he had succeeded in concentrating attention on the method itself and its results. To this extent his judgment in 1861 on how best to respond to *Essays and Reviews* was vindicated in the years to come.[196]

---

[192] From among a large number of notices the best and longest is R.S. Poole, "Modern Commentaries on the Bible," *Macmillan's Magazine* XIII (December 1865) 143-52; & XIV (July 1866) 196-205.

[193] LH II.79.

[194] To give but one example: "It is with a new satisfaction that we discover an editor who is not afraid of the most searching inquiry, and yet is quite content to maintain an honest adherence to the views of his Church." *London Review* (4 November 1865) 493.

[195] *The Christian Advocate and Review* V.52 (June 1865) 362-5, expected it to be of great value to the Church. "His sentiments are orthodox, as those of a Cambridge Divinity Professor must be; and his attachment to the Church of England is patent." *The Athenaeum* 2039 (24 November 1866) 675.

[196] Hengel, "Lightfoot and the Tübingen School," 36, suggests one reason for Lightfoot's success is that he applied his method to the New Testament materials most amenable to it. This may be so, but it needs to be remembered that this was a matter of historical contingency. In taking up St Paul, Lightfoot was responding to the pressures and opportunities of his day. The congruence of his skills with perceived needs was the real basis of his reputation and influence.

The result was the establishment in English Pauline studies of the method advocated in *Essays and Reviews*, and the completion of the transformation begun by Conybeare and Howson. That there could be no going back is indicated by Ellicott's agreeing to include an historical introduction (garnered almost entirely from Lightfoot's work) to a subsequent edition of his own commentary on 'Galatians' in response to the demands of his readers.[197] When a new edition of Smith's *Dictionary of the Bible* appeared in 1893, 30 years after the first, Ellicott's three columns on 'Galatians' had been replaced by 28 columns which not only canvassed the questions Lightfoot had raised for English scholarship, but also reproduced more or less his arguments and conclusions.[198] F.W. Farrar followed up his spectacularly successful *Life of Christ* with a similarly conceived "Life of Paul", dedicated to Lightfoot, "To whom all students of St. Paul's Epistles are deeply indebted".[199] In this change can be seen not only the transition to a critical orthodoxy in English New Testament scholarship, but Lightfoot's important contribution towards it. By causing minimal offence to the contemporary religious mind in giving practical effect to the claims of criticism, without dwelling on the dogmatic implications, he led his countrymen towards their adoption. The wish to mediate the principles and results of criticism was also an important aspect of Lightfoot's other major scholarly achievement, his studies of the Apostolic Fathers.

---

[197] Edwards, "Lightfoot," 74.

[198] G. Salmon, "Galatians, Epistle to the," in *A Dictionary of the Bible* (2nd ed.; eds W. Smith & J.M. Fuller; London: John Murray, 1893) I.II.1101-1115.

[199] F.W. Farrar, *The Life and Work of St Paul* (2 vols; London: Cassel, Peter Calpin, 1879).

Chapter 12

"... not great writers, but great characters": History and the Apostolic Fathers

However important and worthwhile Lightfoot's other works, it is agreed that his greatest scholarly achievement was *The Apostolic Fathers*.[1] At the time Harnack called it the greatest patristics monograph of the nineteenth century, and recent reprints testify to its abiding value.[2] Lightfoot is said to have begun work on the centre piece, on Ignatius, soon after graduation and worked at it for thirty years, but this is difficult to corroborate and may be no more than an inference from the "Preface".[3] A review of the surviving evidence in this area again suggests a more complex story of ebb and flow than that which has been received.[4] Moreover, the celebrated edition of the Apostolic Fathers is the principal monument to a broader interest in the Christian writings of the second century which was to have issued in a "History of Early Christian Literature".[5]

I

It is not surprising that Lightfoot should have been familiar with the writings of the Fathers from the very beginning of his scholarly career. Their use in Anglican theological method was long established, though always a matter of debate.[6] In recent years the study of Christian antiquity had un-

---

[1]   Eg. Lightfoot's "five massive volumes on Clement, Ignatius, and Polycarp will remain a permanent achievement of patristic scholarship". R.M. Grant, *After the New Testament* (Philadelphia: Fortress, 1974) 6.

[2]   Hildesheim: Georg Olms, 1973; and Grand Rapids, Michigan: Baker Book House, 1981, which is the edition used in the present study. Note also J.B. Lightfoot & J.R. Harmer, *The Apostolic Fathers* (second edition; edited and revised by M.W. Holmes; Grand Rapids, Michigan & Leicester: Baker Book House/Apollos, 1990).

[3]   LD 8-9. AF II.1².ix.

[4]   Lightfoot himself says as much when he recalled that "it has engaged my attention off and on in the intervals of other literary pursuits and official duties". AF II.1².ix.

[5]   The only substantive scholarship on this component of Lightfoot's *oeuvre* is L.W. Barnard, "Bishop Lightfoot and the Apostolic Fathers," *Church Quarterly Review* 161 (October-December 1960) 423-35.

[6]   G.V. Bennett, "Patristic Tradition in Anglican Thought, 1660-1900," *Oecumenica* (1971-2) 63-87. S.L. Greenslade, *The English Reformers and the Fathers of the Church* (Oxford: Clarendon Press, 1960); & "The Authority of the Tradition of the Early Church in Early Anglican Thought," *Oecumenica* (1971-2) 9-33. H.R. McAdoo, *The Spirit of*

dergone a significant revival under the impact of the Oxford Movement.[7] As a schoolboy Lightfoot was not unaffected. Prince Lee is said to have been delighted by disclosures of his reading in the Fathers.[8]

At Cambridge the interest developed along different lines. In the hands of Professor Blunt it was less devotional than critical and historical, and anti-Catholic.[9] It was also more concerned with the early Fathers than those of the fourth and fifth centuries. Keenly aware of the differences between the two sets of writers, Lightfoot chose to follow in the Cambridge tradition. He did not aspire so much to be "Deepened By the Study of the Fathers" as to be confirmed and strengthened in the factual basis of his faith through historical scholarship.[10]

This was evident in Lightfoot's first exercise in New Testament criticism. The Apostolic Fathers were used to establish the opinions of the Gentile Church in the period immediately succeeding the Apostolic Age.[11] This was intended as a check upon the theories of speculative criticism, as an answer to those "who tell us that our Christianity is not the same with that of the primitive Church, least of all the Church of the Circumcision".[12] Their evidence could also be turned against critical theories which interpreted some of the New Testament books as post-apostolic creations.[13] From the first Lightfoot turned to the Apostolic Fathers as a critical — and therefore, in his eyes, an apologetical — necessity.

Fundamental historical attitudes were also already at work. Writing of Hort, E.G. Rupp observed: "It was important for him that the New Testament itself is part of historical study and that it must be read within the

---

Anglicanism. A Survey of Anglican Theological Method in the Seventeenth Century (London: Black, 1965); & T.M. Parker, "The Rediscovery of the Fathers in the Seventeenth-century Anglican Tradition," in *The Rediscovery of Newman. An Oxford Symposium* (eds. J. Coulson & A.M. Allchin; London: Sheed & Ward/S.P.C.K., 1967) 31-49.

[7] R.W. Pfaff, "The Library of the Fathers: The Tractarians as Patristic Translators," *Studies in Philology* LXX.3 (July 1973) 329-44; & "Anglo-American Patristic Translations 1866-1900," *Journal of Ecclesiastical History* 28.1 (January 1977) 39-55. For the dynamics of this use of the past, see P.B. Nockles, *The Oxford Movement in Context. Anglican High Churchmanship 1760-1857* (Cambridge: University Press, 1994) ch. 2.

[8] R.A., "Joseph Barber Lightfoot, Bishop of Durham," *The Cambridge Review* (16 January 1890) 134-6.

[9] J.J. Blunt, *A History of the Church During the First Three Centuries* (2nd ed.; London: John Murray, 1857); & *On the Right Use of the Early Fathers* (3rd ed.; London: John Murray, 1869). On Blunt, see *DNB* II.736-8 & 48 above.

[10] R.D. Crouse, ' "Deepened By the Study of the Fathers": The Oxford Movement, Dr Pusey and Patristic Scholarship," *Dionysius* VII (Dec. 1983) 137-47.

[11] LS 193-4. See 284 above.

[12] LS 193.

[13] LS 200.

history of the early church."[14] A similar commitment to historical continuity was behind Lightfoot's almost instinctively turning to the early Fathers when he first encountered Strauss and Baur. As an organic growth, the history of which they were a part could be read backwards to the New Testament age itself to trace the main lines of its development. The study of the New Testament required the study of the early Fathers for its full bearings to be taken.

At the same time early patristics literature offered an exciting field of study for a young scholar anxious to be in touch with new developments.[15] Lightfoot subsequently recalled how his interest had been greatly stimulated by the researches of William Cureton who in 1845 seemed at last to have discovered the original form of the Ignatian letters.[16] More generally, early Christian studies were enlivened by the publication in 1851 of the *Philosophumena* of Hippolytus which was felt to have shed great light on the primitive ages of the Church. The fledgling *Journal of Classical and Sacred Philology* made some attempt to track these developments which promised to have a big effect on how the early history of the Church was written.[17]

Nothing much further is said about the Fathers as such in Lightfoot's *oeuvre* in the late 1850s and early 1860s. Clearly they had been subordinated to the work on St Paul. References to them occur in the commentaries, as special interest attached to their writings.[18] Lightfoot's correspondence suggests that after the appearance of *Galatians* his interest in the Fathers began in earnest. For it was now that he joined the quest for new materials, corresponding and travelling extensively in search of new manu-

----

[14] E.G. Rupp, "Hort and the Cambridge Tradition," in *Just Men. Historical Pieces* (London: Epworth, 1977) 158. Cf. 162-3.

[15] Something of this excitement is reflected at CIRA 251-2. Hengel, "Lightfoot and the Tübingen School," 32-3, details some of these discoveries and their effects.

[16] AF II.1².ix-xi. Cf. the account of the Curetonian discoveries in AF II.1².280-327. For Lightfoot's attitude to Cureton, EWSR 72, 75 n. 1. Cureton gave an account of his engagement with the Ignatian question in *Vindiciae Ignatianae; Or the Genuine Writings of St Ignatius, As Exhibited in the Antient Syriac Version, Vindicated From the Charge of Heresy* (London: Rivingtons, 1846); & *Corpus Ignatianum: A Complete Collection of the Ignatian Epistles, Genuine, Interpolated, and Spurious; Together With Numerous Extracts From Them, As Quoted by Ecclesiastical Writers Down to the Tenth Century; In Syriac, Greek, and Latin: An English Translation of the Syriac Text, Copious Notes, And Introduction* (London: Francis & John Rivington, 1849). On Cureton (1808-1864), see DNB V.325-6.

[17] In addition to reviews of books by scholars such as Döllinger, Baur, Baumgarten and Schaff, each number contained long lists of the contents of foreign journals, and of new books, foreign as well as English. See also E.W. Benson, "On the Martyrdom and Commemorations of Saint Hippolytus," *Journal of Classical and Sacred Philology* I.ii (1854) 188-210; & F.J.A. Hort, On the Date of Justin Martyr," *ibid.* III.viii (June 1856) 155-93.

[18] See G viii-ix for the policy.

scripts.[19] The change coincided with the shift of interest to the latest phase of the New Testament period, and may have been caused by it. Clement furnished an exemplarist christology, though the preexistence and divinity of Christ was not distinctly brought out. Ignatius, on the other hand, transmitted a developed incarnational theology, through which the *Imitatio Christi* praxis was developed. Polycarp was a crucial link in the chain of evidence that authenticated the all-important Fourth Gospel. Lightfoot's main ecclesial and scholarly concerns were drawing him into a deeper engagement with the literary remains of the Apostolic Fathers.

The first fruits appeared as papers (mainly on Ignatius) in the new *Journal of Philology*.[20] A volume on Clement of Rome, the first in a projected edition of the Apostolic Fathers, appeared in 1869.[21] About this time a general article on the "Apostolic Fathers" was written for the first instalment of the *Dictionary of Christian Biography*, although it was not published for many years.[22] Lightfoot was also becoming a reviewer of early patristics materials in journals produced for the educated public.[23] He was at work on editions of Ignatius and Polycarp simultaneously with his contribution towards the New Testament commentary when an event took place that brought the Fathers out of the shadow of Paul and gave them a new prominence and broader function in the life of the Church.

---

[19] The incoming letters from this period reflect Lightfoot's enquiries about, and pursuit of manuscripts of, Clement and Ignatius. His correspondents include P. de Lagarde, G. Salmon, Robert Scott and W. Wright. W. Selwyn to Lightfoot, 16 January 1866, promises to use his influence with a friend of Cardinal Antonelli to secure the information and transcripts Lightfoot needed from the Vatican Library. See also Lightfoot to Westcott, 26 September 1865, which mentions being hard at work on the Syriac Recognitions; & 21 October 1869, which indicates that he had just returned from Ignatian MS work in Paris. Note also that in the Michaelmas term of 1865 Lightfoot conducted a class for B.A.s on the Ignatian Epistles. See Appendix 2 below.

[20] J.B. Lightfoot, "Caius or Hippolytus?" *Journal of Philology* I.1 (1868) 98-112; "Two Neglected Facts Bearing on the Ignatian Controversy," *ibid.* I.2 (1868) 47-55; "Heading of the Paris MS of the Ignatian Epistle to the Romans," *ibid.* II.3 (1869) 157.

[21] J.B. Lightfoot, *S. Clement of Rome* (London & Cambridge: Macmillan, 1869).

[22] [J.B.] L[ightfoot], "Apostolic Fathers," *A Dictionary of Christian Biography* (ed. W. Smith & H. Wace; London: John Murray, 1877-87) I.147-49. Lightfoot also wrote many articles for volume I of this work while he was still (with Westcott) foundation editor. They are listed in the Bibliography.

[23] J.B. Lightfoot, Review of J.G. Müller, *Erklärung des Barnabasbriefes*, *The Academy* III.49 (1 June 1872) 206-7; & Review of *Patrum Apostolicorum Opera. Recensuerunt Oscar de Gebhardt, Adolfus Harnack, Theodorus Zahn. Editio post Dresselianam alteram tertia. Fasciculus I, The Academy* X (29 July 1876) 113-14. Lightfoot was also asked to edit H.L. Mansel's posthumous *The Gnostic Heresies of the First and Second Centuries* (London: John Murray, 1875). See xxiii-xxvi for Lightfoot's 'Preface'.

II

In 1874 W.R. Cassels, a retired Bombay merchant and theological autodidact, published another in the sequence of controversial mid-Victorian books on Christianity.[24] Ostensibly because great questions should be treated dispassionately, uninfluenced by the reputation of the writer, but perhaps because Cassels as an amateur had no such reputation to exploit, *Supernatural Religion* was published anonymously.[25] Divided into two unequal parts, the first was an argument on philosophical grounds against the historicity of miracles. The second began a comprehensive attack on the Biblical canon with an extensive discussion of the Gospel records designed to show that even if miracles were possible, the evidence would not support belief in them.[26] In an atmosphere heavy with theological and ecclesiastical controversy, the wider English public seemed to have been introduced to the world of apocryphal sources and critical New Testament literature with which it had no real previous acquaintance. The effect was immediate and somewhat sensational.[27] Four editions were required in the first year, and a sixth had appeared before the end of 1875.[28]

Not long after its appearance, Lightfoot told Westcott that the book was doing harm.[29] As in the case of Tayler a few years before, he allowed an interruption to his normal literary work to answer immediately yet another dangerous book likely to unsettle English religious opinion. Between December 1874 and May 1877 he published nine papers in rebuttal.[30] Having become increasingly intermittent as the series unfolded, Lightfoot finally abandoned the task. The appearance of a third volume rekindled his interest for a while, and he lost no time in addressing its implications for the 'Acts of the Apostles' in Cambridge lectures.[31] But that was all, and the original plan

---

[24] On Cassels, see DNB. Supplement January 1901 - December 1911, I.322-3.

[25] *Supernatural Religion: An Inquiry Into the Reality of Divine Revelation* (2 vols; London: Longmans, Green & Co., 1874). The fourth edition of 1874 has been used in the present study. The identity of the author was not revealed until many years later.

[26] In 1877 there appeared a third volume which considered the remainder of the New Testament data, and also the Resurrection and Ascension.

[27] On the reaction, see Chadwick, *Victorian Church*, II.70-1; & J.J. Savory, 'Matthew Arnold and "The Author of Supernatural Religion": The Background to *God and the Bible*,' *Studies in English Literature* XVI.4 (Autumn 1976) 677-91.

[28] See the *British Library Catalogue to 1975*, 55.380.

[29] Lightfoot to Westcott, 25 September 1874 (LAC). Cf. EWSR vii-viii.

[30] The articles are listed in the bibliography. They were republished as J.B. Lightfoot, *Essays on a Work Entitled Supernatural Religion* (London: Macmillan, 1889 & 1893²) to which reference is made.

[31] See Appendix 2 below. The third volume seems also to have stimulated J.B. Lightfoot, "Discoveries Illustrating the Acts of the Apostles," *Contemporary Review* 32 (May 1878) 288-96.

"to cover the whole ground, so far as regards the testimony of the first two centuries to the New Testament Scriptures" went unfulfilled.[32]

The usual explanation of Lightfoot's strong initial reaction is his wish to defend his friend Westcott against the charge of disingenuousness.[33] In taking this line scholars have no more than accepted what Lightfoot himself said fifteen years later.[34] His recollection is confirmed by the initial article, which was given over in large part — even though it could be said that "Dr Westcott's honour may be safely left to take care of itself" — to a defence of Westcott's integrity and capacity as a scholar,[35] a matter to which he reverted several times later in the series.[36] But already there was more to it. The good name of several other Christian scholars was also defended.[37] It was legitimate to cavil at the results of honest scholarly investigation, Lightfoot informed the author, but not to impugn the motives that gave rise to it. When the ethics of scholarship were violated, a reviewer was bound to take offence.[38] In taking on *Supernatural Religion* Lightfoot came to the defence of the integrity of Christian Biblical scholarship.

The other side of this motive was the wish to establish where the real authority — moral as well as intellectual — in the matter lay. Against the favourable estimate of other reviewers, Lightfoot pointed to errors of translation which indicated that Cassels lacked even the elementary knowledge of Greek and Latin required of a student of early Christian texts.[39] Some of his arguments indeed were based upon a misconstruction of grammar.[40] Nor did Cassels possess the knowledge of modern languages necessary for the command of the literature on the subject he purported to have.[41] This parade of learning was suspect also because arguments were not always sup-

---

[32] EWSR viii.

[33] Cassels had accused Westcott of deliberate mistranslation in his *Canon of the New Testament* of a passage in Irenaeus bearing on the question of the authenticity of the Fourth Gospel.

[34] EWSR vii-viii.

[35] EWSR 4-6, 11-13, & esp. 20-2, whence the quotation is taken.

[36] EWSR 53-8, 123-4, 137-8.

[37] The honesty of Constantin Tischendorf's textual labours was retrieved from discrediting insinuation: EWSR 5 n. 4; cf. 53-4, 127-9, 138. Though Cassels was hardly to blame for it, Lightfoot utilized the occasion to rebut vigorously the attribution of *Supernatural Religion* to Connop Thirlwall, not only as baseless, but cruelly suggestive of base fraudulence. EWSR 1-2, 3.

[38] Draft of Lightfoot to the Author of *Supernatural Religion*, 26 November 1874. Also EWSR 134 for Lightfoot's thoughts on the etiquette of scholarship.

[39] EWSR 3-9. Cf. 112, 122-3.

[40] EWSR 4-7. Cf. 53-8. He was on occasions extremely confused.

[41] EWSR 5, 19. He was not so well informed as he seemed, and at points showed no acquaintance with the most recent scholarship. Cf. 70-2, 103-4.

ported by his citations.[42] As a controversialist Cassels was unfair and misleading. He considered the weak arguments of apologists and ignored or
evaded their strong ones.[43] Moreover, Cassels did not possess "the higher
qualifications of a critic". Instead of "the discriminating tact and nice balance of judgment necessary for such a work", *Supernatural Religion* exhibited looseness and excessive scepticism.[44] Such a writer was not entitled to
any influence on the questions he addressed.[45]

Lightfoot was spurred on also by his disappointment with contemporary
English intellectual culture in its relation to Theology. Only the year before
he had noted that theological interest in England was at an all time high,
although not directed towards Christian dogmatics.[46] This interest, he was
now forced to conclude, was not matched by critical proficiency. Cassels
was incompetent, but the reviewers, "the leaders of intellectual thought in
this critical nineteenth century", had not seen through his pretensions.[47] With
an irony he seems to have reserved for criticism, Lightfoot savaged the critical reception:

> Out of five reviews or notices of the work which I have read, only one seems to refer to
> our *Supernatural Religion*. The other four are plainly dealing with some apocryphal
> work, bearing the same name and often using the same language, but in its main char-
> acteristics quite different from and much more authentic than the volumes before me.[48]

When the garrulous John Burgon sent him a copy of his proposals for the
further reform of theological study at Oxford,[49] Lightfoot thanked him, adding that the *Supernatural Religion* affair showed the need for such measures
at the present time. He himself had felt constrained to speak out partly because of "despair at the state of theological knowledge in England".[50] The
critical case for Christianity was better than the response to *Supernatural
Religion* suggested.

The importance of these motives emerges from a feature of Lightfoot's
response that has gone unnoticed. Its appearance in *The Contemporary Re-*

---

[42] EWSR 23. He also got the history and bearings of the Ignatian controversy wrong.
Cf. 63-70, 79-80.

[43] EWSR 13-20. Cf. ix, 70-2, 111-12, 123.

[44] EWSR 9-10. Cf. 33-6, 62-3, 88.

[45] This will account for the unusually censorious tone of Lightfoot's language in the
opening paper. Eg.: "his indifference to moods" (6); "the tenses, on which everything
depends, are freely handled in this translation" (7); "it is the very reverse of full and im-
partial" (13); and "all this literary browbeating" (27).

[46] RCC (1873) 227-9.

[47] EWSR 50. "our author ... has resisted evidence which ... would satisfy any jury of
competent critics". Cf. 10 for the quotation in the text.

[48] EWSR 2-3.

[49] J.W. Burgon, *Plea for the Study of Divinity in Oxford* (Oxford & London: James
Parker, 1875).

[50] Lightfoot to Burgon, 2 February 1875 (BLO, MS.Eng.th.d.1-5, ff. 54-5).

view marks it as a contribution to contemporary theological journalism.[51] The organ Lightfoot chose had been founded in 1866 for those to whom "the articles of the Christian faith are not afraid of collision with modern thought in its varied aspects and demands, and scorn to defend their faith by mere reticence, or by the artifices too commonly acquiesced in".[52] It was therefore addressed to what Robert Young has called "the common context", albeit at the very time that context was breaking up.[53] The kinds of issues involved were currently being debated on a grand scale in "The Metaphysical Society" in London and locally at Cambridge in "The Eranus".[54] To establish that advanced criticism did not discredit supernatural religion, Lightfoot at last stepped into the arena of public controversy.[55]

Recognizing that, because of the line he was to take, he might be disregarded on the basis of Cassels' *ad hominem* dismissal of what 'apologists' wrote on the subject, Lightfoot boldly identified himself as such a one and made clear what he thought was at stake:

> If by an 'apologist' is meant one who knows that he owes everything which is best and truest in himself to the teaching of Christianity ... who believes that its doctrines, its sanctions, and its hopes, are truths of the highest moment to the well being of mankind, and who, knowing and believing all this, is ready to use in its defence such abilitities as he has, then a man may be proud to take even the lowest place among the ranks of 'apologists', and to brave any insinuations of dishonesty which an anonymous critic may fling at him.[56]

Moral obligation combined with intellectual conviction to make Lightfoot contest the public standing of Christianity. Indeed, as the controversy unfolded, he linked it with 'the crisis of Christian civilization' in England as he understood it. When Cassels acknowledged his earnestness, Lightfoot retorted:

> He does me no more than justice when he credits me with earnestness. I am indeed in earnest, as I believe him to be. But it seems to me that the motives for earnestness are necessarily more intense in my case than in his; for (to say nothing else), as I read

---

[51] The suggestion to publish there seems to have come from J.B. Paton. J.L. Paton, *John Brown Paton. A Biography* (London: Hodder & Stoughton, 1914) 176. For another sign of the increasing awareness of the importance of journalism in Lightfoot's circle, see Hort to Lightfoot, 26 July 1869, urging him to support the incipient *The Academy*.

[52] *The Wellesley Index to Victorian Periodicals 1824-1900* (ed. W.E. Houghton; Toronto & London: University of Toronto Press/Routledge & Kegan Paul, 1966) I.210-13.

[53] On this, see 18-19 above.

[54] A. Brown, *The Metaphysical Society: Victorian Minds in Crisis, 1869-1880* (New York: Columbia University Press, 1947). For the wider context, see also 126-30 & 157-62 above.

[55] This was not Lightfoot's first contribution to *The Contemporary Review* (for which see 350 below), but it was the first time he used its pages to state his side in a current controversy.

[56] EWSR 22.

history, the morality of the coming generations of Englishmen is very largely dependent on the answers which they give to the questions at issue between us.[57]
The good of society as well as the documentary basis of the faith required
the mobilization of his scholarship against the claims of *Supernatural Religion*.

It is only this last reason which begins to explain the proportions
Lightfoot's rebuttal eventually assumed. In looking back he recalled how
his intention had developed:

> as I advanced with my work, I seemed to see that, though undertaken to redress a
> personal injustice, it might be made subservient to the wider interests of truth.[58]

As was so often the case with Lightfoot, he did not explain what he meant
by this telling statement. But *Supernatural Religion* had a significance beyond itself. At the end of the first article he called it "a handbook of the
critical fallacies of the modern destructive school", which for that reason
"well deserves examination".[59] The matter could not have been more serious:

> The whole tone and spirit of the school in its excess of scepticism must, I venture to
> think, be fatal to the ends of true criticism.[60]

The English public could not be left to think that *Supernatural Religion*
represented either the proper processes or the results of criticism for the
present time.

To this end it was important that Lightfoot establish the true bearings of
contemporary criticism. For this reason he seized the opportunity to continue his rebuttal of the Tübingen School. As its representative in England,
Supernatural Religion — with Tayler's *Character of the Fourth Gospel* —
was the sort of book Lightfoot had tried to head off in 1865 in *Galatians*.[61]
Whereas once it had been necessary to raise the prestige of (or even draw
attention to) German criticism, the need at the present time was to weaken
it.[62] To this end, Lightfoot accused the Tübingen School of that unhealthy
excess of scepticism which was the bane of contemporary critical practice.[63]

---

[57] EWSR 140. Cf. Pure Religion, 1880, 18-21.
[58] EWSR viii.
[59] EWSR 26-7. Cf. 106-7, 110, 115-16.
[60] EWSR 25.
[61] Martin Hengel, "Lightfoot and the Tübingen School," 28, is therefore correct when
he observes:
"When Lightfoot began to write against *Supernatural Religion* in 1874-75, he probably did so not only out of personal concern, because in connection with it close friends
were under suspicion and under attack, but also because of the danger arising out of the
historically untenable criticism which the work contained. He had seen it coming, and
he had incomparable resources for countering it."
[62] EWSR 24 (opposing his estimate to that of Matthew Arnold) & 141.
[63] EWSR 23-5, 82, 141.

It was also indicative of how documents were sometimes assessed for the sake of a theory.[64] More substantively, the specific enquiries frequently impinged upon its views of the Canon of Scripture and the early history of Christianity. It was shown that the alleged antagonism between St Paul and the representatives of Jewish Christianity had no foundation in the documents under investigation.[65] The ranks of Ebionitism, from which the synthesis of Catholic Christianity is said to have sprung, were thinned.[66] Indeed the development it postulated had not really been accounted for.[67] If he was right on these questions, Lightfoot insisted, the Tübingen position would have to be abandoned as untenable,[68] an outcome with devastating implications for *Supernatural Religion*.

In view of the character of the intended audience of this rebuttal of the "modern negative school", it was important that Lightfoot not be seen to decry criticism as such. As a new and manifestly powerful tool in a society that wanted to know the world by science and history, it could not be denied. Lightfoot sought instead to bring it within proper bounds. In particular the captivating linkage with science needed to be qualified:

> It seems to be assumed that, because the sceptical spirit has its proper function in scientific inquiry ... its exercise is equally useful and equally free from danger in the domain of criticism. A moment's reflection however will show that the cases are wholly different. In whatever relates to morals and history — in short, to human life in all its developments — where mathematical or scientific demonstration is impossible, and where consequently everything depends on the even balance of the judicial faculties, scepticism must be at least as fatal to truth as credulity.[69]

Accordingly an important part of Lightfoot's purpose in responding to *Supernatural Religion* was instruction in the true capacity and limits of the critical historical method in the study of the Christianity of the subapostolic period.[70] For it was "high time that the incubus of fascinating speculations should be shaken off, and that Englishmen should learn to exercise their judicial faculty independently".[71]

The frequency with which Lightfoot referred to actual procedures of criticism suggests an intention to educate the English public in their use. In fact

---

[64] EWSR 63-4.

[65] EWSR 11-12, 42, 95-6, 101-2, 219-20, 251, 254-5.

[66] EWSR 151-4.

[67] EWSR 102.

[68] EWSR 89-90, 95-6.

[69] EWSR 26. Cf. 22, 107. On the influence of science on other disciplines, see 20 above.

[70] Cf. B.F. Westcott, "Critical Scepticism," *The Expositor* I (1875) 211-37 (originally a paper written with *Supernatural Religion* in mind for the Church Congress of 1874). Also the "Preface" of the 4th edition of Westcott's *History of the Canon*, dated 1 September 1874.

[71] EWSR 141.

he interwove his papers with four principles which needed to be observed in the study of early Christian literature:

1. Critical theories should not go beyond the data made available by a rigorous induction of verifiable historical facts and an exegesis of the texts controlled by the demands of grammar and contemporary usage.[72]

2. It was necessary to look at things in a straightforward way, avoiding the excessive suspicion of modern criticism.[73]

3. True criticism required reading with a proper historical sense. This entailed realizing "how men in actual life do speak and write now, and might be expected to speak and write sixteen or seventeen centuries ago";[74] and taking the evidence for what it represents, as well as what it says, and interpreting it in its combined force.[75]

4. Simple explanations should be adopted whenever possible. The difficulties of a critical theory should not be greater than those it was framed to remove.[76]

Lightfoot also recommended several controls on critical ingenuity. One was analogy from logic and experience;[77] another, due attention to the genre and purpose of the documents under review;[78] and the third, reference to the actual literary and historical conditions prevailing at the time.[79] Two further caveats were necessary. In criticism it was best to work from the known to the unknown,[80] and the argument from silence needed to be used with great diffidence.[81] Finally, the study of early Christian writings was a field where proof was rarely available. Many questions came down to a balance of probability. Such questions needed to be decided by the cumulative weight of the evidence.[82]

Again Lightfoot commended his procedures on the grounds of their general acceptability. They were of the kind necessary for forming judgments in ordinary life.[83] They were also of the kind that made the writing of his-

---

[72] EWSR 4-6, 12-13, 23, 24-5, 36, 39-40, 50, 51, 52, 75-6, 83, 100-1, 146 n. 1, 169-70, 180-1, 259.

[73] EWSR 22, 25-26.

[74] EWSR 9, 78, 116, 234.

[75] EWSR 53, 219.

[76] EWSR 169-70, 193, 249-50, 257-8, 258-9, 270-1.

[77] EWSR 34, 75-6, 82, 114-15, 117, 120, 147 n. 3, 179, 182, 196, 234, 249.

[78] EWSR 33, 271.

[79] EWSR 15, 53, 89-90, 102, 105-6, 109-10, 121-2, 151, 158 n. 3, 167, 190, 202, 228-9, 236-7, 249-50, 254-5 & 256-7.

[80] EWSR 36, 105-6.

[81] EWSR 32 ff., 84-5, 106-7, 231, 233.

[82] And not by polemical considerations as was often the case in *Supernatural Religion*. EWSR ix.

[83] EWSR 22, 107, 234.

tory possible.[84] His advocacy of them in the formulation of the history of the Canon and the early history of the Church itself was accompanied by the plea for the treatment of extratestamental Christian writings — like the Bible itself — by the standards that would normally be applied to other ancient literature.[85] A secular hermeneutic embodying all these considerations would shed "the light of criticism" to yield respectable results in the use of early patristics evidence for the ultimate benefit of society.

Such procedures, of course, regulated Lightfoot's own historical-exegetical method with its emphasis on documents in relation to their historical contexts. They were also important for the substantive points at issue. Cassels had supplemented a traditional philosophical argument against supernatural religion by denying the historicity of the miracle stories in the Gospels using a criticism that derived from the — congenial for a philosophical attack — speculative approach to the records of early Christianity. Lightfoot himself thought that, as a matter of logic, the critical section of *Supernatural Religion* was superfluous,[86] an observation, it might be suggested, that would apply equally to his own reply. Such a view misunderstands the seriousness Lightfoot assigned to Cassels. By connecting a familiar argument against miracles with the results of higher criticism, he had taken the argument against Christianity on to a new plane. Moreover, it was the critical section which had impressed contemporaries, and there was every likelihood that it would be used independently of the philosophical.[87] It was the novel part of the argument that Lightfoot wanted to refute. To advance the claim that the free use of critical reason operating on early Christian sources actually supported traditional belief, Lightfoot applied his own method to the subject matter covered by *Supernatural Religion*.

To understand this method it is important to recognize that Lightfoot had recently been at work on a history of early Christian literature. The papers against *Supernatural Religion* were in part a product of the research for this project.[88] This accounts for his basic approach, a consideration of each of the major writers of the period. It also left him well placed to develop further his fundamental methodological principle, that the New Testament documents must be considered in relation to the whole of their early church historical context. Given that the point of the controversy was whether the

---

[84] EWSR 22, 107.

[85] EWSR 82, 105, 134, 234, 269-70.

[86] EWSR 26-7.

[87] For an example of one who appreciated this part of the work, see J. Morley, "A Recent Work on Supernatural Religion," *Fortnightly Review* XVI n.s., XXII o.s. (Oct. 1874) 504-18, esp. 516-18.

[88] In attempting to do something like this in *On the Canon of the New Testament* in 1855 Westcott had perhaps been twenty years ahead of his time in English Biblical scholarship.

Gospels were authentic records of the life of Jesus, and that this in turn was seen to depend upon their date, Lightfoot traced the historical relations between the documents of the period for their bearing on the dating of the Gospels. The matter resolved itself into the history of the canon, and in putting his society into possession of it, Lightfoot brought the evidential force of the Fathers of the second century into the prominence he thought it deserved.

However, much of what was known about them came from the *Ecclesiastical History* of the fourth century writer, Eusebius of Caesarea.[89] Before analyzing their extant writings it was necessary to consider how the critic should deal with this "secondary evidence" for the history of the canon. This was because, as almost the only source for the lost ecclesiastical literature of the second century, he was crucial for the whole critical case, whether for or against orthodoxy. Yet there was the problem that this paucity of information on specific points seemed to have permitted, if it did not actually inspire, "the utmost licence of conjecture".[90] For this reason, Lightfoot now maintained,

> The first care of the critic ... should be to inquire with what aims and under what limitations he executed this portion of his work.[91]

The absence of such an inquiry was the first substantive critical deficiency Lightfoot alleged against the case of *Supernatural Religion*. Its confident use of Eusebius' silences was therefore unwarranted.[92] Lightfoot condemned Cassels' method as doubly faulty:

> Not only is it maintained that A knows nothing of B, because he says nothing of B; but it is further assumed that A knows nothing of B, because C does not say that A says anything of B.[93]

On the general point *Supernatural Religion* was again a representative volume. It was a common abuse in the historiography of early Christian literature that these silences were interpreted as a reflection of the state of knowledge about the Gospels in the second century. Eusebius purportedly showed

---

[89] Lightfoot's interest in Eusebius was of long standing. In 1867 he had undertaken to write on him for the *Dictionary of Christian Biography*, "for special reasons". Lightfoot to Lord Arthur Hervey, 24 June 1867 (BLO, MS.Eng.lett.c.297, ff. 167-8). These "special reasons" were not specified, but it may be conjectured that one of them was his preservation of a vast amount of early Christian literature which otherwise will have been entirely lost. See J.B. Lightfoot, "Eusebius of Caearea," *Dictionary of Christian Biography* (ed. W. Smith & H. Wace; London: John Murray, 1877-87) II.308-48. For the regard in which this article is till held see T.D. Barnes, *Constantine and Eusebius* (Cambridge, Massachusetts: Harvard Univerity Press, 1981) v.

[90] PH 404. Cf. EWSR 32-3.

[91] EWSR 33.

[92] For the importance of the argument from silence in Cassels' case, see *Supernatural Religion*, I.212.

[93] EWSR 34.

there was little or no knowledge of the Gospels in the second century, and *ipso facto*, no recognized corpus of Gospels.

Characteristically Lightfoot furnished an alternative perspective on the matter which brought out the true critical bearings of the silences of Eusebius. Importantly this was based on verification wherever possible from extant sources. Thus Lightfoot gathered the references to the canonical writings, and measured them against Eusebius' stated principles of action, in order to establish what the historian had actually done.[94] The analysis showed his "main object was to give such information as might assist in forming correct views respecting the Canon of Scripture".[95] Of the undisputed books, he had preserved only those anecdotes "which he may have found illustrating the circumstances under which they were written".[96] Of the disputed books he recorded every decisive notice. For those in between he mentioned any references to I John and I Peter, perhaps thinking "that this mention would conduce to a just estimate of the meaning of silence in the case of disputed Epistles, as 2 Peter and 2, 3 John". He also recorded the fact that some books had once been treated as Scripture, but were no longer. With these operating principles established, the silences of Eusebius were seen actually to imply authenticity rather than the reverse.[97] Moreover, Cassels' "unqualified denunciations of the uncritical spirit of Eusebius" were answered by the vindication of his method and trustworthiness.[98] Thus a limit was set to speculation in the literary history of early Christianity — Eusebius' silences could no longer be made to mean what a critic wanted them to mean —[99] while the failure to test systematically its major source implied the collapse of much of the argument of *Supernatural Religion* as inadequately founded and misleading.[100]

With the argument from Eusebius' silences brought under critical control, Lightfoot proceeded to his own review of the second century evidence. Of the Apostolic Fathers Clement was too early to be of much use in this connection,[101] but his views on Ignatius and Polycarp, in due course to become the subjects of major editions, were given their first detailed public expression.[102] Their writings were more or less genuine, and an intelligible

---

[94] See more recently R.M. Grant, *Eusebius As Church Historian* (Oxford: Clarendon Press, 1980) ch. XI.

[95] For what follows, EWSR 46-7. Cf. 178.

[96] EWSR 46.

[97] EWSR 51, & 51-3 for the special example of the Fourth Gospel.

[98] EWSR 38, 50-1.

[99] EWSR 51.

[100] EWSR 36, 51.

[101] EWSR 40-1.

[102] EWSR 59-141.

history for both could be written.[103]   They were therefore admissible as witnesses to the traditional view of the origin of the Canon and the early history of the Church.[104]

More important at the time was the opportunity *Supernatural Religion* furnished to give greater prominence to another writer whose significance Lightfoot had come to appreciate at about the same time that he took up Eusebius.[105]   Papias of Hierapolis was important "as one who lived on the confines of the Apostolic age, and seems to have conversed with the personal disciples of the Lord", so that "his traditions and opinions possess an interest which claims the most careful enquiry".[106]   For this very reason the extant fragments of his writings had been canvassed recently by the radical critics, most notably Ernest Renan in the *Vie de Jésus* and Strauss in the *New Life of Jesus*. Because of the "utmost licence of conjecture" evident in this work, Lightfoot made a fresh examination of the Papias-question, showing how, against the now common interpretation of the "Preface" — that Papias had used the oral traditions to frame a Gospel narrative of his own — his work was an exposition of written records which could be identified with the four canonical Gospels, a view which carried their existence as received documents back to an early period in the second century.

All of this was now repeated at greater length because of Cassels' vigorous reaffirmation of the alleged discovery of critical scholarship.[107]   Some careful criticism of the *Chronicon Paschale* of the seventh century was added to remove the martyrdom of Papias from history, and negate thereby the assertion that "a writer who suffered martyrdom under Marcus Aurelius, *ca.* A.D. 165, can scarcely have been a hearer of the Apostles". Against the claim that Papias' "Exposition" was intended as a more complete record of the discourses of Jesus than any previously existing, written to provide "a more reliable source of information regarding Evangelical history" along with his own expositions, Lightfoot defended "explanation" instead of "ennarration" as the proper translation of ἐξήγησις, to make it clear that Papias had written a commentary on a text.[108]   The "interpretations" which he hoped to correct by oral traditions were not Evangelical records, but current books commenting on these records by Gnostic teachers.

---

[103] The difficulty arose in connection with the Ignatian Epistles. Lightfoot was still undecided whether the Curetonian or Vossian recension was genuine, although convinced that one or other was. See further on 364 & 368 below.

[104] For their bearing on this question, see 357 & 360-4 below.

[105] In a response which aspired to cover the whole ground, consideration of Papias took up a quarter of what was eventually published.

[106] J.B. Lightfoot, "Papias of Hierapolis," *The Contemporary Review* V (August 1867) 397-417 (400 for the quote). Cf. EWSR 142, 151.

[107] See esp. *Supernatural Religion,* I.485.

[108] EWSR 156-7.

Papias' testimony did not mention the Third or Fourth Gospels. Cassels predictably inferred that he was unacquainted with them, but again such confident assertions were unjustified by the meagre data.[109] Some indica tions afforded a presumption of familiarity with 'Luke', but they warranted no confidence.[110] On the other hand, circumstantial evidence engendered a high degree of probability in the case of 'John'. From the literature of the period Lightfoot was able to cite five indications that the Fourth Gospel was known to Papias.[111] This furnished a picture quite different from that of *Supernatural Religion*. Instead of being the author of his own "gospel" based on oral tradition, Papias emerged from the investigation as a commentator on the four canonical Gospels concerned to use oral tradition to correct gnostic interpretation, a finding which, in Lightfoot's judgment, tended to authenticate the whole Gospel tradition.

Finally, *Supernatural Religion* required that the critical significance of Irenaeus be made clear. For Lightfoot he was "the most important of all witnesses to the Canonical writings of the New Testament", especially the Gospels.[112] Of the books that he knew, it was clear that:

> He treats them as on a level with the Canonical books of the Old Testament; he cites them as Scripture in the same way; he attributes them to the respective authors whose names they bear; he regards them as writings handed down in the several Churches from the beginning; he fills his pages with quotations from them; ... he assumes an acquaintance with and a recognition of them in his readers.[113]

Yet (in a manner reminiscent of his treatment of Eusebius) Cassels dismissed his evidence with the *ad hominem* "the uncritical character of the Fathers".[114] While the shortcomings of Irenaeus could hardly be ignored,[115] a proper critical evaluation brought out three important characteristics:

1. He was well placed to know the mind of the earlier Church with regard to the Canonical writings.[116]

2. He was not an isolated individual but a representative witness whose evidence incorporated "a whole phalanx of past and contemporaneous authority".[117]

3. Independently corroborated from all around the Mediterranean, he trans-

---

[109] EWSR 181-3, 185.

[110] *Ibid.,* 186.

[111] Lightfoot also put into perspective a passage from a late anonymous author who claimed Papias as John's amanuensis. EWSR 209-14.

[112] EWSR 260. Cf. 52-3, 262-3, 264.

[113] EWSR 261-2.

[114] EWSR 263-4, 268-9. Cf. 53, 104-5.

[115] EWSR 269-70, 271. Cf. 229.

[116] EWSR 264-6. Cf. 96-102, 142, 166, 219.

[117] EWSR 266-8. Cf. 53, 102, 166, 218, 233, 246-8.

mitted the unanimous acceptance of the four Gospels "in a position of exceptional authority".[118]

It followed that there was considerable evidential force in "the authority which Irenaeus attributes to the Four Gospels, the 'Acts of the Apostles', the Epistles of St Paul, several of the Catholic Epistles, and the 'Apocalypse', [which] falls short in no respect of the estimate of the Church Catholic in the fourth or the ninth or the nineteenth century".[119]

More particularly, Irenaeus was the centre piece of the external testimony to 'St John' which Lightfoot now brought before the wider English public for the first time.[120] He testified to the recognition by the Church from the beginning of four Gospels, a fact which carried with it 'St John' of which he not only evinced a particular knowledge but also saw as a foreordained necessity.[121] In this he represented not only the Gallican Church, but also that of Rome and, more importantly, the churches of Asia Minor where the Apostle John spent the last years of his life. Relations with the latter were marked by a constant intercourse, giving a texture and homogeneity to the line of evidence which was the guarantee of the continuity of the tradition from its source. Within it Irenaeus was supported by a number of additional voices — Melito of Sardis, Claudius Apollinaris and Polycrates of Samos — who not only reflected a knowledge of the Gospel, but also a recognition of it as "already a time honoured book".[122] The tradition was also manifestly closely connected with its source. The lives of its leading representatives overlapped with the life of John himself, while Polycarp of Smyrna (Irenaeus' teacher) was his disciple. Owing to the longevity of the main witnesses, the transmission of the tradition to Irenaeus from its origins was uninterrupted. Moeover, there was but one link, and that a double one — Polycarp and Pothinus — connecting the life of St John with Irenaeus. Further, Polycarp, the teacher of Irenaeus, claimed to have followed the teaching of John implicitly, a statement there was no reason to reject.

In advancing this argument, Lightfoot brought before the wider public the development in his method called forth by the need to demonstate the authenticity and genuineness of apostolic documents. To counter the attacks of the Tübingen School and its English representatives, he had turned largely to the external attestation to the New Testament which he interpreted as the history of the reception of the documents in the life of the churches. Properly organized and understood, it created a presumption in favour of authenticity and genuineness which only substantial internal evidence could

---

[118] EWSR 270. Cf. 166-7.
[119] EWSR 261.
[120] EWSR 217-71.
[121] EWSR 263-4.
[122] EWSR 240. Cf. 53.

overturn. While sophisticated in its application, this attitude was in fact an expression in criticism of that component of Lightfoot's general historical outlook which looked to duly accredited facts as making known the conditions of life and regulating expectations accordingly. By setting the testimony to the New Testament on a proper footing, he had aimed to introduce this effect into the discussion of the early history of Christianity. His findings, and the method by which they were achieved, needed to become established in English public doctrine.

Well before the end of 1876 Lightfoot's response to Cassels was virtually completed.[123] The initial impact of *Supernatural Religion* on the English public had passed, and there was some evidence that his own papers had had their intended effect. Lightfoot seemed also to tire of the undertaking, as other scholarly matters pressed in the wake of new manuscript discoveries.[124] Moreover, although he had not covered the entire ground of the subject, he had by this point demonstrated sufficiently both Cassels' critical shortcomings and also the earliness and continuity of the second century testimony to the New Testament documents — especially the Gospels — an achievement he assumed carried their historicity. Having confronted *Supernatural Religion* with the facts which a properly conducted criticism made available, Lightfoot allowed the series to lapse and drew no formal conclusion.[125] On the matter of the bearing for Christian evidences of the second century reception of the New Testament, he had said enough to meet the immediate need.

Within the Church what he had said produced reassurance. Letters flowed in thanking Lightfoot for his achievement.[126] It was envisaged that the substance of the papers would be imparted to candidates for the ministry at the new theological halls for Evangelicals at Oxford and Cambridge, then in the process of formation, partly as a result of the alarm created by *Supernatural Religion*.[127] Liddon wanted them published separately for use as "Apologetica" in the examinations set by the Oxford Board of Theological Studies.[128] The often repeated anecdote about *Supernatural Religion* be-

---

[123] After a break of nine months, almost as an afterthought, Lightfoot published a further paper on the *Diatessaron* of Tatian (in which he argued against *Supernatural Religion* that the tradition that the second century writer Tatian composed a harmony of the four gospels which he named *Diatessaron* could be accepted). EWSR 272-87.

[124] CIRA v-vii.

[125] Significantly he had also abandoned the project of a history of early Christian literature around this time. CIRA vi.

[126] Letters to Lightfoot from Muir (18 January), Mayor (14 February), Carey (7 March), Pullibank (9 March), Dale (18 May) & Abbot (24 August) in 1875; & from F.C. Cook, 2 March 1877.

[127] Bullock, *History of Ridley Hall Cambridge*, I.67-8, 83-4, 120-1. Harford & MacDonald, *Moule*, 91-2.

[128] Liddon to Lightfoot, 15 February 1878.

coming a glut on the second hand market suggests that Lightfoot was also successful in undermining the book in the eyes of the wider reading public.[129]

Lightfoot's effect on the critical reaction was equally important. William Sanday described the effect of the *Contemporary Review* papers upon himself:

> Seeing the turn that Dr Lightfoot's review was taking, and knowing how utterly vain it would be for any one else to go over the same ground, I felt myself more at liberty to follow a natural bent in confining myself pretty closely to the internal aspect of the enquiry. My object has been chiefly to test in detail the alleged quotations from our Gospels, while Dr Lightfoot has taken a wider sweep in collecting and bringing to bear the collateral matter of which his unrivalled knowledge of the early Christian literature gave him such command.[130]

C.A. Row also wrote a reply at the request of the Christian Evidences Society, and followed it with a course of Bampton Lectures in 1877.[131] Such contributions assumed that the appeal to facts benefited Christianity and by doing so adapted the empirical tradition of Christian evidences to historical criticism.[132] In claiming the method for traditional belief in his own work, and by urging Churchmen to concentrate on the history of the communication of the Biblical revelation, Lightfoot led the way in the creation of a new

---

[129] LD 9-10. Cf. 154-5.

[130] W. Sanday, *The Gospels in the Second Century. An Examination of the Critical Part of a Work Entitled 'Supernatural Religion'* (London: Macmillan, 1876) xii. Lightfoot's appreciation was expressed in a letter to Sanday, 27 March 1876 (BLO, MSS.Eng.misc.d.124 (1), ff. 154-5). M.F. Sadler, the High Church Rector of Honiton in Devon, wrote without reference to Lightfoot, but his concentration on Justin Martyr was welcomed by Lightfoot as a useful supplement to his own papers. See M.F. Sadler, *The Lost Gospel and its Contents; Or, The Author of 'Supernatural Religion' Refuted By Himself* (1876); & Lightfoot to Westcott, 19 December 1878 (LAC). On Sadler, see DNB XVII.594; & Crockford's (1882) 950.

[131] C.A. Row, *The Supernatural in the New Testament, Possible, Credible and Historical, or an examination of the validity of some recent objections against Christianity as a Divine Revelation* (London: Norgate, 1875); & *Christian Evidences Viewed in Relation to Modern Thought* (London: Norgate, 1877). On Row, see Crockford's (1882) 939.

[132] Skirmishing with Cassels remained a feature of Anglican apologetics for the next twenty years as the imapact of the critical historical method on the history of the Canon continued to be felt. Eg. H.W. Watkins, *Modern Criticism Considered in its Relation to the Fourth Gospel, Being the Bampton Lectures for 1890* (London: John Murray, 1890). In *The Canon of the New Testament. Its Origin, Development and Significance* (Oxford: Clarendon Press, 1987) 23, B.M. Metzger claims that *The New Testament in the Apostolic Fathers*, By a Committee of the Oxford Society of Historical Theology (Oxford, 1905) was stimulated by the ferment caused by *Supernatural Religion*. No evidence is cited, but it remains a type of the kind of production that came into vogue in late Victorian theology largely under the influence of Lightfoot.

"evidences" theology which was adjusted to the dynamic view of the world forcing itself upon the Church in the "Age of Incarnation".[133]

Not everybody was so impressed.[134] Sophisticated criticism did not have to come to the same findings. From the left of the Broad Church movement, Matthew Arnold ran a parallel series of articles in the same periodical,[135] in which he maintained that the kind of detailed criticism carried out by Lightfoot was inessential, and even misleading.[136] More serious was his study of the manner of quotation in the second century which caused him to endorse Cassels' finding "that there is no evidence of the establishment of our Four Gospels as a Gospel-Canon, or even their existence as they now finally stand at all, before the last quarter of the second century, — nay, that the great weight of evidence is against it".[137] It is this difference which reveals the effect of Lightfoot's historical conception on his method of study in this case. The gap between the alleged date of composition in the four Gospels and unambiguous attestation was bridged by allowances for genre and contemporary interests which neither Cassels nor Arnold acknowledged sufficiently, but most importantly by the representative value of the evidence. Several times Lightfoot affirmed that a development was implied which carried the existence of the Gospels back much earlier in the second century.[138] His empiricalism was applied under the influence of the gradualist expectations of his progressive theology of history.

Nor were the rationalists and freethinkers convinced. In 1882 the aging Samuel Davidson published a new edition of his *Introduction to the New Testament*, in which he claimed the advances made in New Testament research by the Tübingen School were irreversible. He also extolled the learning of *Supernatural Religion* and asserted that the critical reaction led by Lightfoot had left its main positions untouched.[139] Cassels himself was undeterred. Not only did he reply to Lightfoot's early papers,[140] but, unlike Stanley twenty years previously, he did not see himself convicted of inept-

---

[133] For the wider developments in Christian apologetics, see Johnson, "Popular Apologetics," 558-77. See 251-3 above for Lightfoot's intentions in regard to apologetics.

[134] EPIKRISEIS to Lightfoot, 27 September 1875.

[135] Separately published as *God and the Bible*. See *The Complete Prose Works of Matthew Arnold VII* (ed. R.H. Super; Ann Arbor: University of Michigan Press, 1970).

[136] *God and the Bible*, 237-44. Direct contact between the two series was minimal, but to the one direct reference to Lightfoot (307) should probably be added a number of allusions (such as 270).

[137] *Ibid.,* 270.

[138] Eg. EWSR 52-3, 93-5, 96-7, 102, 113, 114.

[139] Hengel, "Lightfoot and the Tübingen School," 40-1, draws attention to Davidson.

[140] He also responded to the reissue of Lightfoot's papers (for which see below) in *A Reply to Dr Lightfoot's Essays* (London: Longmans, 1889).

ness and continued to write criticism.[141] Continuing sales of his books suggest that Cassels still served the free thinking market.[142] In these quarters he had his champions. J.M. Robertson (relying on the German Hegelian and pupil of Baur, Otto Pfleiderer[143]) called Lightfoot "learned yet professionally obscurantist", and affirmed that his refutation had been "wholly inadequate ... leaving the main critical positions standing".[144] There was some wishfulness in this outlook which exaggerated the quality of Cassels' work.[145] But the fact remained that those who did not wish to be convinced felt no necessity to think that competent criticism was against Cassels.

Towards the close of his life Lightfoot returned to *Supernatural Religion* and satisfied the wishes of those who wanted his papers in reply available in a single volume. Republication gave a fresh charge to his influence in the matter. More importantly, Lightfoot made clear what he thought had been at stake in the encounter and how he saw his own role. In what was virtually a last will and testament, he declared that he had been unable "to be indifferent about the veracity of the records which profess to reveal Him, whom I believe to be not only the very truth, but the very Life".[146] In defending the Gospels by reconstructing the history of their reception in the second century, he had regarded himself as συνεργὸς τῇ ἀληθείᾳ. But this retrospectivity had a wider ambit than the essays on *Supernatural Religion*. When it is remembered that these essays were the occasional expression of work done for other projects, and indeed that the series included instalments on Ignatius and Polycarp, Lightfoot's aspiration applied equally to his *magnum opus*, the edition of the Apostolic Fathers.

III

At the tail end of the *Supernatural Religion* controversy Lightfoot brought out an *Appendix* to his edition of Clement of Rome, incorporating new materials discovered by the Metropolitan of Serrae, Philotheos Bryennios.[147]

---

[141] Eg. W.R. Cassels, "The Purpose of Eusebius," *The Hibbert Journal* I (1902-3) 781-8.

[142] The Rationalist Press Association issued a single volume "Popular Edition" in 1905.

[143] See O. Pfleiderer, *The Development of Theology in Germany Since Kant, and its Progress in Great Britain Since 1825* (trans. by J.F. Smith; London: Swann Sonnenschein, 1890) 397. On Pfleiderer, see J.K. Riches, *A Century of New Testament Study* (Valley Forge, Pennsylvania: Trinity Press International, 1993) 7-8.

[144] J.M. Robertson, *A History of Free Thought in the Nineteenth Century* (2 vols; London: Watts, 1929) II.408-9.

[145] Barrett, "Lightfoot," 195, says *Supernatural Religion* is the "most amusing" book of New Testament criticism that he knows.

[146] EWSR ix.

[147] J.B. Lightfoot, *S. Clement of Rome. An Appendix Containing the Newly Recovered Portions. With Introductions, Notes, and Translations* (London: Macmillan, 1877). The Preface is dated 13 April 1877.

Soon afterwards the edition of the Apostolic Fathers replaced the commentary on St Paul as Lightfoot's leading scholarly commitment. The decisive event in this change was the Durham episcopate. With so many new claims upon him, Lightfoot had now to husband his time in order to finish what was already well advanced when he left Cambridge. "Whatever his friends might think or plead [Westcott recalled] he held that his discussion of the Ignatian Epistles was the task of his life."[148] Only by working early in the morning and late at night, and while on vacation, was he able to do so. By 1885 Part II, *SS. Ignatius and Polycarp*, was ready. A revised edition appeared in 1889, and Lightfoot was at work on the remaining components of the new edition of Part I, *S. Clement of Rome*, when he died.[149] Fulfilling his purpose in regard to the Apostolic Fathers was practically the last thing he did.

In the final decade of Lightfoot's life this interest in the Fathers was still chiefly historical and apologetical. In 1878 Lightfoot wrote to Liddon: "I am at present very busy with S. Ignatius; and I trust that my edition, when it appears, may indirectly contribute something to Christian Evidences."[150] The importance of the apologetical motive was acknowledged when *Ignatius and Polycarp* finally appeared seven years later:

> I have been reproached by my friends for allowing myself to be diverted from the more congenial task of commenting on S. Paul's Epistles; but the importance of the position seemed to me to justify the expenditure of much time and labour in 'repairing a breach' not indeed in 'the House of the Lord' itself, but in the immediately outlying buildings.[151]

He had found polemical statement distracting, and now, as with St Paul twenty years earlier, preferred an alternate presentation of the evidence in an impeccably scholarly edition. In addressing the needs of Christian Evidences, scholarship and apologetics came together.

This referred primarily to the bearing of the Apostolic Fathers on the authenticity and date of the canonical writings.[152] Something of their value in this connection had already been drawn out in the rebuttal of *Supernatural Religion*. Carefully guarding against overstatement, Lightfoot now argued that, while the Apostolic Fathers showed no recognition of the New Testament Scriptures by name, their language was leavened with apostolic diction, and fragments of canonical Epistles were embedded in their writings.[153] This meant that already at about the end of the first century their written sources of information were virtually the same as those contained in the New Testament. The implication for the chronology of the New Testament

---

[148] AF I.1.vi.

[149] AF I.1.v-vi.

[150] Lightfoot to Liddon, 19 February 1878 (PHO, Liddon Papers, Envelope 27).

[151] AF II.1².xv.

[152] AF I.1.12. Cf. *ibid.*, 353 f.

[153] AF I.1.9-11; II.1².402-3.

writings was obvious. Contemporaries readily saw that their dates were
pushed down into the first century, seemingly a death-blow to those critical
theories which postulated extensive second century forgery.[154]

Several other closely related matters were in view. For one thing Lightfoot
continued his polemic against the practice of criticism. Again he made it
clear that it was not criticism as such that he opposed. Indeed he stressed
the value and need for criticism as an instrument of "the progress of a sober
and discriminating study of the early records of Christianity".[155] Lightfoot's
own practice, in which the value of evidence and the inferences it warranted
were continually tested, reinforced direct advocacy. But to date the gains
had been achieved at a price,[156] for contemporary criticism was often not
what it should be.[157] Among the shortcomings Lightfoot noted that it was
subjective and arbitrary,[158] confused and captious,[159] excessively sceptical,[160]
inventive,[161] reckless,[162] and inclined to exaggerate its strength because of
its novelty.[163] He also found among critics a tendency to "tricks of exegesis",[164] "disregard of all historical probability",[165] and gratuitous assumptions;[166] to the fallacy of the argument from silence;[167] and to maintain the
preconditions of their own theories.[168] Alternatives to received views often
involved the highly improbable supposition of forgery. Towards the end of
his life, Lightfoot observed with tired resignation: "The caprices of tradition
would not be complete, unless supplemented by the conceits of criticism."[169]

Supernatural Religion itself remained the chief English target, as Lightfoot
extended the critique he had earlier abandoned in order to complete *Ignatius
and Polycarp*.[170] The Rev. J.N. Cotterill was another writer of a similar

---

[154] LD 128-9, 138.

[155] AF I.1.357-8. Cf. "the fuller light of criticism," AF I.1.10. Also AF I.1.385 & 353;
II.1^2.xv. J. Mullooly was "provokingly uncritical" in his *Saint Clement Pope and Martyr
and his Basilica in Rome* (1869), AF I.1.92 n. 3. Cf. the commendation of Duchesne, AF
I.1.393 n. 2.

[156] AF II.1^2.418.

[157] AF I.1.357-8; II.1^2.356.

[158] AF I.1.363, 392.

[159] AF II.1^2.331-3, 341-2.

[160] AF I.1.58.

[161] AF I.1.38 n. 1; II.1^2.413 n. 1.

[162] AF I.1.54-5.

[163] AF I.1.52 n. 3.

[164] AF II.1^2.362.

[165] AF II.1^2.399 n. 1.

[166] AF II.1^2.405-10.

[167] AF II.1^2.580 n. 1.

[168] AF I.1.57 n. 1; II.1^2.579.

[169] AF I.2.477.

[170] AF II.1^2.106 n. 1, 284 n. 1, 285 n. 1; II.2^2.268 n. 3, 437.

temper whose critical efforts needed to be put into proper perspective. Lightfoot first encountered him privately when asked to adjudicate one of his theories.[171] Publication was deprecated on the grounds that, apart from faulty principles of study and facile accusations of forgery, he was yet another specimen of that tendency to suspiciousness which marred contemporary criticism.[172] He was subsequently dismissed as "an utterly crazy critic, who has written a book *Peregrinus Proteus* to prove that the genuine Epistle of Clement was forged in the fifteenth century or thereabouts with other arrant nonsense of the same kind — a strange study as an intellectual phenomenon, from the method in its madness, but worthless otherwise".[173] Lightfoot now expressed this opinion publicly.[174] After exposing the implausibilities of Cotterill's theory, he commented on its significance as yet another illustration of critical perversity. "We live in strange times," Lightfoot suggested in reference to Cotterill's class of critics, "when we are asked to believe that Shakespeare was written by Bacon and Tacitus by a scholar of the renaissance."[175] Ten years after *Supernatural Religion*, there was still a need to bring British criticism under control.

Nevertheless it was with continental criticism that Lightfoot was principally concerned, and the main target was still the Tübingen School which he now pursued with some passion.[176] While Albert Schwegler and Gustav Volkmar were regarded as "extreme critics",[177] Lightfoot's harshest words were reserved for Baur:

> No man has shown himself more ready to adopt the wildest speculations, if they fell in with his own preconceived theories ... especially in his later days — speculations which in not a few cases have been falsified by direct evidence since discovered. Nothing

---

[171] Draft of Lightfoot to an unknown correspondent, 5 July 1876. Cotterill had forced himself upon Lightfoot's attention in connection with the incipient *Dictionary of Christian Antiquities and Biography* project. On Cotterill, incumbent of St Mark's, Portobello, in the diocese of Edinburgh, see Crockford's (1889) 287.

[172] Cotterill nevertheless published *Peregrinus Proteus. An investigation into certain relations subsisting between* De Morte Peregrini *[hitherto attributed to Lucian of Samosata], the two Epistles of Clement to the Corinthians, the Epistle to Diognetus, the Bibliotheca of Photius, and other writings* (1879); & *Modern Criticism and Clement's Epistles to Virgins ... or their Greek Version newly discovered in Antiochus Palaestinensis. With appendix containing newly found versions of fragments attributed to Melito* (1884).

[173] Lightfoot to Benson, 16 September 1884 (BPL, vol. 18, ff. 269-70).

[174] Esp. AF I.1.409-14. At *ibid.*, 409 n. 1 & 413 n. 2 Lightfoot's critique is seasoned by recognition of Cotterill's critical due.

[175] AF I.1.362 n. 2. Cf *ibid.*, 75 n. 2.

[176] The extensive writings on early Christianity by the French *literrateur*, Ernest Renan also attracted frequent comment. On Renan, see H.W. Warman, *Ernest Renan. A Critical Biography* (London: Athlone Press, 1964).

[177] AF I.1.346-7. Volkmar, "with characteristic courage," accepted the identity of the two Clements as "an established fact". AF I.1.52 n. 3.

has exercised a more baneful influence on criticism in the country of critics than the fascination of his name. While he has struck out some lines which have stimulated thought, and thus have not been unfruitful in valuable results, the glamour of his genius has on the whole exercised a fatal effect on the progress of a sober and discriminating study of the early records of Christianity.[178]

Of Adolf Hilgenfeld he had a higher opinion, but his work too could sometimes be dismissed as inadequate and aberrant.[179] Throughout his own edition, Lightfoot noted the errors of judgment, mistakes and critical improbabilities as he sought to erect a definitive critical alternative.[180] More seriously, he alleged that the Tübingen critics were heavily biased in their critical work. The rejection of the Ignatian letters as inauthentic was "an absolute necessity of their theological positon".[181] In turn the Epistle of Polycarp was also rejected since, if it was accepted as genuine, it would carry with it the Ignatian letters.[182] In the practice of the Tübingen School the requirements of the theory rather than an induction of the evidence conditioned critical results.

The Apostolic Fathers were also important to Lightfoot because they permitted further opposition to the substantive views of the Tübingen critics on the history of early Christianity. In two respects this was obvious. First, the Fathers ruled out the alleged conflict between Peter and Paul, which was the presupposition of the Tübingen reconstruction:

> The three Apostolic Fathers more especially are a strong phalanx barring the way ... we have the concurrent testimony of Rome, of Syria, of Asia Minor, to the coordinate rank of the two great Apostles in the estimate of the Christian Church at the close of the first and beginning of the second century.[183]

Secondly, they also represented the state of orthodox theological opinion at the turn of the first century. In the case of Clement, Lightfoot noted in particular the comprehensiveness of his thought. Of the five types of apostolic teaching, all four available to him were recognized in his writings which were marked by the tendency to harmonize and reconcile. Ignatius and Polycarp were different in that both were called upon to face innovations of doctrine. Ignatius rebutted the docetism that was rampant in the Church of his day. In maintaining "the truth of Christ's humanity", his teaching also looked forward:

---

[178] AF I.1.357-8. Cf. I.1.55 n. 2, 68-9; II.1².399 n. 1. On the other hand, Lightfoot could use Baur if need be on a point of fact. Where his judgment proved correct, Lightfoot also pointed it out. See, for example, AF I.1.33-5 & II.1².396 n. 2.

[179] AF I.1.52, with n. 3; II.1².xi, 356 n. 1, 377 n. 2. Hilgenfeld, of course, distanced himself from the Tübingen School from the mid 1850s. See Harris, *Tübingen School*, 238-45.

[180] AF I.1.353-4.

[181] AF II.1².xi-xii.

[182] AF II.1².580, with n. 1. Cf. *ibid.*, I.1.57 n. 1.

[183] AF I.1.9.

for it exhibits plainly enough, though in rougher outline and without preciseness of definition, the same insistence on the twofold nature of Christ — the humanity and the divinity — which distinguished the teaching of the great Athanasius two centuries and a half later.[184]

Polycarp was the foremost of the elders of the second post-apostolic generation who kept alive the oral tradition of Jesus' life and of the apostolic teaching in an age "disturbed by feverish speculations and grave anxieties on all sides".[185] Together the writings of the Fathers incorporated all the elements which lay within the mainstream of Catholic teaching. To summarise his position Lightfoot approvingly quoted Westcott against the Tübingen view that Catholicism was a latter second century synthesis:

They prove that Christianity was Catholic from the very first, uniting a variety of forms in one faith. They show that the great facts of the Gospel narrative, and the substance of the Apostolic letters, formed the basis and moulded the expression of the common creed.[186]

More constructively, the Apostolic Fathers were the key witnesses in the erection of an alternative version of the immediate post New Testament history of Christianity. Their importance followed from their Janus-like stance in relation to the past and the future.[187] They looked backwards to the age of the Apostles, from which they received the deposit of Christian teaching, and forward to the age of theology which elaborated that basic deposit. Each in his own way was an important link in the chain of Christian witness connecting the first century with the period when the Church became more literate and speculative. As representatives of the transitional generation, the Apostolic Fathers testified to the course of Christian life and thought in the murky period between the beginnings of Christianity and the emergence of the Catholic Church. Apart from their theological opinions, Lightfoot drew out their significance in this respect in a number of ways.

Of considerable importance was their character. Each in his own way revealed the continuation of that power of the Gospel to change and sustain lives of diverse types which was so marked in the lives of Paul and John. Clement exhibited its interaction with the Classical temper. His outstanding characteristic was "the calm and equable temper ... the ἐπιείκεια, the 'sweet reasonableness', which pervades his letter throughout".[188] It made him a moderator in the Church. The intensity of passion in Ignatius, by contrast, exhibited the oriental temperament in relation to Christianity. Inside the Church this characteristic led to his determined martyrdom. Not a man of great personal gifts, Polycarp stood out as a man of immovable conviction

---

[184] AF II.1².39.
[185] AF II.1².474.
[186] AF I.1.8.
[187] AF I.1.8-10.
[188] AF I.1.97.

amid "the most tumultuous period in the religious history of the world".[189]
Removed from the extraordinary influences of the first century, they were
the earliest witnesses to the morally transforming power of Christianity
known directly or indirectly through the testimony of the Apostles. Consequently, Lightfoot endorsed the judgment of the French historian, Edmund
De Pressensé: "The Apostolic Fathers are not great writers, but great characters."[190]

In their influence too the Apostolic Fathers testified to the continuous
and progressive life of Christianity and the Church. The spurious documents claiming Clement's authorship indicated "that he was regarded as the
interpreter of the Apostolic teaching and the codifier of the Apostolic ordinances".[191] His reputation as a moderator caused fictitious and anonymous
writings in need of a name to promote their viewpoint to be ascribed to him.
Ignatius left his chief legacy in the manner of his death. "After S. Stephen,
the leader of the band, no martyrdom has had so potent an influence on the
Church as his."[192] His experience established the diction and imagery of
martyrology in the subsequent life of the Church. As 'the elder', Polycarp
was a court of appeal for those who sought confirmation for their view of
the Gospel in the oral tradition of Christ's life.[193] In addition to transmitting
what he had received, each was himself a source of new life in the organic
development of the Church.

The writings of the Apostolic Fathers also reflected the progress achieved
in the internal arrangements and government of the Church. This exhibited
its capacity to develop its organization amid new and changing circumstances,
as chiefly in the case of the Roman episcopate. The nature of Clement's
position, implicit in the modesty of his language, afforded no grounds for
the theory "that the episcopate, as a monarchical office, was developed more
rapidly at Rome than elsewhere".[194] He spoke not in his own name but in
that of his Church. The picture of the power of the Roman Church was
confirmed by Ignatius who assigned to it "a presidency of love". "This
then," Lightfoot concluded, "was the original primacy of Rome — a primacy not of official authority but of practical goodness, backed however by
the prestige and the advantages which were necessarily enjoyed by the church

---

[189] AF II.1².464-5. Cf. *ibid.*, 474-5. Cf. "Apostolic Fathers," 148 col. 2.
[190] AF I.1.7.
[191] AF I.1.102-3. Cf. *ibid.*, 53, 55-6.
[192] AF II.1².37-8.
[193] AF II.1².475.
[194] AF I.1.68-9. For what follows, AF I.1.67-72.

of the metropolis."[195] A generation later, as the career of Polycarp illustrated, this primacy made Rome the general meeting point of Christendom.[196]

Finally, the outward career of the Church, especially in its relations with
the Roman State, was exhibited in the lives and careers of the Apostolic
Fathers.[197] The confusion of Clement the Bishop with Clement the Consul
was an indication of the ground gained. When Paul wrote to the Roman
Church, Christianity had penetrated the imperial household, but only at the
level of the servants.[198] Thirty years later, it had reached the level of the
imperial family itself, which was why the confusion of the two Clements
was possible. From this point the imperial household was the chief centre
of Christianity in the metropolis.[199] This improvement in relations was not
contradicted by the martyrdoms of Ignatius and Polycarp.[200] Lightfoot took
a new line when he argued that the Rescript of Trajan was not the first ordi-
nance against Christians but a modification of the more severe regulations
of predecessors.[201] This meant that during the second century the law against
the Christians lay dormant for long periods:

> Only now and then the panic of a populace, or the bigotry of a magistrate, or the malice
> of some influential personage, awoke it into activity. Sometimes it was enforced against
> one or two individuals, sometimes against collective numbers. But, as a rule, there
> was no disposition to deal hardly with the Christians, who were for the most part peaceful
> and industrious citizens.[202]

While the law against Christianity stood, what happened to Polycarp could
happen to any Christian. Yet the intervals between the persecutions were
longer than the intervals in the period from Nero to Trajan, and "humane
and far-seeing emperors did their best by indirect means to minimize the
application of the law".[203]

In each of these respects the Apostolic Fathers evinced the continuity and
progress of Christianity in the immediate sub-apostolic period. In this way
they illustrated and vindicated Lightfoot's conception of history. What he
expected to find in their writings he found and used. Clement, Ignatius, and
Polycarp, and the developments they represented, were assigned their place

---

[195] AF I.1.71.

[196] AF II.1².451-2. Its importance was underlined by the fact that heretical teachers
also gravitated there.

[197] See the catenae of passages bearing on relations between the Church and Rome: AF
I.1.104-15; & II.1².50-69, 476-545.

[198] P 18-23.

[199] AF I.1.21-63.

[200] AF II.1².31-2 on the uncertainty about the causes of Ignatius' martyrdom; and *ibid.*,
452-5, for the circumstances of Polycarp's.

[201] Noted by A.C. Headlam, "Lightfoot's *Apostolic Fathers*," *Quarterly Review* 182
(October 1895) 376.

[202] AF II.1².17. Cf. *ibid.*, 456-62.

[203] AF II.1².461. Cf. *ibid.*, 16-17.

in that growth prophesied in the twin images of the mustard seed and the leaven. This was just as important to Lightfoot's response to the Tübingen School as his direct criticisms. For ultimately it involved the establishment of his own historical plot against theirs.[204] The Apostolic Fathers were key witnesses in the interpretation of history as the "increasing purpose of God". Through them Lightfoot presented an image of this segment of the Christian past for appropriation by his own age.

The interpretation and evaluation of these writings assumed the clarification of the documentary tradition for each Father by means of the method Lightfoot had made his own. Again he produced an edition, filled with the technicalities of scholarship and arranged along the lines of the commentary on the Pauline Epistles. For each of Clement, Ignatius and Polycarp there was the same sequence of introduction, text and translation with commentary, an occasional excursus on a point of language or history, and dissertations.[205] However, with *The Apostolic Fathers* Lightfoot came closer to fulfilling his intention. As his last major work it also exhibits his mature method both in quantity and quality. This was in response to the challenges of the subject matter,[206] and also the need to model a 'criticism' characterized by "the sober weighing of probabilities [and] careful consideration of evidence" as an alternative to so much that was passed off under this rubric.[207]

The difficulty of the Ignatian problem made Part II of the edition (which appeared first as "the core of the whole") the high point of Lightfoot's achievement with his method. But it is Part I, the posthumous *S. Clement of Rome*, that indicates how it had changed in response to the demands of the materials and the needs of the day. The first edition, prepared directly after *Philippians*, contained thirty and twelve pages of introductory matter for the two epistles, together with the texts and commentary.[208] Apart from publishing new portions of both texts, the *Appendix* eight years later only gave an account of the recent discoveries and gains for scholarship.[209] All this

---

[204] The admiring A.C. Headlam felt the need to mediate Lightfoot's results in a reconstruction of Christianity at the beginning of the second century. Headlam, "Lightfoot's *Apostolic Fathers*," 369-98.

[205] The same procedure was also followed for the main writings associated with or assigned spuriously to Clement and Ignatius. Part of the appeal of the method was its capacity to make such a variety of documents historically intelligible.

[206] In relation to the text of *SS. Ignatius and Polycarp*, he claimed to "have striven to make the materials ... as complete as I could". "Of the introductions, exegetical notes, and dissertations," he continued, "I have spared no pains to make them adequate, so far as my knowledge and ability permitted." AF II.1².xiii.

[207] AF I.1.357.

[208] J.B. Lightfoot, *S. Clement of Rome* (London & Cambridge: Macmillan, 1869).

[209] J.B. Lightfoot, *S. Clement of Rome. An Appendix Containing the Newly Recovered Portions With Introductions, Notes and Translations* (London: Macmillan, 1877).

matter — rationalized and expanded — was retained in the second edition, and, as Westcott observed, the exegetical notes altered little.[210] But much that dealt with the historic relations of I Clement was new and representative of the method used previously in the presentation of Ignatius and Polycarp. The last of his writings, the second edition of Clement was the climax of the development of Lightfoot's historical method.[211]

The biographical component, with which he began, was now more prominent. From only a few lines it had developed into an essay of ninety pages which opened the edition and adumbrated what was to follow.[212] Adhering to the pattern laid down in *Ignatius and Polycarp*, Lightfoot's main questions were: why did Clement write when and as he did? In pursuing answers he again followed by now common procedures by seeking Clement's identity in a study of his name, examining his social background with special reference to how he came to the Christian movement, and tracing his ecclesiastical career and relations. Lightfoot found that he was not to be identified with the consul of the same name, as Baur and other more respectable critics had claimed. Rather he was a freedman of the house of his namesake, of Jewish parentage or a proselyte, an associate of Peter and Paul, a survivor of the Neronic and Domitianic persecutions, third bishop of Rome, and the author of the letter to the Corinthian Church. It was also typical of Lightfoot's method to enquire what it was in the Church that Clement responded to in his letter, and to sum up with a characterization of what he represented to the Church. Perhaps more than anything else this reveals the influence of his biographical conception. The frame of reference was the history of the Church. As men of moment it was important to discover exactly what they had been and how they affected the Church's corporate life. Properly conducted criticism gave access to the historical Clement and permitted some assessment of his character and achievement.

This result of Lightfoot's commitment to "a more authentic tradition" and "the probable results of critical investigation" presupposed the findings of the numerous other investigations which follow. As their basis he added the testimonia to I and II Clement of the first one thousand years of church history,[213] a procedure which drew on his considerable scholarly resources in Greek, Latin and Syriac.[214] Such a review of the evidence facilitated a

---

[210] AF I.1.vi-vii. For I Clement he wrote 158 and 183 pages of notes in the two editions; for II Clement, 48 and 51 pages.

[211] For an account of the contemporary development of the historical method in relation to I Clement in German scholarship, see H. Rollmann, "From Baur to Wrede: The Quest For a Historical Method," *Studies in Religion* 17.4 (1988) 443-54.

[212] CIR 3. AF I.1.14-103.

[213] AF I.1.148-200. Neither CIR nor CIRA contain such testimonia. The rationale of the procedure is explained in AF II.1².135.

[214] Although not in Armenian and Coptic which he had also used for Ignatius.

comprehensive disposal of legendary traditions. In fact the problem of the
pseudo-Clementine literature was so substantial that Lightfoot planned a
separate edition, which he did not live to complete.[215] Yet as an authority
providing information about Clement, the Petro-Clementine cycle could not
be ignored for the present, particularly as it was the only one that seemed to
confuse the bishop with the consul.[216] Accordingly Lightfoot traced it to its
eastern source, and explained its anachronisms and manifest falsities in terms
of origin and purpose. As a fiction invented to disseminate Ebionite views
and claiming Clement's authority in its favour, its information did not deserve to be credited, particularly the alleged imperial relationship.

> Where everything else which he tells us is palpably false, it is unreasonable to set any
> value on this one statement, if it is improbable in itself or conflicts with other evi-
> dence.[217]

On the other hand, the Clementine romance was valuable historically for its
attestation of the reputation Clement enjoyed in the later church as an expositor of apostolic teaching.

The aim of furnishing trustworthy information also required the investigation of special problems. The "most masterly of all his critical essays"
was now included to fix Clement's dates and place in the sequence of Roman bishops.[218] Of the three possibilities only the traditional order, which
placed him third, and assigned a rule in the last decade of the first century,
deserved to be respected.[219] The Clementine romance, which represented
Clement as the immediate successor of Peter, could be dismissed,[220] but the
fourth century Liberian catalogue of popes, which served as the basis for the
Liber Pontificalis (LP), had a certain show of authority and could only be
put aside after lengthy analysis in "The Early Roman Succession". This was
an absolute consideration of all the lists bearing on the question, in which
the main object was to determine the value of the various traditions by establishing the historical relations of the documents. Again Lightfoot was
guided by the organic conception of development, as the comment on the LP
as "not a cast as of molten metal, but a growth as of a tree" makes clear.[221]
The catalogues were divided into families, and the investigation resolved

---

[215] AF I.1.157. Among the Lightfoot Papers there is a memorandum of agreement with
a Mr Richardson to produce an edition of the *Homilies* and the *Recognitions*. Hengel,
"Lightfoot and the Tübingen School," 33 & 47 n. 48, indicates that the projected edition of
the 'Recognitions' did not appear until 1965, Lightfoot's manuscript having passed through
several hands in the meantime.
[216] AF I.1.157-8.
[217] AF I.1.56.
[218] The judgment of Headlam, "Lightfoot's *Apostolic Fathers*," 381.
[219] AF I.1.63-4, 343-4.
[220] AF I.1.64-9, 157-8, 309-10, 343-4, 361.
[221] AF I.1.308-9.

itself into a search for the "progenitor" source out of which the variants arose.

Apart from this major investigation, in the edition of Clement as it stands, the weakest component is the Church historical context. For the writings of one who was its third bishop, this would entail primarily the Church of Rome. What Lightfoot had in mind for this part of the undertaking is evident in two dissertations that were still unfinished at his death. One was an essay on "St Peter at Rome".[222] Lightfoot emphasized that on such a divisive issue his interest was one of history and exegesis rather than theology. Only the facts established by his inductive method would be of use. How these facts were intended to illuminate the text is not at all clear, as Lightfoot died before this could be made explicit. But the inclusion of the dissertation indicates that he considered it useful to furnish what was known about the Church of Rome in the period before Clement. Similarly, for the period that followed, Lightfoot made available what scholarship could provide. For most of the second century this did not amount to a great deal, but the tradition of Hippolytus of Portus brought about a dramatic improvement around the beginning of the third.[223] Lightfoot conceded that the connection with Clement was tenuous, but the questions raised by the life and writings of this later theologian and Church leader at Rome were pursued along the same lines used to illuminate the careers of the Apostolic Fathers themselves. Evidently the organic conception that informed Lightfoot's historical-exegetical method required that a text be placed in its immediate Church historical setting whether there was obvious value in it or not.

Finally, there was the problem of what Clement had actually written. Lightfoot resolved this difficulty by an account of the Clementine tradition, separating genuine from spurious, and assigning each component to its place. The character of the genuine Epistle, and its Roman provenance, early date, and circulation in the Eastern Churches earned for its author the credit for a number of fictitious or anonymous writings "in need of a sponsor".[224] Having explained how such a collection of writings could have gathered around Clement's name, giving some account of the spurious writings was simplest in the case of II Clement. Neither by Clement nor an epistle, it had been accidentally ascribed to him when it was attached to the genuine Epistle in the MSS.[225] While Lightfoot could not determine the authorship, its historical significance as the earliest extant example of a homily, had always war-

---

[222] AF I.2.Appendix A, 480-502.

[223] AF I.2.317-477.

[224] AF I.1.99-103 (99 for the quotation). No fewer than six categories of writings were assigned to Clement in this way.

[225] AF I.1.101, 406; & I.2.197-9.

ranted a full edition along the same lines as the genuine Epistle.[226] Much
more difficult were the other anonymous writings ascribed to Clement which
engendered some difference of denotation throughout the ancient Church
when the "two letters of Clement" were mentioned.[227] Lightfoot therefore
added an account of all the letters ascribed to Clement, so that they might be
sharply differentiated and some confusions in the tradition resolved. After
assigning a date and provenance to the nine extant letters, it was necessary
to point out that other letters circulated in his name were the consequence
and illustration of the tradition which regarded Clement "as the interpreter
of the Apostolic teaching and the codifier of the Apostolic ordinances".[228]

Ordering the Clementine tradition also called for a more extended defence of the authenticity of I Clement.[229] Again this was required because it
had been impugned by the writers of the Tübingen School as a necessity of
their general position. To this end Lightfoot followed the usual procedure
of examining the external evidence for the probability of the matter before
considering the evidence of the text itself. Working outside the New Testament, he was able to add its relation to the canonical documents as a new
criterion.[230] Vindicating I Clement was straightforward compared with the
difficulties faced in the *Ignatius and Polycarp.*[231] As Stephen Pointer has
shown, in that context Lightfoot was able to draw on other criteria.[232] But
the important thing was the final impression. Whatever the problem, his
method was evidently able to resolve it.

The most obvious feature of the new edition of Clement was the scale of
the treatment. This followed from its character as an exhibition of the evidence and processes leading to the results being advanced. The highly problematic nature of the materials required extensive treatment, but it was due
as well to two outside influences working on the method itself.

One was the conception of knowledge arising from the scientific model.[233]
By catering to the penchant for duly classified and catalogued information,
Lightfoot's *Apostolic Fathers* took its place alongside the other big books
of the age, such as Darwin's *The Origin of Species* and H.A.J. Munro's
Lucretius, which sought to found their conclusions on a thorough induction
from the available data. Changing attitudes to knowledge prepared the way
for the effect of the second important influence, the eclipse of literary history by textual work in contemporary historiography. Alongside Lightfoot's

---

[226] ClR 173-212; ClRA 303-42; & AF I.2.191-268.

[227] AF I.1.100, 102, 407-20. Three were admitted to be ninth century forgeries.

[228] AF I.1.103.

[229] AF I.1.36-65. These matters are touched on in ClR 4-5, 9-13.

[230] AF I.1.353, 397.

[231] The standard account is still Neill, *Interpretation of the New Testament*, ch. 2.

[232] Pointer, "Lightfoot as a Christian Historian," 429-39.

[233] Heyck, *Transformation,* esp. ch. 5; & Levine, *Amateur and Professional,* 74-5.

editions of Paul and the Fathers were the numerous schemes for publishing authorities and editions, and the proliferation of textually-based accounts. Under the impetus of German models, history proper was now demanding this approach: verification was through original sources. The effect on Lightfoot was to reinforce and extend his commitment to the text. To be sure, commentary was a long established component of Classical and Biblical study from which his method derived. But the status of the text as the key source of historical investigation coincided with Lightfoot's apologetical intention for his scholarship. Thus the method — responsible criticism of the sources — was a part of the purpose, provision of reliable historical knowledge as the intellectual foundation of Christian belief. As a result Lightfoot raised textual authority to a new level in English Christian historiography, and arguably in that of Christendom itself.

The discovery of new non-literary sources greatly aided Lightfoot's scholarly and apologetical aspirations. Epigraphical and archaeological evidence, already used moderately in the elucidation of Paul, was now given full scope in the resolution of the numerous problems raised by the MS data. Not intended to achieve any literary purpose, inscriptions and artifacts were monuments to the historically real and true. English scholars whose work he helped and used in this area were J.T. Wood and William Ramsay.[234] For Asia Minor he also made extensive use of the French scholar, M. Waddington. However, the major influences behind the appreciation and value of this evidence were the German epigrapher and historian of Rome, Theodor Mommsen, to whom Lightfoot looked as a "truly great scholar"; and his collaborator in the *Corpus Inscriptionum Latinarum*, "the great master of Christian archaeology in Rome", G.B. De Rossi.[235] In following their example, Lightfoot took the English study of early Christianity into the new historical mode they had pioneered.

Of course, Lightfoot did not live to finish *S. Clement* to his own high standard. Even so, with the other components of *The Apostolic Fathers*, it left the impression that the highly complex early literary tradition of Christianity could be reduced to order and explained. Though he had not covered the whole field, Lightfoot had shown that the genuine could be separated from the spurious, and that each component could be assigned a context and function in the life of the early Church. Yet the immediate impact of his

---

[234] Lightfoot's contribution is acknowledged in J.T. Wood, *Discoveries at Ephesus Including the Site and Remains of the Great Temple of Diana* (London: Longmans, Green, & Co., 1877) ix. See also W. Ramsay, "Bishop Lightfoot," *Theology* (Feb. 1933) 75-82.

[235] On whom, see Gooch, *History and Historians*, 510; & O. Marucchi, *Christian Epigraphy. An Elementary Treatise with a Collection of Ancient Christian Inscriptions Mainly of Roman Origin* (trans. by J. Armine Willis; Chicago: Ares, 1974 [first published in 1912]) 46-7.

work was not so dramatic as has often been claimed.[236] Old views died hard, and general criticism and disputation on specific points certainly occurred.[237] But others expressed their appreciation of Lightfoot's achievement. One reviewer claimed that he had cleared a path through the tangled growth of the Christian remains of the second century.[238] He had, moreover, furnished a model of how work was to be done in such a difficult area, even if it was daunting.[239] But it was A.C. Headlam who showed best what Lightfoot had accomplished by "a sober and discriminating study of the early records of Christianity".[240] The facts having been established, he began the work of constructing a picture of Christianity at the beginning of the second century. In due course others built more substantially on the foundation Lightfoot had laid, and his findings became part of the orthodoxy transmitted in theological education.[241]

It was this work of this calibre that earned Lightfoot his ranking with Henry Maine and F.W. Maitland as a Cambridge historian.[242] In a manner similar to theirs in other areas of scholarship, he had used the historical method so to order the Christian writings of the second century that he put a new complexion on his subject. This was the measure of Lightfoot's scholarly importance in *The Apostolic Fathers*. English historiography of the early Church was notoriously weak.[243] Milman had attempted to remedy the deficiency with a providentialist interpretation of Christian history based on literary sources, and written up in the grand literary manner characteristic of mid-century historiography.[244] As such his work represented the pinnacle of early liberal Anglican historiographical achievement. Lightfoot, as

---

[236] LD 139. Neill, *Interpretation of the New Testament*, 55, 56.

[237] Egs: W.D. Killen, *The Ignatian Epistles Entirely Spurious. A Reply to the Right Rev. Dr Lightfoot* (Edinburgh: T. & T. Clark, 1886); & "Bishop Lightfoot's St Clement of Rome," *Church Quarterly Review* XXXII (April 1891) 49-68. Hort, DNB XI.1118. F. Foakes Jackson, *The History of the Christian Church From the Earliest Times to A.D. 461* (London: George Allen & Unwin, 1891, 1914[6]) 115 n. 6, noted, "The views of Bp Lightfoot are not even now generally accepted in England".

[238] "Bishop Lightfoot on the New Testament in the Second Century," *Church Quarterly Review* XXX (April - July 1890) 134-59.

[239] LD 133-5, 138-40. Foakes-Jackson, *History of the Christian Church*, 66 n. 4.

[240] Headlam, "Lightfoot's Apostolic Fathers," 369-98.

[241] Eg. H. Scott Holland, *The Fathers For English Readers. The Apostolic Fathers* (London: S.P.C.K., n.d.); & H.B. Swete, *Patristic Study* (London: Longmans, Green & Co., 1902) ch. II. This volume was part of the 'Handbooks for the Clergy' series.

[242] See Chapter 1 above. On Maine, see Burrow, *Evolution and Society*, ch. 5; & on Maitland, Gooch, *History and Historians*, 376-73.

[243] Earlier in the century Newman had felt the problem, and had been forced to rely on Gibbon.

[244] In his *History of the Jews* (1829), *History of Christianity* (1840) and *History of Latin Christianity* (1855). On Milman, see A. Milman, *Henry Hart Milman, D.D., Dean of St Paul's. A Biographical Sketch* (London: John Murray, 1900).

a representative of this tradition in the next generation, carried forward the same view of the function of history and narrative conception or historical plot. But, partly from personal preference, partly because of the demands of the subject matter, and partly in response to the requirements of the age, he cast his work in the new scientific mould of record history using the method he had fashioned out of precedents in the English Classical humanist tradition and German higher criticism. Thus *The Apostolic Fathers* represents the adjustment of liberal Anglican writing on the early Church to new historiographical and social conditions. In the warmth and strength of its reception by those competent to judge, it completed the establishment of a critical-historical tradition in early Christian studies in England that Lightfoot had spearheaded in the course of his scholarly career.

Lightfoot himself had been optimistic about the effect of constructive work such as his own. At the end of the first stage of the task, before revision of *S. Clement*, he reflected how:

> The destructive criticism of the last half century is ... fast spending its force. In its excessive ambition it has 'o'leapt itself.' ... the immediate effect of the attack has been to strew the vicinity of the fortress with heaps of ruins ... the rebuilding is a measure demanded by truth and prudence alike.[245]

The instrument of this reconstruction was criticism itself, and Lightfoot's final work was a powerful assertion of the textual basis of the historical-critical method over against the more speculative approach of the Tübingen scholars. That it had totally discredited their views was certainly the impression left upon Lightfoot's followers. Equally impressive was the moral dimension of his response. An anonymous reviewer seemed to speak for many:

> There is a spiritual instinct in the studies which he pursued, answering to the use of the imagination in science, and a religious sympathy with the authors expounded, corresponding to common sense and tact in literary criticism. He possessed them both. He had the industry of the most laborious collector of authorities, with an intellect to master and marshal them each in its place, and he possessed powers of feeling and soul that were never overpowered by his learning. He was one of those blessed scholars whose books will long benefit the reading world, not merely because he knew a great deal and thought correctly, but because he was good.[246]

Apart from its intellectual qualities, Lightfoot's criticism and its results were commended by its congruence with the spiritual and moral standards of his constituency. This is a measure of success he himself will have valued. For needs of this order were what the secular hermeneutic of the historical-exegetical method had always been intended to serve.

---

[245] AF II.1².xv.

[246] "Lightfoot's St Clement of Rome," 67. Cf. LD 140-1.

Conclusion

One day in 1883 Lightfoot went walking with G.R. Eden in the park adjacent to Auckland Castle. Eden had just accepted appointment as vicar of the large neighbouring parish of Bishop Auckland. As he contemplated the prospect of his new charge he put to Lightfoot a series of questions concerning the grace of baptism about which he was deeply troubled.[1] Almost 45 years later Eden recalled:

> I pressed him very hard, and plied him with these aspects. He was — *more suo* — silent. Then I stopped him as we were entering the gates, and adjured him, as one about to take up the charge of all these souls, to tell me what he really thought was the truth. With tears in his eyes, he put his hands on my shoulders and said, "My child, I do not know." He begged me not to be too sure of very clear-cut definitions. You know exactly what he would have said. It was like his remarks at Bournemouth in his illness.
> "Things that edify others do not edify me: I feed upon four or five great ideas."[2]

Even in the daily walk for exercise and discussion of some pressing problem with a close friend or associate,[3] the incident is characteristic of his career as a whole, and in several respects furnishes a fitting occasion for bringing this investigation of 'Lightfoot the Historian' to a close.

First, the encounter with Eden indicates how Lightfoot is to be regarded if he is to be seen as more than a student of early Christian literature. For it exhibits him in the role he chose for himself when, very early in his career, he set out to be a clergyman of the established Church, furnishing Christian leadership to the people of England. For two generations he played the part of a spiritual, moral and intellectual guide in public and in private at a time of ecclesiastical controversy and theological unsettlement. The particular group to benefit were young men like Eden — undergraduates at Cambridge, the warehousemen at St Paul's, trainees for the ministry, and (as here) the "sons of the house" at Auckland Castle.[4] But through his publications, addresses, sermons and correspondence, Lightfoot addressed the wider public as well. When Eden appealed to Lightfoot in his perplexity over baptism, he

---

[1]   For the background to Eden's concern, see P. Jagger, *Clouded Witness. Initiation in the Church of England in the Mid-Victorian Period, 1850-1875* (Allison Park, Pennsylvania: Pickwick Publications, 1982).

[2]   R. Wilson, "Lightfoot, Savage and Eden - Sidelights on a Great Episcopate," *Theology* LV.386 (August 1952) 294-9. Cf. LB II.228 for similar remarks at Bournemouth.

[3]   See Wilson, "Life," 171, for the significance of Lightfoot's walking.

[4]   See esp. "Bishop Lightfoot's Influence: His Trust in Young Men," A Paper by the Very Rev. H.E. Savage (Dean of Lichfield, 1909-39), edited with an introductory note by B.S. Benedikz, *Durham University Journal* LXXVII.1, n.s. XLVI.1 (December 1984) 1-6.

did in a personal way what numerous others did less directly on many other occasions. In his efforts "in great things and in small, to be found συνεργὸς τῇ ἀληθείᾳ,"[5] Lightfoot takes his place among those who were self-consciously the leaders of Christian life and thought in England in the mid-Victorian generation.

Second, the incident highlights Lightfoot's influence in this role and its bases. W.R. Ward once commented in passing that the degree of veneration shown to Lightfoot only shows how much reassurance was needed.[6] Certainly amid the so-called 'Victorian crisis of faith', a generation of people were looking for ways to retain the belief system in which they had been brought up. When they turned to Lightfoot for guidance, it was to a well known ecclesiastical leader and scholar of European standing. In each sphere of his Church involvement, he acquired a reputation for practical wisdom, liberality and moderation. It was the same in scholarship. Early in his life Lightfoot had sided with the reaction against dogmatic orthodoxy that began with Coleridge, and thereafter attempted to steer this liberalism in the direction of sounder methods and more defensible results. In his criticism he sought in particular to make the foundations of Christian faith at one with science and history, largely by ensuring that its methods were in accord with the moral ideals which drove Victorian intellectual endeavour and with which it was alleged that Christianity was incompatible. A man with a comprehensive outlook of this order might be relied upon, as Eden plainly expected, to answer difficult questions on matters like baptism with learning, sagacity and probity.[7]

Personal character and style seem to have mattered as much as ecclesiastical and scholarly reputation, and Lightfoot's moral qualities were of the kind that commanded respect in the mid-Victorian age. The typical earnestness and goodness poured out on Eden won the good opinion even of those who could not agree with him. In a time of controversy, moreover, Lightfoot refused to be controversial. He did not like "clear-cut definitions" in theological matters, and he refused to press a point beyond the available evidence. Lightfoot also liked to remain open minded for as long as possible so as to be capable of adapting to new understandings and insights. His usual refusal to take sides, and determination to see what could be said of all, commended him to people on either side of a question. In other words, Lightfoot's characteristic liberal-conservatism gave him influence with both

---

[5] 'A fellow worker in the truth' [trans.]. See the Preface to EWSR ix, dated 2 May 1889.

[6] W.R. Ward, "Faith and Fallacy: English and German Perspectives in the Nineteenth Century," in Helmstadter & Lightman (eds), *Victorian Faith in Crisis*, 39-67, esp. 62.

[7] Cf. the almost contemporaneous estimate of J. Gibb, "Theologians of the Day - Bishop Lightfoot," *Catholic Presbyterian* (March 1882) 177-86.

liberals and conservatives, but prevented him from becoming a leader of either. In practical affairs, finally, he preferred to work through others, delegating to agents, and working in committees or groups wherever possible. Though he exalted the individual, Lightfoot did not exalt himself. This was one reason for his not leaving a bigger impression in the contemporary record. Important as Lightfoot's influence was in mid-Victorian Church life, had he been more forthright, it might have been greater, or at least more manifest.

Another limiting factor was his evasiveness. Although pressed hard, the fact is that Lightfoot refused to answer Eden's question. This was not unusual. On numerous other occasions he avoided people's questions and concerns. While there could be some prudence in this, Lightfoot in fact chose carefully what he would do. But this could become evasion. On his refusal to be more involved in the higher affairs of the Church, his oldest friend commented:

> of late years his caution has grown upon him so exceedingly that I can get nothing out of him. 'I can't advise' has become a fixed phrase with him. The oldness of our friendship has made this rather a trial to me ... One wants to learn his views of things in casual ways, and not by direct interrogation always - for the latter fails, while it's of no use looking for the former. He is what you might call terribly selfish in pursuit of unselfish ends.[8]

And Hort saw clearly the effect of his friend's limitations in theological and intellectual matters:

> Dr Lightfoot is not speculative enough or eager enough to be a leader of thought.[9]

As a result his career is marked by numerous uncompleted projects and missed opportunities. Sometimes he did not see the importance of difficult questions to other people or appreciate how much they will have been helped by a word from him. But in this there was also a certain timidity that caused him to resile from speaking on important questions where his contribution will have been welcomed. Lightfoot's vaunted clarity of speech was not always matched by a willingness to speak. To some extent he was a leader who would not lead.

Another reason for this was a simple lack of interest in the matters causing concern. By his own admission Lightfoot himself was sustained by only a few ideas. Eden gives no indication of what these were, as they were familiar to him and his correspondent. But, when the full range of Lightfoot's writings is taken into account, they can be easily recovered. One was the "vision of God", a conception of Deity that combined immanence and transcendence. God was at once in the world and over it as a loving Father. A second was the understanding of revelation πολυμερῶς καὶ πολυτρόπως into

---

[8] E.W. Benson to Randall Davidson, 15 January 1885, quoted in G.K. Bell, *Randall Davidson Archbishop of Canterbury* (London: Oxford University Press, 1938) 169.
[9] Hort 'To a Friend', 16 January 1868, in LH II.89.

which Lightfoot sought to lead the Victorian Church. In addition to the Scriptures, the immanent God made Himself known in ways humankind could comprehend. Closely related, and partly to sustain this broader view of revelation, was the notion of the Logos, from the mid 1860s Lightfoot's answer to the problem of the God-world relation raised by new discoveries in science and history. The chief of his ideas, however, was the Incarnation, the enfleshment of the Logos in the person of Jesus of Nazareth as the culmination of the history of revelation, to disclose the Father and to secure reconciliation with mankind. This he called the leading idea of Christianity, and to its promotion and acceptance his career as a Churchman was devoted. With this went the life of Christ as the model for humanity. As Lightfoot never tired of saying, Christianity was a life, not adherence to doctrines or obedience of rules.

Together these ideas indicate that, while he may have lacked the subtlety and depth of Westcott and Hort, Lightfoot had a greater theological range and sophistication than has generally been supposed. They also furnish the specific content of the "truth in theology", which, with Westcott, he set himself to propagate as the end of his scholarship and teaching. Each, moreover, was an element in that immanentist model of understanding by which Lightfoot himself understood the world, and which he commended to the Church as a more adequate basis for facing contemporary society. Seen more as rediscoveries of old truths rather than as new breakthroughs, their specific intention was to redirect Church thinking to that more optimistic and inclusive perspective that was needed to meet contemporary apologetical and constructive demands. These ideas also place Lightfoot in the more conservative wing of liberal Anglican thought that functioned as an alternative to 'High', 'Low' and more leftist liberal approaches. His teaching of these ideas made him a proponent of the new outlook as the Church moved from an Atonement to the Incarnational paradigm in the 1860s and 1870s.

Holding these ideas together in a functional whole or system was the further idea of history. For, far from not having such a theory, Lightfoot in fact held to an understanding of history as the domain of "the increasing purpose of God". This was a unitary conception embracing the whole of time and all that happens within time in a framework of progressive spiritual and moral realization leading to fulfilment beyond time. In history the transcendent God draws near as an immanent presence to make Himself known and conform the process to His purpose. As Lightfoot acknowledged, this was an understanding which required all the resources of the doctrine of the Trinity to be in any way intelligible. To promote this end he recalled the attention of the Church to the Logos as the means by which from the beginning God worked in history to reveal himself. This revelation reached its climax when the Word became flesh, a phenomenon that in its impact transformed history to a new potentiality. In the period between the Incarnation and the *eschaton*, the Spirit was working to secure the continuing realization of the revelation in Christ, principally through the Church which existed as the manifestation of His body. This was a theology of history which, in the inclusiveness permitted by the Logos doctrine, was a significant if unsystematic response to the problem of history as it occurred to the Christian consciousness of the early- and mid-Victorian generations. By affirming the value of the whole of terrestrial existence as a factor in the realization of the divine purpose, it clearly set human time within the framework of eternity. Lightfoot's understanding thus presented to the world a supernatural naturalism for its acceptance as the true meaning of history.

Ostensibly based on the whole Bible, it in fact represented a reading determined by his basic liberal Anglican intellectual dispositions and contemporary cultural influences of which he does not appear to have been fully conscious. Consistently with this tradition of thought, it was intended from the beginning to reflect the basis of the essential oneness between Christianity as the "absolute religion" and the society of which it was a part. Specifically, Lightfoot was seeking to demonstrate that the Bible endorsed notions of history cherished in the wider community, and to direct them to their source and outcome in Christianity. In particular, he appropriated for Christianity the popular notion of progress which, he insisted, was ultimately religious in character and cause, a perspective that leaves little scope for the degenerationist and preservationist views mistakenly assigned to him. In reaching this accommodation with contemporary historical thinking, Lightfoot was initially reacting against the narrowness of Churchmen who did not feel the obligation to find how Christianity and the national culture could be held together. But more and more it was also due to a perception that England was facing a crisis in which Christian civilization itself was at stake, so that the elements of the theology of history came to expression in response to assaults on Christianity by its opponents. Increasingly, therefore, it was a means of commending the Bible to the wider society, and thus of defending Christianity and its right to remain the basis of English culture and social organization.

The application of the theology of history along these lines reflected Lightfoot's belief that historical understanding was a theological and cultural resource of the greatest importance for the well being of the English Church and society. At one level, it was the means of realizing the historical capacity and potential of the individuals through whom history is made. At a higher level, it was given providentially in the incarnational scheme as a means of fulfilling the purpose to which it testified. It did so by engendering progressive action in specific situations as it furnished the human intellect with the regulative truths of life and stimulated the imagination to grasp the moral and religious possibilities of each situation. Furnishing the meaning of the whole process and disclosing its central dynamic in turn provided the key to the significance of every activity and moment, and thereby set the participants free to choose for or against the "increasing purpose". Promoting this kind of historical thinking became an important component of Lightfoot's central theological mission. Its standing as an extension of the πολυμερῶς καὶ πολυτρόπως perspective seemed to require such a response from him. But the task was made the more pressing because of the widespread neglect and misuse of history he discerned in both Church and society. Without its correction his community might well squander an important means of managing change to ensure that one of the great epochs of history would continue to advance the course of Christian civilization. More importantly, in the declining sense of the connection between religion and morality, there was a risk that England's place in God's "increasing purpose" would be forfeited. This perception ranged Lightfoot against those liberal reformers who wanted to replace Christianity with a secular ethic as the source of the nation's values and public policy. The need to retain Christianity as "public doctrine" added a polemical edge to Lightfoot's efforts to secure a proper use of history in contemporary England as an important part of his work as Churchman and scholar.

This was a commitment that scholars have not previously recognized. One consequence has been that the conceptual framework to which Lightfoot related his own career has gone unappreciated. However, it is clear that, in line with the programme of optimum historical usage, he interpreted each of the main spheres of his involvement in the life of the contemporary Church and society as part of the setting of God's "increasing purpose". As a result, Lightfoot aspired to Cambridge University becoming a force for national regeneration as "the spiritual power of the nineteenth century". In his outlook Christian ministers were "fellow workers with God", responsible for the destiny of the Church and the "true architects of human progress". Lightfoot's own ministry at St Paul's took place at "the centre of the world's concourse", while Durham was where "the work of the Church of England" was to be done. The Church of England itself was the local manifestation of the historic Church descending through time from Abraham. It was now "the greatest Church of Christendom", and, if it could rise to its destiny, it would be "an ensign to the nations". His self-effacing piety notwithstanding, wherever he happened to be, Lightfoot assigned himself to a place of historic importance where he was in a position to guide the thinking and course taken by Church and nation.

Awareness of their strategic importance guided Lightfoot in what he tried to achieve at his various posts. At Cambridge he engaged in the activities and supported arrangements likely to make the University a fundamental educational, religious and moral influence in the life of the country. In London at St Paul's his hope was to create a spiritual life to match the magnificence of the Cathedral building itself. As a bishop he sought to build up a level of spiritual earnestness and achievement that would rival that of the earliest days of the Church in Durham. Before the Church of England at large Lightfoot advocated a policy of comprehension which, in its many applications, he believed would enable the Church to occupy its rightful place in the life of the nation and rise to its proper eminence in Christendom. An exalted sense of mission led to high ambitions not so much for Lightfoot himself as for the institutions he represented.

The drive to achieve his aims took Lightfoot to the heart of the "great work" of the day. As he sought to assimilate past and present, the framework of history furnished the starting point of his strategizing. At each point Lightfoot began with the role and situation inherited from the past and sought a more progressive future by bringing the reality into closer correspondence with the ideal. At Cambridge he supported changes that would enable it to be the place of moral and intellectual formation it claimed to be. In the process he made some very large concessions, reckoning that it was better for Cambridge to be Christian and national rather than a merely Anglican and sectional institution. The ministry required restoration of the true apostolic paradigm against Tractarian corruptions at the same time as developing new methods as the condition of effectiveness. Paul-like missionary outreach to the working class of London by means of mid-week public lectures in the Cathedral represented one such attempt at innovation. Lightfoot also overhauled the administration of his see, taking the very painful step of dividing it into two dioceses, in order actually to increase the level and efficiency of episcopal supervision. At the national level, he advocated similar flexibility and adaptation to achieve a true catholicity of interest, membership and extent. This continual need to strike a balance between continuity and change as received truths were applied to new situations gave vivid effect to the liberal-conservative ideology inherent in the idealism of the "increasing purpose" perspective.

The other important consequence of not recognizing Lightfoot's commitment to a right use of history has been that one of his key purposes as a Churchman remained to be discerned. In the same way that history was a theological and cultural resource to himself, Lightfoot sought also to make it a possession for others. This required furnishing historical knowledge to those who could make it serve desired ends. While in theory people could discern the required responses for themselves from the structure of historical reality, in practice they needed to be brought into contact with it and alerted to the possibilities. Before the wider Church this was a matter of selecting elements of a tradition which was already well known and directing them to suitable outcomes. At Durham a tradition lay ready to hand, but it had to be activated and enhanced for its power to be felt. While St Paul's had a long and proud history, to some extent a tradition had to be invented to suit a projected constituency. Lightfoot also made some provision for the ongoing availability of this kind of data by strengthening the historical component of theological education at Cambridge. The high point of this endeavour was the Lightfoot Scholarship for History which sought to ensure indefinitely a continuous supply of historians and properly authenticated historical information for the use of both Church and society, in England and beyond.

At a more specific level, Lightfoot appealed to historical knowledge for the benefits it conferred. At numerous points the regulative force of facts was enforced. Lightfoot expected the true nature of the ministry to emerge from a reconstruction of its early history. He appealed to the importance of the lower social orders for the well being of the Church as an aspect of missionary outreach to the working class in London. The preeminence of Aidan in the conversion of England was exalted in Durham as a stimulus to local exertion. Commitment to missionary effort by the contemporary Church was encouraged by the large measure of success achieved by modern missions. Its divisions were put into perspective by disclosure of the conflicts marring the life of the early Church. Confident of their salutary effects, Lightfoot pressed the Church in its organizational arrangements, programmes and aspirations to be in line with the known facts.

In a similar manner he invoked the types which assigned historical entities to their place in God's "increasing purpose". Lightfoot did this for the Church of England itself when he summoned its Jewish prototypes as a way of understanding its position and world wide mission. Anticipations in the early Church pointed to the providential significance of the different varieties of churchmanship it encompassed. At the local level this was most prominent at Durham where the saints and heroes of the northern Church furnished examples of what spiritually minded men and women might achieve for the Church and nation. Cambridge University was identified with a tradition of universities as sources of light to the world around them. As a device for appreciating the true dimensions of its circumstances and formulating suitable responses, historical typology was properly the basis of progressive action.

Most importantly, through both the facts and types of history, and sometimes directly as well, Lightfoot sought to introduce men and women to "the increasing purpose" perspective itself. He did this so that they, like him, would feel the religious and ethical challenge of historical understanding. In perceiving their importance as the link between the past and a better future, Lightfoot hoped that they would sense their independence of the time spirit and resolve to take the progressive action required by the challenges of the present. Within this framework, he envisaged something different for each group addressed. Cambridge undergraduates were being prepared for Christian citizenship and future leadership of the Church. Amid their mundane circumstances, the London warehousemen and people of Durham diocese were introduced to the possibilities of Christian living in the context of eternal purpose. The clergy and lay people who shared his commitment to the Church were being equipped for the decisions they would have to make on her behalf. In taking the same approach at each point Lightfoot was confident that the results would come together under Providence for the benefit of the Church and nation as these men and women reproduced at their own level the spiritual and moral qualities that made for progress.

It is into this setting of Lightfoot's life-purpose and belief in the usefulness of history that his career as a scholar must be set. Assisted by a doctrine of inspiration that recognized the human-historical element in the Biblical text, Lightfoot from the first took up the historical-critical method of studying the New Testament and related writings. It held out the prospect of definite knowledge, the achievement of which even in minute critical subjects he regarded as a form of progressive action. Recent developments in New Testament scholarship called for the marrying of the established Cambridge textual-linguistic method in which he had been nurtured with the 'new' philological approaches encountered in German writers, particularly those of the 'mediating' school. The leading feature of the historical-exegetical method that resulted was the presentation of the best available text in its original literal meaning established by a combination of rigorous grammatical and exegetical analysis with location in the authorial, literary, world and church historical contexts. As his career unfolded Lightfoot was called upon increasingly to determine the status of the texts interpreted in this manner. For this he began with the history of their reception to create a presumption to bring to the evidence of the text itself. The outcome was the characteristic review of external and internal evidence to determine authenticity and genuineness. Although Lightfoot did not complete the programme he set himself, his method of study, in its impulse and development, was one source of coherence in an outwardly dispirate scholarly career.

Another was furnished by the purposes the method served. Lightfoot frequently distinguished between the method and its uses. In its rigorous inductivism, the method was 'secular', and such as might have been used for 'any other book'. This was necessary for it to perform its legitimate functions. One was to furnish definite facts to work on the religious consciousness. Thus the rational study of the basic documents of Christianity was something of benefit to Christianity itself. Properly conceived and executed, the method was a factor to be welcomed in the Church as facilitating the working of the Christian idealist epistemology. The other function was the demonstration that Christian belief was up to the intellectual demands of the day. So understood the historical-critical method was part of the new 'Christian Evidences' Lightfoot advocated as the means of countering attacks on the documents themselves by credible processes. In its acceptance and correction of criticism as a legitimate source of knowledge about incipient Christianity, it was an instrument of truthfulness, and thereby satisfied the requirements of the contemporary moral economy. For his labours to bring Christian scholarship into line with society's intellectual and moral conditions, Lightfoot was happy to be called an 'apologist'. Such work fitted his twin aims of commending modernity to the Church, and retaining Christianity as the religion of modern England.

This agenda suggests that, notwithstanding his pretensions that it was a straightforward secular hemeneutic, Lightfoot's Christian standpoint may have affected his application of the historical method to early Christian texts. The 'hermeneutics of trust' identified by Stephen Pointer was certainly a factor in the adoption of the method,[10] but it was not simply a matter of piety. Behind it was a dual confidence arising from the natural theology in which he had been nurtured. On the one hand, it justified the assurance that the inductive method yielded the facts of the matter. Faith might well be the key necessary to unlock their meaning, but they would be the same facts to any disinterested enquirer. On the other hand, the epistemology of Cambridge natural theology conditioned Lightfoot's attitude towards the documents themselves. These were understood as responses to the phenomenon of Jesus through the eyes of faith. While this left scope for the creative contribution of the writer, Lightfoot saw the Gospels in particular as products of simple observation, and therefore as factual reports. Verification of their authenticity seemed to foreclose the need for further investigation into the manner of their composition, even though Lightfoot's own approach seemed to call for it. C.K. Barrett was right to say that his understanding of reality limited Lightfoot's application of the historical method, but this understanding was that of the Cambridge Christian idealist rather than that of 'a common sense empiricist'.

Lightfoot's conception of history also affected his method and its results. Evidence was frequently arranged to produce developmental sequences in line with the expectation that this is how things happen. The writings of single authors too were ordered according to a similar pattern. The presentation of texts as the consequences of natural causes and themselves in turn a cause also reflected the organic conception of growth. But Lightfoot insisted that the chief factor in the epistolary literature, on which he mainly

---

[10] Pointer, "Lightfoot as a Christian Historian," 426-44.

worked, was the life and death of Christ. Each text therefore was ultimately a response to the Incarnation in the light of circumstances. In turn it transmitted that experience to others, so that it was legitimate to look for the cumulative results. In his own mind free from the need to pursue fundamental research on the Gospels, Lightfoot read early Christian literature as belonging to the tradition of "increasing purpose" arising out of the Incarnation and reflecting that development.

As a result, yet a third source of coherence and wholeness was Lightfoot's subject matter. Despite so many incomplete and unattempted projects, the whole of his scholarly *oeuvre* was concerned with the Christian writings of the first two centuries which he set on an orderly footing. He began with a relatively brief study of Jesus and the Gospels, returning to the subject subsequently only to expound and defend the authenticity and genuiness of the Fourth Gospel, the documentary basis of his theological standpoint. Thereafter he moved on to a major study of St Paul, whom he regarded as the exemplar of incarnational Christianity, concentrating on the speculative writings of the first Roman captivity period. For many years Lightfoot regarded editing St Paul's writings as the work of his life, but circumstances caused this commitment to shift to the edition of the Apostolic Fathers. They were important as the representatives of the Catholic Christianity of the immediate sub-apostolic generations. As such they reflected the impact of a Christ known only by report, but also by their allusions validated the bulk of the New Testament writings as first century productions. This brought to a climax a career-long concern with the documentary basis of incarnational Christianity. Significantly, the structure of Lightfoot's corpus of writings was anticipated in his very first New Testament study. This suggests what is clear in subsequent work, that, while he wrote little on them as such, Jesus and the Gospels were always the ultimate data of his research. Lightfoot's scholarship was at once the exposition and defence of the incarnational foundations of his interpretation of history as the "increasing purpose of God".

It is within this context that Lightfoot's concern with the Tübingen School needs to be placed. It engaged his attention from the first. Strauss was virtually the subject of the Norrisian Prize Essay, and the issues he raised involved some consideration of the views of Baur and others, though at this early stage Lightfoot probably did not know them first hand. Because of their critical importance, he rectified this as he pursued his studies of Paul and the 'Acts of the Apostles'. By the time *Galatians* appeared, Lightfoot saw in the Tübingen School an account of Christian origins radically different from his own incarnational interpretation which he outlined in detail for the first time. His purpose was to undermine any local appeal it might have, but when against the background of the rising crisis of Christian civilization in England the works of Tayler and Cassels suggested he'd been unsuccessful, Lightfoot set out to expose its critical deficiencies, a purpose he carried forward with some vehemence in *The Apostolic Fathers*. In the final decade of his life, he also took several opportunities to assert his view that the progress of scholarship had refuted its views. Throughout his career, Lightfoot had endeavoured to prevent the Tübingen interpretation of Chistian beginnings from becoming influential and adding to the religious malaise in contemporary England.

But his concern with the Tübingen School should not be exaggerated. The evidence of his correspondence, in which the subject hardly occurs, indicates that it was not a preoccupation in his private thinking. Nor were the views of the Tübingen scholars the subject of a direct refutation or mono-graph. The medium of his concern — principally the editions of texts — indicates that it was always pursued in relation to other scholarly agendas, and to that extent was subordinate to them. Moreover, it did not engage Lightfoot's attention uniformly, particularly in his commentaries on St Paul. The Tübingen School was an issue that the presentation of earliest Christiainity in terms of the knowledge of the day raised repeatedly but not continuously. In the early 1860s it was a dangerous alternative to the view of Christian origins Lightfoot was seeking to establish, while in the next two decades it posed the dilemma of how to retain congruence between empirical criticism and Christianity while disposing of its most destructive results. Always it was the manifestation of a deeper problem, the accept-ance of critical scholarship in the life of the Church as an aspect of the larger theological program seeking a broader view of revelation around the Incar-nation. As a continual concern arising because of the pursuit of other objec-tives, the Tübingen School was *a* life problem, but not *the* life problem, of Lightfoot's career as a scholar. Judging from the reaction of contemporaries and the delay in English New Testament scholarship in coming to terms with the issues it raised, Lightfoot was largely successful in solving it.

In having this effect Lightfoot was a transitional figure. From the first in his formal studies he took German scholarship seriously and mediated its methods and results to a public still deeply apprehensive about it. Its im-proved reception was one side of the movement towards the acceptance of critical Biblical study which was largely accomplished by the time of his death. Numerous other factors were involved in this change, and the battles were fought out largely in relation to the Old Testament. In that he coun-tered and discredited radical critical views in his own area of expertise, par-ticularly when *Supernatural Religion* brought them to the attention of the English public, Lightfoot was an important reason for such battles not tak-ing place in relation to the New Testament. But his impact did not rest on a negative achievement. In scholarship, as elsewhere, he furthered the "great work" of the day by synthesizing old and new practices to produce a new method of study. At this level too Lightfoot contributed to keeping Church and society in due relation. By conspicuously demonstrating the benefits of the historical-exegetical method, and exhibiting its congruence with faith and contemporary moral ideals, he commended properly conducted criticism to the Church as a practice that enhanced Christian thought and practice. At the same time the scholarly standard of his work also enabled Christianity to retain a place in a religious and intellectual community where empirical verifiability was the medium of exchange. The claim that Lightfoot actually retarded the development of a more advanced criticism is a perception of hindsight when the need for such a criticism was felt. That criticism of this sort could be contemplated inside the Church itself was due in no small measure to the fact that Lightfoot (along with Westcott and Hort) had established a critical tradition of New Testament study as a legitimate component of its corporate life.

A similar judgment on his significance applies to his career as a Churchman. In each of the areas of his involvement the desire to "bring forth things new and old" induced Lightfoot to initiate or support reforms that modernized the Church of England to enable it to carry out its traditional role. At Cambridge he was instrumental in bringing about the organizational changes required by the nationalization of the University while seeking to retain for the Church as much influence as possible in this new situation. In his own area of professorial responsibility he took the leading part in adjusting theological education to the demands of the age and the changing nature of the University, while the Lightfoot Scholarship created an instrument of historical education of lasting value. In his 'parish' in London he shared in the transformation of the Cathedral from a decorous building into a church reaching out to serve the surrounding community that placed St Paul's in the vanguard of the cathedral reform movement. At Durham, Lightfoot brought Church arrangements more into line with what was being tried elsewhere in response to the dynamics of religious revival and the demand for utility amid the pressures of demographic change and industrialization. The result was such a revival of Church work that admirers at least regarded his episcopacy as a "golden age". On a broader front, Lightfoot was among those who recognized that the contemporary Church of England was called upon to change if it was to achieve the oneness between its faith and society which was its *raison d'être* as the national Church. To this end he advocated modifications to theological method and conceptions which were readily taken up in the next generation as the basis for maintaining the place of the Church of England in the life of the nation. While the supernatural component of Lightfoot's supernatural naturalism was much reduced by his successors, he and his Cambridge associates had made a greater contribution to the 'liberal catholic' consensus of the late-Victorian and Edwardian Church than has usually been allowed.

Lightfoot occupies much the same place in the Victorian historical tradition. By drawing from the Bible a providential pattern which he applied to the whole of history and to which the facts of history were fitted, his outlook relied on literary authority rather than on an examination of history itself. In this dependence on literary authority, Lightfoot's approach, while in other respects employing the methods and sources of empirical historiography, was still fundamentally that of the narrative historians of mid-century rather than that of the record historians whose work was coming increasingly into vogue. Yet he seemed at the same time to have done much to adjust the Christian historical outlook to the broader vistas and naturalistic conceptions that were challenging it with increasing self-confidence. For many Lightfoot's historical supernatural naturalism provided a viable accommodation between ancient faith and the modern world.

If in each of these respects Lightfoot achieved much, he did not succeed in his principal aim, the retention of Christianity as public doctrine. But the belief that this could be done directs attention to the limitations of his historical outlook and approach. With the possible exception of the historical-exegetical method of Biblical study, none of Lightfoot's reforms was particularly innovative, and in some matters, such as the possibility of allowing women to become students at Cambridge, he was opposed to radical change. Because of an exaggerated sense of the practical efficacy of historical understanding and concomitant emphasis on continuity and expectation of organic development, his view of the future was always to a large extent his view of the past. As a result, Lightfoot did not see the disturbing realities lurking behind the contemporary Church revival or anticipate radical change, such as the devastating impact of World War I on his immanentist presuppositions, any better than his contemporaries. More importantly for what he himself hoped to accomplish, it meant that, while his fundamental analysis of English society — that it was in danger of squandering its Christian inheritance — was sound, his remedies were never likely to succeed. This was ironic, for, in his estimate of historical knowledge and reliance on the historical framework of understanding, Lightfoot was in the grip of the *Zeitgeist* in a manner which he deprecated and from which that very historical framework was supposed to deliver him. Yet because of it he was also able to speak in terms and hold out grounds for hope which contemporary Christians who shared his attitudes and assumptions found very appealing.

This is not to say that in his adherence to the progressive tendency of the "increasing purpose" Lightfoot had been naïvely optimistic. A characteristic Victorian tension between hopefulness and anxiety was a feature of much of his career, particularly at the level of the national Church. Because it recognized distractions and diversions from the main pattern of inexorable advancement towards fulfilment of the divine purpose, both were inherent in the theology of history. It also showed that the instrument of Providence could change, so that Lightfoot's fears for Christian England had disturbing historical warrants. In the end, however, his optimism seems to have won out. Towards the end of his life Queen Victoria's first Jubilee and the third Lambeth Conference suggested that the Church of England was in fact fulfilling its destiny, while the progress of scholarship indicated the defeat of the critical theories of the Tübingen School. Before illness affected his temper, Lightfoot was feeling more and more hopeful about the situation he had confronted as Churchman and scholar for almost forty years within the framework of the "increasing purpose of God".

This same triumph of optimism is evident in Lightfoot's personal history. In the spring of 1888 it became clear that his health was failing. Although apparently suffering from overwork, preparations for the third Lambeth Conference precluded a summer holiday. The Conference itself, and the visit of some 60 overseas bishops to Auckland Castle, caused a complete breakdown which necessitated spending the winter at Bournemouth. On his return to Durham, and just two months before his death, Lightfoot reflected in looking back over the previous year:

> it was the strain, both in London and at home, in connexion with this Pan-Anglican gathering, which broke me down hopelessly. I did not regret it then, and I do not regret it now. I should not have wished to recall the past, even if my illness had been fatal. For what after all is the individual life in the history of the Church? Men may come and men may go - individual lives float down like straws on the surface of the waters till they are lost in the ocean of eternity; but the broad, mighty, rolling stream of the Church itself — the cleansing, purifying, fertilising, tide of the River of God — flows on for ever and ever.[11]

This identification of himself with the movement of history by means of the characteristic image of the river of God in the hour of his death matched its announcement on the eve of his professorial career with the equally characteristic image of the rising tide as the "increasing purpose of God". Shortly afterwards Lightfoot left the diocese again, stopping over at Bournemouth where he died on 21 December 1889. As his strength ebbed away, Lightfoot seemed to follow the model of the Venerable Bede, working on his *S. Clement of Rome* as he was able until the last, as the earlier 'leader of the northern Church' had persisted with his translation of the Fourth Gospel right up to his final moment. Even the experience of death was structured according to the types and teaching of his theology of history. Its personal importance was never clearer.

---

[11] DDG III (November 1889) 3-4.

On one occasion Lightfoot commented on the importance of finding the seminal idea from which the career of a great historical personage followed:

> History contains no more valuable lessons than the study of the first conscious outburst in the mind of a great instructor or benefactor of mankind, of the central idea, which enfolds in itself, as the plant is enfolded in the germ, the sum of his teaching or the work of his life. We have thus traced the streams of his manifold energies to their fountainhead. We have made ourselves masters of the stronghold which was the key to his power & influence. We have ascertained the one simple law which regulates the diverse phenomena of his character.[12]

In his own case, the understanding of history as "the increasing purpose of God", enunciated early and ever present thereafter, is entiled to be regarded as this "central idea". To be sure, it was not the chief of the 4-5 ideas off which he fed. That was the Incarnation, the leading fact of the entire Christian dispensation, which the idea of history was intended to comprehend and expound. But "the increasing purpose" was the narrative conception by which Lightfoot organized his thinking and directed it to practical outcomes in each area of his involvement in the life of the Church and society. His personal identification with it, moreover, was a power that led to a life of self-sacrifice and performance of duty in the service of scholarship, the Church and the nation. As his framework of thought and action, the theology of history as "the increasing purpose of God" is the key to the critical biography to which the present investigation is the prolegomenon. When that has been written, perhaps more than a century after his death there will at last be "something sufficient on Lightfoot".

---

[12] Vision, 1877, 8-9.

Appendices

Appendix 1

Lightfoot's Scientific Reading

Among the Lightfoot Papers there is a scrap of paper listing a number of scientific authors and titles. The list bears signs of hurry, and the items seem to have been jotted down at random. There is no indication of the function the list was intended to serve, but it points at least to the level of Lightfoot's awareness of contemporary scientific literature. It is an impressive list, and indicates what an intelligent non-scientist schooled in the Cambridge tradition of natural theology could read in the period before specialization put scientific monographs beyond the reach of this category of student.

The list is reproduced as it appears. It is followed by a fuller citation where the recommended works could be identified.

The List

Herschel's *Outlines of Astronomy*
Bessel's *Populäre Vorlesungen*
Humboldt's *Cosmos*
Airy's *Lectures*
Chalmer's *Astronomical Discourses*
Vestiges of Creation
Indications of a Creator
Sedgwick's *Discourse*
                    Article on *Vestiges*
Hugh Miller's *New Red Sandstone*
                    Lectures etc
Whewell's *Phil.y of Inductive Science*
                    Hist.y of Inductive Science
                    Plurality of Worlds
Lyell's *Geology* both works
Whewell's *Bridgwater Treatise*
Owen
Mrs Somerville
Cuviers
Sumners
Baden Powells
Brewster
Pritchard's *Natural Hist.y of Man*
                    Physical Hist.y of Man

******

From the indications given the works listed appear to be:

John F.W. Herschel, *Outlines of Astonomy*, 1849

Friedrich W. Bessel, *Populäre Vorlesungen über wissenschaftliche Gegenstände*, 1848

Friedrich H.A. von Humboldt, *Kosmos. Entwurf einer physichen Waltbeschreibung*, 1845-62

George B. Airy, *Six Lectures on Astronomy*, 1849

Thomas Chalmers, *Astronomical Discourses, A Series of Discourses on the Christian Revelation viewed in conjunction with the modern Astronomy*,1817

[Robert Chambers], *Vestiges of the Natural History of Creation*, 1844

[William Whewell], *Indicators of the Creator*, 1845

Adam Sedgwick, *A Discourse on the Studies of the University*, 1833

Adam Sedgwick, "*Natural History of Creation*," *Edinburgh Review* 82 (July 1845) 1-85

Hugh Miller, *The Old Red Sandstone; or, new walks in an old field*, 1841

William Whewell, *The Philosophy of the Inductive Sciences, Founded Upon their History*, 1840

William Whewell, *History of the Inductive Sciences*, 1837

William Whewell, *Of the Plurality of Worlds*, 1853

Charles Lyell, *Principles of Geology, being an attempt to explain the former changes of the earth's surface, by reference to causes now in operation*, 1830-3

Charles Lyell, *Elements of Geology*, 1838

William Whewell, *Astronomy and General Physics, Considered with reference to natural theology*, 1833

******

From the remaining names it is clear that Lightfoot was well aware of other significant figures in the scientific community such as Baden Powell and David Brewster, although the fact that he was unable to dash off approximate titles of their books could mean that he was less familiar with them.

Appendix 2

Lightfoot's Cambridge Lectures[1]

Abbreviations:

A = Arts School
E = Easter Term
L = Lent Term
M = Michaelmas Term
T = Trinity College Lecture Room

Year	Term	Venue	Attendance	Subject
1861-2	M			Epistles to Timothy
	L	A		Galatians
	E	A		Colossians
1862-3	M	T		Epistles to Timothy
	E	T		Philippians[2]
1863-4	M	T		Epistles to the Thessalonians
1864-5	M	T		Colossians, Philemon
	E	T		Philippians
1865-6	M	A	84	Epistles to Timothy[3]
	E	A	61	Epistles to the Thessalonians
1866-7	M		89	Colossians and Philemon
	E		45	Ephesians
1867-8	M		65	The Gospel of St John
	L		77	The Gospel of St John[4]
	E		25	
1868-9	M	A	84	The Gospel of St John
	L	A	78	Thessalonians
	E	A	46	Pastoral Epistles
1869-70	M	A	54	Pastoral Epistles
	L		82	Romans[5]
	E		35	
1870-1	M	A	45	Colossians
	L			I Corinthians[6]
1871-2	M	A	72	Acts of the Apostles[6]
	L	A		Acts of the Apostles[7]
	E	A		Acts of the Apostles[7]
1872-3	M	A	65	Introduction to St John's Gospel[8]
	L	A	59	Introduction to St John's Gospel[6]
1873-4	M	A	96	Ephesians[7]
	L	A	53	I Corinthians[8]
1874-5	M	A	83	I Corinthians, from Chapter 5
	L	A	84	I Corinthians[9]

1875-6	M		106	I Peter[7]
	L		130	Epistles to Timothy
1876-7	M	A	191[10]	Romans[6]
	L		115	Romans
1877-8	M		247	The Acts of the Apostles
	L		208	The Acts of the Apostles
1878-9	M		176	The Acts of the Apostles, from XV
	L			The Acts of the Apostles, from XVIII

Notes:

1   The table has been compiled from the *Cambridge Chronicle*; the *Cambridge University Gazette*; the *Cambridge University Reporter;* Cambridge University Archives, Collecteana, UP 30-53; and Cambridge University Library, Cam. Collection, Cam.a.500.1.41-8, and Cambridge University Papers, E 131.

2   Cam.a.500.1.42 lists II Corinthians. The announcement was corrected in the *Cambridge Chronicle* (4 April 1863).

3   In this term Lightfoot also conducted a class twice weekly on the Ignatian Epistles for BAs.

4   Although no formal announcement was made for the Easter term, Lightfoot probably continued the series on the Gospel of John.

5   Again it seems likely that Lightfoot continued the same subject into the next term, although no formal announcement was made to this effect.

6   In these terms Lightfoot also conducted weekly examinations on "Introduction to the New Testament. Criticism of the Text".

7   In these terms Lightfoot's weekly examinations were on "Introduction to the New Testament" using Westcott's *Introduction to the Study of the Gospels* as the text.

8   In these terms the weekly examinations were on"Introduction to the Acts and Epistles". No textbook was prescribed.

9   In this term the weekly examinations were on "The Canon of the New Testament" using Westcott's *History of the Canon* as the textbook.

10   W.H. Thompson to Lightfoot, 31 October 1876, grants permission for the Hall of Trinity College to be used for Lightfoot's lectures. Contrary to what most sources imply, it was only thus late in Lightfoot's Cambridge career that the usual facilities were inadequate for his audiences.

Appendix 3

The Critical Reception of Lightfoot's Scholarship in Germany

The lack of German interest in nineteenth century English theology is well known. As one of the few who were able to penetrate this wall of indifference, Lightfoot was a significant exception. Major journals like the *Theologische Literaturzeitung* and the *Göttingen Gelehrte* carried reviews of his works which evince an appreciation of the genuine signficance of his achievement. An indication of this appreciation more vivid than any survey of these reviews might achieve is the letter written from Leipzig by C.R. Gregory. Himself an authority on the text of the New Testament and an admirer of Lightfoot, he describes Adolf von Harnack's excited reaction to the receipt of Lightfoot's *Clement. Appendix* in 1877:

Waisenhaus Strasse 5 IV l.,
Leipzig, Germany,
13 May 1877

To the Reverend Professor J.B. Lightfoot D.D.:

Dear Sir:

Permit me to thank you heartily for the kind sending of your *S. Clement of Rome. Appendix* which reached me this morning. An uncritical, hasty glance is enough to show its independent value as a contribution to the Clement literature.

You will perhaps be amused if I tell you how Harnack behaved about it: at the same time you will see a pleasant feature in his character. The moment I took my seat at the dinner table to-day, he held up the book: noticing that a few pages in the middle were uncut, I quizzed him on that and told him that my copy had been at once turned through; he defended himself on that point vigorously to our amusement. He kept rushing around to my seat[1] to ask about shades of meaning here and there, of course especially catching up the places wherein you alluded to him. Disposing of soup, he turned to Schürer, and, with a smile at what he knew[2] would make us laugh, said, 'That must have at least eight or nine columns in the *Theologische Literaturzeitung*!' The review question was not settled at once: Harnack said that Gebhardt ought to write it. Schürer said it must be done as quickly as possible in consistency with due accuracy; this is because Schürer thinks so much of you: I really do not believe there is any one in England for whom he has the same respect. As to the time question, you will easily understand how, especially in Germany a review may be delayed. We usually have in printing-order, that is to say in proof, from three to four numbers of the paper ahead; of course not put in place but in the loose proofs. Schürer said that if possible the review ought to be written within eight days: still I hardly think that can be brought about. Harnack let his first course stand: he did not care to do anything but read. When the coffee[3] question came up: Schürer told him he had better go home, that he would only study Clement. Dr

Guthe (the new Old Testament Privatdocent) suggested putting him in a droschhky so that he could read all the way home. Thereupon Harnack confessed that he had read all the way along the street in coming to dinner until he had overtaken Schürer.

The first thing Harnack broke out to me about was his pleasure at having learned your agreement with him as to the relative value of *C* and *A*. In relation to your note on page 305 he said that he, as you also suggest, had not in the least intended to attribute to you the opinion that Clement II was an epistle. Unfortunately, having to preach this afternoon, I was compelled to forgo the "coffee", the real time for talking, and so I can mention no further points.[4]

Hoping that you will find these hurried lines to be an indirect token of the high esteem in which you are held in Leipzig, I remain,

my dear Sir,

with great respect
Your obedient Servant
Caspar Rene Gregory

Harnack's *Hermas* should be done in a few days.

Notes:

1   Schürer sits between him and me.
2   We are always teasing Harnack about his inability to write a short review.
3   In German fashion, after dinner we go to one of two or three coffee-houses and take coffee, read the papers, and in the usual way arrange the affairs of the universe.
4   At one time Harnack said: "He is *four times* as accurate as Gebhardt and I."

Bibliography

The Bibliography is arranged according to the following categories:

A. Primary Sources
    I. The Lightfoot Papers
        a. Auckland Castle, Bishop Auckland
        b. The Dean and Chapter Library, Durham Cathedral
    II. Other Primary Sources
        a. Unpublished
        b. Published
            1. Works By Lightfoot in Chronological Sequence
            2. Editions of Lightfoot's Writings
            3. Materials Concerning Lightfoot by Contemporaries in Chronological Sequence
            4. Short Reviews of Lightfoot's Works in Chronological Sequence
            5. Autobiographies, Biographies and Letters of Contemporaries
            6. Reference Books and Official Publications
            7. Parliamentary Papers
            8. Newspapers and Periodicals
            9. Books and Pamphlets Before 1914
            10. Editions of Sources and Contemporary Works
            11. Articles and Chapters Before 1914

B. Secondary Sources
    I. Materials About, or Containing Significant Discussion of, Lightfoot
    II. Reference Books
    III. Other Books
    IV. Other Articles and Chapters
    V. Other Theses

A. Primary Sources

I. The Lightfoot Papers

At the commencement of the investigation the Lightfoot Papers were thought to consist of a single deposit held in the Dean and Chapter Library, Durham Cathedral. As it proceeded, a second cache was discovered at Auckland Castle, Bishop Auckland. Its existence was suggested by citations in the thesis of D.J. Wilson. First inquiries suggested that these papers had been lost, along with other memorabilia of Lightfoot's episcopate, possibly when part of Auckland Castle was turned into diocesan offices. Subsequent inquiries resulted in the rediscovery of the papers in a cupboard in the Chaplain's office. It is possible that further investigation will lead to the recovery of the additional materials which exist according to oral tradition in the diocese of Durham.

It is obvious that the two sets of papers were originally part of the same deposit. At some point they were separated. The smaller cache at Auckland Castle contains materials bearing on Lightfoot's private and family life. Very few such items remain in the larger set. It would appear that at some time a cull intended to remove these components was begun but not completed. The portion which was finished was transfered to the Dean and Chapter Library, and the remainder left at Auckland Castle. The precise history of the Lightfoot Papers remains to be determined.

Neither set of papers was sorted or catalogued. A provisional arrangement was made along the following lines. Quantities have not been verified and should be regarded as no more than indicative pending proper archival arrangement.

a. Auckland Castle:

Chaplain's Office:

> Correspondence file: "Bishop Lightfoot 1879-1886"
> Correspondence file: "Bishop Lightfoot 1887-1889"
> Newspaper clippings: Bishop Lightfoot's Death and Funeral
> Two envelopes of Lightfoot's correspondence to B.F. Westcott
> Five envelopes of incoming correspondence to Lightfoot, mainly for the years 1877-1879
> One bundle of offprints, printed speeches, sermons etc.

Bishop's Library:

> Address to the Right Reverend Joseph Barber Lightfoot D.D. Lord Bishop of Durham, Visitor to the University of Durham June 6th 1879
> File: "Rev Prof.ʳ Westcott, Trin Coll."
> Bound volume of Lightfoot's personal reading lists (alphabetically arranged)

b. Dean and Chapter Library, Durham Cathedral:

Appointment books and notebooks:

> > Two pocket notebooks used as a journal on the trip to Italy in the winter of 1854-5
> > One pocket notebook dated 1856
> > Two undated memorandum books listing expenses (one is clearly for 1859)
> > Appointment book for 1873
> > Eleven appointment books for the years 1879-1889

'Bishop Lightfoot Manuscripts':

> > A green collapsible box, 19.5 x 37 x 27.5 cm, containing the following in manuscript:
> > > Characteristics of the Epistles of the First Roman Captivity
> > > To the Editor of the Guardian [1881]
> > > Supernatural Religion. IX. Tatian's Diatessaron
> > > Eusebius of Caesarea
> > > Ignatius and Polycarp

Classical lectures and papers:

> > 'Agamemnon': a limp bound volume of unnumbered leaves on the text of Aeschylus' Agamemnon
> > 'The Aeschylean Tetralogy': the introduction to the projected edition of the Aeschylean tetralogy in 41 unbound leaves

Correspondence:

> > Metal deed box containing some four thousand items mainly incoming letters
> > 'The Lady Margaret Professorship. 1875'
> > > Two cardboard boxes, 18.5 x 12 x 4 cm, containing 75 (one by Lightfoot) and 53 (3 by Lightfoot) letters respectively

'Letters of Thanks. Books Etc.'

    Cardboard box, 18.5 x 12 x 4 cm, containing 95 letters

Letters to Bp Lightfoot, while he was (with Dr Westcott) joint-editor for a short while of the Dictionary of Christian Biography

    Hard covered folder containing 135 items, mainly incoming letters 1867-1870

MS Lectures and Papers:

    'The Chapel of St Peter and the Manor House of Auckland' [= HE 182-220]
    'Christian Life in the Second and Third Centuries' [= HE 1-71]
    'Christianity and Paganism' [= S 65-116]
    'Donne the Poet Preacher' [= HE 221-45]
    'Edward I'
    'England During the Latter Half of the Thirteenth Century' [= HE 93-181]
    'England Six Hundred Years Ago'
    'Mill On Religion'

Miscellaneous Papers Arranged and Filed in Envelopes Labelled:

    Addresses as Bishop of Durham I:
        Addresses of Welcome
        Durham Sunday Closing Bill
        Missions: SPG & CMS

    Addresses as Bishop of Durham II:
        Lay Evangelists Admission
        Church of England Temperance Society
        White Cross Association
        Consecration of Cemeteries etc

    Addresses as Bishop of Durham III:
        Confirmation Addresses
        Institution Address

    The Apostolic Fathers: Miscellaneous Papers I
    The Apostolic Fathers: Miscellaneous Papers II
    Auckland Castle: Miscellaneous Papers I
    Auckland Castle: Miscellaneous Papers II
    Cambridge Miscellaneous Papers
    Greek Testament Miscellaneous Papers I
    Greek Testament Miscellaneous Papers II
    Lightfoot Trust Miscellaneous Papers
    Miscellaneous Personal Papers and Effects
    Newcastle Bishopric Papers
    Published Addresses, Sermons & Offprints
    The Revised Version

Lightfoot Fund. MacMillan's Accounts:

    Thirteen bound volumes covering the period from 1889 to 1931

Newspaper Cuttings, Offprints and Reviews Arranged and Filed in Envelopes Labelled:

    1865
    1868
    1869

1870
1871
1872
1873
1875
1876
1877
1878
1879 A
1879 B
1880 A
1880 B
Seaham Harbour Colliery Disaster, 1880
1881
Church Congress, Newcastle 1881
1882
Consecration and Enthronement of Bishop of Newcastle, July-August 1882
1883
1884
1885
1886
1887
1888
1889

Ten File Boxes of Lecture Notes on New Testament Subjects:

St John's Gospel. Genuineness
St John. Notes
Acts
St Paul. Romans
St Paul. I Corinthians
St Paul. Ephesians
St Paul. Thessalonians
St Paul. Pastoral Epistles
Epistles of St Peter
Coptica

Five Limp Bound Books of Unnumbered Leaves:

Acts I-VIII
Acts VIII-XIV
Acts XV-XIX
6 [the manuscript of the Norrisian Prize Essay of 1853]
Undated

Four Box Files of Papers on the Apostolic Fathers Labelled:

Ignatius
Ignatius. For New Edition
Patres Apostolici. Clemens. Clementina
Patres Apostolici. Ignatius & Polycarp

230 Manuscript Sermons and four drafts:
The sermons are written out long hand in separate booklets with each occasion of
delivery set out on the inside cover. The title of each sermon is listed below in chrono-

logical order. Where a sermon was preached more than once, the dates of the first and last occasions of its delivery are given, while the number of times a sermon was preached is indicated in parentheses. It should be noted that the dates furnished are those recorded on the manuscripts. Cross checking with an almanack reveals a number of errors. This suggests that Lightfoot sometimes added the details from memory, and that on occasion his memory failed him. In a few cases a date is supplied in brackets. These dates have been worked out from the available data, such as the occasion in the Church calendar. The italicized portion of each title is the abbreviation by which it is cited in the notes in the text.

The *Sign* of the Prophet Jonah, 16 July 1854 - 29 May 1870 (4)

The *Lord* of Life, 23 July 1854 - 3 May 1868 (25)

St Paul Before Agrippa, 27 August 1854

Members of Christ's Body, 8 October 1854

The *Seal* of the Spirit, 22 October 1854 - 14 October 1860 (2)

Scattering and Increase, 19 November 1854

Jesus of Nazareth Passeth By, 18 February 1855 - February 1866 (20)

Esau, 4 March 1855

The *Veil* Removed, 8 April 1855

Jael, 17 June 1855

The *Spirit* Not of Fear But of Love, 22 July 1855 - 18 October 1862 (11)

The *Disobedient* Prophet, 28 July 1855 - 20 July 1861 (2)

The *Kingdom* of God, 5 August 1855 - 12 September 1859 (4)

Naaman, 19 August 1855 - 12 August 1866 (6)

Christ the Image of God, 26 August 1855

St Thomas, [21 December] 1855

The *Lord* of Life, 27 January 1856

The *Christian Priesthood*, 30 August 1857

I. St Paul's Teaching - 4 Groups of Epistles. Introduction, 2 May [1858]

2. 1st Group. Epistles to the Thessalonians. AD 57, 58. Christ the Judge, 9 May [1858]

3. 2nd Group. Epistles to Corinthians, Galatians, & Romans. AD 57, 58. Christ the Sacrifice, 16 May [1858]

4. 3rd Group. Epistles to Philippians, Colossians & Ephesians. AD 61, 62. Christ the Word, 23 May [1858]

5. 4th Group. Pastoral Epistles. AD 67, 68, 30 May [1858]

The *Kingdom* of God, 6 March 1859

Offenses, 20 November 1859

The *Secrets* of the Heart Revealed, 5 June 1859 - [25 May] 1865 (4)

The *Curse* and the Blessing of Labour, 12 February 1860

Escape For Thy Life, 29 February 1860 - 5 March 1865 (7)

The *Life* Hidden With Christ in God, 22 April 1860

True and False Manliness, [28 October] 1860

All Is Vanity, 14 April, 1861

The *Kingdom* of God, 23 June 1861 - 28 May 1876 (10)

Esau, 10 November 1861 [= CS 3-18]

The *Christian Priesthood*, 3 May 1862 - 15 January 1865 (2)

Our Heavenly Citizenship, 9 October 1862 - 10 June 1866 (6 ?)

The *Life* of Christ the Basis of Christian Belief [and Practice], 16 November 1862 - 21 May 1870 (3)

Joel's Call to Repentance, 3 March 1863 - 28 February 1866 (4)

Stir Up the Gift of God, 6 December 1863

True Blessedness, 28 February 1864 - 12 March 1871 (4)
Life's Pilgrimage, 29 May 1864 - 30 December 1866 (4)
The *Sword* of the Word, 8 August 1864 - 25 January 1865 (2)
The *Morning* and the Night, 27 November 1864
The *Truth* Shall Make You Free, 4 December 1864
Our *Sonship* Realized, 11 December 1864 - 30 December 1866 (2)
The *Lord* Looketh On the Heart, 18 March 1865 - 21 July 1867 (3)
Nathan and David. The Forgiveness of Sin, 19 November 1865 - 4 December [1870] (3)
Divided Allegiance, 25 February 1866 - 15 July 1866 (2)
Thirst Not of Water, 11 March 1866 - 18 April 1869 (3)
Passed from Death to Life/The passage From Death Unto Life, 24 June 1864 - 29 June 1887 (12)
David and Absalom/The Consequences of Sin, 8 July 1866 - 2 October 1870 (3)
The *Message* to Laodicea, 2 December 1866 - 12 May 1872 (4)
Christ Our High Priest, 2 December 1866 - 14 February 1869 (2)
Christ's Little Ones, All Saints Day 1867 - 29 July 1879 (2)
The *People* and the Nations, 27 January 1867 - 19 July 1886 (5)
The Conqueror From Edom, 27 January 1867 - 23 June 1872 (6) [= CS 19-33]
The *Preacher* of Repentance, 6 March 1867 - 24 June 1885 (9)
The *Good Shepherd*, 8 March 1868
Shew Us the Father, 29 November 1868 [= CS 129-49]
Grieve Not the Spirit, 16 May 1869
The *Edifying* of the Body of Christ, 26 October 1869 - 22 July 1879 (2)
Will He Do More Miracles Than These?, 28 November 1869
The *Secrets* of the Heart Revealed, 7 March 1870 - 18 May 1871 (3)
Blessed Are the Pure in Heart, 8 May 1870 [published as 'Purity of Heart', CS 34-47]
The Sword of the Word, 6 November 1870 [= CS 150-71]
The Head and the Body, 13 November 1870 [= CS 172-92]
The *Likeness* of Christ's Death and Resurrection, 8 May 1871 - 25 March 1883 (2)
Christ's Gift of Peace, 14 May 1871 [= SSP 136-49]
The *Teaching* of the Heavens, 21 May 1871
The *Worship* of God in Spirit and in Truth, 28 May 1871 - 1 June 1879 (2)
Consecration of the Voice, 13 June 1871
The Fall of Judas, 3 September 1871 (3) [= SSP 58-74]
The Counsel of Caiaphas, 10 September 1871 - 19 March 1872 (2) [= SSP 75-90]
The *Balance* of Good and Evil, 17 September 1871
The *One Talent* Hidden, 24 September 1871
Two Sowings and Two Harvests, 19 November 1871 [= CS 48-62]
The One God and the Gods Many, 6 December 1871 - 23 November 1873 (2) [= CS 80-95]
Old Things Are passed Away, 7 January 1872 - 1 January 1882 (2)
All Things Are Yours, 21 January 1872 - 22 February 1883 (2)
The *Light* of the Heavenly City, 28 January 1872
The *Sanctification* of Friendship, 3 March 1872
The Holy Trinity, 26 May 1872 [= SSP 287-303]
The Triumph of Failure, 2 June 1872 - 4 December 1887 (23) [= SSP 122-35]
Spiritual Drought, 9 June 1872 - 21 July 1886 (6)
The *Corruptible* and the Incorruptibe Crown, 16 June 1872
The One Taken and the Other Left, 23 June 1872 - 8 July 1888 (20) [= SSP 106-21]

Only Believe, 1 September 1872

Treasure For Self, 8 September 1872 - 26 January 1879 (3)

The *Sympathy* of Our High Priest, 15 September 1872 - 5 December 1886 (34)

The *Sins* of the Fathers Visited on the Children, 22 September 1872

The *Father's* Compassion/Returning Home, 29 September 1872 - 21 December 1879 (3)

The *Eagles* and the Carcase, 5 January - 25 February 1874 (3)

Moral Freedom and Moral Bondage, 12 January 1873 - 28 February 1875 (2)

Hasty Judgment, 19 January 1873 [= SSP 193-205]

The *Sheep* Hear His Voice, 26 January 1873 - 22 January 1888 (14)

Balaam and Balak, 4 May 1873 - 8 May 1881 (3) [= SSP 1-15]

The *Vision* of God, 11 May 1873 - 5 March 1876 (2)

Three Notes of the Spirit, 18 May 1873

Fullness of Life in the Spirit, 7 September 1873 - 11 December 1884 (9)

The *Saving* and Losing of the Soul, 14 September 1873 - 15 March 1874 (2)

Christian Forethought and Unchristian Anxiety, 21 September 1873 [= SSP 164-77]

The *Valley* of Achor, 28 September 1873 - 27 January 1887 (10)

The Wrath of the Lamb, 26 October 1873 - 2 May 1875 (2) [= CS 193-211]

The *Necessity* of Preaching the Gospel, 3 December 1873

Fear Upon Every Soul. 4 January 1874 - 4 January 1880 (2)

The *Right* and the Wrong Knowledge of Christ, 11 January 1874

The *Scene* in the Synagogue at Nazareth, 18 January 1874 - 8 January 1882 (2)

St Paul Our Example, 25 January 1874 [= SSP 218-29]

Risen With Christ, 3 May 1874

Charity Never Faileth, 10 May 1874 - 22 January 1888 (7)

The *Attracting* Power of Christ Lifting Up, 17 May 1874

The *Trisagion*, 31 May 1874 - 5 June 1887 (2)

Depart From Me, 6 September 1874 [marked "altered & preached elsewhere" [= S 17-29: published as "The Consciousness of Sin Heaven's Pathway"]

The *Fire* and the Salt of Sacrifice, 13 September 1874

The *Triumph* of Foolishness, 20 September 1874

Harvest Rejoicing, 27 September 1874 - 28 October 1884 (7)

The *Clerical Office* A Service, 20 December 1874 - 24 September 1881 (2)

The Great Renewal, 3 January 1875 [= SSP 304-14]

Weakness Triumphant in the Gospel, 19 January 1875 - 13 January 1884 (4)

Not Peace But a Sword, 17 January, 1875

God's Witness in Nature, 24 January 1875

Meats Offered to Idols, 31 January 1875

The *Hidden* Life, 9 May 1875 - 13 October 1881 (3)

Another Paraclete, 16 May 1875 - 19 May 1888 (4)

Through a Glass Darkly, 23 May 1875 - 12 June 1881 (2)

Pilate's Question, 30 May 1875 [= SSP 91-105]

The Madness of Paul/Madness and Sanity, 5 September 1875 - 11 November 1877 (2) [= SSP 255-68]

The Mirror of God's Glory, 12 September 1875 - 7 June 1885 (8) [= CS 96-108]

St Paul's One Boast, 19 September 1875 - 18 September 1887 (4)

The *Child* and the Man, 26 September 1875

The Meanness and the Greatness of Man, 21 November 1875 - 13 February 1881 (3) [= CS 229-47]

The *Times* and the Seasons Hidden, 2 January 1876 - 4 January 1880 (2)

The *Mystery* Revealed, 9 January 1876
What Advantageth It?, 19 January 1876
Christ the Power and Wisdom of God, 23 January 1876
True Blessedness, 7 May 1876 [= SSP 178-92]
Christ and the *Samaritan Woman*, 14 May 1876 - 15 December 1885 (4)
The Witness of the Jewish Nation to Christ, 21 May 1876 - 15 May 1887 (5) [= S 29-43: published as "The History of Israel An Argument in Favour of Christianity"]
The Constraining Love of Christ, 3 September 1876 - 31 July 1887 (21) [= SSP 243-54]
If Thine Eye Be Single, 10 September 1876
Lawful and Unlawful Judgments, 24 September 1876
Offences, 22 October 1876 [= CS 248-64]
Folly and Weakness Triumphant, 29 October 1876 [= CS 265-82]
War in the Soul, 14 January 1877 - 24 September 1882 (2)
The Later *Glory* of the Temple, 21 January 1877 - 23 May 1881 (2)
The Spirit and the Letter, 28 January 1877 [= SSP 206-17]
The *Vision* of Isaiah, 6 May 1877
Why Stand Ye Gazing Into Heaven?, 13 May 1877 - 6 June 1886 (4) [= SSP 150-63]
He Shall Take of Mine, 20 May [1877] - [20 May] 1888 (8)
Caesar's Tribute and God's Tribute, 9 September 1877 - 10 July 1887 (6) [= SSP 46-57]
Hunger and Thirst After Righteousness, 16 September 1877 - 21 June 1886 (4)
The *Leaven* of the Pharisees, 23 September 1877
Bearing Fruit, 30 September 1877 - 6 June 1888 (5)
The Whirlwind From the North, 9 October 1877 [= SSO 71-90]
[*What* Is Christianity?], I-IV, 1877[1]
The *Vision* of the King, 6 January 1878 - 9 January 1887 (2)
Vanity of Vanities, 13 January 1878 - 27 November 1881 (4)
What Is That to Thee?, 20 January 1878 - 30 June 1885 (2) [with alterations = OA 149-67]
Untitled sermon on Revelation 3:14 [= The Message to Laodicea ?], 27 January 1878 [= SSP 269-86]
Who Is Against Us?, 5 May 1878 - 4 January 1885 (3)
The Forgiveness of David's Sins/Nathan and David, 12 May 1878 [= SSP 16-30]
The *Consequences* of Sin/David and Absalom, 19 May 1878 [= SSP 31-45]
Teach All Nations, 26 May 1878
Delhi Mission, 1 December 1878 - 11 December 1887 (5)
What Must I Do to Be Saved?" 5 January 1879 [= SSP 230-42: published as "The Philippian Gaoler"]
Not Meat and Drink, 12 January 1879 - 28 June 1889 (2)
Healthy Religion, 19 January - 14 June 1880 (2)
Joseph Butler, 15 May 1879 [= LNC 159-72]
Ordination. *June 1879*
Shew Me Thy Glory, 8 June 1879 [= SSO 91-102]

---

[1]   Four sermons without a title or any indication of occasion. This title has been supplied as an inference from the subject matter. It is conjectured that they are the sermons referred to in RS Hazelbrook to Lightfoot, 29 January 1878, in which case they will have been preached for the Cambridge University Church Society in the Michaelmas Term of 1877.

The *Three Temples*, 23 June 1879 - 8 November 1887 (7)

Lenghten Thy Cords and Strengthen Thy Stakes, 3 November 1879 [= SSO 103-118]

Witnessing to Fact, 30 November 1879 [= SSO 119-130]

Ordination Address. *Advent 1879*

Vision of Isaiah, nd 1880 - 12 February 1888 (14)

Charge to Ordination Candidates I, Trinity 1880 - Advent 1887 (3) [= OA 3-16]

A *Temple* of the Living God, 21 June [1880] - 5 March 1888 (29)

Hope Purifying, 28 June 1880 - 11 May 1885 (5)

Charge to Ordination Candidates II, September 1880 - nd 1888 (3) [= OA 17-29]

The *Pharisee* and the Publican, 18 October - 20 March 1886 (17)

Pure Religion and Undefiled, 14 November 1880 - 22 November 1885 (2)

I Ascend Unto My Father and Your Father, 26 November 1880

The Meeting of Heaven and Earth (Ordination Charge), Advent 1880 - Trinity 1888 (3) [= OA 30-43]

The Value of a Soul, 13 December 1880

Philip's Life and Work, 29 December 1880

The *Sudden Coming* of the Lord, 18 January 1881

Charge to Ordination Candidates IV, Trinity 1881 - Advent 1885 (2) [= OA 44-54]

Both One, 21 June 1881 [= SSO 131-45]

The Death of Bede, 29 June 1881 [= LNC 87-101]

The *House* of God, 23 October 1881

The *Revival* of Dry Bones, 23 November 1881

Charge to Ordination Candidates V, Advent 1881 - Advent 1884 (2) [= OA 55-66]

Andrew Simon Peter's Brother, 1881 - 1886 (2) [= SSO 160-73]

College Gathering 1882

Charge to Ordination Candidates VI, Trinity 1882 - Trinity 1886 (2) [= OA 67-81]

Christian Fellowship, 14 June 1882 - 29 February 1888 (3)

Richard de Bury, 29 June 1882 [= LNC 103-19]

Charge to Ordination Candidates VII, September 1882 - September 1889 [= OA 82-94]

Our *Heavenly* Citizenship, 1 November 1882 - St Peter's Day 1889 (5)

Ordination Charge, *Advent 1882* - Trinity 1887

The *Restored* Temple, 2 February 1883 - 29 July 1887 (6)

Kings and Priests, 7 May 1883 [= SSO 191-203]

White Cross Army, 20 May 1883

St Peter's Temptations, St Peter's Day 1883 [= OA 123-35]

S Cuthbert, 18 July 1883 [= LNC 71-86]

S Oswald, 1 August 1883 [= LNC 19-35]

True Ambition, 21 October 1883 [= CS 317-34]

Bernard Gilpin, 1 May 1884 [= LNC 121-35]

He Hath Not Dealt So With Any Nation, 29 May 1884 [= SSO 204-19]

Twofold Burdens, 29 June 1884 [= OA 136-48]

1. Fellow Workers With God, October 1885 - January 1888 (2) [= OA 214-24]

The Repulsion and Attraction of Christ, October 1885 - January 1888 (2) [= OA 225-40]

Cuddesdon Address III, October 1885 - January 1888 (2) [= OA 241-57]

4. The Partisan Spirit, October 1885 - January 1888 (2) [= OA 258-70]

5. Adventuring the Soul, October 1885 - January 1888 (2) [= OA 271-82]

6 Communication of Self. October 1885 - January 1888 (2) [= OA 283-93]

7. The Unusual Teacher and the Unusual Lesson (?), October 1885 - January 1888 (2)

[= OA 294-308]
Farewell, October 1985 - January 1888 (2) [= OA 309-318]
S. Hilda, 18 November 1885 [= LNC 55-70]
S. Aidan, 7 December 1885 [= LNC 37-54]
Auckland College. 1886
The Passage From Death to Life, 29 June 1887 [= OA 168-82]
Our Citizenship, 1 November 1887 (?) [= S 157-69]
The Celtic Mission of Iona and Lindisfarne, 20 November 1887 [= LNC 1-17]
Auckland Address, 29 June 1888 [= OA 183-93]
The Restoration of Assyria, 8 July 1888 [= SSO 265-80]
John Cosin, 1 August 1888 [= LNC 137-57]
Auckland College. (Commemoration 1889). Not Meat and Drink, 28 June 1889 [= OA 194-213]
Untitled sermon on Isaiah 6:8, n.d.
Untitled sermon on Luke 11: 29, 30, 32, n.d.
Untitled sermon on Acts 15:40, n.d.
Untitled sermon on Colossians, 2:19, n.d.

II. Other Primary Sources

a. Unpublished

Balliol College Oxford:

Jowett Papers

Box E:
Letters, notes, etc. of biographical interest. Letters of Jowett to Stanley, ca. 1840 to 1863

MS 410:
Letters of Jowett to Stanley, from 1841 to the 1860s

Bodleian Library Oxford:

Hort Correspondence
Lightfoot Correspondence
Prince Lee Correspondence
Westcott Correspondence

British Library, London:

Lightfoot (Joseph Barber), Bishop of Durham
Seal, 1879. CXLIV. 40, 41
Letters to Lord Harrowby, 1873
Letter to Sir W.C. James, 1882
Letters to Mary Gladstone, 1883-1885
Letter to A.P. Stanley
Correspondence with W.E. Gladstone, 1870-89
Letter to F.T. Palgrave, 1881

Cambridge University Archives:

Cambridge University Register (CUR)
28.2, Divinity Faculty
28.8, Moral Sciences Tripos
28.10, History Tripos
38.38, Lightfoot Historical Scholarship
39.1, Margaret Professorship of Divinity

39.25.1, The Hulsean Professorship of Divinity
39.25.2, Hulsean Accounts
39.25.3, Hulsean Professorship of Divinity
39.39, Dixie Professorship of Ecclesiastical History
53, Council of the Senate
57.1, Local Examinations and Local Lectures
60, Non-Collegiate Students
112, Revision Syndicate 1849-56. Council and Commission 1856-60

Minute Books of the Council of the Senate
Minutes of the Board of Moral Science Studies
Minutes of the Theological Studies Syndicate
Minutes of the Non-Collegiate Students Admission Syndicate
Minutes of the Divinity School and Additional Buildings Syndicate
Minutes of the University Expences [sic] Syndicate
Minutes of the Museums and Lecture Rooms Syndicate

O.XIV.25-34

Lady Margaret Professorship of Divinity. Votes at Elections to Professorship, 1688-1887, 1907

O.XIV.83-9

Professorial Certificates, 1852-79

O.XIV.90-102

Professorial Certificates, 1852-76

Prem.V.1-3

From the Chancellor, Masters and Scholars of the University of Cambridge to the Trustees of the Selwyn Divinity School, 31 March 1882

Prem.V.2

Lightfoot to Richard Okes, 10 April 1882

Prem.V.4

Selwyn Benefaction Trust: Vouchers for Erection of Divinity Schools, Correspondence, etc

V.C. Corr.V.8 (1-16)

"Compulsory Greek Syndicate", June 1870 - April 1871

UP 5, 15-23

Collecteana. U[niversity] P[apers], 1820-1883

Cambridge University Library

Manuscript Room

Add 2592 70, 984

Lightfoot to H. Bradshaw, 21 May 1869
Lightfoot to H. Bradshaw, 28 March n.y.

Add 2594/X/20

Petition urging completion of the new library buildings

Add 2717 (4) 9

Papers relating to Lancashire Distress, n.d.

Add 5058 p 1

    R. Willis, Correspondence with V.C., etc., 1869

Add 6259 75, 95, 189, 203

    Lightfoot to Taylor, 26 February 1871
    Lightfoot to Taylor, 9 November 1878
    Lightfoot to Taylor, 21 February n.y.
    Lightfoot to Taylor, 10 November n.y.

Add 6377 423

    Lightfoot to Cowell, 29 October n.y.

Add 6580 97

    Lightfoot to the Vice Chancellor, 9 February 1869

Add 6581 275

    Lightfoot to the Vice Chancellor, 17 November 1876

Add 6582 353, 407, 410

    Lightfoot to the Vice Chancellor, 4 May 1877
    Lightfoot to the Vice Chancellor, 8 October 1877
    Lightfoot to the Vice Chancellor, 8 October 1877

Add 6583 553

    Lightfoot to the Vice Chancellor, 10 June 1878

Add 6584 678, 680, 681

    Lightfoot to the Vice Chancellor, 14 February n.y. [1879]
    Lightfoot to the Vice Chancellor, n.d.
    Lightfoot to the Vice Chancellor, 25 February n.y. [1879]

Add 6597 637

    Selections From the Theological Correspondence of F.J.A. Hort

Add 6827 - 6840[2]

    Diaries of Joseph Romilly, vols 13-30, 1851-61

Add 6935 - 6940

    New Testament Revision Company. Minutes of Meetings

Add 6941

    New Testament Revision Company. Register of Attendance 1870-80

Add 8316

    Lightfoot to Arthur Westcott, 6 August 1884

Add 8317 50

    Lightfoot to B.F. Westcott, n.d. 1870

Add 8317 58

    Lightfoot to B.F. Westcott, 5 October [1870]

Add 8317 59

    Lightfoot to E.W. Benson, 28 December n.y.

RA F 35 115-21

    Correspondence of H.R.H. Prince Albert, the Prince Consort, as Chancellor of Cambridge University 1847-186

Rare Book Room

>Cam. Collection
>
>Cambridge Papers
>
>Cambridge University Papers

Main Library

>Cambridge University Examination Papers 1872-1879

Canterbury Cathedral Library and Archives:

Farrar Papers, Bundle 27

Dean and Chapter Library, Durham Cathedral:

Malden Gift

>35 letters to Jenny Barber from J.B. Lightfoot

Durham University. Department of Diplomatic and Palaeography:

Auckland Castle Episcopal Records

>File of "Copies of Printed Matter"
>Box file of correspondence and papers mainly concerning the training of ordinands, ca. 1880-1904 and n.d.
>Volume containing farewell address to the Bishop of Durham from the Clergy of Northumberland, 1882
>Clergy call book 1882
>Volume containing minutes of meetings of bishops, archdeacons and rural deans, 1883-1897

Durham University Library:

Add'l MS 132

>17 letters of Lightfoot to Archdeacon and Mrs Watkins
>4 letters of B.F. Westcott to Archdeacon and Mrs Watkins

MS 274 208 L5

>Geological notes with coloured sections of strata, 2f.

MS 942 81 L 4B2

>Lightfoot to Mrs Mansel, 4 August 1874
>Lightfoot to John Murray, 15 June 1877

SR Cabinet C1 (1873-84) Lightfoot

>6 letters of Lightfoot to various correspondents, concerning subscriptions to appeals, thanks for help, invitations to preach, etc., 1873-1884

SR Cabinet C1 (1876-89) Lightfoot

>12 letters to various correspondents

Emmanuel College Library:

The H.M. Gwatkin Papers

>Testimonial for Gwatkin by Lightfoot
>Hazeltine Manuscript 'Life of Gwatkin'

Girton College Library, Cambridge:

Emily Davies Papers

>ED XVII/GC 5/8 Lightfoot to Emily Davies, 12 December 1872

Keble College Oxford:

Liddon Papers

Lambeth Palace Library London:

Letters and Papers of Edward White Benson Archbishop of Canterbury 1883-1896

Hatch Papers
Jackson Papers
Tait Papers
Wordsworth Papers

Liverpool City Library:

942 Wat 1/42/1 & 942 Wat 1/56/2
Lightfoot to N. Waterhouse, 17 October 1862 & 25 October [1862]

Liverpool Record Office:

Epitaph at St Philip's Church, Liverpool: In Memory of Frances Maria Lightfoot, William Stoker, John Jackson Lightfoot and Ann Matilda Lightfoot
Minute Book of the Liverpool Literary and Philosophical Society 1817-1823
Pedigree of the Barber Family
Probate of the Will of Alice Lightfoot

Pusey House Oxford:

Church Papers
Red Filing Box C. "35 Miscellaneous Letters"
Liddon Papers
Envelope 27: Correspondence. Theological School. Board of Studies

St Paul's Cathedral Library:

Chapter Minute Book 1860-1874
Chapter Minute Book 1870-1915 [Saturday Chapters]
Chapter Minute Book 1874-1889
Chapter Minute Book 1879-1891

Selwyn Divinity School Cambridge:

Minutes of the Board of Theological Studies

University of London Library:

Seeley Papers

Wren Library, Trinity College, Cambridge:

Add Ms.a.63[32-51]

Letters to Seniors (Chapel)

Add Ms.a.63[34]

Lightfoot to W. Whewell, n.d.

Add Ms.a.63[48]

Baron L.N. de Rothschild to Lightfoot, 26 October 1859

Add Ms.a.77[217-23]

Lightfoot to J.L. Hammond

Add Ms.b.17[71]

Lightfoot to J.M. Image, 7 May 1881

Add Ms.b.49[143, 159]

Lightfoot to Mrs F.E. Thompson, 27 March n.y.

Lightfoot to Mrs F.E. Thompson, 11 April 1885

Add Ms.b.49[200]

J.D. Coleridge to Lightfoot, 6 November 1867

Add Ms.b.113[32]

Lightfoot to W. Carus, 1875

Add Ms.c.36[38]

Lightfoot to Henry Jackson, 27 February 1865

Add Ms.c.89[104]

Lightfoot to W. Whewell, 29 November n.y.

Add Ms.c.94[86-7]

Lightfoot to Henry Sidgwick, 28 January 1879
Lightfoot to Henry Sidgwick, 26 April 1879

Bursar's Minutes

From 24 January 1852 to 23 May 1857
From 10 October 1857 to 7 December 1861

College Notices, vol. I

Conclusions 1811 to 1886

Diaries of E.W. Benson

Vol I-IX, 1871-1889

Private Letters of Archbishop Benson

Trinity College Governing Body. Minutes 1857-1860

b. Published

1. Works by Lightfoot In Chronological Sequence

"Hyperides." *Journal of Classical and Sacred Philology* I.i (March 1854) 109-24.

Review of P. Schaff, *History of the Apostolic Church, With a General Introduction to Church History. Journal of Classical and Sacred Philology* II.iv (March 1855) 119-20.

Review of E. Falkener, *A Description of Some Important Theatres and Other Remains in Crete. Journal of Classical and Sacred Philology* II.iv (March 1855) 120.

"The Mission of Titus to the Corinthians." *Journal of Classical and Sacred Philology* II.v (May 1855) 194-205 [= BE 271-84].

Review of C.O. Müller, *Denkmaler der Alten Kunst, Nach der Auswahl und Anordnung. Journal of Classical and Sacred Philology* II.v (May 1855) 240-1.

Review of W. Webster & W.F. Wilkinson, *The Greek Testament, With Notes Grammatical and Exegetical. Journal of Classical and Sacred Philology* II.vi (November 1855) 360-1.

Review of American Bible Union, *The Second Epistle of Peter, the Epistles of John and Judas, and the Revelation: Translated From the Greek, On the Basis of the Common English Version, With Notes. Journal of Classical and Sacred Philology* II.vi (November 1855) 361-3.

Review of W. Blew, *Agamemnon the King: a Tragedy From the Greek of Aeschylus. Journal of Classical and Sacred Philology* II.vi (November 1855) 363-4.

"Recent Editions of St Paul's Epistles." *Journal of Classical and Sacred Philology* III.vii (March 1856) 81-121.

Review of F.A. Paley, *The Tragedies of Aeschylus. Re-edited With an English Commentary. Journal of Classical and Sacred Philology* III.viii (June 1856) 238.

"On the Style and Character of the Epistle to the Galatians." *Journal of Classical and Sacred Philology* III.ix (December 1856) 289-327.

"They That Are of Caesar's Household." *Journal of Classical and Sacred Philology* IV x (March 1857) 57-79.

Review of W.J. Conybeare & J.S. Howson, *The Life and Epistles of St Paul. Journal of Classical and Sacred Philology* IV.x (March 1857) 107-9.

On the Celibacy Question. Privately printed, 26 October, 1857.

"Notes on Some Corrupt and Obscure Passages in the *Helena* of Euripides." *Journal of Classical and Sacred Philology* IV.xi (March 1858) 153-86.

Two flysheets on the Minor Scholarships proposed to be created at Trinity College. Privately printed, 17 & 31 March 1859 [copies in *College Notices*, vol. I, TCC].

"On the Long Walls at Athens." *Journal of Classical and Sacred Philology* IV.xii (December 1859) 294-302.

On the Report of the Syndicate Appointed to Regulate the Examinations of Students Not Members of the University. Privately printed, 6 March, 1860.

"I have just received Mr Roberts' second paper, and I hasten to reply to it ..." Privately printed, 8 March 1860 [copy among the Cambridge University Papers ET 61, CUL].

Christian Progress. A Sermon Preached in the Chapel of Trinity College, Cambridge, at the Commemoration of Benefactors, December 15, 1860. Cambridge & London: Macmillan, 1861.

The Increasing Purpose of God. A Sermon, Preached in the Church of St Olave, Hart Street. On Trinity Monday, May 27, 1861, Before the Corporation of Trinity House. London: Rivingtons, 1861.

"Romans, The Epistle to the," "Thessalonians, First Epistle to the," & "Thessalonians, Second Epistle to the." In *A Dictionary of the Bible.* Ed. W. Smith. London: John Murray, 1863, III.1053-58, 1477-81, 1481-4.

St Paul's Epistle to the Galatians. A Revised Text With Introduction, Notes, and Dissertations, London: Macmillan, 1865 [1957 Zondervan reprint of unnominated edtion].

"The New Professorship." Privately printed, 6 February, 1866.

In Memory of William Whewell. A Sermon Preached in the College Chapel On Sunday, March 18, 1866. London & Cambridge: Macmillan, 1866.

The Mustard Seed and the Leaven. A Sermon Preached On Tuesday, September 18, at St. Paul's Church, Bedford, On Behalf of the Society for the Propagation of the Gospel in Foreign Parts. London & Cambridge: Macmillan, 1866.

"Papias of Hierapolis." *Contemporary Review* 5 (August 1867) 397-417.

"Caius or Hippolytus?" *Journal of Philology* I.1 (1868) 98-112.

"Two Neglected Facts Bearing on the Ignatian Controversy." *Journal of Philology* I.2 (1868) 47-55.

St Paul's Epistle to the Philippians. A Revised Text with Introduction, Notes and Dissertations. London & Cambridge: Macmillan, 1868 [1953 Zondervan reprint of the edition of 1913].

Review of J. Bleek, *An Introduction to the Old Testament. Cambridge University Gazette* 23 (2 June 1869) 184-5.

S. Clement of Rome. London & Cambridge: Macmillan, 1869.

"Heading of the Paris MS of the Ignatian Epistle to the Romans." *Journal of Philology* II.3 (1869) 157.

"M. Renan On the Epistle to the Romans." *Journal of Philology* II.4 (1869) 264-95 [= BE 287-320].

Review of E. Renan, *Saint-Paul. The Academy* I.1 (9 October 1869) 10-11; & I.2 (13 November 1869) 37-8.

Untitled fly-sheet on "the Report of the Great St Mary's Pulpit Syndicate." 14 February, 1871 [copy among the Cambridge University Papers FA 8592, CUL].

"The Evidences of Christianity in Relation to the Current Forms of Scepticism." *Report of the Church Congress* (Nottingham 1871) 76-84.

"The Epistle to the Romans." *The Journal of Philology* III.6 (1871) 193-214 [= BE 352-74].

On a Fresh Revision of the English New Testament. London & New York: Macmillan, 1871, 1891³.

Letter to the Editor. *The Guardian* (10 April 1872) 484.

"Professor Lightfoot On Divinity Degrees." *The Guardian* (22 May 1872) 680.

Review of J.G. Müller, *Erklärung des Barnabasbriefes. The Academy* III.49 (1 June 1872) 206-7.

Letter to the Editor. *The Guardian* (9 October 1872) 1272.

Strength Made Perfect in Weakness. A Sermon Preached In St Paul's Cathedral On Sunday, December 22, 1872, At the Bishop of London's Ordination. Cambridge & London: Macmillan, 1873.

ΠΑΝΤΑ 'ΥΜΩΝ: A Sermon Before the University Church Society. Cambridge: privately printed, n.d. [1873] [= SSO 1-20].

Except It Die. A Sermon Preached in the Chapel of Trinity College, Cambridge, On Sexagesima Sunday, February 16, 1873 Cambridge & London: Macmillan, 1873 [= CS 63-79].

Letter to the Editor. *The Times* (23 May 1873) 12.

"The Drama." In *"The Use and Abuse of the World." Six Sermons Preached ... in the Church of St James's, Piccadilly.* Ed. J.E. Kempe. London: S.P.C.K., 1873 (reprinted as *The Drama.* London: S.P.C.K., 1898) [= SSO 21-37].

Comparative Progress of Ancient and Modern Missions. A Paper Read at the Annual Meeting of the Society for the Propagation of the Gospel in Foreign Parts, April 29, 1873. London: Clay, 1874 [= HE 71-92].

Review of H.J. Holtzmann, *Kritik der Epheser- und Kolosserbriefe auf Grund einer Analyse ihres Verwandtschaftsverhältnisses. The Academy* IV.77 (1 August 1873) 287-9.

"The Present Need and the Best Means of Quickening Interest in Theological Thought." *Report of the Church Congress* (Bath 1873) 227-33.

The Three Temples. An Address Delivered in the Temporary Church of S. Luke's, New Chesterton, Cambridge, On S. Luke's Day, October 18th, 1873, ... On the Occasion of Setting the Memorial Stone of the First Portion of a Permanent Church For S. Luke's District by the Bishop of the Diocese. Cambridge: privately printed, 1873.

"Supernatural Religion. (First Article)." *Contemporary Review* 25 (December 1874) 1-22 [= EWSR 1-31].

"Supernatural Religion (No. II): The Silence of Eusebius." *Contemporary Review* 25 (January 1875) 169-88 [= EWSR 32-58].

"Supernatural Religion (No. III): The Ignatian Epistles." *Contemporary Review* 25 (February 1875) 337-59 [= EWSR 59-88].

"Supernatural Religion (No. IV): Polycarp of Smyrna." *Contemporary Review* 25 (May 1875) 827-66 [= EWSR 89-141].

"Supernatural Religion (No. V): Papias of Hierapolis." *Contemporary Review* 26 (August 1875) 377-403 [= EWSR 142-77].

"Supernatural Religion (No. VI): Papias of Hierapolis." *Contemporary Review* 26 (October 1875) 828-56 [= EWSR 178-216].

Editor of H.L. Mansel, *The Gnostic Heresies of the First and Second Centuries.* London: John Murray, 1875.

Saint Paul's Epistle to the Colossians and Philemon. A Revised Text, With Introductions, Notes, and Dissertations. London: Macmillans, 1875 [1959 Zondervan reprint of the 1879 edition]

"Supernatural Religion (No. VII): The Later School of St John." *Contemporary Review* 27 (February 1876) 471-96 [= EWSR 217-50].

"The New MS of Clement of Rome." *The Academy* IX (20 May 1876) 486.

Review of *Patrum Apostolicorum Opera. Recensuerunt Oscar de Gebhardt, Adolfus Harnack, Theodorus Zahn. The Academy* X.221 (29 July 1876) 113-14.

"Supernatural Religion (No. VIII): The Churches of Gaul." *Contemporary Review* 28 (August 1876) 405-20 [= EWSR 251-71].

The Father of Missionaries. A Sermon Preached on S. Andrew's Day, 1876, Before Members of the University, In S. Michael's Church, Cambridge. Cambridge: privately printed, 1877 [= SSO 38-54].

On the Proposed Grace for Abolishing Compulsory Attendance At Professors' Lectures. Cambridge: University Press, 1877.

S. Clement of Rome. An Appendix Containing the Newly Recovered Portions With Introductions, Notes, and Translations. London: Macmillan, 1877.

All Things To All Men. A Sermon Preached in St Paul's Cathedral on St Mark's Day, At the Consecration of the First Bishop of Truro. London: Macmillan, 1877 [= SSO 55-70].

"Supernatural Religion (No. IX): Tatian's Diatessaron." *Contemporary Review* 29 (May 1877) 1132-43 [= EWSR 272-88].

Letter to the Editor. *The Guardian* (4 July 1877).

"Donne the Poet-Preacher." In *The Classic Preachers of the English Church. Lectures Delivered at St James' Church in 1877*. Series 1. Ed. J.E. Kempe. London: John Murray, 1877 [= HE 221-45].

Articles on Abibas, Ablabius, Aburgius, Acacius (x 4), Achillas, Agapetus (x 2), Alypius, Amphilochius, Anastasius (x 4), Anthimus, Antipater, Antonius, Apion, Apostolic Fathers, Arabianus, Archelaus, Arinthaeus, Asclepiades, Asterius, Atarbius, & Athanasius (bishop of Ancyra); & "Eusebius of Caesarea." In *A Dictionary of Christian Biography, Literature, Sects, and Doctrines*. Ed. W. Smith & H. Wace. London: John Murray, 1877-87, I.7, 11, 12, 14, 15-16, 17, 58, 88, 103-7, 108, 110, 119, 122, 125, 128-30, 147-9, 151, 153, 159, 175, 178, 178-9, 203-4 ; & II.308-48.

"Illustrations of the Acts From Recent Discoveries." *Contemporary Review* 32 (May 1878) 288-96 [= EWSR 291-302].

Address on the Distribution of Scholarships and Prizes of the Liverpool Council of Education in the Concert Room, St George's Hall, Liverpool, January 16, 1879. London: William Tegg & Co., n.d. [1879].

Bought With a Price. Cambridge, 1879 [= CS 283-99].

The Bishop of Durham and the 'Quicumque'. *The Guardian* (27 August 1879) 1216.

"Bishop Lightfoot on Temperance." *Church of England Temperance Chronicle* (20 March 1880) 187.

Inaugural Address. Delivered at the Co-operative Congress, Held at Newcastle-On-Tyne, May 17th, 1880. Manchester: The Central Co-operative Board, 1880.

The Unity of the Church. A Paper Read at the Leicester Church Congress, September 29, 1880. Durham: Andrews & Co., 1880.

"The Last Petition of the Lord's Prayer." *The Guardian* (7, 14, 21 September 1881) [= OFR 269-323].

"Inaugural Address." *Report of the Church Congress* (Newcastle 1881) 12-19.

The Right Rev. The Lord Bishop of Durham, Rev. Canon Ellison, and Mark Knowles ... On Church Temperance Work, With Speech of the Rev. E.H. Perowne, D.D., Vice Chancellor, Chairman at an University Meeting at Cambridge, 22 October, 1881. London: Church of England Temperance Publication Depot, n.d.

"The Cambridge Mission to Delhi. Reprinted from *The Cambridge Review*, November 23, 1881" [copy in Cambridge University Papers MD5, CUL].

"Living Oracles." A Sermon Preached in St Paul's Cathedral at the Anniversary of the British and Foreign Bible Society, By the Right Rev. The Lord Bishop of Durham, Vice President of the Society, On Tuesday, May 2, 1882. London: The Bible House, 1882.

"Many Members and One Body." A Sermon Preached Before the Representative Council of the Scottish Episcopal Church ... On Tuesday, October 10, 1882. Edinburgh: R. Grant & Son, 1882 [= SSO 174-90].

Primary Charge. Two Addresses Delivered to the Clergy of Durham in December 1882. London: Macmillan, 1884.

An Address to Members of the White Cross Army, Delivered in St Mary's Church, Gateshead, May 20, 1883. White Cross Series No. 1; London: Hatchards, 1885.

An Address to Members of the White Cross Army. Delivered at the Lightfoot Institute, March 20th, 1884. London: Hatchards, 1885.

An Address Delivered to the Durham Junior Clerical Society by the Bishop (S. Michael and All Angels, 1884). Cambridge, privately printed, n.d.

"Results of Recent Historical and Topographical Research Upon the Old and New Testament Scriptures." *Report of the Church Congress* (Carlisle 1884) 227-32.

"What Disestablishment Would Involve. A Warning." Address of the Lord Bishop of Durham at the Annual Meeting of the Church Defence Institution, held on June 19, 1885. 1885

"The White Cross." *Contemporary Review* 48 (August 1885) 262-8.

Durham Diocesan Church Conference. Manifesto On Disestablishment. Inaugural Address by the Right Rev. The Lord Bishop of Durham. Newcastle-Upon-Tyne: Andrew Reid, 1885.

The Apostolic Fathers. Part II. S. Ignatius. S. Polycarp. Revised Texts with Introductions, Notes, Dissertations, and Translations. 3 Vols. London: Macmillan, 1885, 1889[2].

"Paul and Festus - A Contrast." In *Expository Sermons On the New Testament*. London: Hodder & Stoughton, 1885, 139-42.

"The Vision of God." In *The Anglican Pulpit of Today*. London: Hodder & Stoughton, 1886, 27-34.

The Bishop of Durham On the Sunday Closing Bill. Speech in the House of Lords, May 11, 1886. Sunday Closing Tracts; New Series No. 17, n.d.

"Inaugural Address." *Journal of the British Archaeological Association* XLIII (March 1887) 1-12.

Lay Evangelists. An Address Delivered by the Bishop of Durham, On Friday, October 22nd, 1886, In Bishopwearmouth Parish Church, When Seven Persons Were Set Apart For This Office. Sunderland, 1887.

A Charge Delivered to the Clergy of the Diocese of Durham, November 25, 1886. London: Macmillan, 1887.

"The Earliest Papal Catalogue." *The Academy* 785 (May 21 1887) 362-3.

The Sermon by the Lord Bishop of Durham, Preached Before the Church Congress, In the Collegiate Church of St Peter, Wolverhampton, On Monday, October 3rd, 1887. London: S.P.C.K., 1887 [= SSO 248-64].

"The Bishop's Inaugural Address." *Durham Diocesan Gazette* I (October 1887) 2-10.

The Threefold Ministry. (From the Writings of the Bishop of Durham). Privately printed, 1888 [= DAA 241-6 & BL 129-39].

An Address, On the Reopening of the Chapel, Auckland Castle, August 1, 1888, By the Bishop of Durham. Bishop Auckland: Cummins, n.d [= LNC 139-57].

"The Bishop of Durham, writing to his diocesan conference from Bournemouth yesterday week." *The Guardian* (27 February 1889) 307.

"The Muratorian Fragment." *The Academy* 907 (21 September 1889) 186-8.

Essays On the Work Entitled Supernatural Religion. London & New York: Macmillan, 1889, 1893[2].

The Apostolic Fathers. Part I. S. Clement of Rome. A Revised Text, with Introductions, Notes, Dissertations, and Translations. London: Macmillan, 1890.

Cambridge Sermons. London: Macmillan, 1890.

"Internal Evidence for the Authenticity and Genuineness of St John's Gospel." *The Expositor* Fourth Series I (1890) 1-21, 81-92, 176-88 [= BE, 1-44].

Leaders of the Northern Church. London: Macmillan, 1890, 1891².

Ordination Addresses and Counsels to Clergy. London: Macmillan, 1890.

Sermons. London: Swan Sonnenschein, 1890.

The Apostolic Fathers ... Revised Texts With Short Introductions and English Translations. Edited and completed by J.R. Harmer. London: Macmillan, 1891.

Sermons Preached in St Paul's Cathedral. London: Macmillan, 1891.

Sermons Preached on Special Occasions. London: Macmillan, 1891.

Dissertations on the Apostolic Age. Reprinted From Editions of St Paul's Epistles. London: Macmillan, 1892.

"Acts of the Apostles." In *A Dictionary of the Bible.* Ed. W. Smith & J.M. Fuller. 2nd ed; London: John Murray, 1893, I.I.25-43.

Biblical Essays. London: Macmillan, 1893.

Notes on the Epistles of St Paul From Unpublished Commentaries. Ed. with an Introductory Note by J.R. Harmer. London: Macmillan, 1895.

Historical Essays. London: Macmillan, 1896.

2. Editions of Lightfoot's Writings

The Apostolic Fathers. Trans. by J.B. Lightfoot & J.R. Harmer. Edited and revised by M.W. Holmes. 2nd ed.; Grand Rapids, Michigan & Leicester: Baker Book House/Apollos, 1990.

Biblical Essays. With an introduction by P.E. Hughes. Grand Rapids, Michigan: Baker Book House, 1979.

The Christian Ministry. Edited with an introduction by P.E. Hughes. Wilton, Connecticut: Morehouse-Barlow Co., 1983.

TRELOAR, G.R. & KAYE, B.N. "J.B. Lightfoot on Strauss and Christian Origins: An Unpublished Manuscript." *Durham University Journal* LXXIX.2 [n.s. XLVIII.2] (June 1987) 165-200.

KAYE, B.N. & TRELOAR, G.R. "J.B. Lightfoot and New Testament Interpretation: An Unpublished Manuscript of 1855." *Durham University Journal* LXXXII.2 [n.s. LI.2] (July 1990) 161-75.

3. Materials Concerning Lightfoot by Contemporaries in Chronological Sequence

ELLIOTT, E.B. "The Rev. E.B. Elliott on Prophetic Articles in the Third Volume of Dr Smith's Dictionary of the Bible." *The Christian Observer* (March 1864) 199-221.

"Dr Lightfoot and his Reviewer," letters by G.W. & W.F. Elgie. *The Churchman* (September 14 1865) 1099; & by "Your Reviewer." *Ibid.* (September 21 1865) 1122.

POOLE, R.S. "Modern Commentaries on the Bible." *Macmillan's Magazine* XIII (December 1865) 143-52; & XIV (July 1866) 196-205.

CUNNINGHAM, R.T. "The Second Epistle of Clement." *British and Foreign Evangelical Review* XXVIII (April 1879) 368-85.

PAROCHUS. *The Bishop of Durham on the Athanasian Creed. The Guardian* (20 August 1879) 1184.

WORDSWORTH, C. *Some Remarks on Bishop Lightfoot's Dissertation on the Christian Ministry.* Edinburgh & London: W. Blackwood & Sons, 1879, 1884².

GIBB, J. "Theologians of the Day." *Catholic Presbyterian* (March 1882) 177-86.

BARBOUR, R.W. *Auckland Castle 1882. Letters of the Rev. R.W. Barbour to his Wife From the Bishop's Palace. Privately printed, n.d.*

LEARY, T.H.L. *Bishop Lightfoot's Defence of the Last Petition of the Lord's Prayer.* London: The Christian Opinion & Revisonist Office, 1882.

HOPKINS, E. *The White Cross Army. A Statement of the Bishop of Durham's Movement.* London: Hatchard's, 1883.

HARNACK, A. von. "Bishop Lightfoot's *Ignatius and Polycarp.*" *The Expositor* 3rd series II (1885) 401-14; III (1886) 9-22 & 175-92.

FULLER, J.M. "The Bishop of Durham on the Ignatian Epistles." *Quarterly Review* 162 (April 1886) 467-500.

MUIR, A.F. "Ignatius and Polycarp: Last Links With the Apostolic Age." *British and Foreign Evangelical Review* XXXV (April 1886) 298-325.

"Bishop Lightfoot's Apostolic Fathers." *The Edinburgh Review* CLXIV (July-October 1886) 100-37.

SANDAY, W. "Bishop Lightfoot." *The Expositor* Third Series IV (July 1886) 13-29.

KILLEN, W.D. *The Ignatian Epistles Entirely Spurious. A Reply to the Right Rev. Dr Lightfoot.* Edinburgh: T. & T. Clark, 1886.

AN ENGLISH PRESBYTER. "The Apostolic Fathers." *The Churchman* I n.s.X (July 1887) 505-19.

[CASSELS, W.R.] *A Reply To Dr Lightfoot's Essays By the Author of "Supernatural Religion."* London: Longmans, 1889.

S. Ignatius the Martyr, Hendon, Sunderland. Service of Consecration. Services and Sermons of the Octave, And Other Matters With Regard to the Church and District of S. Ignatius the Martyr. Consecration By the Right Rev. The Lord Bishop of Durham, D.D., On Tuesday, the 2nd July, 1889 Sunderland, 1889.

BROWNE, G.F. *A Description of the Series of Stained Glass Windows To Be Placed in the Church of S. Ignatius the Martyr, Sunderland, Built By the Late Bishop of Durham, The Right Rev. J.B. Lightfoot, D.D., As a Thank-Offering For God's Mercies Vouchsafed To Him During Seven Years of His Episcopate, 1879-86.* Sunderland, n.d.

"Death of the Bishop of Durham." *Newcastle Daily Chronicle* (Monday 23 December 1889) 4-5.

"Death of the Bishop of Durham." *Newcastle Daily Journal* (Monday, December 23 1889) 5-6.

"The Bishop of Durham." *The Times* (Monday 23 December 1889) [reprinted in *Eminent Persons. Biographies Reprinted From 'The Times'*. London & New York: Macmillan, 1893, IV.203-10].

"Death of the Bishop of Durham." *The Guardian* (24 December 1889) 2013.

"Death of the Bishop of Durham." *The Record* (Friday December 27 1889) 1265-70.

SANDAY, W. "The Bishop of Durham." *The Athenaeum* 3244 (December 28 1889) 894-5.

LAKE, W.C. *Bishop Lightfoot. A Sermon Preached in Durham Cathedral On Sunday, Dec 29th, 1889.* Durham: Andrews & Co., 1890.

"Reminiscences." *The Guardian* (1 January 1890) 6-8.

SANDAY, W. "Bishop Lightfoot." *The Academy* 922 (January 4 1890) 9-10.

R.A. "Joseph Barber Lightfoot, Bishop of Durham." *The Cambridge Review* (January 16 & 23 1890) 134-6, 150-2.

"Report of the Meeting For Procuring a Memorial in Cambridge of the Late Joseph Barber Lightfoot Lord Bishop of Durham." *Cambridge University Reporter* 820 (February 8 1890) 406-20.

Memorial to Bishop Lightfoot. Account of the Meeting Held on the 18th February, 1890, in the Chapter House of Durham Cathedral [copy among the Camb. Uni. Papers, CUL].

FARRAR, F.W. "Bishop Lightfoot." *Contemporary Review* 57 (February 1890) 170-82.

SANDAY, W. "Bishop Lightfoot as an Historian." *English Historical Review* V (April 1890) 208-20.

"Bishop Lightfoot on the New Testament in the Second Century." *Church Quarterly Review* XXX (April - July 1890) 134-59.

Presentation Of a Pastoral Staff to the Bishop of Durham (With Description and Plate). Durham: Andrews & Co., 1890.

BULLOCK, C. *The Two Bishops: A Welcome and a Memory.* London: Home Words, 1890.

WESTCOTT, B.F. *From Strength to Strength: Three Sermons on Stages in a Consecrated Life.* London: Macmillan, 1890.

ARTHUR, T. *The Good Bishop: A Poem.* Newcastle-Upon-Tyne, 1890.

"Bishop Lightfoot's St Clement of Rome." *Church Quarterly Review* XXXII (April 1891) 49-68.

"Bishop Lightfoot." *Durham Directory* (1891) 49-52.

Catalogue of Books Bequeathed to the University of Durham, By Joseph Barber Lightfoot, D.D., Late Lord Bishop. Durham, 1891.

LAMBTON, J.G. "Lord Durham on Bishop Lightfoot." *Illustrated Church News* (Saturday October 29 1892) [copy in the Wren Library, TCC, press mark 103.c.85.8[14]].

[WATKINS, H.W.] "Bishop Lightfoot." *Quarterly Review* 176 (January 1893) 73-105.

CURTEIS, G.H. "Cardinal Newman and Bishop Lightfoot." *Edinburgh Review* 178 (July 1893) 248-65.

BUTLER, E.C. "Bishop Lightfoot and the Early Roman See." *Dublin Review* 4th series 4 (July 1893) 497-514; & (October 1893) 836-57.

"The 'Edinburgh Review' on Newman." *The Spectator* (5 August 1893) 172-3.

HORT, F.J.A. "Lightfoot, Joseph Barber." *Dictionary of National Biography.* Vol. XI. London: Oxford University Press, 1921-2, 1111-19 (originally published in 1893).

[WATKINS, H.W.] *Bishop Lightfoot. Reprinted From the Quarterly Review, With a Prefatory Note by B.F. Westcott.* London: Macmillan, 1894.

PARKS, J.L. "Bishop Lightfoot's Theory of Episcopate." *Sewanee Review* 2 (August 1894) 425-48.

HEADLAM, A.C. "Lightfoot's Apostolic Fathers." *Quarterly Review* 182 (October 1895) 369-98.

FAIRBAIRN, A.M. "Some Recent English Theologians: Lightfoot, Westcott, Hort, Jowett, Hatch." *Contemporary Review* 71 (March 1897) 341-65.

CROSS, J.A. "The Acts of the Apostles. I. A Criticism of Lightfoot and Headlam." *Journal of Theological Studies* o.s. I (1899-1900) 64-75.

MOULE, H.C.G. *"Wise Men and Scribes". A Commemoration Sermon Preached in the Chapel of Trinity College, Cambridge, December 10th, 1907.* Cambridge: Bowes & Bowes, 1907.

BENSON, A.C. "Bishop Lightfoot." *Cornhill Magazine* 103 (May 1911) 672-87 [= *The Leaves of the Tree*, 255-88].

MOULE, H.C.G. *My Cambridge Classical Teachers.* Durham & Newcastle: Andrews & Co./ W.E. Franklin, 1913.

[EDEN, G.R.] "Joseph Barber Lightfoot. A Sermon Preached in Durham Cathedral at the Commemoration of Founders and Benefactors on January 28th, 1926, By The Right Reverend The Lord Bishop of Wakefield." *Durham University Journal* V.24 (1926) 408-12.

EDEN, G.R. & MACDONALD, F.C. (eds). *Lightfoot of Durham. Memories and Appreciations.* Cambridge: University Press, 1932.

D.S.G. "Lightfoot of Durham." *Modern Churchman* XXII.8 (November 1932) 463-66.

RAMSAY, W.M. "Bishop Lightfoot." *Theology* (February 1933) 75-82.

The Society of Christ and the Blessed Mary the Virgin (Durham Diocesan Church Workers) Jubilee Book 1887-1937. 1937

[MACDONALD, F.C.] *The Story of St Peter's Chapel, Auckland Castle, With an Appendix Describing the Windows and Other Features of Interest, Being the Original Draft Manuscript of the Late Frederick Charles MacDonald ... Hon. Canon of Durham.* Revised and completed by H.F. MacDonald. West Hartlepool: G.R. Todd, 1937.

JACKSON, F. FOAKES. "Books Recommended by Bishop Lightfoot." *A History of Church History.* Cambridge: Heffer, 1939, 170-82.

HENSON, H.H. "Bishop Lightfoot." *Bishoprick Papers.* London: Oxford University Press, 1946, 133-40.

SAVAGE, H.E. "Bishop Lightfoot's Influence: His Trust In Young Men." A Paper by the Very Rev. H.E. Savage (Dean of Lichfield, 1909-39). Edited with an introductory note by B.S. Benedikz. *Durham University Journal* LXXVII.1 [n.s. XLVI.1] (December 1984) 1-6.

The Nineteenth Century Painted Glass Windows in St Peter's Chapel Auckland Castle. Undated duplicated pamphlet [copy in the Dean & Chapter Library, Durham Cathedral].

4. Short Reviews of Lightfoot's Works in Chronological Order

Reviews of *Galatians:*
    The Nonconformist (17 May 1865) 405-6.
    The Christian Advocate and Review V.52 (June 1865) 362-5.
    The Churchman (7 September 1865) 1070-71.
    The London Review (4 November 1865) 493-4.
    The Literary Churchman XI.13 (1865) 279-83.
    The Athenaeum 2039 (24 November 1866) 675-6.

Reviews of *Philippians:*
    The Athenaeum 2129 (15 August 1868) 202.
    The Contemporary Review IX (September-December 1868) 444.
    The Literary Churchman (28 November 1868) 487-9.

Reviews of *St Clement of Rome:*
    The Nonconformist (15 September 1869)
    Cambridge University Gazette (8 December 1869) 261.
    The Academy I (9 July 1870) 255.

Reviews of *St Clement of Rome. Appendix:*
    The Literary Churchman (14 July 1877) 273-4.
    The Athenaeum 2602 (8 September 1877) 296.
    The Guardian (28 November 1877) 1653-4.

5. Autobiographies, Biographies and Letters of Contemporaries

ABBOTT, E. & CAMPBELL, L. *Letters of Benjamin Jowett.* London: John Murray, 1899.

ABBOTT, E. & CAMPBELL, L. *The Life and Letters of Benjamin Jowett.* 2nd ed. 2 vols. London: John Murray, 1897.

BAILLIE, A.V. *My First Eighty Years.* London: John Murray, 1951.

BELL, G.K. *Randell Davidson Archbishop of Canterbury.* London: Oxford University Press,1938.

BENSON, A.C. *The Life of Edward White Benson Sometime Archbishop of Canterbury.* 2 vols. London: Macmillan, 1900.

BENSON, A.C. *The Leaves of the Tree. Studies in Biography.* London: Smith, Elder and Co., 1911.

BENSON, A.C. *The Trefoil. Wellington College, Lincoln and Truro.* London: John Murray, 1923.

BICKERSTETH, S. *Life and Letters of Edward Bickersteth Bishop of South Tokyo.* 2nd ed. London: Sampson Low and Co., 1905.

BOBBITT, M.R. *With Dearest Love To All. The Life and Letters of Lady Jebb.* London: Faber and Faber, 1960.

BONNEY, T.G. *Memories of a Long Life.* Cambridge: Metcalfe and Co., 1921.

BROWNE, G. *The Recollections of a Bishop.* London: Smith, Elder and Co., 1915.

BUTLER, J.R.M. *Henry Montagu Butler: Master of Trinity College Cambridge 1886-1918.* London: Longmans, 1925.

CHURCH, M.C. (ed.). *Life and Letters of Dean Church.* London: Macmillan, 1897.

CLARK, J. Willis. *Old Friends at Cambridge and Elsewhere.* London: Macmillan, 1900.

C[OX], W.A., "Charles John Ellicott, Bishop of Gloucester" [copy in CUL, press mark Cam.c.905.14].

CREIGHTON, L. *Life and Letters of Mandell Creighton ... Sometime Bishop of London.* 2 vols. London: Longmans, Green and Co., 1904.

DAVIDSON, R.T. & BENHAM, W. *Life of Archibald Campbell Tait Archbishop of Canterbury.* 2 vols. London: Macmillan, 1891.

GRAHAM, E. *The Harrow Life of Henry Montagu Butler.* London: Longmans, 1920.

GREGORY, R. *Robert Gregory, 1819-1911: Being the Autobiography of Robert Gregory, Dean of St Paul's.* Ed. W.H. Hutton. London: Longmans, 1912.

HARFORD, J.B. & MACDONALD, F.C. *Handley Carr Glyn Moule Bishop of Durham.* London: Hodder and Stoughton, n.d. [1922].

HEITLAND, W.E. *After Many Years. A Tale of Experiences and Impressions Gathered in the Course of an Obscure Life.* Cambridge: University Press, 1926.

HENSON, H.H. *More Letters of Herbert Hensley Henson.* Ed. E.F. Braley. London: S.P.C.K., 1954.

HOLROYD, M. (ed.). *Memorials of the Life of George Elwes Corrie.* Cambridge: University Press, 1890.

HORT, A.F. *Life and Letters of Fenton John Anthony Hort.* 2 vols. London: Macmillan, 1896.

JASPER, R. *Arthur Cayley Headlam. The Life and Letters of a Bishop.* London: Faith Press, 1960.

JEBB, C. *Life and Letters of Sir Richard Claverhouse Jebb.* Cambridge: University Press, 1907.

JOHNSTON, J.O. *Life and Letters of Henry Parry Liddon.* London: Longmans, Green and Co., 1904.

KIDD, B.J. (ed.). *Selected Letters of William Bright*, with an introductory memoir by the Rev. P.G. Medd. London: Wells Gardner and Co., 1903.

KINGSLEY, C. *Charles Kingsley: His Letters and Memories of His Life*, edited by his wife. 2 vols. London: Henry S. King & Co., 1877.

KITCHEN, G.W. *Edward Harold Browne. A Memoir.* London: John Murray, 1895.

LAW, H.W. & LAW, I. *The Book of the Beresford Hopes.* London: Heath Cranton, 1925.

LIDDON, H.P. *Life of Edward Bouverie Pusey.* 4 vols. London: Longmans, Green and Co., 1893.

MACDONNELL, J.C. *The Life and Correspondence of William Connor Magee Archbishop of York.* 2 vols. London: Isbister, 1896.

[MACMILLAN, A.], *Letters of Alexander Macmillan.* Edited with an introduction by his son G.A. Macmillan. Glasgow: printed for private circulation, 1908.

MAJOR, H.D.A. *The Life and Letters of William Boyd Carpenter.* London: John Murray, 1925.

MALAN, A.N. *Solomon Caesar Malan. Memorials of His Life and Writings.* London: John Murray, 1897.

MASON, A.J. *Memoir of George Howard Wilkinson.* 2 vols. London: Longmans, Green and Co., 1909.

MILMAN, A. *Henry Hart Milman, D.D., Dean of St Paul's. A Biographical Sketch*. London: John Murray, 1900.

PARRY, R. St John. *Henry Jackson, O.M.* Cambridge: University Press, 1926.

PATON, J.B. *John Brown Paton. A Biography*. London: Hodder and Stoughton, 1914.

PROTHERO, G.W. *A Memoir of Henry Bradshaw*. London: Kegan Paul, 1888.

PROTHERO, R.E. & BRADLEY, G.G. *The Life and Correspondence of Arthur Penrhyn Stanley, D.D.* 2 vols. London: John Murray, 1893.

RAWNSLEY, H.D. *Harvey Goodwin. Bishop of Carlisle. A Biographical Memoir*. London: John Murray, 1896.

SANDFORD, E.G. (ed.). *Memoirs of Archbishop Temple By Seven Friends*. 2 vols. London: Macmillan, 1906.

S[IDGWICK], A. & S[IDGWICK], E.M. *Henry Sidgwick: A Memoir*. London: Macmillan, 1906.

SIM, A.F. *The Life and Letters of Arthur Fraser Sim. With a Preface by ... Canon Body*. London: Universities Mission, 1896.

STANLEY, A.P. *The Life and Correspondence of Thomas Arnold*. Single vol. ed. London: Ward, Lock & Co., n.d.

STEPHENS, W.R.W. *The Life and Letters of Walter Farqhar Hook*. London: Bentley and Son, 1880.

STUART, J. *Reminiscences*. London: Chiswick Press, 1911.

TURNBULL, H.W. *Some Memories of William Peveril Turnbull One of His Majesty's Inspectors of Schools*. London: S. Bell and Sons, 1919.

WELLDON, J.E.C. *Recollections and Reflections*. London: Cassell, 1915.

WESTCOTT, A. *Life and Letters of Brooke Foss Westcott ... Sometime Bishop of Durham*. 2 vols. London: Macmillan, 1903.

WOOD, J.S. "William Selwyn." *The Eagle* IX (1875) 298-322.

6. Reference Books and Official Publications

Annual Report of the Durham University Association 1884 [copy at Auckland Castle].

BAINES, E. *History, Directory, and Gazeteer, of the County Palatine of Lancaster; With a Variety of Commercial & Statistical Information*. Liverpool: W. Wales & Co., 1824.

BALL, W.W. ROUSE & VENN, J.A. *Admissions To Trinity College, Cambridge. Vol IV. 1801-1850*. London: Macmillan, 1911.

[BRADSHAW, H.] *Statutes For the University of Cambridge and For the Colleges Within It, Made, Published, and Approved (1878-1882) Under the Universities of Oxford and Cambridge Act, 1877, With An Appendix of Acts and Orders*. Cambridge: University Press, 1883.

Cambridge University Calendar 1847-1879.

Cambridge University Reporter 1870-1890.

CLARK, J. Willis, *Endowments of the University of Cambridge*. Cambridge: University Press, 1904.

Conference of Bishops of the Anglican Communion. Holden at Lambeth Palace, in July 1888. Encyclical Letter from the Bishops, With the Resolutions and Reports. London: S.P.C.K., 1888.

Crockford's Clerical Directory.

Dictionary of National Biography.

Durham Diocesan Calendar 1873-1890.

Durham Diocesan Gazette, vols I-IV, 1887-1890.

Durham Diocesan Magazine, vols I-VI, 1881-1886

Gore's Directory of Liverpool and Its Environs. 1829, 1839, 1843.

Gore's Directory and View of Liverpool and Its Environs. 1834.

The Historical Register of the University of Cambridge. Supplement, 1911-20. Cambridge: University Press, 1922.

The Holy Bible ... Revised. Oxford: University Press, 1885.

REDGRAVE, S. *A Dictionary of Artists of the English School.* Amsterdam: G.W. Hissink & Co., 1970 (originally published in 1878).

Reports of the Church Congress 1861-1889.

SCHAFF, P. (ed.). *A Religious Encyclopedia.* 3rd ed. 4 vols. New York: Funk & Wagnalls, 1891.

SMITH, W. (ed.). *A Dictionary of the Bible.* 3 vols. London: John Murray, 1863.

SMITH, W. & WACE, H. (eds). *A Dictionary of Christian Biography, Literature, Sects and Doctrines.* 4 vols. London: John Murray 1877-87.

SMITH, W. & FULLER, J.M. (eds). *A Dictionary of the Bible.* 2nd ed. 3 vols in 4. London: John Murray, 1993.

The Students' Guide to the University of Cambridge. 1862, 1863, 1874, 1880, 1882, 1893.

TANNER, J.R. *The Historical Register of the University of Cambridge.* Cambridge: University Press, 1917.

VENN, J.A. *Alumni Cantabrigienses. Part II. From 1752 to 1900.* 6 vols. Cambridge: University Press, 1940-1954.

White Cross Movement. First Annual Report. London: Hatchards, n.d.

York Journal of Convocation 1879-1890.

7. Parliamentary Papers

Hansard, 3rd series CCLXXXIX (11 June - 3 July 1884) col. 1541-43.

Hansard, 3rd series CCCV (19 April - 24 May 1886) col. 703-21 , 877-78 & 1638-48.

Hansard, 3rd series CCCVI (25 May - 19 June 1886) col. 6-23.

Journals of the House of Lords (CXI - CXXII, 1878/9 - 1890).

Report of the Commissioners appointed to inquire into the state, discipline, studies and revenues of the University and colleges of Cambridge; together with the evidence, and an appendix and index (Graham Commission). 1852-3, xliv.

Report From the Select Committee of the House of Lords On University Tests; Together With the Proceedings of the Committee, Minutes of Evidence, and Appendix. 1871, IX.85.

8. Newspapers and Periodicals[*]

The Academy.
The Athenaeum.
The Cambridge Chronicle.
The Cambridge Gazette.
Church Quarterly Review.
The Contemporary Review.*
The Edinburgh Review.*
The Guardian.
Journal of Classical and Sacred Philology.
Journal of Hellenic Studies.
Journal of Theological Studies.
The Quarterly Review.*
The Times.*

---

[*] An asterisk indicates the use of an index or searching aid rather than personal perusal.

9. Books and Pamphlets Before 1914

ABSOLOM, C.S. *Dr Temple's Essay*. London: Wertheim, Macintosh & Hunt, 1861.

ARNOLD, F. *Oxford and Cambridge*. London: R.T.S., 1873.

BAUR, F.C. *Paul the Apostle of Jesus Christ, His Life and Work, His Epistles and His Doctrine.* 2nd ed. 2 vols. Revised by the Rev. A. Menzies. London & Edinburgh: Williams & Norgate, 1876.

BAUR, F.C. *The Church History of the First Three Centuries*. 3rd ed. 2 vols. Trans. by A. Menzies. London & Edinburgh: Williams & Norgate, 1878.

BENSON, A.C. *The Leaves of the Tree. Studies in Biography*. New York & London: Putnam's, 1911.

BENSON, E.W. *ΣΑΛΠΙΣΕΙ. A Memorial Sermon, Preached After the Death of the Right Reverend James Prince Lee, D.D., First Bishop of Manchester, In His Parish Church of Heaton, Manchester. With An Appendix Containing Memorial Notices of the Late Bishop*. 2nd ed. London & Manchester: Macmillan/Hale & Roworth, 1870.

BLAKELOCK, R. *Observations on the Rev. Dr Temple's Essay on the Education of the World.* London: Nisbet & Co., n.d.

BLUNT, J.J. *The Acquirements and Principal Obligations and Duties of the Parish Priest*. 2nd ed. London: John Murray, 1857.

BLUNT, J.J. *On the Right Use of the Early Fathers*. 3rd ed. London: John Murray, 1869.

BRIGHT, W. *Chapters of Early English Church History*. 2nd ed. Oxford: Clarendon Press, 1888.

BRISTED, C.A. *Five Years in an English University*. 2nd ed. New York: G.P. Putnam & Co., 1852.

BUCKLE, H.T. *History of Civilization in England*. 2 vols. New ed. London: Longmans, Green & Co., 1882.

BURGON, J.W. *Inspiration and Interpretation: Seven Sermons Preached Before the University of Oxford: With Preliminary Remarks: Being an Answer to a Volume Entitled "Essays and Reviews"*. Oxford & London: J.H. & J. Parker, 1861.

BURGON, J.W. *Plea For the Study of Divinity in Oxford*. Oxford & London: James Parker, 1875.

CAMPBELL, L. *On the Nationalisation of the Old English Universities*. London: Chapman & Hall, 1901.

[CASSELS, W.R.] *Supernatural Religion: An Inquiry Into the Reality of Divine Revelation*. 4th ed. 3 vols. London: Longmans, Green & Co., 1874-1877.

CLARK, J.Willis. *Cambridge. Brief Historical and Descriptive Notes*. London: Seeley, Jackson & Holiday, 1881.

CONYBEARE, W.J. & HOWSON, J.S. *The Life and Epistles of St Paul*. London: Longmans, Brown, Green, Longmans & Roberts, 1856.

COOK, F.C. *"Deliver Us From Evil." A Protest Against the Change in the Last Petition of the Lord's Prayer, Adopted in the Revised Version. A Letter to the Bishop of London*. London: John Murray, 1881.

Correspondence Between The Right Rev. The Lord Bishop of Durham and The Rev. and Hon. F.R. Gray, Rector of Morpeth. London: E. Longhurst, 1873.

CREIGHTON, M. *Historical Lectures and Addresses*. Ed. L. Creighton. London: Longmans, Green & Co., 1903.

CURETON, W. *Vindiciae Ignatianae: Or the Genuine Writings of St Ignatius, As Exhibited in the Antient Syriac Version, Vindicated From the Charge of Heresy*. London: Rivingtons, 1846.

CURETON, W. *Corpus Ignatianum: A Complete Collection of the Ignatian Epistles, Genuine, Interpolated, and Spurious; Together With Numerous Extracts From Them, As Quoted by Ecclesiastical Writers Down to the Tenth Century; In Syriac, Greek, and Latin; An English Translation of the Syriac Text, Copious Notes, and Introduction*. London: Francis & John Rivington, 1849.

DALE, R.W. *A Manual of Congregational Principles*. London: Hodder & Stoughton, 1884.

DAVIES, J. LLEWELLYN. *The Proposed Conditions of the Tenure of Fellowships in Trinity College*. Privately printed, 1857 [copy at TCC].

DYKES, J.B. *Eucharistic Truth and Ritual . A Letter to the … Lord Bishop of Durham, occasioned by his Lordship's reply to an address from certain laymen in the diocese*. 2nd ed. London, 1874.

ELLICOTT, CJ. *A Critical and Grammatical Commentary on St Paul's Epistle to the Galatians: With a Revised Translation*. London: John W. Parker & Son, 1854.

ELLICOTT, C.J. *A Critical and Grammatical Commentary on St Paul's Epistle to the Ephesians, with a Revised Translation*. London: J.W. Parker & Son, 1855.

ELLICOTT, C.J. *A Critical and Grammatical Commentary On St Paul's Epistles to the Philippians, Colossians, and to Philemon, With a Revised Translation*. London: John W. Parker & Son, 1857.

ELLICOTT, C.J. (ed.). *Report of the Committee of Bishops On the Revision of the Text and Translation of the Athanasian Creed With an Introduction and Notes by Charles John, Lord Bishop of Gloucester and Bristol*. London: Rivingtons, 1872.

Essays and Reviews. 8th ed. London: Longman, Green, Longman & Roberts, 1861.

EVERETT, W. *On the Cam. Lectures on the University of Cambridge in England*. New ed. London: Ward, Lock & Tyler, 1869.

FARRAR, F.W. *The Life of Christ*. Popular ed. London, Paris & New York: Cassell, Potter, Galpin & Co., 1881.

FARRAR, F.W. *The Life and Work of St Paul*. 2 vols. London: Cassel, Peter Calpin, 1879.

GARBETT, E. *The Bible and its Critics: An Enquiry Into the Objective Reality of Revealed Truths*. London: Seeley & Griffiths, 1861.

GORE, C. *The Ministry of the Christian Church*. 3rd ed., revised. London: Longmans, Green & Co., 1893.

GORE, C. (ed.). *Lux Mundi. A Series of Studies in the Religion of the Incarnation*. 4th ed. London: John Murray, 1890.

HANSELL, E.H. *Notes On the First Essay in the Series Called "Essays and Reviews"*. London: Rivingtons, 1861.

HASTINGS, F. (ed.). *Inspiration. A Clerical Symposium*. London: J. Nisbet, 1884.

HAWKINS, F VAUGHAN. *Peaks, Passes and Glaciers*. 1859.

HEMPHILL, S. *A History of the Revised Version of the New Testament*. London: Elliot Stock, 1906.

HOLLAND, H. SCOTT. *The Fathers For English Readers. The Apostolic Fathers*. London: S.P.C.K., n.d.

HORT, F.J.A. *Two Dissertations. I On MONOΓENHΣ ΘEOΣ In Scripture and Tradition. II On the "Constantinopolitan" Creed and Other Eastern Creeds of the Fourth Century*. Cambridge & London: Macmillan, 1876.

HUNT, J. *Religious Thought in England in the Nineteenth Century*. London: Gibbings & Co., 1896.

JACKSON, F. FOAKES. *The History of the Christian Church From the Earliest Times to A.D. 461*. 6th ed. London: George Allen & Unwin, 1914.

JOWETT, B. *The Epistles of St Paul to the Thessalonians, Galatians, Romans: with Critical Notes and Dissertations.* 2 vols. London: John Murray, 1855. 2nd ed. 2 vols. London: John Murray, 1859.

KENNARD, R.B. *"Essays and Reviews". Their Origin, History, General Character & Significance, Persecution, Prosecution, the Judgment of the Arches Court, - Review of Judgment.* London: Robert Hardwicke, 1863.

LANGFORD, J.A. *Modern Birmingham and its Institutions: A Chronicle of Local Events, From 1841 to 1871.* 2 vols. Birmingham & London, 1873.

LICHTENBERGER, F. *History of German Theology In the Nineteenth Century.* Trans. and ed. by W. Hastie. Edinburgh: T. & T. Clark, 1889.

LIDDON, H.P. *The Divinity of our Lord and Saviour Jesus Christ. Eight Lectures Preached Before the University of Oxford in the Year 1866.* 8th ed. London: Rivingtons, 1878.

MACKAY, R.W. *The Tübingen School and its Antecedents: A Review of the History and Present Condition of Modern Theology.* London & Edinburgh: Williams & Norgate, 1863.

MALAN, S.C. *A Vindication of the Authorised Version of the English Bible, From Charges Brought Against It By Recent Writers.* London, 1856.

MALAN, S.C. *A Plea for the Received Greek Text, and for the Authorised Version of the New Testament, In Answer to Some of the Dean of Canterbury's Criticisms on Both.* London, 1869.

MANSEL, H.L. *The Limits of Religious Thought Examined in Eight Lectures Before the University of Oxford, in the Year MDCCCLVIII, on the Bampton Foundation.* Oxford: John Murray, 1858.

MILL, W.H. *Observations on the Attempted Application of Pantheistic Principles to the Theory and Historic Criticism of the Gospel.* 2nd ed. Cambridge: Deighton, Bell & Co., 1861.

Missions: Their Temporal Utility, Rate of Progress, and Spiritual Foundation, Stated in the Addresses of Lord Napier, Canon Lightfoot, and Bishop Kelly, at the Annual Meeting of the Society for the Propagation of the Gospel, on the 29th April, 1873. London: Macmillan, 1873.

Modern Scepticism. A Course of Lectures Delivered at the Request of the Christian Evidence Society. 4th ed. London: Hodder & Stoughton, 1871.

MOZLEY, J.B. *Eight Lectures on Miracles.* 2nd ed. London: Rivingtons, 1867.

NEANDER, A. *General History of the Christian Religion and Church.* Trans. by J. Torrey. Vol. I. Edinburgh: T. & T. Clark, 1847.

NEANDER, A. *History of the Planting and Training of the Christian Church by the Apostles.* Trans. from the 3rd ed. of the original German by J.E. Ryland. 2 vols. London: H.G. Bohn, 1851.

OXONIENSIS. *An Apology for the Universities; being an attempt to rescue them from the imputation of criminal neglect, which has been recently cast upon them in certain publications issuing from Cambridge.* Oxford, 1841.

PARKER, W.H. *Brief Remarks on the Rev. Dr Temple's Essay, On the "Education of the World".* London: Wertheim, Macintosh & Hunt, n.d.

PERRY, C. *Theological Halls at Oxford and Cambridge. A Letter From The Right Rev. Bishop Perry to the Editor of 'The Christian Observer',* 1878 [copy at CUL].

PFLEIDERER, O. *The Development of Theology in Germany Since Kant, and its Progress in Great Britain Since 1825.* Trans. by J.F. Smith. London: Swann Sonnenschein, 1890.

PICTON, J.A. *Memorials of Liverpool. Historical and Topographical Including a History of the Dock Estate.* 2nd ed. 2 vols. Liverpool & London: G.G. Walmsley/Longmans, Green & Co., 1875.

The Practical Working of the White Cross Movement. A Few Suggestions Founded on the Experience of Three Years' Work. London: Hatchards, 1886.

RAWLINSON, G. *The Historical Evidences of the Truth of the Scripture Records, Stated Anew, With Special Reference to the Doubts and Discoveries of Modern Times*. London: John Murray, 1860.

Replies to "Essays and Reviews". Oxford & London: J.H. & J. Parker, 1862.

Report of the Committee, "Read at a Meeting of the Governing Body, June 9, 1857" [Copy at TCC].

ROW, C.A. *The Supernatural in the New Testament, Possible, Credible and Historical, or an examination of the validity of some recent objections against Christianity as a Divine Revelation*. London: Frederic Norgate, 1875.

ROW, C.A. *Christian Evidences Viewed in Relation to Modern Thought*. 2nd ed. London: Frederic Norgate, 1877.

SANDAY, W. *The Gospels in the Second Century. An Examination of the Critical Part of a Work Entitled 'Supernatural Religion'*. London: Macmillan, 1876.

SANDAY, W. *The Conception of Priesthood in the Early Church and in the Church of England*. London: Longmans, Green & Co., 1898.

SANDYS, J.E. *A History of Classical Scholarship. Vol III. The Eighteenth Century in Germany, and the Nineteenth Century in Europe and the United States of America*. Cambridge: University Press, 1908.

SCHAFF, P. *Germany: Its Universities, Theology and Religion*. Edinburgh: T. & T. Clark, 1857.

SEDGWICK, A. *A Discourse on the Studies of the University of Cambridge. The Fifth Edition, With Additions, and a Preliminary Dissertation*. Cambridge & London: John Deighton/ John Parker, 1850.

[SEELEY, J.R.] *Ecce Homo. A Survey of the Life and Work of Jesus Christ*. 9th ed. London: Macmillan, 1868.

SINCLAIR, W.M. *Memorials of St Paul's Cathedral*. London: Chapman & Hall, 1909.

STANLEY, A.P. *The Epistles of St Paul to the Corinthians*. 2 vols. London: John Murray, 1855.

STEPHEN, L. *Sketches From Cambridge [Reprinted from the Pall Mall Gazette]*. London: Humphrey Milford, 1932.

STORR, V.F. *The Development of English Theology in the Nineteenth Century 1800-1860*. London: Longmans, Green & Co., 1913.

SULLEY, P. *The Hundred of the Wirral*. Birkenhead: B. Haram & Co., 1889.

SWETE, H.B. *Patristic Study*. London: Longmans, Green & Co., 1902.

TAYLER, J.J. *An Attempt to Ascertain the Character of the Fourth Gospel; Especially in its Relation to the First Three*. London & Edinburgh: Williams & Norgate, 1867.

THOMSON, W. (ed.) *Aids to Faith. A Series of Theological Essays. By Several Writers*. London: John Murray, 1861.

TILLYARD, A.I. *A History of University Reform From 1800 to the Present*. Cambridge: W. Heffer & Sons, 1913.

VAUGHAN, D. *Remarks On the Master of Trinity's Second Paper*. Privately printed, 1857 [copy at TCC].

WATKINS, H.W. *Modern Criticism Considered in its Relation to the Fourth Gospel, Being the Bampton Lectures for 1890*. London: John Murray, 1890.

WESTCOTT, B.F. *The Elements of the Gospel Harmony*. Cambridge: Macmillan, 1851.

WESTCOTT, B.F. *A General Survey of the History of the Canon of the New Testament*. 4th ed. London: Macmillan, 1875.

WESTCOTT, B.F. *An Introduction to the Study of the Gospels*. 8th ed. London: Macmillan, 1895.

WESTCOTT, B.F. *The Gospel of the Resurrection: Thoughts on its Relation to Reason and History*. 4th ed. London: Macmillan, 1879.

424 *Bibliography*

WESTCOTT, B.F. *Essays in the History of Religious Thought in the West*. London: Macmillan, 1891.

WESTCOTT, B.F. *On Some Points in the Religious Office of the University*. London: Macmillan, 1873.

WESTCOTT, B.F. *Teacher and Scholar: A Memory and a Hope*. Birmingham: Cornish Brothers, 1893.

WHEWELL, W. *The Elements of Morality, Including Polity*. 2 vols. London: J.W. Parker, 1845.

[WHEWELL, W.] *Notes on the Oxford University Bill in Reference to the Colleges at Cambridge*. Privately printed, 1854 [copy at TCC].

WHEWELL, W. *Remarks on Proposed Changes in the College Statutes*. Privately printed, 1857 [copy at TCC].

WHEWELL, W. *Further Remarks on Proposed Changes in the College Statutes*. Privately printed, 1857 [copy at TCC].

WHEWELL, W. *Remarks on Proposed Changes in the College Statutes. Third Series*. Privately printed, 1857 [copy at TCC].

WHITNEY, J.P. *The Episcopate and the Reformation. Our Outlook*. London: Robert Scott, 1907.

WILLIS, R. & CLARK, J. Willis. *The Architectural History of the University of Cambridge, and of the Colleges of Cambridge and Eton*. Vol. III. Cambridge: University Press, 1886.

WOOD, J.T. *Discoveries at Ephesus Including the Site and Remains of the Great Temple of Diana*. London: Longmans, Green & Co., 1877.

YOUNG, G. *University Tests*. London, 1868 [copy at CUL].

10. Editions of Sources and Contemporary Works

ACTON, J.E.E. DALBERG-. *Historical Essays and Studies*. Ed by J.N. Figgis & R.V. Laurence. London: Macmillan, 1907.

ARNOLD, M. *God and the Bible*. In *The Complete Prose Works of Matthew Arnold VII*. Ed. R.H. Super. Ann Arbor: University of Michigan Press, 1970.

BAUR, F.C. *Ferdinand Christian Baur: On the Writings of Church History*. Ed. & trans. by P.C. Hodgson. New York: Oxford University Press, 1968.

COLERIDGE, S.T. *Confessions of an Inquiring Spirit*. Edited with an introductory note by H. StJ. Hart. London: Black, 1956.

EVANS, G.R. & WRIGHT, J.R. (eds).*The Anglican Tradition. A Handbook of Sources*. London & Minneapolis: S.P.C.K., 1991.

MARUCCHI, O. *Christian Epigraphy. An Elementary Treatise with a Collection of Ancient Christian Inscriptions Mainly of Roman Origin*. Trans. by J. Armine Willis. Chicago: Ares, 1974 [first published in1912].

MILL, J.S. *Essays On Ethics, Religion and Society. The Collected Works of John Stuart Mill X*. Ed. J.M. Robson. Toronto: University Press, 1969.

MILL, J.S. *Autobiography*, with an Introduction by C.V. Shields. New York: Liberal Arts Press, 1957.

MOBERLY, R.C. *Ministerial Priesthood*. Reprinted [from the second edition of 1910] with a new introduction by A.T. Hanson. London: S.P.C.K., 1969.

MOORE, J. (ed.). *Religion in Victorian Britain. Vol III. Sources*. Manchester: University Press, 1988.

STRAUSS, D.F. *The Life of Jesus Critically Examined*. Translated by G. Eliot; edited and with an introduction by P. Hodgson. London: S.C.M., 1973.

WESTCOTT, B.F. *The Gospel According to St John. The Authorised Version with Introduction and Notes*. With a new introduction by A. Fox. London: James Clarke & Co., 1958.

11. Articles and Chapters Before 1914

BENSON, E.W. "On the Martyrdom and Commemorations of Saint Hippolytus." *Journal of Classical and Sacred Philology* I.ii (June 1854) 188-210.

BENSON, E.W. "Cathedral Life and Work." *Quarterly Review* 130 (January 1871) 225-55.

BROWNE, E.H. "Professor Harold Browne on the Cambridge Theological Examinations." *Christian Observer* (January 1862) 69-72.

[CLARK, J WILLIS]. "Half A Century of Cambridge Life." *Church Quarterly Review* XIV (April 1882) 144-76.

CONYBEARE, W.J. "Church Parties." *Edinburgh Review* xcviii (October 1853) 273-342.

CREIGHTON, M. "The Teaching of Ecclesiastical History." *Historical Lectures and Addresses*. Ed. L. Creighton. London: Longmans, Green & Co., 1903, 1-28.

"Dr Temple's Place Amongst the Oxford Essayists." *Christian Observer* LIX.273 n.s. (September 1860) 621-38.

ELLIOTT, E.B. "The Rev. E.B. Elliott On Prophetic Articles in the 3rd Volume of Dr Smith's Dictionary of the Bible." *The Christian Observer* (March 1864) 199-221.

EMMET, J.T. "The Completion of St Paul's." *Quarterly Review* 133 (October 1872), 342-86.

FERGUSSON, J. "St Paul's Cathedral." *Contemporary Review* 24 (October 1874) 750-71.

GREGORY, R. "Are We Better Than Our Fathers?" *The Times* (8, 16 & 23 November, & 1 December 1871).

GREGORY, R. "Some of the Bonds of Society, Past and Present, Material, Social and Moral." *The Times* (30 October, & 7 & 13 November 1872).

HARRISON, F. "Neo-Christianity." *Westminster and Foreign Quarterly Review* LXXIV (October 1860) 293-332.

HORT, F.J.A. "On the Date of Justin Martyr." *Journal of Classical and Sacred Philology* III.viii (June 1856) 155-93.

KINGSLEY, C. "The Limits of Exact Science as Applied to History." *The Roman and the Teuton*. Ed. F.M. Müller. London, 1875, 307-43.

MACAULAY, T.B. "Francis Bacon." *Edinburgh Review* lxv (1837) 1-104.

"Modern German Theology." *The Theologian* I (1845) 76-96.

MOULTON, J.H. "New Testament Greek in the Light of Modern Discovery." *Essays on Some Biblical Questions of the Day by Members of the University of Cambridge*. Ed. H.B. Swete. London: Macmillan, 1909, 461-505.

"Obituary; with Anecdotes of Remarkable Persons." *The Gentleman's Magazine* 81.2 (September 1811) 285.

POOLE, R.S. "Modern Commentaries on the Bible." *MacMillan's Magazine* XIII (December 1865) 143-52; & XIV (July 1866) 196-205.

"The Position and Prospects of the Church in Cambridge." *Church Quarterly Review* XIII (October 1881) 180-204.

'Remarks on the Theory of Dr Temple's Essay on "The Education of the World" in "Essays and Reviews".' *Journal of Sacred Literature* XIV series 3 (October 1861) 13-30.

SANDAY, W. "Marcion's Gospel." *Fortnightly Review* XVII n.s., XXIII o.s. (June 1875) 855-75.

SHIPLEY, A.E. & ROBERTS, H.A. "A Plea For Cambridge." *Quarterly Review* CCV (April 1906) 499-525.

"The Stage and the Pulpit." *Punch* (10 May 1873) 198.

STANLEY, A.P. "Essays and Reviews." *Edinburgh Review* 113 (April 1861) 461-500.

"Strauss - Life of Christ." *Foreign Quarterly Review* 22 (October 1838) 101-34.

"Strauss' Life of Jesus." *The Prospective Review* 2 (1846) 479-520.

"Supernatural Religion." *The Inquirer* (7 November 1874) 720-22.

TYNDALL, J. "Address by the President." *Report of the Forty-Fourth Meeting of the British Association for the Advancement of Science; Held at Belfast in August 1874* (1875) lxvi-xcvii.

WESTCOTT, B.F. "Comte on the Philosophy of the History of Christianity." *Contemporary Review* VI (1867) 399-421.

WESTCOTT, B.F. "Aspects of Positivism in Relation to Christianity." *Contemporary Review* VIII (1868) 371-86.

WESTCOTT, B.F. "Cathedral Work." *Macmillan's Magazine* 21 (January 1870) 246-51; & 21 (February 1870) 308-14.

WESTCOTT, B.F. "Critical Scepticism." *The Expositor* I (1875) 211-37.

WILBERFORCE, S. "Essays and Reviews." *Quarterly Review* 109 (January 1861) 248-305.

B. Secondary Sources

I. Materials About, Or Containing Significant Discussion of, Lightfoot

BARNARD, L.W. "Bishop Lightfoot and the Apostolic Fathers." *Church Quarterly Review* 161 (October-December 1960) 423-35.

BARRETT, C.K. "Joseph Barber Lightfoot." *Durham University Journal* LXIV.3 [XXXIII.3, n.s.] (June 1972) 193-204.

BARRETT, C.K. "*Quomodo Historia Conscribenda Sit.*" *New Testament Studies* 28.3 (July 1982) 303-20.

BARRETT, C.K. "J.B. Lightfoot as Biblical Commentator." In J.D.G. Dunn (ed.), *The Lightfoot Centenary Lectures*, 53-70.

BRUCE, F.F. "J.B. Lightfoot (died 1889): Commentator and Theologian." *Evangel* 7.2 (Summer 1989) 10-12.

BYROM, J.K. "They Were Not Divided." *Theology* LXXVII.652 (October 1974) 536-7.

CONDER, P.C.N. "They Were Not Divided." *Theology* LXXVII.650 (August 1974) 422-31.

DUNN, J.D.G. (ed.). *The Lightfoot Centenary Lectures to Commemorate the Life and Work of Bishop J.B. Lightfoot (1828-89). Durham University Journal*, Extra Complimentary Number for Subscribers (January 1992).

DUNN, J.D.G. "Introduction." In J.D.G. Dunn (ed.), *The Lightfoot Centenary Lectures*, 1-2.

DUNN, J.D.G. "Lightfoot in Retrospect." In J.D.G. Dunn (ed.), *The Lightfoot Centenary Lectures,* 71-94.

EDWARDS, D.L. "Lightfoot and Westcott." In *Leaders of the Church of England 1828-1944.* London: Oxford University Press, 1971, 207-22.

EDWARDS Jr., W.T. "Joseph Barber Lightfoot as an Interpreter of the New Testament." Unpublished Th.D.thesis: Southern Baptist Theological Seminary, 1958.

GASQUE, W. WARD. *A History of the Criticism of the Acts of the Apostles.* Grand Rapids: Eerdmans, 1975, esp. 116-23.

GASQUE, W. WARD. "Nineteenth-Century Roots of Contemporary New Testament Criticism." *Scripture, Tradition and Interpretation.* Eds W. Ward Gasque & W.S. La Sor. Grand Rapids: Eerdmans, 1978, 146-56.

GORANSON, S. ' "Essenes": Etymology From sh.' *Revue Qumran* 11.4 (1984) 483-98.

HEARD, R.G. "Cambridge Biblical Scholarship. Westcott, Lightfoot, and Hort." *Cambridge Review* (15 February 1947) 321-2.

HENGEL, M. "Bishop Lightfoot and the Tübingen School on the Gospel of John and the Second Century." In J.D.G. Dunn (ed.), *The Lightfoot Centenary Lectures*, 23-51.

HOWARD, W.F. "The Cambridge Triumvirate." In *The Romance of New Testament Scholarship.* London: Epworth, 1949, ch 3.

KAYE, B.N. "Lightfoot and Baur on Early Christianity." *Novum Testamentum* XXVI.3 (1984) 193-224.

LOANE, M.L. "Joseph Barber Lightfoot Bishop of Durham." In *Three Faithful Servants*. Blackwood, South Australia: New Creation Publications, 1991, 89-119.

MALDEN, R.H. "Bishop Lightfoot 1828-1889." In *Great Christians*. Ed. R.S. Forman. London: Nicholson & Watson, 1933, 335-47.

MORGAN, R. "Historical Criticism and Christology: England and Germany." In *England and Germany. Studies in Theological Diplomacy*. Ed. S. Sykes. Frankfurt Am Main: Verlag Peter D. Lang, 1982, 80-112.

MORGAN, R. "*Non Angli sed Angeli*: Some Anglican Reactions to German Gospel Criticism." In *New Studies in Theology* I. Eds S. Sykes & J.D. Holmes. London: Duckworth, 1980, 1-30.

NEILL, S. *The Interpretation of the New Testament 1861-1961*. Oxford: University Press, 1964, esp. ch II.

NEWSOME, D. *Godliness and Good Learning. Four Studies on a Victorian Ideal*. London: John Murray, 1961, esp. ch. II.

PICIRELLI, R.E. "The Meaning of *Epignosis*." *The Evangelical Quarterly* 47 (April-June 1975) 85-93.

POINTER, S. "J.B. Lightfoot as a Christian Historian of Early Christian Literature." *The Christian Scholar's Review* XXIII.4 (June 1994) 426-44.

RICHARDS, P.H. "J.B. Lightfoot as a Biblical Interpreter." *Interpretation* 8 (1954) 50-62.

ROBINSON, J.A.T. "J.B. Lightfoot. The Champion of Critical Scholarship." MS Sermon Preached at St Botolph's Church, Cambridge on 7 November 1976 [copy in the Wren Library, TCC].

ROBINSON, J.A.T. "Joseph Barber Lightfoot." In *The Roots of a Radical*. London: S.C.M., 1980, 155-61.

ROBINSON, J.A.T. *Joseph Barber Lightfoot*. Durham: Dean & Chapter of Durham, 1981.

RODD, C.S. "Commentator Supreme." *Expository Times* 104 (January 1993) 128.

SELWYN, E.G. "The University Sermon." *Cambridge Review* (November 11, 1938) 89-90.

THOMPSON, D. "Lightfoot as Victorian Churchman." In J.D.G. Dunn (ed.), *The Lightfoot Centenary Lectures*, 3-21.

TRELOAR, G.R. "JB Lightfoot and St Paul, 1854-65: A Study of Intentions and Method." *Lucas. An Evangelical History Review* 7 (1989) 5-33.

WEBSTER, A.B. "Lightfoot's Ordination Addresses." *Church Quarterly Review* 166 (Jan.-Mar. 1965) 65-74.

WIERSBE, W.W. "Lightfoot: a Devoted Scholar." *Moody Monthly* 76.8 (April 1976) 127-31.

WILSON, D.J. "The Life of J.B. Lightfoot (1829 [sic]-89), with special reference to the training for the ministry." Unpublished Ph.D. thesis: Edinburgh University, 1956.

WILSON, J.C. "The Problem of the Domitianic Date of Revelation." *New Testament Studies* 39 (October 1993) 587-605.

WILSON, R. "Lightfoot, Savage and Eden - Sidelights on a Great Episcopate." *Theology* LV. 386 (August 1952) 294-9.

WRIGHT, N.T. "ἁρπαγμός and the Meaning of Philippians 2:5-11." *Journal of Theological Studies* n.s. 37.2 (October 1986) 321-52.

II. Reference Books

BRIGGS, W.W. & Calder, W.M., III (eds). *Classical Scholarship. A Biographical Encyclopedia*. New York & London: Garland, 1990.

DICKEY, B (ed.). *The Australian Dictionary of Evangelical Biography*. Sydney: Evangelical History Association of Australia, 1994.

HOUGHTON, W.E. *The Wellesley Index to Victorian Periodicals 1824-1900*. 4 vols. Toronto & London: Toronto University Press/Routledge, 1966-87.

LEWIS, D.M. (ed.). *The Blackwell Dictionary of Evangelical Biography 1730-1860*. 2 vols. Oxford: Blackwell, 1995.

III. Other Books

AARSLEFF, H. *The Study of Language in England, 1780-1860.* Princeton: University Press, 1967.

ABRAMS, M.H. *Natural Supernaturalism: Tradition and Revolution in Romantic Literature.* New York: Norton, 1971.

ACTON, H.B. *The Idea of a Spiritual Power.* London: Athlone Press, 1974.

ADAMSON, J.W. *English Education 1789-1902.* Cambridge: University Press, 1964.

ADDINALL, P. *Philosophy and Biblical Interpretation. A Study in Nineteenth-century Conflict.* Cambridge: University Press, 1991.

ALLEN, P. *The Cambridge Apostles. The Early Years.* Cambridge: University Press, 1978.

ALTHOLZ, J.L. *Anatomy of a Controversy. The Debate Over "Essays and Reviews".* Aldershot: Scolar Press, 1994.

ALTICK, R.D. *Lives and Letters. A History of Literary Biography in England and America.* Westport, Connecticut: Greenwood Press, 1979 (originally published in 1965).

ANNAN, N. *Leslie Stephen. His Thought and Character in Relation to his Time.* London: MacGibbon & Kee, 1951.

ANNAN, N. *Leslie Stephen. The Godless Victorian.* New York: Random House, 1984.

ARX, J. von. *Progress and Pessimism. Religion, Politics, and History in Late Nineteenth Century Britain.* Cambridge, Massachusetts: Harvard University Press, 1985.

ATKINSON, R.F. *Knowledge and Explanation in History. An Introduction to the Philosophy of History.* Ithaca, New York: Cornell University Press, 1978.

AVIS, P. *Anglicanism and the Christian Church. Theological Resources in Christian Perspective.* Edinburgh: T. & T. Clark, 1989.

BAIRD, W. *History of New Testament Research. Volume I: From Deism to Tübingen.* Minneapolis: Fortress Press, 1992.

BAMFORD, T. *Thomas Arnold.* London: Cresset Press, 1960.

BARNES, H.E. *A History of Historical Writing.* 2nd revised ed. New York: Dover Publications, 1963.

BARNES, T.D. *Constantine and Eusebius.* Cambridge, Massachusetts: Harvard University Press, 1981.

BARRETT, C.K. *Westcott the Commentator.* Cambridge: University Press, 1959.

BARRETT, P. *Barchester. English Cathedral Life in the Nineteenth Century.* London: S.P.C.K., 1993.

BAUMER, F.L. *Modern European Thought. Continuity and Change in Ideas, 1600-1950.* New York: Macmillan, 1977.

BEALES, D. *History and Biography. An Inaugural Lecture.* Cambridge: University Press, 1981.

BEBBINGTON, D.W. *Evangelicalism in Modern Britain. A History from the 1730s to the 1980s.* London: Unwin Hyman, 1989.

BENEDIKZ, B.S. *Lichfield Cathedral Library. A Handlist of the Papers of the Very Rev. Henry Edwin Savage, D.D., Dean 1909-39, With a Brief Memoir of his Life.* [Birmingham] Birmingham University Library, 1977.

BENTLEY, J. *Ritualism and Politics in Victorian Britain. The Attempt to Legislate for Belief.* Oxford: University Press, 1978.

BEST, G.F. *Westcott and the Miners.* Cambridge: University Press, 1967.

BINNS, L. Elliott-. *Religion in the Victorian Era.* 2nd ed. London: Lutterworth Press, 1946.

BINNS, L. Elliott-. *English Thought 1860-1900. The Theological Aspect.* London: Longmans, Green, & Co., 1956.

BOWEN, D. *The Idea of the Victorian Church. A Study of the Church of England 1833-1889.* Montreal: McGill University Press, 1969.

BOWLER, P. *The Invention of Progress. The Victorians and the Past.* Oxford: Blackwell, 1989.

BRAZILL, W.J. *The Young Hegelians.* New Haven & London: Yale University Press, 1970.

BRENT, R. *Liberal Anglican Politics. Whiggery, Religion, and Reform 1830-1841.* Oxford: Clarendon Press, 1987.

BRIGGS, A. *Victorian People. A Reassessment of Persons and Themes 1851-1867.* Harmondsworth: Penguin, 1965.

BRIGGS, A. *Victorian Cities.* Harmondsworth: Penguin, 1968.

BROCK, W.R. & COOPER, P.H.M. *Selwyn College. A History.* Edinburgh, Cambridge & Durham: Pentland Press, 1994.

BROOKE, C.N.L. *A History of the University of Cambridge. Vol IV. 1870-1990.* Cambridge: University Press, 1993.

BROWN, A. *The Metaphysical Society: Victorian Minds in Crisis, 1869-1880.* New York: Columbia University Press, 1947.

BROWN, C. *Jesus in European Protestant Thought 1778-1860.* Durham, North Carolina: Labrynth Press, 1985.

BUCKLEY, J.H. *The Triumph of Time: A Study of the Victorian Concepts of Time, History, Progress and Decadence.* Cambridge, Massachusetts: Harvard University Press, 1967.

BUDD, S. *Varieties of Unbelief. Atheists and Agnostics in English Society 1850-1960.* London: Heinemann Educational Books, 1977.

BULLOCK, F.W. *The History of Ridley Hall.* 2 vols. Cambridge: University Press, 1941-53.

BULLOCK, F.W.B. *A History of Training for the Ministry of the Church of England in England and Wales From 1800 to 1874.* St Leonard's-On-Sea: Budd & Gillatt, 1955.

BULLOCK, F.W.B. *A History of Training for the Ministry of the Church of England 1875-1974.* London: Home Words, 1976.

BUNTING, I. & BREWSTER, J. *1883-1983. The Eleventh Centenary of the Parish Church in Chester-le-Street.* Chester-le-Street: The Parish Church of St Mary & St Cuthbert, Chester-le-Street, County Durham, [1983].

BURN, W.L. *The Age of Equipoise. A Study of the Mid-Victorian Generation.* London: George Allen & Unwin, 1964.

BURROW, J.W. *Evolution and Society. A Study in Victorian Social Theory.* Cambridge: University Press, 1966.

BURROW, J.W. *A Liberal Descent. Victorian Historians and the English Past.* Cambridge: University Press, 1981.

BURY, P. *The College of Corpus Christi and of the Blessed Virgin Mary. A History From 1822 to 1952.* Cambridge: University Press, 1952.

BUTLER, P. *Gladstone, Church, State and Tractarianism: A Study of his Religious Ideas and Attitudes, 1809-1859.* Oxford: Clarendon Press, 1982.

CAMERON, N.M. de S. *Biblical Higher Criticism and the Defense of Infallibilism in 19th Century Britian.* Lewiston, Queenstown: Edwin Meller, 1987.

CANNON, S.F. *Science in Culture. The Early Victorian Period.* New York: Science History Publications, 1978.

CARPENTER, S.C. *Church and People, 1789-1889. A History of the Church of England From William Wilberforce to Lux Mundi.* London: S.P.C.K., 1933.

CHADWICK, H. *The Vindication of Christianity in Westcott's Thought.* London: Cambridge University Press, 1961.

CHADWICK, O. *Creighton On Luther.* Cambridge: University Press, 1959.

CHADWICK, O. *Westcott and the University.* Cambridge: University Press, 1963.

CHADWICK, O. *The Victorian Church.* Part I, 3rd ed. & Part II, 2nd ed. London: A. & C. Black, 1971-1972.

CHADWICK, O. *The Secularization of the European Mind in the Nineteenth Century.* Cambridge: University Press, 1975.

CHADWICK, O. *Hensley Henson. A Study in the Friction Between Church and State.* Oxford: Clarendon Press, 1983.

CHANDLER, G. *Liverpool.* London: Batsford, 1957.

CHRISTENSEN, T. *The Divine Order. A Study in F.D. Maurice's Theology.* Leiden: Brill, 1973.

CLARK, G.S.R. Kitson. *An Expanding Society. Britain 1830-1900.* Melbourne & Cambridge: Melbourne University Press/Cambridge University Press, 1967.

CLARK, G.S.R. Kitson. *Churchmen and the Condition of England, 1832-1885.* London: Methuen, 1973.

CLARK, G.S.R. Kitson. *The Making of Victorian England.* London: Methuen, 1962.

CLARKE, M.L. *Paley. Evidences for the Man.* London: S.P.C.K., 1974.

CORSI, P. *Science and Religion. Baden Powell and the Anglican Debate, 1800-1860.* Cambridge: University Press, 1988.

COWLING, M. *Religion and Public Doctrine in Modern England.* 2 vols. Cambridge: University Press, 1980-85.

CROWTHER, M.A. *Church Embattled: Religious Controversy in Mid-Victorian England.* Newton Abbot, Devon & Hamden, Connecticut: Archon Books, 1970.

CULLER, A. Dwight. *The Victorian Mirror of History.* New Haven & London: Yale University Press, 1985.

CUMING, G. *The Anglicanism of John Cosin.* Durham: Dean & Chapter of Durham, 1975.

DALE, P.A. *The Victorian Critic and the Idea of History. Carlyle, Arnold and Pater.* Cambridge, Massachusetts: Harvard University Press, 1977.

DAVIE, G.E. *The Democratic Intellect. Scotland and her Universities in the Nineteenth Century.* Edinburgh: University Press, 1961.

DEACON, R. *The Cambridge Apostles. A History of Cambridge University's Elite Intellectual Secret Society.* London: R. Royce, 1985.

DELLHEIM, C. *The Face of the Past. The Preservation of the Medieval Inheritance in Victorian England.* Cambridge: University Press, 1982.

DISTAD, N.M. *Guessing at Truth. The Life of Julius Charles Hare (1795-1855).* Sheperdstown: Patmos Press, 1979.

DUNN, J.D.G. *Testing the Foundations. Current Trends in New Testament Study.* Durham: University of Durham, 1984.

DUNN, J.D.G. *The Parting of the Ways Between Christianity and Judaism and their Significance for the Character of Christianity.* London & Philadelphia: S.C.M./Trinity Press, 1991.

EDEN, T. *Durham.* 2 vols. London: Robert Hale, 1952.

EDWARDS, D. *Leaders of the Church of England 1828-1944.* London: Oxford University Press, 1971.

EISENSTADT, S.N. *Tradition, Change and Modernity.* New York: Wiley, 1973.

ELDRIDGE, C.C. *England's Mission. The Imperial Idea in the Age of Gladstone and Disraeli 1868-1880.* London: Macmillan, 1973.

ELLIS, I. *Seven Against Christ. A Study of "Essays and Reviews".* Leiden: Brill, 1980.

ELLSWORTH, L.E. *Charles Lowder and the Ritualist Movement.* London: Darton, 1982.

ELTON, G. *F.W. Maitland.* London: Wiedenfeld & Nicolson, 1985.

ENGEL, A.J. *From Clergyman to Don. The Rise of the Academic Profession in Nineteenth Century Oxford.* New York: Oxford University Press, 1983.

FALLOWS, W.G. *Mandell Creighton and the English Church.* London: Oxford University Press, 1964.

FISHER, H.A.L. *F.W. Maitland. A Biographical Sketch.* Cambridge: University Press, 1910.

FORBES, D. *The Liberal Anglican Idea of History.* Cambridge: University Press, 1952.

GARDINER, P. (ed.). *Theories of History.* New York: The Free Press, 1959.

GARLAND, M.M. *Cambridge Before Darwin.* Cambridge: University Press, 1980.

GILBERT, A. *Religion and Society in Industrial England. Church, Chapel and Social Change 1740-1914.* London & New York: Longman, 1976.

GILBERT, A. *The Making of Post-Christian Britain. A History of the Secularization of Modern Society.* London & New York: Longman, 1980.

GILL, C. *A History of Birmingham. Vol. I. Manor and Borough to 1865.* London: Oxford University Press, 1952.

GILLEY, S. *Newman and his Age.* London: Darton, Longman & Todd, 1990.

GOOCH, G.P. *History and Historians in the Nineteenth Century.* 2nd ed. London, New York, Toronto: Longmans, Green & Co., 1952.

GRANT, R.M. *After the New Testament.* Philadelphia: Fortress, 1974.

GRANT, R.M. *Eusebius as Church Historian.* Oxford: Clarendon Press, 1980.

GRAVE, S.A. *The Scottish Philosophy of Common Sense.* Oxford: Clarendon Press, 1960.

GRAVE, W.W. *Fitzwilliam College Cambridge 1869-1969. Its History as the Non-Collegiate Institution of the University and its Beginnings as an Independent College.* [Cambridge]: The Fitzwilliam Society, 1983.

GRAY, A. *Cambridge University, an Episodical History.* Cambridge: W. Heffer & Sons, 1926.

GREEN, V.H.H. *Religion at Oxford and Cambridge.* London: S.C.M., 1964.

GREENSLADE, S.L. *The English Reformers and the Fathers of the Church.* Oxford: Clarendon Press, 1960.

HAIG, A. *The Victorian Clergy.* Beckenham & Sydney: Croom Helm, 1984.

HANSON, R.P.C. *The Bible as a Norm of Faith.* Durham: Durham University, 1963.

HÄRDELIN, A. *The Tractarian Understanding of the Eucharist.* Studia historico-ecclesiastica upsaliensia no. 8. Uppsala: Boktryckeri Aktiebolag, 1965.

HARRIS, H. *David Friedrich Strauss and his Theology.* Cambridge: University Press, 1973.

HARRIS, H. *The Tübingen School.* Oxford: Clarendon Press, 1975.

HARRIS, J. *Private Lives Public Spirit. A Social History of Britain 1870-1914.* Oxford: University Press, 1993.

HARVIE, C. *The Lights of Liberalism. University Liberals and the Challenge of Democracy 1860-86.* London: Allen Lane, 1976.

HASTINGS, A. *A History of English Christianity 1920-1990.* 3rd ed. London & Philadelphia: S.C.M./Trinity Press, 1991.

HEENEY, B. *A Different Kind of Gentleman. Parish Clergy as Professional Men in Early and Mid-Victorian England.* Hamden, Connecticut: Archon Books, 1976.

HEESOM, A. *The Foundation of the University of Durham.* Durham: Dean & Chapter of Durham, 1982.

HELMSTADTER, R.J. & LIGHTMAN, B. (eds). *Victorian Faith in Crisis. Essays on Continuity and Change in Nineteenth-Century Religious Belief.* London: Macmillan, 1990.

HENGEL, M. *The Johannine Question.* London & Philadelphia: S.C.M./Trinity International, 1989.

HENSON, H.H. *Bishoprick Papers.* London: Oxford University Press, 1946.

HEYCK, T.W. *The Transformation of Intellectual Life in Victorian England.* London & Canberra: Croom Helm, 1982.

HILTON, B. *The Age of Atonement. The Influence of Evangelicalism on Social and Economic Thought, 1795-1865.* Oxford: Clarendon Press, 1988.

HINCHLIFF, P. *Benjamin Jowett and the Christian Religion.* Oxford: Clarendon Press, 1987.

HINCHLIFF, P. *God and History. Aspects of British Theology 1875-1914.* Oxford: Clarendon Press, 1992.

HOBERMAN, R. *Modernizing Lives. Experiments in English Biography, 1918-1939.* Carbondale and Edwardsville: Southern Illinois University Press, 1987.

HODGSON, P.C. *The Foundation of Historical Theology. A Study of Ferdinand Christian Baur.* New York: Harper & Row, 1966.

HONEY, J.R.S. de S. *Tom Brown's Universe. The Development of the Victorian Public School.* London: Millington, 1977.

HOPKINS, H.E. *Charles Simeon of Cambridge.* London: Hodder & Stoughton, 1977.

HOUGHTON, W.E. *The Victorian Frame of Mind 1830-1870.* New Haven & London: Yale University Press, 1957.

HOUSE, J.W. *North Eastern England. Population Movements and the Landscape Since the Early Nineteenth Century.* University of Durham. King's College Dept of Geography. Research Series no. 1. Newcastle-Upon-Tyne, [1959].

HUGHES, H. Stuart. *Consciousness and Society. The Reorientation of European Social Thought, 1890-1930.* London: MacGibbon & Kee, 1959.

HUTTON, T.W. *King Edward's School Birmingham 1552-1952.* Oxford: Basil Blackwell, 1952.

JAGGER, P. *Clouded Witness. Initiation in the Church of England in the Mid-Victorian Period, 1850-1875.* Allison Park, Pennsylvania: Pickwick Publications, 1982.

JANN, R. *The Art and Science of Victorian History.* Columbus, Ohio: Ohio State University Press, 1986.

JOSAITIS, N.F. *Edwin Hatch and Early Church Order.* Gembloux: Éditions J. Duculot, S.A., 1971.

KELLY, T. *For Advancement of Learning. The University of Liverpool 1881-1981.* Liverpool: University Press, 1981.

KENT, J. *The Unacceptable Face of the Church. The Modern Church in the Eyes of the Historian.* London: S.C.M., 1987.

KENT, J. *William Temple. Church, State and Society in Britain, 1880-1950.* Cambridge: University Press, 1992.

KENYON, J. *The History Men. The Historical Profession in England Since the Renaissance.* London: Wiedenfeld & Nicolson, 1983.

KNIGHTS, B. *The Idea of the Clerisy in the Nineteenth Century.* Cambridge: University Press, 1978.

KORSHIN, P.J. *Typologies in England 1650-1820.* Princeton: University Press, 1982.

KOZICKI, H. *Tennyson and Clio. History in the Major Poems.* Baltimore and London: Johns Hopkins University Press, 1979.

KRENTZ, E. *The Historical Critical Method.* Philadelphia: Fortress Press, 1975.

KÜMMEL, W.G. *The New Testament. The History of the Investigation of its Problems.* Trans. by S.M. Gilmour & H.C. Kee. London: S.C.M., 1973.

LANDOW, G.P. *Victorian Types, Victorian Shadows: Biblical Typology in Victorian Literature, Art and Thought.* Boston: Routledge & Kegan Paul, 1980.

LANGFORD, T. *In Search of Foundations. English Theology 1900-1920.* Nashville: Abingdon, 1969.

LEVINE, P. *The Amateur and the Professional. Antiquarians, Historians, and Archaeologists in Victorian England, 1838-1886.* Cambridge: University Press, 1986.

LIGHTMAN, B. *The Origins of Agnosticism. Victorian Unbelief and the Limits of Knowledge.* Baltimore: Johns Hopkins University Press, 1987.

LIVINGSTON, J.C. *The Ethics of Belief: An Essay on the Victorian Religious Conscience.* Tallahassee, Florida: American Academy of Religion, 1974.

LOWENTHAL, D. *The Past is a Foreign Country*. Cambridge: University Press, 1985.

LÖWITH, K. *Meaning in History*. Chicago & New York: University of Chicago Press, 1949.

McADOO, H.R. *The Spirit of Anglicanism. A Survey of Anglican Theological Method in the Seventeenth Century*. London: Black, 1965.

McCLATCHEY, D. *Oxfordshire Clergy, 1777-1869: A Study of the Established Church and of the Role of its Clergy in Local Society*. Oxford: Clarendon Press, 1960.

McCORD, N. *The Days of Visitation: An Examination of Some Durham Records 1857-1936*. Durham: Dean & Chapter of Durham, 1987.

McCORD, N. *North East England: The Region's Development 1760-1960. An Economic and Social History*. London: Batsford Academic, 1979.

MacDONALD, A. *A Short History of Repton*. London: Ernest Benn, 1929.

MacDONALD, H.D. *Ideas of Revelation. An Historical Study AD 1700 to AD 1860*. London: Macmillan, 1959.

MacDONALD, H.D. *Theories of Revelation. An Historical Study 1860-1960*. London: Allen & Unwin, 1963.

McLACHLAN, H. *The Unitarian Movement in the Religious Life of England*. London: Allen & Unwin, 1934.

McPHERSON, R.G. *Theory of Higher Education in Nineteenth Century England*. Athens: University of Georgia Press, 1959.

MACK, E.C. *Public Schools and British Opinion. An Examination of the Relationship Between Contemporary Ideas and the Evolution of an English Institution*. London: Methuen, 1938.

MAHIEU, D. Le. *The Mind of William Paley. A Philosopher and his Age*. Lincoln & London: University of Nebraska Press, 1976.

MANDELBAUM, M. *History, Man and Reason. A Study in Nineteenth Century Thought*. Baltimore & London: Johns Hopkins Press, 1971.

MARSH, P.T. *The Victorian Church in Decline: Archbishop Tait and the Church of England 1868-1882*. London: Routledge & Kegan Paul, 1969.

METZGER, B.M. *The Canon of the New Testament. Its Origin, Development and Significance*. Oxford: Clarendon Press, 1987.

MEYERHOFF, H. (ed.). *The Philosophy of History in our Time*. New York: Anchor Books, 1959.

MORGAN, R. with BARTON, J. *Biblical Interpretation*. Oxford: University Press, 1988.

MORGAN, R. (ed.). *The Religion of the Incarnation. Anglican Essays in Commemoration of "Lux Mundi"*. Bristol: Bristol Classical Press, 1989.

NEWSOME, D. *A History of Wellington College 1859-1959*. London: John Murray, 1959.

NEWSOME, D. *Two Classes of Men. Platonism and English Romantic Thought*. London: John Murray, 1974.

NEWSOME, D. *On the Edge of Paradise. A.C. Benson the Diarist*. Chicago: University Press, 1980.

NISBET, R. *History of the Idea of Progress*. London: Heinemann, 1980.

NOCKLES, P.B. *The Oxford Movement in Context. Anglican High Churchmanship, 1760-1857*. Cambridge: University Press, 1994.

OLIVER, W.H. *Prophets and Millennialists. The Uses of Biblical Prophecy in England from the 1790s to the 1840s*. [Auckland] Auckland University Press, 1978.

OLOFSSON, F. *Christus Redemptor et Consummator. A Study in the Theology of B.F. Westcott*. Trans. by N. Tomkinson assisted by J. Gray. Studia Doctrinae Christianae Upsaliensia 19. Stockholm: Almquist & Wiksell, 1979.

PALS, D. *The Victorian "Lives" of Jesus*. San Antonio, Texas: Trinity University Press, 1982.

PARKER, C. *The English Historical Tradition Since 1850*. Edinburgh: John Donald, 1990.

PATRICK, G.A. *F.J.A. Hort Eminent Victorian*. Sheffield: Almond Press, 1987.

PICKERING, W.S.F. (ed.). *A Social History of the Diocese of Newcastle 1882-1982*. Stocksfield, Northumberland: Oriel Press, 1981.

PLUMB, J.H. *The Death of the Past*. London: Macmillan, 1969.

POLLOCK, J. *A Cambridge Movement*. London: John Murray, 1953.

PRESTIGE, G.L. *St Paul's in its Glory: A Candid History of the Cathedral 1831-1911*. London: S.P.C.K., 1955.

PREYER, R. *Bentham, Coleridge, and the Science of History*. Bochum-Langendreer: Heinrich Poppinghaus, 1958.

PRICKETT, S. *Romanticism and Religion. The Tradition of Coleridge and Wordsworth in the Victorian Church*. Cambridge: University Press, 1976.

PYM, D. *The Religious Thought of Samuel Taylor Coleridge*. Gerrard's Cross: C. Smyth, 1978.

RAMSEY, A.M. *Durham Essays and Addresses*. London: S.P.C.K., 1956.

RAMSEY, M. *From Gore to Temple. The Development of Anglican Theology Between 'Lux Mundi' and the Second World War*. London: Longmans, 1960.

RAMSEY, I. *Joseph Butler 1692-1752. Author of 'The Analogy of Religion'. Some Features of his Life and Thought*. London: Dr Williams Trust, 1969.

RICHARDSON, A. *The Bible in the Age of Science*. London: S.C.M., 1961.

RICHARDSON, A. *History Sacred and Profane*. London: S.C.M., 1964.

RICHES, J.K. *A Century of New Testament Study*. Valley Forge, Pennsylvania: Trinity Press International, 1993.

RICHTER, M. *The Politics of Conscience. T.H. Green and his Age*. London: Weidenfeld & Nicolson, 1964.

ROBBINS, K. *Nineteenth-Century Britain. Integration and Diversity*. Oxford: Clarendon Press, 1988.

ROBERTSON, J.M. *A History of Free Thought in the Nineteenth Century*. 2 vols. London: Watts, 1929.

ROBIN, A. de Q. *Charles Perry. Bishop of Melbourne. The Challenges of a Colonial Episcopate, 1847-76*. Nedlands, Western Australia: University of Western Australia Press, 1967.

ROGERSON, J.W. *Old Testament Criticism in the Nineteenth Century*. London: S.P.C.K., 1984.

ROPER, H.R. Trevor-. *The Romantic Movement and the Study of History*. London: Athlone Press, 1969.

ROTHBLATT, S. *The Revolution of the Dons. Cambridge and Society in Victorian England*. London: Faber, 1968.

ROTHBLATT, S. *"Tradition and Change" in English Liberal Education. An Essay in History and Culture*. London: Faber & Faber, 1976.

ROWELL, G. *The Vision Glorious. Themes and Personalities of the Catholic Revival in Anglicanism*. Oxford: University Press, 1983.

ROWELL, G. *Hell and the Victorians; a Study of the Nineteenth-century Theological Controversies Concerning Eternal Punishment and the Future Life*. Oxford: Clarendon Press, 1974.

RUSSELL, A. *The Clerical Profession*. London: S.P.C.K., 1980.

RUSSELL, W. *St Paul's Under Dean Church and His Associates*. London, 1922.

RYAN, A. *J.S. Mill*. London & Boston: Routledge & Kegan Paul, 1974.

SACHS, W.L. *The Transformation of Anglicanism. From State Church to Global Communion*. Cambridge: University Press, 1993.

SANDEEN, E.R. *The Roots of Fundamentalism: British and American Millenarianism, 1800-1930*. Chicago: University Press, 1970.

SANDERS, C.R. *Coleridge and the Broad Church Movement*. North Carolina: Duke University Press, 1942.

SANDERSON, M. (ed.). *The Universities in the Nineteenth Century.* London & Boston: Routledge & Kegan Paul, 1975.

SCHNEEWIND, J.B. *Sidgwick's Ethics and Victorian Moral Philosophy.* Oxford: Clarendon Press, 1977.

SHARPE, E. *Understanding Religion.* London: Duckworth, 1983.

SHILS, E. *Tradition.* London: Faber, 1981.

SILBERMAN, N.A. *Digging For God and Country. Exploration, Archaeology, and the Secret Struggle For the Holy Land 1799-1917.* New York: Knopf, 1982.

SIMON, B. & BRADLEY, I. (eds). *The Victorian Public School.* Dublin: Gill & Macmillan, 1975.

SLEE, P.R.H. *Learning and a Liberal Education. The Study of Modern History in the Universities of Oxford, Cambridge and Manchester 1800-1914.* Manchester: University Press, 1986.

SMITH, B.A. *Dean Church. The Anglican Response to Newman.* London: Oxford University Press, 1958.

SMITH, K. Hylson-. *High Churchmanship in the Church of England. From the Sixteenth Century to the Late Twentieth Century.* Edinburgh: T. & T. Clark, 1993.

STEPHEN, B. *Emily Davies and Girton College.* London: Constable & Co., 1927.

STEPHENSON, A.M.G. *Anglicanism and the Lambeth Conferences.* London: S.P.C.K., 1978.

STEPHENSON, A.M.G. *The Rise and Decline of English Modernism.* London: S.P.C.K., 1984.

SWANSTON, H.F.G. *Ideas of Order: The Mid-Nineteenth Century Revival of Anglican Theological Method.* Assen, The Netherlands: Gorcum, 1974.

SYKES, S.W. *The Identity of Christianity. Theologians and the Essence of Christianity From Schleiermacher to Barth.* London: S.P.C.K., 1984.

THOMPSON, D.M. *Nonconformity in the Nineteenth Century.* London & Boston: Routledge & Kegan Paul, 1972.

THOMPSON, J.W. *A History of Historical Writing.* 2 vols. New York: Macmillan, 1942.

THOMPSON, K.A. *Bureaucracy and Church Reform. The Organizational Response of the Church of England to Social Change 1800-1965.* Oxford: Clarendon Press, 1970.

TREVELYAN, G.M. *Trinity College. An Historical Sketch.* Cambridge: University Press, 1943.

TULLBERG, R. McWilliams-. *Women at Cambridge. A Men's University - Though of a Mixed Type.* London: Gollancz, 1975.

TURNER, F.M. *Between Science and Religion. The Reaction to Scientific Naturalism in Late Victorian England.* New Haven & London: Yale University Press, 1974.

TURNER, F.M. *The Greek Heritage in Victorian Britain.* New Haven & London: Yale University Press, 1981.

TURNER, F.M. *Contesting Cultural Authority. Essays in Victorian Cultural Life.* Cambridge: University Press, 1993.

VARLEY, E.A. *The Last of the Prince Bishops: The Episcopate of William Van Mildert (1826-1836).* Durham: Dean & Chapter of Durham, 1986.

VARLEY, E. *The Last of the Prince Bishops. William Van Mildert and the High Church Movement of the Early Nineteenth Century.* Cambridge: University Press, 1992.

VIDLER, A. *F.D. Maurice and Company.* London: S.C.M., 1966.

VOLL, D. *Catholic Evangelicalism. The Acceptance of Evangelical Traditions by the Oxford Movement During the Second Half of the Nineteenth Century.* London: Faith Press, 1963.

WARD, W.R. *Victorian Oxford.* London: Frank Cass & Co., 1965.

WARMAN, H.W. *Ernest Renan. A Critical Biography.* London: Athlone Press, 1964.

WATSON, G. *The English Ideology. Studies in the Language of Victorian Politics.* London: Allen Lane, 1973.

WEBB, C.C.J. *A Study of Religious Thought in England From 1850.* Oxford: Clarendon Press, 1933.

WELCH, C. *A History of Protestant Thought in the Nineteenth Century.* 2 vols. New Haven & London: Yale University Press, 1972-85.

WELCH, E. *The Peripatetic University. Cambridge Local Lectures 1873-1973.* Cambridge: University Press, 1973.

WIENER, M.J. *English Culture and the Decline of the Industrial Spirit, 1850-1980.* Cambridge: University Press, 1981.

WILLIAMS, D. *Genesis and Exodus. A Portrait of the Benson Family.* London: Hamish Hamilton, 1979.

WILLIAMS, N.P. *The Durham Tradition.* London & Oxford: A.R. Mowbray, 1932.

WINSTANLEY, D.A. *Early Victorian Cambridge.* Cambridge: University Press, 1940.

WINSTANLEY, D.A. *Late Victorian Cambridge.* Cambridge: University Press, 1947.

WOODWARD, F.J. *The Doctor's Disciples.* London: Oxford University Press, 1954.

WORMELL, D. *Sir John Seeley and the Uses of History.* Cambridge: University Press, 1980.

WRIGHT, T.R. *The Religion of Humanity. The Impact of Comtean Positivism on Victorian Britain.* Cambridge: University Press, 1986.

YOUNG, G.M. *Portrait of an Age. Victorian England.* Annotated edition by G.S.R. Kitson Clark. London: Oxford University Press, 1977.

IV. Other Articles and Chapters

ADDINALL, P. "Why Read the Bible?" *The Expository Times* 105.5 (February 1994) 136-40.

ALTHOLZ, J.L. "The Warfare of Conscience With Theology." *The Mind and Art of Victorian England.* Ed. J.L. Altholz. Minneapolis: University of Minnesota Press, 1976, 58-77, 184-5.

ALTHOLZ, J.L. 'The Mind of Victorian Orthodoxy: Anglican Responses to *Essays and Reviews,* 1860-64.' *Church History* 51.2 (June 1982) 186-97.

ALTHOLZ, J.L. 'A Tale of Two Controversies: Darwinism in the Debate Over "Essays and Reviews".' *Church History* 63.1 (March 1994) 50-59.

ANDERSON, O. "The Political Uses of History in Mid-Victorian England." *Past and Present* 36 (1967) 87-105.

ANDREWS, J.S. "German Influence on Religious Life in the Victorian Era." *The Evangelical Quarterly* 44 (October-December 1972) 218-33.

ANNAN, N. "Introduction" to the section entitled "Science, Religion, and the Critical Mind." *1859: Entering An Age of Crisis.* Eds P. Appleman, W.A. Madden & M. Wolff. Bloomington: Indiana University Press, 1959, 31-50.

ATKINS, W.M. "The Age of Reform 1831-1934." *A History of St Paul's Cathedral and the Men Associated With It.* Eds W.R. Matthews & W.M. Atkins. London: Phoenix, 1957, 250-99.

AVIS, P. "The Tractarian Challenge to Consensus and the Identity of Anglicanism." *King's Theological Review* 9 (1986) 14-17.

BARR, J. "Jowett and the Reading of the Bible 'Like Any Other Book'." *Horizons in Biblical Theology* 4.2 (December 1982) and 5.1 (June 1983) 1-44.

BARTHOLOMEW, M. "The Moral Critique of Christian Orthodoxy." *Religion in Victorian Britain. Volume II. Controversies.* Ed. G. Parsons. Manchester: University Press, 1988, 166-90.

BEBBINGTON, D. "Religion and Society in the Nineteenth Century." *The Historical Journal* 32.4 (1989) 997-1004.

BECHER, H.W. "The Social Origins and Post-Graduate Careers of a Cambridge Intellectual Elite, 1830-1860." *Victorian Studies* 28.1 (Autumn 1984) 97-127.

BENEDIKZ, B.S. "Henry Edwin Savage – Servant of Christ." *Eastern Churches Newsletter* n.s. 7 (1978) 15-20.

BENEDIKZ, B.S. "Faith and Care: A View of Two Distinguished Lichfield Citizens." *Johnson Society (Lichfield): Transactions* (1981) 14-28.

BENNETT, G.V. "Patristic Tradition in Anglican Thought, 1660-1960." *Oecumenica* (1971-2) 63-87.

BEST, G.F.A. "The Mind and Times of William Van Mildert." *The Journal of Theological Studies* XIV n.s. (1963) 355-70.

BONNER, G.W. "Religion in Anglo-Saxon England." *Religion in England.* Eds S. Gilley & W.J. Sheils. Oxford and Cambridge, Massachusetts: Blackwell, 1994, 24-44.

BOONE, D.R. "Appearing To Conspire: An Episode in the Broad Church Historiography of Nineteenth-century Britain." *Anglican and Episcopal History* LX.4 (December 1991) 493-503.

BONNER, G. "St Cuthbert in Chester-le-Street." Eds G. Bonner, D. Rollason, C. Stancliffe. Woodbridge, Suffolk & Wolfeboro, N.H.: Boydell Press/Boydell & Brewer, 1989, 387-95.

BROOKE, C. *et. al.* "What Is Religious History?" *History Today* 35 (August 1985) 43-52.

BURROW, J.W. "The Uses of Philology in Victorian England." *Ideas and Institutions of Victorian Britain. Essays in Honour of George Kitson Clark.* Ed. R. Robson. London: Bell, 1967, 180-204.

BURROW, J.W. " 'The Village Community' and the Uses of History in Late Nineteenth Century England." *Historical Perspectives. Studies in English Thought and Society in Honour of J.H. Plumb.* Ed. N. McKendrick. London: Europa, 1974, 255-84.

BURROW, J.W. "The Sense of the Past." *The Victorians.* Ed. L. Lerner. New York: Holmes & Meier, 1978, 120-38.

CAM, H. "Stubbs Seventy Years After." *The Cambridge Historical Journal* IX.2 (1948) 129-47.

CAPRA, D. La. "Rethinking Intellectual History and Reading Texts." *History and Theory* 19.3 (1980) 245-76.

CHADWICK, O. "Charles Kingsley at Cambridge." *The Historical Journal* XVIII.2 (1975) 303-25.

CHADWICK, O. "Catholicism." *Theology* LXXVI.634 (April 1973) 171-80.

CLARK, G. Kitson. "The Romantic Element 1830-1850." *Studies in Social History: A Tribute to G.M. Trevelyan.* Ed. J.H. Plumb. London, New York, Toronto: Longmans, Green and Co., 1955, 209-39.

CLARK, G.S.R. Kitson. "A Hundred Years of the Teaching of History at Cambridge, 1873-1973." *The Historical Journal* XVI.3 (1973) 535-53.

CLIVE, J. "The Use of the Past in Victorian England." *Salmagundi* 68-9 (Fall 1985 - Winter 1986) 48-65.

CREED, J.M. "The Study of the New Testament." *Journal of Theological Studies* XLII (1941) 1-11.

CROUSE, R.D. ' "Deepened By the Study of the Fathers": The Oxford Movement, Dr Pusey and Patristic Scholarship.' *Dionysius* VII (December 1983) 137-47.

DODDS, V. "Strauss' English Propagandists and the Politics of Unitarianism, 1841-1845." *Church History* 50 (December 1981) 415-35.

DOWLING, L. "Roman Decadence and Victorian Historiography." *Victorian Studies* 28.4 (Summer 1985) 579-607.

DUFFY, E. "Primitive Christianity Revived: Religious Renewal in Augustan England." *Studies in Church History* 14 (1977) 287-300.

438   *Bibliography*

DYSON, A.O. "Theological Legacies of the Enlightenment: England and Germany." *England and Germany: Studies in Theological Diplomacy.* Ed. S. Sykes. Frankfurt Am Main: Verlag Peter D. Lang, 1982, 45-61.

ELLIS, I. "Schleiermacher in Britain." *Scottish Journal of Theology* 33.5 (October 1980) 417-52.

FRANCIS, M. "The Origins of *Essays and Reviews.* An Interpretation of Mark Pattison in the 1850s." *The Historical Journal* XVII.4 (1974) 797-811.

FRAPPELL, L.O. "The Reformation as Negative Revolution or Obscurantist Reaction: The Liberal Debate on the Reformation in Nineteenth Century Britain." *The Journal of Religious History* 11.2 (December 1980) 289-307.

FREI, H.. "David Friedrich Strauss." *Nineteenth Century Religious Thought in the West.* Eds N. Smart, J. Clayton, S. Katz & P. Sherry. Cambridge: University Press, 1985, I.215-60.

GAUVREAU, M. "Baconianism, Darwinism, Fundamentalism: A Transatlantic Crisis of Faith." *The Journal of Religious History* 13.4 (December 1985) 434-44.

GECK, A. "The Concept of History in E.B. Pusey's First Enquiry Into German Theology and its Background." *Journal of Theological Studies* n.s. 38.2 (October 1987) 387-408.

GEE, H. "Ecclesiastical History." *The Victoria History of the County of Durham.* Ed. W. Page. London: Archibald Constable, 1907, II.1-77.

GIBSON, W.T. "The Social Origins and Education of an Elite: The Nineteenth-Century Episcopate." *History of Education* 20.2 (1991) 95-105.

GIBSON, W.T. "The Professionalization of an Elite: The Nineteenth Century Episcopate." *Albion* 23.3 (Fall 1991) 459-82.

GIBSON, W.T. "Disraeli's Church Patronage: 1868-1880." *Anglican and Episcopal History* LXI.2 (June 1992) 197-210.

GILLEY, S.W. "The Huxley-Wilberforce Debate: A Reconsideration." *Studies in Church History* 17 (1981) 325-40.

GILLEY, S.W. "Western Religious Thought in the Nineteenth Century." *History of European Ideas* 9.1 (1988) 63-9.

GILLEY, S. "The Church of England in the Nineteenth Century." *A History of Religion in Britain. Practice and Belief From Pre-Roman Times to the Present.* Eds S. Gilley & W.J. Sheils. Oxford & Cambridge, Massachusetts: Basil Blackwell, 1994, 291-305.

GOLDIE, M. "Ideology." *Political Innovation and Conceptual Change.* Eds T. Ball *et. al.* Cambridge: University Press, 1989, 266-91.

GOLDSTEIN, D. "J.B. Bury's Philosophy of History: A Reappraisal." *American Historical Review* 82 (1977) 896-919.

GRANT, R.M. "The Apostolic Fathers' First Thousand Years." *Church History* 31 (1962) 421-9.

GREENSLADE, S.L. "The Authority of the Tradition of the Early Church in Early Anglican Thought." *Oecumenica* (1971-2) 9-33.

HAIG, A. "The Church, the Universities and Learning in Later Victorian England." *The Historical Journal* 29.1 (1986) 187-201.

HARDING, A.J. "Sterling, Carlyle, and German Higher Criticism: A Reassessment." *Victorian Studies* 26.3 (1983) 269-85.

HARVEY, V.A. "D.F. Strauss' 'Life of Jesus' Revisited." *Church History* XXX (1961) 191-211.

HILTON, B. "The Role of Providence in Evangelical Social Thought." *History, Society and the Churches. Essays in Honour of Owen Chadwick.* Eds D. Beales & G. Best. Cambridge: University Press, 1985, 215-33.

HINCHLIFF, P. "Ethics, Evolution and Biblical Criticism in the Thought of Benjamin Jowett and John William Colenso." *Journal of Ecclesiastical History* 37.1 (January 1986) 91-110.

HOLMES, J. Derek. "John Henry Newman's Attitude Towards History and Hagiography." *The Downside Review* 92 (1974) 248-64.

HOLMES, J. Derek. "Newman's Reputation and *The Lives of the English Saints.*" *The Catholic Historical Review* LI.4 (1966) 528-38.

JAGGER, P. "The Formation of the Diocese of Newcastle." *A Social History of the Diocese of Newcastle.* Ed. W.S. F. Pickering. Stocksfield, Northumberland: Oriel Press, 1981, 24-52.

JANN, R. "From Amateur to Professional: The Case of the Oxbridge Historians." *Journal of British Studies* 22.2 (1983) 122-47.

JENKINS, H. & JONES, D. Caradog. "Social Class of Cambridge University Alumni of the 18th and 19th Centuries." *British Journal of Sociology* I (1950) 93-116.

JESSE, W. "Cambridge in the 80s." *Cornhill Magazine* CLV (March 1937) 340-56.

JOHNSON, D.A. "Popular Apologetics in Late Victorian England. The Work of the Christian Evidence Society." *The Journal of Religious History* 11.4 (December 1981) 558-77.

KAYE, B.N. "D.F. Strauss and the European Theological Tradition: *Der Ischariotismus unsere Tag?*" *Journal of Religious History* 17.2 (December 1992) 172-93.

KENT, J. "The Study of Modern Ecclesiastical History Since 1930." *The Pelican Guide to Modern Theology.* Eds J. Daniélou, A.H. Couratin & J. Kent. Harmondsworth: Penguin, 1969, 243-369.

LAMPE, G.W.H. "The Bible Since the Rise of Critical Study." *The Church's Use of the Bible Past and Present.* Ed. D. Nineham. London: S.P.C.K., 1963, 125-44.

LIVINGSTON, J.C. "The Religious Creed and Criticism of Sir James Fitzjames Stephen." *Victorian Studies* XVIII.3 (March 1974) 279-300.

McLEOD, H. "Varieties of Victorian Belief." *Journal of Modern History* 64.2 (1992) 321-37.

McGIFFERT, A.C. "The Historical Criticism of Acts in Germany." *The Beginnings of Christianity. Part I. The Acts of the Apostles.* Ed. F. Foakes Jackson & K. Lake. London: Macmillan, 1922, II.363-95.

MacHAFFIE, B.Z. ' "Monument Facts and Higher Critical Fancies": Archaeology and the Popularization of Old Testament Criticism in Nineteenth-Century Britain." *Church History* 50.3 (1981) 316-28.

McLACHLAN, J.O. "The Origin and Early Development of the Cambridge Historical Tripos." *The Cambridge Historical Journal* IX (1947-9) 78-105.

MANSFIELD, B. "Lucien Febvre and the Study of Religious History." *The Journal of Religious History* I.2 (December 1960) 102-11.

MANSFIELD, B. "J.R.H. - A Memoir at Twenty Years." *The Journal of Religious History* XI.1 (June 1980) 3-7.

MARCOMBE, D. "Bernard Gilpin: Anatomy of an Elizabethan Legend." *Northern History* XVI (1980) 20-39.

MAYNARD, W.B. "The Response of the Church of England to Economic and Demographic Change: The Archdeaconry of Durham, 1800-1851." *Journal of Ecclesiastical History* 42.3 (July 1991) 437-62.

MAYOR, S. "Discussion of the Ministry in Late Nineteenth-Century Anglicanism." *Church Quarterly* 2.1 (July 1969) 54-62.

MAYOR, S. "The Anglo-Catholic Understanding of the Ministry: Some Protestant Comments." *The Church Quarterly* 2.2 (October 1969) 152-9.

MOORE, J.R. "The Crisis of Faith: Reformation Versus Revolution." *Religion in Victorian Britain. Vol II. Controversies.* Ed. G. Parsons. Manchester: University Press, 1988, 220-37.

MORGAN, R. "Ferdinand Christian Baur." *Nineteenth Century Religious Thought in the West.* Eds N. Smart, J. Clayton, S. Katz & P. Sherry. Cambridge: University Press, 1985, I.261-89.

MORRISH, P.S. "History, Celticism and Propaganda in the Formation of the Diocese of Truro." *Southern History* 5 (1983) 238-66.

MURPHY, H.R. "The Ethical Revolt Against Christian Orthodoxy in Early Victorian England." *American Historical Review* LX.4 (1955) 800-17.

NEIL, W. "The Criticism and Theological Use of the Bible, 1700-1850." *The Cambridge History of the Bible. The West From the Reformation to the Present Day.* Ed. S.L. Greenslade. Cambridge: University Press, 1963, 238-93.

NEWTON, J.S. "Edward Miall and the Diocese of Durham: The Disestablishment Question in the North-East in the Nineteenth Century." *Durham University Journal* LXXII.2 [n.s. XLI.2] (June 1980) 157-68.

NINEHAM, D. "R.H. Lightfoot and the Significance of Biblical Criticism." *Theology* LXXXVIII.722 (March 1985) 97-105.

O'DAY, R. "The Clerical Renaissance in Victorian England and Wales." *Religion in Victorian Britain. Volume I. Traditions.* Ed. G. Parsons. Manchester: University Press, 1988, 184-212.

O'DAY, R. "The Men From the Ministry." *Religion in Victorian Britain. Volume II. Controversies.* Ed. G. Parsons. Manchester: University Press, 1988, 258-79.

OSBORNE, J.W. "The Endurance of 'Literary' History in Great Britain: Charles Oman, G.M. Trevelyan, and the Genteel Tradition." *Clio* 2.1 (October 1972) 7-17.

PALS, D. "The Reception of *Ecce Homo*." *Historical Magazine of the Protestant Episcopal Church* XLVI.1 (March 1977) 63-84.

PARKER, C. "English Historians and the Opposition to Positivism." *History and Theory* XXII.2 (1983) 120-45.

PARKER, T.M. "The Rediscovery of the Fathers in the Seventeenth-Century Anglican Tradition." *The Rediscovery of Newman. An Oxford Symposium.* Eds J. Coulson & A.M. Allchin. London: Sheed & Ward/S.P.C.K., 1967, 31-49.

PARSONS, G. "Reform, Revival and Realignment: The Experience of Victorian Anglicanism." *Religion in Victorian Britain. Vol I. Traditions.* Ed. G. Parsons. Manchester: University Press, 1988, 14-66.

PARSONS, G. "On Speaking Plainly: 'Honest Doubt' and the Ethics of Belief." *Religion in Victorian Britain. Volume II. Controversies.* Ed. G. Parsons. Manchester: University Press, 1988, 191-219.

PFAFF, R.W. "The Library of the Fathers: The Tractarians as Patristic Translators." *Studies in Philology* LXX.3 (July 1973) 329-44.

PFAFF, R.W. "Anglo-American Patristic Translations 1866-1900." *Journal of Ecclesiastical History* 28.1 (January 1977) 39-55.

PHILLIPS, P.T. "The Concept of a National Church in Late Nineteenth-Century England and America." *Journal of Religious History* 14.1 (June 1986) 26-37.

PREYER, R.O. "The Romantic Tide Reaches Trinity: Notes on the Transmission and Diffusion of New Approaches to Traditional Studies at Cambridge." *Victorian Science and Victorian Values: Literary Perspectives.* Eds J. Paradis & T. Postlewait. New York: New York Academy of Sciences, 1981, 39-68.

RICHARDS, T. "The Image of Victoria in the Year of Jubilee." *Victorian Studies* 31.1 (Autumn 1987) 7-32.

RICHARDSON, A. "The Rise of Modern Biblical Scholarship and Recent Discussion of the Authority of the Bible." *The Cambridge History of the Bible. The West From the Reformation to the Present Day.* Ed. S.L. Greenslade. Cambridge: University Press, 1963, 294-338.

ROACH, J.P.C. "The University of Cambridge." *A History of the County of Cambridgeshire and the Isle of Ely*. Ed. J.P.C. Roach. London: Oxford University Press, 1959, III.210-306.

ROBERTS, M.J.D. "Pressure Group Politics and the Church of England: the Church Defence Institution 1859-1896." *Journal of Ecclesiastical History* 35.4 (October 1985) 560-82.

ROBSON, R. "Trinity College in the Age of Peel." *Ideas and Institutions of Victorian Britain*. Ed. R. Robson. London: Bell, 1967, 312-35.

ROGERSON, J.W. "Philosophy and the Rise of Biblical Criticism: England and Germany." *England and Germany: Studies in Theological Diplomacy*. Ed. S. Sykes. Frankfurt Am Main: Verlag Peter D. Lang, 1982, 63-79.

ROLLMANN, H. "From Baur to Wrede: The Quest For a Historical Method." *Studies in Religion* 17.4 (1988) 443-54.

RUPP, G. "Hort and the Cambridge Tradition." *Just Men. Historical Pieces*. London: Epworth, 1977, 151-66.

RUPP, G. "A Cambridge Centenary. The Selwyn Divinity School, 1879-1979." *The Historical Journal* 24.2 (1981) 417-28.

SAMUEL, R. "The Discovery of Puritanism, 1820-1914: A Preliminary Sketch." *Revival and Religion Since 1700. Essays for John Walsh*. Eds J. Garnett & C. Matthew. London & Rio Grande, Ohio: Hambledon Press, 1993, 201-47.

SAVORY, J.J. "Matthew Arnold and 'The Author of *Supernatural Religion*': The Backgound to *God and the Bible*." *Studies in English Literature* XVI.4 (Autumn 1976) 677-91.

SEMMEL, B. "H.T. Buckle: the Liberal Faith and the Science of History." *British Journal of Sociology* 27.3 (September 1976) 370-86.

SHANNON, R.T. "John Robert Seeley and the Idea of a National Church. A Study in Churchmanship, Historiography, and Politics." *Ideas and Institutions of the Victorians. Essays in Honour of George Kitson Clark*. Ed. R. Robson. London: Bell, 1967, 236-67.

SIMON, A. "Church Disestablishment as a Factor in the General Election of 1885." *The Historical Journal* XVIII.4 (1975) 791-820.

SKINNER, Q. "Meaning and Understanding in the History of Ideas." *History and Theory* VIII (1969) 3-53.

SOFFA, R. "Nation, Duty, Character and Confidence: History at Oxford, 1850-1914." *The Historical Journal* 30.1 (1987) 77-104.

SOLOWAY, R.A. "Church and Society: Recent Trends." *Journal of British Studies* XI.2 (May 1972) 142-59.

STANLEY, B. " 'Commerce and Christianity': Providence Theory, the Missionary Movement, and the Imperialism of Free Trade, 1842-1860." *The Historical Journal* 26.1 (1983) 71-94.

STANLEY, B. "Reactions to the Indian Mutiny." *Studies in Church History* 20 (1983) 277-89.

STRONG, E.W. "William Whewell and John Stuart Mill: Their Controversy About Scientific Knowledge." *Journal of the History of Ideas* XVI.2 (April 1955) 209-31.

SYKES, S.W. & GILLEY, S.W. " 'No Bishop, No Church!' The Tractarian Impact on Anglicanism." *Tradition Renewed. The Oxford Movement Conference Papers*. Ed. G. Rowell. Allison Park, Pennsylvania: Pickwick Publications, 1986, 120-39.

THOMAS, T. "The Impact of Other Religions." *Religion in Victorian Britain. Volume II. Controversies*. Ed. G. Parsons. Manchester: University Press, 1988, 280-98.

THOMPSON, D.M. "The Making of the English Religious Classes." *The Historical Journal* 22.2 (1979) 477-91.

THOMPSON, D.M. "The Emergence of the Nonconformist Social Gospel in England." *Protestant Evangelicalism: Britain, Ireland, Germany and America, c. 1750-c. 1850. Essays in Honour of W.R. Ward*. Studies in Church History Subsidia 7. Ed. K. Robbins. Oxford: Blackwell, 1990, 255-80.

THOMPSON, D.M. "The Christian Socialist Revival in Britain: A Reappraisal." *Revival and Religion Since 1700. Essays For John Walsh.* Eds J. Garnett & C. Matthew. London & Rio Grande, Ohio: Hambledon Press, 1993, 273-95.

TURNER, F.M. "Rainfall, Plagues, and the Prince of Wales. A Chapter in the Conflict of Religion and Science." *Journal of British Studies* XIII.2 (May 1974) 46-75.

TURNER, F.M., & ARX, J. von. "Victorian Ethics of Belief: A Reconsideration." *The Secular Mind.* Ed. W. Wagar. New York: Holmes & Meier, 1982, 83-101.

VANCE, N. "The Ideal of Manliness." *The Victorian Public School. Studies in the Development of an Educational Institution. A Symposium.* Eds B. Simon & I. Bradley. Dublin: Gill and Macmillan, 1975, 115-28.

WALKER, R.B. "Religious Changes in Liverpool in the Nineteenth Century." *Journal of Ecclesiatical History* XIX (1968) 195-211.

WARD, J.M. "The Retirement of a Titan: James Stephen, 1847-50." *Journal of Modern History* XXXI.3 (1959) 189-205.

WARD, W.R. "Oxford and the Origins of Liberal Catholicism in the Church of England." *Studies in Church History* I (1964) 233-52.

WARD, W.R. "Faith and Fallacy: English and German Perspectives in the Nineteenth Century." *Victorian Faith in Crisis. Essays on Continuity and Change in Nineteenth-Century Religious Belief.* Eds R. Helmstadter & B. Lightman. London: Macmillan, 1990, 39-67.

WEBSTER, J. "Ministry and Priesthood." *The Study of Anglicanism.* Eds S. Sykes & J. Booty. London and Philadelphia: S.P.C.K./Fortress Press, 1988, 285-96.

WILLIS, K. "The Introduction and Critical Reception of Hegelian Thought in Britain 1830-1900." *Victorian Studies* 32.1 (Autumn 1988) 85-111.

YEO, R. "An Idol of the Market-Place: Baconianism in Nineteenth Century Britain." *History of Science* XXIII (1985) 251-98.

YOUNG, B.W. "Knock-Kneed Giants: Victorian Representations of Eighteenth-Century Thought." *Revival and Religion Since 1700. Essays for John Walsh.* Eds J. Garnett & C. Matthew. London & Rio Grande, Ohio: Hambledon Press, 1993, 79-93.

YOUNG, R. "The Impact of Darwin on Conventional Thought." *The Victorian Crisis of Faith.* Ed. A. Symondson. London: S.P.C.K., 1970, 13-35.

YOUNG, R. "Natural Theology, Victorian Periodicals and the Formation of a Common Context." *Darwin to Einstein. Historical Studies on Science and Belief.* Eds C. Chant & J. Fauvel. Burnt Mill, Harlow, Essex and New York: Longman in association with the Open University Press, 1980, 69-107.

V. Theses

BUBB, I.M. "The Theology of F.J.A. Hort, in Relation to Nineteenth Century Thought." Unpublished Ph.D. thesis: Manchester University, 1956.

CHARLES, A.O. "The Ministry at St Paul's Under Dean Church as Guide to a Contemporary Pastoral Challenge." Unpublished Diploma thesis: St Augustine's College, Canterbury, 1965 [copy at St Paul's Cathedral Library].

MAYNARD, W.B. "The Ecclesiastical Administration of the Archdeaconry of Durham 1774-1856." Unpublished Ph.D. thesis: Durham University, 1973.

O'DEA, W.G. "Westcott the Theologian." Unpublished M.Litt. thesis: Cambridge University, 1972.

PATRICK, G.A. "A Study of the Writings of F.J.A. Hort, and an Assessment of Him as a Biblical Scholar." Unpublished Ph.D.Thesis: London University, 1978.

PICKARD, A.J. "Liberal Anglicanism 1847-1902. A Study of Class and Cultural Relationships in Nineteenth Century England." Unpublished Ph.D. thesis: University of Birmingham, 1982.

SEDGWICK, P.H. " 'The Character of Christ': The Correlation of Moral Theology and Christology in Anglican Theology, 1830-1870." Unpublished Ph.D. thesis: Durham University, 1983

STANLEY, B. "Home Support for Overseas Missions in Early Victorian England, ca. 1838-1873." Unpublished Ph.D. thesis: Cambridge University, 1979.

THOMAS, P.H.E. "The Lambeth Conferences and the Development of Anglican Ecclesiology 1867-1978." Unpublished Ph.D. thesis: Durham University, 1982.

WHITEHOUSE, R. "Biblical and Historical Criticism in Anglican Theology, 1800-1860. A Study in Authority and Reason in Religion." Unpublished M.Litt. thesis: Bristol University, n.y.

WILLETT, G.T. "The Durham Episcopate of Charles Baring (1807-1879)." Unpublished M.A. thesis: Durham University, 1982.

WINTERNITZ, J. "The Development of the Linguistic Theory of Universal History With Especial Reference to C.C.J. Bunsen, 1830-1880's." Unpublished Ph.D. thesis: University of Sydney, 1979.

YEO, R. "Natural Theology and the Philosophy of Knowledge in Britain, 1819-1869." Unpublished Ph.D. thesis: University of Sydney, 1977.

Index of Authors

Index of Biblical References

Subject Index

Wissenschaftliche Untersuchungen zum Neuen Testament

Alphabetical Index of the First and Second Series

Anderson, Paul N.: The Christology of the Fourth Gospel. 1996. *vol. II/78.*
Appold, Mark L.: The Oneness Motif in the Fourth Gospel. 1976. *vol. II/1.*
Arnold, Clinton E.: The Colossian Syncretism. 1995. *vol. II/77.*
Avemarie, Friedrich and *Hermann Lichtenberger* (Ed.): Bund und Tora. 1996. *vol. 92.*
Bachmann, Michael: Sünder oder Übertreter. 1992. *vol. 59.*
Baker, William R.: Personal Speech-Ethics in the Epistle of James. 1995. *vol. II/68.*
Balla, Peter: Challenges to New Testament Theology. 1997. *vol. II/95.*
Bammel, Ernst: Judaica. vol. I 1986. *vol. 37* – vol. II 1997. *vol. 91.*
Bash, Anthony: Ambassadors for Christ. 1997. *vol. II/92.*
Bauernfeind, Otto: Kommentar und Studien zur Apostelgeschichte. 1980. *vol. 22.*
Bayer, Hans Friedrich: Jesus' Predictions of Vindication and Resurrection. 1986. *vol. II/20.*
Bell, Richard H.: Provoked to Jealousy. 1994. *vol. II/63.*
– No One Seeks for God. 1998. *vol. 106.*
Bergman, Jan: siehe *Kieffer, René*
Betz, Otto: Jesus, der Messias Israels. 1987. *vol. 42.*
– Jesus, der Herr der Kirche. 1990. *vol. 52.*
Beyschlag, Karlmann: Simon Magus und die christliche Gnosis. 1974. *vol. 16.*
Bittner, Wolfgang J.: Jesu Zeichen im Johannesevangelium. 1987. *vol. II/26.*
Bjerkelund, Carl J.: Tauta Egeneto. 1987. *vol. 40.*
Blackburn, Barry Lee: Theios Anēr and the Markan Miracle Traditions. 1991. *vol. II/40.*
Bockmuehl, Markus N.A.: Revelation and Mystery in Ancient Judaism and Pauline Christianity. 1990. *vol. II/36.*
Böhlig, Alexander: Gnosis und Synkretismus. Teil 1 1989. *vol. 47* –Teil 2 1989. *vol. 48.*
Böttrich, Christfried: Weltweisheit – Menschheitsethik – Urkult. 1992. *vol. II/50.*
Bolyki, János: Jesu Tischgemeinschaften. 1998. *vol. II/96.*
Büchli, Jörg: Der Poimandres – ein paganisiertes Evangelium. 1987. *vol. II/27.*
Bühner, Jan A.: Der Gesandte und sein Weg im 4. Evangelium. 1977. *vol. II/2.*
Burchard, Christoph: Untersuchungen zu Joseph und Asenath. 1965. *vol. 8.*
Cancik, Hubert (Ed.): Markus-Philologie. 1984. *vol. 33.*
Capes, David B.: Old Testament Yaweh Texts in Paul's Christology. 1992. *vol. II/47.*
Caragounis, Chrys C.: The Son of Man. 1986. *vol. 38.*
– siehe *Fridrichsen, Anton.*
Carleton Paget, James: The Epistle of Barnabas. 1994. *vol. II/64.*
Ciampa, Roy E.: The Presence and Function of Scripture in Galatians 1 and 2. 1998. *vol. II/102.*
Crump, David: Jesus the Intercessor. 1992. *vol. II/49.*
Deines, Roland: Jüdische Steingefäße und pharisäische Frömmigkeit. 1993. *vol. II/52.*
– Die Pharisäer. 1997. *vol. 101.*
Dietzfelbinger, Christian: Der Abschied des Kommenden. 1997. *vol. 95.*
Dobbeler, Axel von: Glaube als Teilhabe. 1987. *vol. II/22.*
Du Toit, David S.: Theios Anthropos. 1997. *vol. II/91*
Dunn, James D.G. (Ed.): Jews and Christians. 1992. *vol. 66.*
– Paul and the Mosaic Law. 1996. *vol. 89.*
Ebertz, Michael N.: Das Charisma des Gekreuzigten. 1987. *vol. 45.*
Eckstein, Hans-Joachim: Der Begriff Syneidesis bei Paulus. 1983. *vol. II/10.*
– Verheißung und Gesetz. 1996. *vol. 86.*
Ego, Beate: Im Himmel wie auf Erden. 1989. *vol. II/34.*
Eisen, Ute E.: siehe *Paulsen, Henning.*
Ellis, E. Earle: Prophecy and Hermeneutic in Early Christianity. 1978. *vol. 18.*
– The Old Testament in Early Christianity. 1991. *vol. 54.*
Ennulat, Andreas: Die 'Minor Agreements'. 1994. *vol. II/62.*
Ensor, Peter W.: Jesus and His 'Works'. 1996. *vol. II/85.*
Eskola, Timo: Theodicy and Predestination in Pauline Soteriology. 1998. *vol. II/100.*

Feldmeier, Reinhard: Die Krisis des Gottessohnes. 1987. *vol. II/21.*
– Die Christen als Fremde. 1992. *vol. 64.*
Feldmeier, Reinhard and *Ulrich Heckel* (Ed.): Die Heiden. 1994. *vol. 70.*
Fletcher-Louis, Crispin H.T.: Luke-Acts: Angels, Christology and Soteriology. 1997. *vol. II/94.*
Forbes, Christopher Brian: Prophecy and Inspired Speech in Early Christianity and its Hellenistic Environment. 1995. *vol. II/75.*
Fornberg, Tord: siehe *Fridrichsen, Anton.*
Fossum, Jarl E.: The Name of God and the Angel of the Lord. 1985. *vol. 36.*
Frenschkowski, Marco: Offenbarung und Epiphanie. vol. 1 1995. *vol. II/79* – vol. 2 1997. *vol. II/80.*
Frey, Jörg: Eugen Drewermann und die biblische Exegese. 1995. *vol. II/71.*
– Die johanneische Eschatologie. vol. I. 1997. *vol. 96.*
Fridrichsen, Anton: Exegetical Writings. Ed. by C.C. Caragounis und T. Fornberg. 1994. *vol. 76.*
Garlington, Don B.: 'The Obedience of Faith'. 1991. *vol. II/38.*
– Faith, Obedience, and Perseverance. 1994. *vol. 79.*
Garnet, Paul: Salvation and Atonement in the Qumran Scrolls. 1977. *vol. II/3.*
Gese, Michael: Das Vermächtnis des Apostels. 1997. *vol. II/99.*
Gräßer, Erich: Der Alte Bund im Neuen. 1985. *vol. 35.*
Green, Joel B.: The Death of Jesus. 1988. *vol. II/33.*
Gundry Volf, Judith M.: Paul and Perseverance. 1990. *vol. II/37.*
Hafemann, Scott J.: Suffering and the Spirit. 1986. *vol. II/19.*
– Paul, Moses, and the History of Israel. 1995. *vol. 81.*
Hartman, Lars: Text-Centered New Testament Studies. Ed. by D. Hellholm. 1997. *vol. 102.*
Heckel, Theo K.: Der Innere Mensch. 1993. *vol. II/53.*
Heckel, Ulrich: Kraft in Schwachheit. 1993. *vol. II/56.*
– siehe *Feldmeier, Reinhard.*
– siehe *Hengel, Martin.*
Heiligenthal, Roman: Werke als Zeichen. 1983. *vol. II/9.*
Hellholm, D.: siehe *Hartman, Lars.*
Hemer, Colin J.: The Book of Acts in the Setting of Hellenistic History. 1989. *vol. 49.*
Hengel, Martin: Judentum und Hellenismus. 1969, ³1988. *vol. 10.*
– Die johanneische Frage. 1993. *vol. 67.*
– Judaica et Hellenistica. Band 1. 1996. *vol. 90.*
Hengel, Martin and *Ulrich Heckel* (Ed.): Paulus und das antike Judentum. 1991. *vol. 58.*
Hengel, Martin and *Hermut Löhr* (Ed.): Schriftauslegung im antiken Judentum und im Urchristentum. 1994. *vol. 73.*
Hengel, Martin and *Anna Maria Schwemer* (Ed.): Königsherrschaft Gottes und himmlischer Kult. 1991. *vol. 55.*
– Die Septuaginta. 1994. *vol. 72.*
Herrenbrück, Fritz: Jesus und die Zöllner. 1990. *vol. II/41.*
Herzer, Jens: Paulus oder Petrus? 1998. *vol. 103.*
Hoegen-Rohls, Christina: Der nachösterliche Johannes. 1996. *vol. II/84.*
Hofius, Otfried: Katapausis. 1970. *vol. 11.*
– Der Vorhang vor dem Thron Gottes. 1972. *vol. 14.*
– Der Christushymnus Philipper 2,6–11. 1976, ²1991. *vol. 17.*
– Paulusstudien. 1989, ²1994. *vol. 51.*
Hofius, Otfried and *Hans-Christian Kammler:* Johannesstudien. 1996. *vol. 88.*
Holtz, Traugott: Geschichte und Theologie des Urchristentums. 1991. *vol. 57.*
Hommel, Hildebrecht: Sebasmata. vol. 1 1983. *vol. 31* – vol. 2 1984. *vol. 32.*
Hvalvik, Reidar: The Struggle for Scripture and Covenant. 1996. *vol. II/82.*
Kähler, Christoph: Jesu Gleichnisse als Poesie und Therapie. 1995. *vol. 78.*
Kammler, Hans-Christian: siehe *Hofius, Otfried.*
Kamlah, Ehrhard: Die Form der katalogischen Paränese im Neuen Testament. 1964. *vol. 7.*
Kieffer, René and *Jan Bergman* (Ed.): La Main de Dieu / Die Hand Gottes. 1997. *vol. 94.*
Kim, Seyoon: The Origin of Paul's Gospel. 1981, ²1984. *vol. II/4.*
– „The 'Son of Man'" as the Son of God. 1983. *vol. 30.*
Kleinknecht, Karl Th.: Der leidende Gerechtfertigte. 1984, ²1988. *vol. II/13.*

Klinghardt, Matthias: Gesetz und Volk Gottes. 1988. *vol. II/32.*
Köhler, Wolf-Dietrich: Rezeption des Matthäusevangeliums in der Zeit vor Irenäus. 1987. *vol. II/24.*
Korn, Manfred: Die Geschichte Jesu in veränderter Zeit. 1993. *vol. II/51.*
Koskenniemi, Erkki: Apollonios von Tyana in der neutestamentlichen Exegese. 1994. *vol. II/61.*
Kraus, Wolfgang: Das Volk Gottes. 1996. *vol. 85.*
– siehe *Walter, Nikolaus.*
Kuhn, Karl G.: Achtzehngebet und Vaterunser und der Reim. 1950. *vol. 1.*
Laansma, Jon: I Will Give You Rest. 1997. *vol. II/98.*
Lampe, Peter: Die stadtrömischen Christen in den ersten beiden Jahrhunderten. 1987, ²1989.
   vol. II/18.
Lau, Andrew: Manifest in Flesh. 1996. *vol. II/86.*
Lichtenberger, Hermann: siehe *Avemarie, Friedrich.*
Lieu, Samuel N.C.: Manichaeism in the Later Roman Empire and Medieval China. ²1992. *vol. 63.*
Loader, William R.G.: Jesus' Attitude Towards the Law. 1997. *vol. II/97.*
Löhr, Gebhard: Verherrlichung Gottes durch Philosophie. 1997. *vol. 97.*
Löhr, Hermut: siehe *Hengel, Martin.*
Löhr, Winrich Alfried: Basilides und seine Schule. 1995. *vol. 83.*
Luomanen, Petri: Entering the Kingdom of Heaven. 1998. *vol. II/101.*
Maier, Gerhard: Mensch und freier Wille. 1971. *vol. 12.*
– Die Johannesoffenbarung und die Kirche. 1981. *vol. 25.*
Markschies, Christoph: Valentinus Gnosticus? 1992. *vol. 65.*
Marshall, Peter: Enmity in Corinth: Social Conventions in Paul's Relations with the
   Corinthians. 1987. *vol. II/23.*
Meade, David G.: Pseudonymity and Canon. 1986. *vol. 39.*
Meadors, Edward P.: Jesus the Messianic Herald of Salvation. 1995. *vol. II/72.*
Meißner, Stefan: Die Heimholung des Ketzers. 1996. *vol. II/87.*
Mell, Ulrich: Die „anderen" Winzer. 1994. *vol. 77.*
Mengel, Berthold: Studien zum Philipperbrief. 1982. *vol. II/8.*
Merkel, Helmut: Die Widersprüche zwischen den Evangelien. 1971. *vol. 13.*
Merklein, Helmut: Studien zu Jesus und Paulus. vol. 1 1987. *vol. 43.* – vol. 2 1998. *vol. 105.*
Metzler, Karin: Der griechische Begriff des Verzeihens. 1991. *vol. II/44.*
Metzner, Rainer: Die Rezeption des Matthäusevangeliums im 1. Petrusbrief. 1995. *vol. II/74.*
Mittmann-Richert, Ulrike: Magnifikat und Benediktus. 1996. *vol. II/90.*
Niebuhr, Karl-Wilhelm: Gesetz und Paränese. 1987. *vol. II/28.*
– Heidenapostel aus Israel. 1992. *vol. 62.*
Nissen, Andreas: Gott und der Nächste im antiken Judentum. 1974. *vol. 15.*
Noormann, Rolf: Irenäus als Paulusinterpret. 1994. *vol. II/66.*
Obermann, Andreas: Die christologische Erfüllung der Schrift im Johannesevangelium. 1996. *vol. II/83.*
Okure, Teresa: The Johannine Approach to Mission. 1988. *vol. II/31.*
Paulsen, Henning: Studien zur Literatur und Geschichte des frühen Christentums. Ed. by
   Ute E. Eisen. 1997. *vol. 99.*
Park, Eung Chun: The Mission Discourse in Matthew's Interpretation. 1995. *vol. II/81.*
Philonenko, Marc (Ed.): Le Trône de Dieu. 1993. *vol. 69.*
Pilhofer, Peter: Presbyteron Kreitton. 1990. *vol. II/39.*
– Philippi. vol. 1 1995. *vol. 87.*
Pöhlmann, Wolfgang: Der Verlorene Sohn und das Haus. 1993. *vol. 68.*
Pokorný, Petr and *Josef B. Souček:* Bibelauslegung als Theologie. 1997. *vol. 100.*
Prieur, Alexander: Die Verkündigung der Gottesherrschaft. 1996. *vol. II/89.*
Probst, Hermann: Paulus und der Brief. 1991. *vol. II/45.*
Räisänen, Heikki: Paul and the Law. 1983, ²1987. *vol. 29.*
Rehkopf, Friedrich: Die lukanische Sonderquelle. 1959. *vol. 5.*
ein, Matthias: Die Heilung des Blindgeborenen (Joh 9). 1995. *vol. II/73.*
muth, Eckart: Pseudo-Philo und Lukas. 1994. *vol. 74.*
Marius: Syntax und Stil des Markusevangeliums. 1984. *vol. II/11.*
E. Randolph: The Secretary in the Letters of Paul. 1991. *vol. II/42.*
iner: Jesus als Lehrer. 1981, ³1988. *vol. II/7.*
*it des Apostels Paulus. 1994. *vol. 71.*

Rissi, Mathias: Die Theologie des Hebräerbriefs. 1987. *vol. 41.*
Röhser, Günter: Metaphorik und Personifikation der Sünde. 1987. *vol. II/25.*
Rose, Christian: Die Wolke der Zeugen. 1994. *vol. II/60.*
Rüger, Hans Peter: Die Weisheitsschrift aus der Kairoer Geniza. 1991. *vol. 53.*
Sänger, Dieter: Antikes Judentum und die Mysterien. 1980. *vol. II/5.*
– Die Verkündigung des Gekreuzigten und Israel. 1994. *vol. 75.*
Salzmann, Jorg Christian: Lehren und Ermahnen. 1994. *vol. II/59.*
Sandnes, Karl Olav: Paul – One of the Prophets? 1991. *vol. II/43.*
Sato, Migaku: Q und Prophetie. 1988. *vol. II/29.*
Schaper, Joachim: Eschatology in the Greek Psalter. 1995. *vol. II/76.*
Schimanowski, Gottfried: Weisheit und Messias. 1985. *vol. II/17.*
Schlichting, Günter: Ein jüdisches Leben Jesu. 1982. *vol. 24.*
Schnabel, Eckhard J.: Law and Wisdom from Ben Sira to Paul. 1985. *vol. II/16.*
Schutter, William L.: Hermeneutic and Composition in I Peter. 1989. *vol. II/30.*
Schwartz, Daniel R.: Studies in the Jewish Background of Christianity. 1992. *vol. 60.*
Schwemer, Anna Maria: siehe *Hengel, Martin*
Scott, James M.: Adoption as Sons of God. 1992. *vol. II/48.*
– Paul and the Nations. 1995. *vol. 84.*
Siegert, Folker: Drei hellenistisch-jüdische Predigten. Teil I 1980. *vol. 20* – Teil II 1992. *vol. 61.*
– Nag-Hammadi-Register. 1982. *vol. 26.*
– Argumentation bei Paulus. 1985. *vol. 34.*
– Philon von Alexandrien. 1988. *vol. 46.*
Simon, Marcel: Le christianisme antique et son contexte religieux I/II. 1981. *vol. 23.*
Snodgrass, Klyne: The Parable of the Wicked Tenants. 1983. *vol. 27.*
Söding, Thomas: Das Wort vom Kreuz. 1997. *vol. 93.*
– siehe *Thüsing, Wilhelm.*
Sommer, Urs: Die Passionsgeschichte des Markusevangeliums. 1993. *vol. II/58.*
Souček, Josef B.: siehe *Pokorný, Petr.*
Spangenberg, Volker: Herrlichkeit des Neuen Bundes. 1993. *vol. II/55.*
Speyer, Wolfgang: Frühes Christentum im antiken Strahlungsfeld. 1989. *vol. 50.*
Stadelmann, Helge: Ben Sira als Schriftgelehrter. 1980. *vol. II/6.*
Strobel, August: Die Stunde der Wahrheit. 1980. *vol. 21.*
Stuckenbruck, Loren T.: Angel Veneration and Christology. 1995. *vol. II/70.*
Stuhlmacher, Peter (Ed.): Das Evangelium und die Evangelien. 1983. *vol. 28.*
Sung, Chong-Hyon: Vergebung der Sünden. 1993. *vol. II/57.*
Tajra, Harry W.: The Trial of St. Paul. 1989. *vol. II/35.*
– The Martyrdom of St.Paul. 1994. *vol. II/67.*
Theißen, Gerd: Studien zur Soziologie des Urchristentums. 1979, ³1989. *vol. 19.*
Thornton, Claus-Jürgen: Der Zeuge des Zeugen. 1991. *vol. 56.*
Thüsing, Wilhelm: Studien zur neutestamentlichen Theologie. Ed. by Thomas Söding. 1995. *vol. 82.*
Treloar, Geoffrey R.: Lightfoot the Historian. 1998. *vol. II/103.*
Tsuji, Manabu: Glaube zwischen Vollkommenheit und Verweltlichung. 1997. *vol. II/93*
Twelftree, Graham H.: Jesus the Exorcist. 1993. *vol. II/54.*
Visotzky, Burton L.: Fathers of the World. 1995. *vol. 80.*
Wagener, Ulrike: Die Ordnung des „Hauses Gottes". 1994. *vol. II/65.*
Walter, Nikolaus: Praeparatio Evangelica. Ed. by Wolfgang Kraus und Florian Wilk. 1997. *vol. 98.*
Wander, Bernd: Gottesfürchtige und Sympathisanten. 1998. *vol. 104.*
Watts, Rikki: Isaiah's New Exodus and Mark. 1997. *vol. II/88.*
Wedderburn, A.J.M.: Baptism and Resurrection. 1987. *vol. 44.*
Wegner, Uwe: Der Hauptmann von Kafarnaum. 1985. *vol. II/14.*
Welck, Christian: Erzählte 'Zeichen'. 1994. *vol. II/69.*
Wilk, Florian: siehe *Walter, Nikolaus.*
Wilson, Walter T.: Love without Pretense. 1991. *vol. II/46.*
Zimmermann, Alfred E.: Die urchristlichen Lehrer. 1984, ²1988. *vol. II/12.*

For a complete catalogue please write to the publisher Mohr Siebeck,
P.O. Box 2040, D-72010 Tübingen, e-mail postmaster@mohr.de